SUMMON'S COMPENDIUM of DAYS

ALSO BY PARMINDER SINGH SUMMON

Summon's Christian Miscellany

Summon's Bible Miscellany

Summon's Miscellany of Saints and Sinners

SUMMON'S COMPENDIUM *of* DAYS

Being an Essential Digest of Daily History, Biography, Philosophy, Customs and Traditions, Curiosities of Human Nature, and Learned Discourse to Entertain, Elevate & Educate

PARMINDER SINGH SUMMON

SEABURY BOOKS
an imprint of
Church Publishing Incorporated, New York

Summon, Parminder.
Summon's compendium of days : an essential digest of daily history, biography, philosophy, customs and traditions, curiosities of human nature, and learned discourse designed to inspire & entertain / Parminder Singh Summon.
p. cm.
Includes bibliographical references.
ISBN 978-1-59627-057-2 (pbk.)
1. Church history–Chronology. 2. Devotional calendars. 3. Chronology, Historical. I. Title.
BR149.S86 2007
270–dc22
2007019360

Church Publishing, Incorporated.
445 Fifth Avenue
New York, New York 10016

5 4 3 2 1

For David & Jenny Chapman

I will extol thee, my God, O king; and I will bless thy name for ever and ever.

Every day will I bless thee; and I will praise thy name for ever and ever.

Great is the LORD*, and greatly to be praised; and his greatness is unsearchable.*

PSALM 145:1–3

Introduction

*"Time is a sort of river of passing events, and strong is its current;
no sooner is a thing brought to sight than it is swept by
and another takes its place, and this too will be swept away."*

MARCUS AURELIUS ANTONIUS (121–180)

The fast pace of life today means there is little time to appreciate the value of every single day. The advent of "rolling news," the growth of the internet and seemingly insatiable pressure to cram as much as possible into every day often robs us of the chance to slow the torrent of time.

It was not like this in the past, as any antiquated book or grandparent will confirm. Previous generations were familiar with almanacs, handbooks, manuals, yearbooks, and books of days. The purpose of these immensely popular volumes was to share the sheer joy of knowledge for its own sake.

Before the age of jet travel and motorcars, travellers had to use ships and trains to visit faraway places. To help fill the long days at sea or across vast tracts of land, many people packed an extensive "traveller basket" containing treats such as books, candies, and chocolate.

Imagine the year as a long journey into the unknown. We have charts (our experience), milestones (birthdays and anniversaries, for example), measuring devices (our feelings and emotions), and some knowledge of our ports of call. What we often yearn for is a "traveller basket" that can be sampled whenever we fancy.

The purpose of this book is to inspire and entertain by presenting a lively variety of factual information, folklore, and curious characters that demonstrate the diversity of daily history. Items have been selected according to personal preference and with an eye to show the inspirational, instructional, and reflective elements of our past.

The format is simple, consisting of a daily Scripture reading, saints' feast days, a list of notable birthdays, a list of those who died on that day, followed by an account of events and people connected with that day.

As you read about the happenings of each day and the people connected to them, think about your own experiences of this day or the last. What stood out for you? Or maybe you want to detail the ordinary, write a poem or lines of a song you heard, words from your loved ones or something new that you've learned. Think about recording your thoughts and making them part of you own "traveller basket."

Parminder Summon
May 2007

January

Then came old January, wrapped well
In many weeds to keep the cold away;
Yet did he quake and quiver like to quell;
And blow his nayles to warme them if he may;
For they were numb'd with holding all the day
An hatchet keene, with which he felled wood,
And from the trees did lop the needlesse spray.

EDMUND SPENSER–*The Shepheardes Calender* (1579)

Janus am I; oldest of potentates;
Forward I look, and backward, and below
I count, as god of avenues and gates,
The years that through my portals come and go.

I block the roads, and drift the fields with snow;
I chase the wild-fowl from the frozen fen;
My frosts congeal the rivers in their flow,
My fires light up the hearths and hearts of men.

HENRY WADSWORTH LONGFELLOW–*The Poet's Calendar* (1882)

Shakespeare

Perditta: You'd be so lean, that blast of January
Would blow you through and through. Now, my fair'st friend,
I would I had some flowers o' the spring that might
Become your time of day

–William Shakespeare, *The Winter's Tale,* Act IV, Scene 4

January

According to the ancient mythology, Janus was the god of gates and avenues, and in that character held a key in his right hand, and a rod in his left, to symbolize his opening and ruling the year. Sometimes he was represented with four heads, and placed in a temple of four equal sides, with a door and three windows in each side, as emblems of the four seasons and the twelve months over which he presided. The Saxons called this month "Wolf-monat," or Wolf-month, because wolves, impelled by hunger at this season, were wont to prowl and attack.

The Saxons also called this month "Aefter-yula," or After Christmas. In illuminated calendars prefixed to Catholic missals, or service books, January was frequently depicted as a man with fagots or a woodman's axe, shivering and blowing his fingers.

–William Hone, *The Every Day Book* (1825–26)

Proverbs

If January calends be summerly gay,
'Twill be winterly weather till the
calends of May.

The blackest month in all the year
Is the month of Janiveer.

Janiveer–
Freeze the pot upon the fier.

As the day lengthens,
The cold strengthens.

If the grass grows in Janiveer,
It grows the worse for 't all the year.

A January spring
Is worth naething.

Married in January's hoar and rime,
Widowed you'll be before your time.

March in Janiveer,
Janiveer in March, I fear.

*J*ANUARY 1

DAILY READING

Therefore, if anyone is in Christ, he is a new creation;
the old has gone, the new has come! (2 COR 5:17)

FEAST DAYS

ca. 1st cent.	Feast of the Circumcision	Celebrating the circumcision of the Lord
521	Basil	Bishop of Aix, France
ca. 580	Felix	Bishop of Bourges, France

ENTRANCE AND EXIT

b. 1879	Edward Morgan Forster	English writer
b. 1879	William Fox	American founder of 20th Century Fox
b. 1919	Jerome David Salinger	American writer
d. 1969	Ian Fleming	Scottish writer
d. 1972	Maurice Chevalier	French singer
d. 1998	Helen Wills Moody	American tennis star

New Year's Day

The inauguration of the New Year on January 1 began in 1582 with the adoption of the Gregorian calendar in France, Castile, Aragon, Portugal, and the northern states of Italy. The new calendar was not adopted by all nations at that time, but gradually, with Scotland recognizing the new era in 1600 and England in 1752.

From Roman times, the start of the New Year was March 25 and the shift to January 1 only came about through papal decree.

There are many customs and traditions associated with this day, including:

- First Footing in Scotland, where the first person to enter a house has to bring a gift (traditionally coal and whisky) as a portent of good tidings.
- Kirkwall Ba' Game in Scotland, an ancient football game involving the whole village of Kirkwall.
- During the reign of Queen Elizabeth, the custom of presenting Now-Year's gifts to the sovereign was carried to an extravagant height. The queen delighted in gorgeous dresses, in jewellery, in all kinds of ornaments for her person and palaces, and in purses filled with gold coin.
- Burning "Mr. Old Year" is a New Year's tradition in some cities of Colombia.
- In Venezuela, it is good luck to wear yellow underwear on New Year's Day.
- Special rice cakes *(mochi)* are made by the whole family to celebrate New Year's Day in Japan.
- In Vienna, Austria, the tradition is to have a New Year's Concert.
- Many cities hold spectacular fireworks displays to celebrate the beginning of the New Year.

Noteworthy

404 Last gladiator competition in Rome.
1660 Samuel Pepys begins his famous diary.
1898 New York City takes in the boroughs of Manhattan, the Bronx, Brooklyn, Queens, and Staten Island.
1863 Emancipation Proclamation (ending slavery) issued by Lincoln.
1893 Japan adopts the Gregorian calendar.
1901 Australia declares independence from federation of UK colonies.
1923 Union of Soviet Socialist Republics (USSR) is established.
1934 Alcatraz officially becomes a federal prison.
1946 ENIAC, the first computer, is finished by Mauchly/Eckert.
1958 European Community (later to become the European Union) is born.
1973 Britain becomes a member of the European Economic Community.
1981 Greece becomes the tenth member of the European Economic Community.
1993 Czechoslovakia is split into two separate states.
1995 World Trade Organization comes into existence.
2002 Birth of Euro currency.

*J*ANUARY 2

DAILY READING

Have I not commanded you? Be strong and courageous. Do not be terrified; do not be discouraged, for the L*ORD* *your God will be with you wherever you go.* (JOSH 1:9)

FEAST DAYS

330	Gregory of Nazianzus	Bishop of Constantinople
379	Basil the Great	Church father
1837	Caspar Bufalo	Founder of the *Missioners of the Precious Blood*

ENTRANCE AND EXIT

b. 1727	James Wolfe	British general
b. 1857	Martha Carey Thomas	American reformer
b. 1920	Isaac Asimov	Russian writer
d. 18	Publius Ovidius Naso –Ovid	Roman poet
d. 1977	Errol Garner	American musician
d. 1986	Una Merkel	American actor

St. Berchtold's Day

This day honors Duke Berchtold V of Zähringer, who founded Berne, the capital of Switzerland, in 1191. According to legend, he left on a hunt declaring he would name the city after the first animal he killed, which was a bear, or *Bär* in German.

The city of Berne became the eighth member of the Swiss Federation in 1353. Between the fourteenth and sixteenth centuries, it reached the zenith of its power by enlarging its territory and gaining great political influence. The year 1798 saw the invasion of French troops and the collapse of the Ancien Régime of Berne. In 1803 the city became the capital of the Canton of Berne; in 1848 it became the federal capital of Switzerland. As the capital of Switzerland, Berne is the seat of the diplomatic corps and international organizations, including the Universal Postal Union (a specialized agency of the United Nations).

In 1218, the last of the Zähringer line died and Berne came under direct imperial rule. The city was granted various important privileges (self-administration, own court of justice, own market) as a result of which its power and influence gradually grew, and the city evolved into the mightiest city-state north of the Alps (until 1798). Berne, one of the finest examples of medieval civic architecture in Europe, is listed as a UNESCO World Heritage Site.

Unlucky Days

Many cultures ascribe superstitious beliefs and hold that certain days are less favorable than others for important enterprises such as marriage, starting a business, undertaking a journey, or eating certain foods.

According to a calendar from the time of Henry VI (1421–71), there are thirty-two unlucky days:

- 7 in January: 1, 2, 4, 5, 7, 10, and 15.
- 3 in February: 6, 7, and 18.
- 3 in March: 1, 6, and 8.
- 2 in April: 6 and 11.
- 3 in May: 5, 6, and 7.
- 2 in June: 7 and 15.
- 2 in July: 5 and 19.
- 2 in August: 15 and 19.
- 2 in September: 6 and 7.
- 1 in October: 6.
- 2 in November: 15 and 16.
- 3 in December: 15, 16, and 17.

Many "reasons" are given to justify the selection of these dates, but as superstition does not bow to reason, the choice remains arbitrary and inexplicable.

*J*ANUARY 3

DAILY READING

Keep your lives free from the love of money and be content with what you have, because God has said, "Never will I leave you; never will I forsake you." (HEB 13:5)

FEAST DAYS

236	Antherus	Pope
311	Peter Balsam	Governor of Eleutheropolis, Palestine
500	Genovefa	Patron of Paris, France

ENTRANCE AND EXIT

b. 1793	Lucretia Mott	American reformer
b. 1883	Clement Atlee	English statesman
b. 1969	Michael Schumacher	German sportsman
d. 1322	Philip the Tall	King of France
d. 1894	Elizabeth Palmer Peabody	American educator
d. 1992	Dame Judith Anderson	Australian actor

Anna Bowden

"Suttee"–the burning of widows on the funeral pyre of their husbands–was common when English missionary William Carey arrived in India at the beginning of the nineteenth century. It was a practice entirely at odds with Carey's Christian faith, and he sought for many years to end it.

Carey and his helpers succeeded in highlighting the horrors of suttee and eventually it was practiced only in remote areas. Carey's work was furthered by missionaries like Anna Bowden (1852–73), who on this day in 1872 left England for the Madras port town of Conjeeveram.

Anna was born into comfortable surroundings in London and could have chosen the leisured life of a Victorian lady. However, like Moses, she "chose to be mistreated along with the people of God rather than to enjoy the pleasures of sin for a short time" (Heb 11:25). In India she sought to educate children and provide a clinic for local people. But Hindu fanatics attacked the mission compound and killed Anna and her helpers. News of her martyrdom led to a revival and led to the practice of suttee being outlawed.

Martin Luther Outlawed

On this day in 1521, Pope Leo X excommunicated the originator of the Protestant Reformation, Martin Luther, along with his followers. The pope's edict was in a bull called "Decet Romanum": *the Condemnation and Excommunication of Martin Luther, the Heretic, and his Followers.*

This is an extract of from that document, translated from Latin:

> Martin and the rest are excommunicate, accursed, condemned, heretics, hardened, interdicted, deprived of possessions and incapable of owning them. Three days will be given: we pronounce canonical warning and allow one day's notice on the first, another on the second, but on the third peremptory and final execution of our order. This shall take place on a Sunday or some other festival, when a large congregation assembles for worship. The banner of the cross shall be raised, the bells rung, the candles lit and after a time extinguished, cast on the ground and trampled under foot, and the stones shall be cast forth three times, and the other ceremonies observed which are usual in such cases. The faithful Christians, one and all, shall be enjoined strictly to shun these men.
>
> We would occasion still greater confounding on the said Martin and the other heretics we have mentioned, and on their adherents, followers and partisans: hence, on the strength of their vow of obedience we enjoin each and every patriarch, archbishop and all other prelates, that even as they were appointed on the authority of Jerome to allay schisms, so now in the present crisis, as their office obliges them, they shall make themselves a wall of defense for their Christian people.

January 4

DAILY READING

Joshua told the people, "Consecrate yourselves, for tomorrow the Lord will do amazing things among you." (JOSH 3:5)

FEAST DAYS

539	Gregory	Bishop of Langres, France
ca. 750	Rigobert	Archbishop of Rheims, France
1821	Elizabeth Ann Seton	Founder of the Sisters of Charity

ENTRANCE AND EXIT

b. 1809	Louis Braille	French teacher
b. 1813	Sir Isaac Pitman	English inventor of shorthand
b. 1935	Floyd Patterson	American boxer
d. 1854	Thomas Campbell	Irish theologian
d. 1960	Albert Camus	French writer
d. 1990	Alberto Lleras Camargo	President of Colombia

Sir Isaac Newton

Isaac Newton's work on mathematics and physics confirms his status as one of the greatest minds of all time. He was born in Lincolnshire, near Grantham, on December 25, 1642 (January 4 in the Gregorian calendar), and died at Kensington, London, on March 20, 1727. He was educated at Trinity College, Cambridge, and lived there from 1661 till 1696, during which time he produced the bulk of his work in mathematics; in 1696 he was appointed to a valuable government office and moved to London, where he resided till his death.

In character he was religious and conscientious, with an exceptionally high standard of morality. He modestly attributed his discoveries largely to the admirable work done by his predecessors. He summed up his own estimate of his work in the sentence, "I do not know what I may appear to the world; but to myself I seem to have been only like a boy, playing on the sea-shore, and diverting myself, in now and then finding a smoother pebble, or a prettier shell than ordinary, whilst the great ocean of truth lay all undiscovered before me."

In 1687 King James II, having tried to force the university to admit as a master of arts a Roman Catholic priest who refused to take the oaths of supremacy and allegiance, Newton took a prominent part in resisting the illegal interference of the king, and was one of the deputation sent to London to protect the rights of the university. The active part taken by Newton in this affair led to his being elected member for the university in 1689. This parliament only lasted thirteen months, and on its dissolution he gave up his seat. He was subsequently reelected in 1701, but he never took any prominent part in politics.

In 1705 he was knighted. From this time onward he devoted much of his leisure time to theology and wrote at great length on prophecies and predictions, subjects which had always been of interest to him. His evidence before the House of Commons in 1714 on the determination of longitude at sea marks an important epoch in the history of navigation.

Noteworthy

1493 Columbus returned to Spain from the New World with six natives.

1896 Utah becomes forty-fifth state admitted to Union.

1923 Lenin's "Political Testament" calls for removal of Stalin.

1944 Leonard Bernstein's musical *On the Town* opens on Broadway.

1948 Weekly news magazine *Der Spiegel* begins publication in Germany.

1948 Myanmar (Burma) Independence Day.

1951 Chinese and North Korean troops capture Seoul, Korea.

1989 Two Libyan jets are shot down by U.S. aircraft in the Mediterranean.

2000 Charles Schulz, creator of the *Peanuts* comic strip, retires.

2007 Nancy Pelosi becomes the first woman speaker of the U.S. House of Representatives.

*J*ANUARY 5

DAILY READING

But you are a shield around me, O L*ORD;*
you bestow glory on me and lift up my head. (PS 3:3)

FEAST DAYS

303	Martyrs of Egypt	In honor of martyrs in the reign of Diocletian
ca. 459	Simeon Stylites	Syrian hermit
1177	Gerlach of Valkenburg	Patron of domestic animals

ENTRANCE AND EXIT

b. 1855	King Camp Gillette	American inventor
b. 1932	Umberto Eco	Italian writer
b. 1946	Diane Keaton	American actor
d. 1066	Edward the Confessor	English king
d. 1477	Charles the Bald	King of France
d. 1933	Calvin Coolidge	33rd American president

Holy Thorn of Glastonbury

According to legend, Jesus' uncle, Joseph of Arimathea, visited the area around Glastonbury with the Lord and planted the Glastonbury Thorn (Common Hawthorn). It is said that Joseph's staff came from this plant. Many myths relate to this area, and Glastonbury is variously associated with King Arthur's Isle of Avalon and to have been the site of the Holy Grail.

One myth records that Jesus' finger was pricked by the Glastonbury Thorn, and ever since then it has produced red flowers in witness of this incident. For example, the December 1753 edition of *The Gentlemen's Magazine*, records: "A vast concourse of people attended the noted thorn on Christmas-day, new style; but, to their great disappointment, there was no appearance of its blowing, which made them watch it narrowly the 5th of January, the Christmas-day, old style, when it blowed as usual."

There is mention of the Glastonbury Thorn in an anonymous poem called the "Lyfe of Joseph of Arimathea." This relates how the plant was unusual in that it flowered twice in a year, once as normal on "old wood" in spring, and once on "new wood" (the current season's matured new growth) in the winter. This flowering of the Glastonbury Thorn in mild weather just past midwinter was accounted miraculous.

During the seventeenth century, Puritans destroyed the Glastonbury Thorn as part of their campaign against Christmas celebrations. However, some cuttings were taken, and it is said the Glastonbury Thorn was replanted and another cutting was taken to Hertfordshire.

Simeon the Stylite

Simon is the most famous of the stylites or saints who spent their days seated on high platforms or pillars. Born in 392, at age thirteen Simon gave himself over to the service of God in the Syrian Desert. It was the hearing of the Beatitudes as they were read in church that led him to asceticism and caused him to join a monastery. Here the rigors of his mortification of the body proved incompatible with the common life of the brotherhood, so leaving the monastery, he began his discipline as a solitary by shutting himself up in a cell not far from Antioch.

Three years later, he retired to a neighboring height, and there marked out for himself a circular enclosure; to prevent himself from passing beyond this enclosure, he attached himself to a large stone by a chain. After some time he ceased to use the chain, and for four years he stood within the enclosure without lying or sitting down, "snowed upon, rained upon, and scorched." His fame spread far and wide–pilgrims came in large numbers; the sick sought healing; all wished to touch him or to carry off some relic from the saint.

When he later sought solitude away from the crowds that pressed around him, he established himself on a pillar that grew higher and higher above the crowds until it reached sixty feet. He thus lived between heaven and earth for about forty years, preaching and exhorting the crowds from high upon his pillar. Numerous individuals who came to him were converted by his preaching. He died in the year 459.

*J*ANUARY 6

DAILY READING

So we fix our eyes not on what is seen,
but on what is unseen. For what is seen is temporary,
but what is unseen is eternal. (2 COR 4:18)

FEAST DAYS

ca. 210	Martyrs of Africa	In remembrance of those who died by order of Emperor Septimus Severus
11th cent.	Erminold of Prüfening	Benedictine monk
1611	John de Ribera	Archbishop of Valencia, Spain

ENTRANCE AND EXIT

b. 1367	Richard II	King of England
b. 1412	Joan of Arc	French mystic
b. 1854	Sherlock Holmes	English fictional detective
d. 1884	Gregor Mendel	Austrian scientist
d. 1993	Rudolph Nureyev	Russian ballet dancer
d. 1993	Dizzy Gillespie	American musician

Epiphany—The Adoration of the Magi

The last of the twelve days of Christmas is traditionally celebrated with the Feast of Epiphany, also called "The Adoration of the Magi" or "The Manifestation of God." The word epiphany means revelation or sudden unveiling and refers to the revelation given to the Magi as they looked upon the natal star.

The Magi saw, on the night when Christ was born, a bright star, followed it to Bethlehem, and found there the Christ child and brought presents of gold, frankincense, and myrrh. Myrrh is an aromatic gum produced from a thorn bush that grew in Arabia and Ethiopia, and was obtained from a tree in the same manner as frankincense. The significance of myrrh, which is bitter in taste, is that it anticipates the suffering of Jesus on the cross. Frankincense is highly fragrant when burned and was therefore used in worship, where it was burned as a pleasant offering to God in the Old Testament. Gold was the usual offering presented to kings by their subjects, or those wanting to pay respect.

On this day, traditionally carol singers go from house to house, and in many homes the Christmas tree is taken down and in some areas is burnt in a big bonfire. For the children, this is an especially joyous occasion because they are given sweets and chocolate ornaments.

Haxey Hood Game

The villagers of Westwoodside and Haxey in Lincolnshire, England, compete for possession of "the Hood" on this day every year. This tradition started over seven hundred years ago when Lady de Mowbray was out riding and a sudden gust of wind blew her hat off. The local farm laborers chased after it. Lady de Mowbray, so pleased to get her hat back, handed out a few titles.

She named the person who returned her hat the Lord of the Hood. The person who actually caught the hood, but dared not hand it to her, was dubbed the Fool. The rest were called Boggins, apparently because each time the hood changed hands during the chase she squealed in delight "It's boggined again." The game is refereed by the Lord of the Hood, helped by his Chief Boggin, both dressed in scarlet hunting coats and hats decorated with flowers and plumes.

The Haxey Hood Game takes place in a field in Haxey. Proceedings are launched by the Fool from his stone in front of Haxey Parish Church, usually around 2:30 p.m., and include the "smoking" of the Fool. He then leads the crowd up the hill for games for the children and the start of the main game at 3:30 p.m. The Hood, a long leather cylinder, is thrown into the air to launch the proceedings. When it falls, the participants (regulars from the local public houses) swarm around it and attempt to sway the hood out of the field, through the streets, and back to their favorite hostelry for a celebration and the honor of holding it for the coming year.

*J*ANUARY 7

DAILY READING

O Israel, put your hope in the LORD, *for with the* LORD
is unfailing love and with him is full redemption. (PS 130:7)

FEAST DAYS

ca. 960	Reinold	Patron of stonemasons
804	Wittikund	Patron of Westphalia, Germany
1131	Canute Lavard	Patron of Zeeland, Denmark

ENTRANCE AND EXIT

b. 1800	Millard Fillmore	13th American president
b. 1925	Gerald Durrell	English naturalist and writer
b. 1964	Nicholas Cage	American actor
d. 1536	Catherine of Aragon	Queen of England
d. 1943	Nikola Tesla	Croatian scientist
d. 1985	Robert Graves	English writer

St. Distaff's Day

According to ancient tradition, this day was given to playing tricks, as it was the first working day after the twelve days of Christmas. It was called St. Distaff's Day in honor of the rock, which is a *distaff* held in the hand, from where wool was spun by women. Men were in the habit of burning the flax and tow belonging to the women, and women retaliated by drenching the tricksters with buckets of water.

The poet Robert Herrick recalls this custom in this poem:

St. Distaff's day,
or the morrow after Twelfth-day.

Partly work, and partly play,
Ye must on S. Distaff's day:
From the plough soone free your teame,
Then come home and fother them.
If the maides a spinning goe,
Burne the flax, and fire the tow;
Bring in pailes of water then,
Let the maides bewash the men:
Give S. Distaffe all the right,
Then bid Christmas sport good-night.
And next morrow, every one
To his own vocation.

Noteworthy

1558 Calais, the last English possession on mainland France, was recaptured by the French.
1610 Galileo Galilei sighted four of Jupiter's moons.
1785 French aeronaut/balloonist Jean-Pierre Blanchard successfully made the first air crossing of the English Channel from the English coast to France.
1887 Thomas Stevens completed the first worldwide bicycle trip. He travelled 13,500 miles in three years.
1927 Transatlantic telephone service began between New York and London. Thirty-one calls were made on this first day.
1927 In Hinckley, Illinois, the Harlem Globetrotters played their first game.
1942 The World War II siege of Bataan.
1953 President Harry Truman announced the development of the hydrogen bomb.
1975 OPEC agreed to raise crude oil prices by 10 percent, which began a time of world economic inflation.
1989 Crown Prince Akihito became the emperor of Japan following the death of his father, Emperor Hirohito.
1999 President Bill Clinton went on trial before the Senate.

*J*ANUARY 8

DAILY READING

Praise the LORD*! Praise the* LORD*, O my soul!*
I will praise the LORD *as long as I live;*
I will sing praises to my God all my life long. (PSALM 146:1–2)

FEAST DAYS

ca. 410	Severinus	Patron of Austria
ca. 719	Pega of Peakirk	Sister of St. Guthlac
1002	Wulsin of Sherborne	Abbot of Westminster, England

ENTRANCE AND EXIT

b. 1931	Billy Graham	American evangelist
b. 1935	Elvis Presley	American rock star
b. 1947	David Bowie	English rock star
d. 1980	John Lennon	English rock star
d. 1990	Terry Thomas	English actor
d. 1996	François Mitterand	French president

Elvis Presley Day

There is a growing campaign to officially designate this day in honor of Elvis Presley (1935–77). To this end, an online petition has been organized by members of the Elvis Presley Fan Club (The Presley-ites). The petition states:

> To the U.S. Congress:
>
> We, as fans of Elvis Presley, would like a day of recognition on the calendar for Elvis. This will cost the taxpayers nothing and will simply be out on all calendars recognizing Elvis' birthday, January 8th, as Elvis Presley Day.
>
> Elvis was such a wonderful man. He never forgot where he came from and he was always kind and generous to others and to those less fortunate. Elvis gave so much to so many. He has a huge fan base worldwide. Elvis Presley fan clubs keep his love, kindness, and generosity alive in his memory by giving to charities and helping others worldwide. His beautiful voice was a wonderful gift from God that he used to make so many people happy. His talent is immeasurable. The magnitude of Elvis Presley will never be surpassed by any other entertainer. Twenty-seven years after his death, he is still number one. Elvis is the greatest entertainer the world will ever see. Please make January 8th Elvis Presley Day!

Three thousand people have signed the petition so far. There is a ceremony at Graceland on this day every year to mark the King of Rock and Roll's birthday.

St. Pega

The great abbey of Peterborough, England, was consecrated in 664 as part of the kingdom of Mercia. Peterborough became the center of a great religious renaissance in Mercia, with monks and hermits entering the abbey or settling near its grounds.

Pega, sister of St. Guthlac, had her hermitage in the village of Peakirk, near her brother who was a hermit in Croyland. In 714, nearing death, he invited Pega to his funeral. Tradition records that Pega sailed down the River Welland, and cured a blind man from Wisbech en route. Guthlac bequeathed to her his Psalter and scourge, both of which she gave to the monastery that grew up around his hermitage. After Guthlac's death, she is said to have made a pilgrimage to Rome and to have died there. Her relics were kept in a church in Rome and many miracles occurred there.

*J*ANUARY 9

DAILY READING

The LORD *your God did to the Jordan just what he had done to the Red Sea when he dried it up before us until we had crossed over. He did this so that all the peoples of the earth might know that the hand of the* LORD *is powerful and so that you might always fear the* LORD *your God.* (JOSH 4:23–24)

FEAST DAYS

683	Waningus of Fécamp	Benedictine monk
710	Adrian of Canterbury	Benedictine monk
1276	Teobaldo Visconti	Pope Gregory X

ENTRANCE AND EXIT

b. 1728	Thomas Warton	English writer
b. 1898	Gracie Fields	English singer
b. 1941	Joan Baez	American singer
d. 1324	Marco Polo	Italian explorer
d. 1923	Katherine Mansfield	New Zealand writer
d. 1995	Peter Cook	English actor

The Black Nazarene

Every year on this day, thousands of Catholic pilgrims from all over the Philippines gather at the capital, Manila, to take part in the procession of the Black Nazarene (*Nuestro Padre Jesús Nazareno*). This is the largest procession in a nation with many festivals and marches. They all hope that by touching the wooden statue, they will be protected from harm and have a prosperous future. Most in the crowd go barefoot as a sign of humility as they follow the statue. A few dozen people a year pass out and must be taken away by ambulance. And there is at least a small risk of being trampled. The feast and procession, though, are a truly Filipino experience.

The procession originated in the seventeenth century when thousands of men paraded through the district of Quiapo carrying a black wooden statue of Jesus. There is a similar parade on Good Friday as part of the Easter celebrations. The original statue was made by a priest in Mexico and came to Manila in 1606.

One story that accounts for the black statue states that when the icon was on its way to Manila, there was a fire onboard the ship and it became charred in the flames.

The permanent place for the icon is in the St. John the Baptist Church in Quiapo in Manila, where it has been housed since 1787.

Noteworthy

1788 Connecticut became the fifth state to ratify the U.S. Constitution.

1793 First American manned air-balloon flight made by Jean Pierre Blanchard.

1799 Income tax introduced in Britain by Pitt the Younger.

1806 Funeral procession of Admiral Lord Nelson.

1861 Mississippi seceded from the Union.

1913 Birth of Richard Milhous Nixon, the thirty-seventh president of the United States.

1957 British Prime Minister Anthony Eden resigned.

2005 Mahmoud Abbas was elected Palestinian Authority president by a landslide.

2006 *The Phantom of the Opera* became the longest running show on Broadway.

*J*ANUARY 10

DAILY READING

Serve the LORD *with fear and rejoice with trembling. . . .*
Blessed are all who take refuge in him. (PS 2:11–12)

FEAST DAYS

ca. 660	Thomas	Archbishop of Armagh, Ireland
ca. 660	John the Good	Bishop of Milan
1209	William	Archbishop of Bourges, France

ENTRANCE AND EXIT

b. 1945	Rod Stewart	Scottish rock star
b. 1949	George Foreman	American boxer
b. 1952	Pat Benetar	American singer
d. 1645	William Laud	Archbishop of Canterbury
d. 1961	Dashiell Hammett	American writer
d. 1981	Richard Boone	American actor

The Complutensian Polyglot Bible

In 1502, Cardinal Fransisco Ximenez de Cisneros (Archbishop of Toledo in Spain, Primas of Spain, and Grand Inquisitor) had the idea of producing a Bible in Hebrew, Greek, Aramaic, and Latin. This became known as the Complutensian (from the Latin name *Complutum*) of the Spanish city Alcala, where the scholars met and created the Polyglot (meaning "many languages") Bible.

The first section of the Complutensian Polyglot was published on this day in 1514 under the direction of Arnold Guillen de Brocar. It was published as a six-volume set sometime after its completion in 1517. Today, there are fewer than 130 copies surviving. The Old Testament is contained in the first four volumes, and each page consists of three parallel columns of Hebrew (outside), Latin Vulgate (middle), and Greek Septuagint (inside). The Pentateuch also has Aramaic and another Latin translation.

The New Testament forms the fifth volume, and the sixth volume contains Hebrew, Aramaic, and Greek dictionaries, vocabulary lists, and a brief Hebrew grammar.

Before the Polyglot Bible was completed, news of the project reached the Dutch theologian Desiderius Erasmus, who published his rushed edition of the Greek New Testament that became known as the Textus Receptus (Received Text) and formed the foundation of the King James Version published in 1611. Because Erasmus had the patronage of Pope Leo X, full publication of the Polyglot Bible was delayed until 1520, while Erasmus's edition was published in 1516. It was not widely distributed until 1522.

Five months after the completion of the Complutensian Polyglot Bible, Cardinal Jimenez died. He never saw its publication.

William Laud

Archbishop William Laud is a martyred saint of the Anglican Church. However, to Puritan members of Parliament who sent him to be beheaded on Tower Hill on this day in 1645, he was evil incarnate. He was found guilty of attempting to overthrow the Protestant religion.

Laud was the leader of the Arminians and arch persecutor of the Puritans. As England's Primate, Laud shared King Charles I's passion for uniformity. He pushed for standardizing worship in all of his master's dominions by publishing a new prayer book, inspecting churches to enforce the observance of Church of England liturgy, and purging academia of all Puritans. As early as 1625, as a bishop, he had pleased Charles I by writing up a list of churchmen worthy of promotion, with "O" for Orthodox and "P" for Puritan beside each name.

JANUARY 11

DAILY READING

For in Christ Jesus neither circumcision nor uncircumcision has any value. The only thing that counts is faith expressing itself through love. (GAL 5:6)

FEAST DAYS

ca. 5th cent.	Brandan	Irish monk
529	Theodosius the Cenobiarch	Patron of iron workers
ca. 625	Salvius	Bishop of Amiens, France

ENTRANCE AND EXIT

b. 1815	John Macdonald	Canadian prime minister
b. 1903	Alan Paton	South African writer
b. 1952	Ben Crenshaw	American golfer
d. 1843	Francis Scott Key	American composer
d. 1928	Thomas Hardy	English writer
d. 1969	Richmal Crompton	English writer

Burning the Clavie

In Scotland, Old New Year's Eve (January 11) is still celebrated with a fire festival known as "Burning the Clavie" at Burghead on the Moray Firth. The clavier is a half-barrel that is attached to a fisherman's pole. It is filled with wood and tar before being set alight at six in the evening. Carrying the clavie is a sweaty and potentially hazardous task undertaken by ten local men (brochers) whose ancestors over many years have passed on the honor of being part of the clavie crew. Each brocher (traditionally a fisherman) takes it in turn to carry the burning clavie clockwise around the streets of Burghead, occasionally stopping at the houses of former eminent citizens to present a smouldering faggot of the clavie in the doorway to bring the household good luck for the year ahead.

The men proceed to the stone altar of an old fort on the ancient Doorie Hill. The clavie is set down here and more fuel is added until the hillside is ablaze with a beacon of fire.

The superstitious believe that ill luck will fall upon the residents of Burghead if a carrier stumbles. Spectators scramble for pieces of the burning clavie, since its remnants are said to bring good fortune while simultaneously warding off evil. The embers are supposed to be lucky and are collected by the clavie followers. The luck is said to last for a year.

Francis Scott Key (1779–1843)

The American lawyer Francis Scott Key is best known for writing the lyrics to the American National Anthem in 1814. Key had witnessed the Battle of Baltimore, where the British bombarded Fort McHenry. Moved by the American defense, Key wrote a poem called "The Defence of Fort McHenry." Today this is known by its more popular name, "The Star Spangled Banner" and sung to the melody composed by John Stafford Smith:

O say, can you see, by the dawn's early light,
What so proudly we hailed at the twilight's
last gleaming,
Whose broad stripes and bright stars,
through the perilous fight,
O'er the ramparts we watched, were so
gallantly streaming?
And the rockets' red glare, the bombs
bursting in air,
Gave proof through the night that our flag
was still there;
O say, does that star-spangled banner yet
wave
O'er the land of the free and the home of
the brave?

On the shore, dimly seen thro' the mist of
the deep,
Where the foe's haughty host in dread
silence reposes,
What is that which the breeze, o'er the
towering steep,
As it fitfully blows, half conceals, half
discloses?
Now it catches the gleam of the morning's
first beam,
In full glory reflected, now shines on the
stream
'Tis the star-spangled banner. Oh! long may
it wave
O'er the land of the free and the home of
the brave!

*J*ANUARY 12

DAILY READING

You are to help your brothers until the L*ORD gives them rest, as he has done for you, and until they too have taken possession of the land that the* L*ORD your God is giving them. After that, you may go back and occupy your own land, which Moses the servant of the* L*ORD gave you east of the Jordan toward the sunrise.* (JOSH 1:14–15)

FEAST DAYS

690	Benedict Biscop	Patron of Sunderland, England
1768	Bernardo de Corleone	Capuchin friar
1944	Nikola Bunkerd Kitbamrung	Thai priest

ENTRANCE AND EXIT

b. 1729	Edmund Burke	English statesman
b. 1876	Jack London	American writer
b. 1964	Jeff Bezos	American businessman
d.1965	Lorraine Vivian Hansberry	American writer
d. 1976	Agatha Christie	English writer
d. 2003	Maurice Gibb	Australian singer

Aelred of Rievaulx

Aelred (ca. 1120–67), who died on this day in 1167, became a monk at the age of twenty-four. He was from Hexham, in Northumbria, and was educated at Durham. Around 1130, Aelred became a manager in the household of St. David, the pious King of Scotland. Aelred was highly esteemed by the king and was noted for his meekness.

To relinquish entirely all his worldly engagements, he left Scotland and embraced the austere Cistercian order at Rievaulx in Yorkshire, where Walter de L'Espeque had recently (1122) founded a monastery. As a monk under the first abbot, William, Aelred set himself cheerfully to practice the greatest austerities and employed much of his time in prayer and reading. Describing the lives of his brethren, Aelred recorded that they drank nothing but water, ate little, labored hard, slept little–and on hard boards–never spoke, except to their superiors on necessary occasions, and loved prayer. His heart turned with great ardor to the love of God and this made him feel all the Cistercian disciplines as sweetness and light. He had been much delighted, in his youth, with reading Cicero, but after his conversion he devoted himself to Scripture. His thoughts are recorded in his book, *On Spiritual Friendship*.

Around 1142, Aelred traveled as an envoy in the disputed election of William Fitz Herbert to the Archiepiscopate of York. Under Aelred's leadership, the Abbey at Rievaulx prospered to such an extent that it became the largest of its time in England, with 150 monks and 500 lay brothers.

Aelred became a figure of national importance; he preached at Westminster Abbey and wrote a biography of St. Edward the Confessor. Other works include *Life of St. Ninian, Saints of Hexham,* and *Sermons on Isaiah*, which are often considered his finest.

Agatha Christie

Agatha May Clarissa Miller (1890–1976) remains the most popular writer in all genres, and her sales are only second to the works of Shakespeare. The doyenne of mystery writers is famous for creating two of fiction's most famous characters: the Belgian detective Hercule Poirot and the West Country spinster Jane Marple. Her stage play *The Mousetrap* still holds the record for the longest run ever in London, which opened at the Ambassadors Theatre on November 25, 1952, and as of 2007 is still running after more than twenty thousand performances.

She wrote over sixty novels as well as plays, radio plays, and television plays. Her first book, *The Mysterious Affair at Styles*, was published in 1920 and introduced Hercule Poirot. The first Jane Marple adventure, *The Murder at the Vicarage*, was published in 1930. At the height of her fame, she wrote two novels about the last cases featuring Poirot and Marple, to be published after her death. *Curtain: Poirot's Last Case* was published in 1974 and *Sleeping Murder*, featuring Jane Marple, was published in 1975. Christie agreed to them being published before her death, due to popular demand.

January 13

DAILY READING

Be devoted to one another in brotherly love.
Honor one another above yourselves. (ROM12:10)

FEAST DAYS

235	Andrew	Bishop of Trier, Germany
367	Hilary of Poitiers	Doctor of the church
927	Berno	Abbot of Cluny, France

ENTRANCE AND EXIT

b. 1834	Horatio Alger	American writer
b. 1926	Michael Bond	English writer
b. 1977	Orlando Bloom	English actor
d. 1599	Edmund Spenser	English poet
d. 1691	George Fox	English founder of the Quakers
d. 1941	James Joyce	Irish writer

Hilary of Poitiers

St. Hilary of Poitiers (ca. 315–367) was one of the greatest champions of the Catholic faith against Arianism (the teaching that Christ was a created being and not God eternal) in the West. Not much is known about his early life, but it is thought he became an adult convert from paganism, and became Bishop of Poitiers about 350. He is one of the thirty-three Doctors of the Church and is best known for his vigorous opposition to Emperor Constantius II's attempts to impose Arianism on the Western church. He was exiled to Phrygia in 356, but he showed himself so effective a defender and propagator of Catholic belief that he was allowed to return to his diocese in Gaul in 360. He continued to fight the heresy of Arianism in the West till his death about 368. St. Hilary introduced many of the Eastern church's thought to the Western church, including a great theological work *On the Trinity*. For this he is known as the "Athanasius of the West."

Hilary didn't even know about the Nicene Council until years after the event, but he insisted the Western church already held to the Nicene faith, council or no council. For his contributions to the Catholic faith, Pope Pius IX declared him a "Doctor of the Church" in 1851.

Quotes of the Day

"I bought a small toy bear on Christmas Eve 1956. I saw it left on a shelf in a London store and felt sorry for it. I took it home as a present for my wife Brenda and named it Paddington as we were living near Paddington Station at the time. I wrote some stories about the bear, more for fun than with the idea of having them published. After ten days I found that I had a book on my hands. It wasn't written specifically for children, but I think I put into it the kind things I liked reading about when I was young."

–Michael Bond on Paddington Bear

"I got to dress up in funny clothes and run around New Zealand with a bow and arrow for eighteen months, how bad could that be?"

–Orlando Bloom on filming the Lord of the Rings trilogy

"A man of genius makes no mistakes; his errors are volitional and are the portals of discovery."

–James Joyce

*J*ANUARY 14

DAILY READING

"A new command I give you: Love one another. As I have loved you, so you must love one another." (JOHN 13:34)

FEAST DAYS

ca. 340	Macrina the Elder	Patron of widows
346	Barbasymus	Bishop of Selecia
1883	Seraphim of Sarov	Russian hermit

ENTRANCE AND EXIT

b. 1875	Dr. Albert Schweitzer	Swiss theologian
b. 1892	Hal Roach	American film producer
b. 1940	Trevor Nunn	English writer
d. 1898	Lewis Carroll	English writer
d. 1977	Anthony Eden	English Prime Minister
d. 2006	Shelley Winters	American actor

Mallard Day

This day is observed solely at The College of All Souls of the Faithful Departed, Oxford, with merrymaking, chief among which is the eating of the largest and finest mallard the cook can procure. This is because when digging the foundations of the college buildings in 1437, the workmen discovered a splendid mallard in a drain, and it was looked upon it as a sure token of the future prosperity of the new enterprise.

Henry Chichele, Archbishop of Canterbury, and King Henry V1 cofounded All Souls College in 1437. Its original cost was £9500 (approximately £3 million at current prices). £5000 of this was an endowment of property in Kent and Middlesex, ensuring the continued prosperity of the college.

Mallard Day is celebrated by a great feast, and the traditional song to the mallard is sung:

Griffin, bustard, turkey, capon,
Let other hungry mortals gape on;
And on the bones their stomach fall hard,
But let All Souls' men have their
MALLARD.
Oh! by the blood of King Edward,
Oh! by the blood of King Edward,
It was a wopping, wopping MALLARD.

Noteworthy

1783 American congress ratifies peace treaty (Treaty of Paris) between U.S. and UK.
1814 Norway ceded to Sweden by king of Denmark.
1878 Alexander Graham Bell demonstrates his telephone invention.
1907 Earthquake in Jamaica destroys capital of Kingston; 1,000 killed.
1914 Henry Ford inaugurates first assembly line for continuous assembly of cars.
1953 Yugoslavia elects its first president (Marshal Tito).
1969 Russian Soyuz 4 and 5 become first manned spacecraft to interchange astronauts in space.

*J*ANUARY 15

DAILY READING

O L*ORD*, *I have heard of your renown, and I stand in awe, O* L*ORD*,
of your work. In our own time revive it; in our own time make it known;
in wrath may you remember mercy. (HAB 3:2)

FEAST DAYS

342	Paul of Thebes	Patron of weavers
450	John the Cave Dweller	Turkish hermit
ca. 7th cent. BC	Habakkuk	Old Testament prophet

ENTRANCE AND EXIT

b. 1622	Jean-Baptiste Molière	French writer
b. 1914	Hugh Trevor Roper	English historian
b. 1929	Martin Luther King Jr.	American civil rights leader
d. 1993	Sammy Cahn	American musician
d. 1994	Harry Nilsson	American singer
d. 2005	Victoria de los Angeles	Spanish singer

Habakkuk

Habakkuk was an Old Testament prophet who lived in the seventh century BC. During this time, Israel's ten Northern Tribes were defeated by the Assyrians, just before the destruction of Solomon's Temple. His name means "embrace" or "caress." Habakkuk was known as the philosopher prophet and was from the priestly tribe of Levi.

He prophesied over a period of fifty years and struggled with the question of why evil people prosper at the expense of the righteous–"Your eyes are too pure to look on evil; you cannot tolerate wrong. Why then do you tolerate the treacherous? Why are you silent while the wicked swallow up those more righteous than themselves?" (Hab 1:13). As he cried out to God, he realized that God's plan for the purification of his people went far beyond what he could understand. Although God's actions seemed unjust and out of line with human values, Habakkuk reveals that God's actions were a small part of his larger, and perfectly sovereign, plan to bring salvation to Israel.

Habakkuk is also mentioned in the apocryphal story of "Bel and the Dragon," which says that he was carried by an angel to bring food and drink to the prophet Daniel in the lions' den.

The key verse of his book is found in chapter 2, verse 4: "the righteous shall live by his faith"–a call to persevere even when evil appears triumphant. This verse so sparked Martin Luther's heart that it ultimately led to the Protestant Reformation.

Martin Luther King Jr. Day

This day used to be dedicated to the commemoration of the Rev. Martin Luther King Jr., who was assassinated in 1968 while he was leading a workers' strike in Memphis, Tennessee.

The first official Martin Luther King Jr. Day was on Monday, January 20, 1986. However, all through the 1980s, controversy surrounded the idea of a Martin Luther King Jr. Day. Congressmen and citizens had petitioned President Reagan to make January 15, Martin Luther King Jr.'s birthday, a federal holiday. Others wanted to make the holiday on the day he died, while some people did not want to have any holiday at all.

January 15 had been observed as a legal holiday for many years in twenty-seven states and Washington, D.C. Finally, in 1986, President Reagan signed legislation making the third Monday in January a federal legal holiday commemorating the life and example of Dr. Martin Luther King Jr.

*J*ANUARY 16

DAILY READING

I can do everything through him who gives me strength. (PHIL 4:13)

FEAST DAYS

309	Marcellus I	Pope
429	Honore of Arles	Patron against drought
1127	Henry of Coquet	Northumbrian monk

ENTRANCE AND EXIT

b. 1837	Mary Dyer	English missionary
b. 1909	Ethel Merman	American actor
b. 1932	Dian Fossey	American zoologist
d. 1794	Edward Gibbon	English historian
d. 1942	Carole Lombard	American actor
d. 1981	Bernard Lee	English actor

Hampton Court Conference

Elizabeth I, who became queen in 1558 and reigned for forty-five years, sought to establish a state-approved church with Reformation principles. This was in response to religious movements in Europe and growing discord between Protestants and Catholics.

Her successor, James I, had to deal with the demands of Puritans who were keen to rid the church of the remnants of Catholicism. They sent the king a petition signed by ten percent of all the clergy. This urged the king to set the church in order, to rid the church of the remnants of Catholicism.

James called the Puritan leaders together to discuss their ideas when he convened a Court Conference in Hampton Court Palace in 1604.

On this day in 1604 the Puritans were brought to the king's chamber. The Puritans stressed four points:

> The Doctrine of the Church to be according to God's Word;
> Good pastors be planted in churches to preach the same;
> Church government to be ministered according to God's Word;
> The Book of Common Prayer might be suited more to the increase of piety.

As a result, the king authorized a translation of the Scriptures. Fourty-eight godly scholars were convened in three committees. The committees, meeting at Oxford, Cambridge, and Westminster, each took a section of the Bible. When they had completed their work of making a literal translation, their colleagues then reviewed the translation made. Perhaps in no other period have men of such scholarship who were also men of faith been brought together in such a noble cause. The result was the Authorized Version of the Bible.

Noteworthy

1545 Georg Spalatin, German reformer and Luther's coworker and associate, died (b. January 17, 1484).
1547 Ivan the Terrible was crowned Czar of Russia.
1737 "O God of Jacob, by Whose Hand" was written by Philip Doddridge.
1890 The Moody Bible Institute in Chicago was dedicated.
1920 Prohibition began as the Eighteenth Amendment to the U.S. Constitution took effect.
1944 Gen. Dwight D. Eisenhower took command of the Allied invasion force in London.
1992 Civil war in El Salvador ended.
2001 Laurent Kabila, president of the Democratic Republic of Congo, was assassinated.
2003 The space shuttle Columbia and its crew of seven blasted off from Cape Canaveral. The shuttle broke up during its return descent on February 1, killing everyone onboard.
2004 Pop star Michael Jackson pleaded innocent to child molestation charges.
2006 Africa's first elected female head of state, Ellen Johnson Sirleaf, was sworn in as Liberia's new president.

*J*ANUARY 17

DAILY READING

If I rise on the wings of the dawn, if I settle on the far side of the sea, even there your hand will guide me, your right hand will hold me fast. (PS 139:9–10)

FEAST DAYS

356	Anthony the Great	Father of Western monasticism
420	Sabinus	Bishop of Piacenza, Italy
764	Joseph	Bishop of Freising, Germany

ENTRANCE AND EXIT

b. 1706	Benjamin Franklin	American inventor and statesman
b. 1820	Anne Brontë	English writer
b. 1942	Muhammad Ali	American boxer
d. 1893	Rutherford Hayes	19th American president
d. 1911	Francis Galton	English scientist
d. 2005	Virginia Mayo	American actor

Wassailing the Apple Trees

The ancient custom of wassailing fruit trees with hot cider on Old Twelfth Eve (January 17) was popular in many parts of Devonshire. Since ancient times, the apple has been considered the "food of the gods," and wassailing the apple trees has in at least one form continued this reverence for hundreds of years.

The tradition involved the farmer and his men going to the orchard bearing a large can or milk pail full of hot cider with roasted apples hissing in it. They then encircled one of the finest trees and chanted three times the following quaint doggerel rhymes, or some variation thereof:

Here's to thee
Old apple-tree!
Whence thou may bud
And whence thou mayst blow,
And whence thou mayst bear
Apples enow;
Hats full! Caps full!
Bushels, bushels, sacks full!
And my pockets full too!
Huzza! huzza!

Having thus gained a thirst, the men's tankards were filled and they drank success to the next crop. Special blessing and prayers were said to the trees, and thanks given. Finally, a quantity of cider was poured over the tree for luck. Only the most fruitful trees were honored in this way, and any that bore little or no fruit were ignored.

The Wassailing Bowl

The ceremony of wassailing not only occurred in the orchard, but it also came into every house in some areas. A wassailing bowl was prepared, traditionally made from apple wood and sometimes elaborately carved and ornate. The bowl contained a mixture of spices, roasted apples, sugar, and hot ale and in some areas even egg and thick cream floating on the surface, which was known as lamb's wool. The wassailers often carried bunches of greenery, hung with apples, oranges, and brightly colored ribbon. At every house they visited, they would sing a traditional song and ask for alms. In return they would wish everyone good luck for the coming year and let them taste their hot and spicy brew. The song was often sung like this:

Our Wassailing, we do fill
With apples and with spice
Then grant us your goodwill
To taste here once or twice
Of our good Wassailing.

*J*ANUARY 18

DAILY READING

When Jesus came to the region of Caesarea Philippi, he asked his disciples, "Who do people say the Son of Man is?" They replied, "Some say John the Baptist; others say Elijah; and still others, Jeremiah or one of the prophets." "But what about you?" he asked. "Who do you say I am?" Simon Peter answered, "You are the Christ, the Son of the living God." (MATT 16:13–16)

FEAST DAYS

496	Volusian	Bishop of Tours, France
1271	Margaret of Hungary	Daughter of King Bela IV
1272	Fazzio of Verona	Founder of the *Order of the Holy Spirit*

ENTRANCE AND EXIT

b. 1882	Alan Alexander Milne	English writer
b. 1904	Archibald Leach (Cary Grant)	English actor
b. 1955	Kevin Costner	American actor
d. 1862	John Tyler	10th American president
d. 1980	Cecil Beaton	English photographer
d. 1989	Bruce Chatwin	Australian writer

The Confession of St. Peter the Apostle

On this day the Anglican and Roman Catholic Church celebrates the confession of St. Peter. Jesus' response to Peter rewards his faith, "You are Peter, and on this rock will I build my church." This rough fisherman and his brother Andrew were the first disciples called by Jesus. Peter figures prominently in the gospel accounts, often stumbling, impetuous, intense, and uncouth. It was Peter who attempted to walk on the sea, and began to sink; it was Peter who impulsively wished to build three tabernacles on the mountain of the Transfiguration; it was Peter who, just before the crucifixion, three times denied knowing his Lord.

After Pentecost, Peter was the head of the apostles. He spoke first to the crowds that had assembled after the descent of the Holy Spirit at Pentecost; he was the first apostle to perform miracles in the name of the Lord, and he rendered judgment upon the deceitful Ananias and Sapphira. Peter was instrumental in bringing the gospel to the Gentiles.

Tradition holds that Peter died in Rome and that his martyrdom came during the reign of Emperor Nero, probably in 64. He was crucified on the Vatican Hill upside down because he declared himself unworthy to die in the same manner as the Lord. His relics are now enshrined under the high altar of St. Peter's in Rome.

Noteworthy

1460 The bull *Execrabilis* issued by Pope Pius II (1405–64) further established the pope's power.

1778 Capt. James Cook became the first European to discover the Hawaiian Islands, which he dubbed the "Sandwich Islands."

1782 Lawyer and statesman Daniel Webster was born in Salisbury, New Hampshire.

1788 The first English settlers arrived in Australia's Botany Bay to establish a penal colony.

1815 Constantin von Tischendorf, discoverer of the Codex Sinaiticus, was born at Lengenfeld, near Plauen, in the Saxon Vogtland, Germany (d. December 7, 1874).

1919 The World War I peace conference opened in Versailles, France.

1943 The Soviets announced that they had broken the long Nazi siege of Leningrad.

2005 The world's largest commercial jet, an Airbus A380 that can carry 800 passengers, was unveiled in Toulouse, France.

*J*ANUARY 19

DAILY READING

We are not of those who shrink back and are destroyed,
but of those who believe and are saved. (HEB 10:39)

FEAST DAYS

ca. 777	Fillan	Patron against insanity
1095	Wulfstan	Patron of Worcester
1156	Henry of Uppsalla	Patron of Finland

ENTRANCE AND EXIT

b. 1736	James Watt	Scottish inventor
b. 1839	Paul Cézanne	French artist
b. 1946	Julian Barnes	English writer
d. 1954	Sydney Greenstreet	American actor
d. 1998	Carl Perkins	American singer
d. 2000	Hedy Lamarr	American actor

Bishop Wulfstan of Worcester

Wulfstan (or Wulstan) (1008–95) was the founder of Worcester Cathedral. Both his father and mother had embraced monasticism in mature life and their son, after having been educated in the great monastery of Medeshamstead (Peterborough), became a monk at Worcester and, eventually, bishop. Wulfstan, it is said, enjoyed his food and had a particular liking for roast goose. One day, he gave the order for such a bird to be prepared for dinner. He then went about his ordinary business. In due time, he entered the church in a state of extreme hunger. He passed into the chancel, near to which, unfortunately, the kitchen was placed. The savor interfered with his devotions as his thoughts wandered to his dinner, but, fortunately, his conscience reproached him. His resolution was immediate. There and then before the altar, he vowed that, from that time forth, he would never taste meat; and he remained a vegetarian for the rest his life–except on festivals, when he ate fish.

Wulfstan's life was not just of study thoughtful retirement, but of ministering to the common people, supplying the deficiencies of the parochial clergy, and preaching. He rode on horseback, with his retinue of clerks and monks, through his diocese, repeating the Psalter, the litanies, and the office for the dead; his chamberlain always had a purse ready, and "no one ever begged of Wulfstan in vain." In these progresses he came into personal contact with all his flock, high and low–with the rude crowds, beggars and serfs, craftsmen and laborers.

Julian Barnes

The English novelist Julian Barnes was a journalist, contributing to *The Times Literary Supplement, The New Review,* and *The New Statesman,* and was deputy literary editor for the *Sunday Times* before he became a critically acclaimed novelist. His books include:

1980 *Metroland*
–Somerset Maugham Award
1980 *Duffy*
1981 *Fiddle City*
1982 *Before She Met Me*
1984 *Flaubert's Parrot*
–Geoffrey Faber Memorial Prize
1985 *Putting the Boot In*
1986 *Staring at the Sun*
1987 *Going to the Dogs*
1989 *A History of the World in 101/2 Chapters*
1991 *Talking It Over*
–Prix Fémina Étranger (France)
1991 *The Porcupine*
1995 *Letters from London 1990–95*
1996 *Cross Channel*
1998 *England, England*
–Booker Prize for Fiction Shortlist
2000 *Love, etca.*
2002 *Something to Declare: French Essays*
2003 *The Pedant in the Kitchen*
2004 *The Lemon Table*
2005 *Arthur and George*
–Commonwealth Writers Prize

January 20

DAILY READING

There is no fear in love. But perfect love drives out fear,
because fear has to do with punishment.
The one who fears is not made perfect in love. (1 JOHN 4:18)

FEAST DAYS

ca. 250	Fabian	Pope
ca. 288	Sebastian	Patron of archers
473	Euthymius the Great	Bishop of Jerusalem

ENTRANCE AND EXIT

b. 1669	Susanna Wesley	Mother of John and Charles Wesley
b. 1896	George Burns	American actor and comedian
b. 1946	David Lynch	American film director
d. 1936	George V	King of England
d. 1984	Johnny Weissmuller	American actor
d. 1990	Barbara Stanwyck	American actor

The Eve of St. Agnes

Agnes was a fourth-century Christian virgin and martyr, venerated in both the Eastern and Western churches. Her story is told in the works of St. Jerome, Prudentius, St. Ambrose, and Pope Damasus I, although there are conflicting versions of her martyrdom.

When she was around fourteen years of age, she refused marriage to a host of suitors because of her dedication to Christ. She was denounced as a Christian during the reign of Diolcletian and sent to a house of prostitution as her punishment. When a young man ventured to touch her, he lost his sight, but he then regained it in answer to her prayers. Shortly thereafter she was executed and buried on the Via Nomentana in Rome in a catacomb, and a church was built over her tomb about AD 350.

Her feast day is on January 21, and she is often portrayed with a lamb, a symbol of innocence. To this day, on January 21, two lambs are blessed at her church in Rome. Their wool is then woven into palliums (bands of white wool), which the Pope confers on archbishops as a token of their jurisdiction.

There are lots of stories surrounding the legend of St. Agnes, and she has been the subject of paintings, songs, and a long poem by John Keats written in 1820 and poems by Ben Johnson and Alfred Lord Tennyson. It is said that by performing certain rituals, a virgin might see her true love in a dream on the Eve of St. Agnes. These rituals include going without supper; reciting the Pater Noster while pulling a row of pins from your sleeve; taking sprigs of rosemary and thyme and sprinkling them with water, placing a shoe on either side of the bed and saying, "St. Agnes, that's to lovers kind, come, ease the trouble of my mind."

Extract from "The Eve of St. Agnes" by John Keats

They told her how, upon St. Agnes' Eve,
Young virgins might have visions of delight,
And soft adorings from their loves receive
Upon the honey'd middle of the night,
If ceremonies due they did aright;
As, supperless to bed they must retire,
And couch supine their beauties, lily white;
Nor look behind, nor sideways, but require
Of Heaven with upward eyes for all that
they desire.

Extract from "St. Agnes' Eve" by Alfred Lord Tennyson

Deep on the convent-roof the snows
Are sparkling to the moon:
My breath to heaven like vapour goes:
May my soul follow soon!
The shadows of the convent-towers
Slant down the snowy sward,
Still creeping with the creeping hours
That lead me to my Lord:
Make Thou my spirit pure and clear
As are the frosty skies,
Or this first snowdrop of the year
That in my bosom lies.

*J*ANUARY 21

DAILY READING

"It is I; don't be afraid." Then they were willing to take him into the boat, and immediately the boat reached the shore where they were heading. (JOHN 6:20–21)

FEAST DAYS

ca. 112	Publius	Chief of Malta
496	Epiphanius the Peacemaker	Bishop of Pavia, Italy
861	Meginrat	Patron of Swabia, Germany

ENTRANCE AND EXIT

b. 1804	Eliza Roxcy Snow Smith	American poet
b. 1922	Paul Schofield	English actor
b. 1940	Jack Nicklaus	American golfer
d. 1683	Anthony Ashley Cooper	English Earl
d. 1950	George Orwell	English writer
d. 2002	Peggy Lee	American singer

King Louis XVI Executed

The execution of King Louis XVI of France was witnessed by an English priest, Henry Essex Edgeworth, who was living in France on this day in 1793. He recorded this momentous event thus:

> The path leading to the scaffold was extremely rough and difficult to pass; the King was obliged to lean on my arm, and from the slowness with which he proceeded, I feared for a moment that his courage might fail; but what was my astonishment, when arrived at the last step, I felt that he suddenly let go my arm, and I saw him cross with a firm foot the breadth of the whole scaffold; silence, by his look alone, fifteen or twenty drums that were placed opposite to me; and in a voice so loud, that it must have been heard it the Pont Tournant, I heard him pronounce distinctly these memorable words: "I die innocent of all the crimes laid to my charge; I Pardon those who have occasioned my death; and I pray to God that the blood you are going to shed may never be visited on France."
>
> He was proceeding, but the beating of the drums drowned his voice. His executioners then laid hold of him, and an instant after, his head was separated from his body; this was about a quarter past ten o'clock.

After the execution, the people threw their hats up in the air, and cried out *Vive la Nation*! Some of them endeavored to seize the body, but it was removed by a strong guard to the temple, and the lifeless remains of the king were exempted from those outrages which his Majesty had experienced during his life.

Jack Nicklaus

The greatest golfer of all time, Jack Nicklaus still holds the record for the most number of major championship victories (18):

U.S. Masters: 1963, 1965, 1966, 1972, 1975, 1986

British Open: 1966, 1970, 1978

U.S. Open: 1962, 1967, 1972, 1980

U.S. PGA: 1963, 1971, 1973, 1975, 1980

January 22

DAILY READING

When you are brought before synagogues, rulers and authorities, do not worry about how you will defend yourselves or what you will say, for the Holy Spirit will teach you at that time what you should say. (LUKE 12:11–12)

FEAST DAYS

380	Vincent	Archdeacon of Saragossa, Spain
628	Magundat	Patron of goldsmiths
1045	Brithwold of Sarum	Bishop of Ramsbury, England

ENTRANCE AND EXIT

b. 1775	Andre Marie Ampère	French scientist
b. 1788	Lord Byron	English poet
b. 1940	John Hurt	English actor
d. 1901	Victoria	English queen
d. 1973	Lyndon Johnson	36th American president
d. 1994	Telly Savalas	American actor

St. Vincent's Day

In the fourth century, Vincent was archdeacon of the church at Saragossa, Spain, but he also preached there because Valerian, the bishop, had a speech impediment. He appeared with Valerian when they were brought before the Emperor Diocletian. Valerian was sent to be stretched on the rack–his flesh was torn with hooks and he was bound in a chair of red-hot iron; lard and salt were rubbed into his wounds; and amid all this he kept his eyes raised to heaven, and remained unmoved. He was cast into a solitary dungeon, with his feet in the stocks, but the angels of Christ illuminated the darkness and assured Vincent that he was near his triumph. His wounds were now tended to prepare him for fresh torments, and the faithful were permitted to gaze on his mangled body. They came in troops, kissed the open sores, and carried away as relics cloths dipped in his blood. Before the tortures could recommence, the martyr's hour came, and he breathed forth his soul in peace.

The weather on St. Vincent's Day is supposedly indicative of the climate for the rest of the year, as expressed in this traditional rhyme:

Remember on St. Vincent's Day,
If the sun his beams display,
Be sure to mark the transient beam,
Which through the casement sheds a gleam,
For 'tis a token bright and clear
Of prosperous weather all the year.

Noteworthy

1917 President Woodrow Wilson pleaded for an end to war in Europe, calling for "peace without victory."
1922 Pope Benedict XV died.
1944 Allied forces began landing at Anzio, Italy, during World War II.
1970 The Boeing 747 went on its first regularly scheduled commercial flight, from New York to London.
1995 Rose Fitzgerald Kennedy, the mother of President John F. Kennedy, died.
2006 Evo Morales, Bolivia's first native Indian president, took office.

JANUARY 23

DAILY READING

For Christ's love compels us, because we are convinced that one died for all, and therefore all died. And he died for all, that those who live should no longer live for themselves but for him who died for them and was raised again. (2 COR 5:14–15)

FEAST DAYS

ca. 616	John the Almsgiver	Archbishop of Alexandria
702	Colman	Bishop of Lismore, Ireland
1419	Vincent Ferrer	Spanish missionary

ENTRANCE AND EXIT

b. 1832	Edouard Manet	French artist
b. 1930	Derek Walcott	West Indian writer
d. 1944	Rutger Hauer	Dutch actor
d. 1806	William Pitt (the Younger)	English prime minister
d. 1875	Charles Kingsley	English writer
d. 1976	Paul Robeson	American actor

Blaise Pascal–Lettres provinciales

On this day in 1656, Blaise Pascal (1623–62) published the first of his eighteen *Provincial Letters*. The majority attacked the Jesuit theories of grace and moral theology, the rationalism of Descartes, and Montaigne's skepticism, urging a return to the Augustine's doctrine of grace. Pascal was a French polymath–a celebrated writer, religious philosopher, physicist, and mathematician.

At eighteen, Pascal invented a calculating device (the Pascaline) to help his father's tax computations. He made important contributions to geometry and calculus, and developed the theory of probability. In physics, Pascal's law is the basis for all modern hydraulic operations.

On November 23, 1654, Pascal experienced a Christian conversion that would cause his outstanding scientific work to take second place in his pursuits. For the rest of his life, Pascal carried around a piece of parchment sewn into his coat describing how he had experienced God's forgiveness of his sins. From that day forward, Blaise Pascal decided he must live only for God. Pascal wrote that we come to know God's truth not only by reason, but even more through the heart by faith.

Noteworthy

1167 Aben Ezra (Abraham ben Meir ibn Ezra), Jewish poet, grammarian, and commentator, died (b. 1092 or 1093, Toledo, Spain).

1719 Principality of Liechtenstein constituted.

1789 A Catholic academy, now Georgetown University, was founded by Father John Carroll in Washington, D.C., as the first Roman Catholic college in America.

1893 Phillips Brooks, an American Episcopal clergyman, died (b. December 13, 1835).

1901 Francis (Franz) Arnold Hoffmann, one of the founding members of the Missouri Synod, a teacher, pastor, statesman, and cofounder of Republican Party, died (b. June 5, 1822).

1924 First Labour Government formed in England with Ramsay MacDonald as prime minister.

1933 Twentieth Amendment to U.S. Constitution ratified; date of presidential inauguration fixed as January 20.

1943 Tripoli captured by British troops.

*J*ANUARY 24

DAILY READING

Fight the good fight of the faith; take hold of the eternal life, to which you were called and for which you made the good confession in the presence of many witnesses. (1 TIMOTHY 6:12)

FEAST DAYS

ca. 2nd cent.	Macedonius the Barley Eater	Syrian hermit
ca. 268	Zama	Bishop of Bologna, Italy
1622	Francis de Sales	Patron of writers

ENTRANCE AND EXIT

b. 1732	Pierre Augustin Caron de Beaumarchais	French writer
b. 1862	Edith Wharton	American writer
b. 1982	John Belushi	American actor
d. 1527	Felix Manz	Swiss theologian
d. 1895	Lord Randolph Churchill	English politician
d. 1965	Sir Winston Churchill	English Prime Minister

Timothy

In the Julian Calendar this was the feast of St. Timothy, bishop, martyr, and faithful companion of St. Paul.

The fourth-century bishop and historian Eusebius says that Timothy became the first Bishop of Ephesus around AD 50. Born at Lystra in Asia Minor, Timothy's mother Eunice was a Jewess, but his father was a pagan; and though Timothy had read the Scriptures from his childhood, he had not been circumcised as a Jew. He became one of St. Paul's most famous converts and a fervent evangelist.

Paul and Barnabas visited Lystra on their first missionary journey (AD 44–46). Paul was stoned and left for dead by the Jews, and Timothy tended to his wounds. A few years later, Paul returned to Lystra, this time with Silas. By this time, Timothy was already a respected member of the church, as was his grandmother Lois.

In company with St. Paul he visited the cities of Asia Minor and Greece. At Ephesus, he received the two epistles that bear his name, the first written from Macedonia and the second from Rome, in which St. Paul from his prison gives vent to his desire to see his "dearly beloved son."

An apocryphal *Acts of Timothy*, dating from the second century, describes his martyrdom on January 22 in the year 97 (Julian calendar), when protesting at the licentious festivities in honor of Diana of the Ephesians. His relics are believed to have been translated to Constantinople on this day in the year 356.

Noteworthy

41	Claudius I, became Roman Emperor following murder of Caligula.
1236	Henry III married Eleanor of Provence.
1848	Gold discovered at Sutter's Mill, California, by James Wilson Marshall, starting California gold rush.
1908	First Boy Scout Troup founded in Britain by Lord Robert Baden-Powell.
1924	St. Petersburg in Russia renamed Leningrad.
1972	Japanese soldier, Shoichi Yokoi, discovered on Guam jungle believing World War II was still being fought.
1984	Macintosh computer launched by Steven Jobs at Apple Computer.
1986	First photographs from space of Planet Uranus taken from Voyager 2 revealed fifteen moons and eleven rings.
1999	First successful hand transplant performed in Louisville, Kentucky, on Matthew David Scott from New Jersey.

*J*ANUARY 25

DAILY READING

For it is commendable if a man bears up under the pain of unjust suffering because he is conscious of God. (1 PET 2:19)

FEAST DAYS

ca. 65	Confession of St. Paul	Apostle
380	Bretannion	Bishop of Tomi, Romania
660	Ragnobert	Bishop of Autun, France

ENTRANCE AND EXIT

b. 1627	Robert Boyle	Irish scientist
b. 1736	Joseph Louis Lagrange	French mathematician
b. 1981	Alicia Keys	American singer
d. 1947	Al Capone	American gangster
d. 1990	Ava Gardner	American actor
d. 2005	Philip Johnson	American architect

Burns Night

On this day, Scots throughout the world celebrate the life and works of one of their best-loved sons, the bard Robert Burns (1759–96). The traditional form of celebration is by holding Burns Suppers. A Burns Night supper usually begins with Burns's own Selkirk Grace: "Some hae meat and canna eat, And some wad eat that want it; But we hae meat and we can eat, And sae the Lord be thankit."

The menu usually consists of cock-a-leekie soup (or Scotch broth) and haggis with "tatties and neeps" (potatoes and turnips), and Tipsy Laird (sherry trifle) followed by oatcakes and cheese, all washed down with liberal tots of quality Scotch whisky.

The haggis is "piped" in–brought in ceremoniously by the chef accompanied by a piper–and "addressed" with Burns's own poem–"Address to a Haggis"–before being cut and served.

Traditional speeches include numerous references to the genius of Burns, recitations of his poems and the glory of Scotland.

Traditional Haggis Recipe –Robert H. Christie (1911)

Clean a sheep's pluck thoroughly. Make incisions in the heart and liver to allow the blood to flow out, and parboil them, letting the windpipe lie over the side of the pot to permit the phlegm and blood to disgorge from the lungs; change the water after a few minutes boiling for fresh water. Another half hour's boiling will be sufficient; but throw back the half of the liver to boil until it will grate easily.

Take the heart, the half of the liver and the lungs, trimming away all skins and black-looking parts, and mince them together along with a pound of good beef suet. Grate the other half of the liver. Have eight onions peeled and scalded in two waters, which chop and mix with this mince. Toast some oatmeal before the fire till it is of a light brown colour and perfectly dry. Less than two teaspoonfuls of meal will do for this quantity of meat. Spread the mince on a board and strew the meal lightly over it, with a high seasoning of pepper, salt, a little cayenne and marjoram, well mixed.

Have a sheep's stomach perfectly clean, and see that there is no thin part in it in case of its bursting. Put in the meat with a half-pint of good beef gravy, or as much strong broth and the juice of a lemon or a little good vinegar as will make a thick stew. Be careful not to fill the bag too full so as to allow the meat room to swell. Press out the air and sew up the bag; prick it with a large needle when it first swells in the pot, to prevent bursting; let it boil slowly for three hours if large.

Traditional Haggis Recipe

Fair fa' your honest, sonsie face,
Great chieftain o' the pudden race

–Robert Burns

JANUARY 26

DAILY READING

After they prayed, the place where they were meeting was shaken. And they were all filled with the Holy Spirit and spoke the word of God boldly. (ACTS 4:31)

FEAST DAYS

ca. 96	Titus	Bishop of Crete
648	Conan of Iona	Bishop of Isle of Man
1943	Michael Kozal	Bishop of Wloclawek, Poland

ENTRANCE AND EXIT

b. 1880	Douglas MacArthur	American general
b. 1925	Paul Newman	American actor
b. 1961	Wayne Gretsky	Canadian ice hockey star
d. 1828	Lady Caroline Lamb	English writer
d. 1949	Peter Marshall	Scottish theologian
d. 1998	Shinichi Suzuki	Japanese violinist

Australia Day

On this day in 1788, Admiral Arthur Phillip, Governor-Designate of New South Wales led the English First Fleet into Sydney Cove to establish the Australian colony. The party consisted of a few free men, but mostly convicts who had left England in May 1787.

This momentous event is today remembered as the founding of the modern nation of Australia. It is a national holiday in Australia celebrated by official parades, lunches, dinners, awards, and historical reenactments. Families enjoy barbecues with friends or family, enjoy a day at the beach, join community celebrations, or play sports like cricket. This is the biggest national celebration in the country.

One of the most prominent ceremonies is the award for the Australian of the Year. This has been awarded annually since 1960 and the winner in 2007 was the scientist and writer Professor Tim Flannery. Previous winners have included cricketer Steve Waugh (2004), tennis player Pat Rafter (2002), and the actor Paul Hogan (1985).

Australian National Anthem

"Advance Australia Fair" was formally adopted as the National Anthem in 1974; previously it was "God Save the Queen" and the unofficial anthem is "Waltzing Matilda."

"Advance Australia Fair"
by Pete Dodds McCormick

Australians all let us rejoice,
For we are young and free;
We've golden soil and wealth for toil;
Our home is girt by sea;
Our land abounds in nature's gifts
Of beauty rich and rare;
In history's page, let every stage
Advance Australia Fair.
In joyful strains then let us sing,
Advance Australia Fair.

Beneath our radiant Southern Cross
We'll toil with hearts and hands;
To make this Commonwealth of ours
Renowned of all the lands;
For those who've come across the seas
We've boundless plains to share;
With courage let us all combine
To Advance Australia Fair.
In joyful strains then let us sing,
Advance Australia Fair.

*J*ANUARY 27

DAILY READING

But we have this treasure in jars of clay to show that this all-surpassing power is from God and not from us. (2 COR 4:7)

FEAST DAYS

ca. 3rd cent.	Julian	Bishop of Le Mans, France
555	Maire	Founder of Bodon Abbey, France
672	Vitalianus	Pope

ENTRANCE AND EXIT

b. 1756	Wolfgang Amadeus Mozart	Austrian composer
b. 1885	Jerome Kern	American composer
b. 1964	Bridget Fonda	American actor
d. 1901	Giuseppe Verdi	Italian composer
d. 1972	Mahalia Jackson	American singer
d. 1989	Thomas Sopwith	English aircraft designer

International Holocaust Memorial Day

The United Nations designated January 27 as International Holocaust Memorial Day in 2005. This date was chosen to coincide with the anniversary of the liberation of the Auschwitz-Birkenau concentration and extermination camp, seen as a powerful symbol of the horrors of the Holocaust.

The objectives of the day are to:

- To provide a national mark of respect for victims of Nazi persecution.
- To raise awareness and understanding of the Holocaust as a continuing issue for humanity.
- To reflect on recent genocides that raise similar issues.
- To assert a continuing commitment to oppose racism, anti-Semitism, victimization, and genocide.
- To promote a democratic society that respects and celebrates diversity.
- To highlight the values of universal human dignity and good citizenship.

This is a somber day to remember and learn from the lessons of the past. It provides an opportunity to commemorate all those who were victims of the Holocaust and Nazi persecution, as well as the victims of racism and discrimination in other genocides.

In the United Kingdom, Prime Minister Tony Blair announced the establishment of Holocaust Memorial Day in 2000 and the first commemoration took place in 2001.

First they came for the communists, and I did not speak out—because I was not a communist;
Then they came for the socialists, and I did not speak out—because I was not a socialist;
Then they came for the trade unionists, and I did not speak out—because I was not a trade unionist;
Then they came for the Jews, and I did not speak out—because I was not a Jew;
Then they came for me—and there was no one left to speak out for me.

—Friedrich Gustav Emil Martin Niemöller (1892–1984), German theologian

*J*ANUARY 28

DAILY READING

I pray that out of his glorious riches he may strengthen you with power through his Spirit in your inner being. (EPH 3:16)

FEAST DAYS

814	Charles the Great	King of the Franks
1159	Amadeus of Lausanne	Chancellor of Burgundy
1274	Thomas Aquinas	Angelic Doctor

ENTRANCE AND EXIT

b. 1457	Henry VIII	King of England
b. 1856	Rueben Archer Torrey	American evangelist
b. 1981	Elijah Wood	American actor
d. 1596	Sir Francis Drake	English explorer
d. 1937	William Butler Yeats	Irish poet
d. 1986	Christa McAuliffe	American astronaut

Dr. Rueben Archer Torrey

Dr. Rueben Archer Torrey (1856–1928) was born on this day in 1856 in Hoboken, New Jersey. For many years, he was associate to the great evangelist Dwight L. Moody, one of the great Christian leaders of his era. Torrey was educated at Yale and also at various German universities. During his early years, he went through a time of extreme skepticism, but emerged as a staunch preacher of the faith.

He was the second president of the Moody Bible Institute, succeeding its founder in 1899. He wrote many books addressing the fundamentals of the Christian faith, including *How to Pray*, *The Deity of Jesus Christ*, *How to Work for Christ*, and *How to Be Inexpressibly Happy*.

Following in the steps of D. L. Moody, Torrey conducted a worldwide preaching tour and in Australia, became known as "the man with God a'back of him." He visited many countries, including Japan, India, New Zealand, England (several times), and Germany. At each crusade many hundreds of people came to faith. After his travels, Torrey turned his attention to assisting the Bible Institute of Los Angeles, where he led the Church of the Open Door.

From 1924 to 1928, he devoted his time to holding Bible conferences, giving special lectures at the Moody Bible Institute among other places. He made his home in Biltmore, North Carolina. He passed on quietly at Asheville, North Carolina.

St. Thomas Aquinas

St. Thomas was born of noble parents at Aquino in Italy, in 1226. At the age of nineteen he joined the Dominicans at Naples, where he was studying. Seized by his brothers on his way to Paris, he suffered two years' captivity in their castle of Rocca-Secca; but neither the caresses of his mother and sisters nor the threats and stratagems of his brothers could shake him in his vocation.

While St. Thomas was in captivity, his brothers endeavored to entrap him into the sin of fornication, but the attempt only ended in the triumph of his purity. Snatching from the hearth a burning brand, the saint drove from his chamber the woman whom they had there concealed. Then marking a cross upon the wall, he knelt down to pray, and forthwith, being rapt in ecstasy, an angel girded him with a cord, in token of the gift of perpetual chastity that God had given him. The pain caused by the girdle was so sharp that St. Thomas uttered a piercing cry, which brought his guards into the room. But he never told this to anyone other his confessor, a little while before his death.

From this came the confraternity of the "Angelic Warfare" for the preservation of the virtue of chastity. Having at length escaped, St. Thomas went to Cologne to study under Blessed Albert the Great, and after that to Paris, where for many years he taught philosophy and theology. The Catholic Church named him the Angelic Doctor and recognized the rarest gifts of intellect were combined in him with the tender piety.

*J*ANUARY 29

DAILY READING

Now to him who is able to do immeasurably more than all we ask or imagine, according to his power that is at work within us, to him be glory in the church and in Christ Jesus throughout all generations, for ever and ever! Amen. (EPH 3:20–21)

FEAST DAYS

ca. 320	Valerius	Bishop of Treves, Germany
523	Blath of Kildare	Cook
ca. 570	Gildas	British historian

ENTRANCE AND EXIT

b. 1820	George III	King of England
b. 1862	Frederick Delius	English composer
b. 1916	Victor Mature	American actor
d. 1888	Edward Lear	English writer
d. 1963	Robert Frost	American writer
d. 1980	Jimmy Durante	American comedian

"Tell Me the Old, Old Story"

On this day in 1866, the English evangelical poet Arabella Katherine Hankey (1834–1911) composed the words of one of the most loved hymns—"Tell Me the Old, Old Story."

Arabella grew up in Clapham, London, and her father was a prominent banker. Her family belonged to an evangelical group known as the Clapham Sect. They strongly supported the abolition of slavery in England and promoted missionary endeavors.

As a teenager, Arabella she taught Sunday school and began a Bible class for girls who clerked in the shops of London. She went to South Africa to work as a nurse and to bring home her invalid brother. While there she traveled through the "up country" by ox cart, and this experience increased her interest in foreign missions.

Three years after she wrote the words to "Tell Me the Old, Old Story," the highly respected music teacher and choral conductor William Fischer composed the tune to the hymn. The lyrics are similar to another Hankey hymn, "I Love to Tell the Story," because they come from the same original poem that Hankey composed whilst recuperating from a long illness.

Speaking of the purpose behind the hymn she said, "God's remedy for sin is something I want to understand, and I want to hear it often, lest I forget it. As weak as I am, I cannot think too well or too fast. I need to have the story explained to me as a little child."

Tell Me the Old, Old Story

Tell me the old, old story, Of unseen things above,
Of Jesus and His glory, Of Jesus and His love.
Tell me the story simply, As to a little child,
For I am weak and weary, And helpless and defiled.

Refrain:
Tell me the old, old story,
Tell me the old, old story,
Tell me the old, old story
Of Jesus and His love.

Tell me the story slowly, That I may take it in—
That wonderful redemption, God's remedy for sin.
Tell me the story often, For I forget so soon;
The early dew of morning Has passed away at noon.

Tell me the story softly, With earnest tones and grave;
Remember, I'm the sinner Whom Jesus came to save.
Tell me the story always, If you would really be,
In any time of trouble, A comforter to me.

Tell me the same old story When you have cause to fear
That this world's empty glory Is costing me too dear.
Yes, and when that world's glory Is dawning on my soul,
Tell me the old, old story—"Christ Jesus makes thee whole."

JANUARY 30

DAILY READING

But he said to me, "My grace is sufficient for you,
for my power is made perfect in weakness."
Therefore I will boast all the more gladly about my weaknesses,
so that Christ's power may rest on me. (2 COR 12:9)

FEAST DAYS

451	Arementarius	Bishop of Pavia, Italy
680	Bathild	Patron of widows
ca. 1100	Adelelmus	Patron of servants

ENTRANCE AND EXIT

b. 1882	Franklin Delano Roosevelt	32nd American president
b. 1937	Vanessa Redgrave	English actor
b. 1941	Richard Cheney	American vice president
d. 1649	Charles I	King of England
d. 1948	Orville Wright	American flight pioneer
d. 2006	Coretta Scott King	American civil rights pioneer

The Rise of the Bohemian Corporal

January 30th is notable because on this day Adolph Hitler, "the Bohemian corporal," was helped to power by a coalition of conservative politicians in 1933. Franz von Papen persuaded President von Hindenburg to nominate Hitler as Reich Chancellor. Days later he was asked to form a new government.

Within a month of his leadership, Hitler virtually ousted the conservatives from any real participation in government. He abolished free trade unions, eliminating the communists, Social Democrats, and Jews from any role in political life and sweeping opponents into concentration camps.

The Reichstag fire of February 27, 1933, provided him with the perfect pretext to begin consolidating the foundations of a totalitarian one-party state. Special "enabling laws" were forced through the Reichstag to legalize the regime's tactics.

It was the last election that Hitler allowed. Before the end of 1933, Hitler had effectively abolished civil liberties. The Nazi's were the sole power of Germany. Now they could pursue and execute the ideals that Adolf Hitler so openly wrote of barely nine years before.

Noteworthy

1847 Yerba Buena changes name to San Francisco.

1933 Lone Ranger radio program premieres on WXYZ in Detroit.

1948 On his way to prayers, Mahatma Gandhi is shot three times in the chest by Hindu extremist Nathuram Godse in Delhi.

1965 British state funeral for Winston Churchill draws a million mourners.

1969 Beatles' last record/film session together on roof of Apple Studios, London; they record "Get Back."

1991 The first major ground battle of the Gulf War is fought at the frontier port of Khafji in Saudi Arabia; eleven U.S. Marines are killed, seven of them by friendly fire.

2003 Richard Reid, the "shoe bomber," is sentenced to life in prison.

2005 Iraqis vote in their country's first free election in a half century.

*J*ANUARY 31

DAILY READING

In the presence of God and of Christ Jesus, who is to judge the living and the dead, and in view of his appearing and his kingdom, I solemnly urge you: proclaim the message; be persistent whether the time is favorable or unfavorable; convince, rebuke, and encourage, with the utmost patience in teaching. (2 TIM 4:1–2)

FEAST DAYS

632	Aedan	Bishop of Ferns, Ireland
1533	Louisa Albertoni	Franciscan miracle worker
1888	John Bosco	Patron of apprentices

ENTRANCE AND EXIT

b. 1797	Franz Peter Schubert	Austrian composer
b. 1915	Thomas Merton	French theologian
b. 1971	Minnie Driver	English actor
d. 1892	Charles Haddon Spurgeon	English theologian
d. 1974	Samuel Goldwyn	American film producer
d. 2006	Moira Shearer	Scottish actor

The Prince of Preachers

The largest megachurch of the Victorian Age was the Metropolitan Tabernacle in London England, which could accommodate seven thousand people. It was led by the popular Baptist minister Charles Haddon Spurgeon (1834–92), affectionately known as the "Prince of Preachers."

It is difficult to overstate the influence of Spurgeon. He preached his first sermon at sixteen years of age in a small cottage living room to a few people; years later he addressed over 23,500 in one service. It is estimated that in thirty-eight years of ministry he preached to more than ten million people–before the invention of modern transport, radios, microphones, or recording equipment.

He started Spurgeon's College, which graduated over nine hundred students while he was living, and it is still going strong today. He had sixty-six separate organizations in the church working under his direction, and many other ministries outside the premises.

He wrote over 140 separate books, three of which sold over a million copies while he has still living. One of these publications was a twenty-five-year compilation of 3,561 sermons, *The Metropolitan Tabernacle Pulpit*, a collection bound in sixty-three volumes. Beside these writings, he often wrote as many as five hundred letters a week–before there was a typewriter.

Samuel Goldwyn

As well as being a famous film producer, Sam Goldwyn has acquired a reputation for his mangling of the English language. This is a list of some of his best known verbal fluffs (although it is impossible to determine which ones can be definitely attributed to him):

"Gentlemen, include me out."

"Anyone who goes to a psychiatrist ought to have his head examined."

"They stayed away in droves."

"A bachelor's life is no life for a single man."

"Let's have some new clichés."

"Don't improve it into a flop!"

"Give me a smart idiot over a stupid genius any day."

"I don't want yes-men around me. I want everyone to tell the truth, even if it costs them their jobs."

"You fail to overlook the crucial point."

"Never make forecasts, especially about the future."

"I don't care if it doesn't make a nickel. I just want every man, woman, and child in America to see it."

"I had a great idea this morning, but I didn't like it."

February

And lastly, came cold February, sitting
In an old waggon, for he could not ride,
Drawne of two fishes, for the season fitting,
Which through the flood before did softly slyde
And swim away; yet had he by his side
His plough and harnesse fit to till the ground,
And tooles to prune the trees before the pride
Of hasting prime did make them burgeon round.

EDMUND SPENSER–*The Shepheardes Calender* (1579)

I am lustration, and the sea is mine!
I wash the sands and headlands with my tide;
My brow is crowned with branches of the pine;
Before my chariot-wheels the fishes glide.
By me all things unclean are purified,
By me the souls of men washed white again;
E'en the unlovely tombs of those who died
Without a dirge, I cleanse from every stain.

HENRY WADSWORTH LONGFELLOW–*The Poet's Calendar* (1882)

Proverbs ~

"February fills the dyke
Either with the black (rain) or white (snow)."

"A' the months o' the year
Curse a fair Februeer."

February ~

It is thought that February derives its name from the Roman word *Februare* meaning to expiate or purify. Religious purification ceremonies took place at the beginning of this month. Our Saxon ancestors called this month *Sol-monatt* (son month) and later *Sprout-Kale* as many of these vegetables grew at this time.

February is the shortest month because the Emperor Augustus added a day to August (the month named for him) from February which used to have thirty days in a leap year and twenty-nine at other times.

In the Northern Hemisphere, February is often cold and wet with much of the grip of the winter and a few signs of spring.

A Valentine to My Wife ~

You are as fair and sweet and tender,
   Dear brown-eyed little sweetheart mine,
As when, a callow youth and slender,
   I asked to be your Valentine.

What though these years of ours be fleeting?
   What though the years of youth be flown?
I'll mock old Tempus with repeating,
   "I love my love and her alone!"

And when I fall before his reaping,
   And when my stuttering speech is dumb,
Think not my love is dead or sleeping,
   But that it waits for you to come.

So take, dear love, this little token,
   And if there speaks in any line
The sentiment I'd fain have spoken,
   Say, will you kiss your Valentine?

–Eugene Field (1850–1895)

FEBRUARY 1

DAILY READING

O Lord, let your ear be attentive to the prayer of this your servant
and to the prayer of your servants who delight in revering your name.
Give your servant success today by granting him favor
in the presence of this man. (NEH 1:11)

FEAST DAYS

656	Sigebert III	King of Austrasia
1163	John of the Grating	Bishop of Aleth
1645	Henry Morse	English martyr

ENTRANCE AND EXIT

b. 1843	Sir John Isaac Thornycroft	English inventor
b. 1918	Dame Muriel Spark	English writer
b. 1967	Laura Dern	American actor
d. 1885	Sidney Gilchrist Thomas	English inventor
d. 1976	Werner Karl Heisenberg	German scientist
d. 1966	Joseph Frank (Buster) Keaton Jr.	American actor

St. Brigit

The Patron of Ireland, St. Brigit (or St. Bride) was born in 453, shortly after St. Patrick, the daughter of an Irish prince and a druidic slave. As she grew up she became remarkable for her piety and was the first nun in Ireland. She built her first cell under a large oak, which had perhaps been the site of pagan worship in earlier times, and from whence it was named Kildara (modern day Kildare), or the cell of the oak.

The convent developed into a center of learning and spirituality, famed for its illuminated manuscripts. The most famous of which, the Book of Kildare, was one of the finest of all illuminated Irish manuscripts that was, tragically, lost over three hundred years ago.

Details of Bride's life are unclear, but a poem ascribed to her gives us a picture of her character:

I long for a great lake of ale
I long for the meats of belief and pure piety
I long for flails of penance at my house
I long for them to have barrels full of peace
I long to give away jars full of love
I long for them to have cellars full or mercy
I long for cheerfulness to be in their drinking
I long for Jesus too to be there among them.

Tradition records that St. Brigit died at Kildare on this day in 525 and was buried at the same site as St. Patrick. It is customary to carry on Brigit's tradition of sharing with the poor by baking a cake and offering it to needy people.

Deep Impact

In 2002 journalists were excited by an announcement from NASA and the U.S. Airforce's Linear Observatory. Astronomers revealed that a two-kilometer asteroid (NT7) was due to collide with our planet on February 1, 2019, at 11:47 a.m., at an impact velocity of eighteen miles a second. NT7 was first spotted on July 9, 2002. A deep impact could wipe out an entire continent, plunge the world into a nuclear winter, or take humanity to the brink of extinction. The odds of an impact in 2019 have been estimated to be one in 75,000.

Astronomers initially calculated at least seven potential impact dates beginning in 2019. Only one, February 1, 2060, has yet to be ruled out, but astronomers expect to dismiss that threat as well after more observations of the asteroid are made. A full-scale evaluation of NT7 will be made by the International Astronomical Union, the main international body responsible for announcing such risks. Objects the size of NT7 only hit the Earth every one or two million years.

*F*EBRUARY 2

DAILY READING

"Sovereign Lord, as you have promised, you now dismiss your servant in peace. For my eyes have seen your salvation, which you have prepared in the sight of all people, a light for revelation to the Gentiles and for glory to your people Israel." (LUKE 2:29–32)

FEAST DAYS

ca. 651	Adalbald d'Ostrevant	Patron of large families
880	Theodoric	Bishop of Ninden, Germany
1640	Joan de Lestonnac	Patron of widows

ENTRANCE AND EXIT

b. 1859	Henry Havelock Ellis	English physician and writer
b. 1915	Abba Eban	Israeli politician
b. 1962	Garth Brooks	American singer
d. 1907	Dimitri Mendeleyev	Russian scientist
d. 1970	Bertrand Russell	English mathematician
d. 1995	Donald Pleasance	English actor

Candlemas Day

According to a proclamation by Henry VIII in 1539, "On Candlemas Daye it shall be declared, that the bearynge of candels is done in the memorie of Christe the spirituall lyghte, whom Simeon dyd prophecye as it is redde in the Churche that daye."

This festival celebrates the presentation of the Lord in the Temple at Jerusalem and the Purification of the Virgin Mary. It also includes Simeon's prophecy when he blessed the Lord in the temple. Apparently, in consequence of the celebration of Mary's purification by candle-bearing, it became customary for women to carry candles with them, when, after recovery from childbirth, they went to be church.

The traditional prayer for Candlemas Day is:

> O Lord Jesu Christ, blesse thou this creature of a waxen taper at our humble supplication, and, by the vertue of the holy crosse, poure thou into it an heavenly benediction; that as thou hast graunted it unto mans use for the expelling of darknes, it may receave such a strength and blessing, thorow the token of thy holy crosse, that in what places soever it be lighted or set, the Divil may avoid out of these habitacions, and tremble for feare, and fly away discouraged, and presume no more to unquiete them that serve thee, who with God.

In Scotland, it is a custom for children to bless their teachers with gifts. Each school selects a king and queen, who reside over drinks and biscuits and are the guests of honor at a bonfire.

Another Scottish tradition is the "Candlemass Ba" football game between different parts of a town. In Jedburgh, this game is in the River Jed.

Weather Forecasting

The Romans adopted February 2nd as "Hedgehog Day." The Christian festival of Candlemas assimilated pagan customs including those associated with weather forecasting. An old English song claims:

> If Candlemas be fair and bright,
> Come, winter, have another flight.
> If Candlemas brings clouds and rain,
> Go, winter, and come not again.

In the nineteenth century, Germans immigrants to Pennsylvania looked to hedgehogs or groundhogs to predict the beginning of spring. If this day was sunny, the hedgehog or groundhog would emerge from hibernation. Seeing its shadow, the creature would run back in to continue its hibernation, thus indicating the continuation of winter. However, if the animal stays outside, then it is a prediction that spring has begun and good weather is on its way.

Today, Groundhog Day is celebrated by thousands of people who descend on the town of Punxsutawney, Pennsylvania, to observe whether the animal (named Phil) will emerge from or remain in its lair. The first Groundhog Day was in 1886, and its popularity has grown every year, particularly after the 1993 Bill Murray film *Groundhog Day*.

FEBRUARY 3

DAILY READING

God looks down from heaven on the sons of men to see
if there are any who understand, any who seek God. (PS 53:2)

FEAST DAYS

576	Lawrence the Illuminator	Patron of blind people
865	Ansgar	Patron of Denmark
1192	Margaret of England	Benedictine nun

ENTRANCE AND EXIT

b. 1821	Elizabeth Blackwell	American physician
b. 1950	Morgan Fairchild	American actor
b. 1956	Nathan Lane	American actor
d. 1924	Woodrow Wilson	28th American president
d. 1935	Hugo Junkers	German aircraft designer
d. 1989	John Cassavetes	American film director

Blessing the Throat

On this day in many Roman Catholic Churches, the ceremony of Blessing the Throat is performed. Two long candles are blessed and lit in the form of a St. Andrew's Cross. Sufferers from throat ailments kneel while the ribboned cross is laid under their chins, and their throats are gently stroked with the ends of the candles. As the candles touch the sufferers, the priest says to each in turn, "May the Lord deliver you from the evil of the throat, and from every other evil."

This ceremony derives from the life of St. Blaise, who was Bishop of Sebaste in Armenia. The most popular account of this saint–*The Acts of St. Blaise*–place his martyrdom in the reign of the Emperor Licinius around 316. Before becoming a bishop, Blaise may have been a physician, and it is thought that he, under divine command, fled to the Armenian mountains to escape Licinius's persecution of Christians.

He lived for some time in caves with wild animals, who he blessed and healed as the need arose. He is reputed to have rescued a pig from a wolf's fangs and restored it. For these actions, he is known as one of the patron saints of wild animals.

His most famous healing took place on his way to trial. A child who had swallowed a fish bone was about to die through choking. St. Blaise touched the child's throat and dislodged the bone, thus saving the child's life. For centuries after this act, St. Blaise has been invoked for every kind of throat ailment. It was common for country priests to remove throat obstructions by holding the sufferer in both hands and saying, "Blaise, the martyr and servant of Jesus Christ, commands thee to pass up and down."

Four Chaplains Day

On February 3, 1943, the U.S. ship *Dorchester* was torpedoed by a German U boat. On board were four chaplains from the Army Chaplain Corps. Unlike most of the other sailors, the four chaplains had gone to bed with their life jackets on. When the torpedo hit, many of the sailors could not find their life jackets in time. In an act of incredible selflessness, the four chaplains gave their own life jackets to other sailors, knowing that by doing so, they would go down with the sinking ship. Witnesses testified that the last they saw of the four chaplains, they had their arms together and were praying as the ship sank.

This act of courage was recognized with the award of posthumous medals of heroism and a special stamp, issued in 1948. Today, February 3rd is designated by the United States Congress as "Four Chaplains Day."

The four chaplains were:

• George L. Fox	Methodist minister
• Alexander D. Goode	Rabbi
• Clark V. Poling	Minister of the Dutch Reformed Church
• John P. Washington	Roman Catholic priest

FEBRUARY 4

DAILY READING

Grace to all who love our Lord Jesus Christ
with an undying love. (EPH 6:24)

FEAST DAYS

ca. 375	Isidore of Pelusium	Theologian
ca. 538	Theophilus the Penitent	Archdeacon of Adana, Cilicia
1302	Andrew Corsini	Apostle of Florence

ENTRANCE AND EXIT

b. 1749	Thomas Earnshaw	English inventor
b. 1906	Clyde William Tombaugh	American astronomer
b. 1973	Oscar De La Hoya	Mexican boxer
d. 211	Lucius Septimius Severus	Roman Emperor
d. 1983	Karen Carpenter	American singer
d. 2007	Barbara McNair	American actor

Giambattista della Porta

The Neapolitan scholar Giambattista della (John Baptist) Porta (b. 1535), who died on this day in 1615, was a great student of the natural and physical world. He visited most of his known world to gather and perfect the knowledge utilized in his many writings. His first work, *Magiae naturalis* (*Natural Magick*) was first published in 1558 in parts (written, according to the author, when he was fifteen years old). It was later expanded to twenty books and published as one volume in 1584.

Natural Magick became a great bestseller–it was translated from the original Latin into the principal European languages and republished in the Latin edition in many places for a hundred years. It is a work on cosmology, geology, optics, plant products, medicines, poisons, and cooking. It includes sections on the transmutation of the metals; distillation; artificial gems; the magnet and its properties; known remedies for a host of ailments; cosmetics used by women; fires; and clandestine writing.

In the treatment of these subjects Porta includes statements of the ancients from the time of Theophrastus and Aristotle, as well as the contemporary knowledge of his own time. The value of this book today is that it gives the reader a perspective of early scientists and the way they understood their universe. His information is definite and practical, and his work shows him to be a conscientious and scholarly student of literature, ancient and contemporary.

The Smithfield Martyr

On this day in 1555, Rev. John Rogers was burned at the stake at Smithfield, London. He was the first martyr during the reign of Mary I. He was the editor of the English Bible, published (1537) under the pseudonym Thomas Matthew.

A graduate of Cambridge University (1526), Rogers was made rector of Holy Trinity, Queenhithe, London. Two years later he became a chaplain to English merchants at Antwerp, where he was influenced by William Tyndale.

In 1553 when Mary I became queen, Rogers preached an anti-Catholic sermon warning against "pestilent Popery, idolatry and superstition" and was immediately placed under house arrest. In January 1554, he was sent him to Newgate, where he was imprisoned for a year. With ten other prisoners he was brought before a council in Southwark in January 1555 for examination, and within a week he was sentenced to death by burning for his heretical views.

His martyrdom is recorded in *Foxe's Book of Martyrs.*

FEBRUARY 5

DAILY READING

Haughty eyes and a proud heart,
the lamp of the wicked, are sin! (PROV 21:4)

FEAST DAYS

ca. 250	Agatha	Patron of breast cancer
ca. 710	Indract	Irish prince
1015	Adelaide of Bellich	Benedictine nun

ENTRANCE AND EXIT

b. 1788	Sir Robert Peel	English prime minister
b. 1840	John Boyd Dunlop	Scottish inventor
b. 1962	Jennifer Jason Leigh	American actor
d. 45 BC	Cato	Roman philosopher
d. 1973	John Heyburn Gibbon	American surgeon
d. 1991	Ira Dean Jagger	American actor

A Lively Experiment

On this day in 1631, the English clergyman Roger Williams (1603–84) landed at Boston, New England, having left London in 1630 aboard the *Lyon* with his wife, Mary.

A law and theology student from Cambridge University, Williams was opposed to the established church. He left England and continued to challenge the religious order in Boston so that by 1635, he was banished from the Massachusetts Bay Colony for his "dissident beliefs." He founded Providence at the tip of Narragansett Bay in the spring of 1632. Williams was a keen proponent of the notion that church and state should be separate. He also supported freedom of conscience to worship in whatever way suited people.

In 1643, Williams sailed to England to obtain a charter for the new Rhode Island colony. The charter he received granted independence "comfortable to the laws of England and liberty of the conscience." When efforts were made to revoke this charter, Williams returned to England to have it confirmed. King Charles II granted Rhode Island a favorable new charter "to hold forth a lively experiment that a most flourishing civil state may stand and best be maintained with full liberty of religious concernments."

Because of Williams's policy of religious toleration, Rhode Island became a haven for refugees from bigotry. Most notable among these were the Quakers from Boston. When the Narragansett Tribe joined the King Philip War in 1675, Williams served as captain of the forces defending Providence. Thereafter, he participated in the politics of the colony until his death in 1683. He is remembered as one of the notable champions of democracy and religious freedom in the colonies.

Williams died at Providence in March or April 1684.

The Father of Pietism

The Lutheran theologian Philipp Jacob Spener (b. 1635), who died on this day in 1705, is considered the Father of pietism. Pietism was a Protestant movement that emphasized heartfelt religious devotion, Bible study, prayer, ethical purity, charitable activity, and pastoral theology rather than sacramental or dogmatic precision.

In 1670, Spener began to bring together small groups in "little churches" of believers for prayer, study, and talk. Spener was an inspiration to others as "house churches" sprang up all over Germany. He departed from the Orthodox Church because he viewed his little "churches" not as a new religion, but as an extension of the Reformation.

FEBRUARY 6

DAILY READING

Seek good, not evil, that you may live. Then the LORD *God Almighty will be with you, just as you say he is.* (AMOS 5:14)

FEAST DAYS

311	Dorothy of Caesarea	Patron of newlyweds
540	Vedast	Patron of Arras, France
1597	Paul Miki	Nagasaki martyr

ENTRANCE AND EXIT

b. 1564	Christopher Marlowe	English playwright
b. 1911	Ronald Reagan	40th American president
b. 1968	Molly Ringwald	American actor
d. 1685	Charles II	King of England
d. 1783	Lancelot "Capability" Brown	English landscape designer
d. 1952	George VI	King of England

Waitangi Day

Today is National Day in New Zealand, celebrating the treaty signed at Waitangi between the Maori and the British Crown on this day in 1840. Over five hundred chiefs from various Maori tribes met with representatives of Queen Victoria to establish the founding document of the modern nation.

Some tribes refused to sign the treaty, and many early settlers simply ignored the provisions for caring for the indigenous people. This led to strained relations between the Maori and the colonizers.

In recent times, Waitangi Day has witnessed Maori protests, arrests, scuffles, and demands for better treatment of Maori people. Some people are uncomfortable about celebrating Waitangi Day and choose not to attend any official events, instead treating the day as a pleasant summer holiday to spend with family and friends.

There is also an increasing campaign for Waitangi Day to be renamed "New Zealand Day," as in fact it was known briefly in the 1970s. As an increasingly multicultural society, many feel that this would more accurately reflect the modern New Zealand nation.

No one knows how the Maori came to colonize New Zealand, but some historians think they sailed from Hawaii over eight hundred years ago.

Noteworthy

1778 The United States gained official recognition from France as the two nations signed the Treaty of Amity and Commerce and the Treaty of Alliance in Paris.

1788 Massachusetts became the sixth state to ratify the U.S. Constitution.

1933 The Twentieth Amendment to the Constitution was declared in effect. The amendment moved the start of presidential, vice-presidential, and congressional terms from March to January.

1959 The U.S., for the first time, successfully test-fired a Titan intercontinental ballistic missile from Cape Canaveral.

1971 NASA Astronaut Alan B. Shepard used a six-iron that he had brought inside his spacecraft and swung at three golf balls on the surface of the moon.

1987 President Ronald Reagan turned seventy-six years old this day and became the oldest U.S. president in history.

2000 In Finland, Foreign Minister Tarja Halonen became the first woman to be elected president.

2001 Ariel Sharon was elected Israeli prime minister.

*F*EBRUARY 7

DAILY READING

I urge you, brothers, by our Lord Jesus Christ
and by the love of the Spirit, to join me in my struggle
by praying to God for me. (ROM 15:30)

FEAST DAYS

319	Theodore the General	Patron of soldiers
722	Richard	King of Wessex
1846	Giovanni Maria Mastai-Ferretti	Pope Pius IX

ENTRANCE AND EXIT

b. 1478	Sir Thomas More	English politician
b. 1908	Buster Crabbe	American actor
b. 1960	James Spader	American actor
d. 1779	William Boyce	English composer
d. 1998	Carl Dean Wilson	American musician
d. 1999	Hussein I bin Talal	King of Jordan

Charles Dickens

On this day in 1812, Charles John Huffam Dickens, the popular English novelist, was born to John and Elizabeth Dickens in a small terraced house at 1 Mile End Terrace, Landport, Portsea. The house is now a museum and place of pilgrimage for his admirers.

In 1824 when his father was imprisoned for debt, he was sent to work at a Warren's Blacking Factory at Hungerford Market. Three years later, the young Charles began work as a solicitor's clerk, subsequently becoming a freelance reporter at Doctor's Commons Courts. In 1836 he married Catherine Hogarth, the daughter of his friend George Hogarth. The same year saw the publication of *The Pickwick Papers*. Dickens created many memorable characters, and it is believed that his book *David Copperfield* was based on his own upbringing.

His novels made him a superstar of his age, and he traveled to America and Italy as news of his fame spread. Today, he is still the novelist that defines the Victorian era with his vivid descriptions of poverty, education, and Christmas traditions. He pioneered the practice of public readings and these added to his success.

Dickens's final public readings took place in London in 1870. He suffered a stroke after a full day's work on *Edwin Drood*, and died on June 9. He was buried at Westminster Abbey and the last episode of the unfinished *Mystery of Edwin Drood* appeared in September.

Popular Quotes from Dickens' Novels

"Change begets change. Nothing propagates so fast."

–*Martin Chuzzlewit*

"It is a melancholy truth that even great men have their poor relations."

–*Bleak House*

"Oliver Twist has asked for more!"

–*Oliver Twist*

"Annual income twenty pounds, annual expenditure nineteen nineteen and six, result happiness. Annual income twenty pounds, annual expenditure twenty pounds ought and six, result misery."

–*David Copperfield*

"It was always said of him, that he knew how to keep Christmas well, if any man alive possessed the knowledge. May that be truly said of us, and all of us! And so, as Tiny Tim observed, 'God Bless Us, Every One!'"

–*A Christmas Carol*

"It was the best of times, it was the worst of times, it was the age of wisdom, it was the age of foolishness, it was the epoch of belief, it was the epoch of incredulity, it was the season of Light, it was the season of Darkness, it was the spring of hope, it was the winter of despair, we had everything before us, we had nothing before us, we were all going direct to Heaven, we were all going direct the other way–in short, the period was so far like the present period, that some of its noisiest authorities insisted on its being received, for good or for evil, in the superlative degree of comparison only."

–*A Tale of Two Cities*

*F*EBRUARY 8

DAILY READING

What a wretched man I am! Who will rescue me from this body of death? Thanks be to God—through Jesus Christ our Lord! (ROM 7:24–25)

FEAST DAYS

570	Honoratus	Bishop of Milan
ca. 900	Cuthman	Patron of bachelors
1537	Gerolamo Miani	Patron of orphans

ENTRANCE AND EXIT

b. 1820	William Tecumseh Sherman	American general
b. 1828	Jules Gabriel Verne	French writer
b. 1953	Mary Steenburgen	American actor
d. 1587	Mary Tudor	Queen of Scotland
d. 1921	Peter Alekseyevich Kropotkin	Russian scientist
d. 2007	Anna Nicole Smith	American actor

The Devil's Footprints

A sensation occurred on this day in 1885. Following a light snowfall in Topsham, Lympstone, Exmouth, Teignmouth, and Dawlish, in Devon, villagers woke up to a vast number of mysterious tracks covering many miles.

The *London Times* of February 6, reported the incident thus:

> The tracks were in all kinds of unaccountable places: in gardens enclosed by high walls, and up on the tops of houses, as well as in the open fields. There was in Lympstone scarcely one unmarked garden. And, because they occurred in single lines, the marks are said to have been "more like those of a biped than of a quadruped"—as if a biped would place one foot precisely ahead of another—unless it hopped—but then we have to think of a thousand, or of thousands. It is said that the marks were generally 8 inches in advance of each other. At Dawlish a number of persons sallied out, armed with guns and other weapons, for the purpose, if possible, of discovering and destroying the animal which was supposed to have been so busy in multiplying its footprints. As might have been expected, the party returned as they went.
>
> The impression of the foot closely resembles that of a donkey's shoe, and measured from an inch and a half, in some instances, to two and a half inches across.
>
> On Sunday last the Rev. Mr. Musgrave alluded to the subject in his sermon and suggested the possibility of the footprints being those of a kangaroo, but this could scarcely have been the case, as they were found on both sides of the River Este. At present it remains a mystery, and many superstitious people in the above towns are actually afraid to go outside their doors after night.

Noteworthy

356 For the third time since the Council of Nicea (325), Athanasius (ca. 293–373) went into exile. The defender of orthodoxy was out of favor as Arianism, a heresy condemned at the council, ran rampant throughout the Empire. He would be exiled twice more before he died.

1693 The College of William and Mary was founded in Williamsburg, Virginia, under Anglican auspices for the purpose of educating Anglican clergymen.

1851 James Alexander Haldane (b. July 14, 1768), Scottish evangelist, died.

1861 The Confederate States of America was formed.

1878 Martin Buber, Jewish religious philosopher, was born in Vienna, Austria (d. June 13, 1965).

1924 The first U.S. execution to make use of gas took place in Nevada State Prison.

1952 Queen Elizabeth II ascended to the British throne. Her father, George VI, had died on February 6.

1956 First red London double-decker buses go into service.

1974 The three-man crew of the Skylab space station returned to Earth after eighty-four days.

1980 President Jimmy Carter announced a plan to reintroduce draft registration.

2005 Ariel Sharon and Mahmoud Abbas agreed on a ceasefire in first step toward Israeli and Palestine peace.

*F*EBRUARY 9

DAILY READING

Because your love is better than life,
my lips will glorify you. (PS 63:3)

FEAST DAYS

ca. 249	Apollonia	Patron of dentists
556	Sabinus	Bishop of Canosa, Italy
1225	Raynald	Bishop of Nocera, Italy

ENTRANCE AND EXIT

b. 1773	William Henry Harrison	9th American president
b. 1926	Garret FitzGerald	Irish prime minister
b. 1945	Maria (Mia) Farrow	American actor
d. 1670	Frederik III	King of Denmark
d. 1981	Bill Haley	American rock star
d. 2002	Princess Margaret	Sister of Queen Elizabeth II

Bishop John Hooper

On this day in 1555, Bishop John Hooper (b. 1495) was burned alive at the stake in Gloucester for being an unrepentant heretic. He was one of the many martyrs of the Roman Catholic Queen Mary. John Hooper became Bishop of Gloucester in 1550. On arriving in the diocese, he was deeply disappointed with the local clergy. He found that 168 of them could not even repeat the Ten Commandments and that forty-one couldn't find the Lord's Prayer in the Bible.

The bishop became an outspoken critic of many church practices in general, including the veneration of the saints and the church hierarchy. His fate was sealed with the accession of Queen Mary in 1553.

This is an extract from his last letter written to his supporters from his prison cell in Gloucester:

> But now is the time of trial, to see whether we fear God or man. It was an easy thing to hold with Christ while the Prince and world held with Him; but now the world hateth Him, it is the true trial who be His. Wherefore, in the name and in the virtue, strength, and power of His Holy Spirit, prepare yourselves in any case to adversity and constancy. Let us not run away when it is most time to fight. Remember, none shall be crowned but such as fight manfully; and *he that endureth to the end shall be saved.* You must now turn all your cogitations from the peril you see, and mark the felicity that followeth the peril, either victory in this world of your enemies, or else a surrender of this life to inherit the everlasting kingdom.

The Patron Saint of Dentists

St. Apollonia, the patron saint of dentists, is often pictured carrying what look like pliers. She was one of a group of virgin martyrs who suffered in Alexandria around 249 during a local uprising against Christians, and she was tortured mercilessly. Supposedly all of her teeth were violently shattered, or pulled out one by one. This is before she threw herself vigorously into the fire that sealed her martyrdom.

February 10

DAILY READING

The tongue that brings healing is a tree of life,
but a deceitful tongue crushes the spirit. (PROV 15:4)

FEAST DAYS

543	Scholastica	Patron against storms
1157	William of Malval	Patron of the Philippines
1344	Clare of Rimini	Italian noble

ENTRANCE AND EXIT

b. 1824	Samuel Plimsoll	English reformer
b. 1950	Mark Spitz	American swimmer
b. 1955	Greg Norman	Australian golfer
d. 1954	Wilhelm Schmidt	German scientist
d. 1992	Alex Haley	American writer
d. 2005	Arthur Miller	American writer

The Marriage of Queen Victoria

Alexandrine Victoria (1819–1901) became Queen Victoria in 1837 because none of George III's sons older than her father, the Duke of Kent, produced a legitimate heir. Her reign remains the longest in British history. On February 10, 1840, Victoria married Prince Albert of Saxe-Coburg-Gotha, and this marriage, which ended with his death in 1861 at the age of forty-two, was happy and produced nine children. The queen never recovered from the death of her husband, and her remaining years were marked by depression.

The children from the marriage were:

Victoria (Vicky), Princess Royal (1840–1901), as dowager Empress of Germany (married Frederick [Fritz] of Prussia, 1858)

Albert Edward (Bertie), Prince of Wales (1841–1910), as King Edward VII (married Princess Alexandra of Denmark, 1863)

Alice (1843–78) as Grand Duchess of Hesse-Darmstadt (married Prince Louis of Hesse-Darmstadt, 1862)

Alfred (Affie) (1844–1900) as Duke of Edinburgh and Saxe-Coburg-Gotha (married Princess Marie of Russia, 1874)

Helena (Lenchen) (1846–1923) as Princess Helena of Schleswig-Holstein (married Prince Christian of Schleswig-Holstein, 1866)

Louise (1848–1939) as Dowager Duchess of Argyll (married Marquess of Lorne, 1871)

Arthur (1850–1942) as Duke of Connaught (married Princess Louise of Prussia, 1879)

Leopold (1853–84) as Duke of Albany (married Princess Helena of Waldeck-Pyrmont, 1882)

Beatrice (1856–1944) as Princess Beatrice of Battenberg (married Prince Henry of Battenberg, 1886)

Queen Victoria died on January 22, 1901.

St. Scholastica's Day Riots

The often uneasy relationship between students and local residents saw one of its worst eruptions in Oxford on St. Scholastica's Day 1355. The trouble began when some students and priests in the Swindlestock (or Swyndlestock) Tavern at Carfax complained about the quality of the wine. The landlord John de Bereford (who was also the mayor) responded to their complaint with "stubborn and saucy language," whereupon a student threw a quart pot at his head. The subsequent riot lasted three days. The townsmen rang the bell of Carfax Tower to summon reinforcements who came armed with various weapons. The chancellor immediately ordered the ringing of St. Mary's bell, whereupon the scholars of the university mustered with bows and arrows.

On the third day, two thousand or so country people joined in on the side of the townsmen and sixty-three students were killed.

For the following five hundred years (until 1855) on February 10, the mayor and sixty-three citizens were obliged to process in penitence to St. Mary's Church, to bow before the vice-chancellor, and to pay a fine of a penny each.

FEBRUARY 11

DAILY READING

Do not let any unwholesome talk come out of your mouths, but only what is helpful for building others up according to their needs, that it may benefit those who listen. (EPH 4:29)

FEAST DAYS

450	Lazarus	Bishop of Milan
ca. 6th cent.	Gobnata	Irish abbess
817	Paschal I	Pope

ENTRANCE AND EXIT

b. 1847	Thomas Edison	American inventor
b. 1936	Burt Reynolds	American actor
b. 1969	Jennifer Aniston	American actor
d. 731	Gregory II	Italian pope
d. 1963	Sylvia Plath	English poet
d. 2006	Peter Benchley	American writer

First Vision at Lourdes

On this day in 1858, a fourteen-year-old French peasant girl, Bernadette Soubirous, had an experience that changed her life and the town of Lourdes where she lived. While gathering firewood with her sister Tionette and a friend Jeanne Abadie, Bernadette saw a vision of the Virgin Mary in a grotto. She claimed that the "beautiful lady" asked her to return to the grotto every day for fifteen days. Further visions followed, and Bernadette's story caused a sensation with the townspeople, although some doubted her. However, she soon had a large number of people following her on her daily journey, some out of curiosity and others who firmly believed that they were witnessing a miracle.

Bernadette's credibility was increased when she claimed that she had been instructed to dig in the ground with her hands, which resulted in the discovery of an underground spring. The water was soon found to have healing powers, and the grotto at Lourdes became a haven for the sick and afflicted from all over the world.

The apparitions at Lourdes were approved by the Holy See in 1862, which further increased the popularity of the town as a center for spiritual, physical, and mental healing.

Bernadette died in 1879 and was declared a saint by Pope Pius XI in 1933.

Noteworthy

1878 The first U.S. bicycle club, Boston Bicycle Club, was formed.

1929 The Lateran Treaty was signed. Italy now recognized the independence and sovereignty of Vatican City.

1943 Gen. Dwight David Eisenhower was selected to command the Allied armies in Europe.

1945 The Yalta Agreement was signed by U.S. President Franklin Roosevelt, British Prime Minister Winston Churchill, and Soviet leader Josef Stalin.

1979 Nine days after the Ayatollah Ruhollah Khomeini returned to Iran (after fifteen years in exile), power was seized by his followers.

1989 Rev. Barbara C. Harris became the first woman to be consecrated as a bishop in the Episcopal Church.

1990 Nelson Mandela was freed after twenty-seven years in captivity.

1990 In Tokyo, Japan, James "Buster" Douglas knocked out Mike Tyson in the tenth round to win the heavyweight championship.

2000 Great Britain suspended self-rule in Northern Ireland.

*F*EBRUARY 12

DAILY READING

Instead, speaking the truth in love,
we will in all things grow up into him who
is the Head, that is, Christ. (EPH 4:15)

FEAST DAYS

ca. 704	Aethelweald of Lindisfarne	Commissioned *Lindisfarne Book of Gospels*
ca. 900	Bendedict Revelli	Bishop of Albenga, Itlay
1584	John Nutter	Catholic martyr

ENTRANCE AND EXIT

b. 1567	Thomas Campion	English writer and physician
b. 1809	Charles Darwin	English scientist
b. 1980	Christina Ricci	American actor
d. 1554	Lady Jane Grey	Queen of England
d. 1804	Immanuel Kant	German philosopher
d. 2000	Charles Schulz	American cartoonist

Lincoln Day

This date used to be a national holiday in America in honor of the sixteenth president of America, Abraham Lincoln (1809–65). However, this is now incorporated into President's Day, which takes place on the third Monday of February. However, some states still observe this day as a separate legal holiday, while other states have adopted President's Day as a dual celebration of George Washington and Abraham Lincoln.

To add to the confusion, some states observe Lincoln Day from a political perspective, as Lincoln was the first Republican president, best known for leading the Union for the duration of the Civil War and signing the Emancipation Proclamation. These Lincoln Days are fundraising events for the Republicans and occur throughout the year and with greater frequency in the run up to state and presidential elections.

The great man himself was born in humble circumstances in Hodgenville, Kentucky. Lincoln's log cabin now has National Historic Site status and is a popular place for visitors. In 2005, the Abraham Lincoln Presidential Library and Museum was opened in Springfield, Illinois, and is now a major tourist attraction.

In one of the last acts of the Civil War, Lincoln was fatally wounded on April 14, 1865, while at a play called *Our American Cousin* at Ford's Theater, Washington, D.C. His assailant was John Wilkes Booth, a Confederate spy.

The Borrowed Days of February

According to ancient custom, February 12, 13, and 14 are said to be "borrowed" from January—that is, the weather on these days can remind one more of winter than spring. If these days all prove stormy, the year will be favored with good weather; but if it is fine, the year will be foul and unfavorable. In the Scots tongue, these three days are called *faoilteach*, and the word *faoilteach* means unfavorable weather.

*F*EBRUARY 13

DAILY READING

Submit to one another out of reverence for Christ. (EPH 5:21)

FEAST DAYS

ca. 1st cent.	Agabus the Prophet	Companion of St. Paul
ca. 590	Stephen	Abbot at Rieti, Italy
703	Ermengild of Ely	Daughter of King Erconbert of Kent

ENTRANCE AND EXIT

b. 1942	Peter Tork	American singer
b. 1950	Peter Gabriel	English singer
b. 1974	Robbie Williams	English singer
d. 1542	Catherine Howard	Queen of England
d. 1883	Richard Wagner	German composer
d. 2002	Waylon Jennings	American singer

Blessing of the Salmon Nets

Just before midnight on this day, the ceremony of Blessing of the Salmon Nets takes place at Pedwell Beach, Northumbria. It is not known how long this practice has been observed, but fishermen are well represented in the Lord's disciples, and many seafarers demonstrate piety in Catholic and Protestant counties. For example, in the Hebridean Isle of Barra, fishermen would always carry holy water with them on their boats and sprinkle the nets with it before fishing. On the west coast of Ireland, priests still bless the fishing boats and nets at the beginning of every season, and this custom extends far away in the Pacific and Indian oceans.

The vicar of the local village of Norham along the banks of the River Tweed conducts a simple service of blessing upon the fishermen and their families. Prayers are said for bountiful harvest and protection against the elements. At the conclusion of the beautiful little ceremony, the nets splash into the dark waters, and the first catch belongs to the church as it has done for centuries.

Similar ceremonies take place for local fishing fleets around the mainland of Brittany before the annual sardine fisheries start, and throughout the year in Spain.

Many festivals of blessing were held around the coasts of Britain by local guilds and confraternities before the English Reformation. But these were largely abandoned. Then in the nineteenth century, similar festivals were started up again, and are nowadays usually celebrated on Ascension Day.

William and Mary

On this day, the English parliament recognized William III of Orange and his wife Mary Stuart as King and Queen, replacing the Roman Catholic James II. William landed with an army at Torbay in November 1688. He promised to defend the liberty of England and the Protestant religion, and marched unopposed on London. James fled ignominiously to France. Parliament then met, denounced James, and offered the throne to William and his wife Mary as joint sovereigns.

William had little to commend him, being short, asthmatic, and stooped. He could not handle a horse or sword until full grown. Nonetheless, he overcame all of these physical setbacks to present a dashing and inspiring figure on horseback in the thick of the battle. His success in life came from the care he took to eat simply, drink little, and obtain plenty of sleep.

As King William III of England, he accomplished far more for the welfare of the English people than had most of his native-born predecessors. His reign marked the transition from the personal government of the Stuarts to the parliamentary rule of the Hanoverians. Control of the army was transferred to Parliament, a better system of finance was introduced, and the Bank of England was established.

*F*EBRUARY 14

DAILY READING

Love must be sincere. Hate what is evil; cling to what is good. (ROM 12:9)

FEAST DAYS

ca. 269	Valentine	Patron of lovers
827	Cyril the Philosopher	Patron of Bulgaria
885	Methodius	Apostle of the Slavs

ENTRANCE AND EXIT

b. 1766	Thomas Robert Malthus	English clergyman
b. 1864	Israel Zangwill	English writer
b. 1960	Meg Tilly	American actor
d. 1400	Richard II	King of England
d. 1779	Capt. James Cook	English navigator
d. 1975	Sir Pelham Grenville Wodehouse	English writer

St. Valentine

Little is known about this celebrated saint, but it is thought he was a fourth-century Roman who was martyred during the reign of Claudius II. His feast day supercedes the ancient Roman festival of Lupercalia when young men and women drew lots for one another.

Valentine is the lover's saint and in former times, it was the custom for men to send presents to their sweethearts. In some places, it was the tradition that the gentleman's valentine was the first lady he saw on Valentine's Day and vice versa for ladies.

In England in the eighteenth century, the eve of St. Valentine's Day was celebrated thus: an equal number of maids and bachelors came together, with each writing their true love's name or some feigned name upon separate tickets. These were rolled up and lots were drawn so that each girl was randomly matched to each lad and each lad matched to each girl. By this means everyone had two partners, but the lad had to select the valentine. The couples then spent the next few days feasting and dancing.

Many songs, poems, and ballads were sung on St. Valentine's Day, including this invocation to the saint:

> Hast, friendly Saint! to my relief,
> My heart is stol'n, help! stop the thief!
> My rifled breast I search'd with care,
> And found Eliza lurking there.
> Away she started from my view,
> Yet may be caught, if thou pursue;
> Nor need I to describe her strive–
> The fairest, dearest maid alive!
> Seize her–yet treat the nymph divine
> With gentle usage, Valentine!
> Then, tell her, she, for what was done,
> Must bring my heart, and give her own.

Samuel Pepys noted Valentine's Day, 1667, thus: "This morning came up to my wife's bedside (I being up dressing myself) little Will Mercer to be her valentine, and brought her name written upon blue paper in gold letters, done by himself, very pretty; and we were both well pleased with it. But I am also this year my wife's valentine, and it will cost me £5: but that I must have laid out if we had not been valentines."

FEBRUARY 15

DAILY READING

Obey your leaders and submit to their authority.
They keep watch over you as men who must give an account.
Obey them so that their work will be a joy, not a burden,
for that would be of no advantage to you. (HEB 13:17)

FEAST DAYS

120	Faustinus	Patron of Brescia, Italy
120	Jovita	Patron of Brescia, Italy
1302	Andrew of Anagni	Patron against demons

ENTRANCE AND EXIT

b. 1564	Galileo Galilei	Italian astronomer and physicist
b. 1951	Jane Seymour	English actor
b. 1954	Matthew Groening	American animator
d. 1965	Nat King Cole	American singer
d. 1984	Ethel Merman	American singer
d. 2001	Burt Kennedy	American writer

Susan Browwell Anthony

> At the election of President and Vice President of the United States, and members of Congress, in November 1872, Susan B. Anthony, and several other women, offered their votes to the inspectors of election, claiming the right to vote, as among the privileges and immunities secured to them as citizens by the fourteenth amendment to the Constitution of the United States. For this act, the women, fourteen in number, were arrested and held to bail, and indictments were found against them severally, under the 19th Section of the Act of Congress of May 30, 1870 (16 St. at L. 144.), charging them with the offense of "knowingly voting without having a lawful right to vote."

This was how the American suffragist and Christian temperance leader, Susan B. Anthony (born today in 1820), was indicted of daring to vote when voting by women was not allowed.

Susan's first involvement in the world of reform was in the temperance movement. In 1849, Susan gave her first public speech for the Daughters of Temperance and then helped found the Woman's State Temperance Society of New York, one of the first organizations of its time.

In 1851 she went to Syracuse to attend a series of antislavery meetings. During this time Susan met Elizabeth Cady Stanton, became fast friends, and joined Stanton and Amelia Bloomer in their campaigns for women's rights.

In 1854, she devoted herself to the antislavery movement, serving from 1856 to the outbreak of the Civil War in 1861. Here, she served as an agent for the American Anti-slavery Society. Afterward, she collaborated with Stanton and published the New York liberal weekly, *The Revolution* (1868–70), which called for equal pay for women.

In 1872, Susan demanded that women be given the same civil and political rights that had been extended to black males under the Fourteenth and Fifteenth Amendments.

Thus, she led a group of women to the polls in Rochester to test the right of women to vote. She was arrested two weeks later and while awaiting trial, engaged in highly publicized lecture tours and in March 1873, she tried to vote again in city elections. After being tried and convicted of violating the voting laws, Susan succeeded in her refusal to pay the fine. From then on she campaigned endlessly for a federal woman suffrage amendment through the National Woman Suffrage Association (1869–90) and the National American Woman Suffrage Association (1890–1906) and by lecturing throughout the country.

In 1888 she organized the International Council of Women and in 1904 the International Woman Suffrage Alliance. Although Anthony did not live to see the consummation of her efforts to win the right to vote for women, the establishment of the Nineteenth Amendment, which gave women the right to vote, owes much to her efforts.

FEBRUARY 16

DAILY READING

Anyone who receives instruction in the word must share all good things with his instructor. (GAL 6:6)

FEAST DAYS

ca. 1st cent.	Onesimus	Companion of St. Paul
ca. 305	Juliana of Nicomedia	Patron against sickness
1487	Bernard of Scammacca	Dominican priest

ENTRANCE AND EXIT

b. 1497	Philip Melanchthon	German reformer
b. 1822	Sir Francis Galton	English scientist
b. 1959	John McEnroe	American tennis player
d. 1279	Afonso III	King of Portugal
d. 1917	Octave Mirbeau	French writer
d. 1990	Keith Harding	American artist

Black Earth Man

The German Protestant reformer and supporter of Martin Luther Philip Melanchthon (1497–1560) had his Latin surname (which means Black Earth) conferred on him by his humanist tutor, Johannes Reuchlin, in 1509.

Melanchthon was a brilliant student and became the first professor of Greek Literature at the University of Wittenberg at just twenty-one years of age. At Wittenberg, he first met Martin Luther and became a great supporter of his views. Indeed in 1520 he wrote, "I would rather die than be separated from Luther."

And Luther also valued his comrade. After attending Melanchthon's lectures on Greek, Luther wrote, "I thank my good Phillip for teaching us Greek. I am older than he. But this does not prevent me from learning from him. I say frankly that he understands more than I, which I am not ashamed of. Therefore, I think much of the young man and will not hear a word against him." This sealed the friendship between Luther and Melanchthon, who was fourteen years his junior. The friendship lasted until Luther's death.

From 1519 until his death Melanchthon devoted himself to studying the gospel as well as reformed theology. In doing so, he laid the foundation for Lutheran education. By nature he was moderate, conscientiousness, cautious, and peaceable; but these qualities were sometimes said to only be lack of decision, consistence, and courage. Often, however, his actions showed not anxiety for his own safety but concern for the welfare of the community, and for the quiet development of the church.

Onesimus

According to *Easton's Bible Dictionary*, Onesimus was "a slave who, after robbing his master Philemon at Colosse, fled to Rome, where he was converted by the apostle Paul, who sent him back to his master with the epistle which bears his name. In it he beseeches Philemon to receive his slave as a 'faithful and beloved brother.'"

Paul offers to pay to Philemon anything his slave had taken, and to bear the wrong he had done him. He was accompanied on his return by Tychicus, the bearer of the Epistle to the Colossians.

> I am sending him—who is my very heart—back to you. I would have liked to keep him with me so that he could take your place in helping me while I am in chains for the gospel. But I did not want to do anything without your consent, so that any favor you do will be spontaneous and not forced. Perhaps the reason he was separated from you for a little while was that you might have him back for good—no longer as a slave, but better than a slave, as a dear brother. He is very dear to me but even dearer to you, both as a man and as a brother in the Lord. (Philm 1:12–16)

*F*EBRUARY 17

DAILY READING

Humble yourselves, therefore, under God's mighty hand, that he may lift you up in due time. Cast all your anxiety on him because he cares for you. (1 PET 5:6–7)

FEAST DAYS

ca. 450	Loman	Bishop of Trim, Ireland
661	Finan	Monk at Iona
ca. 6th cent.	Fortchern	Patron of bell ringers

ENTRANCE AND EXIT

b. 1934	Barry Humphries	Australian comedian
b. 1963	Michael Jordan	American sports star
b. 1981	Paris Hilton	American socialite
d. 1673	Jean Baptiste Poquelin-Molière	French writer
d. 1909	Geronimo	Apace chief
d. 1968	Sir Donald Wolfit	English actor

Giordano Bruno

The Italian priest, philosopher, cosmologist, and poet Giordano Bruno (1548–1600) was taken out into the Campo dei Fiori in Rome on this day, and taken to the stake as an unrepentant heretic. His tongue spiked for silence, he was stripped, then burned alive. His ashes were scattered to the winds of Rome; his books were burned and his name erased, along with all true mention of him in textbooks of history, science, and literature.

He had suffered eight years imprisonment and sustained torture in order to get him to recant. His crime was to question the Catholic Church's belief that the Earth was the center of the universe. His theories of the infinite universe and the multiplicity of worlds, in which he rejected the traditional geocentric (or Earth-centered) astronomy and intuitively went beyond the Copernican sun-centered theory, which still maintained a finite universe with a sphere of fixed stars.

In his autobiography, he wrote:

> I, the Nolan [Bruno was born in Nola, Italy], in order to free men's minds, seek to unchain the human spirit and understanding from its stifling prison room. Freed again, the human spirit and understanding will, as if through peepholes, aim again at the far distant stars. The authorities of Faith would cut off your wings so you cannot fly to pierce the clouds of their illusions. This they would do because one who can be free of their illusions, will be able to see what is real.

Noteworthy

1801 The House of Representatives broke an electoral tie between Thomas Jefferson and Aaron Burr, choosing Jefferson to be president.

1904 Giacomo Puccini's opera *Madama Butterfly* had its world premiere at La Scala in Milan, Italy.

1996 World chess champion Garry Kasparov beat IBM supercomputer "Deep Blue," winning a six-game match in Philadelphia.

2005 Iraq's electoral commission certified the results of the January 30 elections and allocated 140 of 275 National Assembly seats to the United Iraqi Alliance, giving the Shiite-dominated party a majority in the new parliament.

FEBRUARY 18

DAILY READING

Give thanks to the LORD, for he is good;
his love endures forever. (PS 107:1)

FEAST DAYS

451	Flavian	Patriarch of Constantinople
676	Colman	Bishop of Lindisfarne
1820	Francis Regis Clet	Chinese martyr

ENTRANCE AND EXIT

b. 1784	Niccolo Paganini	Italian composer
b. 1954	John Travolta	American actor
b. 1974	Yevgeny Kafelnikov	Russian tennis star
d. 1564	Martin Luther	German reformer
d. 1982	Ngaio Marsh	New Zealand writer
d. 2003	Johnny Paycheck	American singer

Martin Luther

As the church remembers Martin Luther (1483–1564) on this day, it seems appropriate to reproduce below his definition of faith taken from his *Introduction to St. Paul's Epistle to the Romans* (1522):

> Faith cannot help doing good works constantly. It doesn't stop to ask if good works ought to be done, but before anyone asks, it already has done them and continues to do them without ceasing. Anyone who does not do good works in this manner is an unbeliever. He stumbles around and looks for faith and good works, even though he does not know what faith or good works are. Yet he gossips and chatters about faith and good works with many words.
>
> Faith is a living, bold trust in God's grace, so certain of God's favor that it would risk death a thousand times trusting in it. Such confidence and knowledge of God's grace makes you happy, joyful and bold in your relationship to God and all creatures. The Holy Spirit makes this happen through faith. Because of it, you freely, willingly and joyfully do good to everyone, serve everyone, suffer all kinds of things, love and praise the God who has shown you such grace. Thus, it is just as impossible to separate faith and works as it is to separate heat and light from fire! Therefore, watch out for your own false ideas and guard against good-for-nothing gossips, who think they're smart enough to define faith and works, but really are the greatest of fools. Ask God to work faith in you, or you will remain forever without faith, no matter what you wish, say or can do.

The Pilgrim's Progress

One of the greatest classics of English literature, *The Pilgrim's Progress* was published on this day in 1678. John Bunyan wrote this epic from Bedford prison in 1675, where he was serving time for violating the Conventicle Act. This act forbade the holding of religious services outside the control of the Church of England.

The Pilgrim's Progress was immediately popular and published in two parts. Today, it has been translated into more than one hundred languages and remains one of the most popular works of allegorical literature.

FEBRUARY 19

DAILY READING

He who despises his neighbor sins,
but blessed is he who is kind to the needy. (PROV 14:21)

FEAST DAYS

ca. 295	Gabinus	Roman noble
ca. 345	Mesrop the Teacher	Missionary to Armenia
ca. 452	Odran	Companion of St. Patrick

ENTRANCE AND EXIT

b. 1473	Nicolas Copernicus	Polish astronomer
b. 1960	Prince Andrew	Duke of York
b. 1967	Benicio Del Toro	Puerto Rican actor
d. 1414	Thomas Arundel	Archbishop of Canterbury
d. 1990	Michael Powell	English film director
d. 2001	Stanley Kramer	American film director

The Pythians

The Order of Knights of Pythias is an international fraternity founded by Justus Rathbone in Washington, D.C., on February 19, 1864. Their primary object is to promote friendship among men and to relieve suffering. The watchwords of the organization are friendship, charity, and benevolence.

The Order bases itself on the Greek story of the friendship between Damon and Pythias. Damon had opposed the pretensions of the king of Syracuse, who had gained the throne by fraud, and as a result he was condemned to death. Pythias became a hostage for Damon, while the latter was permitted his liberty to bid his wife and child goodbye. Each was willing to die to save the other's life.

The Order began as a way to heal the wounds and allay the hatred of the Civil War. President Abraham Lincoln, being advised of the contents of the ritual and its teaching, said: "The purposes of your organization are most wonderful. If we could but bring its spirit to all our citizenry, what a wonderful thing it would be. It breathes the spirit of Friendship, Charity and Benevolence."

The Pythians is dedicated to the cause of universal peace and is pledged to the promotion of understanding among men of goodwill as the surest means of attaining it.

The National Federation of Women's Institutes

Although the Women's Institute is considered quintessentially English, the movement actually began in Canada on this day in 1897. Adelaide Hoodless (1857–1910) inspired by the Farmer's Institute began the Women's Institute as a branch of that body. Her purpose was to promote rural education for women, share cooking and homemaking skills, and provide a regular forum for discussion of all things rural.

The idea took root in England in 1915, and today there are over one thousand branches with over six hundred members.

FEBRUARY 20

DAILY READING

Learn to do right! Seek justice,
encourage the oppressed. (ISA 1:17)

FEAST DAYS

456	Eleuthere	Bishop of Tournai, Belgium
743	Eucherius	Bishop of Orleans, France
1154	Wulfric	English hermit

ENTRANCE AND EXIT

b. 1925	Robert Altman	American film director
b. 1963	Charles Barkley	American sportsman
b. 1967	Kurt Cobain	American singer
d. 1437	James I	King of Scotland
d. 1920	Robert Peary	American explorer
d. 2005	Hunter Stockton Thompson	American writer

Death of an Emperor

The Holy Roman Emperor Joseph II (1741–90), who died on this day in mysterious circumstances, ruled from 1780 to 1790 over the Austrian Habsburg lands. He tried to be a wise ruler and act for the good of all his subjects. To this end, he ordered the spread of education, the reduction of religious orders, and the promotion of unity by the compulsory use of the German language. However, his moves against the excesses of Catholicism induced Pope Pius VI to visit him in 1782. The emperor received the pope politely, and showed himself a good Catholic, but refused to be influenced.

In 1781, Joseph issued the *Edict on Idle Institutions*, which began the closure of monasteries. Eventually about seven hundred monasteries closed and their assets were used to support schools and charities. The number of monks dropped from 65,000 to 27,000. His view was that service to God was the same as service to the state.

He was also responsible for the *Patent of Toleration*, a series of church reforms that aimed to give religious freedoms to non-Catholics. However, under pressure from his Catholic advisers and mindful of the papal power, these measures were eventually revoked shortly before his death. By this time around sixty thousand Protestants had joined the Reformed Church and established congregations in over seventy parishes.

Extract from the Patent of Toleration *(1781)*

> Convinced on the one hand by the harmfulness of all coercion of conscience and on the other hand of the great benefit for religion and the state of a true Christian toleration, we have found ourselves persuaded to allow adherers to the Augsburg and Helvetian confessions to perform a religious practice appropriate to their religion. . . . The Roman-Catholic religion alone should continue to have precedence in regard to public religious practices.
>
> 1. . . . Concerning the churches, we expressly enjoin, where it is not already so, that there should be no bell ringing, no bells, no towers and no public entrance from the street. . . .
>
> 7. Non-Catholics are permitted real estate and property, rights of citizenship and craftsmanship, academic titles and civil employment . . . and they are to be urged to no other oath than to that which is appropriate to their religious principles, nor to the attendance of the processions or functions of the dominant religion. . . .

FEBRUARY 21

DAILY READING

We give thanks to you, O God, we give thanks,
for your Name is near; men tell of your wonderful deeds. (PS 75:1)

FEAST DAYS

ca. 676	Gundebert	Bishop of Sens, France
1561	Robert Southwell	English martyr
1794	Noel Pinot	French martyr

ENTRANCE AND EXIT

b. 1801	John Henry Newman	English clergyman
b. 1924	Robert Mugabe	President of Zimbabwe
b. 1946	Tyne Daly	American actor
d. 1554	Hieronymus Bock	German priest and scientist
d. 1677	Benedict de Spinoza	Dutch philosopher
d. 1919	Mary Edwards Walker	American physician

International Mother Language Day

In 1999, UNESCO declared this day as International Mother Language Day. This promotes "linguistic diversity and multilingual education that strengthen the unity and cohesion of societies." It is a celebration of the world's six thousand languages and dialects.

Each year has its own theme, and in 2006 it was Languages and Cyberspace. UNESCO Director General Koichiro Matsuura, noted:

> Cyberspace constitutes an essential dimension for the expression and the promotion of languages, and the presence of a language on the Web is only possible if a number of political, social and technical conditions are met. UNESCO is duty bound to facilitate the creation of those conditions in a coordinated manner at the national, regional and international levels and will willingly continue to play its role most actively as a laboratory of ideas, a catalyst and an international advocate, by facilitating discussion, negotiation and effective and sustainable multilateral action which holds out hope for all.

Previous themes for this day have included Braille and Sign Languages, Children and Languages, and Disappearing Languages.

John Henry Newman (1801–90)

The English Anglican priest who converted to Catholicism in 1847 was a notable preacher and much loved writer. These are his rules for writing sermons:

1. A man should be earnest, by which I mean he should write not for the sake of writing, but to bring out his thoughts.
2. He should never aim at being eloquent.
3. He should keep his idea in view, and should write sentences over and over again until he has expressed his meaning accurately, forcibly, and in a few words.
4. He should aim at being understood by his hearers or readers.
5. He should use words which are likely to be understood. Ornament and amplification will come spontaneously in due time, but he should never seek them.
6. He must creep before he can fly, by which I mean that humility which is a great Christian virtue has a place in literary composition.
7. He who is ambitious will never write well, but he who tries to say simply what he feels, what religion demands, what faith teaches, what the Gospel promises, will be eloquent without intending it, and will write better English than if he made a study of English Literature.

FEBRUARY 22

DAILY READING

Therefore each of you must put off falsehood and speak truthfully to his neighbor, for we are all members of one body. (EPH 4:25)

FEAST DAYS

139	Telesforo	Pope
895	John	Saxon monk
1297	Margaret of Cortona	Patron of tramps

ENTRANCE AND EXIT

b. 10,000 BC	Pebbles Flintstone	Cartoon character
b. 1788	Arthur Schopenhauer	German philosopher
b. 1975	Drew Barrymore	American actor
d. 1521	Amerigo Vespucci	Spanish astronomer
d. 1636	Santorio Santorio	Italian physician
d. 1987	Andy Warhol	American artist

Founder's Day

Today is the joint birthday of Lord Robert (1857–1941) and his wife Olave Baden-Powell (1889–1977). Scouts and Guides remember this day as Founder's Day (Scouts) and Thinking Day (Guides) to celebrate the life and work of the Chief Scout and Chief Guide of the World.

Over twenty-eight million scouts and fifteen million guides from one hundred nations hold parties and special events on this day.

As 2007 is the 150th anniversary of Lord Baden-Powell, there will be special activities for this occasion. A national service of thanksgiving will be held at Westminster Abbey and both youth movements will join together to promote the message of unity and adventure.

Lord Baden-Powell served as a lieutenant general in the Army and was posted to India and Africa. He saw action in the Second Boer War in South Africa and took part in the defense of the Mafeking. He also served for three years in the Secret Intelligence Service.

He married Olave in 1912, and she shared her husband's enthusiasm for directing young people to purposeful activity. In 1930, she was elected Chief of the Girl Guides. Thinking Day is an opportunity for members to consider the meaning of Guiding and Scouting and about Scouts and Guides in all the countries of the world. Many troops use it as an opportunity to study about other countries and cultures.

St. Peter's Chair

According to the great hagiographer Alban Butler (1710–73):

> St. Peter, before he went to Rome, founded the see of Antioch is attested by many Saints. It was just that the Prince of the Apostles should take this city under his particular care and inspection, which was then the capital of the East, and in which the faith took so early and so deep root as to give birth in it to the name of Christians. St. Chrysostom says that St. Peter made there a long stay; St. Gregory the Great, that he was seven years Bishop of Antioch; not that he resided there all that time, but only that he had a particular care over that Church. If he sat twenty-five years at Rome, the date of his establishing his chair at Antioch must be within three years after Our Saviour's Ascension; for in that supposition he must have gone to Rome in the second year of Claudius. In the first ages it was customary, especially in the East, for every Christian to keep the anniversary of his Baptism, on which he renewed his baptismal vows and gave thanks to God for his heavenly adoption: this they called their spiritual birthday. The bishops in like manner kept the anniversary of their own consecration, as appears from four sermons of St. Leo on the anniversary of his accession or assumption to the pontifical dignity; and this was frequently continued after their decease by the people, out of respect for their memory. St. Leo says we ought to celebrate the chair of St Peter.

*F*EBRUARY 23

DAILY READING

Accept him whose faith is weak, without passing judgment on disputable matters. (ROM14:1)

FEAST DAYS

303	Serenus the Gardener	Patron of bachelors
ca. 5th cent.	Zebinus	Syrian hermit
1011	Willigis	Archbishop of Mainz, Germany

ENTRANCE AND EXIT

b. 1792	Sir Joshua Reynolds	English artist
b. 1817	Sir George Watts	English artist
b. 1963	Michael Saul Dell	American businessman
d. 1931	Dame Nellie Melba	Australian opera singer
d. 1965	Stanley Laurel	English comedian
d. 1976	Laurence Stephen Lowry	English artist

The Cato Street Conspiracy

The Cato Street Conspiracy was a plot to assassinate the British cabinet and so overthrow the government on this day in 1820. The conspirators rented a disused stable in Cato Street from which to launch their attack, and it was during their last meeting there before the planned attack that the authorities became aware of their plans. The leader of the conspiracy, Arthur Thistlewood, stabbed and killed one of the arresting policemen during the assassination attempt.

A reward of £1,000 was immediately offered for Thistlewood, and the next morning he was captured at a friend's house at No. 8 White Street, Little Moorfields.

Thistlewood and his fellow conspirators were sent to the Tower. On the 20th of April, Thistlewood was condemned to death after three days' trial; and on May 1st, he and his four principal accomplices: Ings, Brunt, Tidd, and Davidson, who had been severally tried and convicted, were hanged at the Old Bailey. The remaining six pleaded guilty; one received a pardon and five were transported to Australia for life. To efface recollection of the conspiracy, Cato Street was renamed Homer Street.

The stable at Cato Street enjoyed a brief fame as a tourist attraction. As *The Sunday Observer* (March 3, 1820) reported, "The premises in Cato Street . . . was visited by several thousand persons" and noted that the "blood of poor Smithers (the policeman) was still visible on the floor, and seemed to be avoided with a sort of reverential awe."

George Frederic Handel

The German Baroque composer who was born on this day in 1685 became a British citizen in 1727. His most famous work is *Messiah*, an oratorio he wrote in just twenty-four days. A devout Christian, Handel believed the work to be divinely inspired. In the summer of 1741 Handel, at the peak of his musical powers but depressed and in debt, began setting Charles Jennens's biblical libretto to music at his usual breakneck speed. It is said that while Handel was writing *Messiah*, his valet would often find him weeping silently at his desk, overcome by the beauty and majesty of the music that was flowing from his pen. It was first performed at a charity concert on Fishamble Street, Dublin, in 1742.

FEBRUARY 24

DAILY READING

Therefore, there is now no condemnation for those who are in Christ Jesus, because through Christ Jesus the law of the Spirit of life set me free from the law of sin and death. (ROM 8:1–2)

FEAST DAYS

489	Modestus	Bishop of Trier, Germany
586	Pratexatatus	Bishop of Rouen, France
1137	Adela	Daughter of William the Conqueror

ENTRANCE AND EXIT

b. 1500	Charles V	Holy Roman Emperor
b. 1943	George Harrison	English rock star
b. 1955	Steve Jobs	American businessman
d. 1799	Georg Christoph Lichtenberg	German scientist
d. 1800	Henry Cavendish	English scientist
d. 1994	Dinah Shore	American singer

St. Matthias's Day

St. Matthias used to be observed in the Roman Catholic Church on this day until it was moved in the twentieth century to May 14. However, the Episcopal and Lutheran traditions observe his feast on this day. The vigil of his feast was distinctive in that, in leap year, it moved to the traditional leap day of February 24, with the feast one day later. In the Eastern Orthodox Church, his feast is celebrated on August 9.

Matthias was chosen to be an apostle to replace the traitor Judas Iscariot, according to Acts 1:23–26: "So they proposed two men: Joseph called Barsabbas (also known as Justus) and Matthias. Then they prayed, 'Lord, you know everyone's heart. Show us which of these two you have chosen to take over this apostolic ministry, which Judas left to go where he belongs.' Then they cast lots, and the lot fell to Matthias; so he was added to the eleven apostles."

All further information concerning Matthias is uncertain. He may have preached the gospel in Judea, then in Ethiopia, and was crucified. Another tradition maintains that Matthias was stoned at Jerusalem by the Jews, and then beheaded. It is said that St. Helena brought the relics of St. Matthias to Rome, and that a portion of them was at Trier, Germany.

Noteworthy

1582 Pope Gregory XIII issued a papal bull outlining his calendar reforms, paving the way for the Gregorian calendar. This meant that October 4, 1582, had to be followed by October 15.

1821 Mexico declared its independence from Spain.

1920 The Nazi party held its first meeting of importance in Munich.

1981 Buckingham Palace announced the engagement of Britain's Prince Charles to Lady Diana Spencer.

2005 Pope John Paul II underwent an operation to insert a tube in his throat to relieve breathing problems.

2006 South Dakota lawmakers approved a ban on nearly all abortions.

FEBRUARY 25

DAILY READING

Sing to the LORD a new song, for he has done marvelous things; his right hand and his holy arm have worked salvation for him. (PS 98:1)

FEAST DAYS

369	Caesarius of Nanzianzen	Greek Father of the Church
616	Ethelbert	King of Kent
ca. 710	Walburga	Patron of sailors

ENTRANCE AND EXIT

b. 1841	Pierre Auguste Renoir	French artist
b. 1873	Enrico Caruso	Italian singer
b. 1966	Tea Leoni	American actor
d. 1899	Paul Julius Reuter	German journalist
d. 1983	Thomas Lanier Williams III	American writer
d. 2001	Sir Donald Bradman	Australian cricketer

Sister Elizabeth Fedde

On this day, the Lutheran Church honors Sister Elizabeth Fedde (b. 1850), who died on this day in 1921. She spent her formative years in Flekkefjord, Norway, where she endured harsh conditions. On her thirty-second birthday, Sister Elizabeth received a letter from her brother-in-law, Gabriel Fedde, challenging her to set up a ministry in New York City for Norwegian seamen there. Three months later, she left for American and arrived in April 1883.

Weeks later, she founded the Norwegian Relief Society in a boarding house with three small rooms rented for a price of $9 per month and located at 109 Williams Street, near the Seaman's Church. She made a particular point of visiting the sick and distressed, often writing in a journal about her experiences.

Two years later Sister Fedde established a training facility for fellow workers in a house consisting of just nine beds. This expanded to become the Lutheran Medical Center, a much needed institution for the health and well-being of local people.

Sister Fedde also served in Minnesota, Minneapolis, and Chicago establishing hospitals and volunteer-caring ministries that involved hundreds of people.

The Greatest Batsman

Sir Donald George Bradman (1908–2001) is regarded as the greatest ever batsman. At test level, he averaged over 99 runs per innings and scored 334 runs at Headingly during the Ashes Test Match on July 11, 1930. It was the first time that any player had scored more than 300 runs at test level in a single day.

DONALD GEORGE BRADMAN (1908–2001)—Career Test Batting and Fielding Figures

	Batting & Fielding
Matches	52
Innings	80
Not Out	10
Runs	6,996
Highest Score	334
Average	99.94
100s	29
50s	13
Caught	32
Stumped	0

FEBRUARY 26

DAILY READING

Come, let us sing for joy to the LORD;
let us shout aloud to the Rock of our salvation. (PS 95:1)

FEAST DAYS

326	Alexander	Bishop of Alexandria
ca. 6th cent.	Victor	French hermit
1270	Isabelle	Patron of sick people

ENTRANCE AND EXIT

b. 1839	Sir John Pentland Mahaffy	Irish writer
b. 1829	Levi Strauss	American businessman
b. 1979	Corinne Bailey Rae	American singer
d. 1878	Pietro Angelo Secchi	Italian priest and astronomer
d. 1930	Mary Whiton Calkins	American educator
d. 1994	William Hicks	American comedian

Moral Sense

Anthony Ashley Cooper who was born on this day in 1671 (d. 1713) was the third Earl of Shaftesbury. He is renowned as being an outstanding philosopher who began the "moral sense" school of philosophy that attracted many adherents, including Adam Smith and David Hume.

Cooper defined the moral sense as the ability to understand the value of one's actions. During childhood the moral sense is unrefined and primarily emotional, but through education and use the moral sense can be refined to distinguish between right and wrong.

In 1711, Cooper published *Characteristicks of Men, Manners, Opinions, Times*, which became the most reprinted book in Europe. Cooper believed that everything in the world was created by a morally perfect God and that the world God created is the best of all possible ones. Any evil we observe, according to Cooper, is only apparent or subordinate, not real or ultimate. He drew a distinction between goodness and virtue arguing that goodness is something that is within not only humans but also animals. This is because a creature is good if its affections promote the well-being of the system of which it is a part, and animals are just as capable of possessing this type of affection as humans. Merit, on the other hand, is within the reach of humans alone because it is tied to a special kind of affection that only humans possess.

According to Cooper, the ultimate end of religion (which encompasses virtue, beauty, and true understanding) was to know one's part in the grand order of the cosmos.

Noteworthy

1802 Author Victor Hugo was born in Besancon, France.

1815 Napoleon Bonaparte escaped from the island of Elba to begin his second conquest of France.

1848 The Second French Republic was proclaimed.

1919 Congress established Grand Canyon National Park in Arizona.

1929 President Calvin Coolidge signed a measure establishing Grand Teton National Park.

1952 Prime Minister Winston Churchill announced that Britain had developed its own atomic bomb.

1993 A bomb built by Islamic extremists exploded in the parking garage of New York City's World Trade Center, killing six people and injuring more than one thousand.

1995 Barings PLC, Britain's oldest investment banking firm, collapsed after a securities dealer, Nick Leeson, lost more than $1.4 billion.

2000 Pope John Paul II visited Mount Sinai in Egypt, revered as the place where Moses received the Ten Commandments.

*F*EBRUARY 27

DAILY READING

Stop trusting in man, who has but a breath in his nostrils. Of what account is he? (ISA 2:22)

FEAST DAYS

ca. 600	Leander	Bishop of Seville, Spain
1198	Emmanuel	Bishop of Cremona, Italy
1601	Anne Line	Patron of widows

ENTRANCE AND EXIT

b. 1861	Rudolf Steiner	Austrian philosopher
b. 1932	Elizabeth Taylor	English actor
b. 1980	Chelsea Clinton	Daughter of President Clinton
d. 1706	John Evelyn	English writer
d. 1993	Lillian Diana de Guiche (Gish)	American actor
d. 2002	Spike Milligan	Irish comedian and writer

John Evelyn

"I was born at Wotton in the County of Surrey about twenty minutes past two in the morning, after my father had been married about seven years and that my mother had borne him three children; viz. two daughters and one son, about the 33rd year of his age, and the 23rd of my mother's."

Historians are indebted to English gentleman and country lover John Evelyn for his accounts of daily life during momentous times. Evelyn was a contemporary of Samuel Pepys and his long life extended over the reigns of the last three Stuart kings (Charles I, Charles II, and James II), the English Civil War, the Commonwealth, Cromwell's Protectorate, and the Glorious Revolution of 1688.

His journal comprises over seven hundred pages, commencing in 1641 until a few weeks before his death. Here are some extracts:

> June 18, 1657: I saw at Greenewich a sort of Catt brought from the East Indies, shaped & snouted much like the Egyptian Ratoone, in the body like a Monkey, & so footed: the eares & taile like a Catt, onely the taile much longer, & the Skin curiously ringed, with black & white: With this taile, it wound up its body like a Serpent, & so got up into trees, & with it, would also wrap its whole body round; It was of a wolly haire as a lamb, exceedingly nimble, & yet gentle, & purr'd as dos the Cat.
>
> May 29, 1658: This day came in his Majestie Charles the 2d to London after a sad, & long Exile, and Calamitous Suffering both of the King and Church: being 17 yeares: This was also his Birthday, and with a Triumph of above 20000 horse and foote, brandishing their swords and shouting with unexpressable joy: The wayes straw'd with flowers, the bells ringing, the streetes hung with Tapissry, fountaines running with wine: The Major, Aldermen, all the Companies in their liveries, Chaines of Gold, banners; Lords & nobles, Cloth of Silver, gold and vellvet every body clad in, the windos and balconies all set with Ladys, Trumpets, Musick, & myriads of people flocking the streetes & was as far as Rochester, so as they were 7 houres in passing the Citty, even from 2 in the afternoone 'til nine at night: I stood in the strand, & beheld it, & blessed God: And all this without one drop of bloud, & by that very army, which rebell'd against him: But it was the Lords doing, *et mirabile in oculis nostris*: for such a Restauration was never seene in the mention of any history, antient or modern, since the returne of the Babylonian Captivity, nor so joyfull a day, & so bright, ever seene in this nation: this hapning when to expect or effect it, was past all humane policy.
>
> September 15, 1685: I went to Lond: accompanied Mr. Pepys (Secretary of the Admiralty) to Portsmouth, Whither his Majestie was going. Wee tooke Coach & 6 horses, late after dinner, yet got to Bagshot that night: I went & made a Visite to Mrs. Grahames, some time Maide of honor to the queen Dowager, now wife to Ja: Gr: Esquire of the Privie-purse to the King: very importunate she was that I would sup, & abide there that night: but being oblig'd by my companion, I return'd to our Inn, after she had shew'd me her house which was very commodious, as she was an excellent housewife, a prudent & vertuous Lady: Her eldest sonn, was now sick there of the small pox, but in a likely way of recovery; & other of her Children ran about, & among the infected, which she said let them do on purpose that they might whilst young, passe that fatal dissease, which she fancied they were to undergo one time or other, & that this would be the best: The severity of this cruel dissease so lately in my poore family confirming much of what she affirm'd.

February 28

DAILY READING

I myself am convinced, my brothers, that you yourselves are full of goodness, complete in knowledge and competent to instruct one another. (ROM 15:14)

FEAST DAYS

ca. 6th cent.	Ermine	Irish priest
1399	Hedwig	Queen of Poland
1936	Daniel Brottier	French army chaplain

ENTRANCE AND EXIT

b. 1901	Linus Pauling	American scientist
b. 1909	Stephen Spender	English poet
b. 1947	Stephanie Beacham	English actor
d. 1916	Henry James	American writer
d. 1986	Olof Palme	Swedish Prime Minister
d. 2007	Arthur Schlesinger Jr.	American historian

Anna Julia Hayward Cooper

In 2006, the General Convention of Episcopal Church provisionally approved this day to commemorate the life and work of Anna Julia Hayward Cooper (ca. 1859–1964). She was a high school principal, the fourth African American woman to receive a doctorate, and a woman who spoke her mind eloquently and forcefully. Writing more than one hundred years ago, she argued that just as white men cannot fully understand the consciousness of black men, neither can black men completely comprehend black women's experience–and that it is black women who mark the progression of society.

Anna was born in Raleigh, North Carolina, to an enslaved woman and a white man, presumably her mother's master. She was educated at St. Augustine Normal School and Collegiate Institute, a school founded by the Episcopal Church. A passionate advocate for African American women, Cooper assisted in organizing the Colored Women's League and the first Colored Settlement House in Washington, D.C. She wrote and spoke widely on issues of race and gender, and took an active role in national and international organizations founded to advance African Americans.

Prayer: "Almighty God, you inspired your servant Anna Julia Hayward Cooper with the love of learning and the skill of teaching: Enlighten us more and more through the discipline of learning, and deepen our commitment to the education of all your children; through Jesus Christ our Lord, who lives and reigns with you and the Holy Spirit, one God, for ever and ever. Amen."

Noteworthy

1861 The Territory of Colorado was organized.

1954 Scientists James D. Watson and Francis H. C. Crick at Cambridge University discovered the double-helix structure of DNA.

1974 The United States and Egypt reestablished diplomatic relations after a seven-year break.

1975 A subway train smashed into the end of a tunnel in London's Underground, killing more than forty people.

1991 Allied and Iraqi forces suspended their attacks as Iraq pledged to accept all United Nations resolutions concerning Kuwait.

2005 Lebanon's pro-Syrian prime minister, Omar Karami, resigned amid large anti-Syria street demonstrations in Beirut.

*F*EBRUARY 29

DAILY READING

Better is one day in your courts than a thousand elsewhere;
I would rather be a doorkeeper in the house of my God
than dwell in the tents of the wicked. (PS 84:10)

FEAST DAYS

ca. 433	John Cassian	Desert Father
992	Oswald	Archbishop of York

ENTRANCE AND EXIT

b. 1896	William Wellman	American film director
b. 1928	Sidney Edmond Jocelyn (Joss) Ackland	English actor
b. 1960	Antony Robbins	American businessman
d. 1604	John Whitgift	Archbishop of Canterbury
d. 1868	Ludwig I	King of Barvaria
d. 2004	Jerome Lawrence	American writer

Mother Ann Lee

Ann Lee, or "Mother Ann" as she became known to her followers, was born on February 29, 1736, in Manchester, England, the daughter of a blacksmith. At the tender age of eight, she became employed in a cotton factory, and afterward was a cutter of hatter's fur. She was also employed as a cook in the Manchester infirmary, where she was distinguished for her "neatness, faithfulness, prudence, and good economy."

She joined the United Society of Believers in Christ's Second Appearing, commonly known as the Shakers, in Manchester. In 1774 she persuaded her husband, brother (William) and six other followers to emigrate with her to the America, where they settled at present day Watervliet, in New York. Under her leadership, the Shaker movement in the United States grew to include thousands of people.

They sought with some success to attract converts to a gospel of pacifism, celibacy, racial and gender equality, and industrious communal living. Mother Ann herself endured persecution and even physical attacks when traveling to evangelize.

She died in Watervliet on September 8, 1784.

Testimony of Ann Lee

I love the day that I first received the Gospel. I call it my birthday. I cried to God, without intermission, for three days and three nights, that he would give me true desires. And when I received a gift of God, I did not go away and forget it, and travel no further; but I stood faithful, day and night, warring against all sin, and praying to God for deliverance from the very nature of sin. And other persons need not expect to find power over sin without the same labor and travel of soul.

Soon after I set out to travel in the way of God, I labored a-nights in the work of God. Sometimes I labored all night, continually crying to God for my own redemption. Sometimes I went to bed and slept; but in the morning, if I could not feel that sense of the work of God that I did before I slept, I would labor all night. This I did many nights, and in the daytime I put my hands to work, and my heart to God; and when I felt weary and in need of rest, I labored for the power of God, and the refreshing operations thereof would release me, so that I felt able to go to my work again.

Many times, when I was about my work, I have felt my soul overwhelmed with sorrow. I used to work as long as I could keep it concealed, and then would go out of sight, lest any one should pity me with that pity which was not of God. In my travel and tribulation my sufferings were so great, that my flesh consumed upon my bones, bloody sweat pressed through the pores of my skin, and I became as helpless as an infant. And when I was brought through, and born into the spiritual kingdom, I was like an infant just born into the natural world. They see colors and objects, but they know not what they see. It was so with me; but before I was 24 hours old, I saw, and I knew what I saw.

–From *Shakers Compendium of the Origin, History, Principles, Rules and Regulations, Government and Doctrines of the United Society of Believers in Christ's Second Appearing (1859)*

First, Sturdy March with brows full sternly bent
And armed strongly, rode upon a ram,
The same which over Hellespontus swam;
Yet in his hand a spade he also hent,
And in a bag all sorts of weeds ysame,
Which on the earth he strewed as he went,
And fill'd her womb with fruitfull hope of nourishment.

EDMUND SPENSER–*The Shepheardes Calender* (1579)

I Martius am! Once first, and now the third!
To lead the Year was my appointed place;
A mortal dispossessed me by a word,
And set there Janus with the double face.
Hence I make war on all the human race;
I shake the cities with my hurricanes;
I flood the rivers and their banks efface,
And drown the farms and hamlets with my rains.

HENRY WADSWORTH LONGFELLOW–*The Poet's Calendar* (1882)

Shakespeare

SOOTHSAYER
Beware the ides of March.

CAESAR
What man is that?

BRUTUS
A soothsayer bids you beware the ides
of March.

CAESAR
Set him before me; let me see his face.

CASSIUS
Fellow, come from the throng;
look upon Caesar.

CAESAR
What say'st thou to me now?
speak once again.

SOOTHSAYER
Beware the ides of March.

CAESAR
He is a dreamer; let us leave him: pass.

–JULIUS CAESAR, Act 1, Scene II

March

March derives its name from the Roman god of war, Mars, as it was a favorable time to set out for war. Mars was the Roman god of war, identified with the Greek Ares. As a god, Romans ranked Mars second only to Jupiter. A Roman legend had it that Mars was the father of Romulus and Remus, founders of the city of Rome.

After January was added to the calendar, March alternated with it several times in being the year's first month.

Proverb

In like a lion,
Out like a lamb

Refers to the weather at the beginning and end of March as it is often blustery to begin with and the month frequently ends with calm weather.

Perdita: For the flowers now, that frighted thou let'st fall
From Dis's waggon! daffodils,
That come before the swallow dares, and take
The winds of March with beauty; violets dim,
But sweeter than the lids of Juno's eyes
Or Cytherea's breath;

–*A Winter's Tale,* Act 4, Scene IV

MARCH 1

DAILY READING

As far as the east is from the west, so far has he removed our transgressions from us. (PS 103:12)

FEAST DAYS

ca. 647	Swithbert	Apostle to the Frisians
ca. 856	Leo	Bishop of Rouen, France
1367	Roger Lefort	Bishop of Limoges, France

ENTRANCE AND EXIT

b. 1611	John Pell	English mathematician
b. 1810	Frédéric Chopin	Polish composer
b. 1954	Ronald Howard	American actor and film director
d. 1633	George Herbert	English writer
d. 1984	Jackie Coogan	American actor
d. 2001	Joseph Cyril Bamford	English industrialist

St. David's Day

David, the patron saint of Wales (where he is known as Dewi Sant), was born around AD 542, in Pembrokeshire, South Wales. He is thus the only one of the British saints to be patron of his home country. His mother, Non, was later canonized in her own right, and his father was Sant, son of Ceredig Prince of Cardigan, which makes David, according to legend, the uncle of King Arthur.

Despite his noble birth, he soon took to the monastic life and was noted for his austerity: He drank only water, not the beer and wine that was usual at the time, and worked long hours and studied hard. He was a colleague of St. Columba and St. Finnegan and rose rapidly within the clergy and became famous in his own lifetime. David founded a monastery in the town of Menevia (later renamed in his honor) and even went on a pilgrimage to Jerusalem, a long and hazardous journey in those days. He was known as a powerful orator, and many legends grew up about miraculous events around him. The most famous is one that tells how the people at the back of the crowd were unable to hear him preach so he spread a handkerchief on the ground and stood on it. The ground under his feet swelled up and everyone could hear and see him; local legend points to the isolated hills just outside the town of St. Davids, at Llandewi Brefi (Llandewi means "David's church") as being the hills created on that occasion.

David died on March 1st in AD 589, and he was canonized in 1120; his feast has been celebrated on the anniversary of his death ever since.

World Book Day

March 1, 2007, is the tenth anniversary of World Book Day in the UK. The organizers carried out a survey to find out the top ten books the nation "could not live without." Over two thousand people responded, and the results were:

1. *Pride and Prejudice*–Jane Austen, 20 percent
2. *Lord of the Rings*–J. R. R. Tolkein, 17 percent
3. *Jane Eyre*–Charlotte Bronte, 14 percent
4. Harry Potter books–J. K. Rowling, 12 percent
5. *To Kill a Mockingbird*–Harper Lee, 9.5 percent
6. The Bible, 9 percent
7. *Wuthering Heights*–Emily Brontë, 8.5 percent
8. *1984*–George Orwell, 6 percent
9. *His Dark Materials*–Philip Pullman, 6 percent
10. *Great Expectations*–Charles Dickens, .55 percent

March 2

DAILY READING

Salvation is found in no one else, for there is no other name under heaven given to men by which we must be saved. (ACTS 4:12)

FEAST DAYS

672	Chad	Patron of Lichfield
1127	Charles the Good	Son of King Cnut
1282	Agnes	Patron of Prague

ENTRANCE AND EXIT

b. 1904	Theodor Geisel (Dr. Seuss)	American writer and illustrator
b. 1931	Mikhail Sergeyevich Gorbachev	Russian leader
b. 1950	Karen Carpenter	American singer
d. 1791	John Wesley	English founder of Methodism
d. 1939	Howard Carter	English Egyptologist
d. 1998	Henry Steele Commager	American historian

Texas Independence Day

On March 2, 1836, the state of Texas declared independence from Mexico by issuing a "Unanimous Declaration of Independence."

The declaration is similar in tone to the American Declaration of Independence and states the reasons for the break away, namely that

> Government has ceased to protect the lives, liberty and property of the people, from whom its legitimate powers are derived, and for the advancement of whose happiness it was instituted, and so far from being a guarantee for the enjoyment of those inestimable and inalienable rights, becomes an instrument in the hands of evil rulers for their oppression.
>
> . . . in consequence of such acts of malfeasance and abdication on the part of the government, anarchy prevails, and civil society is dissolved into its original elements. In such a crisis, the first law of nature, the right of self-preservation, the inherent and inalienable rights of the people to appeal to first principles, and take their political affairs into their own hands in extreme cases.

The document was signed by fifty-four delegates, and Texas retained its independence for ten years from this point. The President of the Independence Convention was Richard Ellis, a Methodist who also founded La Grange College in Franklin County, Alabama. Eillis County in Texas is named after him.

St. Chad

The church celebrates the life of St. Chad on this day. He was a miracle worker who is reputed to have purified spring water by praying in a well at Lichfield. Chad was from Northumbria, and received his training in the monastic life partly in Ireland and partly at Lindisfarne. In 664 he succeeded his brother Cedd as Abbot of Lastingham. Later in the same year he was appointed Bishop of York by King Oswy. Now Wilfrid had already been nominated to the see of York by Oswy's son, and had gone to Gaul to be consecrated. There were thus two contending claimants to the bishopric of York. Owing to irregularities in Chad's consecration, he apparently resigned from York at the prompting of Theodore and retired to Lastingham.

Wilfrid got York, but Chad was soon afterward compensated with the bishopric of Mercia, whose seat he established at Lichfield. During his Mercian episcopate he founded a monastery at Barrow-on-Humber in Lincolnshire. He died in 672.

MARCH 3

DAILY READING

He is the image of the invisible God,
the firstborn over all creation. (COL 1:15)

FEAST DAYS

ca. 536	Titian	Bishop of Brescia, Italy
ca. 728	Christicola	Bishop of Leinster, England
1955	Katharine Drexel	Founder, the Sisters of the Blessed Sacrament for Indians and Colored

ENTRANCE AND EXIT

b. 1841	Sir John Murray	Scottish scientist
b. 1847	Alexander Graham Bell	Scottish inventor
b. 1958	Miranda Richardson	English actor
d. 1703	Robert Hooke	English scientist
d. 1879	William Kingdon Clifford	English philosopher
d. 1987	Danny Kaye	American actor

St. Winwaloe

The sixth-century abbot St. Winwaloe (also called Wonnow and Wynwallow) was born at Ploufragen, in Brittany, France. At the age of fifteen, he entered the monastery on Lauren Island under Abbot Budoca. When he came to Cornwall, he lived in a cell in the shelter of Castle Hill. He is known in France as Guenole, and it was he who founded the monastery at Landevennec in Brittany on land donated by Prince Gallo. Winwaloe died there.

There are at least four churches in Cornwall, England, dedicated to him. He is also connected with an English proverb about weather:

First theres David
Then theres Chad
Next comes Winwaloe
Roaring mad

Robert Hooke (1635–1703)

The scientist and philosopher Robert Hooke possessed a natural curiosity and a brilliant mind. He lived in an age of great scientists, such as Newton, and his achievements are impressive. For example, he was among the first to:

- refer to cells in living matter.
- study fossils and hypothesize that they were extinct species.
- observe Jupiter's Red Spot and deduce that the planet rotated.
- observe the rotation of Mars.
- work out the number of vibrations of each musical note.
- observe lunar craters.
- publish a book on microscopy.
- explain the shape of crystal in terms of the packing of its component parts.
- postulate a wave theory of light.
- propose the inverse square relationship for gravity.
- devise a law relating to weight and stretching.

He is also credited with many inventions, including the:

- first anemometer, a device for measuring wind speed and direction.
- first recording weather station.
- universal joint.
- spirit level.
- first modern telescope.
- air pump.
- iris diaphragm used in cameras.
- sash window.

*M*ARCH 4

DAILY READING

It is not good to have zeal without knowledge,
nor to be hasty and miss the way. (PROV 19:2)

FEAST DAYS

254	Lucius I	Pope
ca. 614	Leonard	Bishop of Avranches, France
1484	Casimir	Patron of Poland

ENTRANCE AND EXIT

b. 1678	Antonio Vivaldi	Italian composer
b. 1823	Sir William Siemens	English inventor
b. 1968	Patsy Kensit	English actor
d. 1832	Jean-François Champollion	French Egyptologist
d. 1915	William Willett	English builder
d. 1994	John Candy	American actor

Zachary Taylor (1784–1850)

On this day in 1849, America was without a president for a day because Zachary Taylor, the twelfth president, refused to take the Oath of Office on a Sunday. No one else was sworn in for just the day, and there was no constitutional crisis because everyone was aware this was just a temporary delay.

The incident shows that Zachary Taylor really lived his faith and refused to bend his principles to the demands of office.

Although Taylor was known as "Old Rough and Ready" while in the army, Taylor was not so tough as president. He was nominated by the Whigs and elected because of his military reputation and southern roots, not because of his politics. He had a political pedigree though, being a second cousin of James Madison, a fourth cousin once removed of Robert E. Lee, and a fourth cousin three times removed of Franklin D. Roosevelt.

Taylor kept his old warhorse named Whitney on the White House lawn. People would pluck hairs from it for souvenirs.

Shortly after breaking ground for the Washington Monument on July 4, 1850, Zachary Taylor, a hero of the Mexican War, fell ill after eating some cherries. He died having served just sixteen months in office. Abraham Lincoln gave the eulogy at his funeral.

In 1991 Taylor's remains were exhumed because some historians wanted to know whether he had died from arsenic poisoning, as they suspected foul play. However, forensic examination of hair and fingernail samples ruled out this theory.

Jean-François Champollion

The archaeological world is greatly indebted to the French Egyptologist Jean-François Champollion (1790–1832), who is best known for his work on the Rosetta Stone. This block of black basalt stone, measuring three feet, nine inches long, two feet, four and half inches wide, and eleven inches thick contains three distinct bands of writing. It was found near Alexandria in 1799 by French soldiers under Napoleon's command.

A skilled linguist, Champillion had studied the earliest translation of the Greek text on the Rosetta Stone by Stephen Weston in London in April 1802. As a result of his studies and his fluency in many languages, including Hebrew, Arabic, Syriac, Chaldean, Chinese, Coptic, Ethiopic, Sanskrit, Pahlevi, and Persian, Champillion was able to decipher the text of the Rosetta Stone. Thus, it became possible to make sense of the hieroglyphics, and this proved to be a valuable key in understanding ancient Egyptian culture. Today, the Rosetta Stone is located in the British Museum, London.

*M*ARCH 5

DAILY READING

We know also that the Son of God has come and has given us understanding, so that we may know him who is true. And we are in him who is true—even in his Son Jesus Christ. He is the true God and eternal life. (1 JOHN 5:20)

FEAST DAYS

ca. 530	Kieran	First Bishop of Ossory, Ireland
ca. 540	Carthage the Elder	Bishop of Ossory, Ireland
1374	John Joseph of the Cross	Patron of Ischia, Italy

ENTRANCE AND EXIT

b. 1133	Henry II	King of England
b. 1940	Samantha Eggar	English actor
b. 1958	Andrew Gibb	Australian singer
d. 1625	James I	King of England
d. 1980	Jay Silverheels	American actor
d. 2003	Hardy Amies	English fashion designer

The Map Maker

According to the cartographers Carl Moreland and David Bannister, Gerardus Mercator (also known as Gerhard Kremer) is as important as Ptolemy, the ancient scholar from Alexandria in Egypt, in extending our understanding of the world. The quality of his maps made them a copy source for generations of mapmakers. He is best known for a new mapping technique that bears his name, the Mercator projection.

Mercator was born in Rupelmonde in Flanders on this day in 1512 and studied geography, cartography, and mathematics at the University of Leuven (Louvain) in Belgium. He published his first map (of the Holy Land) in 1537. From 1537 to 1540 Gerardus Mercator surveyed and mapped Flanders. In 1538 he published his first world map. It was based on the Ptolemy map. The maps by Ptolemy had been completely lost in Europe during the dark Middle Ages. Thanks to Arab scholars, some of the Ptolemy maps were saved and came back to Europe during the Renaissance period.

In 1552 Gerardus Mercator moved to Duisburg to evade religious persecution. In 1554 he produced a map of six panels of Europe. In 1568 Mercator used a new way of displaying a map with ninety-degree parallel lines for the latitudes and meridians. This new technique was actually not invented by Mercator. But he was the first cartographer to apply it. The Mercator projection was a great progress for navigation on sea. Its disadvantage is the disproportion of size. The closer the area toward the poles, the larger it is in size. Greenland, for instance, is shown sixteen times larges than in reality.

Mercator's main work, a three-volume world atlas, was published in several editions from 1585 on and beyond his death in 1594. Mercator was the first to use the word *atlas*.

Noteworthy

1770 The Boston Massacre took place as British soldiers, taunted by a crowd of colonists, opened fire, killing five people.

1867 An abortive Fenian uprising against English rule took place in Ireland.

1868 The Senate was organized into a court of impeachment to decide charges against President Andrew Johnson.

1933 The Nazi Party won 44 percent of the vote in German parliamentary elections, enabling it to join with the Nationalists to gain a slender majority in the Reichstag.

1953 Soviet dictator Josef Stalin died at age seventy-three after twenty-nine years in power.

1970 A nuclear nonproliferation treaty went into effect after forty-three nations ratified it.

1997 Representatives of North Korea and South Korea met for first time in twenty-five years, for peace talks in New York.

2001 Vice President Dick Cheney underwent an angioplasty for a partially blocked artery after going to a hospital with chest pains.

March 6

DAILY READING

Every word of God proves true; he is a shield to those who take refuge in him. (PROV 30:5)

FEAST DAYS

ca. 680	Kyneburga	Saxon princess
776	Chrodegand	Bishop of Metz, France
1298	Helen	Polish princess

ENTRANCE AND EXIT

b. 1475	Michelangelo di Lodovico Buonarroti Simoni	Italian artist
b. 1806	Elizabeth Barrett Browning	English writer
b. 1972	Shaquille O'Neal	American sportsman
d. 1683	Guarino Guarini	Italian mathematician
d. 1900	Gottlieb Daimler	German engineer
d. 1986	Georgia O'Keefe	American artist

Louisa May Alcott

Celebrated author Louisa May Alcott (b. 1832) died on this day in 1888, three days after the death of her distinguished father, Bronson Alcott. She was born in Germantown, Pennsylvania, but moved to Boston, Massachusetts, where her father was a teacher.

Her most famous work, *Little Women*, was semi-autobiographical and was published in 1868. Alcott wrote the novel quickly, writing a chapter a day, and modeled the character of Jo on herself and Jo's sisters Meg, Beth, and Amy after her own sisters. Many events in the book were happenings in the lives of the Alcott sisters. In particular, both the fictional and real sisters often found themselves playing in imaginary worlds and acting out plays and storylines quite frequently as a means of entertainment.

Although Louisa and her editor considered the story "flat," the response of the public was overwhelmingly positive. It was the first novel of its kind, being straightforward and true to life rather then existing solely to expound religious didacticism or male views on how girls ought to behave.

She also became active in the women's suffrage movement and the temperance movement.

Little Women *Quotes*

Beth could not reason upon or explain the faith that gave her courage and patience to give up life, and cheerfully wait for death. Like a confiding child, she asked no questions, but left everything to God and nature, Father and Mother of us all, feeling sure that they, and they only, could teach and strengthen heart and spirit for this life and the life to come.

. . . for when women are the advisers, the lords of creation don't take the advice till they have persuaded themselves that it is just what they intended to do. Then they act upon it, and, if it succeeds, they give the weaker vessel half the credit of it. If it fails, they generously give her the whole.

He looked like an Italian, was dressed like an Englishman, and had the independent air of an American–a combination which caused sundry pairs of feminine eyes to look approvingly after him, and sundry dandies in black velvet suits, with rose-colored neckties, buff gloves, and orange flowers in their buttonholes, to shrug their shoulders, and then envy him his inches.

MARCH 7

DAILY READING

These commandments that I give you today are to be upon your hearts. Impress them on your children. Talk about them when you sit at home and when you walk along the road, when you lie down and when you get up. (DEUT 6:6–7)

FEAST DAYS

203	Perpetua	Patron of martyrs
ca. 340	Paul the Simple	Hermit
845	Theophilus	Bishop of Nicomedia, Turkey

ENTRANCE AND EXIT

b. 1792	Sir John Herschel	English astronomer
b. 1908	Anna Magnani	Italian actor
b. 1944	Sir Ranulph Fiennes	English explorer
d. 1274	St. Thomas Aquinas	Italian philosopher and theologian
d. 1999	Stanley Kubrick	American film director
d. 2006	Gordon Parks	American film director

British and Foreign Bible Society

In 1802, Rev. Thomas Charles traveled from Wales to London to plead with the Religious Tract Society for Bibles in the Welsh tongue. He had given his last copy away, but unfortunately the society was not able to help him. However, his request was considered by one of the society's members, Rev. Joseph Hughes. He began to convince his fellow members of the need to provide Bibles to as many people as possible in their own tongue.

Thus it was that on this day in 1804, the British and Foreign Bible Society was formed, the first of many such organizations across the world. The inaugural meeting was in a London tavern and was attended by three hundred people. The first Scripture translation took place in 1804 when St. John's Gospel was published in the Canadian Mohawk language. By 1904 the Society had supplied nearly 181 million copies of the Scriptures; spent nearly £14 million on the translation, production, and distribution of Scriptures; and employed one thousand colporteurs and Bible women–over half of them in India and China.

Today, the Bible Society works with over one hundred and forty national Bible Societies across the world and has produced over forty million Bibles and New Testaments in over one hundred languages.

Thomas Aquinas

St. Thomas Aquinas (1224–74) was a Dominican priest, theologian, and philosopher. Called the Doctor Angelicus (the Angelic Doctor), Aquinas is considered one the greatest Christian philosophers to have ever lived. Two of his most famous works, the *Summa Theologiae* and the *Summa Contra Gentiles*, are the finest examples of his work on Christian philosophy.

He presented five arguments for the existence of God:

The Argument from Motion
As nothing can move itself, then the first object in motion needed a mover. That first mover was God.

The Argument from Causation of Existence
As nothing can be the cause of itself (nothing can create itself), then the first cause must be God.

The Argument from Contingent and Necessary Objects
There must exist a being which is necessary to cause contingent beings. That being is God.

The Argument from Degrees and Perfection
St. Thomas concluded that for any given quality (e.g., goodness, beauty, knowledge) there must be an perfect standard by which all such qualities are measured. These perfections are contained in God.

The Argument from Intelligent Design
Aquinas states that common sense tells us that the universe works in such a way, that one can conclude that is was designed by an intelligent designer, God. In other words, all physical laws and the order of nature and life were designed and ordered by God, the intelligent designer.

MARCH 8

DAILY READING

Charm is deceitful, and beauty is vain, but a woman who fears the LORD is to be praised. (PROV 31:30)

FEAST DAYS

642	Julian	Bishop of Toledo, Spain
871	Humphrey	Bishop of Therouanne, France
1550	John of God	Patron of alcoholics

ENTRANCE AND EXIT

b. 1921	Cyd Charisse	American actor
b. 1943	Lynn Redgrave	English actor
b. 1969	Andrea Parker	American actor
d. 1874	Millard Fillmore	13th American president
d. 1971	Harold Clayton Lloyd	American actor and director
d. 2001	Dame Ninette de Valois	Irish ballerina

International Women's Day

March 8th has been observed as International Women's Day since 1909 when the Socialist Party of America organized a commemoration to celebrate the "economic, political and social achievements of women." It is an official holiday in many Eastern countries, including the official holiday in Russia, Armenia, Azerbijan, Bulgaria, Macedonia, Moldova, and Ukraine. It is traditional for men in these countries to see men honoring their mothers, wives, girlfriends, and colleagues with flowers and small gifts.

Since 1975, this day has been officially recognized by the United Nations, although in 1977 it also recognized that "a United Nations Day for Women's Rights and International Peace be observed on any day of the year by Member States, in accordance with their historical and national traditions."

Most years have a theme to focus activities raise awareness of particular issues. Recent themes have included:

2007 Ending Impunity for Violence against Women and Girls
2006 Women in Decision Making
2005 Gender Equality beyond 2005: Building a More Secure Future
2004 Women and HIV/AIDS

Noteworthy

1702 Queen Anne accedes to throne of England upon the death of King William III to reign until 1714.
1917 Russian Revolution (February Revolution) begins at Petrograd under new Gregorian calendar.
1932 Depression–Wall Street reaches lowest point at 41.22.
1949 Vietnam proclaims independence within French Union.
1971 Joe Frazier beats Muhammad Ali for heavyweight boxing championship at New York.
1976 Largest meteorite fall in recorded history near Chinese city of Kirin. One stone weighed 3,902 lbs.

March 9

DAILY READING

O Lord, you are my God; I will exalt you and praise your name, for in perfect faithfulness you have done marvelous things, things planned long ago. (IS 25:1)

FEAST DAYS

ca. 390	Pacian	Bishop of Barcelona
686	Bosa of York	Benedictine monk
1440	Frances of Rome	Patron of car drivers

ENTRANCE AND EXIT

b. 1934	Yuri Gagarin	Russian cosmonaut
b. 1940	Raul Julia	American actor
b. 1943	Bobby Fischer	American chess grandmaster
d. 1888	Wilhem I	Prussian king
d. 1992	Menachem Begin	Israeli prime minister
d. 1994	Fernando Rey	Spanish actor

Gregory of Nyssa

St. Gregory of Nyssa (ca. 330–ca. 395) was a younger sibling in a family that gave the church many years of service and at least five saints. Before entering the monastery of his brother Basil the Great, Gregory was a rhetorician. He may have been married, although some scholars believe that his treatise *On Virginity* argues against that. He became Bishop of Nyssa ca. 371 and was accused by the Arians of mismanagement. He was deposed in 376.

On the death of the Arian, Valens, two years later, he was restored to his see. He attended the first Council of Constantinople in 381, after which he traveled in Transjordan (Arabia) to settle disputes in the churches.

In his approach to the Scriptures, he was heavily influenced by Origen, and his writings on the Trinity and the Incarnation build on and develop insights found in germ in the writings of his brother Basil. But he is chiefly remembered as a writer on the spiritual life, on the contemplation of God, not only in private prayer and meditation, but also in corporate worship and in the sacramental life of the Church.

His treatise *On the Making of Man* deals with God as Creator, and with the world as a good thing, as something that God takes delight in, and that ought to delight us. His *Great Catechism* is esteemed as a work of systematic theology. His commentary on the *Song of Songs* is a work of contemplative, devotional, and mystical theology.

During a trip to Jerusalem, he was forced to defend his Christology, although he was then and is now well known for his Trinitarian theology. In 394, he attended a synod in Constantinople and is thought to have died shortly after that, when mention of him in church records ceases.

Mladentzi: The Day of the Holy Forty Martyrs

In Orthodox countries on this day, Christians remember the forty holy martyrs who were executed in Armenia for confessing their faith. They were soldiers who perished after being made to stand naked in icy water.

A legend of the Bulgarians from the village of Zelenovka, Tavria, tells how, on this day, God drives forty red-hot spits into the earth to warm it, and "the sun turns towards summer" and people can sow and plant.

Traditionally, on this day, every housewife cooks forty red peppers stuffed with rice (*Pulneni chushki*) and people try to eat forty different things.

MARCH 10

DAILY READING

In your hearts, set apart Christ as Lord.
Always be prepared to give an answer to everyone
who asks you to give the reason for the hope that you have.
But do this with gentleness and respect. (1 PET 3:15)

FEAST DAYS

ca. 172	Caius	Missionary preacher
483	Simplicius	Pope
ca. 1380	John of the Holy Trinity	Florentine monk

ENTRANCE AND EXIT

b. 1772	Friedrich von Schlegel	German writer
b. 1940	Chuck Norris	American actor
b. 1947	Kim Campbell	19th president of Canada
d. 37	Tiberius Claudius Nero	Roman Emperor
d. 1985	Konstantin Chernenko	Russian leader
d. 1988	Andrew Gibb	Australian singer

A Woman Called Moses

Reverently called "Moses" by the hundreds of slaves she helped to freedom and the thousands of others she inspired, Harriet Tubman (1820–1913) became the most famous leader of the Underground Railroad to aid slaves escaping to free states or Canada.

Born into slavery in Bucktown, Maryland, Tubman escaped her own chains in 1849 to find safe haven in Philadelphia, Pennsylvania. She did so through the Underground Railroad, an elaborate and secret series of houses, tunnels, and roads set up by abolitionists and former slaves. "When I found I had crossed the [Mason-Dixon] line, I looked at my hands to see if I were the same person," Tubman later wrote. "The sun came like gold through the tree and over the field and I felt like I was in heaven." She would spend the rest of her life helping other slaves escape to freedom.

After her escape, Tubman worked as a maid in Philadelphia and joined the large and active abolitionist group in the city. In 1850, after Congress passed the Fugitive Slave Act, making it illegal to help a runaway slave, Tubman decided to join the Underground Railroad. Her first expedition took place in 1851, when she managed to thread her way through the backwoods to Baltimore and return to the North with her sister and her sister's children. From that time until the onset of the Civil War, Tubman traveled to the South about eighteen times and helped close to three hundred slaves escape. In 1857, Tubman led her parents to freedom in Auburn, New York, which became her home as well.

Harriet Tubman died March 10, 1913, and in 1990 President George H. W. Bush declared March 10th Harriet Tubman Day.

Alexander Graham Bell

Alexander Graham Bell's notebook entry for March 10, 1876, describes the first successful experiment with the telephone, during which he spoke through the instrument to his assistant, Thomas A. Watson, in the next room. Bell writes, "I then shouted into M [the mouthpiece] the following sentence: 'Mr. Watson–come here–I want to see you.' To my delight he came and declared that he had heard and understood what I said."

This first telephone communication took place in Boston, Massachusetts. The phone was made of a wooden stand, a funnel, a cup of acid, and copper wire that transmitted his voice to Mr. Watson listening in on a receiver in another room.

Bell was born into a family deeply interested in speech and hearing. Both his father and grandfather were teachers of elocution, and throughout his life Bell had a keen interest in teaching the deaf to speak.

*M*ARCH 11

DAILY READING

The Lord your God is God; he is the faithful God,
keeping his covenant of love to a thousand generations of those
who love him and keep his commands. (DEUT 7:9)

FEAST DAYS

598	Constantine of Cornwall	Cornish prince
639	Sophronius	Patriarch of Jerusalem
1539	Joannes de Fabriano	Italian hermit

ENTRANCE AND EXIT

b. 1819	Sir Henry Tate	English sugar magnate
b. 1916	Harold Wilson	British prime minister
b. 1963	Alexandra Kingston	English actor
d. 1897	Henry Drummond	Scottish evangelist
d. 1955	Sir Alexander Fleming	Scottish scientist
d. 1971	Philo Taylor Farnsworth	American inventor

St. Matthew Passion

On March 11, 1829, the great and the good of Prussia assembled at the Singakademie in Berlin to hear twenty-year-old wunderkind Felix Mendelssohn (1809–47) conduct an obscure work by a neglected composer.

The king of Prussia was in attendance, so were the poet Heinrich Heine, the philosopher Friedrich Hegel, and the virtuoso violinist Nicolo Paganini. The demand for tickets was such that hundreds of people were turned away at the door.

The unknown work was Bach's *St. Matthew Passion*. First performed in Leipzig either in 1727 or 1729, the *Passion*, now considered by many to be the greatest piece of music ever composed, had not been heard in public since Bach's death in 1750.

Mendelssohn's performance was so successful that it became legendary and is now seen as starting the Bach Revival. Had it not been for that performance, the *St. Matthew Passion* we love today might never have seen the light of day.

The ramifications of the 1829 performance were enormous. In that year, *St. Matthew Passion* was performed over three hundred times all over the world, from Manchester to Cologne to America.

Mendelssohn never wavered in his Christian faith and saw the *St. Matthew Passion* as a great work of Christian significance. He gave a second performance on March 29, Bach's birthday.

Unrest in Nottinghamshire

On this day in 1811, a group of Nottinghamshire framework knitters led by Ned Ludd attacked the village of Arnold in Nottinghamshire and destroyed the new hosiery machines. They felt their livelihoods were threatened by mechanization and were determined to halt the process. It was the start of years of riots against machinery, and many local people were sympathetic to the "Luddites," although today the term is used to refer to someone opposed to technology and change.

Lord Byron, whose home Newstead Abbey was in Nottinghamshire, was one of the Luddite sympathizers, and he wrote a poem about them in 1816:

SONG FOR THE LUDDITES

As the Liberty lads o'er the sea
Bought their freedom, and cheaply,
with blood,
So we, boys, we
Will die fighting, or live free,
And down with all kings but King Ludd!

When the web that we weave is complete,
And the shuttle exchanged for the sword,
We will fling the winding sheet
O'er the despot at our feet,
And dye it deep in the gore he has pour'd.

Though black as his heart its hue,
Since his veins are corrupted to mud,
Yet this is the dew
Which the tree shall renew
Of Liberty, planted by Ludd!

MARCH 12

DAILY READING

He has given us his very great and precious promises,
so that through them you may participate in the divine nature
and escape the corruption in the world caused by evil desires. (2 PET 1:4)

FEAST DAYS

295	Maximillian	Roman soldier
817	Theopanes the Chronographer	Greek abbot
1253	Seraphine	Patron of spinners

ENTRANCE AND EXIT

b. 1932	Andrew Young	American politician
b. 1946	Liza Minnelli	American actor
b. 1948	James Taylor	American singer
d. 1914	George Westinghouse	American inventor
d. 1942	Sir William Bragg	English scientist
d. 1971	Eugene Lindsay Opie	American scientist

Gregory the Great

On this day, the Anglican Church celebrates the life of Gregory the Great, who died on this day in 604. Gregory was a Roman of noble birth, and while still young was governor of Rome. On his father's death he gave his great wealth to the poor and for some years lived as a perfect monk. The pope drew him from his seclusion to make him one of the seven deacons of Rome, and he did great service to the church for many years as Nuncio to the imperial court at Constantinople.

While still a monk, Gregory saw some boys who were for sale in Rome and heard with sorrow that they were pagans. "And of what race are they?" he asked. "They are Angles." "Worthy indeed to be Angels of God." He got leave from the pope and set out to convert the English. He sent St. Augustine and other monks to England, and they began the Christianization of the people.

On the death of Pope Pelagius II, Gregory was compelled to take the government of the church, and for fourteen years his pontificate was a perfect model of ecclesiastical rule. He healed schisms; revived discipline, and saved Italy by converting the wild Arian Lombards who were laying it waste. He aided in the conversion of the Spanish and French Goths, who were also Arians, and kindled anew in Britain the light of the faith, which the English had put out in blood. He is famous for establishing the Gregorian chant, and the church reveres him as one of her four great doctors. His feast day is celebrated on September 3 by the Roman Catholic, the date of his papal consecration.

Moving Pictures

On this day in 1923, the Phonofilm, the first motion picture with a sound-on-film track, was demonstrated at a press conference in Hollywood. It was developed in 1920 by Dr. Lee De Forest, who also invented the radio tube in 1907. Dancers and musicians were shown on the film with music, but without voice dialogue. The sound was imaged in a narrow margin alongside the picture frames on the film. De Forest's process came several years before the 1928 film *The Jazz Singer*, but that film used the Warner Vitaphone system. The Vitaphone system attempted to synchronize its sound from a record player turntable connected to the film projector. The De Forest process read a series of light and dark areas on the film itself, using a photocell to convert to audio.

*M*ARCH 13

DAILY READING

"Is not God in the heights of heaven?
And see how lofty are the highest stars!" (JOB 22:12)

FEAST DAYS

ca. 656	Mochoemoc	Irish monk
712	Gerald	Lindisfarne monk
842	Heldrad	Benedictine monk

ENTRANCE AND EXIT

b. 1733	Joseph Priestly	English scientist and clergyman
b. 1855	Percival Lowell	American astronomer
b. 1956	Dana Delany	American actor
d. 1842	Henry Shrapnel	English inventor
d. 1901	Benjamin Harrison	23rd American president
d. 2006	Lois Maureen Stapleton	American actor

Discovery of Uranus

The discovery of the seventh planet from the sun is attributed to Frederick William Herschel on this day in 1781. He was an avid amateur astronomer, telescope maker, music teacher, and composer. The first recorded sighting of Uranus was in 1690 by the Astronomer Royal John Flamsteed, but he failed to notice its motion and so entered it into his star catalog as *34 Tauri*. In the course of the next century, several other astronomers recorded its position. The most unfortunate of these was Pierre Le Monier, who observed Uranus eight times in four weeks but failed to realize it was a planet.

At first, Herschel thought it was a comet and named it Georgium Sidus (George's Star), in honor of George III, but its motion was unlike that of a comet. When news of Herschel's observations reached Astronomer Royal Nevil Maskelyne, he suggested that it might be a planet. Mathematical confirmation of this proposal created a sensation, making Herschel the most celebrated astronomer of his day, and he was appointed King's Astronomer.

Other than in Britain, where the new planet was referred to as the Georgian Planet for nearly sixty years, there was great resistance to Herschel's suggested name for the planet. The newly created United States and France, recently and still at war with Britain, particularly found the name anathema, and it was quickly christened Herschel. Eventually, a multitude of suggestions based on mythological figures was resolved in favor of Ouranos, the Greek god of the heavens, transliterated to the present Uranus.

By 1787, Herschel had also observed the Uranian satellites Titania and Oberon, which were later given these names by his son, John Herschel.

Discovery of Pluto

On this day in 1930, the Lowell Observatory in Flagstaff, Arizona, announced the discovery of the ninth planet, Pluto. Its discoverer was Clyde William Tombaugh (1906–97). Few astronomers have scanned the sky with such minute detail as Tombaugh.

In 1929, Tombaugh was hired as a junior astronomer to join in the search for a "Planet X" beyond Neptune. Working through the nights in a cold, unheated dome, he made pairs of exposures of portions of the sky with time intervals of two to six days. These were scrutinized under a device called a blink comparator in hopes of detecting a small shift in position of one of the hundreds of thousands of points of light–the sign of a planet among a field of stars. During his work, he photographed 65 percent of the sky and spent thousands of hours examining millions of star images, most with the blink comparator. As well as Pluto, he discovered several star clusters, a comet, and more than a hundred asteroids.

Dr. Tombaugh, the former farm boy with a fondness for corny jokes and puns, delighted in recounting the tale of his discovery of Pluto, which he compared to finding a needle in a haystack. It was tedious work but better than pitching hay on his father's farm, he liked to say: "I'd had my hay day."

In August 2006, astronomers at the International Astronomical Union decided that Pluto was not a planet but a "dwarf planet," a new prototype object under the orbit of Neptune.

MARCH 14

DAILY READING

By standing firm you will gain life. (LUKE 21:19)

FEAST DAYS

558	Lubinus	Patron of innkeepers
968	Matilda	Patron of Saxony
1308	James Capocci	Bishop of Naples

ENTRANCE AND EXIT

b. 1808	Johann Strauss the Elder	Austrian composer
b. 1897	Albert Einstein	German scientist
b. 1933	Michael Caine	English actor
d. 1883	Karl Marx	German philosopher
d. 1932	George Eastman	American actor
d. 1975	Susan Hayward	American actor

Eysteinn Ásgrímsson

The medieval monk Eysteinn Ásgrímsson (1310–61), who died on this day, is best known for producing one of the finest religious poems produced in Roman Catholic Iceland. *Lilja* (*The Lily*) is a comprehensive survey of Christian belief about the fall of Satan, the creation, the first sin, and the birth, life, and passion of Christ, followed by twenty-five stanzas on contrition and a prayer to the Virgin Mary. Ásgrímsson abandoned traditional poetic forms and wrote *Lilja* as a rapid, vivid narrative that remained the most ambitious and popular of the Icelandic religious poems until the appearance of the Lutheran passion hymns of the seventeenth century.

Little is known about Ásgrímsson's life, but it is thought that he lived in Thykkvabaer. In 1349 he was imprisoned for thrashing his abbot and perhaps for a breach of chastity as well. That same year, he was made an official of the Skálholt bishopric, and he attended the bishop on a mission to the remote villages of Iceland.

Matilda of Saxony

According to the Catholic Encyclopaedia (1913), St. Matilda (c. 895–968) was the daughter of Count Dietrich of Westphalia and Reinhild of Denmark. She was also known as Mechtildis and Maud. She was raised by her grandmother, the Abbess of Eufurt in a convent. Matilda married Henry the Fowler, son of Duke Otto of Saxony, in the year 909. He succeeded his father as Duke in the year 912 and in 919 succeeded King Conrad I to the German throne. She was noted for her piety and charitable works. She was widowed in the year 936, and supported her son Henry's claim to his father's throne. When her son Otto (the Great) was elected, she persuaded him to name Henry Duke of Bavaria after he had led an unsuccessful revolt. She was severely criticized by both Otto and Henry for what they considered her extravagant charities. She resigned her inheritance to her sons, and retired to her country home but was called to the court through the intercession of Otto's wife, Edith. When Henry again revolted, Otto put down the insurrection in the year 941 with great cruelty. Matilda censored Henry when he began another revolt against Otto in the year 953 and for his ruthlessness in suppressing a revolt by his own subjects; at that time she prophesized his imminent death. When he did die in 955, she devoted herself to building three convents and a monastery, and spent most of the declining years of her life at the convent at Nordhausen she had built. She died at the monastery at Quedlinburg on March 14 and was buried there with Henry.

George Eastman

"Light makes photography. Embrace light. Admire it. Love it. But above all, know light. Know it for all you are worth, and you will know the key to photography."

*M*ARCH 15

DAILY READING

Have not I commanded you? Be strong and courageous.
Do not be terrified; do not be discouraged,
for the Lord your God will be with you wherever you go. (JOSH 1:9)

FEAST DAYS

ca. 1st cent.	Longinus	Roman soldier
1660	Louise de Marillac	Founder of the Daughters of Charity
1880	Clemens Mary Hofbauer	Apostle of Vienna

ENTRANCE AND EXIT

b. 44 BC	Julius Caesar	Roman Emperor
b. 1838	Alice Cunningham Fletcher	American scientist
b. 1935	Jimmy Swaggart	American evangelist
d. 1950	Alice Stone Blackwell	American reformer
d. 1975	Aristotle Onassis	Greek magnate
d. 1994	Mae Zetterling	Swedish actor

Ides of March

In the complicated world of the Roman calendar, there were forty-five public festivals. Most months had days sacred to Jupiter, known as "ides," and in March, May, July, and October, the ides fell on the 15th. To the superstitious, the ides were unlucky days, similar to Friday the 13th today.

It is thought that Julius Caesar was assassinated on the ides of March, an event featured in Shakespeare's tragedy:

Caesar: Who is it in the press that calls on me?
I hear a tongue, shriller than all the music
Cry "Caesar!" Speak. Caesar is turn'd to hear.
Soothsayer: Beware the ides of March.

–Act 1, scene II

Brutus: Remember March, the ides of March remember:
Did not great Julius bleed for justice' sake?
What villain touch'd his body, that did stab,
And not for justice? What, shall one of us
That struck the foremost man of all this world
But for supporting robbers, shall we now
Contaminate our fingers with base bribes,
And sell the mighty space of our large honours
For so much trash as may be grasped thus?
I had rather be a dog, and bay the moon,
Than such a Roman.

–Act 4, scene III

Noteworthy

221 Liu Bei, a Chinese warlord and member of the Han royal house, declares himself emperor of Shu-Han, claiming his legitimate succession to the Han dynasty.

351 Constantius II elevates his cousin Gallus to Caesar, and puts him in charge of the Eastern part of the Roman Empire.

1545 First meeting of the Council of Trent.

1672 Charles II of England issues the Royal Declaration of Indulgence.

1892 Liverpool Football Club founded by John Houlding.

1917 Tsar Nicholas II of Russia abdicates himself and his son from the Russian throne and his brother the Grand Duke becomes Tsar.

1939 World War II: Nazi troops occupy the remaining part of Bohemia and Moravia; Czechoslovakia ceases to exist.

2004 Announcement of the discovery of 90377 Sedna, the farthest natural object in the solar system so far observed.

*M*ARCH 16

DAILY READING

Therefore, as God's chosen people, holy and dearly loved, clothe yourselves with compassion, kindness, humility, gentleness and patience. (COL 3:12)

FEAST DAYS

ca. 366	Abraham Kidunaia	Missionary priest
ca. 560	Finian the Leper	Disciple of St. Columba
794	Meningaud	Bishop of Wurzburg

ENTRANCE AND EXIT

b. 1750	Caroline Lucretia Herschel	German astronomer
b. 1932	Ronnie Walter Cunningham	American astronaut
b. 1953	Isabelle Huppert	French actor
d. 1941	John Murray	Canadian scientist
d. 1963	William Henry Beveridge	English economist
d. 1971	Thomas Dewey	American politician

The Fictional Saint

It is thought that the legend of St. Urho was created in 1956 by Richard Mattson, a retail store manager from Virginia, as a rival to St. Patrick. His joke story of the patron saint of Finland quickly gained credence, and today St. Urho's day is celebrated in Finnish centers in Virginia, Minnesota, and New York, as well as cities in Finland on March 16.

Mattson's story was a simple retelling based on the legend of St. Patrick, who is said to have expelled snakes from Ireland. In Mattson's version, St. Urho was famous for driving poisonous frogs from Finland! In some later versions, it is supposed to be grasshoppers rather than frogs.

It is thought that Mattson named the saint after Urho Kekkonen became the president of Finland in March 1956. According to Mattson, Urho was a powerful man who gained his strength from fish soup (*kalla mojakka*) and sour whole milk (*feelia sour*).

There are varied rituals and ceremonies on St. Urho's day that include Finnish national dishes, dressing up as grasshoppers, and wearing the saint's colors–purple and green. It is a day to party and celebrate all things Finnish. There is even an "Ode to St. Urho" that is sometimes recited:

Ooksie, kooksie kollme vee
Santia Urho is the boy for me
He chase out the hopper as big as birds
Never before have I heard those words.

He really told those bugs of green.
Bravest Finn I ever seen.
Some celebrate for St. Pat and his snake
But that Urho boy got what it takes.

He got tall and strong on feelia sour
And ate kalla mojakkaa every hour.
Thats why that guy could chase those beetles
That crew as thick as jack pine needles.

So lets give a cheer
in our very best way
On the sixteenth of March
St. Urho's Day!

Incidentally, Finland's official national patron saint is Henry of Uppsalla.

*M*ARCH 17

DAILY READING

The Lord is my shepherd, I shall not be in want.
He makes me lie down in green pastures,
he leads me beside quiet waters,
he restores my soul. (PS 23:1–3)

FEAST DAYS

ca. 1st cent.	Joseph of Glastonbury	Patron of undertakers
461	Patrick	Patron of Ireland
580	Agricola	Bishop of Chalon-sur-Saône

ENTRANCE AND EXIT

b. 1846	Kate Greenaway	English artist
b. 1919	Nathaniel King Cole	American singer
b. 1972	Melissa Auf der Maur	Canadian singer
d. 1871	Robert Chambers	Scottish theologian
d. 1956	Irène Joliot-Curie	French scientist
d. 1995	Ronnie Kray	English gangster

Patrick's Confession of Faith

On this day that celebrates St. Patrick, it is appropriate to reprint his confession:

> I, Patrick, a sinner, a most simple countryman, the least of all the faithful and most contemptible to many, had for father the deacon Calpurnius, son of the late Potitus, a presbyter, of the settlement of Bannaven Taburniae; he had a small villa nearby where I was taken captive. I was at that time about sixteen years of age. I did not, indeed, know the true God; and I was taken into captivity in Ireland with many thousands of people, according to our deserts, for quite drawn away from God, we did not keep his precepts, nor were we obedient to our presbyters who used to remind us of our salvation. And the Lord brought down on us the fury of his being and scattered us among many nations, even to the ends of the earth, where I, in my smallness, am now to be found among foreigners.
>
> And there the Lord opened my mind to an awareness of my unbelief, in order that, even so late, I might remember my transgressions and turn with all my heart to the Lord my God, who had regard for my insignificance and pitied my youth and ignorance. And he watched over me before I knew him, and before I learned sense or even distinguished between good and evil, and he protected me, and consoled me as a father would his son.
>
> Therefore, indeed, I cannot keep silent, nor would it be proper, so many favours and graces has the Lord deigned to bestow on me in the land of my captivity. For after chastisement from God, and recognizing him, our way to repay him is to exalt him and confess his wonders before every nation under heaven:
>
> For there is no other God, nor ever was before, nor shall be hereafter, but God the Father, unbegotten and without beginning, in whom all things began, whose are all things, as we have been taught; and his son Jesus Christ, who manifestly always existed with the Father, before the beginning of time in the spirit with the Father, indescribably begotten before all things, and all things visible and invisible were made by him. He was made man, conquered death and was received into Heaven, to the Father who gave him all power over every name in Heaven and on Earth and in Hell, so that every tongue should confess that Jesus Christ is Lord and God, in whom we believe. And we look to his imminent coming again, the judge of the living and the dead, who will render to each according to his deeds. And he poured out his Holy Spirit on us in abundance, the gift and pledge of immortality, which makes the believers and the obedient into sons of God and co-heirs of Christ who is revealed, and we worship one God in the Trinity of holy name.

Proverbs from the Emerald Isle

A drink precedes a story.

Time is a great storyteller.

A friend's eye is a good mirror.

It is not a secret if it is known by three people.

The man with the boots does not mind where he places his foot.

If you do not sow in the spring, you will not reap in the autumn.

*M*ARCH 18

DAILY READING

May the God of hope fill you with all joy and peace
as you trust in him, so that you may overflow
with hope by the power of the Holy Spirit. (ROM 15:13)

FEAST DAYS

386	Cyril of Jerusalem	Doctor of the Church
588	Frigidian	Bishop of Lucca, Italy
978	Edward the Martyr	Son of King Edgar the Peaceful

ENTRANCE AND EXIT

b. 1858	Rudolph Christian Karl Diesel	German inventor
b. 1869	Neville Chamberlain	English prime minister
b. 1893	Wilfred Owen	English soldier and poet
d. 1745	Sir Robert Walpole	English prime minister
d. 1871	Augustus de Morgan	English mathematician
d. 2001	John Phillips	American singer

National Biodiesel Day

National Biodiesel Day is sponsored by the American Soybean Association and the National Biodiesel Board. It honors the foresight of Rudolph Diesel (1858–1913) in recognizing the "valuable role of vegetable oil based fuel."

Rudolph Diesel ran his prototype combustion engine on peanut oil. A year before his death, Diesel said, "The use of vegetable oils for engine fuels may seem insignificant today, but such oils may become, in the course of time, as important as petroleum and the coal tar products of the present time."

There is great interest in replacing fossil fuels with alternative fuels. In his State of the Union Address in January 2006, President Bush acknowledged this need:

> Keeping America competitive requires affordable energy. And here we have a serious problem: America is addicted to oil, which is often imported from unstable parts of the world. The best way to break this addiction is through technology.
>
> We must also change how we power our automobiles. We will increase our research in better batteries for hybrid and electric cars, and in pollution-free cars that run on hydrogen. We'll also fund additional research in cutting-edge methods of producing ethanol, not just from corn, but from wood chips and stalks, or switch grass. Our goal is to make this new kind of ethanol practical and competitive within six years.

Extract from Neville Chamberlain's Historic Speech to the Nation

September 3, 1939, 11:15 a.m.

> I am speaking to you from the Cabinet Room at 10 Downing Street. This morning the British Ambassador in Berlin handed the German Government an official note stating that unless we heard from them by eleven o'clock, that they were prepared at once to withdraw their troops from Poland, a state of war would exist between us. I have to tell you now that no such undertaking has been received, and consequently this county is at war with Germany.
>
> You can imagine what a bitter blow it is to me that all my long struggle to win peace has failed. Yet I cannot believe that there is anything more or anything different that I could have done and that would have been more successful.

MARCH 19

DAILY READING

The fruit of the Spirit is love, joy, peace, patience, kindness, goodness, faithfulness, gentleness and self-control. Against such things there is no law. (GAL 5:22–23)

FEAST DAYS

640	Leontius	Bishop of Saintes, France
668	Lanold	Roman priest
774	Alcmund	English prince

ENTRANCE AND EXIT

b. 1813	David Livingstone	Scottish missionary
b. 1821	Richard Francis Burton	English explorer
b. 1947	Glenn Close	American actor
d. 1702	King William III	Prince of Orange
d. 1950	Edgar Rice Burroughs	American writer
d. 1997	Willem De Kooning	American artist

Thomas Ken

Thomas Ken (b. 1637), who died on this day in 1711, was the conscientious and fearless Bishop of Bath and Wells. He was educated at Winchester College and Hart Hall, Oxford. He completed his BA degree in 1661 and his MA degree in 1664. In 1662, he was ordained and served as curate of Little Easton in Essex for three years, but returned to Winchester as domestic chaplain to Bishop Morley. While he was there, he prepared his "Manual of Prayers for Use of the Scholars of Winchester College, 1674," for the boys of the school.

He wrote the hymns "Awake My Soul" and "All Praise to Thee," which were published in his *Manual of Prayers*. In 1679, he went to The Hague as the chaplain to Princess Mary, later Queen Mary, wife of William II of Orange. He was dismissed a year later because he incurred William's displeasure because of his candid criticism.

He was appointed bishop in 1685 by Charles II and dispensed with the customary consecration dinner, choosing to donate £100, which would have been the cost, to charity. Eight days later King Charles II died from a stroke. James II, who succeeded Charles II, was impressed with Ken. He considered him to be the most eloquent Protestant preacher of his time, but Ken was one of the seven bishops imprisoned at the Tower of London for refusing to read at the King's command the Declaration of Indulgence.

Thomas Ken wrote the lyrics to the popular hymn "Praise God from Whom All Blessings Flow" in 1674. Today it is sung as the doxology in many churches:

Praise God, from Whom all blessings flow;
Praise Him, all creatures here below;
Praise Him above, ye heavenly host;
Praise Father, Son, and Holy Ghost.

David Livingstone

"If a commission by an earthly king is considered a honor, how can a commission by a Heavenly King be considered a sacrifice?"

March 20

DAILY READING

Like newborn babies, crave pure spiritual milk,
so that by it you may grow up in your salvation,
now that you have tasted that the Lord is good. (1 PET 2:2–3)

FEAST DAYS

1st cent.	Archippus	Companion of St. Paul
687	Herbert of Derwentwater	Companion of St. Cuthbert
703	Wulfram of Fontenelle	Patron of Abbeville, France

ENTRANCE AND EXIT

b. 43 BC	Ovid	Roman poet
b. 1917	Dame Vera Lynn	English singer
b. 1958	Holly Hunter	American actor
d. 1413	Henry IV	King of England
d. 1964	Brendan Behan	Irish writer
d. 2004	Juliana	Queen of Netherlands

St. Cuthbert

St. Cuthbert is one of the best loved Anglo Saxon saints. He was born around AD 634 in the Scottish borderlands and worked as a shepherd. Tradition records that one night, by the River Leader, he became aware of a great light, stretching between earth and sky. The light faded, and Cuthbert was left to wonder the meaning of the vision he had witnessed.

He later discovered that on that same night, August 31, 651, Aiden, Bishop of Lindisfarne, had died. To the young shepherd, the vision seemed to be a challenge and a call to serve God. He entered the Monastery of Old Melrose–one of the parent seats of the Celtic Church and founded by Aiden–and there he followed thirteen years of monastic life.

Bede tells us that Cuthbert had the gift of healing and so, wherever he went, people would flock to him. In 664, the Synod of Whitby was held to settle the differences in church life between Celtic and Roman. Cuthbert, although trained in the Celtic Church, followed the decision of the synod and accepted the Roman system.

Cuthbert was sent to Lindisfarne as prior and won the respect of his monks and of the people he met in his mission work. He was consecrated bishop on Easter Day 685, at York, and became Bishop of Lindisfarne, thus following in Aiden's footsteps. He died in 687 and was buried on March 20 in the little church of St. Peter. In 883, his remains were buried in Chester-le-Street and, in 996, his remains finally came to rest in Durham Cathedral.

Noteworthy

1593 The Augsburg Confession (Unaltered) was officially adopted by Sweden as a result of the Decree of Uppsala.

1804 Cephas Bennett, missionary to Burma, was born in Homer, New York (d. 1885).

1806 Arthur Tozer Russell, hymn translator, was born at Northampton, England (d. 1874).

1885 Christopher Wordsworth, Anglican clergyman and hymnist and nephew of the English poet William Wordsworth, died in Lincoln, England (b. 1807).

1889 Albrecht Ritschl (b. 1822), a leading German Protestant theologian of the latter half of the nineteenth century, died.

1897 Frank Sheed, Roman Catholic lay theologian and founder of Sheed and Ward, publishers of books in the areas of biography, history, philosophy, theology, and literature, was born.

1928 Fred M. Rogers, American Presbyterian clergyman and host of public television's longest-running children's program, *Mr. Rogers' Neighborhood*, was born in Latrobe, Pennsylvania (d. February 27, 2003).

*M*ARCH 21

DAILY READING

Blessed is the man who trusts in the Lord, whose confidence is in him.
He will be like a tree planted by the water that sends out its roots by the stream.
It does not fear when heat comes; its leaves are always green.
It has no worries in a year of drought. (JER 17:7–8)

FEAST DAYS

370	Serapion the Scholastic	Bishop of Thmius, Egypt
c. 547	Benedict	Founder of the Benedictine Order
1487	Nicholas von Flüe	Swiss hermit

ENTRANCE AND EXIT

b. 1685	Johann Sebastian Bach	German composer
b. 1917	Yigael Yadin	Israeli archaeologist
b. 1962	Rosie O'Donnell	American actor
d. 1556	Thomas Cranmer	Archbishop of Canterbury
d. 1617	Pocahantas–Mrs. Jean Rolfe	Native American princess
d. 1988	Patrick Steptoe	English scientist

Vernal Equinox Day

Today is a national holiday in Japan to mark the vernal equinox, when the sun crosses the equator, making night and day equal in length. Japanese people pay their respects to ancestors by visiting and cleaning ancestral graves and offering flowers and incense to console ancestral spirits. They also take family walks and show their affection for all living things.

Following Vernal Equinox Day or *Shunbun no Hi*, days gradually get longer and nights shorter. There's an old saying that the chill of winter finally disappears after *Shunbun no Hi*, and temperatures do get higher from around this time. Cherry blossoms–the most popular symbol of spring in Japan–begin to bloom, first in the south and then in the colder parts of the country in the north.

In the Northern Hemisphere, today is the start of spring, a season of new life and renewal. In the Julian calendar, this period was associated with the start of the New Year and many people undertook new resolutions and enterprises at this time.

The Death of Thomas Cranmer

Archbishop Thomas Cranmer (1489–1556) was the main impetus behind the Protestant Reformation in England, the establishment of the Church of England, and the creation of the first English Prayer Book (1549). Cranmer was accused of heresy under the reign of Queen Mary and imprisoned in the Tower of London. This is an extract of an eyewitness account of his execution:

> On Saturday 21 of March, was his day appointed to die. When praying was done, he stood up, and, having leave to speak, said, "Good people, I had intended indeed to desire you to pray for me; which because Mr Doctor hath desired, and you have done already, I thank you most heartily for it. And now will I pray for myself, as I could best devise for mine own comfort, and say the prayer, word for word, as I have here written it." And he read it standing: and after kneeled down, and said the Lord's Prayer; and all the people on their knees devoutly praying with him. . . .
>
> And then rising, he said, "Every man desireth, good people, at the time of their deaths, to give some good exhortation, that other may remember after their deaths, and be the better thereby. So I beseech God grant me grace, that I may speak something, at this my departing, whereby God may be glorified, and you edified. . . . And now I come to the great thing that troubleth my conscience more than any other thing that ever I said or did in my life: and that is, the setting abroad of writings contrary to the truth. Which here now I renounce and refuse, as things written with my hand, contrary to the truth which I thought in my heart, and written for fear of death, and to save my life, if it might be: and that is, all such bills, which I have written or signed with mine own hand since my degradation: wherein I have written many things untrue. And forasmuch as my hand offended in writing contrary to my heart, therefore my hand shall first be punished: for if I may come to the fire, it shall be first burned. And as for the pope, I refuse him, as Christ's enemy and antichrist, with all his false doctrine."

*M*ARCH 22

DAILY READING

"Whoever drinks the water I give him will never thirst. Indeed, the water I give him will become in him a spring of water welling up to eternal life." (JOHN 4:14)

FEAST DAYS

484	Octavian	Priest at Carthage
745	Harlandis	First abbess of Arland, Belgium
1946	Clemens August von Galen	Nazi martyr, Bishop of Munster, Germany

ENTRANCE AND EXIT

b. 1599	Sir Anthony Van Dyck	Flemish painter
b. 1868	Robert Andrews Millikan	American scientist
b. 1976	Reese Witherspoon	American actor
d. 1832	Johann Wolfgang von Goethe	German writer
d. 1960	Agnes Arber	English botanist
d. 2001	William Hanna	American animator

World Day for Water

World Water Day is an initiative that grew out of the 1992 United Nations Conference on Environment and Development (UNCED) in Rio de Janeiro. The United Nations General Assembly designated March 22 of each year as the World Day for Water by adopting a resolution. Nations were invited to devote the day to highlight the crucial issues surrounding water availability and quality.

Under the leadership of the Food and Agriculture Organization (FAO), the 2007 theme is "Coping with Water Scarcity." The theme highlights the significance of cooperation and importance of an integrated approach to water resource management of water at international, national, and local levels. The UN estimates that by 2025 nearly two billion people will face absolute water shortage.

The theme was decided among all members of UN Water at the World Water Week in Stockholm in August 2006. FAO acts as coordinator, on behalf of all the UN Agencies and Programs members of UN-Water for the celebration of World Water Day 2007. It is assisted by the Secretariat for UN-Water, which is based in New York, and which is serving as point of contact within the UN system for freshwater-related issues.

Over one hundred events have been planned for World Water Day in over fifty nations, including conferences, workshops, exhibitions, and political lobbying.

Agnes Arber

The Cambridge botanist Agnes Arber, (née Robertson February 23, 1879–March 22, 1960) was a renowned plant morphologist and anatomist, historian of botany, botanical bibliographer, and philosopher of biology. This stature was achieved as a result of innumerable papers and eight books, including: *Herbals* (1912, 1938, 1986); *Water Plants* (1920); *Goethe's Botany* (1946); *The Natural Philosophy of Plant Form* (1950); and *The Mind and the Eye* (1954).

She is best known outside botany because of her *Herbals* book and is also significant to women's studies because she was the first woman botanist and only the third woman overall elected to the Royal Society, in 1946.

Arber was greatly influenced by the British morphologist Ethel Sargant (October 28, 1863–January 16, 1918), who for the last six years of her life lived in nearby Girton in the Old Rectory. Agnes is buried next to her husband, Newell Arber, at St. Andrew's Parish Church in Girton.

MARCH 23

DAILY READING

Blessed is the man who perseveres under trial, because when he has stood the test, he will receive the crown of life that God has promised to those who love him. (JAS 1:12)

FEAST DAYS

ca. 460	Gwinear	Irish miracle worker
1606	Turibius de Mongrovejo	Archbishop of Lima, Peru
1702	Joseph Oriol	Spanish missionary

ENTRANCE AND EXIT

b. 1769	William Smith	English geologist
b. 1900	Erich Fromm	American scientist
b. 1962	Sir Steve Redgrave	English sportsman
d. 1555	Julius III	Italian Pope
d. 1842	Stendahl	French writer
d. 1994	Giulietta Masina	Italian actor

World Meteorological Day

Every year on March 23, the World Meteorological Organization (WMO) and the worldwide meteorological community celebrate the foundation of WMO on this day in 1950 as a specialized agency of the United Nations System.

In recent years, there has been renewed interest in the climate and the environmental conditions in the polar regions, which has some important historical antecedents, since these regions have traditionally played a crucial role in world weather.

In 2007, the theme is "Polar Meteorology: Understanding Global Impacts," in recognition of the importance of, and as a contribution to, International Polar Year, which is being cosponsored by WMO and the International Council for Science (ICSU).

The 2007 theme will provide valuable contributions to the assessment of climate change and its impacts. Although the polar regions are generally distant from widely populated zones, there is a great need for reliable weather forecasts in these areas. Around the Arctic, forecasts are needed for the protection of indigenous communities and in support of maritime operations, as well as for oil and gas exploration and production. In the Antarctic, reliable forecasts are required for complex air and marine logistical operations, as well as in support of scientific research programs and the expanding tourism industry.

Gregory the Illuminator

On this day, the Armenian Church celebrates the feast of St. Gregory, called the "Enlightener" or "Illuminator." Gregory was from a noble family and was educated in Caesarea, then a Christian center. He entered the service of King Tiridates of Armenia and after much persecution succeeded in converting the king in AD 301.

Tiridates in turn helped Gregory to convert the whole country to Christianity. In some regions this took place with relative ease; in others evangelization met great resistance. With the help of the King, Gregory destroyed the pagan sanctuaries and crushed the armed opposition of the pagan priests. Gregory was formally designated as the supreme head of the church, and was sent to Caesarea to be ordained a bishop. He thus became the first in an unbroken line of 131 catholicoi (or "universal bishops") of the Armenian Church.

Gregory was also instrumental in the conversion of the neighboring countries of Georgia and Albania. He built the first Christian cathedral in Vagharshapat, near Mount Ararat, then the capital of Armenia.

*M*ARCH 24

DAILY READING

I tell you the truth, unless a kernel of wheat falls to the ground and dies, it remains only a single seed. But if it dies, it produces many seeds. (JOHN 12:24)

FEAST DAYS

304	Irenaeus of Sirmium	Bishop of Pannonia, Hungary
ca. 712	Hildelith	Anglo Saxon princess
1382	Catherine of Sweden	Patron of miscarriages

ENTRANCE AND EXIT

b. 1834	William Morris	English poet
b. 1874	Harry Houdini	American magician
b. 1970	Lara Flynn Boyle	American actor
d. 1603	Elizabeth I	Queen of England
d. 1953	Mary	Queen of England
d. 1990	An Wang	Chinese scientist

Archbishop Oscar Romero

On July 9, 1998, the Archbishop of Canterbury, in the presence of Queen Elizabeth II, unveiled statutes of ten twentieth-century martyrs outside the West Front of Westminster Abbey, London. One of the martyrs was Oscar Romero (1917–1980), Archbishop of San Salvador, who is commemorated by the Roman Catholic and Anglican Church on this day.

In 1977, Romero became the Archbishop of San Salvador. At this time, the peasants were forming small Christian communities and began to see themselves as victims of unjust treatment and started to work for land reform. El Salvador's land-owning class and government began to take notice of the peasant movement.

Priests and lay members of the small Christian communities were killed, and Archbishop Romero was one of the only bishops to speak out against what was happening. He made the world aware of what was taking place in his country, was nominated for a Nobel Peace Prize, and received a number of honorary degrees. He revealed that he had received death threats in response to his outspokenness and activism. He knew that his life was in great danger.

Oscar Romero was assassinated on March 24, 1980, while presiding at the Eucharist. The day before he had publicly called on soldiers to ignore their orders to kill peasants and asked the government to let the peasants' voices be heard.

Archbishop Oscar Romero Quotes

If they don't let us speak, if they kill all the priests and the bishop too, and you are left a people without priests, each one of you must become God's microphone, each one of you must become a prophet.

You can tell the people that if they succeed in killing me, that I forgive and bless those who do it. Hopefully, they will realize they are wasting their time. A bishop will die, but the church of God, which is the people, will never perish.

We may never see the end results, but that is the difference between the master builder and the worker. We are workers, not master builders; ministers, not messiahs. We are prophets of a future not our own.

Greek Independence Day

A Proclamation by the President of the United States of America:

> On Greek Independence Day, we celebrate our special ties of friendship, history, and shared values with Greece.
>
> Our country has welcomed generations of Greek immigrants, and we are grateful for their talents, wisdom, and creativity. We honor the Greek spirit that values family and education, public service and faith. Their strong record of public service has also strengthened our democracy, and their contributions have made America a better place.
>
> NOW, THEREFORE, I, GEORGE W. BUSH, President of the United States of America, by virtue of the authority vested in me by the Constitution and laws of the United States, do hereby proclaim March 25, 2005, as Greek Independence Day: A National Day of Celebration of Greek and American Democracy. I call upon all Americans to observe this day with appropriate ceremonies and activities.

MARCH 25

DAILY READING

In the sixth month, God sent the angel Gabriel to Nazareth, a town in Galilee, to a virgin pledged to be married to a man named Joseph, a descendant of David. The virgin's name was Mary. (LUKE 1:26)

FEAST DAYS

ca. 30	Dismas	One of the thieves crucified with Jesus
ca. 720	Hermeland	French priest
1732	Lucia Filippini	Founder of the Pious Matrons

ENTRANCE AND EXIT

b. 1908	Sir David Lean	English film director
b. 1942	Aretha Franklin	American singer
b. 1965	Sarah Jessica Parker	American actor
d. 1918	Claude Débussy	French composer
d. 1991	Eileen Joyce	Australian pianist
d. 2006	Buck Owens	American singer

Lady Day

Today is the Feast of the Annunciation, popularly known as Lady Day in honor of the Virgin Mary. The Feast of the Annunciation marks the visit of the angel Gabriel to the Virgin Mary, during which he told her that she would be the mother of Jesus Christ, the Son of God. Since it occurs nine months before the birth of Jesus on Christmas Day, the Annunciation marks the actual incarnation of Jesus Christ–the moment that Jesus was conceived and that the Son of God became the son of the Virgin. The festival has been celebrated since the fifth century AD.

In his *Golden Legend* (1275) Jacobus de Voragine, Archbishop of Genoa wrote:

> This blessed Annunciation happened the twenty fifth day of the month of March, on which day happened also, as well to fore as after, these things that hereafter be named. On that same day Adam, the first man, was created and fell into original sin by in obedience, and was put out of paradise terrestrial. After, the angel showed the conception of our Lord to the glorious Virgin Mary. Also that same day of the month Cain slew Abel his brother. Also Melchisedech made offering to God of bread and wine in the presence of Abraham. Also on the same day Abraham offered Isaac his son. That same day St. John Baptist was beheaded, and St. Peter was that day delivered out of prison, and St. James the more, that day beheaded of Herod. And our Lord Jesu Christ was on that day crucified, wherefore that is a day of great reverence.

From the twelfth century to 1752, this day also marked the formal beginning of the year, prior to the adoption of the Gregorian calendar in England.

Waffle Day

In Sweden, Lady Day is known as *Varfrudagen*, which sounds like the Swedish for waffles–*vaffeldagen*. Traditionally, country people would put aside indoor winter tasks such as wood cutting, spinning, and weaving to prepare for spring planting. And their menu would include spring foods such as *frasvafflor* or crisp waffles.

*M*ARCH 26

DAILY READING

If we confess our sins, he is faithful and just and will forgive us our sins and purify us from all unrighteousness. (1 JOHN 1:9)

FEAST DAYS

ca. 651	Braulio	Patron of Aragon, Spain
ca. 743	Liudger	Apostle of Saxony
1144	William of Norwich	Patron of torture victims

ENTRANCE AND EXIT

b. 1874	Robert Frost	American poet
b. 1911	Tennessee Williams	American writer
b. 1985	Keira Knightley	English actor
d. 1982	Walt Whitman	American poet
d. 1945	David Lloyd George	British prime minister
d. 2005	James Callaghan	British prime minister

The Prince of People

Today, the people of Hawaii celebrate Prince Jonah Kuhio Kalanianaole (1871–1922) Day, which honors the birthday of Hawaii's second delegate to Congress. Prince Kuhio was born in Koloa, Kauai. He was the youngest of three sons of Kauai High Chief David Kahalepouli Piikoi and Princess Kinoiki Kekaulike. He served as the Territory of Hawaii's delegate to the U.S. Congress from 1903 to 1921. With John Wise, John Lane, and Noah Alulii, they formed the first Hawaiian civic club in 1917 to stimulate civic efforts and education within the Hawaiian community and promote Hawaiian culture.

Kuhio was often called Ke Ali'i Makaainana (Prince of People) and is well known for his efforts to preserve and strengthen the Hawaiian people. He was in line to become king before the monarchy was overthrown in 1893. Kuhio is best remembered for his successful effort to get Congress to pass the 1920 Hawaiian Homes Commission Act, which provides homesteads for native Hawaiians. It was his dream to save the rapidly declining Hawaiian race from extinction. His plan was to return tenement dwellers to the land and encourage them to be self-sufficient farmers, ranchers, and homesteaders on leased parcels of reserved land.

He died of heart disease at the age of fifty and was buried at the royal mausoleum in Nuuanu Valley on Oahu. A new statue honoring Prince Kuhio was dedicated in 2002 at his birthplace.

Noteworthy

1027 John XIX crowns Conrad II the Salier Roman German emperor.
1147 Jewish community in Cologne fast to commemorate anti-Jewish violence.
1526 King François I returns captured land to France.
1534 Lübeck accepts free Dutch ships into the East Sea.
1636 University of Utrecht opening ceremony.
1668 England takes control of Bombay, India.
1692 King Maximilian installed as land guardian of South Netherlands.
1780 First Sunday newspapers issued—*The British Gazette* and *Sunday Monitor.*
1790 Congress passes Naturalization Act, which requires two-year residency.
1793 The Holy Roman Empire declares war on France.
1799 Napolean captures Jaffa Palestine.
1830 *Book of Mormon* published by Joseph Smith.
1885 Eastman Dry Plate Co. in Rochester, New Hork, manufactures first movie film.
1933 Adolf Hitler orders boycott of all Jewish businesses in Germany.
1994 Talk show hostess Ricki Lake weds Rob Sussman.
2000 Former KGB agent Vladimir Putin elected as Russian leader.

*M*ARCH 27

DAILY READING

For it has been granted to you on behalf of Christ
not only to believe on him, but also to suffer for him. (PHIL 1:29)

FEAST DAYS

5th cent.	Augusta di Serravalle	German martyr
749	John of Damascus	Church father
1197	William Tempier	Bishop of Poitiers, France

ENTRANCE AND EXIT

b. 1845	Wilhelm Conrad Röntgen	German scientist
b. 1863	Sir Henry Royce	English industrialist
b. 1970	Mariah Carey	Canadian singer
d. 1625	James I	King of England
d. 1997	Sir Malcolm Brown	English geologist
d. 2002	Dudley Moore	English actor

Discovery of Florida

The famous Spanish explorer Juan Ponce de Léon (ca. 1460–1521) was inspired by Christopher Columbus's voyage to the Americas in 1492. In fact, many historians think that he was part of Columbus's second expedition across the Atlantic in 1493.

In 1502 Ponce de Léon sailed to the West Indian island of Hispaniola, where he played a key role in containing a native uprising against Spanish rule. As a reward for his service, the Spanish governor of Hispaniola placed Ponce de Léon in charge of the eastern part of the island.

On March 3, 1513, Ponce de Léon left Puerto Rico on a search for the fabled Fountain of Youth. He sailed past the Bahamas and, on March 27, he first saw the mainland of Florida. Ponce de Léon called the new land *Tierra La Florida*, because he discovered it on Palm Sunday (*Pascua Florida* in Spanish). On April 2, he landed just north of present-day St. Augustine, and remained there for six days.

He spent several months exploring the Florida coastline, continuing his search for the Fountain of Youth. He returned to Puerto Rico in October, disappointed that he had been unable to locate the Fountain. The following year Ponce de Léon traveled to Spain, where the King granted him permission to settle in Florida.

After several more years in Puerto Rico, Ponce de Léon left for Florida with two ships and two hundred men in early 1521. Shortly after landing on Florida's west coast, they were attacked by Seminole Indians. Ponce de Léon was struck by an arrow during the attack and was immediately taken to Cuba, where he died. He was buried in Puerto Rico.

George Matheson

The Scottish clergyman and hymn writer, George Matheson (1842–1906) was born on this day. He is best remembered for his hymn, "O Love That Will Not Let Me Go," written on June 6, 1882, to mark the occasion of his sister's marriage. He recalled what led to his composition:

> I was alone in the manse at that time. Something happened to me, which was known only to myself, and which caused me the most severe mental suffering. The hymn was the fruit of that suffering. It was the quickest bit of work I ever did in my life. I had the impression of having it dictated to me by some inward voice rather than of working it out myself.

O Love That Will Not Let Me Go

O Love that wilt not let me go,
I rest my weary soul in thee;
I give thee back the life I owe,
That in thine ocean depths its flow
May richer, fuller be.

O light that foll'west all my way,
I yield my flick'ring torch to thee;
My heart restores its borrowed ray,
That in thy sunshine's blaze its day
May brighter, fairer be.

O Joy that seekest me through pain,
I cannot close my heart to thee;
I trace the rainbow through the rain,
And feel the promise is not vain,
That morn shall tearless be.

O Cross that liftest up my head,
I dare not ask to fly from thee;
I lay in dust life's glory dead,
And from the ground there blossoms red
Life that shall endless be.

*M*ARCH 28

DAILY READING:

My salvation and my honor depend on God;
he is my mighty rock, my refuge. (PS 62:7)

FEAST DAYS

440	Sixtus III	Pope
ca. 750	Gundelindis	Daughter of the Duke of Alsace
ca. 915	Tutilo von Gallen	Benedictine monk

ENTRANCE AND EXIT

b. 1483	Raphael	Italian painter
b. 1515	St. Teresa of Avila (Teresa de Cepeda y Ahumada)	Spanish Carmelite nun
b. 1936	Mario Vargas Llosa	Peruvian writer
d. 1969	Dwight David Eisenhower	34th American president
d. 1980	Jesse Owens	American athlete
d. 2004	Sir Peter Ustinov	English actor and writer

St. Alkelda

Little is known about St. Alkelda, whose feast day is celebrated on March 28. There are two churches dedicated to her at the villages of Middleham and Giggleswick in Yorkshire. According to legend, she was a chaste Saxon princess, killed by Vikings at Middleham in Yorkshire. In a window of the church there, overlooking the site of her shrine, the lady is represented as being strangled by two Danish women. Her holy well, where she was martyred, still stands near the church and has always been believed to have healing virtues. The Old English name for spring or well is *keld* and the name Alkelda is very much like *haeligkeld*–Old English for "holy well."

Some believe that local wells and springs around Giggleswick and its church were places of pilgrimage during the Middle Ages. A cast lead figurine (ca. Iron Age) was found at nearby Bank Well, suggesting a site sacred from pagan times. Rivers, wells, and springs were sacred places for the Celtic peoples. It was the custom of the early Christian church to "baptise unto Christ" any site formerly used for pagan practices.

As a patron saint of Giggleswick, Alkelda does not appear in a written record until the later Middle Ages. But yet Alkelda is herself a powerful symbol of a Christian presence since Anglo-Saxon times.

St. Teresa of Avila

St. Teresa Avila (1515–82) was one of the great Christian mystics. Overcoming physical ailments, she became fully absorbed in her devotion to God. As well as founding an order of Carmelite nuns (the Discalced Carmelites), she was an accomplished poet and this is one of her best known poems:

Christ Has No Body

Christ has no body now on earth
 but yours,
No hands but yours, No feet but yours,
Yours are the eyes through which is to
 look out
Christ's compassion to the world;
Yours are the feet with which he is to go
 about doing good;
Yours are the hands with which he is to
 bless men now.

*M*ARCH 29

DAILY READING

God made him who had no sin to be sin for us,
so that in him we might become the righteousness of God. (2 COR 5:21)

FEAST DAYS

327	Jonah of Hubaham	Persian monk
6th cent.	Gwladys	Welsh hermit
6th cent.	Gwynllyw	Welsh hermit

ENTRANCE AND EXIT

b. 1790	John Tyler	10th American president
b. 1943	Eric Idle	English actor
b. 1943	John Major	British prime minister
d. 1912	Robert Falcon Scott	English explorer
d. 1987	Lee Marvin	American actor
d. 2004	Alistair Cooke	English broadcaster

Borrowed Days of March

According to the almanackist, Robert Chambers, the Borrowed Days are the three last days of March. The popular notion is that they were borrowed by March from April, with a view to the destruction of a parcel of unoffending young sheep—a purpose, however, in which March was not successful. The whole affair is conveyed in a rhyme thus given at the firesides of the Scottish peasantry:

March said to Aperill,
I see three hoggs [hoggets, sheep] upon a hill,
And if you'll lend me dayes three,
I'll find a way to make them dee [die].
The first o' them was wind and weet,
The second o' them was snaw and sleet,
The third o' them was sic a freeze,
It froze the birds' nebs [legs] to the trees:
When the three days were past and gave,
The three silly hoggs came hirpling [limping] hame.

Noteworthy

1638 Swedish colonists found what later will become Wilmington, Delaware.
1864 Britain cedes the Ionian Islands to Greece.
1867 British North America act establishes Dominion of Canada.
1871 Royal Albert Hall opened.
1882 Knights of Columbus founded.
1886 Coca-Cola invented.
1929 Women get the vote in Britain.
1973 Last regular American troops leave South Vietnam.
1979 President Idi Amin of Uganda deposed.
1989 Louvre Pyramid inaugurated.

MARCH 30

DAILY READING

Surely he took up our infirmities and he carried our sorrows,
yet we considered him stricken by God,
smitten by him, and afflicted. (ISA 53:4)

FEAST DAYS

ca. 260	Rieul	Bishop of Senlis, France
ca. 649	John of the Ladder	Mount Sinai hermit
660	Zozimus	Bishop of Syracuse, Italy

ENTRANCE AND EXIT

b. 1135	Moses Maimonides	Jewish philosopher
b. 1820	Anna Sewell	English writer
b. 1945	Eric Clapton	English musician
d. 1956	Edmund Clerihew Bentley	English writer
d. 1986	James Cagney	American actor
d.1992	Manolis Andronicos	Greek archaelogist

Seward's Folly

On March 30, 1867, U.S. Secretary of State William Henry Seward (1801–72) signed an agreement with Baron Edouard Stoeckl, the Russian Ambassador to the United States. The agreement, derided in America as "Seward's Folly" and "Seward's Icebox" ceded possession of the vast territory of Alaska to the United States for the sum of $7.2 million. Few citizens of the U.S. could fathom what possible use or interest the 586,000 square miles of land would have for their country.

In a speech given at Sitka on August 12, 1868, however, Secretary Seward claimed he did not doubt "that the political society to be constituted here, first as a Territory, and ultimately as a state or many States, will prove a worthy constituency of the Republica."

Many settlers came to Alaska with the expectation that the territory would follow the path of the Western states to official state status. The First Organic Act did not provide for eventual representative government, however, and Alaska was consigned to a territorial status much like that of the Newfoundland fisheries of the seventeenth-century British Empire. Although some reports had been circulated about the wealth of furs, seals, fish, and minerals to be found in Alaska, the conventional wisdom was that Alaska was just too remote to inspire much interest.

Then, in 1872, gold was discovered in southeast Alaska and further gold strikes in the Klondike region led to thousands of prospectors seeking their fortune.

Clerihews

Edmund Clerihew Bentley (1875–1956) was a crime writer and friend of G. K. Chesterton. He is also known for inventing a humorous verse form–the Clerihew–that expresses opinions about famous people in a succinct rhyme. For example:

Sir Humphrey Davy
Abominated gravy.
He lived in the odium
Of having discovered sodium.

Dante Alighieri
Seldom troubled a dairy.
He wrote the Inferno
On a bottle of Pernod.

The people of Spain think Cervantes
Equal to half-a-dozen Dantes;
An opinion resented most bitterly
By the people of Italy.

I doubt if King John
Was a sine qua non.
I could rather imagine it
Of any other Plantagenet.

MARCH 31

DAILY READING

But God chose the foolish things of the world to shame the wise;
God chose the weak things of the world to shame the strong. (1 COR 1:27)

FEAST DAYS

ca. 251	Acacius the Wonder Worker	Bishop of Hither, Turkey
ca. 424	Benjamin	Persian martyr
1046	Guy	Benedictine monk

ENTRANCE AND EXIT

b. 1732	Franz Joseph Haydn	Austrian composer
b. 1948	Al Gore	American vice president
b. 1971	Ewan McGregor	Scottish actor
d. 1703	Johann Christoph Bach	German composer
d. 1855	Charlotte Brontë	English writer
d. 1993	Brandon Lee	American actor

The Father of Modern Philosophy

Rene Descartes who was born on this day in 1596 in Tours, France, was a contemporary of Galileo and Desargues. A brilliant philosopher, scientist, writer, and mathematician, Descartes was educated at a Jesuit college, where he was a friend of the mathematician Marin Mersenne.

In 1617, Descartes joined the army of Prince Maurice of Orange, then at Breda. Walking through the streets there, he saw a placard in Dutch that excited his curiosity, and stopping the first passer, asked him to translate it into either French or Latin. The stranger, who happened to be Isaac Beeckman, the head of the Dutch College at Dort, offered to do so if Descartes would answer it; the placard being, in fact, a challenge to all the world to solve a certain geometrical problem. Descartes worked it out within a few hours, and a warm friendship between him and Beeckman was the result.

In 1628 Cardinal de Berulle, the founder of the Oratorians, met Descartes, and was so much impressed by his conversation that he urged on him the duty of devoting his life to the examination of truth. Descartes agreed, and the better to secure himself from interruption moved to Holland, where for twenty years he gave up all his time to philosophy and mathematics. Descartes maintained that science may be compared to a tree; metaphysics is the root, physics is the trunk, and the three chief branches are mechanics, medicine, and morals, these forming the three applications of our knowledge, namely, to the external world, to the human body, and to the conduct of life.

Descartes most famous statement is *Cogito ergo sum*–I think, therefore I am found–in *Principles of Philosophy*.

Noteworthy

1146 Bernard of Clairvaux (1090–1153) preached for the Second Crusade at Vezelay, France.

1492 By royal edict of Ferdinand II (1452–1516), all Jews were expelled from Spain.

1567 Philip of Hesse (b. November 13, 1504), the most eminent of the Protestant princes during the Reformation, died.

1631 John Donne, English divine, metaphysical poet, and priest, died (b. 1572).

1856 In Mexico, the property of the clergy was seized by the government.

1860 Rodney "Gypsy" Smith, popular nineteenth-century American evangelist, was born (d. August 4, 1947).

1901 Sir John Stainer, composer, died in Verona, Italy (b. June 6, 1840).

1901 The first Lutheran confirmation (eight confirmands) took place at San Pedro, Pelotas, Brazil.

Next came fresh April, full of lustyhed,
And wanton as a kid whose horne new buds;
Upon a bull he rode, the same which led
Europa floting through th' Argolick fluds:
His horns were gilden all with golden studs,
And garnished with garlands goodly dight
Of all the fairest flowers and freshest buds
Which th' earth brings forth; and wet he seem'd in sight
With waves, through which he waded for his love's delight.

EDMUND SPENSER–*The Shepheardes Calender* (1579)

I open wide the portals of the Spring
To welcome the procession of the flowers,
With their gay banners, and the birds that sing
Their song of songs from their aerial towers.
I soften with my sunshine and my showers
The heart of earth; with thoughts of love I glide
Into the hearts of men; and with the Hours
Upon the Bull with wreathed horns I ride.

HENRY WADSWORTH LONGFELLOW–*The Poet's Calendar* (1882)

Proverbs ~

A cold April
The barn will fill

An April flood
Carries away the frog and his brood

April showers
Make May flowers

When April blows his horn
It's good for both hay and corn.

April ~

The derivation of the name of this month is disputed. Most sources point to *aperio*, the Latin word meaning "I open," signifying the opening of Spring flowers. A few sources maintain that April stems from aphrilis, corrupted from Aphrodite, a Greek name for Venus. Still others believe the month's name may have originated from that of a sky-god named Aper or Aprus.

Shakespeare ~

CAPULET:
Such comfort as do lusty young men feel
When well-apparell'd April on the heel
Of limping winter treads, even such delight
Among fresh female buds shall you this night
Inherit at my house; hear all, all see,
And like her most whose merit most shall be.

–*Romeo and Juliet,* Act 1, Scene II

SERVANT:
Yet I have not seen
So likely an ambassador of love:
A day in April never came so sweet,
To show how costly summer was at hand,
As this fore-spurrer comes before his lord.

–*The Merchant of Venice,* Act 2, Scene IX

April 1

DAILY READING

The fool says in his heart,
"There is no God." (PS 14:1)

FEAST DAYS

ca. 180	Melito of Asia	Bishop of Sardis, Turkey
1194	Hugh of Bonnevaux	Exorcist
1574	Catherine Tomas	Patron of Valldemossa, Spain

ENTRANCE AND EXIT

b. 1578	William Harvey	English physician
b. 1929	Milan Kundera	Czech writer
b. 1973	Stephen Fleming	New Zealand cricketer
d. 1204	Eleanor of Aquitaine	Queen of England
d. 1922	Charles I	Emperor of Austria
d. 2004	Carrie Snodgress	American actor

April Fools' Day

The origins of April Fools' Day are uncertain. Some maintain that it began in 1564 with the introduction of the Gregorian calendar in France, when peasants refused to believe the New Year would begin on January 1 and not March 25. For this they were labeled fools, and pranks were played on them.

Whatever the origins, many countries and regions celebrate April Fools' Day. For instance:

- In Devon, England, pranks are played in the afternoon. The day there was known as "Tailpipe Day," because it was a custom to pin an inscription "Please kick me" to the coattails of an unsuspecting victim.
- In Cheshire, England, an April Fool is a "April gawby" or "gobby or gob."
- In Mexico, the day for pranks is on December 28. *El Dia de los Inocentes* was set aside as a day for Christians to mourn Herod's slaughter of innocent children.

Extract From A Paschal Homily

We should understand, beloved, that the paschal mystery is at once old and new, transitory and eternal, corruptible and incorruptible, mortal and immortal. In terms of the Law it is old, in terms of the Word it is new. In its figure it is passing, in its grace it is eternal. It is corruptible in the sacrifice of the lamb, incorruptible in the eternal life of the Lord. It is mortal in his burial in the earth, immortal in his resurrection from the dead.

The Law indeed is old, but the Word is new. The type is transitory, but grace is eternal. The lamb was corruptible, but the Lord is incorruptible. He was slain as a lamb; he rose again as God. He was led like a sheep to the slaughter, yet he was not a sheep. He was silent as a lamb, yet he was not a lamb. The type has passed away; the reality has come. The lamb gives place to God, the sheep gives place to a man, and the man is Christ, who fills the whole of creation. The sacrifice of the lamb, the celebration of the Passover, and the prescriptions of the Law have been fulfilled in Jesus Christ. Under the old Law, and still more under the new dispensation, everything pointed toward him.

Both the Law and the Word came forth from Zion and Jerusalem, but now the Law has given place to the Word, the old to the new. The commandment has become grace, the type a reality. The lamb has become a Son, the sheep a man, and man, God.

The Lord, though he was God, became man. He suffered for the sake of those who suffer, he was bound for those in bonds, condemned for the guilty, buried for those who lie in the grave; but he rose from the dead, and cried aloud: Who will contend with me? Let him confront me. I have freed the condemned, brought the dead back to life, raised men from their graves. Who has anything to say against me? I, he said, am the Christ; I have destroyed death, triumphed over the enemy, trampled hell underfoot, bound the strong one, and taken men up to the heights of heaven: I am the Christ.

Come, then, all you nations of men, receive forgiveness for the sins that defile you. I am your forgiveness. I am the Passover that brings salvation. I am the lamb who was immolated for you. I am your ransom, your life, your resurrection, your light, I am your salvation and your king. I will bring you to the heights of heaven. With my own right hand I will raise you up, and I will show you the eternal Father.

April 2

DAILY READING

Now as Jesus was going up to Jerusalem, he took the twelve disciples aside and said to them, "We are going up to Jerusalem, and the Son of Man will be betrayed to the chief priests and the teachers of the law. They will condemn him to death and will turn him over to the Gentiles to be mocked and flogged and crucified. On the third day he will be raised to life!" (MATT 20:17–19)

FEAST DAYS

ca. 390	Urban	Bishop of Langres, France
1507	Francis of Paola	Patron of sailors
1945	Vilos Amor	Bishop of Gyor, Hungary

ENTRANCE AND EXIT

b. 1805	Hans Christian Andersen	Danish writer
b. 1947	Camille Anna Paglia	American writer
b. 1961	Keren Jane Woodward	English singer
d. 1502	Arthur	Prince of England
d. 1987	Bernard "Buddy" Rich	American musician
d. 2005	Karol Józef Wojtyła	Pope John Paul II

The Greatest Medieval King

Charles the Great (Charlemagne) (742–814), King of the Franks, Roman Emperor, and Defender of the Faith, was born on this day in 742 in France. He came to the throne in 768, and in 772 declared war against the Saxons, for the extension of the Christian faith.

In 774, Charlemagne's armies overthrew the kingdom of the Lombards. He secured the pope's favor by confirming the gift that Pepin (his father) had made to the papalsee, of the Exarchate of Ravenna.

In 800, Charlemagne undertook an Italian campaign to support Pope Leo III against the rebellious Romans. When Charlemagne on Christmas Day was worshipping in St. Peter's Church, the pope unexpectedly, as it appeared, set a crown upon his head, and, amid the acclamations of the people, saluted him as Carolus Augustus, emperor of the Romans. After this Charlemagne still extended and confirmed his conquests both in Spain and Germany.

He zealously endeavored to promote education, agriculture, arts, manufactures, and commerce. He projected great national works, one of which was a canal to connect the Rhine and Danube. He required his subjects to plant certain kinds of fruit trees, the cultivation of which was thus extended northward in Europe. His own domains were an example of superior cultivation. He had a school in his palace for the sons of his servants. Learned men were encouraged to come to his court. His fame spread to all parts of the world.

Pope John Paul II

"Do not abandon yourselves to despair. We are the Easter people and hallelujah is our song."

April 3

DAILY READING

Let us fix our eyes on Jesus, the author and perfecter of our faith, who for the joy set before him endured the cross, scorning its shame, and sat down at the right hand of the throne of God. (HEB 12:2)

FEAST DAYS

ca. 304	Irene	Patron of girls
ca. 304	Agape	Sister of St. Irene
ca. 304	Chionia	Sister of St. Irene

ENTRANCE AND EXIT

b. 1593	George Herbert	English writer
b. 1822	Dr. Edward Everett Hale	American church leader
b. 1986	Amanda Laura Bynes	American actor
d. 1859	Washington Irving	American writer
d. 1991	Henry Graham Greene	English writer
d. 1999	Lionel Bart	English composer

St. Richard of Chichester

Richard, Bishop of Chichester (1197–1253), is celebrated on this day by the Anglican Church. He and his brother became orphans when Richard was very young. Richard gave up his studies to help his brother save the family farm from going to ruin. He worked so hard that his grateful brother wanted to give the farm to him, but Richard returned to his studies.

Richard went to Oxford University and eventually became its chancellor. Later, St. Edmund, who was Archbishop of Canterbury, gave him assignments in his diocese. Although he was made the Bishop of Chichester, England, King Henry III refused to recognize his appointment. Henry also threatened the people of Chichester with punishment if they offered Richard hospitality. However, when the pope threatened to excommunicate the king, he stopped interfering and let the new bishop alone.

As bishop, St. Richard did his duties well. He was always gentle and kind with the people. He was courageous and confronted people when they were doing wrong and did not repent.

It is said that when St. Richard became ill, he foretold his death, because God had let him know the exact place and time when he would die. His friends, including Father Simon of Tarring, were at his bedside.

He was proclaimed a saint by Pope Urban IV in 1262.

Prayer of St. Richard

Thanks be to Thee, my Lord Jesus Christ
For all the benefits Thou hast given me,
For all the pains and insults Thou hast
borne for me.
O most merciful Redeemer, friend and
brother,
May I know Thee more clearly,
Love Thee more dearly,
Follow Thee more nearly,
Day by day.

Love

Love bade me welcome; yet my soul
drew back,
Guilty of dust and sin.
But quick-eyed Love, observing me
grow slack
From my first entrance in,
Drew nearer to me, sweetly questioning
If I lack'd anything.

"A guest," I answer'd, "worthy to be here":
Love said, "You shall be he."
"I, the unkind, ungrateful? Ah, my dear,
I cannot look on Thee."
Love took my hand and smiling did reply,
"Who made the eyes but I?"

"Truth, Lord; but I have marr'd them:
let my shame
Go where it doth deserve." "And know you
not," says Love, "Who bore the blame?"
"My dear, then I will serve."
"You must sit down," says Love, "and taste
my meat."
So I did sit and eat.

—George Herbert (1595–1633)

APRIL 4

DAILY READING

In Christ we have redemption through his blood, the forgiveness of sins, in accordance with the riches of God's grace. (EPH 1:7)

FEAST DAYS

549	Tigernach	Bishop of Clogher, Ireland
636	Isidore of Seville	Patron of the Internet
1589	Benedict the Moor	Patron of Palermo, Sicily

ENTRANCE AND EXIT

b. 397	Ambrose	Italian bishop
b. 1950	Christine Lahti	American actor
b. 1973	David Blaine	American magician
d. 1774	Oliver Goldsmith	English writer
d. 1986	Martin Luther King	American civil rights leader
d. 1992	Samuel Herman (Sammy) Reshevsky	American chess grandmaster

"A Liberty to Tender Consciences"

On April 4, 1660, the future King Charles II issued the Declaration of Breda. He was in exile in the city of Breda in the Netherlands and the declaration was his manifesto for the restoration of the monarchy. The declaration promised freedom from persecution for all his subjects and laid the foundations for the English constitution.

This is an extract from the Declaration of Breda:

> Charles, by the grace of God, King of England, Scotland, France and Ireland, Defender of the Faith, &ca. To all our loving subjects, of what degree or quality soever, greeting.
>
> If the general distraction and confusion which is spread over the whole kingdom doth not awaken all men to a desire and longing that those wounds which have so many years together been kept bleeding, may be bound up. all [*sic*] we can say will be to no purpose; however, after this long silence, we have thought it our duty to declare how much we desire to contribute thereunto; and that as we can never give over the hope, in good time, to obtain the possession of that right which God and nature hath made our due. . . .
>
> And because the passion and uncharitableness of the times have produced several opinions in religion, by which men are engaged in parties and animosities against each other (which, when they shall hereafter unite in a freedom of conversation, will be composed or better understood), we do declare a liberty to tender consciences, and that no man shall be disquieted or called in question for differences of opinion in matter of religion, which do not disturb the peace of the kingdom; and that we shall be ready to consent to such an Act of Parliament, as, upon mature deliberation, shall be offered to us, for the full granting that indulgence.

On May 8, 1660, Parliament restored the monarchy and declared that Charles II was King of England, Scotland, France, and Ireland.

De Spritu Sancto

> Who will give this Fount to my breast? Let it spring up in me, let that which gives eternal life flow upon me. Let that Fount overflow upon us, and not flow away. For Wisdom says: "Drink water out of thine own vessels, and from the founts of thine own wells, and let thy waters flow abroad in thy streets." How shall I keep this water that it flow not forth, that it glide not away? How shall I preserve my vessel, lest any crack of sin penetrating it, should let the water of eternal life exude? Teach us, Lord Jesus, teach us as Thou didst teach Thine apostles, saying: "Lay not up for yourselves treasures upon the earth, where rust and moth destroy, and where thieves break through and steal."
>
> –*St. Ambrose of Milan*

April 5

DAILY READING

He died for all, that those who live should no longer live for themselves but for him who died for them and was raised again. (2 COR 5:15)

FEAST DAYS

660	Dervel the Mighty	Welsh hermit
1127	Albert	Bishop of Montecorvino, Italy
1419	Vincent Ferrer	Patron of builders

ENTRANCE AND EXIT

b. 1588	Thomas Hobbes	American philosopher
b. 1937	Colin Powell	American politician
b. 1963	Jimmy Osmond	American singer
d. 1794	Georges Danton	French politician
d. 1964	Douglas MacArthur	American general
d. 1997	Allen Ginsberg	American poet

Matoaka

On this day in 1614, the Algonquin Princess Matoaka, also known as Pocahontas, married the English tobacco planter John Rolfe in Jamestown, Virginia. Thus began a period of peaceful relations between the colonists and indigenous people.

Pocahontas was called Lady Rebecca Rolfe and on January 30, 1615, the marriage produced a child, Thomas Rolfe. According to Rolfe, Pocahontas had saved his life when he was about to be killed by Algonquin warriors. They subsequently fell in love, married, and returned to Plymouth, England. They were also presented before King James I in London.

In March 1617, they were preparing to return to Jamestown when Pocahontas became ill. On March 21, she succumbed to her illness and died at age twenty-one. She is buried at St. George's Church, Gravesend.

This is an account of her wedding preparations to John Rolfe by the governor of Virginia, Capt. John Smith, an English sailor and writer:

Master John Rolfe, an honest Gentleman, and of good behaviour, had beene in love with Pocahontas, and she with him, and she acquainted her brother with it. The news of this mariage came soone to the knowledge of Powhatan [Pocahontas' father], a thing acceptable to him, as appeared by his sudden consent, for within ten daies he sent Opachisco, an old Uncle of hers, and two of his sons, to see the manner of the mariage, and to doe in that behalfe what they were requested, for the confirmation thereof, as his deputie. And ever since wee have had friendly trade and commerce, as well with Powhatan himselfe, as all his subjects.

Noteworthy

2348 BC Noah's ark grounded on Mount Ararat (calculated date).
1541 Start of the Diet of Regensburg to restore religious unity in Germany between the Roman Church and the Protestants.
1553 Antonius Corvinus (Rabe), pastor in Hessen, dies (b. 1501).
1614 Second parliament of King James I begins session.
1621 *Mayflower* sails from Plymouth on a return trip to England.
1742 Christian Wilhelm Gericke, Lutheran missionary in India, born.
1792 George Washington casts first presidential veto.
1811 Robert Raikes, English philanthropist and founder of Sunday schools, dies (b. 1735).
1895 Oscar Wilde loses libel case against Marquess of Queensberry.
1896 First modern Olympic Games officially open in Athens.
1927 Swimmer Johnny Weissmuller set records in the 100- and 200-meter freestyle.
1939 Membership in Hitler Youth becomes obligatory.
1971 Mount Etna erupts in Sicily, Italy.
1973 Pioneer 11 is launched to Jupiter.

April 6

DAILY READING

Therefore confess your sins to each other and pray for each other so that you may be healed. The prayer of a righteous man is powerful and effective. (JAS 5:16)

FEAST DAYS

720	Gennard	French hermit
1203	William of Eskhill	Patron of Abelholt, Denmark
1813	Zefirino Agostini	Italian priest

ENTRANCE AND EXIT

b. 1773	James Mill	Scottish economist
b. 1928	James Watson	American scientist
b. 1947	John Ratzenberger	American actor
d. 1199	Richard I	King of England
d. 1528	Albrecht Durer	German artist
d. 1998	Tammy Wynette	American singer

Tartan Day

Since 1987, Scots have celebrated their history, culture, and global links on April 6. The date is appropriate since on April 6, 1320, the Declaration of Arbroath asserted Scottish sovereignty and independence from England.

Millions of Scottish people are part of the Diaspora in America, Canada, Australia, and New Zealand. For example, there are over eleven million people of Scottish descent in America alone. Around the world, many communities take part in parades, festivals, and concerts celebrating Scottish heritage.

The Declaration of Arbroath was made to Pope John XXII by Scottish nobility. This is an extract:

> We know from the chronicles and books of the ancients we find that among other famous nations our own, the Scots, has been graced with widespread renown. They journeyed from Greater Scythia by way of the Tyrrhenian Sea and the Pillars of Hercules, and dwelt for a long course of time in Spain among the most savage tribes, but nowhere could they be subdued by any race, however barbarous. Thence they came, twelve hundred years after the people of Israel crossed the Red Sea, to their home in the west where they still live today.
>
> The King of kings and Lord of lords, our Lord Jesus Christ, after His Passion and Resurrection, called them, even though settled in the uttermost parts of the earth, almost the first to His most holy faith. Nor would He have them confirmed in that faith by merely anyone but by the first of His Apostles the most gentle Saint Andrew, the Blessed Peter's brother, and desired him to keep them under his protection as their patron forever.
>
> May it please you to admonish and exhort the King of the English, who ought to be satisfied with what belongs to him since England used once to be enough for seven kings or more, to leave us Scots in peace, who live in this poor little Scotland, beyond which there is no dwelling-place at all, and covet nothing but our own. We are sincerely willing to do anything for him, having regard to our condition, that we can, to win peace for ourselves.

Noteworthy

202 Irenaeus, Greek church father, died.

1249 King Louis IX of France was taken prisoner by Muslims during the Seventh Crusade.

1520 Italian painter and architect, Raffaello Sanzio, died (b. April 6, 1483).

1759 The last active performance by Georg Friedrich Handel (1685–1759) took place. It was a production of *The Messiah*.

1830 The Church of Jesus Christ of Latter Day Saints (Mormon) was founded by Joseph Smith in Manchester, New York.

1851 Anglican churchman and Archbishop of Westminster Henry E. Manning (1808–92) converted to Roman Catholicism.

1893 The Mormons dedicated their Salt Lake City temple in Utah after forty years of construction.

1932 Eric Liddell (1902–45), the Olympic athlete whose story was told in the film *Chariots of Fire*, made his evangelistic debut by sharing his testimony with a group of men in Armadale, Scotland.

APRIL 7

DAILY READING

I have been crucified with Christ and I no longer live,
but Christ lives in me. The life I live in the body,
I live by faith in the Son of God,
who loved me and gave himself for me. (GAL 2:20)

FEAST DAYS

ca. 6th cent.	Goran	Cornish hermit
816	George the Younger	Bishop of Mitylene, Greece
1595	Henry Walpole	English Catholic martyr

ENTRANCE AND EXIT

b. 1506	Francis Xavier	Spanish missionary
b. 1770	William Wordsworth	English poet
b. 1969	Jack Black	American actor
d. 1614	Doménicos Theotokópoulos –El Greco	Spanish artist
d. 1947	Henry Ford	American industrialist
d. 1994	Kurt Cobain	American rock star

The Canterbury Tales

Geoffrey Chaucer's masterpiece, *The Canterbury Tales*, was published on this day in 1499.

The Canterbury Tales is a collection of short stories from pilgrims on their way to visit the shrine of St. Thomas a Beckett at Canterbury. The format is similar to other "books within a book," such as *The Decameron* and *The Arabian Nights*.

The pilgrims are a fascinating cross-section of feudal, ecclesiastical, and urban medieval society, including such characters as a knight, a cook, carpenter, miller, priest, franklin, prioress, pardoner, lawyer, merchant, clerk, and physician. The language of *The Canterbury Tales* is close to Old English and suggests the project began over a hundred years before publication. Chaucer originally intended to feature two stories from character that would have produced 124 tales. However, the final version has only twenty-four stories.

The Canterbury Tales remains a rich source of information about the traditions, personalities, and hierarchy of medieval England. Chaucer created a colorful world of high and low morals, tears and laughter, faith and faults that forms a masterpiece of beautiful poetry, acute observation, and sustained quality.

Extract from the Prologue to
The Canterbury Tales:

Whan that aprill with his shoures soote
The droghte of march hath perced to
the roote,
And bathed every veyne in swich licour
Of which vertu engendred is the flour;
Whan zephirus eek with his sweete breeth
Inspired hath in every holt and heeth
Tendre croppes, and the yonge sonne
Hath in the ram his halve cours yronne,
And smale foweles maken melodye,
That slepen al the nyght with open ye
(so priketh hem nature in hir corages);
Thanne longen folk to goon on pilgrimages,
And palmeres for to seken straunge strondes,
To ferne halwes, kowthe in sondry londes;

Noteworthy

1541 Spanish Roman Catholic missionary and founder of the Jesuits, Francis Xavier (1506–52), and three companions departed Lisbon, Portugal, for Goa.

1546 Friedrich Myconius, friend and coworker of Martin Luther and reformer of Thuringia, died.

1677 Johann Ernst Gruendler, missionary to India, was born in Weissensee, Germany.

1770 William Wordsworth, English romantic poet, was born (d. April 23, 1850).

1884 C. H. Dodd, English Congregational clergyman and New Testament scholar, was born (d. September 21, 1973).

1917 James Hope Moulton (b. October 11, 1863), English Methodist clergyman and biblical Greek scholar, died.

1953 Swedish diplomat and Christian statesman Dag Hammarskjöld (1905–61) was elected Secretary General of the United Nations.

April 8

DAILY READING

If, when we were God's enemies, we were reconciled to him through the death of his Son, how much more, having been reconciled, shall we be saved through his life. (ROM 5:10)

FEAST DAYS

ca. 1st cent.	Herodian	Bishop of Patras, Greece
1215	Albert of Jerusalem	Bishop of Bobbio, Italy
1816	Julia of Billiart	Patron against sickness

ENTRANCE AND EXIT

b. 563	Gautama Buddha	Indian religious leader
b. 1918	Betty Ford	American First Lady
b. 1938	Kofi Annan	Ghanian statesman
d. 1835	Baron Wilhelm von Humboldt	German philosopher
d. 1973	Pablo Picasso	Spanish artist
d. 1994	Walter Arnold	German theologist

Chalmers of New Guinea

The Scottish missionary and explorer James Chalmers was born in 1841 in the town of Ardishaig, Scotland. He was brutally murdered on this day in 1901 during a missionary trip to Goaribari Island, New Guinea.

James studied theology at Cheshunt College from 1859 and was ordained in 1865. With his new wife, James took up his first missionary appointment in Rarotonga (New Zealand) arriving in 1867. The natives named him "Tamate." He was known by this name until his death.

The Rarotonga Christian mission was well established. He reorganized an existing training institution and set about educating native children.

James encouraged self-government and independence of European influence once a native work was well established. He wrote: "So long as the native churches have foreign pastors, so long will they remain weak and dependent."

In 1877 James was assigned to New Guinea, which was, at the time, a largely unexplored island. Besides introducing the gospel, James accomplished the seemingly impossible goal of promoting peace among the tribes all along the coast.

The news of Tamate's martyrdom was the cause of worldwide grief and lamentation. His coworker wrote: "I have wept much. My father Tamate's body I shall not see again, but his spirit we shall certainly see in heaven, if we are strong to do the work of God thoroughly and all the time, till our time on earth shall finish."

Pablo Picasso (1881–1973) Quotes

God is really only another artist. He invented the giraffe, the elephant, and the cat. He has no real style. He just keeps on trying other things.

Art is a lie that makes us realize truth.

Everything you can imagine is real.

Some painters transform the sun into a yellow spot; others transform a yellow spot into the sun.

Every child is an artist. The problem is how to remain an artist once we grow up.

Are we to paint what's on the face, what's inside the face, or what's behind it?

The world today doesn't make sense, so why should I paint pictures that do?

Inspiration exists, but it has to find us working.

April 9

DAILY READING

The Son is the radiance of God's glory and the exact representation of his being, sustaining all things by his powerful word. After he had provided purification for sins, he sat down at the right hand of the Majesty in heaven. (HEB 1:3)

FEAST DAYS

ca. 619	John the Almoner	Patriarch of Alexdandria
870	Hedda	Abbot of Peterborough
1374	Antony Pavoni	Patron of lost articles

ENTRANCE AND EXIT

b. 1821	Charles Baudelaire	French writer
b. 1898	Paul Robeson	American actor
b. 1957	Sevériano Ballesteros	Spanish golfer
d. 1483	Edward IV	King of England
d. 1626	Francis Bacon	English philosopher
d. 1945	Dietrich Bonhoeffer	German theologian

St. Casilda

St. Casilda of Toledo, whose feast day is celebrated on April 9 by the Catholic Church, was thought to have been the daughter of a Muslim king of Toledo. She died around 1050, aged nearly one hundred years.

Legend records that her father forbade her to have anything to do with Christianity, but she secretly fed her father's Christian captives. She resisted her father's angry outbursts and became an anchorite in the city of Brivesca, in the province of Burgos, Spain.

Her conversion came after a miraculous healing when she made a pilgrimage to the shrine of St. Vicenzo in northern Spain. After local Arab doctors were unable to cure her she sought the healing waters of the shrine. In response to her healing, she became a Christian and lived a life of solitude and penance not far from the miraculous spring.

She is portrayed in paintings as a Saracen maiden carrying roses in her lap. Sometimes she is pictured as a Saracen princess with roses or as bread changed to roses in memory of a miracle she is supposed to have performed. Casilda is the patron of Saragossa, Toledo, and Burgos. She is invoked in time of war and is also the patron against sterility.

A Modern Martyr

Dietrich Bonhoeffer (1906–45) was a German Lutheran theologian who was an outspoken opponent of Adolf Hitler and the Nazi regime during their rise to power in 1933. Bonhoeffer joined the Confessing Church, which resisted the Nazi attempt to impose anti-Semitism on the church and society. Leaving Berlin in protest, he spent two years (1933–35) as pastor of German-speaking congregations in London. Called back to Germany in 1935, Bonhoeffer became director of a seminary of the Confessing Church at Finkenwald, Pomerania. This "illegal" enterprise was eventually closed by the Gestapo; after the start of World War II, Bonhoeffer joined in the political resistance to Hitler, which that led to his imprisonment in April 1943 in Berlin. On April 9, 1945, Bonhoeffer was hanged in the Nazi concentration camp at Flössenberg.

April 10

DAILY READING

At just the right time, when we were still powerless,
Christ died for the ungodly. (ROM 5:6)

FEAST DAYS

ca. 376	Bademus	Persian martyr
1012	Marcarius of Antioch	Patron of Ghent, Belgium
1625	Michael de Sanctis	Spanish monk

ENTRANCE AND EXIT

b. 1512	James V	Scottish king
b. 1583	Hugo Grotius	Dutch theologian
b. 1988	Haley Joel Osment	American actor
d. 879	Louis II	French king
d. 1966	Evelyn Waugh	English writer
d. 1995	Morarji Desai	Prime minister of India

Salvation Army

Methodist minister William Booth, who was born on this day in 1829, founded the Christian Revival Society in the East End of London. Shortly afterward, the society changed its name to the Christian Mission. The name was changed again, to the Salvation Army in 1878.

A powerful preacher, Booth was moved to evangelize the poor people around Whitechapel with compassion as well as words. Although there were over five hundred charitable bodies trying to help the people of the East End, Booth's fervent "fire and brimstone" sermons had a powerful impact.

Booth came up with the notion of a "salvation army" as a body of committed Christians fighting the scourge of poverty and sin. This military metaphor found ready acceptance by alcoholics, gamblers, drug addicts, and prostitutes. By 1912, the army was represented in over fifty countries.

Although the army does not have any sacraments, it insists that members refrain from alcohol, smoking, illicit drugs, and gambling. All members become "soldiers" of the army, and salvationist roles include: auxiliary captain (mature person beyond the age for full officer training), cadet (trainee officer), candidate (member accepted for officer training), chief of staff (second in command), sergeant major (local officer), envoy (visiting officer), general (overall leader), local officer (voluntary worker), officer (paid member), and sergeant (officer with specific duties).

Today, the Salvation Army provides practical help for over one million needy people in 109 countries, has over 25,000 members, 107,000 employees, and over 1,500 shops. The Salvation Army provides social programs, addiction dependency support, education programs, health programs, and emergency disaster response services.

"While women weep, as they do now, I'll Fight; while little children go hungry, as they do now, I'll Fight; while men go to prison, in and out, in and out, as they do now, I'll Fight; while there is a poor lost girl upon the streets, while there remains one dark soul without the light of God, I'll Fight, I'll fight to the very end!"

—*William Booth*

Hugo Grotius

Hugo de Groot of Holland, better known by his Latin name Hugo Grotius, is an almost legendary figure today in several respects. Born in Delft on Easter Day in 1583, he was a child prodigy, and joined the University of Leyden at the age of twelve, earning his doctorate by the age of fifteen. By the year 1607, he had been appointed "Advocate-Fiscal" of Holland, an office that could be said to have functioned as Attorney-General, Public Prosecutor, and Sheriff. Dutch children still remember him, due to his daring escape from prison in a trunk after being arrested for being on the wrong side of a politicoreligious controversy. He fled to France, where the king hailed him as "the miracle of Holland."

He is best known today, however, as one of the pioneering figures in the field of modern international law (called by many "the father of modern international law"); he was one of the first modern theorists to systematically propose the existence of norms in the conduct of relations between states.

April 11

DAILY READING

He himself bore our sins in his body on the tree,
so that we might die to sins and live for righteousness;
by his wounds you have been healed. (1 PET 2:24)

FEAST DAYS

ca. 92	Antipas	Bishop of Pergamum
ca. 550	Isaac	Syrian monk
1079	Stanislaus	Patron of Poland

ENTRANCE AND EXIT

b. 146	Septimus Severus	Roman Emperor
b. 1722	Christopher Smart	English poet
b. 1923	Theodore Isaac Ruben	American writer
d. 1240	Llywelyn ab Iorwerth the Great	Welsh prince
d. 1987	Primo Levi	Italian writer
d. 1992	James Brown	American actor

St. Stanislaus

According to the Catholic Encyclopaedia (1913) St. Stainislaus was a Bishop and martyr, born at Szczepanów, in the Diocese of Krakow, July 26, 1030. He is patron of Poland and the city and Diocese of Krakow and was invoked in battle. In pictures he is given the episcopal insignia and the sword. Larger paintings represent him in a court or kneeling before the altar and receiving the fatal blow. At the time of his canonization, a life appeared written by a Dominican called Father Vincent which contains much legendary matter.

His parents, Belislaus and Bogna, pious and noble Catholics, gave him a religious education. Lambert Zula, Bishop of Krakow, ordained him priest and made him pastor of Czembocz near Krakow, canon and preacher at the cathedral, and later, vicar-general. After the death of Lambert he was elected bishop, but accepted only on explicit command of Pope Alexander II.

He worked with great energy for his diocese, and inveighed against vices among high and low, regardless of consequences. Boleslaw II had become King of Poland and the renown he had gained by his successful wars he now sullied by atrocious cruelty and unbridled lust. Moreover, the bishop had several serious disputes with the king about a piece of land belonging to the Church that was unjustly claimed by Boleslaw, and about some nobles, who had left their homes to ward off various evils threatening their families and who were in consequence cruelly treated by the king.

Stanislaus spared neither tears nor prayers and admonitions to bring the king to lead a more Christian life. All being in vain, Boleslaw was excommunicated and the canons of the cathedral were instructed to discontinue the Divine Offices in case the king should attempt to enter. The king was furious and sent guards to kill the saint. These dared not obey, so Boleslaw slew him during the Holy Sacrifice. The body was at first buried in the chapel, but in 1088 it was transferred to the cathedral by Bishop Lambert II. St. Stanislaus was canonized in 1253 by Innocent IV at Assisi.

Noteworthy

1079 Polish bishop of Krakow, Stanislaus was martyred (b. ca. 1030).

1506 The foundation stone of the new St. Peter's Basilica was laid under the patronage of Pope Julius II.

1562 Huguenots in France signed a manifesto declaring they would take up arms in defense of Protestants.

1598 King Henry IV of France issued the Edict of Nantes, which recognized non-Catholic religions in France, granted freedom of conscience to Protestants, and ended the persecution of the Huguenots.

1816 The first African American bishop in America, Richard Allen (1760–1831), was ordained in Philadelphia by Francis Asbury to head the new African Methodist Episcopal Church.

1836 English philanthropist George Mueller (1805–98) opened his famous orphanage on Wilson Street, Bristol, in two rented houses.

APRIL 12

DAILY READING

[Jesus] said to them all: "If anyone would come after me, he must deny himself and take up his cross daily and follow me." (LUKE 9:23)

FEAST DAYS

337	Julius I	Pope
371	Zeno	Patron of Verona
372	Sabas	Patron of lectors

ENTRANCE AND EXIT

b. 1550	Edward de Vere	Earl of Oxford
b. 1950	David Cassidy	American singer
b. 1979	Claire Danes	American actor
b. 1859	John Emde	German evangelist
d. 1945	Franklin Delano Roosevelt	32nd American president
d. 1989	Sugar Ray Robinson	American boxer

Cosmonauts Day

On April 12, 1961, the first manned spaceship left our planet from the Baikonur cosmodrome in the Soviet Union. This was the beginning of the space race. The cosmonaut, Major Yuri Gagarin, told the press:

> Dear friends, compatriots, and people of all countries and continents! In a few minutes a mighty ship will carry me aloft to distant space. What can I say to you in these last moments before the launch? At this instant the whole of my life seems to be condensed into one wonderful moment. I want to dedicate this first cosmic flight to the people of communism–the society which the Soviet people are now already entering upon. To be the first to enter the cosmos, to engage, single-handed, in an unprecedented duel with nature–could one dream of anything more!

Gagarin blazed a trail that has now become a road to the cosmos. Today, space pilots live and work for months aboard space stations, and Soviet and American spacemen work together.

But Yuri Gagarin's 108-minute flight in spacecraft *Vostok* represented not only a triumph of science and engineering, but also a bursting of the "bounds of possibility," the breaking of a psychological barrier. It was literally a flight into the unknown.

Gagarin died in 1968 aged just thirty-four when his aircraft crashed in a training flight. In Russia, today is celebrated as Cosmonauts' Day, in honor of Yuri Gagarin and his achievements.

England and Scotland Unite

April 12, 1654, was the first time that Scotland and England became united under a single constitution under the Protectorate of Oliver Cromwell. The union (which also incorporated Ireland) lasted barely five years, for while the political union survived the remainder of the Protectorate, it effectively collapsed in 1659–60 and was reversed at the restoration of the monarchy.

This is an extract from the Constitution establishing the Union:

> His Highness the Lord Protector of the Commonwealth of England, Scotland and Ireland, &c., taking into consideration how much it might conduce to the glory of God and the peace and welfare of the people in this whole island, that after all those late unhappy wars and differences, the people of Scotland should be united with the people of England into one Commonwealth and under one Government, and finding that in December, 1651, the Parliament then sitting did send Commissioners into Scotland to invite the people of that nation unto such a happy Union, who proceeded so far therein that the shires and boroughs of Scotland, by their Deputies convened at Dalkeith, and again at Edinburgh, did accept of the said Union, and assent thereunto; for the completing and perfecting of which Union, be it ordained, and it is ordained by his Highness the Lord Protector of the Commonwealth of England, Scotland and Ireland, and the dominions thereto belonging, by and with the advice and consent of his Council, that all the people of Scotland, and of the Isles of Orkney and Shetland, and of all the dominions and territories belonging unto Scotland, are and shall be, and are hereby incorporated into, constituted, established, declared and confirmed one Commonwealth with England.

APRIL 13

DAILY READING

For all have sinned and fall short of the glory of God. (ROM 3:23)

FEAST DAYS

585	Hermengild	Patron against drought
655	Martin I	Pope
ca. 838	Guinoc	Scottish bishop

ENTRANCE AND EXIT

b. 1743	Thomas Jefferson	3rd American president
b. 1906	Samuel Beckett	Irish writer
b. 1963	Gary Kasparov	Russian chess grandmaster
d. 1728	Samuel Molyneux	English astronomer
d. 1941	Annie Jump Cannon	American astronomer
d. 2006	Dame Muriel Spark	Scottish writer

The Most Hated Woman in America

Madalyn Murray O'Hair, who was born on this day in 1919, was the founding president of American Atheists in 1963, a group campaigning for the separation of church and state. She was referred to as "the most hated woman in America" by *Life* magazine in 1964 after her campaign to ban school prayer was approved by the U.S. Supreme Court in 1963.

She was murdered in 1995 after being kidnapped with her son Jon Garth Murray and granddaughter Robin Murray O'Hair by her former office manager, David Walters. Walters was trying to recover money he claimed was owed to him by Madalyn.

The bodies remained hidden until 2001, when police found their dismembered remains near San Antonio, Texas.

Madalyn's son William (the father of Robin) announced his conversion to Christianity on Mother's Day in 1980 and became a fundamentalist Baptist minister. This led to a permanent estrangement between mother and son. A self-described advocate for "family-friendly legislation," William Murray went to live in Washington, D.C., and wrote books, such as *Let Us Pray: A Plea for Prayer in Our Schools, My Life Without God*, and *The Church Is Not for Perfect People.*

The Last Martyr Pope

Pope Martin I was born in Umbria and succeeded Theodore I in July 649. He reigned for six years and died from starvation at Cherson in the Crimea.

Almost his first official act as Pope was to summon the First Lateran Synod to deal with the Monothelites, who believed Christ had no free will and whom the church considered heretical. His failure to condemn this heresy led to Emperor Constans II arresting Martin and imprisoning him in Constantinople along with Maximus the Confessor.

After suffering an exhausting imprisonment and many alleged public indignities, he was ultimately banished to Cherson, where he died in September 655. He was the last pope to suffer martyrdom.

April 14

DAILY READING

Christ died for our sins according to the Scriptures. (1 COR 15:3)

FEAST DAYS

1342	Anthony	Patron of Vilna, Lithuania
1342	Eustace	Patron of Vilna, Lithuania
1669	Benezet the Bridge Builder	Patron of bachelors

ENTRANCE AND EXIT

b. 1578	Philip III	King of Spain and Portugal
b. 1904	Sir John Gielgud	English actor
b. 1977	Sarah Michelle Gellar	American actor
d. 911	Sergius III	Italian Pope
d. 1986	Simone de Beauvoir	French writer
d. 1995	Burl Ives	American singer

Titanic *Hero*

Shortly before midnight on April 14, 1912, the merchant liner *Titanic* struck an iceberg off the coast of Newfoundland. Two and a half hours later the ship sank, with a loss of 1,523 lives. Only around 705 people survived. Bodies of 306 people were recovered by the White Star–chartered *Mackay-Bennett.*

The Reverend John Harper was one of those who perished. He was the pastor of Walworth Road Baptist, London, and was on his way to Moody Church Chicago to preach for three or four months, as he had done previously. He traveled with his daughter, Nana (age six), and her nurse, Jessie Leith, both of whom survived. Other survivors recalled that Harper gave his life to allow the women and children to be rowed away to safety.

In 1916, a survivor recounted Harper's final moment. He recalled that when he was drifting alone on a spar that awful night, the tide brought Mr. Harper also on a piece of wreck near him. He said that Mr. Harper asked him if he was saved and when he told him he wasn't, Mr. Harper said, "Believe on the Lord Jesus Christ, and thou shall be saved." He said the waves then bore Mr. Harper away, but strangely brought him back a little later and Mr. Harper then asked, "Are you saved now?" The man said that when he said that he couldn't honestly say that he was, Mr. Harper repeated, "Believe on the Lord Jesus Christ, and thou shalt be saved." The man said that shortly after Mr. Harper went down, he, being there alone in the night with two miles of water under him, accepted Christ as his personal saviour. He saw himself as John Harper's last convert.

The Old Believers

Russian Archpriest Avvakum (1620–82) was the leader of a movement of traditionalists that broke away from the Russian Orthodox Church known as the "Old Believers." He was martyred on this day in 1682 by being burned alive, having spent several years in prison for circulating his autobiography. This is an account of his suffering from his autobiography, translated from the Russian:

> I was locked up three days, and neither ate nor drank. Locked there in darkness I bowed down in my chains, maybe to the east, maybe to the west. No one came to me, only the mice and the cockroaches; the crickets chirped and there were fleas to spare. It came to pass that on the third day I was voracious, that is, I wanted to eat, and after Vespers there stood before me, whether an angel or whether a man I didn't know and to this day I still don't know, but only that he said a prayer in the darkness, and taking me by the shoulder led me with my chain to the bench and sat me down, and put a spoon in my hands and a tiny loaf, and gave a dab of cabbage soup to sip–my it was tasty, uncommonly good! And he said unto me, "Enough, that wil suffice thee for thy strengthening." And he was gone. The doors didn't open, but he was gone! It's amazing if it was a man, but what about an angel? Then there's nothing to be amazed about, there are no barriers to him anywhere.

April 15

DAILY READING

Give everyone what you owe him. If you owe taxes, pay taxes; if revenue, then revenue; if respect, then respect; if honor, then honor. (ROM 13:7)

FEAST DAYS

ca. 584	Ruadhan	Apostle of Erin
679	Hunna the Holy Washerwoman	Patron of washerwomen
1607	Cesar de Bus	Patron of catechists

ENTRANCE AND EXIT

b. 1452	Leonardo da Vinci	Italian artist
b. 1469	Guru Nanak	Indian founder of Sikhism
b. 1959	Emma Thompson	English actor
d. 1865	Abraham Lincoln	16th American president
d. 1980	Jean-Paul Sartre	French philosopher
d. 1990	Greta Garbo	Swedish actor

The Leper of Molokai

On May 11, 1873, the steamer Kilauea deposited thirty-three-year-old Father Joseph Damien de Veuster on the landing at Molokai in the Hawaiian Islands. The islands were ravaged with leprosy, the "separating sickness" that came with increased trading links in the seventeenth century. King Kamehameda V established a leprosarium on the island of Molokai and in 1866 over 140 sufferers were banished to the island. Here they were isolated, and the rest of the population forgot about them.

However, the Catholic Church did not forget, and Bishop Maigret sent Father Joseph to minister to the lepers of Molokai. The plan was to send ministers on a rota basis to help the lepers, but Father Joseph knew he was to stay with them after just a few days and he wrote back: "I am bent on devoting my life to the lepers. It is absolutely necessary for a priest to live here. The afflicted are coming here by the boatloads."

For the next sixteen years, Father Damien served the growing leper community with Christ-like devotion. He cleaned wounds, bandaged ulcers, amputated gangrenous limbs, built shelters, laid pipelines for fresh water, dug graves, and constructed over 1,600 coffins.

A few days before he died on April 15, 1889, he said, "The work of the lepers is in good hands and I am no longer necessary, so I shall go up yonder."

On June 4, 1995, Father Joseph was beatified by Pope John Paul II, and today his memory is honored by a statue that stands in the Rotunda of the U.S. Capitol Building.

Noteworthy

1800 James Ross discovers north magnetic pole.
1961 Yuri Gagarin, the first man in space, is awarded the Order of Lenin.
1982 The Muslims who murdered President Sadat of Egypt are executed.
1986 American warplanes bomb Tripoli, Libya, in retaliation for Libyan terrorism.
1998 The leader of the Khmer Rouge regime, Pol Pot, dies at the age of seventy-three.
1999 In Algeria, former Foreign Minister Abdelaziz Bouteflika is elected president.
1999 In Rawalpindi, Pakistan, a panel of two Lahore High Court judges convict former Prime Minister Benazir Bhutto and her husband, Asif Ali Zardari, of corruption.

APRIL 16

DAILY READING

Let no debt remain outstanding, except the continuing debt to love one another, for he who loves his fellowman has fulfilled the law. (ROM 13:8)

FEAST DAYS

304	Chrysogonus	Greek martyr
665	Fructuosus	Archbishop of Braga, Portugal
ca. 1186	Drogo	Patron of unattractive people

ENTRANCE AND EXIT

b. 1889	Sir Charles Spencer Chaplin	English actor
b. 1963	Jimmy Osmond	American singer
b. 1965	Martin Lawrence	American actor
d. 1788	George-Louis Leclerc de Buffon	French scientist
d. 1828	Francisco Goya y Lucientes	Spanish artist
d. 1914	George William Hill	American astronomer

The Beggar of Perpetual Adoration

The French mystic St. Benedict Joseph Labre (1748–83) spent years wandering through Europe dressed in rags and in perpetual adoration at cathedrals, especially in Rome. He is the patron of beggars, bachelors, tramps, and people rejected by religious orders. He was supposed to have the gift of bilocation (being in two places at once) and levitation.

This is a list of some of his maxims:

- Everything may be done by the help of God, provided we have a sincere goodwill.
- To communicate through obedience is better and more pleasing to God than to abstain from it through humility.
- We offend God, because we do not know his greatness.
- God afflicts us because he loves us; and it is very pleasing to him, when in our afflictions he sees us abandon ourselves to his paternal care.
- Where fraternal charity is concerned, everything should be sacrificed.
- However much we suffer for the love of Jesus crucified, it is but little.
- If there were only one person to be condemned, each should fear to be that one.
- The providence of God is never wanting to him who confides in God as he ought.
- A poor man does not seek a bed in order to sleep, he throws himself down anywhere.
- The poor should not drink wine: it is not necessary; water suffices to appease thirst.

Pioneer Aviator

Harriet Quimby (1875–1912) made history on this day in 1912 by being the first woman to fly solo across the English Channel. Unfortunately, her brief career as an aviator came to an end. On July 1, 1912, at an aviation exhibition near Quincy, Massachusetts, Harriet and her "manager of the air" made a publicity stunt flight over the bay. As hundreds of spectators watched from below, Harriet and her passenger fell from the craft when it suddenly pitched forward and crashed into the bay.

Harriet Quimby was born in Michigan and relocated to San Francisco in 1900. Harriet never married, but she supported herself and her parents through her journalism work. By the last two years of her life, Harriet Quimby had become New York's sweetheart, frequently in the public eye. Fascinated by the challenge of flying an airplane, Harriet took flying lessons during 1911, and became the first woman to get a license in the United States. As soon as Harriet got her license to fly, she went on exhibition in the U.S. and Mexico.

April 17

DAILY READING

Abram believed the L*ORD, and he credited it to him as righteousness. He also said to him, "I am the* L*ORD, who brought you out of Ur of the Chaldeans to give you this land to take possession of it."* (GEN 15:6–7)

FEAST DAYS

ca. 756	Waldo of Fontenelle	French monk
1117	Gervinus	German monk
1367	James of Cerqueto	Italian hermit

ENTRANCE AND EXIT

b. 1586	John Ford	English writer
b. 1894	Nikita Khrushchev	Russian politician
b. 1972	Muttiah Muralitharan	Sri Lankan cricketer
d. 1790	Benjamin Franklin	American statesman
d. 1998	Linda Eastman McCartney	Wife of Sir Paul McCartney
d. 1997	Chaim Herzog	President of Israel

Adventures in Archaeology

Sir Charles Leonard Woolley, who was born in London on this day in 1860, was the son of a clergyman. He considered a clerical career, but eventually decided to practice archaeology. Graduating from Oxford University, Woolley is best known for his excavations at Ur of the Chaldees, the city that Abraham left at the call of God.

He learned his trade while working as assistant keeper of the Ashmolean Museum at Oxford from 1905 until 1907. In the field he worked with T. E. Lawrence from 1912 to 1914 and later in 1919 excavated Carchemish, the Hittite city, and in Sinai. From there he went to work in Tel el Armana with the Egypt Exploration Society.

He began working at Ur (in modern day Iraq) in 1922 in a joint venture between the British Museum and the University of Pennsylvania. Ur was the royal burial site of many Mesopotamian rulers, and Woolley discovered amazing pieces of gold and silver jewellery, cups, and written documents in his excavations of the tombs. One of his most sensational discoveries came in 1925 when the Royal Cemetery was excavated. Dating to about 2,500 BC, the cemetery produced some of the most beautiful Sumerian artifacts to survive from ancient Mesopotamia. They included the Royal Standard of Ur and the Ram in the Thicket.

Woolley was knighted in 1935. The crime writer Agatha Christie married his assistant Max Mallowan in 1930, and her book *Murder in Mesopotamia* was inspired by the discoveries at Ur.

Noteworthy

69 After the First Battle of Bedriacum, Vitellius becomes Roman Emperor.

1492 Spain and Christopher Columbus sign a contract for him to sail to Asia to get spices.

1521 Martin Luther speaks to the assembly at the Diet of Worms, refusing to recant his teachings.

1861 American Civil War: Virginia secedes from the Union.

1924 Metro-Goldwyn-Mayer studios is formed from a merger of Metro Pictures, Goldwyn Pictures, and the Louis B. Mayer Company.

1935 Sun Myung Moon claims to have a revelation from Jesus telling him to complete his mission from almost 2,000 years ago.

1941 World War II: Yugoslavia surrenders to Germany.

1961 Bay of Pigs Invasion: A group of CIA financed and trained Cuban refugees lands at the Bay of Pigs in Cuba with the aim of ousting Fidel Castro.

1970 Apollo program: The ill-fated Apollo 13 spacecraft returns to Earth safely.

1984 Police Constable Yvonne Fletcher is killed by automatic gunfire coming from the Libyan People's Bureau in central London.

1986 Treaty signed ending Three Hundred and Thirty-Five Years' War between the Netherlands and the Isles of Scilly.

April 18

DAILY READING

For the message of the cross is foolishness to those who are perishing, but to us who are being saved it is the power of God. (1 COR 1:18)

FEAST DAYS

526	Eusebius	Bishop of Fano, Italy
ca. 7th cent.	Laserian	Irish hermit
850	Perfecto	Spanish priest

ENTRANCE AND EXIT

b. 1480	Lucrezia Borgia	Italian royal
b. 1740	Sir Francis Baring	English banker
b. 1963	Conan O'Brien	American comedian
d. 1161	Theobald	Archbishop of Canterbury
d. 2002	Thor Heyerdahl	Norwegian explorer
d. 2003	Edgar Frank Codd	British scientist

St. Cyprian Baptized

April 18, 246, was the eve of Easter, and is traditionally thought to be the day of St. Cyprian's baptism. Cyprian was born around 200 in the city of Carthage in North Africa to a prominent pagan family.

While quite young he displayed talents in oratory and could have become a philosopher. The writings of Tertullian led to him becoming a Christian and, when he was baptized, he experienced a spiritual renewal that led to him giving away his possessions to the poor. He wrote, "A second birth created me a new man by means of the Spirit breathed from heaven." Such was the power of his baptism that many were impressed by his new life and just two years later there was a clamor for him to be made a bishop.

During the reign of Emperor Decius (249–51), Christians faced many persecutions and the church needed shepherds of the caliber of St. Cyprian to care for them. Cyprian had already won respect as an able and wise leader of the church, so that when Pope Fabian of Rome was martyred, his clergy turned to Cyprian for advice. Together with the Carthaginians, they persuaded him to go into hiding in order to preserve himself for further service to the church. He remained in close contact with his flock, exhorting them in letters to turn to prayer as their only sure weapon, and entreating the priests to look out for the weak and to use whatever possessions he had left to help the poorer Christians resist the temptation of material advantage to join the pagans.

Cyprian was executed for his faith in 258.

Late Night with Conan O'Brien

Conan O'Brien has been presenting this show for over fourteen seasons (over nine hundred episodes), since 1993. It's an entertaining mix of music, comedy, and chat show and has collected many awards, including Emmys, the Writers Guild of America, the PGA Golden Laurel Awards, and the Teen Choice Awards.

APRIL 19

DAILY READING

Christ has indeed been raised, the first fruits of those who have fallen asleep. (1 COR 15:20)

FEAST DAYS

814	George	Bishop of Pisidian Antioch
1054	Leo IX	Pope
1602	James Duckett	Catholic martyr

ENTRANCE AND EXIT

b. 1772	David Ricardo	English economist
b. 1903	Eliot Ness	American special agent
b. 1987	Maria Sharapova	Russian tennis player
d. 1824	George Gordon Byron	English poet
d. 1882	Charles Darwin	English naturalist
d. 1989	Daphne Du Maurier	English writer

St. Elphege

St. Elphege (also known as Alphege or Godwine) was born in the year 954, of a noble Saxon family. He lived as a hermit near Bath, where he founded a community under the rule of St. Benedict and became its first abbot. At thirty years of age he was chosen Bishop of Winchester.

In 1005 he became the twenty-ninth Archbishop of Canterbury and immediately went to Rome to receive the pallium (symbol of metropolitan jurisdiction) from Pope John XVIII. Around 1009, he called the Council of Enham in a futile effort to halt the social demoralization caused by the devastating Danish invasions.

In 1011, when the Danes landed in Kent and took the city of Canterbury, putting all to fire and sword, St. Elphege was captured and carried off in the expectation of a large ransom. He was unwilling that his ruined church and people should be put to such expense, and was kept in a loathsome prison at Greenwich for seven months. While so confined some friends came and urged him to lay a tax upon his tenants to raise the sum demanded for his ransom. "What reward can I hope for," said he, "if I spend upon myself what belongs to the poor? Better give up to the poor what is ours, than take from them the little which is their own."

As he still refused to give ransom, the enraged Danes fell upon him in a fury, beat him with the blunt sides of their weapons, and bruised him with stones until one, whom the saint had baptized shortly before, put an end to his sufferings by the blow of an axe. He died on Easter Saturday, April 19, 1012, his last words being a prayer for his murderers. His body was first buried in St. Paul's, London, but was afterward transferred to Canterbury by King Canute. A church dedicated to St. Elphege still stands upon the place of his martyrdom at Greenwich.

Noteworthy

1587 Sir Francis Drake sinks the Spanish fleet in Cadiz harbor.
1775 American Revolutionary War begins.
1839 The Treaty of London establishes Belgium as a kingdom.
1904 Much of Toronto, Ontario, Canada, is destroyed by fire.
1909 Joan of Arc receives beatification.
1933 President Franklin D. Roosevelt announces that the United States will be abandoning the gold standard.
1951 Gen. Douglas MacArthur retires from the military.
1954 Constituent Assembly of Pakistan decides Urdu and Bengali to be national languages of Pakistan.
1956 Actress Grace Kelly marries Rainier III of Monaco.
1993 The fifty-day siege of the Branch Davidian building outside Waco, Texas, ends when a fire breaks out. Eighty-one people die.
1995 Oklahoma City bombing: The Alfred P. Murrah Federal Building in Oklahoma City, Oklahoma, is bombed, killing 168.
1999 The German Bundestag returns to Berlin.
2005 Joseph Cardinal Ratzinger elected Pope Benedict XVI on the second day of the Papal conclave.

APRIL 20

DAILY READING

But thanks be to God! He gives us the victory through our Lord Jesus Christ. (1 COR15:57)

FEAST DAYS

689	Caedwalla	King of Wessex
1317	Agnes	Patron of Montepulciano, Italy
1322	Simon Rinalducci	Augustinian preacher

ENTRANCE AND EXIT

b. 121 BC	Marcus Aurelius Antonius	Roman Emperor
b. 1889	Adolf Hitler	German leader
b. 1972	Carmen Electra	American actor
d. 1314	Bertrand de Goth	Pope Clement V
d. 1912	Bram Stoker	Irish writer
d. 1998	Trevor Huddleston	English missionary

Rump Parliament Dissolution

On this day in 1653, Oliver Cromwell dissolved the so-called "rump" Parliament of fifty-three members who were supposed to administer government in the new commonwealth following the overthrow of Charles I. They were deliberating on a bill for the future representation, in which they should have a permanent place, when Cromwell resolved to make an end of them.

Cromwell, having ordered a company of musketeers to follow him, entered the House in plain black clothes and gray worsted stockings and, sitting down, listened for a while to their proceedings. Stepping into the floor of the House, and clapping on his hat, he declared, "It is not fit you should sit here any longer–you have sat too long for any good you have been doing lately. You shall now give place to better men."

He called in his musketeers and dismissed the Parliament thus, "Some of you are corrupt, unjust persons–how can you be a parliament for God's people? Depart, I say, and let us have done with you. Go!" This has been paraphrased as "In the name of God, go!" by today's tabloids when they press for a public figure to depart.

From that time Oliver Cromwell began his five and a half year rule as Lord Protector of England, Scotland, and Ireland.

James Ramsay

The naval surgeon, Anglican priest, and leading slavery abolitionist James Ramsay died on this day in 1789, aged fifty-five. It was as a surgeon onboard the British warship *Arundel* that Ramsay first saw the terrible effects of slavery. As a result, he left the navy and entered into the Anglican ministry in 1761. He was sent to serve in the West Indies, where he had further contact with slaves. In 1784, he published *Essay on the Treatment and Conversion of African Slaves in the British Sugar Colonies* and began to work with other abolitionists such as Thomas Clarkson and William Wilberforce. In 1787 he was one of the founders of the Committee for Abolition of the African Slave Trade. Although he died before he saw the abolition of the slave trade, Ramsay was one of its chief campaigners and his influence led to the end of this dread practice.

April 21

DAILY READING

Jesus said, "I give them eternal life, and they shall never perish; no one can snatch them out of my hand." (JOHN 10:28)

FEAST DAYS

ca. 640	Beuno	Welsh prince
ca. 740	Ethelwald	Bishop of Lindisfarne
1894	Conrad Birndorfer	Capuchin priest

ENTRANCE AND EXIT

b. 1816	Charlotte Brontë	English writer
b. 1923	John Mortimer	English writer
b. 1926	Elizabeth II	Queen of United Kingdom
d. 1109	Peter Abelard	French philosopher
d. 1910	Samuel Clemens (Mark Twain)	American writer
d. 2003	Nina Simone	American singer

St. Anselm

Today is the feast day of St. Anselm, Archbishop of Canterbury from 1093 to 1109. He was a notable theologian and the original proposer of the Ontological Argument. This implies that if we can conceive of God, then God exists; otherwise it would not be possible to imagine the actual existence of God.

Anselm was born at Aosta, in Piedmont, about the year 1033, and exhibited from a very early age a strongly marked love for learning and a monastic life. At fifteen, he was forbidden by his father to enter religion, but left his home and went to various schools in France. Eventually, he became a monk at Bec in Normandy. The fame of his sanctity in this cloister led King William II to name him to the vacant see of Canterbury.

Although he endured much opposition from King William, he remained much sought after for his teaching and is today recognized as the Father of Scholasticism, a system of philosophy that attempts to join faith to reason by synthesizing theology with classical Greek and Roman thought.

During the last years of his life, his health was entirely broken. Having for six months labored under a hectic decay, with an entire loss of appetite, under which disorder he would be carried every day to assist at holy Mass, he happily expired, laid on sackcloth and ashes, at Canterbury, on the 21st of April 1109. He was buried in his cathedral.

By a decree of Pope Clement XI, in 1720, he is honored among the Doctors of the church.

Noteworthy

1440 The Prussian Confederation is formed.

1804 The first self-propelling steam locomotive makes its outing at the Pen-y-Darren ironworks in Wales.

1848 Karl Marx publishes the *Communist Manifesto.*

1885 The newly completed Washington Monument is dedicated.

1916 World War I: In France the Battle of Verdun begins.

1952 Language Martyrs' Day, marking language revolution in then East Pakistan (now, Bangladesh).

1953 Francis Crick and James D. Watson discover the structure of the DNA molecule.

1972 The Soviet unmanned spaceship Luna 20 lands on the Moon.

1995 Steve Fossett lands in Leader, Saskatchewan, Canada, becoming the first person to make a solo flight across the Pacific Ocean in a balloon.

2004 The first European political party organization, the European Greens, is established in Rome.

April 22

DAILY READING

Since the creation of the world, God's invisible qualities–his eternal power and divine nature–have been clearly seen, being understood from what has been made, so that men are without excuse. (ROM 1:20)

FEAST DAYS

202	Leonidas	Egyptian philosopher
ca. 613	Theodore of Sikion	Patron for and against rain
770	Opportuna	French nun

ENTRANCE AND EXIT

b. 1754	Henry Fielding	English writer
b. 1899	Vladimir Nabokov	Russian writer
b. 1950	Peter Frampton	English singer
d. 536	Agapitus I	Italian pope
d. 1778	James Hargreaves	English inventor
d. 1994	Richard Milhouse Nixon	37th American president

Earth Day

The first Earth Day took place on April 22, 1970, as a result of the efforts of U.S. Senator Gaylord Nelson (Wisconsin) to raise environmental awareness and celebrate the diversity of life on Earth.

Today, over 175 countries observe Earth Day, and a charity called the Earth Day Network (www.earthday.org) promotes activities in relation to this event. The organizers claim this is the largest secular holiday in the world, but this has not been independently confirmed.

Activities for Earth Day include:

- Workshops on topics such as global warming.
- Environmental education projects in schools and colleges.
- Energy audits for companies and schools.
- Political campaigning.
- Special sermons for churches.
- Interfaith Power and Light program to encourage use of renewable energy.
- Water for Life events to celebrate clean water and campaign for clean water to be available to all communities.

Gaylord Nelson Honored

The founder of Earth Day, Senator Gaylord Nelson, was honored in September 1995 when President Clinton awarded him the Presidential Medal of Freedom. This is an extract from the citation:

> The Presidential Medal of Freedom is the highest honor given to civilians in the United States. . . . Twenty-five years ago this year, Americans came together for the very first Earth Day. . . . They came together . . . because of one American–Gaylord Nelson. As the father of Earth Day . . . he inspired us to remember that the stewardship of our natural resources is the stewardship of the American Dream. He is the worthy heir of the tradition of Theodore Roosevelt. . . . And I hope that Gaylord Nelson's shining example will illuminate all the debates in this city for years to come.

April 23

DAILY READING

It is written, "As surely as I live," says the Lord,
"every knee will bow before me;
every tongue will confess to God." (ROM 14:11)

FEAST DAYS

ca. 500	Ibar	Disciple of St. Patrick
997	Adalbert	Apostle of Bohemia
1262	Giles	Disciple of St. Francis of Assisi

ENTRANCE AND EXIT

b. 1564	William Shakespeare	English playwright
b. 1775	Joseph Mallord William Turner	English artist
b. 1981	Lady Gabriella Marina Alexandra Ophelia Windsor	English royal
d. 1616	William Shakespeare	English playwright
d. 1695	Henry Vaughan	Welsh poet
d. 1915	Rupert Brooke	English poet

St. George

April 23 is the feast day of St. George (ca. 275–81), patron of England, Canada, Ethiopia, Georgia, Greece, Montenegro, Portugal, Serbia, Libya, Lithuania, Malta Lebanon, Barcelona, Valencia, Istanbul, Ljubljana, Moscow, Venice, Ferrara, Limburg, Aragon, and Genoa.

According to the hagiographer Alban Butler, George was born in Cappadocia, to Christian parents. In early youth he chose a soldier's life, and soon obtained the favor of the Emperor Diocletian, who advanced him to the grade of tribune. When, however, the Diocletian began to persecute the Christians, George rebuked him at once sternly and openly for his cruelty and threw up his commission.

In consequence, George was subjected to a lengthened series of torments, and was finally beheaded. There was something so inspiring in the defiant cheerfulness of the young soldier that many Christians felt a personal share in this triumph of Christian fortitude; and as years rolled on St. George became a type of successful combat against evil, the slayer of the dragon, the darling theme of camp song and story, until "so thick a shade his very glory round him made" that his real lineaments became hard to trace.

Even beyond the circle of Christendom he was held in honor, and invading Saracens taught themselves to except from desecration the image of him they hailed as the "White-horsed Knight."

Slaying the Dragon

According to legend, St. George slayed a dragon in Silene, a city in Libya. The Archbishop of Genoa, Jacobus de Voragine, recalled the feat in his *Golden Legend* in 1275:

> The dragon appeared and came running to them, and St. George was upon his horse, and drew out his sword and garnished him with the sign of the cross, and rode hardily against the dragon which came towards him, and smote him with his spear and hurt him sore and threw him to the ground. And after said to the maid: Deliver to me your girdle, and bind it about the neck of the dragon and be not afeard.
>
> When she had done so the dragon followed her as it had been a meek beast and debonair. Then she led him into the city, and the people fled by mountains and valleys, and said: Alas! Alas! We shall be all dead.
>
> Then St. George said to them: No doubt ye no thing, without more, believe ye in God, Jesu Christ, and do ye to be baptized and I shall slay the dragon.
>
> Then the king was baptized and all his people, and St. George slew the dragon and smote off his head, and commanded that he should be thrown in the fields, and they took four carts with oxen that drew him out of the city.

APRIL 24

DAILY READING

You know that it was not with perishable things such as silver or gold that you were redeemed from the empty way of life handed down to you from your forefathers, but with the precious blood of Christ, a lamb without blemish or defect. (1 PET 1:18–19)

FEAST DAYS

ca. 394	Gregory	Patron of Elvira, Spain
729	Egbert	Northumbrian bishop
ca. 852	Diarmuid	Archbishop of Armagh, Ireland

ENTRANCE AND EXIT

b. 1815	Anthony Trollope	English writer
b. 1889	Sir Stafford Cripps	English statesman
b. 1942	Barbara Streisand	American singer and actor
d. 1731	Daniel Defoe	English writer
d. 1986	Wallis Simpson	Duchess of Windsor
d. 1993	Oliver Tambo	South African politician

The Eve of St. Mark

The eve of the feast of St. Mark (April 24), like St. John's Eve and All Hallows Eve, was traditionally marked with many country rituals. On this day, one belief was that everyone who was fated to be married or to die in the coming year would pass the parish church porch in solemn procession. So superstitious people used to gather for this parade of wraiths to see if their death or marriage was imminent.

The poet John Keats wrote about this custom in his poem called "The Eve of St Mark":

Upon a Sabbath-day it fell;
Twice holy was the Sabbath-bell
That call'd the folk to evening prayer;
The city streets were clean and fair
From wholesome drench of April rains;
And, on the western window panes,
The chilly sunset faintly told
Of unmatur'd green vallies cold,
Of the green thorny bloomless hedge,
Of rivers new with spring-tide sedge,
Of primroses by shelter'd rills,
And daisies on the aguish hills.
Twice holy was the Sabbath-bell:
The silent streets were crowded well
With staid and pious companies,
Warm from their fire-side orat'ries,
And moving with demurest air
To even-song and vesper prayer.

Noteworthy

1547 The Schmalcaldic League, an alliance of German Lutheran princes, was crushed by Charles V in the Battle of Muehlberg.

1575 Jacob Boehme, German Lutheran pietist and mystic, was born near Goerlitz (d. 1624).

1576 Vincent de Paul, founder of the Lazarist Fathers and the Sisters of Charity, was born in Pouy, Landes, France (d. September 27, 1660).

1649 The Toleration Acts were passed in Maryland under the administration of Protestant deputy governor William Stone. They provided for religious freedom for all Christians, including Roman Catholics.

1920 Eliza E. Hewitt (b. June 28, 1851), American Presbyterian Sunday school leader and hymn writer, died.

1944 In *United States v. Ballard* the U.S. Supreme Court ruled that no governmental agency can determine "the truth or falsity of the beliefs or doctrines" of anyone.

1982 William Cameron ("Uncle Cam") Townsend, founder of the Wycliffe Bible Translators, died (b. July 9, 1896).

APRIL 25

DAILY READING

To them God has chosen you to make known among
the Gentiles the glorious riches of this mystery,
which is Christ in you, the hope of glory. (COL 1:27)

FEAST DAYS

ca. 68	Mark the Evangelist	Apostle
ca. 489	Macaille	Bishop of Croghan, Ireland
ca. 857	Heribaldus	Bishop of Auxerre, France

ENTRANCE AND EXIT

b. 1284	Edward II	King of England
b. 1940	Al Pacino	American actor
b. 1969	Renée Zellweger	American actor
d. 1744	Anders Celsius	Swedish scientist
b. 1800	William Cowper	English writer
d. 1995	Ginger Rogers	American actor and dancer

ANZAC Day

On this day in 1915, Commonwealth troops from Australia and New Zealand landed along the Turkish peninsula at Gallipoli in an attempt to open up the Eastern front and eventually capture Constantinople. Turkey was allied to Germany, and it would have been a vital blow to the Germans.

However, ANZAC (Australian and New Zealand Army Corps) troops met fierce resistance from Turkish troops, and over eight thousand soldiers were killed, with casualties three times that number.

The Battle of Gallipoli seared into the national psyche of both Australia and New Zealand and helped to build national identity in a time of great loss.

On April 25, 1916, the Australian government observed the first ANZAC Day to remember the sacrifice of troops at Gallipoli. There were patriotic rallies, church services, and reunions of survivors.

In 1981, the Australian director Peter Weir and Australian star Mel Gibson made a film about the ANZAC action called *Gallipoli.*

Today ANZAC Day is the official day of remembrance observed wherever there are Australian or New Zealand communities. It has grown to be an observance encompassing all Australian and New Zealand service in all conflicts. A special service is held at dawn to set the tone for the day, and there are displays of poppies and special events of thanksgiving and commemoration.

St. Mark the Evangelist

According to legend, the Apostle Mark was a Levite and served at the wedding in Cana that Jesus attended. He is supposed to have poured the water that Jesus transformed into wine.

St. Mark is said to have accompanied St. Peter to Rome, where Peter ordained him bishop and sent him to Alexandria, where his first convert was the shoemaker Annianus. Thus, he is the patron of shoemakers. Around 68, he was martyred in Alexandria by a heathen mob.

Mark's gospel was probably the earliest, written just thirty years after the death of Jesus. It was written for Greeks as is evident from the explanation of Jewish traditions.

APRIL 26

DAILY READING

You have shaken the land and torn it open;
mend its fractures, for it is quaking. (PS 60:2)

FEAST DAYS

ca. 620	Clarence	Bishop of Vienne, France
ca. 790	Paschasius	French hermit
1146	John	Bishop of Valence, France

ENTRANCE AND EXIT

b. 1889	Ludwig Wittgenstein	German philosopher
b. 1894	Rudolph Hess	German Nazi leader
b. 1900	Charles Richter	American scientist
d. 1865	John Wilkes Booth	American assassin
d. 1951	Arnold Sommerfeld	German scientist
d. 1984	Count Basie	American band leader

The Richter Magnitude Scale (1900–1985)

The American seismologist Charles Richter from the California Institute of Technology developed a logarithmic scale to measure the magnitude of an earthquake. The Richter Magnitude Scale measures the waves of energy released emanating from an earthquake as measured by data from seismographs.

There is more than one chart to represent the Richter scale. This is a basic one:

Richter Magnitude	Earthquake Effects
< 3.5	Generally not felt, but recorded
< 6.0	Slight damage to well constructed building; major damage to poorly constructed buildings
6.1–6.9	Major destruction up to 100 km of epicenter
7.0–7.9	Major event, serious damage
> 8.0	Great earthquake, serious damage over several hundred km

Notable Earthquakes

August 24, 70: Mount Vesuvius, Italy, erupts, burying Pompeii and Herculaneum. Thousands killed.

January 23, 1556: Shaanxi province, China. Deadliest earthquake in history kills approx. 830,000 people.

April 18, 1906: The famous San Francisco earthquake and fire. 7.8 on the Richter scale (retrospective).

December 16, 1920: Gansu province, China, approx. 200,000 killed. 8.6 on the Richter scale (retrospective).

September 1, 1923: Tokyo and Yokahoma, Japan. 8.3 magnitude (retrospective) earthquake destroys 1/3 of Tokyo and most of Yokohama. Over 140,000 killed.

May 22, 1927: Xining, China: 8.3 magnitude earthquake (retrospective). Approx. 200,000 killed.

May 22, 1960: Strongest earthquake ever recorded, at 9.5 magnitude, occurs off the coast of Chile.

December 26, 2004: An earthquake measuring 9.0 on the Richter scale off the coast of Sumatra, Indonesia, creates the deadliest Tsunami in history. The waves reach numerous Asian and African countries. More than 225,000 killed, millions homeless.

October 2, 2005: Kashmir, Pakistan, a 7.6 magnitude earthquake kills more than 80,000 people.

APRIL 27

DAILY READING

The Son of Man came to seek
and to save what was lost. (LUKE 19:10)

FEAST DAYS

ca. 490	Asicus	Patron of Elphin, Ireland
1304	Pietro Armengaudio	Italian martyr
1565	Catherine Cosie	Greek martyr

ENTRANCE AND EXIT

b. 1889	Sergei Prokofiev	Russian composer
b. 1904	Cecil Day-Lewis	Irish writer
b. 1959	Sheena Easton	Scottish singer
d. 1521	Ferdinand Magellan	Portuguese explorer
d. 1932	Hart Crane	American poet
d. 1998	Carlos Castaneda	American writer

Paradise Lost *Sold*

On this day in 1667, one of the greatest poems in the English language, *Paradise Lost* was sold by its author John Milton (1608–74) to the publisher Samuel Simmons for a mere £5 advance and another £5 once 1,300 copies were sold. John Milton was impoverished because he had supported Cromwell in the Civil War, served as a minister in Cromwell's government, and had been arrested after the restoration of the monarch. He was fined for his support for Cromwell, and his works were publicly burned. This opprobrium was heaped upon a man who had lost his sight in 1651.

It took eighteen months for *Paradise Lost* to sell 1,300 copies, but by this time it was recognized as being a work of unparallel genius. Today, *Paradise Lost* has sold millions of copies and ranks alongside the works of Shakespeare, Chaucer, and the King James Bible.

Paradise Lost, published in ten parts has the grand theme of the fall and expulsion of Man from Eden. It deals with universal subjects of temptation, sin, redemption, and the ultimate triumph of good over evil.

The second edition of *Paradise Lost* is noted for its poetic preface by Andrew Marvell, the leading metaphysical poet, and an extract is given below:

When I beheld the Poet blind, yet bold,
In slender Book his vast Design unfold,
Messiah Crown'd, Gods Reconcil'd Decree,
Rebelling Angels, the Forbidden Tree,
Heav'n, Hell, Earth, Chaos, All;
  the Argument
Held me a while misdoubting his Intent,
That he would ruine (for I saw him strong)
The sacred Truths to Fable and old Song,
(So Sampson groap'd the Temples Posts
  in spight)
The World o'rewhelming to revenge
  his Sight.
Yet as I read, soon growing less severe,
I lik'd his Project, the success did fear;
Through that wide Field how he his way
  should find
O're which lame Faith leads
  Understanding blind;
Lest he perplext the things he would explain,
And what was easie he should render vain.
Or if a Work so infinite he spann'd,
Jealous I was that some less skilful hand
(Such as disquiet alwayes what is well,
And by ill imitating would excell)
Might hence presume the whole
  Creations day
To change in Scenes, and show it in a Play.

April 28

DAILY READING

I know that my Redeemer lives, and that in the end he will stand upon the earth. (JOB 19:25)

FEAST DAYS

ca. 1st cent.	Vitalis of Milan	Patron of Thibodeaux, Louisana
639	Gerard	English pilgrim
1716	Louis Marie de Montfort	French theologian

ENTRANCE AND EXIT

b. 1442	Edward IV	King of England
b. 1758	James Monroe	5th American president
b. 1974	Penelope Cruz	Spanish actor
d. 1842	Sir Charles Bell	Scottish scientist
d. 1945	Benito Mussolini	Italian leader
d. 1992	Olivier Messiaen	French composer

St. Peter-Louis-Marie Chanel

According to the Catholic Encyclopaedia, Peter Chanel (1802–41), whose feast is celebrated on this day, suffered martyrdom on this day in 1841 on the island of Tonga.

Chanel, who upon his ordination in 1827 sought to serve overseas, was of French descent. In 1831 he joined the Society of Mary, and in 1836 he embarked for Oceania (the Pacific Islands). He was assigned by his bishop to the Island of Futuna, near as Tonga, and landed in November 1837.

He was the first Christian missionary ever to set foot there, and met with almost insurmountable difficulties among the natives. Nevertheless, after two years of faithful service, he began to see the results of his efforts, when Niuluki, king and also pontiff of the island, already jealous of the progress of the new religion, was exasperated by the conversion of his son and daughter.

At Niuluki's instigation, one of the ministers gathered some of the enemies of Christianity, and Peter was cruelly assassinated without uttering a word of complaint. Through his death, the venerable martyr obtained what he had so ardently desired and earnestly worked for, the conversion of Futuna.

When news of his martyrdom reached his church, two more missionaries resumed his work, and reaped what Peter had sown, with many people converted to Christianity.

In 1857 Peter was declared Venerable by Pius IX, and on November 17, he was beatified by Leo XIII.

Salisbury Cathedral

On this day in 1220, Bishop Richard Poore laid the foundation stone of one of England's greatest buildings, Salisbury Cathedral. The bishop brought in priests, clerks, canons, and senior clergy to carry out the work of the cathedral. Depending on their place in the hierarchy, they were given varying amounts of land around the cathedral and along the riverbank. Lower clergy were allotted an acre and half upon which to build their dwellings, and the senior clergy were given twice that measure. The land upon which the clergy dwellings were built is the Cathedral Close.

The main cathedral building was finished in 1258, and in 1331 the Close was walled with stone taken from the original Norman cathedral at Old Sarum. Many of the old medieval buildings still remain within the Close. The Close is the largest in Britain, and Salisbury Cathedral has the tallest spire in Britain at 123 m (404 ft.). The church is dedicated to Mary and contains Europe's oldest working clock (1326).

April 29

DAILY READING

[There is] a time to weep and a time to laugh,
a time to mourn and a time to dance. (ECCL 3:4)

FEAST DAYS

744	Wilfrid the Younger	Bishop of York
1109	Hugh	Patron of Cluny, France
1380	Catherine	Patron of Siena

ENTRANCE AND EXIT

b. 1769	Arthur Wellesley	Duke of Wellington
b. 1954	Jerry Seinfeld	American comedian
b. 1970	Uma Thurman	American actor
d. 1768	Georg Brandt	Swedish scientist
d. 1980	Alfred Hitchcock	English film director
d. 2006	John Kenneth Galbraith	American economist

International Dance Day

International Dance Day was created in 1982 by the International Dance Committee of the International Theatre Institute, UNESCO. The date commemorates the birthday of Jean-Georges Noverre (1727–1810), the creator of modern ballet. The intention of International Dance Day is to bring all dance together to cross all political, cultural, and ethnic barriers and bring people together in peace and friendship with a common language–dance.

Every year a message from a well-known dance personality is circulated throughout the world. This is the official message of International Dance Day 2007 from the German choreographer, Sasha Waltz:

One dances on birthdays, at weddings, on the streets, in living rooms, on the stage, behind the scenes. To communicate joy, sorrow, as ritual and borderline experience.

Dance is a universal language: emissary for a peaceful world, for equality, tolerance and compassion. Dance teaches us sensibility, consciousness and to pay attention to the moment.

Dance is the manifestation of our being alive. Dance is transformation. Dance locates the soul, dance affords the body a spiritual dimension.

Dance enables us to feel our body, to rise above, to go beyond, to be another body.

To dance is to participate actively in the vibration of the universe.

St. Hugh of Cluny

According to the hagiographer Alban Butler, St. Hugh (1024–1109) was of royal blood, being related to the sovereign house of the dukes of Burgundy. He was educated by Hugh, Bishop of Auxerre, his great-uncle. From his infancy he was exceedingly given to prayer and meditation, and his life was remarkably innocent and holy. One day, hearing an account of the wonderful sanctity of the monks of Cluny, under St. Odilo, he was so moved that he set out that moment and begged to join them. He became a monk in 1039, being sixteen years old. His extraordinary virtue, especially his admirable humility, obedience, charity, sweetness, prudence, and zeal, gained him the respect of the whole community; and upon the death of St. Odilo, in 1049, though only twenty-five years old, he succeeded to be head of the great abbey of Cluny, a position he held for sixty-two years. He was canonized twelve years after his death by Pope Calixtus II.

APRIL 30

DAILY READING

Speaking the truth in love, we will in all things grow up into him who is the Head, that is, Christ. (EPH 4:15)

FEAST DAYS

ca. 397	Lawrence	Italian priest
1131	Adjutor	Patron of swimmers
1572	Antonio Ghisleri	Pope Pius V

ENTRANCE AND EXIT

b. 1662	Mary II	Queen of England
b. 1946	Carl Gustav XVI	King of Sweden
b. 1982	Kirsten Dunst	American actor
d. 1883	Edouard Manet	French artist
d. 1984	Arthur Travers Harris	British air marshall
d. 1989	Sergio Leone	Italian film director

Walpurgisnacht

This is the eve of the feast of St. Walburga celebrated in Germany and Sweden. Her feast day is actually February 25, but in Sweden and Finland this is celebrated on May 1 (the day when she was canonized in 779).

According to tradition, Walburga was born in Devon around 710, the daughter of St. Richard of Wessex. Her uncle was the great St. Boniface (Archbishop of Mainz) and her brothers were St. Winnebald and St. Willibald, who would later become Abbot of Heidenheim and Bishop of Eichstätt respectively.

In 720, she entered the at Wimborne (Dorset) under the direction of St. Tatta. Around the same time, her brothers embarked on a pilgrimage to Heidenheim. Winnebald joined a Benedictine monastery in Rome and Willibald traveled to the Holy Land. Her uncle St. Boniface was busy consolidating the church in Germany, establishing monasteries and bishoprics. In 750 St. Walburga traveled to Germany to assist her kinsmen in this great work. It is said that, as she crossed the Channel, a terrible storm arose, which was stopped only by Walburga's prayers–the miracle was traditionally commemorated at Eichstätt on August 4.

St. Walburga died on February 25, 779, and was buried at Heidenheim. Traditionally, Walpurgisnacht is a time for witches to host spring festivities before the goodness of Walburga overtakes them.

Noteworthy

313 Emperor Licinius unified the whole of the Eastern empire under his own rule.

1527 Henry VIII and King Francis of France signed the Treaty of Westminster.

1563 All Jews were expelled from France by order of Charles VI.

1789 George Washington took office as first elected U.S. president.

1812 Louisiana admitted as the eighteenth U.S. state.

1849 The republican patriot and guerrilla leader Giuseppe Garabaldi repulsed a French attack on Rome.

1900 Casey Jones was killed while trying to save the runaway train "Cannonball Express."

1930 The Soviet Union proposed a military alliance with France and Great Britain.

1943 The British submarine HMS *Seraph* dropped "the man who never was," a dead man the British planted with false invasion plans, into the Mediterranean off the coast of Spain.

1945 Adolf Hitler and Eva Braun committed suicide. They had been married for one day. One week later Germany surrendered unconditionally.

1967 Muhammad Ali was stripped of his world heavyweight boxing championship when he refused to be inducted into the U.S. military service.

1980 Terrorists seized the Iranian Embassy in London.

1991 An estimated 125,000 people were killed in a cyclone that hit Bangladesh.

Then came faire May, the fayrest mayd on ground,
Deckt all with dainties of her seasons pryde,
And throwing flow'res out of her lap around:
Upon two brethren's shoulders she did ride,
The twinnes of Leda; which on either side
Supported her, like to their soveraine Queene.
Lord! how all creatures laught, when her they spide,
And leapt and daunc't as they had ravisht beene!
And Cupid Selfe about her fluttred all in greene.

EDMUND SPENSER–*The Shepheardes Calender* (1579)

Hark! The sea-faring wild-fowl loud proclaim
My coming, and the swarming of the bees.
These are my heralds, and behold! my name
Is written in blossoms on the hawthorn-trees.
I tell the mariner when to sail the seas;
I waft o'er all the land from far away
The breath and bloom of the Hesperides,
My birthplace. I am Maia. I am May.

HENRY WADSWORTH LONGFELLOW–*The Poet's Calendar* (1882)

Proverbs ~

Be it weal or be it woe,
Beans blow before May doth go.

Come it early or come it late,
In May comes the cow-quake.

The haddocks are good,
When dipped in May flood.

May ~

May is thought to have been named in honor of the Roman Senate or *Maiores*, the body charged with compiling and protecting the constitution of Rome. Among Anglo-Saxon races, this month was known as *Milchi* or *Tri-Milchi* in recognition of cattle being able to give milk three times a day.

Chaucer ~

Embroider'd was he, as it were a mead
All full of freshe flowers, white and red.
Singing he was, or fluting all the day;
He was as fresh as is the month of May.
Short was his gown, with sleeves long and wide.
Well could he sit on horse, and faire ride.

–*Canterbury Tales*, The Prologue

May 1

DAILY READING

Without faith it is impossible to please God,
because anyone who comes to him must believe that he exists
and that he rewards those who earnestly seek him. (HEB 11:6)

FEAST DAYS

ca. 1st cent.	Joseph the Worker	Husband of Mary
ca. 705 BC	Jeremiah	Old Testament prophet
ca. 1383	Panacea de Muzzi	Patron of shepherds

ENTRANCE AND EXIT

b. 1218	King Rudolph I	King of Germany
b. 1769	Arthur Wellesley	Duke of Wellington
b. 1923	Joseph Heller	American writer
d. 1904	Antonin Dvórak	Czech composer
d. 1965	Spike Jones	American film director
d. 1994	Ayrton Senna	Brazilian racing driver

May Day

Throughout Europe, May Day is a time to celebrate the onset of flowers and blossom. In the sixteenth century it was still customary for the local people to go out into the woods and gather flowers and hawthorn branches, which they brought home about sunrise, with accompaniments of horn and tabor, and all possible signs of joy and merriment. With these spoils they would decorate every door and window in the village. By a natural transition of ideas, they gave to the hawthorn bloom the name of the May; they called this ceremony "bringing home the May"; they spoke of the expedition to the woods as "going a-Maying."

According to custom, a towering maypole was set up on the village green. This pole, usually made of the trunk of a tall birch tree, was decorated with bright field flowers. The villagers then danced and sang around the maypole, accompanied by a piper. When the sun rose, the maypole was decked with leaves, flowers, and ribbons while dancing and singing went on around it. The May Queen was chosen from the pretty girls of the village to reign over the May Day festivities. Crowned on a flower-covered throne, she was drawn in a decorated cart by the young to the village green. She would be crowned there right on the green spot. She was set in an arbor of flowers and often the Morris dancing was performed around her, rather than around the maypole.

These dances are still performed in England. For example, the May Day procession at Padstow, Cornwall, features a central figure, called "Oss"–a man disguised as a horse and wearing a face mask. Washing the face with May dew was yet another custom. There was a belief among the women in England that washing in May dew would restore beauty.

May Day as a special day for workers originated in the 1830s when workers throughout America and Europe began campaigns to limit the number of hours worked per week. Today, May Day celebrations include parades by trade unions in solidarity of workers throughout the world.

Jeremiah the Prophet

Jeremiah is one of the most important prophets of the Old Testament. He was called to prophecy in 627 BC and warned the people of Israel of the destruction they were bringing upon themselves by failing to heed to the word of God. His predictions are incorporated in the books of Jeremiah and Lamentations. In 586 BC, Jerusalem was destroyed by the Babylonian King Nebuchadnezzar II, and the Israelites were exiled to Babylon.

May 2

DAILY READING

This is the confidence we have in approaching God:
that if we ask anything according to his will, he hears us.
And if we know that he hears us—whatever we ask—
we know that we have what we asked of him. (1 JOHN 5:14–15)

FEAST DAYS

373	Athanasius of Egypt	Bishop of Alexandria
ca. 460	Germanus	Bishop of Auxerre, France
926	Wibroda	Benedictine nun

ENTRANCE AND EXIT

b. 1729	Catherine II	Russian Empress
b. 1859	Jerome Klapka Jerome	English writer
b. 1975	David Beckham	English footballer
d. 1519	Leonardo da Vinci	Italian artist
d. 1972	John Edgar Hoover	American FBI director
d. 1999	Oliver Reed	English actor

Jerome K. Jerome

The humorist, essayist, and novelist Jerome K. Jerome (1859–1927) was born on this day in Walsall, Staffordshire. His most famous work is *Three Men in a Boat* (1889), which describes the humorous adventures of three friends and their pet dog on a rowing holiday on the River Thames. His father was renowned as a nonconformist preacher and was deacon at the Bridge Street Congregational Church in Walsall.

On leaving school at the age of fourteen, Jerome worked as a railway clerk at Euston Station. He became an actor, but also tried his hand at teaching and journalism. In 1885, he published *On the Stage and Off* and followed this a year later with *Idle Thoughts of an Idle Fellow*. From 1892 he edited and contributed to magazines such as *The Idler* and a weekly magazine called *Today*, but he was forced to sell his interests in 1897 following an expensive libel action. He went on to concentrate on the theater, and one of his best plays, modeled on J. M. Barrie, is *The Passing of the Third Floor Back* (1907).

In 1927 Jerome K. Jerome returned to the place of his birth to be conferred with the honor of Freeman of the Borough of Walsall. At the presentation dinner in his honor, Jerome said: "This Freedom of the Borough, it is the people's knighthood. I take it you have conferred upon me the Knighthood of Walsall, and I shall always be proud of my spurs."

He died a few months later, following a stroke.

Athanasian Creed

The Athanasian Creed is one of the four authoritative creeds of the Catholic Church. The Anglican Church and some Protestant Churches also hold it to be authoritative. Tradition holds that Athanasius was the author of this creed. The most famous statement of this document asserts the doctrine of the Trinity:

> And the catholic faith is this: That we worship one God in Trinity and Trinity in Unity; Neither confounding the persons nor dividing the substance. For there is one person of the Father, another of the Son, and another of the Holy Spirit. But the Godhead of the Father, of the Son, and of the Holy Spirit is all one, the glory equal, the majesty coeternal. Such as the Father is, such is the Son, and such is the Holy Spirit.

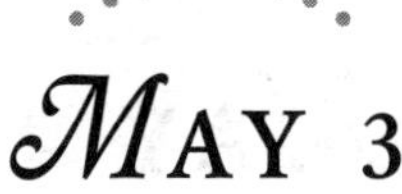

*M*AY 3

DAILY READING

Be joyful in hope, patient in affliction,
faithful in prayer. (ROM 12:12)

FEAST DAYS

ca. 62	James the Less	Apostle
ca. 80	Philip	Apostle
1010	Ansfrid	Bishop of Utrecht

ENTRANCE AND EXIT

b. 1898	Golda Meir	Israeli prime minister
b. 1903	Bing Crosby	American singer
b. 1939	Samantha Eggar	English actor
d. 1481	Mohammed II	Sultan of Turkey
d. 1606	Henry Garnett	English Gunpowder Plot conspirator
d. 1926	Napoleon V	French royal

Discovery of the True Cross

On this day in 614, the Empress Helena, mother of Constantine the Great, claimed to have discovered the true cross on which Jesus was crucified. Tradition records that Helena went to Jerusalem, and there compelled the Jews give up to her this and other crosses, and that its identity was established by a miracle. The body of a dead man was placed on each of the crosses, and when it touched the true one, the dead man immediately came to life. The cross was entrusted to the charge of the Bishop of Jerusalem and soon became an object of pilgrimage–and a source of profit, for small pieces were cut from it and given to the pilgrims, who made liberal offerings. In this manner the whole cross would naturally have been soon used up, but such a result was averted: It was found that the wood of the cross possessed the power of reproducing itself, and that, however much was cut off, the substance was not diminished.

When the Empress Helena discovered the cross, she also obtained possession of the four nails with which Christ's body was attached to it, the spear that pierced his side, and other articles. The largest pieces of it were then preserved in Paris, Poitiers, and Rome.

The discovery was controversial, and many were not convinced of it. In 1561 John Calvin observed that so great a quantity of fragments of the true cross were scattered among the Christian churches in his time, that they would load a large ship. Also, whereas the original cross could be carried by one man, it would take three hundred men to support the weight of the existing fragments of it.

St. James the Less

He is so called to distinguish him from the other apostle of the same name, the son of Zebedee. He is also known by the title of James the Just. He was thought to have been the son of Alpheus and Mary and seems to have been born some years before Jesus.

In the New Testament, he is the author of the book that bears his name. In the book of James, which he wrote in Greek, he refuted false teachers and exhorted believers to live out their faith. He added excellent precepts of a holy life and exhorted the faithful not to neglect anointing with oil those who suffer from ill health.

MAY 4

DAILY READING

If my people, who are called by my name, will humble themselves and pray and seek my face and turn from their wicked ways, then will I hear from heaven and will forgive their sin and will heal their land. (2 CHRON 7:14)

FEAST DAYS

ca. 304	Florian	Patron of firefighters
1038	Godard	Bishop of Hildesham, Germany
1535	Augustine Webster	Carthusian monk

ENTRANCE AND EXIT

b. 1796	Horace Mann	American writer
b. 1825	Thomas Henry Huxley	English scientist
b. 1928	Hosni Mubarak	Egyptian president
d. 1891	Sherlock Holmes	English fictional detective
d. 1980	Josip Broz Tito	Yugoslav president
d. 1997	Vijayananda Dahanayake	Sri Lankan president

Star Wars Day

Fans of the Star Wars sagas need little excuse to dress up as characters from the six movies, see all six movies in one sitting, recite well-known passages, enact key scenes, produce their own homage films, and jam bulletin boards and blog sites to share the excitement with other adherents.

Today is a special day for such fans, as it is the unofficial day to celebrate everything to do with Star Wars. The main reason seems to be that "May the fourth" sounds like the start of the Star Wars catch phrase, "May the force be with you."

However, there are lots of occasions to celebrate the Star Wars franchise, and the appellation of this day in honor of Star Wars is still to be fully realized. Fans in different states and countries chose to celebrate Star Wars on different days, and there are conventions throughout the year in many countries.

Sherlock Holmes

The world's foremost consulting detective continues to fascinate and delight. His many adventures were recorded by Sir Arthur Conan Doyle and include the following:

Novels

A Study in Scarlet (1887)
The Sign of the Four (1890)
The Hound of the Baskervilles (1902)
The Valley of Fear (1904)

Short Stories

The Adventures of Sherlock Holmes (1892)
–collection containing

A Scandal in Bohemia (1891) • The Red Headed League (1891) • A Case of Identity (1891) • The Boscombe Valley Mystery (1891) • The Five Orange Pips (1891) • The Man with the Twisted Lip (1891) • The Adventure of the Blue Carbuncle (1892) • The Adventure of the Speckled Band (1892) • The Adventure of the Engineer's Thumb (1892) • The Adventure of the Noble Bachelor (1892) • The Adventure of the Beryl Coronet (1892) • The Adventure of the Copper Beeches (1892)

Memoirs of Sherlock Holmes (1894)
–collection containing

Silver Blaze (1892) • The Yellow Face (1893) • The Stock Broker's Clerk (1893) • The Gloria Scott (1893) • The Musgrave Ritual (1893) • The Reigate Puzzle (1893) • The Crooked Man (1893) • The Resident Patient (1893) • The Greek Interpreter (1893) • The Naval Treaty (1893) • The Final Problem (1893)

The Return of Sherlock Holmes (1904)
–collection containing

The Adventure of the Empty House (1903) • The Adventure of the Norwood Builder (1903) • The Adventure of the Dancing Men (1903) • The Adventure of the Solitary Cyclist (1903) • The Adventure of the Priory School (1904) • The Adventure of Black Peter (1904) • The Adventure of Charles Augustus Milverton (1904) • The Adventure of the Six Napoleons (1904) • The Adventure of the Three Students (1904) • The Adventure of the Golden Pince-Nez (1904) • The Adventure of the Missing Three-Quarter (1904) • The Adventure of the Abbey Grange (1904) • The Adventure of the Second Stain (1904)

MAY 5

DAILY READING

Do not be anxious about anything, but in everything,
by prayer and petition, with thanksgiving, present your request to God.
And the peace of God, which transcends all understanding,
will guard your hearts and your minds in Christ Jesus. (PHIL 4:6–7)

FEAST DAYS

ca. 300	Jovinian	Lector of the church at Auxerre, France
1220	Angelo of Jerusalem	Carmelite martyr
1844	Edmund Ignatius Rice	Founder of the Congregation of Christian Brothers

ENTRANCE AND EXIT

b. 1747	Leopold II	King of Belgium
b. 1813	Søren Aaby Kierkegaard	Danish philosopher
b. 1818	Karl Heinrich Marx	German writer
d. 1821	Napoleon Bonaparte	French Emperor
d. 1827	Frederik Augustus I	King of Saxony
d. 1981	Bobby Sands	Irish hunger striker

Edmund Ignatius Rice

Edmund Rice (1762–1844) was beatified by Pope John Paul II in 1996 in Rome. In his peroration, the pope stated:

> Here we have an outstanding model of a true lay apostle and a deeply committed Religious. . . . Today, his spiritual sons, the Christian Brothers and the Presentation Brothers, continue his mission: a mission which he himself described in this simple and clear intention: "Trusting in God's help, I hope to be able to educate these boys to be good Catholics and good citizens."

Edmund Rice was born in Kilkenny, Ireland. He was the fourth son of nine children, and his father leased 180 acres of farmland to provide for the family. His family was regarded as being comfortably well off for that time. They were very religious and highly respected in the community for their generosity to the poor. In his family home, Edmund learned what it is to care for and share with others.

However, there was little Catholic education and Edmund and his brothers and sisters were taught at home. In 1790 he joined a religious confraternity, and two years later he founded a society for orphans and devoted his time to helping prisoners. Edmund was opposed to slavery and would regularly help slaves heading to America escape from the boats in Waterford harbor and hide in local homes.

Edmund founded the Christian Brothers to enable children to receive a Catholic education. He was encouraged by Thomas Hussey, the Bishop of Waterford. From the start, Edmund saw the Christian Brothers' schools as a way of helping local children find employment, so the curriculum was structured to deliver practical skills such as carpentry.

Edmund died in 1844, his motto for the Christian Brothers was "faith and fatherland."

Søren Kierkergaard Quotes

"Seek first God's Kingdom, that is, become like the lilies and the birds, become perfectly silent then shall the rest be added to you."

—*Christian Discourses*

"Faith is against understanding, faith is on the other side of death."

—*For Self Examination*

"The person who is deceived by the world can still hope that he will not be disappointed some other time under other circumstances, but the person who deceives himself is continually deceived even if he flees to the farthest limits of the world, because he cannot escape himself."

—*Upbuilding Discourse*

MAY 6

DAILY READING

Confess your sins to each other and pray for each other so that you may be healed. The prayer of a righteous man is powerful and effective. (JAS 5:16)

FEAST DAYS

ca. 69 BC	Evodius	Bishop of Antioch
ca. 4th cent.	Protegenes	Bishop of Carrhae, Syria
ca. 7th cent.	Edbert	Bishop of Lindisfarne

ENTRANCE AND EXIT

b. 1758	Maximilien Robespierre	French leader
b. 1856	Sigmund Schlomo Freud	Austrian father of psychoanalysis
b. 1953	Anthony Charles Lynton Blair	British prime minister
d. 1638	Cornelius Jansen	Dutch theologian
d. 1910	Edward VII	King of England
d. 2002	Pim Fortuyn	Dutch politician

Battle of Ethadune

On this day in 878, King Alfred the Great (849–99) defeated the pagan Viking leader Guthrum at Ethadune (modern-day Edington) in Wiltshire, England. This famous victory ensured that the Christian faith would remain alive in England instead of being overwhelmed by the pagan gods of the Danes. Guthrum agreed to be baptized a Christian and to stay north and east of the River Thames, in an area called the Danelaw. However, the Danes broke the peace, and Alfred renewed the war. He won London in 886. All the English people not subject to the Danes recognized Alfred as their ruler and paid him homage. The old, independent Anglo-Saxon kingdoms began to merge under the rule King Alfred the Great.

Alfred was the youngest son of King Ethelwulf of Wessex and was born in Wantage, Oxfordshire. His biographer, the Welsh writer Asser, records that Alfred was a keen scholar and that he visited Rome twice, where the pope acknowledged the status of the royal house of Wessex.

Alfred became king in 871 at the death of his brother Ethelred. The West Saxons had been at war with the Danes for many years. After several losing battles, Alfred made peace with the invaders. But the Danes renewed their attacks and defeated Alfred at the Battle of Chippenham in 877.

After the Battle of Ethadune in 878, Alfred built forts and boroughs (fortified towns) at strategic points along the coast as protection against further invasions. He also issued a code of laws to restore peaceful government.

Under his influence, the *Anglo-Saxon Chronicle* began to be compiled. It is now the main source for Anglo-Saxon history up to 1154.

Extracts from The Ballad of the White Horse: Book VIII: Ethandune: The Last Charge *by G. K. Chesterton*

"Brothers at arms," said Alfred,
"On this side lies the foe;
Are slavery and starvation flowers,
That you should pluck them so?

"For whether is it better
To be prodded with Danish poles,
Having hewn a chamber in a ditch,
And hounded like a howling witch,
Or smoked to death in holes?

"Or that before the red cock crow
All we, a thousand strong,
Go down the dark road to God's house,
Singing a Wessex song?

"To sweat a slave to a race of slaves,
To drink up infamy?
No, brothers, by your leave, I think
Death is a better ale to drink,
And by all the stars of Christ that sink,
The Danes shall drink with me."

MAY 7

DAILY READING

Be joyful always; pray continually; give thanks in all circumstances, for this is God's will for you in Christ Jesus. (1 THESS 5:16–18)

FEAST DAYS

304	Duje	Bishop of Salona, Croatia
721	John of Beverley	Bishop of Hexham, England
ca. 1095	Gisella	Queen of Hungary

ENTRANCE AND EXIT

b. 1812	Robert Browning	English poet
b. 1840	Peter Ilyich Tchaikovsky	Russian composer
b. 1901	Gary Cooper	American actor
d. 1825	Antonio Salieri	Italian composer
d. 1940	George Lansbury	English politician
d. 1989	Guy Williams	American actor

William of Rubrouc

A year before the celebrated traveler Marco Polo set out on his quest, a Flemish Franciscan monk, William of Rubrouch (ca. 1210–ca. 1270), set out to preach the gospel in the Mongol Empire. The detailed report of his eleven-thousand-mile journey is considered the most authentic description of the Mongol Empire in the thirteenth century.

William was sent by King IX of France and left Constantinople on this day in 1253. The king had heard that the Mongol leader Sartak was a Christian, and he determined to encourage him in his newfound faith.

From Constantinople, William crossed the Black Sea, traversed the Crimea, and then continued eastward. He discovered that Sartak was not a Christian and was directed to the Great Khan Mangu in the heart of Mongolia. In midwinter William's party reached the eastern point of Lake Alakul, south of Lake Balkasch, and near this the court of the khan, which they arrived at on Easter 1254. Williams discussed theology with the Great Khan and was allowed to preach at his court for nearly nine months and baptized nearly sixty believers.

William arrived back at Acre in May 1255 and produced a detailed report of his adventures for King Louis. He suggested further missions, and although this was not possible for many years, William's journey opened up remote Asia to the West for the first time.

Garry Cooper–Popular Movies

1930 *The Texan*
1932 *A Farewell to Arms*
1935 *The Lives of the Bengal Lancer*
1936 *Mr. Deeds Goes to Town*
1937 *The Plainsman*
1938 *The Adventures of Marco Polo*
1938 *The Cowboy and the Lady*
1939 *Beau Geste*
1941 *Meet John Doe*
1948 *Good Sam*
1949 *Task Force*
1952 *Springfield Rifle*
1954 *Vera Cruz*
1957 *Love in the Afternoon*

MAY 8

DAILY READING

Make the most of every opportunity. Let your conversation be always full of grace, seasoned with salt, so that you may know how to answer everyone. (COL 4:5–6)

FEAST DAYS

ca. 515	Gibrian	Irish hermit
615	Boniface IV	Pope
ca. 1417	Julian of Norwich	English mystic

ENTRANCE AND EXIT

b. 1737	Edward Gibbon	English historian
b. 1884	Harry S. Truman	33rd American president
b. 1926	David Attenborough	English broadcaster
d. 1794	Antoine Lavoisier	French scientist
d. 1994	George Peppard	American actor
d. 1999	Sir Dirk Bogarde	English actor

Victory in Europe (VE) Day

World War II began on September 3, 1939. During the first year of the six-year campaign, the people of Britain endured evacuation, rationing, terrifying air raids, and the real threat of invasion. Britain stood alone against the forces of Nazi Germany. By the end of 1940, the Soviet Union joined Britain to oppose the Nazi threat, and in later years America supplied troops, ammunition, and intelligence. The Germans surrendered to Allied Forces on this day in 1945, and Victory in Europe was announced. All over Britain, Europe, and Russia, millions of people filled the streets of cities, towns, and villages to celebrate the victory.

Two days of celebration were declared–today to celebrate the British stand, and May 9 to celebrate the Russian triumph. King George VI led the national celebrations and spoke to his subjects from Buckingham Palace:

> Let us think what it was that has upheld us through nearly six years of suffering and peril. The knowledge that everything was at stake: our freedom, our independence, our very existence as a people; but the knowledge also that in defending ourselves we were defending the liberties of the whole world; that our cause was the cause not of this nation only, not of this Empire and Commonwealth only, but of every land where freedom is cherished and law and liberty go hand in hand. In the darkest hours we knew that the enslaved and isolated peoples of Europe looked to us, their hopes were our hopes, their confidence confirmed our faith. We knew that, if we failed, the last remaining barrier against a worldwide tyranny would have fallen in ruins. But we did not fail. We kept faith with ourselves and with one another, we kept faith and unity with our great allies. That faith, that unity have carried us to victory through dangers which at times seemed overwhelming.

Extract from Winston Churchill's Speech to the People in London

> So we came back after long months from the jaws of death, out of the mouth of hell, while all the world wondered. When shall the reputation and faith of this generation of English men and women fail? I say that in the long years to come not only will the people of this island but of the world, wherever the bird of freedom chirps in human hearts, look back to what we've done and they will say "do not despair, do not yield to violence and tyranny, march straightforward and die if need be–unconquered."

Sixty years after VE day, President George W. Bush made a visit to Holland at the American Military Cemetary to remember the American war dead. This is part of his address:

> On this peaceful May morning we commemorate a great victory for liberty, and the thousands of white marble crosses and Stars of David underscore the terrible price we pay for that victory. For the Americans who rest here, Dutch soil provides a fitting home. It was from a Dutch port that many of our pilgrim fathers first sailed for America. It was a Dutch port that gave the American flag its first gun salute. It was the Dutch who became one of the first foreign nations to recognize the independence of the new United States of America.

*M*AY 9

DAILY READING

There is now no condemnation for those who are in Christ Jesus, because through Christ Jesus the law of the Spirit of life in Christ has set me free from the law of sin and death. (ROM 8:1–2)

FEAST DAYS

389	Gregory of Nazianzus	Doctor of the Church
ca. 501	Gerontius	Bishop of Cervia, Italy
1879	Teresa of Jesus Gerhardinger	Founder of the School Sisters of Notre Dame

ENTRANCE AND EXIT

b. 1873	Howard Carter	English archaelogist
b. 1904	Sir Henry Morton Stanley	Welsh journalist
b. 1934	Alan Bennett	English writer
d. 1805	Friedrich von Schiller	German writer
d. 1957	Ezio Pinza	Italian singer
d. 1986	Sherpa Tenzing Norgay	Nepalese mountaineer

Crown Jewels Stolen

Thomas Blood is one of history's most daring criminals. During the English Civil War, he was a spy for Cromwell's forces and was rewarded with land in lieu of wages. After the monarchy was restored, he twice tried to kidnap James Butler, the Lord Lieutenant of Ireland, from Dublin Castle in 1663. Both attempts failed, and Blood escaped to Holland dressed as a Quaker.

His most famous criminal activity was an attempt to steal the Crown Jewels from the Tower of London on this day in 1671. Over several months, Blood befriended Talbot Edwards, the Keeper of the Crown Jewels. Eventually, he persuaded Edwards to show him (and his accomplices) the Crown Jewels. When they were let into the Jewel Chamber, Edwards was quickly bound and gagged. Blood and his gang made off with the Crown Jewels, but somehow, Edwards managed to sound the alarm. They were all captured before they left the Tower.

Ironically, Blood and his gang were kept prisoner in the Tower. Everyone thought they would hang at Tyburn, but Blood insisted on a meeting with the king. The outcome of that meeting, which took place on July 18, 1671, was that, although Blood and his gang were guilty of treason, they were pardoned by the king. In addition, Blood was granted a sum of £500 (a great deal of money at that time) a year for the rest of his life. One explanation for this curious turn of events is that Blood may have served King Charles II as a double agent, and his crime was thus overlooked. Another explanation is that he persuaded the king that he wanted to sell the Crown Jewels to bring much needed money into the king's treasury.

Blood died in 1680 in London, but such was his reputation for trickery that his remains were exhumed in 1684 to confirm his identity.

Noteworthy

1607 First Protestant religious service celebrated in America at Cape Henry, Virginia.
1933 Nazi bonfire in Berlin burns twenty-five thousand books, including the Holy Bible.
1936 Ethiopia annexed by Italy under Mussolini.
1945 Britain's Channel Islands liberated from German occupation.
1962 First James Bond film, *Dr. No* opens.
1994 Nelson Mandela chosen as South Africa's first black president.

MAY 10

DAILY READING

If your brother sins against you, go and show him his fault,
just between the two of you. If he listens to you,
you have won your brother over. (MATT 18:15)

FEAST DAYS

ca. 1st cent.	Simon the Zealot	Apostle
603	Comgall	Irish monk
1569	John of Avila	Patron of Andalusia, Spain

ENTRANCE AND EXIT

b. 1812	Frances Elizabeth Cox	English hymn translator
b. 1859	Wilhelm Wrede	German theologian
b. 1960	Paul David Hewson (Bono)	Irish rock star
d. 238	Gaius Julius Verus Maximinus	Roman Emperor
d. 1920	John Wesley Hyatt	American inventor
d. 1973	Bruce Lee	American actor

Abbot Comgall

The much-loved Irish abbot Comgall (ca. 517–603) was the founder of the monastery of Bangor, Belfast. He was also a pupil of St. Fintan, who lived as a hermit on the shore of Lough Erne at Cluain Eidnech Monastery. The rule at this monastery was reportedly so severe that several monks died. However, under Comgall's leadership, the Bangor monastery grew to accommodate over three thousand monks.

Comgall joined Columba in his mission to Scotland to evangelize the Picts, and when Columba died, Comgall remarked, "My soul-friend has died, and I am without a head; so you too are without a head, for a man without a soul-friend is a body without a head."

In Scotland, Comgall lived on the isle of Tiree, and he founded a monastery at Land of Heth. Many miracles are attributed to Comgall. For instance, he is said to have restored a blind man's sight by pressing saliva to his eyes, an imitation of one of Jesus' miracles. In later life, he is said to have spat into a beggar's pocket, where a gold ring immediately appeared.

Comgall died in 603 from the harsh conditions he imposed upon himself and his followers. His relics were kept at Bangor, but in 823 were desecrated by Danish raiders.

Frances Elizabeth Cox

Francis Elizabeth Cox was among the important English translators of the nineteenth century and, together with Catherine Winkworth, she translated German hymns into English. In 1841, she published forty-nine translations of German hymns in *Sacred Hymns from the German.*

Jesus Lives!

Jesus lives! no longer now
Can thy terrors, death, appall us;
Jesus lives! by this we know
Thou, O grave, canst not enthrall us.
Alleluia!

Jesus lives! henceforth is death
But the gate of life immortal;
This shall calm our trembling breath,
When we pass its gloomy portal.
Alleluia!

Jesus lives! for us He died;
Then, alone to Jesus living
Pure in heart may abide,
Glory to our Savior giving.
Alleluia!

Jesus lives! our hearts know well
Naught from us His love shall sever;
Life, nor death, nor powers of hell
Tear us from His keeping ever.
Alleluia!

Jesus lives! to Him the throne
Over all the world is given;
May we go where He is gone,
Rest and reign with Him in heaven.
Alleluia!

Words: Christian F. Gellert, 1751 (*Jesus lebt, mit ihm auch ich*); translated from German to English by Frances Elizabeth Cox, *Sacred Hymns from the German*, 1841.

May 11

DAILY READING

Be kind and compassionate to one another, forgiving each other, just as in Christ God forgave you. (EPH 4:32)

FEAST DAYS

303	Anthimus	Roman priest
ca. 457	Mammertus	Archibishop of Vienne, France
995	Mayeul	Archdeacon of Macon, France

ENTRANCE AND EXIT

b. 1888	Israel Isidore Berlin (Irving Berlin)	American composer
b. 1904	Salvador Dalí	Spanish artist
b. 1963	Natasha Richardson	English actor
d. 1812	Spencer Perceval	British prime minister
d. 1812	John Bellingham	Spencer Perceval's assassin
d. 1981	Bob Marley	Jamaican rock star

British Prime Minister Assasinated

On this day in 1812, the Prime Minister and Chancellor of the Exchequer Spencer Perceval (1762–1812) was shot and killed by John Bellingham (1776–1812). Bellingham's motives remain a subject of intense debate: Was he insane, was he a spy, or was he driven by denial of justice?

Bellingham had been a dealer specializing in marine products since his teens. He visited Russia in 1803, and while still in port, suffered the loss of his vessel, the *Soluere*. Although the ship was insured by Lloyds of London, they refused to pay because they suspected fraud. Unable to return home and facing legal proceedings, Bellingham was imprisoned. Although he sought the help of the British ambassador, the government declined to act, and this may have led to Bellingham feeling bitter against the authorities and the government in particular.

After his return from Russia, Bellingham demanded compensation from the government for his losses. He appealed to Spencer Perceval, but was turned away. Enraged by this "betrayal," Bellingham concealed a gun in his specially adapted coat and awaited the arrival of the prime minister at the House of Commons. At 5:15 p.m., Spencer Perceval came into the lobby, and Bellingham fired a single bullet into his chest from a distance of four feet. Then he calmly gave himself up.

At his trial, Bellingham said, "My family was ruined and myself destroyed, merely because it was Mr Perceval's pleasure that justice should not be granted; sheltering himself behind the imagined security of his station, and trampling upon law and right in the belief that no retribution could reach him."

He was sentenced to death by hanging, and at 5 a.m. on Monday, May 18, 1812, the sentence was duly carried out at Newgate Prison, London.

City of Miskolc

Since 1992, May 11th has been an official holiday in the historic city of Miskolc, Hungary. The holiday commemorates Miskolc achieving city status in 1909 when King Franz Joseph granted Miskolc its official coat of arms. On this day, Miskolc presents awards to its citizens for sporting, civil, heroic, artistic, and scientific endeavours.

MAY 12

DAILY READING

A wife of noble character who can find? She is worth far more than rubies. . . .
She watches over the affairs of her household and does not eat the bread of idleness.
Her children arise and call her blessed; her husband also, and he praises her. (PROV 31:27–28)

FEAST DAYS

ca. 290	Pancras	Patron of children
ca. 5th cent.	Diomma	Irish evangelist
805	Athelhard	Archbishop of Canterbury

ENTRANCE AND EXIT

b. 1828	Dante Gabriel Rossetti	English artist
b. 1842	Jules Massanet	French composer
b. 1929	Burt Bacharach	American composer
d. 1957	Erich von Stroheim	Austrian film director
d. 1967	John Masefield	English poet laureate
d. 2001	Perry Como	American singer

King Athelhard

King Athelhard (or Athelbald) of Mercia was an abbot in Louth, Lincolnshire, and a bishop at Winchester (although this is disputed by historians). He became the fourteenth Archbishop of Canterbury in 793.

During his lifetime, England was divided into three states (Northumbria, Mercia, and Wessex), each with its own church center, at York (Northumbria), Canterbury (Mercia), and Lichfield (Wessex). However, the division created political and ecclesastical tensions, and eventually the see of Lichfield was not recognized following the death of its supporter, King Offa. Athelhard, who had been the Archbishop of Lichfield, was therefore proposed as the new Archbishop of Canterbury.

In 747, Athelard was present at the Second Church Council of Cloveshoe, in Northamptonshire. The council is an important part of church history because for the first time priests were ordered to learn and explain to the people in their own tongue the Creed, the Lord's Prayer, and the offices of Mass and Baptism. The need to set a good example was apparent, as Athelhard had been accused of allowing powerful laymen to take over the monasteries, allowing the drunkenness of the clergy, and allowing the monks to wear extravagant clothes.

During King Athelhard's occupancy of the see of Canterbury, the principle of bishops electing their leader was established. They also had to promise obedience to the Archbishop of Canterbury, thus confirming the primacy of Canterbury over all other metropolitan sees. The first record of this appears in 796.

Noteworthy

1870 Manitoba joins Canadian federation.
1873 First postcard issued in United States.
1926 General Strike ends in Britain.
1937 Coronation of King George VI.
1943 German U-boat sinks American cargo ship at the mouth of the Mississippi River.
1949 Berlin blockade lifted.
1971 Mick Jagger marries Bianca Perez Morena de Macias.
1982 Security guards foil an assassination attempt on Pope John Paul II on his visit to Fatima, Portugal.

May 13

DAILY READING

I write these things to you who believe in the name of the Son of God so that you may know that you have eternal life. (1 JOHN 5:13)

FEAST DAYS

454	John the Silent	Miracle worker and exorcist
ca. 686	Erkenwald of London	Patron against gout
ca. 970	Merwenna	First abbess of Rumsey, England

ENTRANCE AND EXIT

b. 1767	John VI	King of Portugal
b. 1842	Sir Arthur Sullivan	English composer
b. 1950	Stevie Wonder	American singer
d. 1832	Georges Cuvier	French scientist
d. 1884	Cyrus Hall McCormick	American inventor
d. 1997	Laurie Lee	English writer

Abbotsbury Garland Day

The charming tradition of making flower garlands, putting them in boats, or carrying them round in a village procession in Abbotsbury, Dorset, began in the early nineteenth century. At that time, Abbotsbury still had its own small fishing fleet, and the festival took place on this day because it is May Day in the Julian calendar, a traditional time for merrymaking. Following a procession, led by the May Queen and her attendants, the garlands were taken from the boats into the village church for a service of blessing. Here thanks were offered to God for the harvest of the sea and the safekeeping of fishermen.

After the procession and the church service, children spent the rest of the day at the beach, as Garland Day was a local holiday.

Around 1954, a local policeman tried to halt the procession, claiming that children were begging in the streets. However, local villagers took their protests to the Chief Constable, and the policeman was transferred.

The modern Garland Day is kept alive by village children who make two separate sets of garlands, one of wild flowers and one of flowers from the garden. These are taken round the village to be admired, the bell-shaped garlands carried on poles between two children, and donations are happily accepted for their pains. After World War I, garlands were also placed at the war memorial.

Stevie Wonder–Popular Albums

Year	Album Title	Label
1962	*A Tribute to Uncle Ray*	Motown
1962	*The Jazz Soul of Little Stevie Wonder*	Motown
1963	*Workout Stevie, Workout*	Tamla
1963	*Little Stevie Wonder*	Motown
1968	*For Once in My Life*	Motown
1970	*Talk of the Town*	Motown
1970	*Signed, Sealed & Delivered*	Motown
1972	*Talking Book*	Motown
1976	*Songs in the Key of Life*	Motown
1976	*Portrait*	EMI
1979	*Journey Through the Secret Life of Plants*	Motown
1980	*Hotter Than July*	Motown
1984	*The Woman in Red*	Motown
1995	*Conversation Peace*	Motown
1995	*Natural Wonder–Live*	Motown

MAY 14

DAILY READING

You created my inmost being; you knit me together in my mother's womb.
I praise you because I am fearfully and wonderfully made;
your works are wonderful, I know that full well. (PS 139:13–14)

FEAST DAYS

ca. 80	Matthias	Apostle
306	Boniface of Tarsus	Patron of bachelors
637	Carthage	Patron of Waterford, Ireland

ENTRANCE AND EXIT

b. 1885	Otto Klemperer	German conductor
b. 1944	George Lucas	American movie mogul
b. 1969	Cate Blanchett	Australian actor
d. 1844	Henry John Heinz	American food manufacturer
d. 1936	Viscount Edmund Allenby	English field marshall
d. 1998	Frank Sinatra	American singer

Birth of a Nation

On Friday, May 14, 1948 (5th Iyar, 5708 in the Hebrew calendar), the ancient nation of Israel was reborn. The United Nations had debated the Palestine question for many months before coming to the decision to allow Israel to be declared a new nation within its ancient borders. Years of Zionist dreams culminated in this moment, but within twenty-four hours, neighboring nations attacked Israel, determined to destroy the nation at birth.

Premier David Ben-Gurion stood before the masses gathered in Tel Aviv and declared Israel's independence. This is an extract of his speech:

The Land of Israel was the birthplace of the Jewish people. Here their spiritual, religious and political identity was shaped. Here they first attained to statehood, created cultural values of national and universal significance and gave to the world the eternal Book of Books.

After being forcibly exiled from their land, the people remained faithful to it throughout their Dispersion and never ceased to pray and hope for their return to it and for the restoration in it of their political freedom.

This recognition by the United Nations of the right of the Jewish people to establish their State is irrevocable.

This right is the natural right of the Jewish people to be masters of their own fate, like all other nations, in their own sovereign State.

Noteworthy

264 English barons triumph over King Henry III at the Battle of Lewes.
1610 King Henry IV of France assassinated in Paris.
1643 King Louis XIV (The Sun King), age four years, eight months, ascends throne of France.
1796 World's first vaccination against smallpox, developed by British physician Edward Jenner.
1940 Home Guard formed in Britain.
1994 Jericho handed over to Palestinian rule by Israel.
1998 108 million Americans tune in for finale of *Seinfeld* TV series.

MAY 15

DAILY READING

As you do not know the path of the wind, or how the body is formed in a mother's womb, so you cannot understand the work of God, the Maker of all things. (ECCL 11:5)

FEAST DAYS

ca. 650	Dympna	Patron of therapists
ca. 1043	Hallvard	Patron of Oslo, Norway
1130	Isidore	Patron of farmers

ENTRANCE AND EXIT

b. 1886	Emily Dickinson	American poet
b. 1909	James Mason	English actor
b. 1937	Madeleine Albright	American politician
d. 1773	Alban Butler	English hagiographer
d. 1967	Edward Hopper	American artist
d. 2003	Robert Stack	American actor

Alban Butler

Theologians, teachers, and students owe much to the Reverend Alban Butler (1710–73), author of the definitive work on saints: *Lives of the Saints*. Alban Butler, a man of gentle and tolerant temper, was born in Northampton and sent to the English college in Douay, France, when he was eight. There he became noted for his studious habits, especially his love of reading. With a passion for sacred biography, he began to direct his reading to the collection of materials for his *Lives of the Saints*. He became professor of philosophy, and then of divinity, at Douay, and on his return to England in 1746, he was given a living in Staffordshire.

After three years, he was appointed chaplain to the Duke of Norfolk. After thirty years' research, he published his *Lives of the Saints* in 1750. He submitted the manuscript to Challoner, the vicar apostolic of the London district, who recommended the omission of all the notes, on which Butler had expended years of research. Like a good Catholic he yielded to the advice, but in the second edition he was allowed to restore them. He was ultimately chosen president of the English college of St. Omer's, France, where he died in 1773. However, his greatness lives on in his published works, and his *Lives of the Saints* remains a primary reference for anyone interested in traditions and tales about notable and little-known saints.

Emily Dickinson (1830–86) Poem

Success Is Counted Sweetest

Success is counted sweetest
By those who ne'er succeed.
To comprehend a nectar
Requires sorest need.

Not one of all the purple host
Who took the flag to-day
Can tell the definition,
So clear, of victory,

As he, defeated, dying,
On whose forbidden ear
The distant strains of triumph
Break, agonized and clear.

MAY 16

DAILY READING

The LORD your God is with you, he is mighty to save.
He will take great delight in you, he will quiet you with his love,
he will rejoice over you with singing. (ZEPH 3:17)

FEAST DAYS

ca. 577	Brendan	Patron of sailors
ca. 1210	Adam	Benedictine monk
1393	John of Nepomuk	Patron of Czechoslavakia

ENTRANCE AND EXIT

b. 1804	Elizabeth Palmer Peabody	American reformer
b. 1905	Henry Fonda	American actor
b. 1953	Pierce Brosnan	Irish actor
d. 1861	John Stevens Henslow	British botanist
d. 1947	Sir Frederick Gowland Hopkins	British scientist
d. 1990	Sammy Davis Jr.	American singer

Martyrs of Sudan

In June 2006, the Episcoplian Church at its 75th General Convention meeting in Columbus, Ohio, provisionally approved this day to remember the martyrs of Sudan.

The Rt. Rev. William Gregg, Bishop of Eastern Oregon, proposed that the Martyrs of Sudan feast should be included in the Episcopalian calendar as one of its "Lesser Feasts and Fasts" on a trial basis.

The UN and the US State Department has declared that the Sudan is the most devastated country in the world today. Everything in southern Sudan has been destroyed including the villages, schools, and churches, and there is no infrastructure. No building has remained standing in an area the size of Alaska. Of a southern population of 6 million, two-thirds of the people are internally displaced with another million in exile throughout Africa and the world, including the bishops of twenty-two of the twenty-four dioceses. There are over eighty Sudanese ministries in the US.

In 1983 it was estimated that only 5 percent of the population of the south was Christian. Today nearly 90 percent are either Episcopalian or Roman Catholic. The bishops, most notably Roman Catholic Bishop Paride Taban and Episcopal Bishop Nathaniel Garang, are clear when they say that "we live only on the mercy of God . . . whether we live or die we are the Lord's . . . we have had nothing else but the grace of God and his guidance."

The Gospel takes on a radically different meaning when it is experienced in communities of trauma. The writings of the New Testament were formed in such a context and they speak with an obvious power that is not easily accessed by communities of comfort, stability and privilege. The faith and conviction of Sudanese Christians is an amazing witness to the world and the Church.

The collect for the Martyrs of Sudan is given below:

> O God, you who will not be defeated and who is steadfast in the midst of persecution, by your providence the blood of the martyrs is the seed of the Church: Grant that we who remember before you the blessed martyrs of the Sudan, may, like them, be steadfast in our faith in Jesus Christ, to whom they refuse to abandon, even in the face of death, and by their sacrifice brought forth a plentiful harvest, through Jesus Christ our Lord, who lives and reigns with you and the Holy Spirit, one God, for ever and ever. Amen.

The readings are from Psalm 116:10–17 and from the New Testament book of Hebrews (10:32–39).

Noteworthy

1633 Charles I crowned King of Scotland at Edinburgh.
1791 James Boswells *Life of Samuel Johnson* published.
1817 First steamboat on the Mississippi, *Washington*, goes into service.
1920 Roman Catholic Church canonizes Joan of Arc.
1975 Junko Tabei, age thirty-five, of Japan becomes first woman to conquer Mt. Everest; reaches the summit at 12:30 p.m.
1991 Queen Elizabeth II addresses U.S. Congress, the first British monarch to do so.

May 17

DAILY READING

Oh, the depth and riches of the wisdom and the knowledge of God! How unsearchable his judgments, and his paths beyond tracing out. (ROM 11:33)

FEAST DAYS

ca. 540	Madron	Cornish hermit
1045	Bruno	Bishop of Wurzburg, Austria
1618	Pascal Bayon	Patron of cooks

ENTRANCE AND EXIT

b. 1444	Alessandro di Mariano Filipepi (Sandro Botticelli)	Italian artist
b. 1749	Edward Jenner	English physician
b. 1935	Dennis Potter	English writer
d. 1575	Matthew Parker	English theologian
d. 1840	Niccolo Paganini	Italian composer
d. 1900	Ayatollah Ruhollah Khomeini	Iranian leader

Edward Jenner

The English surgeon Edward Jenner (1749–1823) is famous for his discovery of the vaccination for smallpox. In May 1796, Jenner found a young dairymaid, Sarah Nelmes, who had fresh cowpox lesions on her hand. Using the cowpox from Sarah's lesions, he inoculated a young smallpox sufferer, James Phipps. Over the next nine days James became slightly ill, but on the tenth day he recovered. Jenner carried out a further "inoculation" on James, and this time noted that he was completely protected from smallpox. In 1798 Jenner, having added further cases, published privately his findings in a slender book called *An Inquiry into the Causes and Effects of the Variolae Vaccinae.*

The reaction to Jenner's discovery was not immediately favorable. He went to London seeking volunteers for vaccination but, in a stay of three months, was not successful. When he did obtain volunteers, difficulties arose with obtaining cowpox vaccine, and others tried to take the credit from Jenner. However, eventually vaccination rapidly proved its value, and Jenner became intensely active promoting it. The procedure spread rapidly to America and the rest of Europe and soon was carried around the world.

Jenner was born in Berkeley, Gloucestershire, the son of a clergyman and acquired a love of nature that remained with him all his life. On completing his apprenticeship at the age of twenty-one, he went to London and became the house pupil of John Hunter, who was on the staff of St. George's Hospital and soon became one of the most prominent surgeons in London.

After studying in London, Jenner returned to country practice in Berkeley and enjoyed substantial success. He was capable, skillful, and popular. In addition to practicing medicine, he played the violin in a musical club, wrote light verse, and as a naturalist, made many observations, particularly on the nesting habits of the cuckoo and on bird migration.

Sandro Botticelli

The Italian artist Sandro Botticelli (1445–1510) was attracted in later life to the Catholic Church. He was so convicted of the irreligious nature of his earlier works that he burned most of them at the Bonfire of the Vanities. However, Botticelli was a prolific painter, and his surviving works include:

Madonna and Child with an Angel

Adoration of the Magi

St. Sebastian

The Birth of Christ

St. Augustine

Venus and Mars

The Birth of Venus

Madonna of the Pomegranate

Salome with the Head of St. John the Baptist

Lamentation over the Dead Christ with Saints

Last Communion of St. Jerome

Portrait of Dante

The Mystical Nativity

MAY 18

DAILY READING

God is not unjust; he will not forget your work and the love you have shown him as you have helped his people and continue to help them. (HEB 6:10)

FEAST DAYS

944	Elviga	Wife of King Edmund I
1161	Eric the Lawgiver	King of Sweden
1587	Felix of Cantalice	Capuchin monk

ENTRANCE AND EXIT

b. 1897	Frank Capra	American film director
b. 1920	Karol Wojtyla	Pope John Paul II
b. 1949	Rick Wakeman	English rock star
d. 1675	Jacques Marquette	French missionary
d. 1911	Gustav Mahler	Austrian composer
d. 1980	Ian Curtis	English rock star

The Christian Good of Scotland

On this day in 1843, the Scottish social reformer, evangelical preacher, and lecturer in moral philosophy, economics, and theology, Thomas Chalmers (1780–1847) led four hundred evangelical ministers to leave the Church of Scotland and form the Free Church. Chalmers referred to this separation as the "Disruption." Chalmers enjoyed a reputation unparalleled since John Knox in his devotion to establishing a vibrant expression of Christianity in Scotland. He had a number of vivid sayings such as "the Christian good of Scotland," "the expulsive power of a new affection," and "show me a people-going minister and I will show you a church-going people."

Chalmers's fame was such that his name was used in support of many causes, from creation theories to the prevention of cruelty to animals. A theology chair and the home of the Faculty of Divinity Graduate School and Centre for the Study of Christianity in the Non-Western World are named after him at the University of Edinburgh. North American interest in Chalmers remains substantial, as subsequent generations have discovered his views about science, Calvinism, church and state, church union, the ambiguities of social welfare, or the relationship between religious and national identity.

Chalmers was the first moderator of the Free Church of Scotland General Assembly. One of his challenges was to provide for the material and spiritual needs of his ministers. He established a Sustentation Fund and managed finances of the Free Church so well that the movement began to spread quickly. The Free Church congregations provided more than £300,000–a considerable sum at that time.

Toward the end of his life, he started work on two books, *Institutes of Theology* and *Daily Scripture Readings*. On the night of May 30, 1847, he died in his sleep.

Noteworthy

1291 Saracens defeat Christians in Acre, the last Christian stronghold in the Holy Land.
1631 John Winthrop elected governor of Massachusetts in the first election in America.
1756 Britain declares war on France.
1900 Tonga proclaimed a British protectorate.
1944 Independence of Iceland proclaimed.
1980 Mount St. Helens volcano erupts, killing fifty-seven people.

MAY 19

DAILY READING

The wisdom that comes from heaven is first of all pure; then peace-loving, considerate, submissive, full of mercy and good fruit, impartial and sincere. Peacemakers who sow in peace raise a harvest of righteousness. (JAS 3:17–18)

FEAST DAYS

988	Dunstan	Archbishop of Canterbury
1303	Ivo	Patron of orphans
1740	Theophilus	Franciscan monk

ENTRANCE AND EXIT

b. 1879	Lady Nancy Astor	English politician
b. 1925	Malcolm Little (Malcolm X)	American leader
b. 1945	Pete Townshend	English rock star
d. 1536	Anne Boleyn	English queen
d. 1898	William Gladstone	British prime minister
d. 1984	Sir John Betjeman	English poet laureate

Revised Version of the Bible

A new version of the complete Bible–the Revised Version (or the English Revised Version)–was published on this day in 1885. The Revised Version of the Bible is the only officially authorized revision of the King James Version. In 1870, a convocation of Episcopal clergymen at Canterbury, England, appointed 101 eminent Bible scholars from various denominations in Britain and America to undertake the work. They began in 1879, and the New Testament was published in 1881, followed by the Old Testament four years later. In the New Testament alone, more than thirty thousand changes were made, over five thousand of them on the basis of a better Greek text.

The translators aimed "to adapt King James' version to the present state of the English language without changing the idiom and vocabulary," and "to adapt it to the present standard of Biblical scholarship." Further, it was to be "the best version possible in the nineteenth century, as King James' version was the best which could be made in the seventeenth century." To those ends, the Greek text used to translate the New Testament was more liberal and believed by some to be of higher reliability than the *Textus Receptus* used for the KJV.

Other important enhancements introduced in the RV include arrangement of the text into paragraphs, printing Old Testament poetry in indented lines, and the inclusion of notes to alert the reader to variations in wording in ancient manuscripts.

The American Standard Edition, based on the Revised Version, was published in 1901.

Defiled Is My Name Full Sore

Defiled is my name full sore,
Through cruel spyte and false report
That I may say for evermore,
Farewell, my joy! adiewe comfort!
For wrongfully ye judge of me,
Unto my fame a mortall wounde;
Say what ye lyst it will not be,
Ye seek for that can not be found.

O death! rocke me on slepe,
Bring me on quiet reste;
Let passe my very guiltiness goste
Our of my careful brest:
Toll on the passinge bell,
Ringe out the doleful knell,
Let the sounde my dethe tell,
For I must dye,
There is no remedy,
For now I dye.

Alone, in prison stronge,
I wayle my destenye;
Wo worth this cruel hap that I
Should taste this miserye.
Toll on the passinge bell, &c.

Farewell my pleasures past,
Welcum my present payne;
I fele my torments so increse,
That lyfe cannot remayne.

Cease now the passinge bell,
Rong is my doleful knell
For the sound my deth doth tell:
Death doth draw nye,
Sound my end dolefully,
For now I dye.

–Anne Boleyn (1504–36)

MAY 20

DAILY READING

May the God who gives endurance and encouragement give you a spirit of unity among yourselves as you follow Christ Jesus, so that with one heart and mouth you may glorify the God and Father of our Lord Jesus Christ. (ROM 15:5–6)

FEAST DAYS

778	Theodore	Bishop of Pavia, Italy
793	Ethelbert	King of East Anglia
1501	Columba	Patron of Perugia, Italy

ENTRANCE AND EXIT

b. 1799	Honore de Balzac	French writer
b. 1946	Cher	American singer
b. 1958	Ronald Prescott Reagan	Son of President Reagan
d. 1506	Christopher Columbus	Spanish explorer
d. 1690	John Eliot	English missionary
d. 2002	Stephen Jay Gould	American scientist

The Apostle to the Indians

The American colonial clergyman John Eliot (1604–90) was born at Widford, Hertfordshire, the son of a middle-class farmer. John Eliot graduated from Jesus College, Cambridge, in 1622 and then ministered alongside Rev. Thomas Hooker at Little Baddow, Chelmsford. Under Hooker's influence, Eliot became a Puritan and decided to emigrate to America, settling in Boston in 1631.

Shortly after his arrival, John Eliot was ordained to preach at Roxbury, Massachusetts. He developed an interest in Indian language and customs, and began to preach to the Indians in 1646, at first in English but within a year in their own tongue, Algonquian. He published a catechism for them in 1654, and by 1658 had translated the Bible into Algonquian, the first Bible to be printed in North America. A revised edition was published in 1685. Eliot also wrote *The Christian Commonwealth* (1659), *Up-bookum Psalmes* (1663), *The Communion of Churches* (1665), *The Indian Primer* (1669), and *The Harmony of the Gospels* (1678), and was a major contributor to the *Bay Psalm Book.*

Eliot planned towns for Indian converts, away from the white towns, in areas where they could preserve their own language and culture and live by their own laws. Eliot had fourteen towns with thousands of inhabitants, but they were scattered in an Indian rebellion, and although four communities were restored, they did not continue long.

He died in 1690, aged eighty-five, his last words being "welcome joy!" His grandson, Jared Eliot, became a noted pastor and agriculture writer.

Noteworthy

1867 Foundation stone at Royal Albert Hall, London, laid by Queen Victoria.
1895 U.S. income tax declared unconstitutional.
1919 Volcano eruption in central Java kills over sixteen thousand.
1927 Charles Lindbergh, age twenty-five, takes off on first solo nonstop flight to Paris from Long Island, New York.
1956 Americans drop hydrogen bomb over Bikini atoll.
1977 Original Orient Express makes its last journey between Paris and Istanbul.
1990 Hubble Space Telescope sends first photos back to earth.

MAY 21

DAILY READING

I appeal to you, brothers, in the name of our Lord Jesus Christ, that all of you agree with one another so that there may be no divisions among you and that you may be perfectly united in mind and thought. (1 COR 1:10)

FEAST DAYS

1170	Godric of Finchale	English hermit
1861	Charles Joseph Eugene de Mazenod	Founder of the Oblates of Mary Immaculate
1928	Toribio Romo González	Martyr of the Cristero Wars

ENTRANCE AND EXIT

b. 1471	Albrecht Durer	German artist
b. 1780	Elizabeth Fry	English reformer
b. 1917	Raymond Burr	American actor
d. 1471	King Henry VI	English king
d. 1632	Otto Blumhardt	German missionary
d. 2000	John Gielgud	English actor

The Poet of Methodism

On this day in 1738, Charles Wesley (1707–88) found salvation. It was Pentecost Sunday, and he was in London with his brother John. Charles was recovering from a recurrence of illness in the home of some Moravians near St. Paul's Cathedral. Charles was deeply affected by the Christian testimonies and concern of his Christian hosts. He opened his Bible at Isaiah 40:1: "Comfort ye, comfort ye my people, saith your God." His journal entry for this day reads: "I now found myself at peace with God, and rejoiced in hope of loving Christ. . . . I saw that by faith I stood, by the continual support of faith. . . . I went to bed still sensible of my own weakness . . . yet confident of Christ's protection."

On the following day, Charles's strength began to return, and he began a glorious ministry that produced over six thousand hymns. Exactly a year later, Charles wrote perhaps his most famous hymn, "O for a Thousand Tongues to Sing," which he recommended for singing "on the anniversary of one's conversion."

Many of Charles Wesley's hymns began as poems and were put to music by many composers. "O for a Thousand Tongues to Sing" first appeared in 1740 in *Hymns & Sacred Poems*, and in 1828 Carl G. Glaser added the original melody.

Charles Wesley remained a hymn writer to the end. When he lay dying in 1788, he dictated these lines to his wife, Sally:

In age and feebleness extreme,
Who shall a helpless worm redeem?
Jesus, my only hope Thou art,
Strength of my failing flesh and heart,
O, could I catch a smile from Thee
And drop into eternity!

O for a Thousand Tongues to Sing

O for a thousand tongues to sing
My great redeemer's praise,
The glories of my God and King,
The triumphs of His grace.

My gracious Master and my God,
Assist me to proclaim,
To spread thro' all the earth abroad,
The honors of Thy name.

Jesus the name that charms our fears,
That bids our sorrows cease.
'Tis music in the sinner's ears,
'Tis life and health, and peace.

He breaks the pow'r of canceled sin,
He sets the pris'ner free;
His blood can make the foulest clean;
His blood availed for me.

Hear him ye deaf; His praise, ye dumb,
Your loosened tongues employ;
Ye blind behold your Savior come;
And leap, ye lame, for joy.

*M*AY 22

DAILY READING

You, my brothers, were called to be free.
But do not use your freedom to indulge the sinful nature;
rather, serve one another in love. (GAL 5:13)

FEAST DAYS

836	Aigulf	Bishop of Bourges, France
1397	John of Cetina	Franciscan missionary
1538	John Forest	Confessor to Queen Catherine of Aragon

ENTRANCE AND EXIT

b. 1813	Richard Wagner	German composer
b. 1859	Sir Arthur Conan Doyle	Scottish writer
b. 1907	Baron Laurence Olivier	English actor
d. 337	Constantine the Great	Roman Emperor
d. 1885	Victor Hugo	French writer
d. 1972	Dame Margaret Rutherford	English actor

Sir Arthur Conan Doyle

The Scottish physician, writer, cricketer, historian, war correspondent, sailor, spiritualist, skier, and amateur detective, Sir Arthur Conan Doyle (1859–1930) created the world's most famous consulting detective, Sherlock Holmes. Doyle studied medicine at the University of Edinburgh, where he met Dr. Joseph Bell, a teacher with extraordinary deductive reasoning power. He based the character of Sherlock Holmes on Dr. Bell.

The first Sherlock Holmes story, *A Study in Scarlet*, was published in *Beeton's Christmas Annual* in 1887. Starting in 1891, a series of Holmes stories appeared in *The Strand* magazine. The success of Holmes enabled Doyle to leave his medical practice in 1891 and devote himself to writing, but the author soon grew weary of his creation. In *The Final Problem*, he killed off both Holmes and his nemesis, Dr. Moriarty, but had to revive them later due to popular demand.

Doyle's first book was written at the age of six and illustrated by the author. Throughout his school years at the Jesuit School at Stonyhurst, Doyle was known as a great storyteller. He would invent a character at the beginning of a term, and keep up a marvelous series of adventures that would hold his character on the stage until vacation arrived. His first published story was during his years as a medical student, and the three guineas he received for it gave him the necessary conviction that he could write for a living.

After his son died in World War I, Doyle became a dedicated spiritualist. A statue has been erected in Sir Arthur Conan Doyle's honor at Crowborough Cross in Crowborough, Sussex, where Sir Arthur lived for twenty-three years. There is also a statue of Sherlock Holmes in Picardy Place, Edinburgh, Scotland–close to the house where Conan Doyle was born.

Noteworthy

1216 Louis VIII of France invades England.
1892 Dr. Sheffield invents the toothpaste tube.
1906 Orville and Wilbur Wright receive patent on their airplane.
1972 Richard Nixon becomes first U.S. president to visit Moscow.

MAY 23

DAILY READING

Each of us should please his neighbor for his good, to build him up. (ROM 15:2)

FEAST DAYS

1118	Ivo	Bishop of Chartres, France
1764	John Baptist de Rossi	Italian miracle worker
1828	Joan Antide Thouret	Founder of the Institute of the Daughters of Saint Vincent de Paul

ENTRANCE AND EXIT

b. 1707	Carolus Linnaeus	Swedish scientist
b. 1882	Douglas Fairbanks Jr.	American actor
b. 1951	Anatoly Karpov	Russian chess grandmaster
d. 1498	Gioralamo Savonarola	Italian reformer
d. 1701	"Captain" William Kidd	Scottish pirate
d. 1906	Henrik Johan Ibsen	Nowegian playwright

Gioralamo Savonarola

On this day in 1498, the Italian reformer Gioralamo Savonrola (1452–98) was strangled, along with two others, and burned on the orders of Pope Alexander Borgia. Savonarola's "crime" was to expose the corrupt lives of the clergy. He openly resisted the despotism of the Medici family and sided with the people, prophecying judgment and woe for his adversaries. The lives led by the clergy and the papal court he pronounced infernal, and sure to sweep the church to perdition if repentance were not early sought and found. Under his influence, Florence became a center of a great revival.

The pope tried to silence Savonarola by offering to make him a cardinal. Savonarola refused this, and the pope used other tactics. He got the monks to speak out against Savonarola, then excommunicated him, and finally arrested him.

Savonarola was born in the Italian city of Ferrara and, for a time, lived in a Dominican monastery. At the age of thirty-eight, he went to the city of Florence and began his great work of religious reform. Savonarola was a man of great natural force of character, well fitted to be a reformer, and he derived his main energies from his divine calling. It is alleged that Savonarola had frequent conversations with God, and it was said the devils who infested his convent trembled at his sight, and in vexation never mentioned his name without dropping some of its syllables.

Martin Luther regarded Savonarola as a pioneer of the Reformation because of his work to reform public morals. The doctrinal reformation began about twenty years later.

Anatoly Karpov

The Russian chess grandmaster Anatoly Karpov is considered the one of the best positional players of chess. He dominated the world of the chess for over a decade (1975–85), and with more than 160 tournament wins, he has won more times than any other chess player. This is a timeline of his life and career:

1951 Anatoly Evgenievich Karpov was born in Zlatoust, Russia.
1955 Learned to play chess at age four with his father, Evgeny Stepanovich.
1966 Became Soviet National Master.
1969 World Junior Champion.
1970 Became a grandmaster.
1975 World Champion after defeating American Bobby Fisher.
1976 Became Soviet Champion.
1978 Defeated Viktor Korchnoi to regain World Championship.
1981 Defeated Viktor Korchnoi again to regain World Championship.
1983 Became Soviet Champion.
1985 Lost world title to Gary Kasparov.
1987 Draw World Championship match with Kasparov in Seville, Spain.
1990 Lost World Championship to Kasparov.
1993 Won FIDE World Champion after defeating Jan Timman.
1996 Successful defense of World Championship title against Gata Kamsky.
1998 Successful defense of World Championship title against Viswananthan Anand.
1999 Refused to defend the World Champion title.

MAY 24

DAILY READING

Be devoted to one another in brotherly love.
Honor one another above yourselves. (ROM 12:10)

FEAST DAYS

ca. 1st cent.	Manaen	Friend of Herod Antipas
1177	John of Montfort	Knight Templar of Jerusalem
1636	John del Prado	Member of the Barefooted Franciscans of the Strict Observance

ENTRANCE AND EXIT

b. 1686	Daniel Farenheit	German scientist
b. 1819	Alexandrina Victoria	Queen of England
b. 1941	Bob Dylan	American singer
d. 1870	Jackson Kemper	American bishop
d. 1974	Duke Ellington	American jazz musician
d. 1995	Harold Wilson	British prime minister

Jackson Kemper

When Wisconsin bishop and missionary Jackson Kemper (1789–1870) died on this day in 1870, he was deeply mourned by many people throughout the country. David Jackson Kemper graduated from Columbia College in 1809, and as soon as he became old enough to be ordained, he became a deacon in 1811 in Philadelphia. He served in the Philadelphia area for twenty years, and during vacation periods (1812, 1814, 1819, and 1820), he served as border missionary in the western parts of Pennsylvania, Virginia, and eastern Ohio.

In 1834, under the auspices of the Domestic and Foreign Missionary Society of the Protestant Episcopal Church, he undertook a trip to Wisconsin to report on the native Indian settlement established by Reverend Cadle. At the general convention of the American church in 1835, Dr. Kemper was elected its first missionary bishop, his field being the "Northwest," out of which have since been formed the dioceses of Missouri, Indiana, Wisconsin, Minnesota, Iowa, Kansas, and Nebraska. Early in the winter of 1835, he reached St. Louis, which was his headquarters. Because of the itinerant nature of his ministry, Kempner barely had a home, and throughout much of the remainder of his life he wandered far and wide upon his laborious mission; "his saddle-bags contained his worldly goods–his robes, his communion service, his Bible, and his prayer-book."

In 1854, he was elected bishop of Wisconsin, but still insisted on remaining a missionary, and for four years thereafter traveled much in the Indian Territory and Kansas.

Kemper wrote a journal detailing his labors, and thus we know about his daily trials and triumphs.

Extract from Jackson Kemper's Journal of a Tour to Green Bay, 1834

July 15

The Indians whom we saw yesterday & today were dressed most fantastically. Some in dirty blankets without shirts, some with one legging blue and the other red, some painted red & another brown around the eyes, with rays say of white and red. Some with red on the cheek bone with black stripes. Two had hats. The hair of all black & shining & thick. Some had several long plaits in front tied at the end with ribbons. Some with ear rings & nose rings–& one with worsted hoops more that 3 inc[he]s wide. Some had calico shirts–most had blue cloth rappers edged with red–the leggings were generally red. Some had turbans of dark party col[oure]d handkerchiefs on their heads–most were without any covering on the head but were ornamented by ribbons or feathers stuck together most fantastically, generally eagle feathers–sometimes a profusion of ribbons with them. The few women we saw were modest in their appearance & dress & had not many colours–their heads were uncovered. Some of the boys had only a piece of an old blanket & made a great display of their naked legs. A chief called Old Wing made his appearance with the skin like that of a cat in his hand. He is said to be 80 yrs old & was the Ottawa chief that assisted the Americans during the last war. He looked very old & comical–cleaner than any of the rest–had on a round hat with a silver band–a large medal on his breast &c. Almost all the men looked very ugly & very dirty. Very few spoke to us or were noticed by any one. It appears they might very generally take up the expression, No one cares for my soul.

May 25

DAILY READING

My dear brothers, take note of this: Everyone should be quick to listen, slow to speak and slow to become angry. (JAS 1:19)

FEAST DAYS

417	Zenobius	Bishop of Florence, Italy
735	Venerable Bede	Father of English history
1085	Gregory VII	Pope

ENTRANCE AND EXIT

b. 1889	Igor Sikorsky	American engineer
b. 1939	Sir Ian McKellen	English actor
b. 1963	Mike Myers	Canadian actor
d. 1681	Pedro Calderón	Spanish writer
d. 1934	Gustav Holst	English composer
d. 2005	Ismail Merchant	Indian film producer

The Return of the King

After Oliver Cromwell's death in 1658, the English republican experiment faltered because of continued resistance from the Royalists and the ineffectual rule of his son and successor, Richard Cromwell.

The leaders of the English commonwealth led by Gen. George Monck met with Charles II and arranged to restore him in exchange for a promise of amnesty and religious toleration for his former enemies. On this day in 1660, Charles II landed at Dover and marched into London on May 29, his thirtieth birthday, and assumed the throne a year later, thus ending eleven years of republican rule.

Charles II was known as the "Merry Monarch," as he was an easy-going, fun-loving king, and represented a complete contrast to the restrictive rule of Cromwell. Charles II favored horseracing and was a great patron of the arts and sciences. Theaters reopened after having been closed during the protectorship of Oliver Cromwell, Puritanism lost its momentum, and the bawdy Restoration Comedy became a recognizable genre.

In 1649, Charles II had vainly attempted to save his father's life by presenting Parliament a signed blank sheet of paper, thereby granting whatever terms were required. However, Oliver Cromwell was determined to execute Charles I, and on January 30, 1649, the king was beheaded in London.

After his father's death, Charles was proclaimed king of Scotland and parts of Ireland and England, and traveled to Scotland to raise an army. In 1651, he invaded England but was defeated by Cromwell at the Battle of Worcester. Charles escaped to France, and later lived in exile in Germany and then in the Spanish Netherlands.

Oliver Cromwell was posthumously convicted of treason, and his body disinterred from its tomb in Westminster Abbey and hanged from the gallows at Tyburn.

Noteworthy

AD 597	St. Augustine arrives in Britain from Rome.
1768	Capt. James Cook sets sail on first voyage to Australia.
1895	Oscar Wilde sentenced to two years imprisonment for homosexuality.
1950	First passenger cars allowed on new Brooklyn-Battery Tunnel in New York City.
1953	World's first atomic shell fired in Nevada.
1963	Formation of the Organization of African Unity.
1976	George Lucas's *Star Wars* opens across America.
1985	Hurricane kills over eleven thousand people in Bangladesh.

MAY 26

DAILY READING

God did not send his Son into the world to condemn the world, but to save the world through him. (JOHN 3:17)

FEAST DAYS

1595	Philip Romolo Neri	Founder of the Congregation of the Oratory
1645	Mariana de Paredes y Flores	Patron of the Americas
1747	Pedro Sanz	Chinese martyr

ENTRANCE AND EXIT

b. 1886	Asa Yoelson (Al Jolson)	American actor
b. 1907	John Wayne	American actor
b. 1966	Helena Bonham Carter	English actor
d. 1702	Samuel Pepys	English writer
d. 1976	Martin Heidiegger	German philosopher
d. 1995	Isadore "Friz" Freleng	American animator

National Sorry Day

On this day in 1997, the Australian Parliament received a report called *Bringing Them Home*, which presented painful evidence of the removal of thousands of Aboriginal and Torres Strait Islander children from their families. The report recommended that a national "Sorry Day" be held as part of a "journey of healing to acknowledge, reflect, and apologize for this wrong."

The first National Sorry Day held on May 26, 1998, and a huge range of community activities took place across Australia. For example, Sorry Books, in which people could record their personal feelings, were presented to representatives of the indigenous communities.

This is part of the Sorry Day Statement for 2006:

> Sorry Day is a day to learn about the aspects of our history which non-Indigenous Australians tend to forget, but Indigenous people remember–the destruction of Indigenous culture through massacre, disease, neglect, and the removal of children. A day to search together for ways to overcome the continuing impact of this history. A day to recognise the extent of discrimination towards Indigenous Australians today, and discover how to work for a fair go.
>
> It is a day to challenge our Governments, Federal and State. It is shameful that Indigenous Australians die 20 years younger than the wider population when our medical authorities all agree that dramatic improvements are well within our capacity.
>
> It is shameful that so few of the recommendations of the *Bringing Them Home* report are yet to be implemented–including a Federal apology.
>
> It is a day for each of us to commit ourselves to enabling Indigenous Australia to flourish. We can all help bridge the gulf of misunderstanding and mistrust. It may be through: getting to know a neighbour, or through confronting racism in our workplace, or through organising a Sorry Day event, or by participating in a Sorry Day event.
>
> That is the purpose of Sorry Day.

Extract from Samuel Pepys's Dairy

The noted diarist, gossip and statesman Samuel Pepys (1633–1703) has left a fascinating account of significant and ordinary events in England in the seventeenth century. For instance, this is an excerpt from his entry for May 26 1668:

> Up by four o'clock; and by the time we were ready, and had eat, we were called to the coach, where about six o'clock we set out, there being a man and two women of one company, ordinary people, and one lady alone, that is tolerably handsome, but mighty well spoken, whom I took great pleasure in talking to, and did get her to read aloud in a book she was reading, in the coach, being the King's Meditations and then the boy and I to sing, and so about noon come to Bishop's Stafford, to another house than what we were at the other day, and better used. And here I paid for the reckoning 11s., we dining together, and pretty merry; and then set out again, sleeping most part of the way; and got to Bishopsgate Street before eight o'clock, the waters being now most of them down, and we avoiding the bad way in the forest by a privy way, which brought us to Hodsden; and so to Tibalds, that road, which was mighty pleasant.

*M*AY 27

DAILY READING

I consider my life worth nothing to me, if only I may finish the race and complete the task the Lord Jesus has given to me— the task of testifying to the gospel of God's grace. (ACTS 20:24)

FEAST DAYS

302	Julius of Dorostorum	Roman soldier
605	Augustine of Canterbury	Patron of England
1300	James of Nocera	Italian monk

ENTRANCE AND EXIT

b. 1648	St. Antoine Daniel	French missionary
b. 1867	Arnold Bennett	English writer
b. 1922	Christopher Lee	English actor
d. 1910	Robert Koch	German scientist
d. 1964	Jawaharlal Nehru	1st president of India
d. 2001	Victor Kiam	American businessman

St. Antoine Daniel

St. Antoine Daniel (1601–48) was a Jesuit missionary to the Huron Indians in Canada. He joined the Jesuits at Rouen in 1621, studied theology at the Collège in Clermont (1627–30), taught humanities (1630–31), and was minister at the Collège in Eu (1631–32).

In 1633, he went to Quebec to begin studying the Huron language. In 1634, he came to the Huronia region and translated many prayers into the Huron language and put them to music. Father Daniel's plan to move Huron children to Quebec for schooling was reconsidered because they were undisciplined. Nevertheless, in 1635 Daniel founded the first boy's college in North America at Quebec.

In 1638, Father Daniel returned to Huronia, where he relieved Father Brebuef at the mission Teanaostaye near Hillsdale, Limcoe County, Ontario, and also stayed at the mission Cahiaguie on Lake Couchiching. In June of 1648, Father Daniel prophetically spoke to the natives at St. Marie mission as he confessed and prepared for death before he returned to Teanaostaye.

In July 1648, the Iroquois Indians attacked the chapel led by Father Daniel. "Flee," said the missionary to his congregation, "and keep the faith to your dying breath." As for himself, his life belonged to the souls in his charge. He left the chapel and strode toward the enemy, who were astonished by such courage. When the first moment of stupefaction had passed, his body was riddled with arrows. A bullet struck him in the chest, passing through his body, and he fell uttering the name of Jesus. After desecrating his body, the Iroquois threw it into the fire that was consuming the chapel. As the first martyr of Huronia, Father Daniel, even after his death, inspired in his brother missionaries a wealth of tenderness and encouragement.

Noteworthy

1703 Czar Peter the Great proclaims St. Petersburg the new Russian capital.
1904 Triumph of Japanese Navy over Russians in the Battle of Tsushima.
1919 First airplane crosses Atlantic.
1937 Golden Gate Bridge opens in San Francisco.
1941 German battleship *Bismarck* sunk in France with a loss of 2,300 lives.
1998 United Nations indicts Slobodan Milosevic as a war criminal.

MAY 28

DAILY READING

Rejoice with those who rejoice;
mourn with those who mourn. (ROM 12:15)

FEAST DAYS

555	Germanus	Bishop of Paris, France
1008	Bernard of Menton	Founder of St. Bernard dogs rescue service
1541	Margaret Pole	Ward of King Henry VIII

ENTRANCE AND EXIT

b. 1759	William Younger the Pitt	British prime minister
b. 1908	Ian Fleming	English writer
b. 1944	Gladys Knight	American singer
d. 1843	Noah Webster	American lexicographer
d. 1849	Anne Brontë	English writer
d. 1998	Phil Hartman	American actor

Indian Removal Act

On this day in 1830, President Andrew Jackson's administration passed the Indian Removal Act, which had been approved by Congress by one vote. Since the settlement of Europeans had taken root, relations between them and the native Indians had steadily deteriorated. Jackson was convinced that the only solution to the Indian "problem" was the complete removal of all natives beyond the Mississippi, and now he had the law with which to accomplish it. No people would be more affected by this than the Cherokee Indians.

The Cherokee nation covered the Georgia-Tennessee border. They were the richest and most advanced of all Indian tribes. They had learned early to be farmers and had grown 40,000 acres worth of crops, along with running 22,000 cattle and 7,200 horses.

The Cherokees endeavoured to live in peace with their white neighbors. But the white settlers began to take more and more of their land. The Cherokees took their case to the United States Supreme Court. That court declared that the Cherokee were a people of a "domestic, dependant nation" and that the state of Georgia had no right to impose its laws over them. Although the Indians won their case, enforcement was another matter.

After many years of increasing hostility and pressure, in 1838 the Cherokee nation were put on the road and forced to march over a thousand miles of difficult terrain to Oklahoma. About four thousand Cherokees died on the road, and the long march became known as the Trail of Tears.

Anne Brontë Novels

The English writer Anne Brontë (1820–49) was the sister of novelists Charlotte and Emily Brontë. The youngest of six children, Anne was born in the village of Thornton, Yorkshire, and educated largely at home. Her best known works are *Agnes Grey* (1847) and *The Tenant of Wildfell Hall* (1848).

May 29

DAILY READING

From everlasting to everlasting the LORD's love is with those who fear him, and his righteousness with their children's children. (PS 103:17)

FEAST DAYS

352	Maximinus	Bishop of Trier, Germany
927	Gerald	Bishop of Macon, France
1207	Bona of Pisa	Patron of air hostesses

ENTRANCE AND EXIT

b. 1630	Charles II	English king
b. 1917	John Fitzgerald Kennedy	35th American president
b. 1959	Rupert Everett	English actor
d. 1829	Sir Humphrey Davy	English inventor
d. 1911	Sir William Schwenck Gilbert	English librettist
d. 1942	John Barrymore	American actor

International Day of UN Peacekeepers

On this day the United Nations pays tribute to "all the men and women who have served and continue to serve in UN peacekeeping operations for their high level of professionalism, dedication and courage and honours those who have lost their lives in the cause of peace." The General Assembly established UN Peacekeepers Day in 2002 when it adopted resolution 57/129.

In 2006, Secretary-General of the United Nations Kofi Annan gave this address to mark this day:

> On this day, we pay tribute to the professionalism, dedication and courage of all the men and women serving in United Nations peacekeeping operations, and honour the memory of those who have lost their lives in the cause of peace. The days of lightly armed peacekeepers conducting foot patrols along ceasefire lines between sovereign States are long over. UN peacekeeping operations are now increasingly complex and multi-dimensional, going beyond monitoring a ceasefire to actually bringing failed States back to life, often after decades of conflict. More peacekeepers died in the service of the United Nations in 2005 than in any other year in the last decade with 124 peacekeepers from 46 countries losing their lives to violence, disease and accidents. A further 32 have fallen in the line of duty so far in 2006.

The sight of UN Peacekeepers in their trademark blue helmets has become familiar all over the world, as they take on the difficult task of maintaining stability in hostile areas, providing an opportunity for restoration and renewal. The efforts of UN Peacekeepers were recognized in 1998 by the award of the Nobel Peace Prize.

Noteworthy

1453 Fall of Constantinople to Turks ends Byzantine Empire.
1721 South Carolina incorporated as a Royal Colony.
1790 Rhode Island thirteenth state admitted to the Union.
1848 Wisconsin thirtieth state admitted to the Union.
1942 Bing Crosby records "White Christmas."
1953 Sir Edmund Hillary conquers Mount Everest.

May 30

DAILY READING

In God, whose word I praise, in God I trust;
I will not be afraid. What can mortal man do to me? (PS 56:4)

FEAST DAYS

1016	Walstan	Patron of farmers
1431	Joan of Arc	Patron of France
1582	Lawrence Richardson	English martyr

ENTRANCE AND EXIT

b. 1896	Howard Winchester Hawks	American film maker
b. 1908	Melvin Jerome Blanc	American voice artist
b. 1909	Benny Goodman	American musician
d. 542	Arthur Pendragon	King of England
d. 1593	Christopher Marlowe	English writer
d. 1960	Boris Pasternak	Russian writer

King Arthur

According to ancient English tradition, King Arthur died on this day. During Arthur's lifetime, Britain was at war with the Saxons and was ruled by Arthur's father, Uther Pendragon. According to the historian Geoffrey of Monmouth, Uther fell in love with the Duke of Cornwall's wife, Igerna. This led to civil war and Uther laid siege to Cornwall. Uther used his magician, Merlin, to win Igerna, and their child was Arthur.

As well as crushing the Saxons, Arthur triumphed over the Picts and Scots. He went on to conquer Ireland, Iceland, Norway, and Denmark, placing over them all kings chosen from among his own chieftains. He also ruled over France for nine years.

Arthur's conquests roused the wrath of Rome, and Lucius Tiberius, the "procurator" of the republic of Rome, summoned Arthur to restore to Rome the provinces that he had unjustly usurped on the Continent, and also to pay the tribute that Britain had formerly paid to the Imperial power.

Enraged at this demand, Arthur raised an army to go to Italy, leaving his kingdom to his nephew Modred. Arthur and his men endured many adventures on the Continent, including Arthur slaying a Spanish giant in Brittany. Although Arthur triumphed over the Romans, his kingdom was usurped by Modred, who gained the support of the Saxons.

Arthur defeated Modred at Winchester but was mortally wounded. He was carried to the Isle of Avallon (Glastonbury) to be cured of his wounds. but all the efforts of the physicians were in vain, and he died and was buried there. According to legend, King Arthur will one day be raised to life to rescue Britain at the time of her direst need.

Howard Winchester Hawkes

The film maker Howard Hawkes (1896–1977) is notable for his mastery of many genres of film including westerns, comedies, film noir, musicals, historical epics, science fiction, war and adventure, prison dramas, aviation films and gangster movies. In a long career, he worked with many stars and his work includes:

1930 *The Dawn Patrol*
1938 *Bringing Up Baby*
1939 *Only Angels Have Wings*
1940 *His Girl Friday*
1946 *The Big Sleep*
1948 *Red River*
1953 *Gentlemen Prefer Blondes*
1959 *Rio Bravo*
1962 *Hatari!*
1965 *Red Line 7000*
1967 *El Dorado*

MAY 31

DAILY READING

The Lord himself will come down from heaven, with a loud command, with the voice of the archangel and with the trumpet call of God, and the dead in Christ will rise first. After that, we who are still alive and are left will be caught up together with them in the clouds to meet the Lord in the air. And so we will be with the Lord forever. (1 THESS 4:16–17)

FEAST DAYS

ca. 1st cent.	Aurelia Petronilla	Patron of mountaineers
1341	James the Venetian	Patron of Forli, Italy
1524	Camilla Battista Varani	Poor Clare nun

ENTRANCE AND EXIT

b. 1819	Walt Whitman	American writer
b. 1930	Clint Eastwood	American actor
b. 1965	Brooke Shields	American actor
d. 1809	Franz Joseph Haydn	Austrian composer
d. 1962	Adolf Eichmann	German leader
d. 1983	Jack Dempsey	American boxer

John Hus

The great religious reformer John Hus(s) was burned at the stake along with his works on this day in 1416. His crime had been to challenge the Catholic Church to reform the poor example of the clergy and return to biblical doctrine. As the flames began to engulf him, Hus proclaimed, "In 100 years, God will raise up a man whose calls for reform cannot be suppressed." His ashes were gathered and cast into the nearby Rhine River.

Almost exactly 100 years later, in 1517, Martin Luther nailed his famous 95 Theses of Contention onto the church door at Wittenberg, Germany. The prophecy of John Hus was thus fulfilled.

Like Luther, John Hus was ordained as a Roman Catholic priest. Like Luther, Hus began to denounce various church abuses in his sermons. His disputes with authority concerned theological issues and matters of church discipline and practice. For instance, only the priest was allowed to drink from the Eucharist cup. Huss wanted a return to the New Testament practice of all believers sharing the Eucharist bread and wine. Hus also taught that the office of the pope did not exist by divine command, but was established by the church so that things might be done in an orderly fashion.

He also held that church officials ought to exercise spiritual powers only, and not be earthly governors. For this, he was excommunicated by his archbishop in 1412. In 1414 he was summoned to the Council of Constance, with the emperor guaranteeing his personal safety even if he was found guilty. He was tried, and ordered to recant certain heretical doctrines. His refusal sealed his fate.

The followers of John Hus and his fellow martyr Jerome of Prague became known as the Czech Brethren and later as the Moravians. The Moravian Church survives to this day, and has had a considerable influence on the Lutheran movement.

Final Declaration of Jan (John) Hus(s)

I, Jan Hus, in hope a priest of Jesus Christ, fearing to offend God, and fearing to fall into perjury, do hereby profess my unwillingness to abjure all or any of the articles produced against me by false witnesses. For God is my witness that I neither preached, affirmed, nor defended them, though they say that I did. Moreover, concerning the articles that they have extracted from my books, I say that I detest any false interpretation which any of them bears. But inasmuch as I fear to offend against the truth, or to gainsay the opinion of the doctors of the Church, I cannot abjure any one of them. And if it were possible that my voice could now reach the whole world, as at the Day of Judgment every lie and every sin that I have committed will be made manifest, then would I gladly abjure before all the world every falsehood and error which I either had thought of saying or actually said!

I say I write this of my own free will and choice.

Source: Herbert B. Workman and R. Martin Pope, eds., *The Letters of John Hus* (London: Hodder and Stoughton, 1904).

June

And after her came jolly June, array'd
All in green leaves, as he a player were;
Yet in his time he wrought as well as play'd,
That by his plough-irons mote right well appeare.
Upon a crab he rode, that him did bare
With crooked crawling steps an uncouth pase,
And backward-yode, as bargemen wont to fare
Bending their force contrary to their face;
Like that ungracious crew which faines demurest grace.

EDMUND SPENSER—*The Shepheardes Calender* (1579)

Mine is the Month of Roses; yes, and mine
The Month of Marriages! All pleasant sights
And scents, the fragrance of the blossoming vine,
The foliage of the valleys and the heights.
Mine are the longest days, the loveliest nights;
The mower's scythe makes music to my ear;
I am the mother of all dear delights;
I am the fairest daughter of the year.

HENRY WADSWORTH LONGFELLOW—*The Poet's Calendar* (1882)

June ~

The temperature of the air is still mild, and in our climate sometimes too chilly; but when the season is fine, this is, perhaps, the most delightful month of the year. The hopes of spring are realized, yet the enjoyment is but commenced: we have all summer before us; the cuckoo's two notes are now at what may be called their ripest,–deep and loud; so is the hum of the bee; little clouds lie in lumps of silver about the sky, and sometimes fall to complete the growth of the herbage; the pea, the blue and yellow nightshade, the fox-glove, the mallow, white briony, wild honeysuckle, and the flower of the hip or wild rose, which blushes through all the gradations of delicate red and white. The leaves of the hip, especially the young ones, are as beautiful as those of any garden rose. Towards evening, the bat and the owl venture forth, flitting through the glimmering quiet; and at night, the moon looks silveriest, the sky at once darkest and clearest; and when the nightingale, as well as the other birds have done singing, you may hear the undried brooks of the spring running and panting through their leafy channels.

–William Hone, *The Every Day Book* (1825–26)

Shakespeare ~

To me, fair friend, you never can be old,
For as you were when first your eye I eyed,
Such seems your beauty still. Three winters cold
Have from the forests shook three summers' pride,
Three beauteous springs to yellow autumn turn'd
In process of the seasons have I seen,
Three April perfumes in three hot Junes burn'd,
Since first I saw you fresh, which yet are green.
Ah! yet doth beauty, like a dial-hand,
Steal from his figure and no pace perceived;
So your sweet hue, which methinks still doth stand,
Hath motion and mine eye may be deceived:
For fear of which, hear this, thou age unbred;
Ere you were born was beauty's summer dead.

–Sonnet CIV

Proverbs ~

Mist in May and heat in June,
Make the harvest right soon.

June brings tulips, lilies, roses,
Fills the children's hands with posies.

Marry when June roses grow,
Over land and sea you'll go.

A dripping June
Puts all things in tune.

June 1

DAILY READING

I saw the Holy City, the new Jerusalem, coming down out of heaven from God, prepared as a bride, beautifully dressed for her husband. And I heard a loud voice from the throne saying, "Now the dwelling of God is with men, and he will live with them. They will be his people, and God himself will be with them and be their God. He will wipe every tear from their eyes. There will be no more death or mourning or crying or pain, for the old order of things has passed away." (REV 21:2–4)

FEAST DAYS

ca. 100	Justin Martyr	Patron of philosophers
849	Wistan of Evesham	Prince of Mercia, England
1571	John Storey	English martyr

ENTRANCE AND EXIT

b. 1801	Brigham Young	American Mormon leader
b. 1878	John Masefield	English writer
b. 1937	Morgan Freeman	American actor
d. 1868	James Buchanan	15th American president
d. 1941	Sir Hugh Walpole	English writer
d. 1968	Helen Keller	American writer

The Glorious First of June

> Early on 1 June 1794, the signal was made to form the line of battle. . . . At eight the action began, and the firing from the enemy was very smart before we could engage the ship that came to our turn to engage, as every ship is to have one because our line is formed ahead, and theirs is formed also. . . . I believe we were the ninth or tenth ship; our lot fell to an 80 gun ship, so we would not waste our powder and shot by firing at other ships, though I am sorry to say they fired very smartly at us and unluckily killed two men before we fired a gun, which so exasperated our men that they kept singing out, "For God's sake, brave Captain, let us fire!"

Thus wrote Admiral Sir William Parker about the first naval battle of the French Revolutionary Wars fought between a British fleet under Admiral Richard Howe and a French fleet commanded by Rear Admiral Villart-Joyeuse.

Howe's fleet attacked the French line and broke it in several places, and the action turned into a general melee, during which six French ships were captured and one, the *Vengeur di Peuple*, sank after a four-hour onslaught. The French withdrew and returned to Brest. The British fleet was in no condition to pursue, with two ships, *Defence* and *Marlborough*, having to be towed home.

Although the British could claim a victory, so could the French as their grain fleet managed to reach Brest safely. However, France never again tried to run such a fleet through the British blockade.

Noteworthy

1599 Shakespeare's Globe Theatre opens in Southwark, London.
1792 Kentucky is fifteenth state admitted to the Union.
1796 Tennessee is sixteenth state admitted to the Union.
1857 Royal Navy destroys Chinese fleet in second Anglo-Chinese War.
1869 Thomas Alva Edison patents his electric vote recorder.
1888 First seismograph exhibited at Lick Observatory, University of California.
1944 Colossus II, the first working computer by Alan Turing, begins operations.
1967 Beatles release *Sgt. Pepper's Lonely Hearts Club Band* album.

JUNE 2

DAILY READING

Christ was sacrificed once to take away the sins of many people; and he will appear a second time, not to bear sin, but to bring salvation to those who are waiting for him. (HEB 9:28)

FEAST DAYS

ca. 303	Eramus	Bishop of Formiae, Italy
657	Eugene I	Pope
ca. 1150	John of Ortega	Spanish hermit

ENTRANCE AND EXIT

b. 1840	Thomas Hardy	English writer
b. 1857	Sir Edward Elgar	English composer
b. 1904	Johnny Weissmuller	American actor
d. 1882	Guiseppe Garibaldi	Italian politician
d. 1962	Vita Sackville West	English writer
d. 1987	Andres Segovia	Spanish musician

Nikolai of Japan

On this day in 1861, Russian Orthodox missionary Nikolai Ivan Dimitrovich Kasatkin (1836–1912) arrived in Japan to serve as a chaplain to the Russian embassay.

At that time, Christianity was forbidden in Japan, and he had to work in secret to present the gospel. It took nearly eight years before his first three converts were baptized.

Nikolai was committed not only to winning converts, but to building churches. He trained converts to become priests and lay workers in the Orthodox tradition. He established a Japanese synod that met every two years.

Nikolai had a long-term vision. It wasn't enough for him to build a huge church, or have a lot of followers. He saw beyond himself. He built churches, and encouraged converts to study and begin their own ministries. He didn't make the ministry all about himself–he made sure he trained disciples of Christ, so that they could have a part in the work Christ was doing in Japan.

By 1873, Christianity was legal in Japan, and by the time of Nikolai's death the Japanese church had over thirty thousand converts.

Noteworthy

1895 Japan takes formal possession of Formosa (Taiwan) from China.
1896 Guglielmo Marconi receives U.S. patent on his invention of radio.
1924 Congress gives full citizenship to all Native Americans.
1953 First televised coronation of a royal monarch–Queen Elizabeth II.
1979 Pope John Paul II visits Poland.

JUNE 3

DAILY READING

A gentle answer turns away wrath,
but a harsh word stirs up anger. (PROV 15:1)

FEAST DAYS

618	Kevin	Patron of blackbirds
1886	Mbaga Tuzinde	Ugandan martyr
1919	Diego Oddi	Franciscan monk

ENTRANCE AND EXIT

b. 1771	Sidney Smith	English clergyman
b. 1865	George V	King of England
b. 1925	Tony Curtis	American actor
d. 1875	George Bizet	French composer
d. 1963	Angelo Giuseppe Roncalli	Pope John XXIII
d. 2001	Anthony Quinn	American actor

Sidney Smith

The Reverend Sidney Smith (1771–1845) was a man who was universally loved and had no recorded personal enemies. He was a parson, founder of the *Edinburgh Review*, promoter of the cause of Catholic emancipation, and passionate proponent of the abolition of slavery.

Throughout his life as a parson in Yorkshire and Somerset, and later as Dean of St. Paul's Cathedral, Sidney was admired for his conversational wit and humanity.

Sidney Smith came from Suffolk and was educated at Winchester School. In 1772, he went to Oxford and studied classics with a view to being a doctor or lawyer (he studied medicine and anatomy in his spare time). However, he became a minister because his father refused to pay for his further studies.

In 1802, he became the founding editor of *Edinburgh Review* and used that outlet to prick the consciences of those who were in positions of power. Although he was a minister of the Church of England, this did not blind him to the corruption within the church itself–the chain of nepotism that allowed members of some families to obtain positions within the church regardless of merit or even vocation. Nor did his own position prevent him from commenting on what he saw as its "iniquities," neither to the lack of humanity he perceived in some of the church's leading lights. "I must believe in the Apostolic succession," he once remarked. "There being no other way of accounting for the descent of the Bishop of Exeter from Judas Iscariot."

The Wit of Sidney Smith

Poverty is no disgrace to a man, but it is profoundly inconvenient.

Thank God for tea! What would the world do without tea! I am glad I was not born before tea.

I never read a book before reviewing it; it prejudices a man so.

I have, alas, only one illusion left, and that is the Archbishop of Canterbury.

Live always in the best company when you read.

There are three sexes–men, women, and clergymen.

June 4

DAILY READING

Yours, O LORD, is the greatness and the power and the glory and the majesty and the splendor, for everything in heaven and earth is yours. Yours, O LORD, is the kingdom; you are exalted as head over all. (1 CHRON 29:11)

FEAST DAYS

325	Metrophanes	Bishop of Byzantium
ca. 594	Petroc	Patron of Cornwall, England
939	Aldegrin of Baume	Benedictine monk

ENTRANCE AND EXIT

b. 1738	George III	King of England
b. 1932	John Drew Barrymore Jr.	American actor
b. 1975	Angelina Jolie	American actor
d. 1798	Giacomo Girolamo Casanova	Italian writer
d. 1941	Wilhelm II	German Kaiser
d. 1968	Dorothy Gish	American actor

Balloon Flight Pioneers

French opera singer Marie Elisabeth Thible made history on this day in 1784 by making the first free female flight. Madame Thible made her ascent in a Montgolfier balloon, named *Le Gustave* in honor of the Swedish king, Gustav III, who witnessed the ascent. The balloon reached a height of 8,500 feet (2,591 meters) in a flight lasting 45 minutes.

Madame Thible's achievement occurred exactly a year after the Montgolfier brothers launched the first hot air balloon.

Joseph Michel and Jacques Étienne Montgolfier constructed a globe-shaped balloon of sackcloth with three thin layers of paper inside. The envelope could contain nearly 28,000 cubic feet of air and weighed 500 pounds. It was constructed of four pieces (the dome and three lateral bands) held together by some 1,800 buttons. A reinforcing "fish net" of cord covered the outside of the envelope.

On June 4, 1783, they flew this craft as their first public demonstration at Annonay in front of a group of dignitaries from the Etats particulars. Its flight covered two kilometers, lasted ten minutes, and had an estimated altitude of 1,600 to 2,000 meters.

Word of their success quickly reached Paris. Étienne went to the capital to make further demonstrations and to solidify the brothers' claim to the invention of flight.

After many trials, on September 19, 1783, the brothers launched the *Aerostat Réveillon*. The basket contained a sheep, a duck, and a rooster, and King Louis XVI and Marie Antoinette witnessed the demonstration. The flight lasted approximately eight minutes, covered two miles, and obtained an altitude of about 1,500 feet. The animals survived the trip unharmed.

Noteworthy

- 1844 Hunters kill last two Great Auk on the island of Eldey in Iceland.
- 1944 Allies enter Rome.
- 1971 Yehudi Menuhin's 250-year-old Stradivarius sells for record $200,000 at Sotheby's.
- 1989 Massacre by police against students in Tiananmen Square, Beijing, ends.

June 5

DAILY READING

Encourage one another and build each other up,
just as in fact you are doing. (1 THESS 5:11)

FEAST DAYS

362	Dorotheus	Bishop of Tyre, Lebanon
574	Boniface	Apostle of Germany
1402	Ferdinand	Son of King John 1 of Portugal

ENTRANCE AND EXIT

b. 1723	Adam Smith	Scottish economist
b. 1883	John Maynard Keynes	English economist
b. 1971	Mark Wahlberg	American actor
d. 1916	Horatio Kitchener	English general
d. 1993	Conway Twitty	American singer
d. 2004	Ronald Reagan	40th American president

World Environment Day

In 1972, the United Nations General Assembly designated this day as World Environment Day (WED) to encourage greater awareness of environmental issues and protection of the planet and its resources. Every year has a special theme to highlight particular aspects of the environment. Each year a city is selected to spearhead the WED campaign.

The theme for 2006 was "Deserts and Desertification," and the chosen city was Algiers. UN General Secretary Kofi Annan made the following comments in his WED press statement:

> Desertification is hard to reverse, but it can be prevented. Protecting and restoring drylands will not only relieve the growing burden on the world's urban areas, it will contribute to a more peaceful and secure world. It will also help to preserve landscapes and cultures that date back to the dawn of civilisation and are an essential part of our cultural heritage. I urge governments and communities everywhere to focus on the challenges of life on the desert margins so the people who live there can look forward to a future of peace, health and social progress.

World Environment Day—Themes and Cities

Year	Theme	City
2005	Green Cities–Plan for the Planet	San Francisco
2004	Wanted! Seas and Oceans –Dead or Alive?	Barcelona
2003	Water–Two Billion People Are Dying for It!	Beirut
2002	Give Earth a Chance	Shenzhen
2001	Connect with the World Wide Web of Life	Torino and Havana
2000	The Environment Millennium –Time to Act	Adelaide
1999	Our Earth–Our Future–Just Save It!	Tokyo
1998	For Life on Earth–Save Our Seas	Moscow
1997	For Life on Earth	Seoul
1996	Our Earth, Our Habitat, Our Home	Istanbul
1995	We the Peoples: United for the Global Environment	Pretoria
1994	One Earth, One Family	London
1993	Poverty and the Environment –Breaking the Vicious Circle	Beijing
1992	Only One Earth, Care and Share	Rio de Janeiro
1991	Climate Change–Need for Global Partnership	Stockholm
1990	Children and the Environment	Mexico City

JUNE 6

DAILY READING

I pray that you, being rooted and established in love, may have power, together with all the saints, to grasp how wide and high and deep is the love of Christ, and to know this love that surpasses knowledge—that you may be filled to the measure of all the fullness of God. (EPH 3:17–19)

FEAST DAYS

ca. 540	Jarlath	Patron of Tuam, Ireland
ca. 7th cent.	John	Bishop of Verona, Italy
1146	Falco	Benedictine monk

ENTRANCE AND EXIT

b. 1799	Alexander Pushkin	Russian poet
b. 1875	Thomas Mann	German writer
b. 1956	Björn Borg	Swedish tennis star
d. 1862	Turner Ashby	American general
d. 1941	Louis Chevrolet	American car designer
d. 1961	Carl Jung	Swiss psychologist

D-Day—The Longest Day

On this day in 1944, Supreme Allied Commander Gen. Dwight D. Eisenhower launched the Allied invasion of northern France, Operation Overlord, code named D-Day. It remains the largest amphibious military operation in history.

By daybreak, over eighteen thousand British and American parachutists were already on the ground. At 6:30 a.m., American troops came ashore at Utah and Omaha beaches on the Normandy coast. At Omaha, the U.S. First Division battled high seas, mist, mines, burning vehicles—and German coastal batteries, including an elite infantry division. Many wounded Americans ultimately drowned in the high tide.

British divisions landed at Gold, Juno, and Sword beaches and Canadian troops who landed at Juno met with heavy German fire, but by the end of the day they were able to liberate several coastal villages. Despite the German resistance, Allied casualties overall were relatively light. The United States and Britain each lost about a thousand men, and Canada 355. Before the end of the day 155,000 Allied troops landed in Normandy.

Field Marshal Montgomery, commander of Britain's Twenty-first Army Group, claimed later that the invasion had come off exactly as planned. That was not quite correct because, for example, the town of Caen was not taken on the first day, as scheduled.

The D-Day invasion has been the basis for several movies, from *The Longest Day* (1962), which boasted an all-star cast that included Richard Burton, Sean Connery, and John Wayne, to *Saving Private Ryan* (1998), which included some of the most grippingly realistic war scenes ever filmed.

Noteworthy

1520 Henry VIII and Francis I confer at Field of the Cloth of Gold near Calais.
1523 Gustavus Vasa ascends throne of Sweden.
1833 Andrew Jackson becomes first U.S. president to ride in a railroad train.
1844 YMCA (Young Men's Christian Organization) founded in London.
1954 First Eurovision song contest.
1962 Beatles meet producer George Martin for the first time.
1968 Senator Robert F. Kennedy assassinated.

JUNE 7

DAILY READING

Before the mountains were born or you brought forth the earth
and the world, from everlasting to everlasting you are God.
For a thousand years in your sight are like a day that has
just gone by, or like a watch in the night. (PS 90:2, 4)

FEAST DAYS

1066	Gotteschalk	Patron of translators
1159	Robert of Newminster	Benedictine monk
1302	Meriadoc	Welsh hermit

ENTRANCE AND EXIT

b. 1761	John Rennie	Scottish engineer
b. 1848	Paul Gaugin	French artist
b. 1940	Tom Jones	Welsh singer
d. 1329	Robert the Bruce	King of Scotland
d. 1954	Alan Turing	English mathematician
d. 1967	Dorothy Parker	American writer

Dunmow Flitch Trials

The Dunmow Flitch Trials regularly took place on this day in ancient times, but more recently the date has moved to July. The trials have a history dating back to the 1104 and are a celebration of marriage. In that year, the Augustinian Priory of Little Dunmow (in the county of Essex) awarded a flitch (side) of bacon to Lord of the Manor, Reginald Fitzwalter, and his wife for their devotion to one another after one year and one day of marriage. This became an annual competition or trial for local villagers to prove their devotion to their spouses and be rewarded with the Dunmow Flitch.

By the fourteenth century, the Dunmow Flitch had achieved far-reaching notoriety. The author William Langland, who lived on the Welsh borders, mentions it in his 1362 book, *The Vision of Piers Plowman*, in a manner that implies general knowledge of the custom among his readers. Chaucer, writing less than half a century later, alludes to the Dunmow Flitch Trials in "The Wife of Bath's Tale."

However, is it not until 1445 that the winners of the Flitch were officially recorded. The earliest record we have of a successful claimant to the Dunmow Flitch is Richard Wright, who traveled from Norwich to try his marital harmony and take home the bacon. The win is recorded in documents from the Priory of Little Dunmow still held by the British Museum.

The Dunmow Flitch Oath

You do swear by custom of confession
That you ne'er made nuptual transgression
Nor since you were married man and wife
By household brawls or contentious strife
Or otherwise in bed or at board
Offended each other in deed or in word
Or in a twelve months time and a day
Repented not in thought in any way
Or since the church clerk said amen
Wish't yourselves unmarried again
But continue true and desire
As when you joined hands in holy quire.

JUNE 8

DAILY READING

The Sovereign LORD is my strength;
he makes my feet like the feet of a deer,
he enables me to go on the heights. (HAB 3:19)

FEAST DAYS

ca. 514	Gildard	Bishop of Rouen, France
545	Medard	Bishop of Rouen, France
1154	William	Archbishop of York

ENTRANCE AND EXIT

b. 1867	Frank Lloyd Wright	American architect
b. 1916	Francis Crick	English scientist
b. 1955	Tim Berners Lee	English computer scientist
d. 632	Muhammed	Founder of Islam
d. 1809	Thomas Paine	American writer
d. 1845	Andrew Jackson	7th American president

The Ten Articles of Religion

In 1536, Thomas Cranmer, Archbishop of Canterbury during the reign of King Henry VIII, published the Ten Articles of Religion. This document was a major step in the separation of England from the Church of Rome and led the way to defining the Church of England.

The Ten Articles referred to baptism, the authority of Scripture, the sacraments, justification by faith, and the observance of holy festivals.

In that same year, Henry moved quickly to dissolve monasteries and convents in England, thus nullifying any protest at his divorce of Anne Boleyn and doubling his annual income. Henry owed his newly discovered spiritual authority to Parliament. Had he kept the monastic lands, he might have been wealthy enough to rule without Parliamentary appropriations. But he sold numerous tracts to the gentry in order to finance a useless war with Scotland (1542) and other projects.

However, Henry's personal faith seldom strayed farther from Catholic orthodoxy than politics required. After he had jettisoned his first wife, the pope, and Latin Mass, he desired little further change in doctrine of liturgy. But many of his subjects wanted change, and Protestantism flourished despite royal disapproval. Henry vacillated between doing nothing and giving in to anti-Catholic feeling. Between 1536–37 he issued the Ten Articles and Bishop's Book; in 1538, the Great Bible, a new English translation; in 1539 and 1543, the Catholic-leaning Six Articles and King's Book, respectively. By supporting both Protestant and Catholic causes, Henry hoped to balance, and eventually neutralize, extreme religious sentiment.

Noteworthy

1709 First paper currency in America issued in New York City.
1789 James Madison first proposes Bill of Rights.
1861 Tennessee becomes eleventh and last state to secede from the Union.
1869 Vacuum cleaner patented by I. W. McGaffrey of Chicago.
1912 Universal Studios founded by Carl Laemmle.
1946 Victory Day celebration in Britain.

June 9

DAILY READING

"Wide is the gate and broad is the road that leads to destruction, and many enter through it. But small is the gate and narrow the road that leads to life, and only a few find it." (MATT 7:13–14)

FEAST DAYS

597	Columba	Apostle of the Picts
599	Baithen of Iona	Biographer of St. Columba
1666	Henry the Shoemaker	Founder of the *Frères Cordonniers*

ENTRANCE AND EXIT

b. 1781	George Stephenson	English engineer
b. 1891	Cole Porter	American composer
b. 1963	Johnny Depp	American actor
d. 1870	Charles Dickens	English writer
d. 1964	Lord William Maxwell Aitken Beaverbrook	English politician
d. 1976	Sybil Thorndike	English actor

St. Columba

The Irish missionary St. Columba (or Colm Cille) established a monastery in Iona. Iona is just off the western coast of Scotland, opposite the mountains of Mull. From this small island, the gospel spread over Scotland and the north of England.

According to the Venerable Bede, in 565 Columba left Ireland on his missionary expedition. The monks were learned men who practiced calligraphy and produced wonderful copies of the Psalter and Gospels.

Columba was a great miracle worker, and many stories relate to his adventures. For example, according to St. Adamnan's account of Columba:

> By virtue of his prayer, he healed several persons suffering under various diseases. He expelled innumerable hosts of malignant spirits, whom he saw with his own eyes and beginning to bring deadly distempers on his monastic brotherhood. Partly by mortification, and partly by a bold resistance, he subdued the furious rage of wild beasts. He hoisted his sail when the breeze was against him to confound the Druids, and made as rapid a voyage as if the wind had been favourable The surging waves, also, at times rolling mountains high in a great tempest, became quickly at his prayer quiet and smooth, and his ship, in which he then happened to be, reached the desired haven in a perfect calm.

Columba is supposed to have rid Loch Ness of a monster by making the sign of the cross over the waters. Columba died in 597, the same year Augustine came to Canterbury to convert the English. In America, Columba is the founding patron of the Knights of Saint Columba.

Charles Dickens Characters

According to the *Dictionary of British Literary Characters*, the Victorian writer Charles Dickens created 989 characters in his books. Some of the most popular characters include:

David Copperfield	Tiny Tim
Uriah Heep	Jacob Marley
Wilkins Micawber	Fagin
Agnes Wickfield	Oliver Twist
Philip Pirrip	Noah Claypole
Abel Magwitch	Bill Sykes
Wemmick	The Artful Dodger
Ebenezer Scrooge	Mr. Bumble
Bob Cratchitt	Martin Chuzzlewit
Nicholas Nickleby	Seth Pecksniff

June 10

DAILY READING

Bear with each other and forgive whatever grievances you may have against one another. Forgive as the Lord forgave you. (COL 3:13)

FEAST DAYS

523	Brigid of Ireland	Patron of scholars
1270	Amata	Dominican nun
1315	Henry	Patron of Treviso, Italy

ENTRANCE AND EXIT

b. 1688	James Edward Stuart	The Old Pretender
b. 1915	Saul Bellow	American writer
b. 1922	Judy Garland	American actor
d. 1836	Andre Marie Ampere	French mathematician
d. 1934	Frederick Delius	English composer
d. 1967	Spencer Tracey	American actor

Witchcraft in Salem

In 1692, fifty-eight-year-old Bridget Bishop became one of the first Salem "witches" to be hanged.

In February of that year, two young girls began to experience fits and hysterics. A doctor concluded that the children were suffering from the effects of witchcraft.

A month later, Sarah Goode, Sarah Osborne, and Tituba, an Indian slave from Barbados, became the first Salem residents to be charged with the capital crime of witchcraft. By June a special court was convened under Chief Justice William Stoughton to judge the accused. The outcome led to thirteen more women and four men being found guilty and hanged. Five others died in jail.

In October of 1692, Gov. William Phipps of Massachusetts ordered the Court of Oyer and Terminer dissolved and replaced with the Superior Court of Judicature, which forbid the type of sensational testimony allowed in the earlier trials. Executions ceased, and the Superior Court eventually released all those awaiting trial and pardoned those sentenced to death, effectively ending the Salem Witch Trials.

Noteworthy

1652 First mint in America established at Boston.

1682 First recorded tornado in America near New Haven, Connecticut.

1727 On the death of George I, George II proclaimed king of Britain.

1829 First Oxford vs. Cambridge boat race—won by Oxford.

1846 Rubber tire patented in England by Robert William Thomson.

1865 Wagner's opera *Tristan and Isolde* first performed in Munich.

1940 Italy declares war on Britain and France—World War II.

1967 Six Day War between Israel and Arabs ends.

June 11

DAILY READING

Be still, and know that I am God;
I will be exalted among the nations,
I will be exalted in the earth. (PS 46:10)

FEAST DAYS

ca. 61	Barnabas	Apostle
1915	Ignazio Maloyan	Armenian martyr
1930	Paula Frassinetti	Patron of sickness

ENTRANCE AND EXIT

b. 1864	Richard Strauss	German composer
b. 1910	Jacques Cousteau	French oceangrapher
b. 1959	Hugh Laurie	English actor
d. 1488	James III	King of Scotland
d. 1979	John Wayne	American actor
d. 2001	Timothy McVeigh	American terrorist

St. Barnabas Day

St. Barnabas Day is associated with the summer solstice because in the Julian calendar, the date coincided with the longest day in the year. An old saying links the solstice with St. Barnabas thus: "Barnaby Bright, Barnaby Bright: the longest day and the shortest night."

It was the custom on this day to deck churches and houses with "Barnaby garlands" of roses and sweet woodruff. Sometimes the garlands also included the pink ragged robin, also known as Wild Williams.

> When Barnabas smiles both night and day
> Poor Ragged Robin blooms in the hay
> At St. Barnabas, the scythe in the meadow.

St. Barnaby also had a thistle named after him: *Centaurea solstitialis*, confirming his association with the solstice. In Denmark, this was the end of the contract year, and masters and servants were free to renegotiate their contracts or part ways.

Barnabas was not one of the twelve apostles, but is mentioned in the book of Acts as a companion of St. Paul. According to tradition, Barnabas went to live with the Christians in Jerusalem after selling his estate and giving the money to the apostles.

The apocryphal *Epistle of Barnabas* was probably written not by Barnabas, but by Gnostic disciples eager to reassert the Jewish background to the New Testament after the destruction of the Temple in Jerusalem in AD 70.

According to legend, he was martyred in Salamis in 61.

Acts 11:22–30

. . . they sent Barnabas to Antioch. When he arrived and saw the evidence of the grace of God, he was glad and encouraged them all to remain true to the Lord with all their hearts. He was a good man, full of the Holy Spirit and faith, and a great number of people were brought to the Lord.

Then Barnabas went to Tarsus to look for Saul, and when he found him, he brought him to Antioch. So for a whole year Barnabas and Saul met with the church and taught great numbers of people. The disciples were called Christians first at Antioch.

During this time some prophets came down from Jerusalem to Antioch. One of them, named Agabus, stood up and through the Spirit predicted that a severe famine would spread over the entire Roman world. (This happened during the reign of Claudius.) The disciples, each according to his ability, decided to provide help for the brothers living in Judea. This they did, sending their gift to the elders by Barnabas and Saul.

June 12

DAILY READING

The heavens declare the glory of God; the skies proclaim the work of his hands. Day after day they pour forth speech; night after night they display knowledge. (PS 19:1–2)

FEAST DAYS

1248	Placid	Cistercian monk
1479	John of Sahagun	Patron of Salamanca, Spain
1835	Gaspar Bertoni	Founder of the Stigmatines

ENTRANCE AND EXIT

b. 1819	Charles Kingsley	English writer
b. 1924	George Herbert Walker Bush	41st American president
b. 1929	Anne Frank	Nazi victim
d. 1963	Medgar Evers	American civil rights leader
d. 1982	Dame Marie Rambert	English ballet dancer
d. 2003	Gregory Peck	American actor

Charles Kingsley

Victorian novelist, Christian Socialist, poet, and amateur naturalist Charles Kingsley (1819–75) grew up in Bristol and graduated from Magdalene College, Cambridge, in 1838. In July 1839 he met Frances (Fanny) Grenfell, with whom he fell almost immediately in love. He took up Holy Orders in 1842 when he became curate of Eversley Church in Hampshire, which he served for the rest of his life.

Kingsley was a supporter of the Chartist movement that campaigned for better conditions for poor people and was instrumental in the formation of the Christian Socialist movement. Kingsley's lifelong interest was in improving the lot of common people.

Kingsley wrote many pamphlets and books promoting Christian Socialism and also wrote historical fiction, exposing the clash of Christianity with Greek culture, for example.

His most famous work was *The Water Babies*, which was serialized in *Macmillan's Magazine* 1862–63, then published in 1863. It is the story of Tom, a young boy who is a chimney sweep employed by the brutal bully Mr. Grimes. Falling down a chimney, Tom finds himself in the presence of a girl called Ellie. Her cleanliness and neatness makes Tom aware for the first time of his own dirty blackened body. He is chased out of Ellie's house and falls into the river, where he enters a magical underwater world and becomes a water-baby. Like Lewis Carroll's *Adventures in Wonderland* or T. H. White's *The Sword in the Stone*, this tale explores the possibilities of an alternative world following certain transformations. *The Water Babies* touches upon most of Kingsley's favorite themes: the working conditions of the poor; education; sanitation and public health; water pollution; and evolutionary theory. It remains a landmark children's tale depicting these serious issues in an entertaining way.

Anne Frank–Key Dates

June 12, 1929: Anne Frank is born in Frankfurt am Main.

March 1931: The Frank family moves to number 24 Ganghoferstrasse.

September 15, 1933: Otto Frank establishes the company Opekta-works.

February 1934: Anne Frank moves to Amsterdam.

Summer 1941: Anne and her older sister Margot attend the Jewish Lyceum in Amsterdam.

June 12, 1942: Anne Frank receives a diary for her thirteenth birthday.

July 6, 1942: The Frank family goes into hiding at the Secret Annex at number 263 Prinsengracht.

August 4, 1944: The people from the Secret Annex are discovered.

August 8, 1944: Transported to the concentration camp at Westerbork.

October 1944: Anne and Margot are taken to the concentration camp at Bergin-Belsen.

March 1945: Anne and Margot Frank die in Bergin-Belsen.

JUNE 13

DAILY READING

If you then, though you are evil, know how to give good gifts to your children, how much more will your Father in heaven give the Holy Spirit to those who ask for him. (LUKE 11:13)

FEAST DAYS

1138	Gerard of Clairvaux	Benedictine monk
1231	Anthony of Padua	Doctor of the Church
1839	Augustine of Huy	Vietnamese martyr

ENTRANCE AND EXIT

b. 1865	Walter Butler Yeats	Irish poet
b. 1893	Dorothy Leigh Sayers	English writer
b. 1937	Eleanor Holmes Norton	American writer
d. 323 BC	Alexander the Great	King of Macedonia
d. 1965	Martin Buber	German theologian
d. 1987	Geraldine Page	American actor

Dorothy Leigh Sayers

Dorothy L. Sayers (1893–1957), Catholic writer and creator of detective Lord Peter Wimsey, was born in Oxford and became one of the first women to receive a degree from Oxford University.

Her first novel, *Whose Body?* was published in 1923. It introduced the world to the educated and fanciful Lord Peter Wimsey, a complex, intriguing character, comic and lighthearted at times, but plagued with nightmares and nervous disorders from his service in World War I.

Sayers was enchanted with Wimsey, although she herself had an unhappy romance in the early 1920s and had a child in 1924. Two years later, she married Scottish journalist Oswald Atherton Fleming, who became an invalid not long afterward. With G. K. Chesteron, Sayers founded the Detection Club, a group of mystery writers. She edited an important anthology called *Great Short Stories of Detection, Mystery and Horrors* from 1928 to 1934. She numbered among her friends T. S. Eliot and C. S. Lewis.

After the late 1930s, she grew tired of detective fiction, and returned to her academic roots, writing scholarly treatises on aesthetics and theology, as well as translations of Dante. Sayers died on December 17, 1957.

Christ the Companion

When I've thrown my books aside, being petulant and weary,
And have turned down the gas, and the firelight has sufficed,
When my brain's too stiff for prayer, and too indolent for theory,
Will You come and play with me, big Brother Christ?

Will You slip behind the book-case? Will you stir the window-curtain,
Peeping from the shadow with Your eyes like flame?
Set me staring at the alcove where the flicker's so uncertain,
Then suddenly, at my elbow, leap up, catch me, call my name?

Or take the great arm-chair, help me set the chestnuts roasting,
And tell me quiet stories, while the brown skins pop,
Of wayfarers and merchantmen and tramp of Roman hosting,
And how Joseph dwelt with Mary in the carpenter's shop?

When I drift away in dozing, will You softly light the candles
And touch the piano with Your kind, strong fingers,
Set stern fugues of Bach and stately themes of Handel's
Stalking through the corners where the last disquiet lingers?

And when we say good-night, and You kiss me on the landing,
Will You promise faithfully and make a solemn tryst:
You'll be just at hand if wanted, close by here where we are standing,
And be down in time for breakfast, big Brother Christ?

–Dorothy L. Sayers

June 14

DAILY READING

Our citizenship is in heaven. And we eagerly await a Savior from there, the Lord Jesus Christ. (PHIL 3:20)

FEAST DAYS

853	Felix	Spanish martyr
866	Joseph the Hymnographer	Bishop of Salonica, Greece
ca. 870	Caeran the Devout	Irish monk

ENTRANCE AND EXIT

b. 1928	Che Guevara	Argentine revolutionary leader
b. 1946	Donald Trump	American tycoon
b. 1969	Steffi Graf	German tennis star
d. 1594	Orlando di Lasso	German composer
d. 1946	John Logie Baird	Scottish inventor
d. 1986	Jorge Luis Borges	Argentine writer

National Flag Day—America

On this day in 1777, the Continental Congress "resolved, that the flag of the thirteen United States be thirteen stripes, alternate red and white: That the union be thirteen stars, white in a blue field, representing a new constellation." Because the resolution was not specific, there were a number of variations of the thirteen-star flag.

The national flag, which became known as the "Stars and Stripes," was based on the "Grand Union" flag, a banner carried by the Continental Army in 1776 that also consisted of thirteen red and white stripes. Historians dispute whether the story of Philadelphia seamstress Betty Ross designing the U.S. flag is true or a myth.

With the entrance of new states into the United States after independence, new stripes and stars were added to represent these additions to the Union. However, in 1818, Congress enacted a law stipulating that the thirteen original stripes be restored, and only stars be added to represent new states. On June 14, 1877, the first Flag Day observance was held on the hundredth anniversary of the adoption of the Stars and Stripes. As instructed by Congress, the U.S. flag was flown from all public buildings across the country.

Flag Day—the anniversary of the Flag Resolution of 1777—was officially established by the proclamation of President Woodrow Wilson on May 30, 1916. While Flag Day was celebrated in various communities for years after Wilson's proclamation, it was not until August 3, 1949, that President Truman signed an Act of Congress designating June 14 of each year as National Flag Day.

Many communities across America celebrate Flag Day with official ceremonies and parades, sports events, and lectures on the history of the American flag.

American Pledge of Allegiance

I Pledge Allegiance to the flag of the United States of America
and to the Republic for which it stands,
one Nation under God,
indivisible, with liberty and justice for all.

—*Francis Bellamy*
(see September 8 entry)

June 15

DAILY READING

The father of a righteous man has great joy;
he who has a wise son delights in him. (PROV 23:24)

FEAST DAYS

ca. 303	Vitus	Patron of dancers
1053	Bardo	Archbishop of Mainz, Germany
1827	Yolanda	Daughter of Bela IV, King of Hungary

ENTRANCE AND EXIT

b. 1843	Edvard Grieg	Norwegian composer
b. 1937	Waylon Jennings	American singer
b. 1941	Harry Nilsson	American singer
d. 1849	James Polk	11th American president
d. 1885	Rosalio de Castro	Spanish writer
d. 1966	Ella Fitzgerald	American singer

Magna Carta—The Charter of Liberties

> John, by the grace of God King of England, Lord of Ireland, Duke of Normandy and Aquitaine, and Count of Anjou, to his archbishops, bishops, abbots, earls, barons, justices, foresters, sheriffs, stewards, servants, and to all his officials and loyal subjects, Greeting.

Thus begins the Magna Carta, the Charter of Liberties agreed on this day in 1215 on the banks of the Thames at Runnymede meadow, England. The Magna Carta is a crucial document in England's history and probably the best known of all documents surviving from medieval England.

The Magna Carta came about because of a bargain struck between King John and the English barons who wanted to limit the king's oppressive power. This foundational agreement was granted because of a desire for reform, and wrung from a king whose position had been weakened by his disastrous campaigns in Flanders and France the year before. Historically, the Magna Carta can be understood only by reference to the turbulent history of the times in the context of a feudal system. King John tried to rescind the Magna Carta by seeking annulment from Pope Innocent III. However, both men died in the following year.

In 1216, the Great Charter's fate was in doubt, with a nine-year-old boy as the new king Henry III. Yet the Charter took root and was quickly reissued, again in 1217, and in its definitive 1225 version. When in 1258 the great men of the kingdom had grown impatient with Henry's incompetent rule, baronial reformers sought to revive the 1215 Charter's provision for a committee of barons to supervise the king. Among their reform proposals was a demand that Henry "faithfully keep and observe the charter of the liberties of England."

Some Provisions from the Magna Carta

Clause 1: The English Church shall be free, and shall have its rights undiminished, and its liberties unimpaired.

Clause 6: Heirs may be given in marriage, but not to someone of lower social standing. Before a marriage takes place, it shall be made known to the heir's next-of-kin.

Clause 8: No widow shall be compelled to marry, so long as she wishes to remain without a husband. But she must give security that she will not marry without royal consent, if she holds her lands of the Crown, or without the consent of whatever other lord she may hold them of.

Clause 16: No man shall be forced to perform more service for a knight's "fee," or other free holding of land, than is due from it.

Clause 35: There shall be standard measures of wine, ale, and corn (the London quarter), throughout the kingdom. There shall also be a standard width of dyed cloth, russett, and haberject, namely two ells within the selvedges. Weights are to be standardised similarly.

Clause 39: No free man shall be taken or imprisoned, or dispossessed or outlawed or exiled or in any way ruined, except by the lawful judgement of his peers or by the law of the land.

June 16

DAILY READING

Like as a father pitieth his children,
so the LORD pitieth them that fear him. (PS 103:13, KJV)

FEAST DAYS

551	Aurelian the Sinner	Bishop of Arles, France
ca. 6th cent.	Curig	Bishop of Llanbadarn, Wales
1106	Benno	Patron of anglers

ENTRANCE AND EXIT

b. 1890	Stan Laurel	English actor
b. 1937	Erich Segal	American writer
b. 1938	Joyce Carol Oates	American writer
d. 1722	John Churchill	1st Duke of Marlborough
d. 1958	Imre Nagy	Hungarian prime minister
d. 1977	Wernher von Braun	German scientist

Bloomsday

Since 1954, fans of James Joyce (Gaelic: *Seamus Seoighe*) have designated this day as Bloomsday, in honor of the protagonist, Leopold Bloom in Joyce's masterpiece *Ulysses*, published in Paris in 1922.

Bloomsday is a national holiday in Ireland and activities include academic conferences, public readings from *Ulysses*, guided journeys around the book's locations, and celebrations to mark one of Dublin's most gifted sons. Bloomsday is also celebrated throughout the world with street festivals, Irish food and music, and public readings.

James Joyce (1882–1941) was the eldest of ten children, born into a poor family. He was educated at University College, Dublin, and was a noted autodidact. *Ulysses* was written during the period of World War I and was serialized in the American journal *Little Review*. The whole novel takes place on June 16, 1904, the day Joyce met and fell in love with Nora Barnacle.

Ulysses was banned in America shortly after it began appearing in *Little Review* because it was considered obscene. The ban wasn't lifted until 1933.

In *Ulysses*, Joyce used a revolutionary stream of consciousness style coupled with parody, jokes, and virtually every other literary technique to present his characters. He used the framework of Homer's *Odyssey* to chart the journey of Leopold Bloom through explores various areas of Dublin life, dwelling on its squalor and monotony. *Ulysses* remains one of the most challenging books in world literature, and its multifaceted, kaleidoscopic presentation of philosophical themes, structures, history, and styles continues to fascinate and exasperate in equal measure.

Noteworthy

1567 Mary, Queen of Scots, was imprisoned in Lochleven Castle in Scotland.

1897 The United States signed a treaty of annexation with Hawaii.

1963 The first female space traveler, Valentina Tereshkova, was launched into orbit aboard Vostok 6.

1992 Former Defense Secretary Caspar Weinberger was indicted on felony charges in the Iran-Contra affair.

2000 Empress dowager Nagako, widow of Japan's Emperor Hirohito, died in Tokyo at age ninety-seven.

2004 The independent commission investigating the September 11, 2001, attacks said no evidence existed that al-Qaida had strong ties to Saddam Hussein.

2005 European Union leaders put on hold plans to unite their twenty-five nations under a single constitution.

June 17

DAILY READING

Sing to God, sing praise to his name, extol him who rides on the clouds—his name is the LORD*—and rejoice before him. A father to the fatherless, a defender of widows, is God in his holy dwelling.* (PS 68:4–5)

FEAST DAYS

ca. 610	Botolph	Patron of Huntingdonshire, England
1250	Teresa of Portugal	Cistercian nun
1697	Gregorio Barbarigo	Bishop of Padua, Italy

ENTRANCE AND EXIT

b. 1703	John Wesley	English evangelist
b. 1882	Igor Stravinsky	Russian composer
b. 1946	Barry Manilow	American singer
d. 1719	Joseph Addison	English politician
d. 1999	Basil Hume	English cardinal
d. 2001	Thomas Winning	Scottish cardinal

John Wesley

John Wesley (1703–91), the founder of Methodism, was the son of a Church of England clergyman. Being in London on May 24, 1738, he went "very unwillingly" to a meeting in Aldersgate Street. Listening to the preacher expound from the Epistle to the Romans, "at about a quarter before nine o'clock," light flashed upon his mind, and he was converted. Until that evening, he used to say, that although a teacher of others, he had never known real faith.

Wesley followed the example of George Whitefield, and he dedicated his life to open air preaching. His early efforts were directed to supplement the services of the Church of England, but gradually he superseded them.

For fifty years he rose at four in the morning, summer and winter, and was accustomed to preaching a sermon at five, an exercise he esteemed "the healthiest in the world." This early devotion, he said, "is the glory of the Methodists. Whenever they drop it they will dwindle away to nothing." Traveling did not suspend his industry. "Though I am always in haste," he says of himself, "I am never in a hurry, because I never undertake any more work than I can go through with perfect calmness of spirit. On other days, I never spend less than three hours, and frequently ten or twelve, alone." In this way he found time to read much and to write voluminously. In eating and drinking he was very abstemious. Suppers he abhorred, and sometimes for years he never tasted animal food. Once for three or four years he lived almost exclusively on potatoes.

He built chapels, organized a ministry and worship, allowed laymen to preach, and at last found himself at the head of a great and independent religious community, which in 1790 numbered 76,000 in Great Britain and 57,000 in America.

Barry Manilow International Fan Club —Top Ten Songs

1. "Even Now"
2. "Mandy"
3. "Weekend in New England"
4. "Could It Be Magic?"
5. "Copacabana (at the Copa)"
6. "Somewhere in the Night"
7. "I Write the Songs"
8. "Looks Like We Made It"
9. "This One's for You"
10. "Can't Smile without You"

JUNE 18

DAILY READING

Fathers, do not exasperate your children; instead, bring them up in the training and instruction of the Lord. (EPH 6:4)

FEAST DAYS

373	Ephrem the Syrian	Church father
ca. 940	Guy	Benedictine monk
1164	Elisabeth of Schonau	Abess

ENTRANCE AND EXIT

b. 1901	Anastasia Romanov	Russian duchess
b. 1915	Red Adair	American engineer
b. 1942	Paul McCartney	English pop star
d. 1835	William Cobbett	English writer
d. 1936	Maxim Gorky	Russian writer
d. 1959	Ethel Barrymore	American actor

Second Anglo-American War

On this day in 1812, President James Madison signed a declaration of war against Great Britain. This declaration was a response to the British economic blockade of France, the induction of American seaman into the British Royal Navy against their will, and the British support of hostile Indian tribes along the Great Lakes frontier.

A faction of Congress, known as the "War Hawks," had been advocating war with Britain for several years, and had not hidden their hopes that a U.S. invasion of Canada might result in significant territorial land gains for the United States. In the months after President Madison proclaimed the state of war, American forces launched a three-point invasion of Canada, all of which were decisively unsuccessful.

In 1814, with Napoleon Bonaparte's French Empire collapsing, the British were able to allocate more military resources to the American war, and in August, Washington, D.C., fell to the British troops, who burned the White House. However, in September of that same year, Thomas Macdonough's American naval force won an impressive victory at the Battle of Plattsburg Bay on Lake Champlain, forcing the invading British army to retreat into Canada. The American victory led to peace negotiations in Ghent, Belgium, and on December 24, 1814, the Treaty of Ghent was signed, formally ending the War of 1812.

By the terms of the agreement, all conquered territory was to be returned, and a commission would be established to settle the boundary of the U.S. and Canada.

Noteworthy

1429 Battle of Patay—major victory of French led by Joan of Arc over English in Hundred Years War.

1744 First recorded cricket match in England; Kent beat England team by one wicket at Finsbury, London.

1815 Napoleon defeated at Waterloo by Duke of Wellington.

1928 Amelia Earhart became first woman to fly Atlantic Ocean.

1953 Egypt became a republic.

1970 Edward Heath elected British prime minister.

1983 Sally Ride, aboard the space shuttle *Challenger*, became first U.S. woman astronaut launched into space.

June 19

DAILY READING

Husbands, love your wives, just as Christ loved the church and gave himself up for her to make her holy. (EPH 5:25–26)

FEAST DAYS

ca. 1st cent.	Jude Thaddeus	Brother of St. James the Lesser
559	Innocent	Bishop of Le Mans, France
ca. 827	Hildegrin	Benedictine nun

ENTRANCE AND EXIT

b. 1566	James I (VI of Scotland)	King of England
b. 1861	Earl Haig	Scottish general
b. 1947	Salman Rushdie	Indian writer
d. 1937	Sir James Matthew Barrie	Scottish writer
d. 1991	Jean Arthur	American actor
d. 1993	Sir William Gerald Golding	English writer

The Statue of Liberty

The Statue of Liberty arrived in New York harbor on this day in 1885. It was a gift of friendship from the people of France to the people of the United States. Originally known as "Liberty Enlightening the World," the statue was proposed in 1865 by French historian Edouard Laboulaye, chairman of an antislavery society, to commemorate the Franco-American alliance during the U.S. War of Independence.

The Statue of Liberty was the creation of French sculptor Frederic Auguste Bartholdi. The 46-meter statue is in the form of a woman with an uplifted arm holding a torch.

On the 1877, the anniversary of the birthday of George Washington, the U.S. Congress approved the use of a site on Bedloe's Island suggested by Bartholdi. In May of 1884, the statue was completed in France; three months later the cornerstone for its pedestal was laid in New York. The Statue of Liberty was packed in 214 packing cases. Its copper sheets were reassembled, and the last rivet of the monument was driven in on October 28, 1886, during a dedication ceremony attended by U.S. President Grover Cleveland.

In 1903, on the pedestal were inscribed lines from "The New Colossus," a famous sonnet by American poet Emma Lazarus that welcomed immigrants to the United States with this declaration:

> Give me your tired, your poor,
> Your huddled masses yearning to breathe free,
> The wretched refuse of your teeming shore.
> Send these, the homeless, tempest-tossed
> to me.
> I lift my lamp beside the golden door.

In 1892, Ellis Island, next to Bedloe's Island, opened as the chief entry station for immigrants to the United States. For the next thirty-two years, more than twelve million immigrants were welcomed into New York harbor by "Lady Liberty." In 1924, the Statue of Liberty was made a national monument.

Books by William Golding

The Double Tongue (1995)

Fire Down Below (1989)

Close Quarters (1987)

A Moving Target (1984)

Rites of Passage (1980)

Darkness Visible (1979)

The Pyramid (1967)

The Spire (1964)

Free Fall (1959)

Brass Butterfly (1958)

Pincher Martin (1956)

The Inheritors (1955)

Lord of the Flies (1954)

Recognition:

1979 Winner–James Tait Black Memorial Prize for Fiction–*Darkness Visible*

1980–Booker Prize–*Rites of Passage*

1983–Nobel Laureate–Nobel Prize in Literature

JUNE 20

DAILY READING

What good is it for a man to gain the whole world, yet forfeit his very soul? (MARK 8:36)

FEAST DAYS

ca. 304	Alban	First British martyr
ca. 6th cent.	Govan	Welsh hermit
537	Silverius	Pope

ENTRANCE AND EXIT

b. 1819	Jacques Offenbach	French composer
b. 1909	Errol Flynn	American actor
b. 1967	Nicole Kidman	Australian actor
d. 1837	William IV	English king
d. 1923	Pancho Villa	Mexican revolutionary leader
d. 1947	Benjamin "Bugsy" Siegel	American gangster

St. Alban

The first English martyr St. Alban lived in the Roman city of Verulamium (present day St. Albans in Hertfordshire). The Venerable Bede records that as a pagan, Alban gave shelter to Amphibalus, a Christian priest fleeing from persecution. Influenced by the priest's prayer and teaching, he became a Christian.

When the authorities discovered Amphibalus' hiding place, Alban exchanged clothes with him. The priest escaped, but Alban was bound and taken before the judge. The judge was furious at the deception, and ordered that Alban should receive the punishment due to the priest, if he had indeed become a Christian.

Alban declared his Christian faith, saying, "I worship and adore the true and living God, who created all things." Despite flogging he refused to sacrifice to the Roman gods and was sentenced to death.

He was brought out of the town, across the river and up a hill to the site of execution, where his head was cut off. According to legend, on the hill a spring of water miraculously appeared to give the martyr a drink. The legend also states that moved by St. Alban's witness, the original executioner refused to carry out the deed, and after his replacement had killed Alban, his eyes dropped out.

Bede records that "when the peace of Christian times was restored a beautiful church worthy of his martyrdom was built, where sick folk are healed and frequent miracles take place to this day" (about 760). In later years the church also contained the shrine of Amphibalus.

The Alban Prayer–St. Albans Cathedral, Hertfordshire

Almighty God,
We thank you for this place built to
your glory
and in memory of Alban, our first martyr:
Following his example in the fellowship
of the saints,
may we worship and adore the true and
living God,
and be faithful witnesses to the Christ,
who is alive and reigns, now and for ever.
AMEN

June 21

DAILY READING

He who dwells in the shelter of the Most High
will rest in the shadow of the Almighty. (PS 91:1)

FEAST DAYS

ca. 1st cent.	Terence	Bishop of Iconium, Turkey
379	Eusebius	Bishop of Samosata, Syria
ca. 6th cent.	Aaron	Welsh hermit

ENTRANCE AND EXIT

b. 1639	Increase Mather	American theologian
b. 1905	Jean Paul Satre	French philosopher
b. 1948	Ian McEwan	Scottish writer
d. 1527	Niccolo Machiavelli	Italian politician
d. 1652	Inigo Jones	English architect
d. 1908	Nicolai Rimsky-Korsakov	Russian composer

Summer Solstice

In the Northern Hemisphere, this day marks the summer solstice: when the sun is at its most northern point in the sky, creating the longest day. The word "solstice" comes from the Latin *sol sistere,* meaning "sun stand still." The summer and winter solstices are the longest and shortest days of the year. The summer solstice should not be confused with Midsummer Day, which occurs on June 24. Because of the solstice, today is traditionally celebrated as the first "official" day of summer.

This was originally the day on which people celebrated midsummer. There is still a famous summer solstice celebration at Stonehenge, the ancient stone circle on Salisbury Plain in Wiltshire. A group of white-robed Druids gather at Stonehenge to watch the sun rising. As it comes up, the sun rises exactly over the Heel Stone, one of the stones that lie outside the main circle at Stonehenge.

Many famous poets have written poems about the sun. For example, here is a poem by Robert Louis Stevenson, called "The Summer Sun."

Great is the sun, and wide he goes
Through empty heaven without repose;
And in the blue and glowing days
More thick than rain he showers his rays.

Though closer still the blinds we pull
To keep the shady parlour cool,
Yet he will find a chink or two
To slip his golden fingers through.

Above the hills, along the blue,
Round the bright air with footing true,
To please the child, to paint the rose,
The gardener of the World, he goes.

Noteworthy

17 BC Hannibal wins Battle at Lake Trasimene in Italy–the third major battle of the Second Punic War.

1887 Queen Victoria's Golden Jubilee celebrated.

1788 The U.S. Constitution came into effect as New Hampshire became the ninth state to ratify it.

1977 Menachem Begin became Israel's sixth prime minister.

1989 Original script of *Citizen Kane* sold at a New York auction for a record $210,000.

1990 Worst earthquake ever in Northern Iran; 7.7 quake levels villages, killed 40,000, injured 60,000.

1997 The Women's National Basketball Association founded.

June 22

DAILY READING

The Lord will keep you from all harm—he will watch over your life; the Lord will watch over your coming and going both now and forevermore. (PS 121:7–8)

FEAST DAYS

1164	Eberhard	Archbishop of Salzburg, Austria
1535	Thomas More	Patron of Pensacola, Florida
1535	John Fisher	Patron of Rochester, New York

ENTRANCE AND EXIT

b. 1906	Samuel "Billy" Wilder	American film director
b. 1910	Sir John Hunt	English mountaineer
b. 1949	Meryl Streep	American actor
d. 1956	Walter de la Mare	English writer
d. 1965	David Selznick	American film producer
d. 1987	Fred Astaire	American actor and dancer

Third Ecumenical Council

On this day in 431, the Emperor Theodosius the Younger convened the Third Ecumenical Council, also known as the Council of Ephesus, since it was held in that city in Asia Minor. Over two hundred bishops came together to resolve a controversy that had divided the church into two main camps. Theodore of Mopsuestia, supported by Nestorius, Archbishop of Constantinople, held to what has become known as the Nestorian heresy. He taught that there were two separate persons in the Incarnate Christ, the one divine and the other human. The opposite camp was represented by Cyril, Archbishop of Alexandria, who taught that the Incarnate Christ was a single person, at once God and Man.

Theodosius believed that the strength of his empire depended upon true worship of God without the intermingling of falsehood. The council condemned the doctrines of Nestorius, because he overstated the human nature of Christ at the expense of the divine, teaching that the Virgin Mary gave birth to a man (Jesus Christ), and not God (the "Logos" and Son of God).

The council reiterated the orthodox teaching that Jesus Christ is one person, not two separate "people." The council decreed that Lord Jesus Christ, the Son of God is perfect God and perfect Man with a rational soul and body. The union of the two natures of Christ took place in such a fashion that one did not "confound" the other. After the Council, most of Theodore's works were burnt, but his teaching remained persuasive to many; indeed Nestorianism is alive and well to this very day.

Films Directed by Billy Wilder

Buddy Buddy (1981)
Fedora (1978)
The Front Page (1974)
Avanti! (1972)
The Private Life of Sherlock Holmes (1970)
The Fortune Cookie (1966)
Kiss Me, Stupid (1964)
Irma la Douce (1963)
The Apartment (1960)
Some Like It Hot (1959)
Witness for the Prosecution (1957)
Love in the Afternoon (1957)
The Spirit of St. Louis (1957)
The Seven Year Itch (1955)
Sabrina (1954)
Stalag 17 (1953)
Ace in the Hole (1951)
Sunset Blvd. (1950)
A Foreign Affair (1948)
The Emperor Waltz (1948)
The Lost Weekend (1945)
Death Mills (1945)
Double Indemnity (1944)
Five Graves to Cairo (1943)
The Major and the Minor (1942)
Mauvaise Graine (1934)

JUNE 23

DAILY READING

Those who hope in the Lord will renew their strength. They will soar on wings like eagles; they will run and not grow weary, they will walk and will not be faint. (ISA 40:31)

FEAST DAYS

ca. 262	Agrippina	Patron against storms
679	Ethelreda	Patron of Cambridge University
1976	Basil Hopko	Czech martyr

ENTRANCE AND EXIT

b. 1894	Edward VIII	King of England
b. 1912	Alan Turing	English mathematician
b. 1957	Frances McDormand	American actor
d. 1537	Pedro de Mendoza	Spanish explorer
d. 1995	Jonas Salk	American scientist
d. 1998	Maureen O'Sullivan	Irish actor

Vox Piscis—*Book Fish*

English Reformer and Protestant martyr John Frith (1503–33) was suspected of heresy and imprisoned in Oxford in 1532. He was a follower of Martin Luther and Desiderius Erasmus. He was also a close associate of William Tyndale, the first person to translate the Bible into English. It was a time of immense social and religious upheaval in Europe.

Frith's great crime had been to distribute contraband Protestant books. He was confined in a fish storage cellar in Oxford, where the overpowering stench of fish had caused a few fellow prisoners to die. He was later moved to a tower and then burned alive at the stake. During his time in prison, Frith wrote a theological book that has been the center of one of the strangest mysteries known to the literary world.

On Midsummer Eve in 1626 in the market place in Cambridge, a fishmonger was gutting a fish and discovered a small book in the stomach of the fish. The cover and a few pages had been partially digested by the fish, but the middle section of the book was still intact. The book turned out to be the theological work Firth had written whilst in prison. It is unknown how the lost book got inside the fish's stomach. Some believe the book was thrown from the tower into a river, where it lay dormant for over one hundred years before being swallowed by the cod. An eyewitness wrote:

> I saw all with mine own eyes, the fish, the maw, the piece of sail-cloth, the book, and observed all I have written; only I saw not the opening of the fish, which not many did, being upon the fish-woman's stall in the market, who first cut off his head, to which the maw hanging, and seeming much stuffed with somewhat, it was searched, and all found as aforesaid.

The book was reprinted in 1627 by Cambridge University, amidst much attention from academics and clergy. The preface was written by Thomas Goad, a Cambridge graduate and chaplain to Archbishop George Abbot.

Noteworthy

1683 William Penn signs peace treaty with Indians.
1793 French Revolution begins.
1845 Republic of Texas annexed by United States.
1868 Typewriter patented by Christopher Latham Sholes.
1951 British spies Donald McLean and Guy Burgess flee to USSR.
1956 Gen. Gamal Abdel Nasser elected president of Egypt.
1993 Dr. Andrew Wiles proves 350-year-old Fermat's Last Theorem.

JUNE 24

DAILY READING

The Lord is faithful, and he will strengthen and protect you from the evil one. (2 THESS 3:3)

FEAST DAYS

ca. 30	John the Baptist	Jewish prophet
ca. 880	Henry	Benedictine monk
1193	Bartholomew	Patron of Farne, Northumbria

ENTRANCE AND EXIT

b. 1842	Ambrose Bierce	American writer
b. 1895	Jack Dempsey	American boxer
b. 1915	Sir Frederick Hoyle	English astronomer
d. 79	Vespasian	Roman Emperor
d. 1908	Grover Cleveland	22nd and 24th American president
d. 1987	Jackie Gleason	American actor

Midsummer Day

On this day, the Catholic Church celebrates the Nativity of John the Baptist as a Solemnity, the highest degree for a religious festival. Midsummer Day is celebrated by many nations. For example, in Seattle, America, there is a large Summer Solstice Parade, which in recent years has included painted naked cyclists.

In Great Britain, since the thirteenth century, Midsummer Day was celebrated with the lighting of bonfires, feasting, and merrymaking. This was dropped after the Reformation, but persisted in rural areas up until the nineteenth century before petering out. The Chester Midsummer Watch Parade and Chester Mystery Plays were performed until 1675.

In Denmark, this was the day when medieval wise men and women would gather special herbs that they needed for the rest of the year to cure people. It has been celebrated since the times of the Vikings by visiting healing water sources and making a large bonfire to ward away evil spirits.

In Italy, the feast of St. John the Baptist has been celebrated in Florence from medieval times, with festivals sometimes lasting the three days from June 21 to 24. St. John the Baptist is the patron saint of Florence.

In Sweden, Midsummer Day is the most important holiday of the year, and one of the most uniquely Swedish in the way it is celebrated, even if it has been influenced by other countries long ago. Traditional events include raising and dancing around a huge maypole, and eating the year's first potatoes, pickled herring, sour cream, and possibly the first strawberries of the season. Drinking songs are also important at this feast, and many drink heavily.

A Midsummer Night's Dream *—Famous Lines*

"The course of true love never did run smooth." (act 1, scene 1)

"Love looks not with the eyes, but with the mind, and therefore is winged Cupid painted blind." (act 1, scene 1)

"That would hang us, every mother's son." (act 1, scene 2)

"I'll put a girdle round about the earth in forty minutes." (act 2, scene 1)

"My heart is true as steel." (act 2, scene 1)

"The true beginning of our end." (act 5, scene 1)

—William Shakespeare

JUNE 25

DAILY READING

"Can anyone hide in secret places so that I cannot see them?"
declares the L*ORD.* *"Do not I fill heaven and earth?"*
declares the L*ORD.* (JER 23:24)

FEAST DAYS

460	Prosper	Secretary to Pope Leo the Great
1150	Henry Zdick	Bohemian prince
1391	Guy Marmaladi	Grand Inquisitor

ENTRANCE AND EXIT

b. 1796	Nicholas I	Russian czar
b. 1852	Antonio Gaudi	Spanish architect
b. 1924	Sidney Lumet	American film director
d. 1897	Margaret Oliphant	Scottish writer
d. 1908	Stanford White	American architect
d. 2003	Lester Maddox	American politician

Eliphalet Nott

The educator and clergyman Eliphalet Nott (1773–1866) was born in Ashford, Connecticut, but was left a poor orphan while still a child. He overcame this misfortune by applying himself rigorously to education, although his only collegiate education consisted of a period of less than a year at Brown University. He passed all the baccalaureate examinations and gained an honorary Master of Arts degree.

In 1804 he became the fourth president of Union College in Schenetady, New York, where he served for the rest of his life. He was also president of Rensselaer Polytechnic from 1829 to1845. He found Union College to be very low on funds but succeeded in placing it on a sound financial footing. He amassed a large fortune through patents on his heating inventions, including a stove that burned anthracite coal. Having rehabilitated Union College by raising lottery funds, Nott bequeathed $550,000 of his fortune to that institution. In 1845 Nott introduced the first college course in civil engineering.

A supporter of the temperance movement, Nott's publications include *Counsels to Young Men* (1810) and *Lectures on Temperance* (1847).

Nott's sixty-two-year term set a record for American college presidencies. At Union College, he is remembered by the Nott Memorial, a sixteen-sided building located on the center of the quad. A popular tradition (regarded as an "unofficial graduation requirement") among students at Union is the "Naked Nott Run," which involves streaking a full circuit around the Nott Memorial.

Noteworthy

1788 Virginia becomes tenth of original thirteen states to ratify Constitution and be admitted to the Union.
1867 Barbed wire patented.
1876 Custer's last stand in Battle of Little Bighorn, Montana.
1910 Igor Stravinsky's ballet score for *The Firebird* first performed at Paris Opera.
1917 Thirty thousand American troops land in northwest France in World War I.
1950 North Korea invades South Korea.
1967 Beatles sing "All You Need Is Love" to 350 million viewers in 26 countries.
1981 Microsoft incorporated by Bill Gates and Paul Allen.
1991 Croatia and Slovenia declare independence from Yugoslavia.
1993 Kim Campbell becomes first female prime minister of Canada.

June 26

DAILY READING

Do not seek revenge or bear a grudge against one of your people, but love your neighbor as yourself. I am the Lord. (LEV 19:18)

FEAST DAYS

ca. 800	John	Bishop of the Goths, Russia
1941	Andrij Ishcak	Russian martyr
1975	Josemaria Escrivra	Founder of Opus Dei

ENTRANCE AND EXIT

b. 1824	William Thompson (Lord Kelvin)	Scottish scientist
b. 1898	Wilhelm Messerschmitt	German engineer
b. 1970	Chris O'Donnell	American actor
d. 363	Julian the Apostate	Roman Emperor
d. 1793	Rev. Gilbert White	English naturalist
d. 1939	Ford Maddox Ford	English writer

The Reverend Gilbert White

The Reverend Gilbert White (1720–93), author of the world-famous *Natural History and Antiquities of Selborne* (1789), was a pioneering naturalist, who recorded his observations of nature drawn from life, rather than from knowledge gained from dead specimens. His own notes were supplemented by an exchange of letters with Thomas Pennant and Daines Barrington, two friends who were also naturalists.

Gilbert White took holy orders in 1747, and became curate of his hometown of Selborne in 1756. Selborne was a village of one straggling street, about fifty miles from London, situated in a corner of Hampshire, bordering on Sussex.

His careful studies from 1765 covered a wide range of natural history subjects around the parish. He detailed the flora, and the habits and lives of the local mammals, birds, and insects.

His book is one of the most popular books in the English language. The exact, but engagingly written, scientific descriptions of the commonplace creatures of the English countryside appealed to generations of homesick administrators of the British Empire.

White's meticulous studies yielded many discoveries. For example, in 1767 he noticed that the harvest mouse (*Micromys minutes*), the smallest European mouse, with a body only two inches long, was a different species from other mice. In a letter to Thomas Pennant he wrote, "I have procured some of the mice mentioned in my former letters, a young one and a female with young, both of which I have preserved in brandy. From the colour, shape, size, and manner of nesting, I make no doubt but that the species is nondescript [not known to science]."

United Nations Charter

On June 26, 1945, the fifty member nations agreed the Charter of the United Nations. The preamble is given below:

> WE THE PEOPLES OF THE UNITED NATIONS DETERMINED to save succeeding generations from the scourge of war, which twice in our lifetime has brought untold sorrow to mankind, and to reaffirm faith in fundamental human rights, in the dignity and worth of the human person, in the equal rights of men and women and of nations large and small, and to establish conditions under which justice and respect for the obligations arising from treaties and other sources of international law can be maintained, and to promote social progress and better standards of life in larger freedom, AND FOR THESE ENDS to practice tolerance and live together in peace with one another as good neighbours, and to unite our strength to maintain international peace and security, and to ensure, by the acceptance of principles and the institution of methods, that armed force shall not be used, save in the common interest, and to employ international machinery for the promotion of the economic and social advancement of all peoples, HAVE RESOLVED TO COMBINE OUR EFFORTS TO ACCOMPLISH THESE AIMS Accordingly, our respective Governments, through representatives assembled in the city of San Francisco, who have exhibited their full powers found to be in good and due form, have agreed to the present Charter of the United Nations and do hereby establish an international organization to be known as the United Nations.

JUNE 27

DAILY READING

Whoever wants to save his life will lose it,
but whoever loses his life for me will find it. (MATT 16:25)

FEAST DAYS

ca. 1st cent.	Crescens	Companion of St. Paul
ca. 1st cent.	Joanna the Myrrhbearer	Wife of Chusa, steward to King Herod Antipas
444	Cyril	Archbishop of Alexandria

ENTRANCE AND EXIT

b. 1818	James Lloyd Breck	American clergyman
b. 1880	Helen Adams Keller	American writer
b. 1955	Isabelle Adjani	French actor
d. 1844	Joseph Smith	American religious leader
d. 2001	Jack Lemmon	American actor
d. 2002	John Entwhistle	English rock star

James Lloyd Breck

James Lloyd Breck (1818–76) was a clergyman, missionary, and educator. He grew up in Philadelphia and graduated from Rev. Dr. Muhlenberg's Academy, Flushing, New York. In 1841, with two classmates, J. H. Hobart and William Adams, he came to Nashotah, Wisconsin, as a missionary. Under the direction of Bishop Jackson Kemper, the three men founded Nashotah House, a theological seminary located thirty miles west of Milwaukee.

The other seminary founded by Breck–Seabury, in Fairbault, Minnesota–is no longer there, but merged with Western Seminary in 1883 to become Seabury-Western Theological Seminary. Breck grew disenchanted with seminary life and, after establishing Seabury, he started a mission to the Chippewa people, that was eventually run by native priests.

In one of his letters to his mother, written in December 1842, he described his progress in bringing Christian teaching to Native Americans:

> Brother Adams and myself work four hours, except when we are teaching or doing Missionary labor. We must all work for our board. This is the only way in which they will feel that it is their duty to labor and study, and the only way in which our people will feel their duty to the Church, and to ourselves as the clergy of the same. We rise at 5am. Matins at 6. The Morning Service of the Church at 9. On Wednesdays and Fridays, the Litany at 12. On Thursdays the Holy Eucharist at the same hour of 12. The Evening Service of the Church at 3, and Family Prayer or Vespers at 6:30 or 7 pm. Our students labor between 7 and 9 in the morning, and 1 and 3 in the afternoon.

Breck went on to establish a cathedral and a school named after him in Minneapolis. In 1867 he moved to California and at Bernicia founded the Missionary College of St. Augustine, and later St. Mary's of the Pacific, a school for girls.

Helen Keller Quotes

Helen Keller was deaf and blind from infancy due to a severe illness. She overcame these barriers to become an accomplished student, campaigner, and educator for the disabled. Her life remains an inspiration to many people today. Here are some quotes from Helen Keller that give a glimpse into her character:

"All the world is full of suffering. It is also full of overcoming."

"As selfishness and complaint pervert the mind, so love with its joy clears and sharpens the vision."

"Character cannot be developed in ease and quiet. Only through experience of trial and suffering can the soul be strengthened, ambition inspired, and success achieved."

"Faith is the strength by which a shattered world shall emerge into the light."

"I can see, and that is why I can be happy, in what you call the dark, but which to me is golden. I can see a God-made world, not a manmade world."

"I long to accomplish a great and noble task, but it is my chief duty to accomplish small tasks as if they were great and noble."

"It is a terrible thing to see and have no vision."

June 28

DAILY READING

The Lord is not slow in keeping his promise, as some understand slowness. He is patient with you, not wanting anyone to perish, but everyone to come to repentance. (2 PET 3:9)

FEAST DAYS

ca. 202	Irenaus	Bishop of Lyons, France
1654	John Southworth	Catholic martyr
1847	Catherine Gerosa	Founder of the Sisters of Charity of Lovere

ENTRANCE AND EXIT

b. 1577	Peter Paul Rubens	Flemish artist
b. 1712	Jean Jacques Rousseau	French philosopher
b. 1926	Mel Brooks	American writer
d. 1836	James Madison	4th American president
d. 1889	Maria Mitchell	American astronomer
d. 1975	Rod Serling	American writer

The Shot Heard around the World

On this day in 1914 at around 10 a.m. on Franz Joseph Street in Sarajeve, a Bosnian-Serb called Gavrilo Princip (1894–1918) fired a shot that killed Archduke Franz Ferdinand and his wife, Sophie. In doing so, he set in motion the wheels of the First World War. Princip was a member of the Serbian Black Hand partisan academy and had been recruited in 1912, along with two others–Nedjelko Cabrinovic and Danilo Ilic–to carry out the assassination.

After the shooting, Princip was arrested but during interrogation gave few details about the Black Hand organization. While some of the defendants expressed remorse over their crime, Princip maintained his silence about the Black Hand with a stoic detachment. His final statement in court was short: "In trying to insinuate that someone else has instigated the assassination, one strays from the truth. The idea arose in our own minds, and we ourselves executed it. We have loved the people. I have nothing to say in my defense."

Princip was found guilty. Whether he would receive the death penalty or a prison term hinged on his exact birthday. One account had him turn twenty days before the crime, another that he turned twenty a few days after. The court gave Princip the benefit of the doubt, and sentenced him to twenty years in prison. He died in the hospital of Theresienstadt prison on April 28, 1918, from tuberculosis of the bone.

Within a month of the assassination of the Archduke, France, Great Britain, Belgium, Germany, Austria, and Turkey were at war. By the end of the conflict, dozens of nations would be at war with some ten million soldiers dead and twenty-one million more wounded. Five years later, on June 28, 1919, Germany and the Allies signed the Treaty of Versailles, formally ending the war and providing for the creation of the League of Nations.

Noteworthy

1687 William Phipps is first American knighted by King James II.
1838 Queen Victoria's coronation at Westminster Abbey, London.
1910 First zeppelin airliner crashes.
1967 After Six Day War, Jerusalem reunited under Israeli control.

June 29

DAILY READING

The LORD *will fulfill his purpose for me; your love, O* LORD, *endures forever—do not abandon the works of your hands.* (PS 138:8)

FEAST DAYS

ca. 67	Paul	Apostle to the Gentiles
ca. 67	Peter	Apostle to the Jews
ca. 380	Syrus	Bishop of Genoa, Italy

ENTRANCE AND EXIT

b. 1900	Antoine de Saint-Exupery	French writer
b. 1901	Nelson Eddy	American actor
b. 1941	Stokely Carmichael	American activist
d. 1852	Henry Clay	American secretary of state
d. 1861	Elizabeth Barrett Browning	English writer
d. 2003	Katherine Hepburn	American writer

St. Peter's Day and St. Paul's Day

In the Catholic Church, this Holy Day of Obligation commemorates the martyrdom of the two great apostles—St. Peter and St. Paul—assigned by tradition to the same day of June in the year 67. It is thought they had been imprisoned in the famous Mamertine Prison of Rome, and both had foreseen their approaching death. St. Peter was crucified; St. Paul, a Roman citizen, was slain by the sword.

The two apostles share another feast—the Feast of the Dedication of the Basilicas of Peter and Paul on November 18.

Peter, the chief of the apostles was a Galilean fisherman, called to be an apostle by Jesus. Although an unlearned man, Peter was candid, eager, and loving. In his heart, first of all, his conviction grew, and then from his lips came the spontaneous confession: "Thou art the Christ, the Son of the living God!" Although he failed the Lord by denying him three times, Jesus commanded him to be a good shepherd of his flock. The New Testament contains many references to St. Peter—he is mentioned over 160 times. But it is after Pentecost that he stands out in the full grandeur of his office. He sees to the replacement of the fallen disciple; he admits the Jews by thousands into the fold; and in the person of Cornelius, opens it to the Gentiles.

Paul, whose father was Roman and mother Jewish, was a native of Tarsus in Cilicia. A Pharisee from the tribe of Benjamin, Paul had great claims to be a "Hebrew of the Hebrews." His famous conversion on the Damascus road transformed his mission from persecuting Christians to becoming one of Christianity's most powerful missionaries. He made at least three missionary journeys in a twelve-year period (45–57) from Antioch to Jerusalem to start churches and establish sound doctrine. Although he sought the conversion of Jews, they rejected him, so Paul presented the gospel to the Gentiles. The Acts of the Apostles gives a detailed account of his efforts throughout Asia Minor.

Popular Nelson Eddy Movies

The Girl of the Golden West (1938)
Sweethearts (1938)
Let Freedom Ring (1939)
Balalaika (1939)
New Moon (1940)
The Chocolate Soldier (1941)
I Married an Angel (1942)
Phantom of the Opera (1943)
Willie the Operatic Whale (1946)
Northwest Outpost (1947)
The Desert Song (1955)

*J*UNE 30

DAILY READING

The L*ORD will be king over the whole earth.*
On that day there will be one L*ORD,*
and his name the only name. (ZECH 14:9)

FEAST DAYS

623	Bertrand	Bishop of Le Mans, France
ca. 718	Erentude	Benedictine nun
1066	Theobald	Camaldolese monk

ENTRANCE AND EXIT

b. 1792	Thomas Edmondson	English inventor
b. 1817	John Hooker	English botanist
b. 1966	Mike Tyson	American boxer
d. 1660	William Oughtred	English mathematician
d. 1966	Margery Allingham	English writer
d. 1973	Nancy Mitford	English writer

William Oughtred

English clergyman and mathematician William Oughtred (1575–1660) is recognised as the inventor of the slide rule in 1622. He is also credited as introducing the "x" symbol for multiplication as well as the abbreviations "sin" and "cos" for the sine and cosine functions.

Oughtred attended his local school, Eton, and from there went to King's College, Cambridge. Although very little mathematics was taught at either institution, Oughtred was passionate about numbers, as is evident from his diary entry from this day in 1593, "the time which over and above those usuall studies I employed upon the mathematicall sciences I redeemed night by night from my naturall sleep, defrauding my body, and inuring it to watching, cold, and labour, while most others tooke their rest."

Oughtred was ordained in 1603 and became the rector of Albury, near Guildford in Surrey. In 1628 he was appointed by the Earl of Arundel to instruct his son in mathematics.

His most famous work is *Clavis Mathematicae* (*The Key to Mathematics*), published in 1631. Like all Oughtred's works, it was very condensed, containing only eighty-eight pages. It included a description of Hindu-Arabic notation and decimal fractions and a considerable section on algebra.

In 1622, Oughtred produced his first slide, an instrument that plotted a logarithmic scale along a single, straight two-foot-long stick. He added and subtracted lengths by using a pair of dividers, operations that were equivalent to multiplying and dividing.

He corresponded with some of the most eminent scholars of his time on mathematical subjects, and his house was generally full of pupils from all quarters. It is said that he died in 1660 in a sudden fit of excitement upon hearing the news of the vote at Westminster for the restoration of Charles II.

Noteworthy

1859 French acrobat Blondin crossed Niagara Falls on a tightrope as 5,000 spectators watched.

1934 Adolf Hitler began his "blood purge" of political and military leaders in Germany.

1936 The novel *Gone with the Wind*, by Margaret Mitchell, was published.

1963 Pope Paul VI was crowned the 262nd head of the Roman Catholic Church.

1971 Three Soviet cosmonauts aboard Soyuz 11 were found dead inside their spacecraft after it returned to Earth.

2004 The international Cassini spacecraft entered Saturn's orbit after a nearly seven-year journey.

Then came hot July, boiling like to fire,
That all his garments he had cast away.
Upon a lyon raging yet with ire
He boldly rode, and made him to obey:
(It was the beast that whilom did forray
The Nemæan forest, till the Amphitrionide
Him slew, and with his hide did him array:)
Behind his backe a sithe, and by his side
Under his belt he bore a sickle circling wide.

EDMUND SPENSER–*The Shepheardes Calender* (1579)

My emblem is the Lion, and I breathe
The breath of Libyan deserts o'er the land;
My sickle as a sabre I unsheathe,
And bent before me the pale harvests stand.
The lakes and rivers shrink at my command,
And there is thirst and fever in the air;
The sky is changed to brass, the earth to sand;
I am the Emperor whose name I bear.

HENRY WADSWORTH LONGFELLOW–*The Poet's Calendar* (1882)

July ~

According the Chamber's Book of Days (1869), 'July was originally the fifth month of the Roman year, and thence denominated Quintilis. In the Alban Calendar, it had a complement of thirty-six days. Romulus reduced it to thirty-one, and Numa to thirty days, and it stood thus for many centuries. At length, it was restored to thirty-one days by Julius Caesar, who felt a personal interest in it as his natal month. After the death of this great reformer of the calendar, Mark Antony changed the name to July, in honour of the family-name of Caesar. This month he selected for such honorary distinction, when the sun was generally most potent, the more effectually to denote that Julius was the emperor of the world, and therefore the appropriate leader of one-half of the year. Our Saxon ancestors called July 'Hey Monath', 'because therein they usually mowed and made their hay-harvest; and also 'Maed Monath', from the meads being then in their bloom'.

Proverbs ~

If the first of July, it be rainy weather,
'Twill rain, more or less, for four weeks
together.

Hot July brings cooling showers,
Apricots and gillyflowers.

Those who in July are wed,
Must labor for their daily bread.

Bow-wow dandy fly,
Brew no beer in July.

Shakespeare ~

BUCKINGHAM
Sir,
I am thankful to you; and I'll go along
By your prescription: but this top-proud fellow,
Whom from the flow of gall I name not but
From sincere motions, by intelligence,
And proofs as clear as founts in July when
We see each grain of gravel, I do know
To be corrupt and treasonous.

–*King Henry VIII*, Act 1, Scene 1

POLIXENES
If at home, sir,
He's all my exercise, my mirth, my matter,
Now my sworn friend and then mine enemy,
My parasite, my soldier, statesman, all:
He makes a July's day short as December,
And with his varying childness cures in me
Thoughts that would thick my blood.

–*Winter's Tale*, Act 1, Scene II

JULY 1

DAILY READING

By the grace given me I say to everyone of you: Do not think of yourself more highly than you ought, but rather think of yourself with sober judgment, in accordance with the measure of faith God has given you. (ROM 12:3)

FEAST DAYS

ca. 6th cent.	Servanus	Archbishop of West Fife, Scotland
1180	Bernard	Patron of Valencia, Spain
1784	Blessed Junipero Serra	Apostle of California

ENTRANCE AND EXIT

b. 1646	Gottfried Leibniz	Mathematician
b. 1872	Louis Bleriot	Pioneer aviator
b. 1906	Estée Lauder	Business woman
d. 1896	Harriet Beecher Stowe	Author
d. 1925	Erik Satie	French composer
d. 1997	Robert Mitchum	Actor

Gideons International

In 1898, John H. Nicholson of Janesville, Wisconsin, came to the Central Hotel at Boscobel, Wisconsin, for the night. The hotel being crowded, it was suggested that he take a bed in a double room with Samuel E. Hill of Beloit, Wisconsin. The two men soon discovered that both were Christians, and that John, as a twelve-year-old boy, had promised his dying mother that he would read God's Word and pray daily. It had been his custom for many years to read the Bible before retiring for the night. During their evening devotions, they became convinced of the need to form an association for Christian commercial travelers.

They called a meeting in Janesville, Wisconsin, on July 1, 1899, in the YMCA and established Gideons International. They chose the name Gideon after an Old Testament leader who, with a few chosen men, did a great work for God. Today, 150,000 Gideon members work in 179 countries placing a total of over 60 million copies of the Word of God annually, as well as witnessing personally for Christ. Internationally, over 1 billion Bibles have been presented.

Canada Day

As July 1st has been the National Day of Canada (or Dominion Day) since 1867, it seems appropriate to reproduce the Canadian National Anthem in that nation's two main languages, English and French:

English:
O Canada!
Our home and native land!
True patriot love in all thy sons command.
With glowing hearts we see thee rise,
The True North strong and free!
From far and wide, O Canada,
We stand on guard for thee.
God keep our land glorious and free!
O Canada, we stand on guard for thee.
O Canada, we stand on guard for thee.

Français:
Ô Canada!
Terre de nos aïeux,
Ton front est ceint de fleurons glorieux!
Car ton bras sait porter l'épée,
Il sait porter la croix!
Ton histoire est une épopée
Des plus brillants exploits.
Et ta valeur, de foi trempée,
Protégera nos foyers et nos droits,
Protégera nos foyers et nos droits.

July 2

DAILY READING

The heart is deceitful above all things and beyond cure. Who can understand it? "I the LORD search the heart and examine the mind, to reward a man according to his conduct, according to what his deeds deserve." (JER 17:9–10)

FEAST DAYS

ca. 570	St. Monegundis	Hermit of Tours, France
1139	St. Otho	Bishop of Bamberg, Germany
1489	Thomas Cranmer	Archbishop of Canterbury

ENTRANCE AND EXIT

b. 1724	Frederick Klopstock	German poet
b. 1877	Hermann Hesse	Author
b. 1947	Larry David	Writer and comedian
d. 1566	Michael Nostradamus	Mystic physician
d. 1591	Robert "Old" Scarlett	Sexton of Peterborough Cathedral
d. 1997	James Stewart	Actor

"Old Scarlett"

Visitors to Britain's cathedrals and churches are accustomed to seeing memorials to nobility and royalty, but it is rare to find monuments to people of a more humble background. This is not the case in the East Anglican cathedral city of Peterborough, where a gravedigger by the name of "Old Scarlett" is something of a local folk hero.

Robert Scarlett died in 1591 at the age of ninety-eight, having spent much of his life as the sexton at Peterborough Cathedral. Not only does his memory live on in a portrait above the great west door of the twelfth-century cathedral, but he also enjoys the distinctly English honor of having a Peterborough pub, the "Old Scarlett," named after him. Legend suggests that he may have been the inspiration for the gravedigger in Shakespeare's *Hamlet*. That is pure speculation, but there is no doubt about his main claim to fame–that during his long career he buried two queens in the cathedral: Katherine of Aragon and Mary, Queen of Scots.

Battle of Marston Moor

On the evening of July 2, 1644, the largest conflict of the English Civil War was fought between the Royalists and Parliamentarians at Marston Moor, near York, England.

The Parliamentarian forces were led by Oliver Cromwell who, in alliance with Scottish generals, attacked Prince Rupert's army at night. The Parliamentarians began by singing psalms and, under Cromwells's disciplined leadership, eventually inflicted a heavy defeat on the Royalists, who suffered over 3,000 fatalities.

An eyewitness report by a member of the Eastern Association (from Cromwell's side) states that the brigade "had a hard pull of it, for they were charged by Rupert's bravest both in front and flank . . . but they pressed on . . . dispersing the enemies foot (soldiers) almost as fast as they charged them. . . ." Another eyewitness stated that "Colonel Russell, Colonel Montagu and Colonel Pickering (from Cromwell's side), stood as a wall of brass and let fly small shot like hail upon the enemy, and not a man of their whole brigade killed. . . ."

Although this is an exaggeration, since Cromwell's men certainly suffered some loses, victory at Marston Moor eventually led to the city of York falling to Parliamentarian forces after a long siege.

July 3

DAILY READING

Righteousness exalts a nation,
but sin is a disgrace to any people. (PROV 14:34)

FEAST DAYS

ca. 6th cent.	St. Guntheim	Brittany abbot
72	St. Thomas	Apostle
ca. 8th cent.	St. Guthagon	Hermit of Oosterkerk, Holland

ENTRANCE AND EXIT

b. 1423	Louis XI	King of France
b. 1883	Franz Kafka	Czech writer
b. 1962	Tom Cruise	Actor
d. 1792	Ferdinand	Duke of Brunswick
d. 1845	Joel Chandler Harris (Uncle Remus)	Author
d. 1971	Jim Morrison	Lead singer, the Doors

St. Thomas the Apostle

Little is known about St. Thomas the Apostle, but it is thought that he was born in the Galilean city of Pansada and was a fisherman. Hearing the good tidings of Jesus Christ, he left all and followed after him. "Thomas, being once weaker in faith than the other apostles," says St. John Chrysostom, "toiled through the grace of God more bravely, more zealously and tirelessly than them all, so that he went preaching over nearly all the earth, not fearing to proclaim the Word of God to savage nations."

The church tradition that claims Thomas preached in "India" was widely spread in both East and West and is to be found in such writers as Ephraem Syrus, Ambrose, Paulinus, Jerome, and later Gregory of Tours. However, it is difficult to discover any adequate support for the long-accepted belief that St. Thomas pushed his missionary journeys as far south as Mylapore, not far from Madras. In that region you can still find a granite bas-relief cross with a Pahlavi (ancient Persian) inscription dating from the seventh century, and the tradition that it was here that St. Thomas laid down his life is locally very strong.

On the Malabar, or west coast, of southern India, a body of Christians still exists using a form of Syriac for its liturgical language as a link to Thomas. Preaching the gospel earned St. Thomas a martyr's death. For having converted the wife and son of the governor of the Indian city of Meliapur [Melipur], Thomas was locked up in prison, suffered torture, and finally, after being pierced with five spears, he departed to the Lord.

Noteworthy

529 The second Synod of Orange convened in Arausio in southern France.

1721 Hans Egede (1686–1758), Lutheran Apostle of Greenland, landed in Greenland with a party of forty-six people.

1840 Søren Kierkegaard was examined for his theological degree at the University of Copenhagen.

1878 First African-American Lutheran congregation was organized in Little Rock, Arkansas.

1880 Prussia declared that clergy are subordinate to the state.

1904 Theodor Herzl (b. May 2, 1860), Hungarian-born journalist and founder of political Zionism, died.

1907 Pope Saint Pius X (1835–1914) formally condemned the modernist intellectual movement within the Roman Catholic Church.

1936 Charles Theodore Benze, Lutheran seminary professor, died (b. September 19, 1865).

1960 Alfred H. Ackley (b. January 21, 1887), American Presbyterian clergyman and hymn writer, died.

July 4

DAILY READING

Blessed is the nation whose God is the LORD. (PS 33:12)

FEAST DAYS

ca. 180	St. Namphanion	The Archmartyr
397	St. Martin	Bishop of Tours, France
ca. 870	St. Odo the Good	Archbishop of Canterbury

ENTRANCE AND EXIT

b. 1826	Stephen Foster	American songwriter
b. 1872	Calvin Coolidge	30th American president
b. 1885	Louis B. Meyer	Founder of MGM studios
d. 1826	John Adams	2nd American president
d. 1826	Thomas Jefferson	3rd American president
d. 1831	James Monroe	5th American president

A long train of abuses and usurpations . . .

In 1776 after two days of debate, the Second Continental Congress of America agreed its declaration of independence from Great Britain and the rule of King George III. This formal separation and formation into an independent nation was a great milestone in the history of America and its anniversary is much celebrated every year.

This is an extract of the Declaration of Independence signed by the fifty-six leaders of America:

> IN CONGRESS, July 4, 1776.
>
> The unanimous Declaration of the thirteen united States of America,
>
> When in the Course of human events, it becomes necessary for one people to dissolve the political bands which have connected them with another, and to assume among the powers of the earth, the separate and equal station to which the Laws of Nature and of Nature's God entitle them, a decent respect to the opinions of mankind requires that they should declare the causes which impel them to the separation.
>
> We hold these truths to be self-evident, that all men are created equal, that they are endowed by their Creator with certain unalienable Rights, that among these are Life, Liberty and the pursuit of Happiness.–That to secure these rights, Governments are instituted among Men, deriving their just powers from the consent of the governed, –That whenever any Form of Government becomes destructive of these ends, it is the Right of the People to alter or to abolish it, and to institute new Government, laying its foundation on such principles and organizing its powers in such form, as to them shall seem most likely to effect their Safety and Happiness. Prudence, indeed, will dictate that Governments long established should not be changed for light and transient causes; and accordingly all experience hath shewn, that mankind are more disposed to suffer, while evils are sufferable, than to right themselves by abolishing the forms to which they are accustomed. But when a long train of abuses and usurpations, pursuing invariably the same Object evinces a design to reduce them under absolute Despotism, it is their right, it is their duty, to throw off such Government, and to provide new Guards for their future security.–Such has been the patient sufferance of these Colonies; and such is now the necessity which constrains them to alter their former Systems of Government. The history of the present King of Great Britain is a history of repeated injuries and usurpations, all having in direct object the establishment of an absolute Tyranny over these States.

St. Martin of Tours

St. Martin is one of the Catholic Church's greatest saints and there are many stories relating his fame. It is said that on one occasion, the Emperor Valentinian came to see him, but failed to respect him by rising from his chair. However, he quickly arose when the chair suddenly burst into flames. Another time, Martin saw a shivering beggar and shared his own cloak with the stranger.

Another story related that while Bishop of Tours, Martin he converted his whole area to Christianity.

St. Martin is the patron of beggars, vintners, soldiers, tailors, reformed alcoholics, and innkeepers. He is also the patron saint of Mainz (Germany), France, Foiano della Chiana (Italy), and Buenos Aires (Argentina). The official memorial of St. Martin is on November 11, but he is also remembered on this day, as in 372 he was made Bishop of Tours, and this day is the anniversary of the relocation of his bones from Rome to Tours.

July 5

DAILY READING

Give thanks to the L*ORD, call on his name;*
make known among the nations what he has done
and proclaim that his name is exalted. (ISA 12:4)

FEAST DAYS

ca. 300	Grace	Patron of Cornwall
462	Athansius	Bishop of Jerusalem
1387	Peter of Luxembourg	Bishop of Metz, France

ENTRANCE AND EXIT

b. 1794	Sylvester Graham	American inventor
b. 1810	Phineas Taylor Barnum	American showman
b. 1911	Georges Jean Raymond Pompidou	French president
d. 1761	Cardinal Domenico Silvio Passionei	Vatican librarian
d. 1826	Sir Thomas Stamford Bingley Raffles	Founder of Singapore
d. 2002	Theodore Samuel Williams	American baseball player

The Poet of Bran and Pumpkins

Sylvester Graham (1794–1851), a Presbyterian minister from Connecticut, is best known for his creation of the Graham cracker. He also put forth the idea that certain foods and behaviors are detrimental to both physical and spiritual health. It is not enough to practice moderation in all things, he claimed, because some things are simply not good, either for spiritual or physical reasons, or both. These theories made Graham a central figure in the health reform movement of the 1800s.

He invented the Graham Cracker in 1829, but it wasn't until after his death that the National Biscuit Company (Nabisco) made the product available across America. Nabisco achieved even greater success with their Honey Maid line, introduced in 1925, which boosted the original flavor through the addition of honey.

In 1830, Graham was made general agent for the Pennsylvania Temperance Society, and he began to study human physiology and diet. He advocated bread at least twelve hours old, made of the whole of the wheat, and coarsely ground. He also recommended hard mattresses, open bedroom windows, cold shower baths, loose and light clothing, daily exercise, vegetables and fruits, rough (whole-grain) cereals, pure drinking water, and cheerfulness at meals. He taught that temperance included both physical and moral reform.

In 1837, Sylvester Graham wrote his *Treatise on Bread and Bread Making*, which advocated the use of Graham flour, made from coarsely ground whole-wheat kernels, and instructed wives to bake their own bread. He influenced John Kellogg to take up the cause of health reform, and Ralph Waldo Emerson referred to Sylvester Graham as the "poet of bran and pumpkins."

Tynwald Day

According to the Isle of Man authorities, its government, known as the Tynwald, is the oldest democratically elected parliament in the world. It celebrated its millennium on this day in 1979.

The *Manx Quarterly* (the Isle of Man magazine) reports that originally the Tynwald was an annual gathering of commoners presided over by feudal lords to enact laws and make judgments on issues affecting all islanders.

Today, Tynwald Day is the official national day of the Isle of Man. This small isle off the northwest coast of England sees great celebration every July 5. A formal procession consisting of His Excellency the Lieutenant Governor, members of parliament, the judiciary, Church members, and other prominent Manx men and women gather at the Chapel of St. John the Baptist for a ceremony of remembrance and thanksgiving.

After a service the Governor sits on the summit together with the President of Tynwald, Legislative Council, and the officers in attendance. There then follow a number of traditional and ancient ceremonies, followed by the proclaiming of Laws which have been made during the last year in both Manx and English. Then island residents, who have exhausted all normal channels of appeal, present their grievances to Tynwald in a custom right dating back more than 1,000 years. The Court of Tynwald hears these grievances and makes decisions based on its ancient laws and customs.

JULY 6

DAILY READING

"All we like sheep have gone astray; we have turned every one to his own way; and the Lord hath laid on him the iniquity of us all." (ISA 53:6, KJV)

FEAST DAYS

ca. 740 BC	Isaiah	Old Testament prophet
ca. 370	St. Julian	Anchoret
1585	Thomas Alfield	Catholic martyr

ENTRANCE AND EXIT

b. 1866	Helen Beatrix Potter	Children's author
b. 1921	Nancy Reagan	American First Lady
b. 1946	George W. Bush	American president
d. 1535	Sir Thomas More	Chancellor of England
d. 1932	Kenneth Grahame	Scottish writer
d. 1971	Louis Armstrong	American band leader

The Prophet Isaiah

Isaiah was born during the reign of the King Uzziah of Judah, and it was during the last year of his reign that he received the call to the prophetic office. His name means "Jehovah saves," or "Jehovah is salvation." His call was constantly to have faith in the one who alone could save the land and its inhabitants. He challenged and inspired the people of Judah at times when hope seemed dead. His ministry was a long one, stretching at least forty years through the reigns of King Uzziah, Jothan, Ahaz, and Hezekiah. Isaiah's father's name was Amoz, and there is a Jewish tradition that he was a brother of King Amaziah; in which case Isaiah would be the cousin of King Uzziah. He was married, and he himself called his wife "the prophetess" (Isa 8:3). He had two children: one named Shear-jashubl, which means "a remnant shall return," and the other Maher-shalalhashbaz, which means "haste ye to the spoil." These names were given to them as portents of what was to come and also as a reinforcement of the prophet's predictive message.

Apart from this, there is little else known of his personal history except what is found in the book itself. Tradition records that Isaiah was martyred under the order of King Manasseh by being sawed in two.

Isaiah's prophecy, the longest of all the Old Testament prophecies, divides naturally into two parts: chapters 1–39 and 40–66. In addition to these two separate parts, the prophecy also divides into nine sections:

1. Prophecies centered on Judah and Jerusalem (chapters 1–12).
2. Prophecies against foreign and and hostile nations (chapters 13–23).
3. Isaiah's apocalypse: judgments of Jehovah against the world's sin (chapters 24–27).
4. Prophecies concerning the relation of Judah and Jerusalem to Egypt and Assyria (chapters 28–33).
5. Prophecies proclaiming the doom of Edom and the redemption of Israel (chapters 34–35).
6. Historical appendix: Isaiah's life and activity during the reign Hezekiah (chapters 36–39).
7. Deliverance from the dominion of Babylon (chapters 40–48).
8. Redemption through suffering and sacrifice (chapters 49–57).
9. The triumph and the universal dominion of Jehovah (chapters 58–66).

Malawi Independence Day

On July 6, 1964, the British Commonwealth territory of Nyassaland in the heart of Africa, became the independent nation of Malawi.

The word Malawi means haze or reflected light, in reference to the sun rising over the country's main body of water, Lake Nyasa. Malawi is known as the "warm heart of Africa."

In celebration of Malawi Independence Day, here are some terms in Chichewa, the official language of that country:

Hello	Moni
How are you?	Muli Bwanji?
I'm fine	Ndili bwino
What is your name?	Dzani lako ndani?

*J*ULY 7

DAILY READING

As for God, his way is perfect; the word of the LORD *is flawless. He is a shield for all who take refuge in him.* (PS 18:30)

FEAST DAYS

ca. 450	St. Palladius	Apostle of Scotland
705	Hedda	Bishop of Wessex
1304	Niccolo Boccasini	Pope Benedict XI

ENTRANCE AND EXIT

b. 1887	Marc Chagall	Russian artist
b. 1911	Gustav Mahler	Austrian composer
b. 1940	Ringo Starr	English pop star
d. 1791	Dr. Thomas Blacklock	Scottish poet
d. 1816	Richard Brinsley Sheridan	English satirist
d. 1930	Sir Arthur Conan Doyle	English writer

The Blind Poet

Thomas Blacklock (1721–91) was a Scottish poet born at Annan in Dumfrieshire. When not quite six months old, he lost his sight because of smallpox, and his career is largely interesting as that of one who achieved what he did in spite of this disability.

Shortly after his father's death in 1740, some of Blacklock's poems began to be handed about among his acquaintances and friends, who arranged for his education at the grammar school, and subsequently at the university of Edinburgh, where he was a student of divinity. His first volume of poems was published in 1746. In 1754 he became deputy librarian for the Faculty of Advocates, by the kindness of David Hume, the famous philosopher. Blacklock was among the first friends of Robert Burns in Edinburgh, being one of the earliest to recognize his genius. He was influential in inducing Burns to abandon his intention to emigrate, and may be credited, therefore, with saving for his country and humanity at large one of the most gifted of his country's sons. In 1762 he was ordained minister of the church of Kirkcudbright, and in 1767 the degree of Doctor in Divinity was conferred on him by Marischal College, Aberdeen.

This is one of his most well-known poems:

Death Levels All

One night I dream'd, and dreams may oft prove true,
That to this foolish world I bade adieu.
With solemn rites, and decent grief deplored,
My friends to mother earth her gift restor'd.
But O! eternal insult to my shade,
Close by a vile plebeian corse was laid!
Enrag'd, confin'd, I try'd to shift my ground;
But all attempts were unsuccessful found
"Begone, gross lump," I cry'd in high disdain,
"No slave of abject birth shall here remain.
Be distant far, to nobler names give way,
And mix with vulgar dust thy sordid clay."
"Thou fool, thou wretch!" a hollow voice reply'd,
"Now learn the impotence of wealth and pride;
Hereditary names and honours, here,
With all their farce and tinsel, disappear.
In these dark realms Death's reptile heralds trace
From one sole origin all human race:
On all the line one equal lot attends:
From dust it rises and to dust descends.
Her pale Ambition, quitting pomp and form,
Admits her last-best counsellor, a worm.
Here Nature's charter stands confirm'd, alone;
The grave is less precarious than the throne.
Then seek not here preeminence and state,
But own and bless th' impartial will of Fate;
With life, its errors and its whims resign,
Nor think a beggar's title worse than thine."

JULY 8

DAILY READING

I will bow down toward your holy temple and will praise your name for your love and your faithfulness, for you have exalted above all things your name and your word. (PS 138:2)

FEAST DAYS

ca. 689	Totnan	Patron of whitewashers
975	Edgar the Peaceful	Patron of widowers
1872	Peter dei Paganelli di Montemagno	Pope Eugene III

ENTRANCE AND EXIT

b. 1838	Count Ferdinand von Zeppelin	German aviator
b. 1839	John Davison Rockefeller Sr.	American industrialist
b. 1908	Nelson Rockefeller	41st American vice president
d. 1115	Peter the Hermit	First Crusade preacher
d. 1623	Alessandro Ludovisi	Pope Gregory XV
d. 1822	Percy Bysshe Shelley	English poet

Peter the Hermit

Peter the Hermit was a priest of Amiens, in France. According to legend, Christ appeared to him in the Church of the Holy Sepulchre before 1096, and bade him to start the First Crusade to recapture Jerusalem. The story is difficult to verify, though it appears in the pages of William of Tyre. He may or may not have been present at Pope Urban's great sermon in Clermont in 1095 that urged the recapture of Jerusalem, but he was certainly one of the preachers of the First Crusade after that sermon.

He soon leapt to fame as an emotional revivalist preacher: even his donkey became an object of popular adoration, and thousands of peasants eagerly took the cross at his bidding. The crusade of the *pauperes* (Poor People), which forms the first act in the First Crusade, was his work, and he himself led one of the five sections of the *paupers* to Constantinople, starting from Cologne and arriving at Constantinople at the end of July 1096. Here he joined the only other section that had succeeded in reaching Constantinople–that of Walter the Penniless; and with the joint forces, he crossed to the Asiatic shore in the beginning of August. The *pauperes* began hostilities against the Turks, and Peter returned to Constantinople, either in despair at their recklessness, or in the hope of procuring supplies. In his absence, the army was cut to pieces by the Turks, and during the winter of 1096–97, he was left in Constantinople without any followers to wait for the coming of the princes.

In 1099 he is recorded as treasurer of the alms at the siege of Arca (March), and as leader of the processions in Jerusalem that preceded the battle of Ascalon (August). At the end of the year, he went to Laodicea and sailed from there to the West. From this time he disappears, but Albert of Aix records that he died in 1151, as prior of a church of the Holy Sepulchre that he had founded in France.

Noteworthy

- 1497 Vasco da Gama set sail from Lisbon in search of a sea route to India.
- 1792 France declared war on Prussia.
- 1796 America's first passport issued to Francis Maria Barrere.
- 1815 Louis XVIII re-entered Paris as King of France after Napoleon's defeat at Waterloo.
- 1858 British declared peace in India.
- 1887 *Wall Street Journal* first published by Charles H. Dow and Edward Jones.
- 1924 Adolf Hitler resumed leadership of National Socialist Party.
- 1932 Dow Jones Industrial Average slipped to record low of 41.22 having fallen 89 percent in 3 years.
- 1976 New York Bar Association expelled Richard Nixon.

JULY 9

DAILY READING

O righteous God, who searches minds and hearts, bring to an end the violence of the wicked and make the righteous secure. (PSALM 7:9)

FEAST DAYS

1539	Adrian Fortescue	Cousin of Anne Boleyn
1572	John of Cologne	Gorkum martyr
1842	Antoninus Fantosati	Martyr of China

ENTRANCE AND EXIT

b. 1919	Sir Edward Heath	British prime minister
b. 1937	David Hockney	English artist
b. 1956	Tom Hanks	American actor
d. 68 BC	Claudius Caesar Augustus Germanicus	Roman Emperor Nero
d. 1797	Edmund Burke	Irish statesman
d. 1850	Zachary Taylor	12th American president

The Nineteen Martyrs of Gorkum

The Protestant Reformation gained its foothold in the Netherlands in opposition to the Catholicism of the Spanish princes of the country. Anti-Spanish and Calvinist soldiers joined together with a band of pirates and laid siege to the city of Gorkum (the Netherlands), capturing it in June 26, 1572, after a struggle. For reprisal because of the city's determined defense, they gathered all members of the clergy in Gorkum into one prison and set about taking revenge on the priests for their own grievances against the Spanish crown.

The priests were tortured, subjected to all kinds of indignities, and offered their freedom if they would abjure Catholic teaching on the primacy of the pope.

After ten days, the priests were thrown half-naked into the hold of a ship and taken to the city of Briel. After being exhibited to the curious townspeople, who paid to see the spectacle, and tortured, the nineteen priests and followers were hanged in an old barn at deserted Ruggen Monastery on the outskirts of Briel.

Their bodies, mutilated before or after death, were callously thrown into a ditch. The nineteen martyrs included eleven Franciscans (called Recollects), two Premonstratensians, one Dominican, one canon regular of St. Augustine, and four secular priests.

The scene of the martyrdom soon became a place of pilgrimage, and accounts of several miracles, supposedly performed by the martyrs' intercession and relics, were used for their beatification and published by the Bollandists. Most of their relics are kept in the Franciscan church at Brussels to which they were secretly conveyed from Briel in 1616.

Mysterium Cosmographicum

On this day in 1595, the great astronomer and mathematician Johannes Kepler published *Mysterium cosmographicum* (*Mystery of the Cosmos*), one of the first works in support of the new Copernican system of the cosmos. While teaching in Graz he demonstrated the periodic conjunction of Saturn and Jupiter in the zodiac and he realized that regular polygons bound one inscribed and one circumscribed circle at definite ratios, which, he reasoned, might be the geometrical basis of the universe. Kepler found that each of the five Platonic solids could be uniquely inscribed and circumscribed by spherical orbs; nesting these solids, each encased in a sphere, within one another would produce six layers, corresponding to the six known planets–Mercury, Venus, Earth, Mars, Jupiter, and Saturn. By ordering the solids correctly–octahedron, icosahedron, dodecahedron, tetrahedron, cube–Kepler found that the spheres could be placed at intervals corresponding (within the accuracy limits of available astronomical observations) to the relative sizes of each planet's path, assuming the planets circle the Sun.

As he indicated in the title, Kepler thought he had revealed God's geometrical plan for the universe. His first manuscript of *Mysterium cosmographicum* contained an extensive chapter reconciling heliocentrism with biblical passages that seemed to support geocentrism. With the support of his mentor, Michael Maestlin, Kepler received permission from the Tubingen university senate to publish his manuscript, pending removal of the Bible exegesis and the addition of a simpler, more understandable description of the Copernican system as well as Kepler's new ideas.

July 10

DAILY READING

He who began a good work in you will carry it on to completion until the day of Christ Jesus. (PHIL 1:6)

FEAST DAYS

ca. 370	Januarius	African martyr
ca. 370	Felix	African martyr
690	Amalburga	Patron of Ghent

ENTRANCE AND EXIT

b. 1509	John Calvin	French theologian
b. 1834	James McNeil Whistler	American artist
b. 1871	Marcel Proust	French writer
d. 1099	Rodrigo Díaz de Vivar (El Cid)	Spanish nobleman
d. 1941	Jelly Roll Morton	American bandleader
d. 1989	Mel Blanc	American voice artist

John Calvin

John Calvin (1509–64) was a French Protestant reformer regarded generally as second in importance only to Martin Luther as a key figure in the Protestant Reformation.

At fourteen he was sent to Paris to study theology, and there he developed a particular interest in the writings of Augustine. In about 1534, he underwent a sudden conversion and became an ardent Protestant. He went to Basel in Switzerland, where he wrote and published the first edition of his *Institutes of the Christian Religion*, a work of systematic theology that provided a detailed logical account of grace.

This doctrine was rooted in Calvin's experience of God's grace at work in his own heart. He was unwilling to attribute grace to anything but the mercy of God, and determined never to claim that he has done anything more or better than Judas Iscariot to deserve a better destiny.

In 1536, he became one of the preachers in the city of Geneva, in 1538 he was banished, and in 1541 returned in triumph, and established a "Reformed" or "Presbyterian" form of church government. The cultural impact of that model has extended beyond the church to influence modern democratic political theory. In the sixteenth century, new social institutions emerged to replace the deteriorating ones that had once held medieval civilization together. Many of these new institutions were influenced by Calvin's model.

Calvin's theology has been neatly summed up in the five main points of his teaching, known by the acronym TULIP:

Total Depravity (also known as Total Inability and Original Sin)
Unconditional Election
Limited Atonement (also known as Particular Atonement)
Irresistible Grace
Perseverance of the Saints (also known as Once Saved Always Saved)

He died peacefully in Geneva on May 27, 1564.

The Man of a Thousand Voices

Melvin Jerome Blanc (1908–89) was the leading voice artist of his generation and is famed for his work in giving voice to many cartoon creations. Known as the "man of a thousand voices," Blanc enjoyed a lengthy career beginning with his first feature, *Picador Porky* in 1937.

In 1961, Blanc was revived out of a coma, arising from a near fatal car accident, by recordings of Bugs Bunny and Porky Pig. His other main credits include giving voice to:

Barney Rubble

Captain Caveman

Daffy Duck

Elmer Fudd

Foghorn Leghorn

Marvin the Martian

Pepe Le Pew

Road Runner

Speedy Gonzales

Sylvester

Tweety Pie

Wile E. Coyote

Woody Woodpecker

Yosemite Sam

JULY 11

DAILY READING

Ah, Sovereign L*ORD*, *you have made the heavens*
and the earth by your great power and outstretched arm.
Nothing is too hard for you. (JER 32:17)

FEAST DAYS

ca. 320	Pelagia	Martyr
547	Benedict	Founder of monastic order
ca. 690	John	Bishop of Bergamo, Italy

ENTRANCE AND EXIT

b. 1274	Robert I (the Bruce)	King of Scotland
b. 1767	John Quincy Adams	6th American president
b. 1920	Yul Brunner	Russian-born U.S. actor
d. 1804	Alexander Hamilton	American statesman
d. 1937	George Gershwin	American composer
d. 2000	Robert Runcie	Archbishop of Canterbury

Benedict of Nursia

Benedict, the founder of Western monasticism, was born at Nursia in Italy, around AD 480. He was sent to Rome for his studies, but was repelled by the dissolute life of most of the populace, and withdrew to a solitary life. A group of monks asked him to be their abbot, but some of them found his rule too strict, and he returned to solitary living. Again, other monks called him to be their abbot, and he agreed, founding twelve communities over an interval of some years. His most famous founding was Monte Cassino, an abbey that stands to this day as the motherhouse of the worldwide Benedictine order.

When Totila the Goth visited Benedict, he was so awed by his presence that he fell on his face before him. Benedict raised him from the ground and rebuked him for his cruelty, telling him that it was time that his iniquities should cease. Totila asked Benedict to remember him in his prayers and departed, to exhibit from that time an astonishing clemency and chivalry in his treatment of conquered peoples.

Benedict drew up a rule of life for monastics, a rule that he called "a school of the Lord's service, in which we hope to order nothing harsh or rigorous." The Rule gives instructions for how the monastic community is to be organized, and how the monks are to spend their time. An average day includes about four hours to be spent in liturgical prayer (called the *Divinum Officium*–the Divine Office), five hours in spiritual reading and study, six hours of labor, one hour for eating, and about eight hours for sleep.

The spirit of St. Benedict's Rule is summed up in the motto of the Benedictine Confederation: *Pax ora et labora*–Peace, Pray and Work.

A Benedictine monk takes vows of "obedience, stability, and conversion of life." That is, he vows to live in accordance with the Benedictine Rule, not to leave his community without grave cause, and to seek to follow the teaching and example of Christ in all things.

St. Benedict spent the rest of his life realizing the ideal of monasticism that he had drawn out in his Rule. He died at Monte Cassino in Italy. In 1964, Pope Paul VI named him Patron Protector of Europe.

Noteworthy

1220 London Bridge collapses during fire in which 3,000 die.
1460 Yorkists defeat Lancastrians at Northampton and capture King Henry VI.
1553 Lady Jane Grey crowned Queen of England to reign for only nine days.
1790 American capital moved from New York to Philadelphia.
1890 Wyoming becomes 44th state admitted to Union.
1900 Paris Metro opens.
1925 Scopes "Monkey Trial" begins.
1940 The Battle of Britain begins when 70 German bombers attack docks in South Wales; Luftwaffe bombs continue for 114 days.
2002 Rubens's *Massacre of the Innocents* sells for all time record of £49.5 million at Sotheby's London.

July 12

DAILY READING

Jesus answered, "It is written: 'Man does not live on bread alone, but on every word that comes from the mouth of God.'" (MATT 4:4)

FEAST DAYS

ca. 66	Fortunatus	Patron of Udine, Italy
ca. 67	Paulinus of Antioch	First bishop of Lucca, Tuscany
1626	John Tanaka	Nagasaki martyr

ENTRANCE AND EXIT

b. 100 BC	Gaius Julius Caesar	Roman Emperor
b. 1817	Henry David Thoreau	American writer
b. 1937	Bill Cosby	American actor
d. 1536	Desiderius Erasmus	Christian scholar
d. 1704	Titus Oates	Anglican minister
d. 1850	Robert Stevenson	English inventor

Desiderius Erasmus

The great Dutch scholar and humanist Desiderius Erasmus (1466–1536) was born at Rotterdam, the illegitimate son of a physician's daughter by a man who afterward turned monk. He was called Gerrit Gerritszoon (Dutch for Gerard Gerardson) but adopted the name Desiderius Erasmus. He attended the school of the "Brothers of the Common Life" at Deventer. On his parents' death, his guardians insisted on his entering a monastery, and he spent six years at the Augustinian college of Stein near Gouda. This austere experience of the clerical life made Erasmus fiercely opposed to the monks as he believed a retreat from the real world was not the way to acquire holiness.

In 1516 he published his annotated New Testament, virtually the first Greek text, and in 1519 his edition on St. Jerome in nine folio volumes. In both of these works the aim of Erasmus was to introduce a more rational conception of Christian doctrine, and to emancipate men's minds from the frivolous and pedantic methods of the Scholastic theologians. But when the Lutheran revolution came, he found himself in the most embarrassing position. Those of the old order fell upon him as the author of all the new troubles. The Lutherans assailed him for his cowardice and inconsistency in refusing to follow up his opinions to their legitimate conclusions. In 1521 he left Louvain, where the champions of the old faith had made his stay unendurable, and he spent nearly the rest of his life at Basel.

The Voice that Breathed O'er Eden

On this date in 1857, the English churchman and writer John Keble (1792–1866) wrote the words to the popular wedding hymn, "The Voice that Breathed O'er Eden," for the marriage of Lucy Maud Montgomery (author of *Anne of Green Gables*) to Ewan Macdonald, a Presbyterian minister.

The voice that breathed o'er Eden, that earliest wedding day,
The primal wedding blessing, it hath not passed away.
Still in the pure espousal of Christian man and maid
The Holy Three are with us, the threefold grace is said.

For dower of blessèd children,
For love and faith's sweet sake,
For high mysterious union
Which naught on earth may break.

Be present, awful Father, to give away this bride
As Thou gav'st Eve to Adam, a helpmate at his side.
Be present, Son of Mary, to join their loving hands
As Thou didst bind two natures in Thine eternal bands.

Be present, Holy Spirit, to bless them as they kneel,
As Thou for Christ, the Bridegroom, the heav'nly Spouse dost seal.
O spread Thy pure wing o'er them, let no ill power find place
When onward to Thine altar their hallowed path they trace.

To cast their crowns before Thee in perfect sacrifice,
Till to the home of gladness with Christ's own Bride they rise.
To Father, Son, and Spirit, eternal One and Three,
And was and is forever, all praise and glory be.

July 13

DAILY READING

God exalted him to the highest place and gave him the name that is above every other name, that at the name of Jesus every knee should bow, in heaven and on earth and under the earth, and every tongue confess that Jesus Christ is Lord, to the glory of God the Father. (PHIL 2:9–11)

FEAST DAYS

ca. 700	Mildred	Patron of Minster, England
ca. 750	Turiaf	Bishop of Dol, Brittany
1896	James of Voraigne	Author of *The Golden Legend*

ENTRANCE AND EXIT

b. 1527	John Dee	English alchemist
b. 1793	John Clare	English poet
b. 1942	Harrison Ford	American actor
d. 1712	Richard Cromwell	Lord Protector of England
d. 1762	Dr. James Bradley	English astronomer
d. 1951	John C. Fremont	American explorer

The Golden Legend

Much of our knowledge of saints derives from *The Golden Legend*, a compilation of heroic deeds by famous saints such as George, Valentine, and Christopher. The author of this medieval best seller was James (or Jacobus) of Voragine.

Born in Lombardy in 1230, James became provincial of the Dominicans of Lombardy at a remarkably early age. He was later sent to Genoa by Pope Nicholas V to reintegrate that city, then under interdict for political reasons, into the Catholic Church. Eventually, and much against his will, he became archbishop. As archbishop, he endowed a number of hospitals and repaired the city's decaying parish churches. Soon after his death, he was revered locally as a saint; although never formally canonized, he was beatified in 1896.

Although based on the work of earlier hagiographers, in particular Vincent of Beauvais, Jean de Mailly, and Bartholomew of Trent, James's *The Golden Legend* rapidly eclipsed all previous works of its kind in the West and dominated the genre for centuries; from 1470 to 1530 it was the most printed book in Europe.

It begins with an elaboration of the events recounted in the Gospels, especially the life of Christ, but also includes episodes from the Old Testament and stories of the lives of the saints, and of the birth, childhood, and death of the Virgin Mary drawn from numerous sources. It is arranged in accordance with feast days.

The Golden Legend was frequently copied and translated, and when printing was introduced was still more popular. It was a highly important and accessible source for painters of religious subjects, especially for the lives of the saints.

Noteworthy

1105 Rashi (b. February 22, 1040), medieval Jewish Bible scholar, died.

1519 The second session of the Leipzig Debate between Johan Eck and Martin Luther closed.

1520 A riot broke out among Wittenberg University students, which Luther blamed on inflammatory remarks by the university rector, Peter Burkhard. Luther was present at the meeting addressed by the rector but left when he saw "that Satan was presiding over the meeting."

1521 Luther's writings were burned at Antwerp.

1813 Adoniram Judson (1788–1850), missionary and Bible translator, arrived in Burma.

1900 China's Boxer Rebellion against foreigners and Chinese Christians erupted.

1983 The U.S. space probe Pioneer 10 became the first spacecraft to leave the solar system as it crossed the orbit of Neptune.

1997 A jury voted unanimously to give Timothy McVeigh the death penalty for his role in the Oklahoma City bombing.

2005 A jury acquitted Michael Jackson of molesting a 13-year-old cancer survivor at his Neverland ranch.

JULY 14

DAILY READING

"If you obey my commands, you will remain in my love, just as I have obeyed my Father's commands and remain in his love." (JOHN 15:10)

FEAST DAYS

ca. 505	Optatian	Bishop of Brescia, Italy
1610	Francis Solano	Patron of Argentina
1656	Kateri Tekakwitha	First Native American to be beatified

ENTRANCE AND EXIT

b. 1805	John Frederick Lewis	English artist
b. 1912	Woody Guthrie	American songwriter
b. 1913	Gerald Ford Jr.	38th American president
d. 1881	Billy the Kid	American outlaw
d. 1965	Adlai E. Stevenson I	23rd American vice president
d. 2000	Sir Mark Oliphant	Australian nuclear physicist

She Who Moves Forward

Kateri Tekakwitha was the first Native American to become a saint. She was a born into the Turtle Clan of the Iroquois tribe in 1656 along the southern bank of the Mohawk River near a village called Ossernenon. It is thought that her mother was a Christian and her name, Tekakwitha, means "she who moves forward," or "she who puts things in order."

Before her fifth birthday, Kateri survived a smallpox epidemic that claimed the lives of her parents and baby brother. But the disease impaired her vision and scarred her face. Following the death of her parents, she was raised by tribal parents.

In 1667 the area was visited by Jesuit missionaries (known as the Blackrobes), and she came to a knowledge of the Christian faith through this contact. The Blackrobes established a mission nearby, and despite tribal opposition, she was baptized on April 5, 1676, taking the name Kateri (Iroquois for Catherine).

She suffered persecution from her tribe and eventually had to flee the encampment with the help of other Christian Indians. She remained a steadfast Christian despite much opposition and died on April 17, 1680, at twenty-four years of age.

The case for her canonization was started in 1884 under Pope Leo XIII, and Pope John Paul II beatified her on June 22, 1980. She is recognized as the patron saint of ecologists, exiles, orphans, and people ridiculed for their faith.

First American World Fair

On this day in 1853, just two years after the first world's fair in London's Crystal Palace, New York hosted America's first world's fair. The Fair was held in New Yorks's own "Crystal Palace," a smaller replica of the London building. The site was an area known as Reservoir Square on 42nd Street near 5th Avenue.

The New York Crystal Palace was in the shape of a Greek cross, with each of the arms being of equal length. The center of the building was surmounted by a large dome which was 100 feet in diameter. According to the *New York Times*,

> Our advances in the study of Nature should stand forth in the niches of the temple and embody the progress of the American mind. Let the great West and the great South roll their voices along the Palace aisles, and tell the world what stuff they are made of and what strides they have taken in the arts of business of life. . . . The impulse which this exhibition will give to the mechanical and artistic glories of this country is insignificant when compared with the moral power which it may exert over the fortunes of our happy Union.

One of the attendees to the Fair was the poet, Walt Whitman, who wrote the following lines:

The Song of the Exposition

. . . a Palace,
Lofter, fairer, ampler than any yet,
Earth's modern wonder, History's Seven out stripping,
High rising tier on tier, with glass and iron facades,
Gladdening the sun and sky–enhued in the cheerfulest hues,
Bronze, lilac, robin's-egg, marine and crimson
Over whose golden roof shall flaunt, beneath thy banner, Freedom.

JULY 15

DAILY READING

Get rid of all moral filth and the evil that is so prevalent and humbly accept the word planted in you, which can save you. (JAS 1:21)

FEAST DAYS

830	Haruch	Bishop of Werden, Germany
862	Swithin	Bishop of Winchester, England
927	Edith of Tamworth	Sister of King Athelstan, England

ENTRANCE AND EXIT

b. 1606	Rembrandt Harmenszoon van Rijn	Dutch artist
b. 1919	Dame Iris Murdoch	Playwright
b. 1946	Linda Ronsdtadt	American singer
d. 1015	Vladimir the Great	Prince of Kiev
d. 1904	Anton Chekhov	Russian writer
d. 1997	Gianni Versace	Italian fashion designer

St. Swithin's Day

According to John Brand's *Popular Antiquities* (1806), St. Swithin was a man equally noted for his uprightness and humility. So far did he carry the latter quality that on his deathbed he requested to be buried, not within the church, but outside in the churchyard, on the north of the sacred building, where his corpse might receive the eaves droppings from the roof, and his grave be trodden by the feet of passersby. His lowly request was complied with, and in this neglected spot his remains reposed till about a hundred years afterward, when a fit of indignation seized the clergy at the body of so pious a member of their order being allowed to occupy such a position; on an appointed day they all assembled to convey it with great pomp into the adjoining cathedral of Winchester. When they were about to commence the ceremony, a heavy rain burst forth, and continued without intermission for the next forty days. The monks interpreted this tempest as a warning from heaven of the blasphemous nature of their attempt to contravene the directions of St. Swithin, and instead of disturbing his remains, they erected a chapel over his grave, at which many astounding miracles were performed. From this circumstance, it is stated, arose the popular belief of the anniversary of the attempted translation of St. Swithin being invested with a prophetic character in reference to the condition of the weather for the ensuing six weeks.

Popular Works By Anton Chekhov (1860–1904)

DRAMA NA OKHOTE, 1884–85–*The Shooting Party*

IVANOV, 1887–*Ivanov*

LEBEDINAIA PESNIA, 1888–*The Swan Song*

STEP, 1888–*The Steppe*

SKICHNAIA ISTORIIA, 1889–*A Boring Story*

PREDLOZHENIE, 1889–*The Proposal*

SVADBA, 1889–*The Wedding*

TRAGIK PONEVOLE, 1890–*The Reluctant Tragedian*

DUEL, 1891–*The Duel*

POPRYGUNIA, 1892–*The Grasshopper*

IUBILEI, 1892–*The Anniversary*

CHERNYI MONAKH, 1894–*The Black Monk*

MOYA ZHIZN, 1895–*My Life*

CHAIKA, 1896–*The Seagull*

DYADYA VANYA, 1897–*Uncle Vanya*

MUZHIKI, 1897–*The Peasants*

CHELOVEK V FUTLIARE, 1898–*Man in a Case*

DUSHECHKA, 1899–*The Darling*

TRI SESTRY, 1901–*Three Sisters*

ARKHIEREI, 1902–*The Bishop*

VISHNYOVY SAD, 1904–*The Cherry Orchard*

"To judge between good or bad, between successful and unsuccessful would take the eye of a God."

–*Anton Chekhov*

JULY 16

DAILY READING

In Christ, all the fullness of the Deity lives in bodily form,
and you have been given fullness in Christ,
who is the head over every power and authority. (COL 2:9–10)

FEAST DAYS

ca. 6th cent.	Helier	Hermit of Jersey
866	Irmengard	Daughter of King Louis of Germany
1645	Andre de Soveral	Brazilian martyr

ENTRANCE AND EXIT

b. 1723	Sir Joshua Reynolds	English artist
b. 1821	Mary Baker Eddy	Founder of Christian Science
b. 1911	Ginger Rogers	American actor and dancer
d. 1486	Andrea del Sarto	Italian artist
d. 1953	Hilaire Belloc	French writer
d. 1990	Sir Stephen Spender	English writer

Christian Science

Christian Science healing is a method of spiritual healing based on the beliefs of the Christian Science, or Church of Christ, Scientist, Church. Adherents hold that the material world is a false reality and that health is a condition of mind, God, and truth. Thus, Christian scientists believe that ill health can be cured by spiritual education and prayer.

Founder Mary Baker Eddy was born in New Hampshire into a family of strict Christian practice and Puritan values. Baker was ill for much of her childhood and early adult life. She explored medical therapies popular in her time, including homeopathy, and found no relief for her chronic illness.

Between 1862 and 1865 Baker was a patient of a charismatic healer named Phineas Parkhurst Quimby. A former hypnotist, Quimby developed a philosophy of mental healing based on the belief that he had rediscovered the secret of Jesus' ability to heal the sick. It is thought that Quimby's ideas may have influenced Baker in the development of her philosophy of Christian Science healing, although she herself denied it.

She called her method Christian Science, and believed that she had found the one and only "truth." In 1875 Mary Baker published *Science and Health*. This book, revised by Baker Eddy over the next thirty-five years, is the fundamental document explaining the doctrine of Christian Science healing.

Mary Baker Eddy died in 1910. At the time of her death, there were about 1,200 Christian Scientist congregations in the United States.

In addition to its practices of spiritual healing, Christian Science is best known today for its publishing activities, spearheaded by the international newspaper the *Christian Science Monitor* founded by Eddy in 1908. Each congregation also provides a public Christian Science Reading Room where the public may read Christian Science literature and ponder spiritual matters.

Extract from No and Yes *by Mary Baker Eddy*

Disease is more than *imagination*; it is a human error, a constituent part of what comprise the whole of mortal existence,–namely, material sensation and mental delusion. But an erring sense of existence, or the error of belief, named disease, never made sickness a stubborn reality. On the ground that harmony is the truth of being, the Science of Mind-healing destroys the feasibility of disease; hence error of thought becomes fable instead of fact. Science demonstrates the reality of Truth and the unreality of the error. A self-evident proposition, in the Science of Mind-healing, is that disease is unreal; and the efficacy of my system, beyond other systems of medicine, vouches for the validity of that statement. Sin and disease are not scientific, because they embody not the idea of divine Principle, and are not the phenomena of the immutable laws of God; and they do not arise from the divine consciousness and true constituency of being.

The unreality of sin, disease, and death, rests on the exclusive truth that being, to be eternal, must be harmonious. All disease must be–and can only be–healed on this basis. All true Christian Scientists are vindicating, fearlessly and honestly, the Principle of this grand verity of Mind-healing.

July 17

DAILY READING

I am not ashamed of the gospel, because it is the power of God for the salvation of everyone who believes. (ROM 1:16)

FEAST DAYS

821	Kenelm	Mercian prince
1246	Hugh the Little	Patron of torture victims
1794	Sister Mary Henrietta of Providence	Carmelite martyr of Compeigne, France

ENTRANCE AND EXIT

b. 1674	Isaac Watts	English hymn writer
b. 1763	John Jacob Astor	American financier
b. 1952	David Hasselhoff	American actor
d. 1790	Adam Smith	Scottish economist
d. 1912	Henri Poincaré	French mathematician
d. 1959	Billie Holiday	American jazz singer

The Father of English Hymnody

According to the *Dictionary of National Biography* (1899), Isaac Watts, pastor, preacher, poet, and hymn writer, was the "father of English Hymnody." Watts was born in Southampton, the eldest of nine children. His facility in English verse showed itself very early, and he was educated in an academy at Stoke Newington. Here he excelled in classics, logic, Hebrew, and divinity.

After leaving the academy in 1694, he spent two and a half years at home, and commenced the composition of his hymns. The first of these, "Behold the Glories of the Lamb," was produced as an improvement on the hymns of William Barton and others then sung in the Southampton Chapel. Several other pieces followed; they were circulated in manuscript, and given out line by line when sung.

Watts was one of the most popular writers of the day. His educational manuals–the *Catechisms* (1730) and the *Scripture History* (1732)–were still standard works in the middle of the last century. His philosophical books, especially *Logic* (1725), had a long circulation; so also had his *World to Come* (1738) and other works of popular divinity.

In the early years of the last century, the annual output of Watts's hymns, notwithstanding all the wealth of hymn production arising out of Methodism, was still 50,000 copies. The two staple volumes, subsequently often bound together, were the *Hymns* (1707; 2nd ed. 1709) and the *Psalms of David* (1719). The total number of hymns produced by Watts must be about six hundred. The most well known include "Jesus Shall Reign Where'er the Sun"; "When I Survey the Wondrous Cross"; "Come, Let Us Join Our Cheerful Songs"; and "Our God, Our Help in Ages Past." The characteristics of his hymns are tender faith, joyousness, and serene piety.

Isaac Watts died in 1748, and a monument has been erected to him in Westminster Abbey

When I Survey the Wondrous Cross

When I survey the wondrous cross
On which the Prince of glory died,
My richest gain I count but loss,
And pour contempt on all my pride.

Forbid it, Lord, that I should boast,
Save in the death of Christ my God!
All the vain things that charm me most,
I sacrifice them to His blood.

See from His head, His hands, His feet,
Sorrow and love flow mingled down!
Did e'er such love and sorrow meet,
Or thorns compose so rich a crown?

His dying crimson, like a robe,
Spreads o'er His body on the tree;
Then I am dead to all the globe,
And all the globe is dead to me.

Were the whole realm of nature mine,
That were a present far too small;
Love so amazing, so divine,
Demands my soul, my life, my all.

July 18

DAILY READING

I will praise you with an upright heart
as I learn your righteous laws. (PS 119:7)

FEAST DAYS

ca. 6th cent.	Goneri	Hermit of Brittany
1183	Bruno	Bishop of Segni, Italy
1838	Frederick of Holland	Patron of Utrecht, Netherlands

ENTRANCE AND EXIT

b. 1811	William Makepeace Thackeray	English author
b. 1848	William Gilbert Grace	English cricketer
b. 1918	Nelson Mandela	South African president
d. 1100	Godfrey of Bouillon	Leader of the First Crusade
d. 1817	Jane Austen	English author
d. 1997	James Goldsmith	Financier

Godfrey of Bouillon

Godfrey of Bouillon was the French Duke of Lower Lorraine who became famous as the leader of the First Crusade who seized Jerusalem from the rule of the Moors. In 1095, Pope Urban II called upon Christians to regain control of Jerusalem. Godfrey almost literally sold all he had to respond to this call. Along with his brothers Eustace and Baldwin (the future Baldwin I of Jerusalem), he led a German contingent along "Charlemagne's road" through Hungary to Constantinople, starting in August 1096. He was the first of the crusading princes to arrive and pay homage of Emperor Alexius.

In 1099 the mass of the crusaders became weary of the political factions that divided some of their leaders. Godfrey, who was more of a pilgrim than a politician, became the natural representative of this feeling. He was thus able to force the reluctant crusaders to march to Jerusalem, and he took a prominent part in the siege of that city. His division was the first to enter when the city was captured, and Godfrey was made ruler of Jerusalem in 1099. He assumed the title not of king, but of "Protector of the Holy Sepulchre." During his short reign, Godfrey had to contend with Prince Raymund, the Arabs of Egypt, and the Patriarch Dagobert.

Because he had been the first ruler in Jerusalem, Godfrey was idolized in later sagas, being depicted as the sole leader of the crusades, the king of Jerusalem, and the legislator who laid down the assizes of Jerusalem.

In reality he would seem to have been a quiet, pious, hard-fighting knight, who was chosen to rule in Jerusalem because he had no dangerous qualities and no obvious defects.

Extract from "The King of Brentford's Testament"

The noble King of Brentford
  Was old and very sick,
He summon'd his physicians
  To wait upon him quick;
They stepp'd into their coaches
  And brought their best physick.

They cramm'd their gracious master
  With potion and with pill;
They drench'd him and they bled him;
  They could not cure his ill.
"Go fetch," says he, "my lawyer,
  I'd better make my will."

The monarch's royal mandate
  The lawyer did obey;
The thought of six-and-eightpence
  Did make his heart full gay.
"What is't," says he, "your Majesty
  Would wish of me to-day?"

"The doctors have belabor'd me
  With potion and with pill:
My hours of life are counted,
  O man of tape and quill!
Sit down and mend a pen or two,
  I want to make my will."

—William Makepeace Thackeray

JULY 19

DAILY READING

"Do not fear, for I am with you; do not be dismayed, for I am your God. I will strengthen you and help you; I will uphold you with my righteous right hand." (ISA 41:10)

FEAST DAYS

ca. 445	Arsenius	Hermit
787	Jerome	Bishop of Pavia, Italy
1679	William John Plessington	Catholic martyr

ENTRANCE AND EXIT

b. 1834	Edgar Degas	French painter
b. 1922	George McGovern	American senator
b. 1947	Brian May	English pop star
d. 1573	Dr. John Caius	Founder of Caius College, Oxford
d. 1814	Capt. Matthew Flinders	Explorer
d. 2002	Alan Lomax	American musicologist

Arsenius the Great

Arsenius was born to two rich parents in AD 350 in Rome. His father was a senator and judge. His parents sent Arsenius to the teachers of the church, and he was ordained a deacon by Damasus, the Bishop of Rome.

According to legend, Damascus recommended the erudite Arsenius to Emperor Theodosius the Great in 383, who appointed him tutor of his sons. Arsenius was rewarded with money and servants, honor and possessions. After a decade of luxury and influence, he kept hearing the voice of God telling him that only by abandoning it all could he be saved.

In 395 he abandoned the court and joined the monks in Alexandria, Egypt. On the death of Theodosius, he became a desert monk in the Wadi Natrun. There he was tutored in the eremitical customs by St. John the Short. Initially suspicious of his dedication, St. John tested Arsenius's humility by throwing his bread upon the floor. When Arsenius ate it, undismayed, St. John became convinced of his devotion.

The simple maxims for which he was known and the doings recorded of him are characteristic of the desert fathers, marked by strict self-discipline and shrewdness about human nature. He constantly repeated: "I have always something to repent having spoken, but never for having held my tongue." Arsenius feared damnation because of his former self-centered ways.

In art he is shown weaving baskets of palm leaves, which was a common occupation of the desert monks.

St. Macrina the Younger

On this day, the Eastern Orthodox Church remembers St. Macrina the Younger (c. 330–d.379), who is noted as being the sister of two of the Fathers of the Eastern Church: St. Basil (c. 323–d.379) and St. Gregory (c. 335–c. 395). St. Gregory wrote a biography about his sister and records this prayer by her at the end of her life:

> O God eternal, to Whom I have been attached from my mother's womb, Whom my soul has loved with all its strength, to Whom I have dedicated both my flesh and my soul from my youth up until now-do Thou give me an angel of light to conduct me to the place of refreshment, where is the water of rest, in the bosom of the holy Fathers. Thou that didst break the flaming sword and didst restore to Paradise the man that was crucified with Thee and implored Thy mercies, remember me, too, in Thy kingdom; because I, too, was crucified with Thee, having nailed my flesh to the cross for fear of Thee, and of Thy judgments have I been afraid. Let not the terrible chasm separate me from Thy elect. Nor let [986 A] the slanderer stand against me in the way; nor let my sin be found before Thy eyes, if in anything I have sinned in word or deed or thought, led astray by the weakness of our nature. O Thou Who hast power on earth to forgive sins, forgive me, that I may be refreshed and may be found before Thee when I put off my body, without defilement on my soul. But may my soul be received into Thy hands spotless and undefiled, as an offering before Thee.

July 20

DAILY READING

If we walk in the light, as he is in the light, we have fellowship with one another, and the blood of Jesus, his Son, purifies us from all sin. (1 JOHN 1:7)

FEAST DAYS

ca. 100	Joseph Barsabas	Mentioned in the Acts of the Apostles
ca. 300	Margaret of Antioch	Patron of pregnant women
ca. 300	Wilgefortis	Patron of difficult marriages

ENTRANCE AND EXIT

b. 1304	Francesco Petrarch	Italian poet and scholar
b. 1889	John Charles Walsham Reith	Founder of the BBC
b. 1947	Carlos Santana	Musician
d. 1903	Vincenzo Pecci	Pope Leo XIII
d. 1923	Pancho Villa	Mexican revolutionary
d. 1937	Guglielmo Marconi	Italian inventor

The July 20th Plot

Claus Graf von Stauffenberg (1907–44) sacrificed himself for his country. He was one of those professional German officers whom Hitler never truly understood for in every way he was the opposite of Hitler. He was an aristocrat from a long line of noblemen, a devout Catholic, a brilliant scholar, an accomplished horseman, and a lover of music and poetry.

Stauffenberg belonged to the organizational department of the Army High Command. He was high enough in rank to have direct access to Hitler. Often he had stood three feet from the man he regarded as "the enemy of humanity." He was often plagued by treasonable thoughts, so he joined a group of conspirators, including his brother Berthold von Stauffenberg and his cousin, Caesar von Hofacker.

On April 7, 1943, Stauffenberg's staff car was riddled with bullets from a low-flying airplane in Tunisia. He lost an eye, his right hand, and two fingers of his left hand. He then was flown to a military hospital in Munich. During his recovery, he told friends who came to visit that he had made the decision to sacrifice himself in order to kill Hitler.

Bodyguards, all of them excellent marksmen, protected Hitler. His timetable was nearly always changed at the last minute, and in fact, he was rarely where people expected him to be. The conspirators decided against shooting him; if the first shot missed, it was highly unlikely they would get a second chance. So they turned to time bombs.

Several attempts failed, mostly because Hitler changed his schedule, and on one occasion a bomb placed in Hitler's plane failed to detonate. On July 20, 1944, Count von Stauffenberg made his last attempt.

He planted a bomb during a meeting at Hitler's headquarters in East Prussia, which is now Poland. The bomb, in a briefcase, exploded, but Hitler survived virtually unscathed. He was protected from the force of the blast by a conference table.

Shortly after the failed assassination attempt, Stauffenberg and other army officers implicated in the plot were rounded up, and on July 21 they were executed on Hitler's orders.

Francesco Petrarch—Sonnet

Io non fut d'amar voi lassato unquanco.

Tired, did you say, of loving you? Oh, no!
I ne'er shall tire of the unwearying flame.
But I am weary, kind and cruel dame,
With tears that uselessly and ceaseless flow,
Scorning myself, and scorn'd by you. I long
For death: but let no gravestone hold in view
Our names conjoin'd: nor tell my passion
strong
Upon the dust that glow'd through life
for you.
And yet this heart of amorous faith
demands,
Deserves, a better boon; but cruel, hard
As is my fortune, I will bless Love's bands
For ever, if you give me this reward.

JULY 21

DAILY READING

I have chosen the way of truth;
I have set my heart on your laws. (PS 119:30)

FEAST DAYS

ca. 204	Zoticus	Bishop of Comana, Italy
ca. 290	Victor of Marseilles	Patron of millers
ca. 590	Simeon of Emesa	Holy Fool

ENTRANCE AND EXIT

b. 1899	Ernest Hemingway	American author
b. 1945	Wendy Cope	English poet
b. 1952	Robin Williams	American actor
d. 1796	Robert Burns	Scottish poet
d. 1928	Ellen Terry	English actor
d. 2000	George Macaulay Trevelyan	English historian

Simeon the Holy Fool

Throughout the history of the church, there have been holy people who poked fun at Christians who were feeling a little too self-righteous. Their stories, still revered in the Greek and Russian Orthodox Churches, sound absurd.

St. Simeon Silos, the patron of Holy Fools, retreated to the Syrian desert in the sixth century to devote his life to prayer. A few decades later, Simeon returned to Edessa a changed man. Simeon would throw nuts at the priests during the worship service and publicly ate sausage on Good Friday, which is not only a fast day, but at that time no one ate meat during the season of Lent.

In the main town square, he wrapped his arms around the dancing girls and went skipping and dancing across the arena. In the streets, he tripped people up, developed a theatrical limp, and dragged himself around on his buttocks. In the bath house, he ran naked into the crowded women's section. On solemn fasting days he feasted riotously, consuming vast amounts of beans–with predictable and hilarious results. In his lifetime, Simeon was regarded as a madman, as an unholy scandal.

Yet, there was another side to Simeon. The seemingly nutty monk also helped people in the town. Simeon's saintly deeds were done in secret, never when someone else might notice and he never took credit later. And no one could dispute that Simeon was a very holy person, even the priests he pelted with nuts on Sunday. Simeon just poked fun at every attempt people made to make themselves feel holier than others.

National Day in Belgium

Belgium is an ancient and yet still young nation. Although Belgians were first mentioned about 2,000 years ago by Julius Caesar in his book on the Gallic Wars, for many centuries, Belgium was part of other nations, including France and Germany.

The Independant State of Belgium was born on October 4, 1830, although National Day is celebrated on July 21. This is because on this day in 1831, King Leopold I took the constitutional oath as the first King of Belgium.

The Belgian National Anthem is known as the "Song of Brabant" and is reproduced here in its two versions:

Official French-language text:

O Belgique, ô mère chérie,
A toi nos cœurs, à toi nos bras,
A toi notre sang, ô Patrie !
Nous le jurons tous, tu vivras !
Tu vivras toujours grande et belle
Et ton invincible unité
Aura pour devise immortelle :
le Roi, la Loi, la Liberté !
le Roi, la Loi, la Liberté ! (2x)

Official Dutch-language text:

O dierbaar België, O heilig land der Vad'ren,
Onze ziel en ons hart zijn u gewijd.
Aanvaard ons kracht en bloed van ons ad'ren,
Wees ons doel in arbeid en in strijd.
Bloei, o land, in eendracht niet te breken;
Wees immer uzelf en ongeknecht,
Het woord getrouw, dat g' onbevreesd moogt spreken,
Voor Vorst, voor Vrijheid en voor Recht. :|
Voor Vorst, voor Vrijheid en voor Recht. (2x)

JULY 22

DAILY READING

"What about you?" Jesus asked. "Who do you say that I am?" Simon Peter answered, "You are the Christ, the Son of the living God." (MATT 16:15–16)

FEAST DAYS

ca. 100	Mary Magdalene	Jesus' anointer
ca. 306	Plato	Martyr
1679	Phillip Evans	English martyr

ENTRANCE AND EXIT

b. 1822	Gregor Mendel	Austrian botanist
b. 1844	William Spooner	English clergyman
b. 1930	Sister Madonna Buder	American triathlete
d. 1932	Florenz Zeigfield	American theater manager
d. 1934	John Dillinger	American gangster
d. 1967	Carl Sandburg	American author

Mary Magdalene

Mary Magdalene (meaning she was from Magdala) is mentioned in the Gospels as being among the women of Galilee who followed Jesus and his disciples. She was present at his crucifixion and burial, and went to the tomb on Easter Sunday to annoint his body. She was the first to see the risen Lord, and to announce his resurrection to the apostles. Accordingly, she is referred to in early Christian writings as "the apostle to the apostles."

Mary Magdalene, Mary of Bethany (sister of Martha and Lazarus), and the unnamed penitent woman who anointed Jesus' feet (Luke 7:36–48) are sometimes wrongly supposed to be the same woman. From this, plus the statement that Jesus had cast seven demons out of her (Luke 8:2) has risen the traditional belief that she had been a prostitute before she met Jesus.

Because of the assumption that Mary Magdalene had been a spectacular sinner, and also perhaps because she is described as weeping at the tomb of Jesus on the resurrection morning, she is often portrayed in art as weeping, or with eyes red from having wept. From this appearance we derive the English word "maudlin," meaning "effusively or tearfully sentimental." There is a Magdalen College at Oxford and a Magdalene College at Cambridge (different spelling), both pronounced "Maudlin."

Noteworthy

1796 The city of Cleveland was founded by Gen. Moses Cleaveland.

1933 American aviator Wiley Post completed the first solo flight around the world in seven days, eighteen and a half hours.

1943 American forces led by Gen. George S. Patton captured Palermo, Sicily.

1946 Jewish extremists blew up a wing of the King David Hotel in Jerusalem, killing about 100 people.

1981 Turkish extremist Mehmet Ali Agca was sentenced in Rome to life in prison for shooting Pope John Paul II.

1994 O.J. Simpson pleaded innocent to the slaying of his ex-wife, Nicole, and her friend, Ronald Goldman.

2003 Saddam Hussein's sons Odai and Qusai were killed when U.S. forces stormed a villa in Mosul, Iraq.

2003 Months after her prisoner-of-war ordeal, Pvt. 1st Class Jessica Lynch returned home to a hero's welcome in Elizabeth, West Virginia.

2004 The September 11th commission issued a report saying America's leaders failed to grasp the gravity of terrorist threats before the 9/11 attacks.

JULY 23

DAILY READING

Jesus said, "Let the little children come to me, and do not hinder them, for the kingdom of heaven belongs to such as these." (MATT 19:14)

FEAST DAYS

ca. 150	Apollinaris	Patron of Germany
ca. 303	Phocas	Patron of gardners
1372	Bridget of Sweden	Partron of Sweden

ENTRANCE AND EXIT

b. 1888	Raymond Chandler	American author
b. 1893	Dr. Karl Menninger	American scientist
b. 1912	Michael Wilding	English actor
d. 1885	Gen. Ulysses S. Grant	18th American president
d. 1918	Joseph Henry Gilmore	American hymn writer
d. 2001	Eudora Welty	American writer

"He Leadeth Me"

Joseph Henry Gilmore was born in Boston, Massachusetts, on April 29, 1834. He graduated from Phillips-Andover Academy in 1854. In 1858 he received a Bachelor of Arts degree and in 1861 a Master of Arts degree from Brown University. He attended Newton Theological Institution in 1861 and served as pastor of a Baptist church in Fisherville, New Hampshire.

He wrote the popular hymn "He Leadeth Me" in 1862. Three years later, Henry was invited to preach a sermon at the Second Baptist Church in Rochester. "I picked up a church hymnal to see what songs they sang and was surprised to have the book fall open to the very song I had written three years earlier," he wrote.

"When I returned home, I related this experience to my wife. 'I do not understand it,' I said. 'My words had been set to music by Dr. William B. Bradbury; yet I had not given the words to anybody.' My wife smiled and said, 'I can explain it, Joseph. I felt that the words would bless the hearts of people in these troublesome times so I sent the poem to *The Watchman* and *Reflector*. I am glad to know that they have printed it.'"

He Leadeth Me

He leadeth me, O blessed thought!
O words with heav'nly comfort fraught!
Whate'er I do, where'er I be
Still 'tis God's hand that leadeth me.

Refrain:
He leadeth me, He leadeth me,
By His own hand He leadeth me;
His faithful foll'wer I would be,
For by His hand He leadeth me.

Sometimes 'mid scenes of deepest gloom,
Sometimes where Eden's bowers bloom,
By waters still, o'er troubled sea,
Still 'tis His hand that leadeth me.

Lord, I would place my hand in Thine,
Nor ever murmur nor repine;
Content, whatever lot I see,
Since 'tis my God that leadeth me.

And when my task on earth is done,
When by Thy grace the vict'ry's won,
E'en death's cold wave I will not flee,
Since God through Jordan leadeth me.

A Prayer of St. Bridget of Sweden

One Our Father, One Hail Mary. O Jesus Christ! Eternal Sweetness to those who love Thee. Joy surpassing all joy and all desire. Salvation and Hope of all sinners. Who hast proved that Thou hast no greater desire than to be among men, even assuming human nature at the fullness of time for the love of men, recall all the sufferings Thou hast endured from the instant of Thy Conception and especially during Thy Passion, as it was decreed and ordained from all Eternity in the Divine Plan. Remember, O Lord, that during the Last Supper with Thy disciples, having washed their feet, Thou gavest them Thy Most Precious Body and Blood and while at the same time Thou didst sweetly console them, Thou didst foretell them Thy coming Passion. Remember the sadness and bitterness which Thou didst experience in Thy Soul as Thou Thyself bore witness saying, "My soul is sorrowful even unto death."

JULY 24

DAILY READING

Good will come to him who is generous and lends freely,
who conducts his affairs with justice. (PS 112:5)

FEAST DAYS

ca. 400	Declan	Bishop of Ardmore, Ireland
1224	Christina the Astonishing	Patron of the mentally ill
1594	John Boste	English martyr

ENTRANCE AND EXIT

b. 1725	John Newton	English hymn writer
b. 1862	Martin van Buren	8th American president
b. 1898	Amelia Earhart	American aviator
d. 1802	Alexander Dumas, Père	French author
d. 1980	Peter Sellers	English actor
d. 1991	Isaac Bashevis Singer	Polish author

Amazing Grace

John Newton, who converted to Christianity in 1748, led an adventure-filled life as a master of a slave ship. He wrote of his experiences in his autobiography, *An Authentic Narrative*, published in 1764. He found salvation on board *The Greyhound*, a merchant ship bound from Africa to Liverpool.

On rough seas, the vessel was about to sink, but in desperation Newton began to pray, and the crew eventually made it to Liverpool. In his autobiography, Newton recorded the deliverance thus:

> When we came into this port our very last victuals were boiling in the pot: and before we had been there two hours, the wind, which seemed to have been providentially restrained till we were in a place of safety, began to blow with great violence, so that if we had continued at sea that night in our shattered, enfeebled condition, we must have gone to the bottom. About this time I began to know that there is a God that hears and answers prayer.

Following retirement from the sea, Newton became Surveyor of the Tides in Liverpool, during which time he studied Greek, Hebrew, and theology. Newton was ordained as a priest in the Church of England in 1764.

Today, John Newton is best known as the author of the world-famous hymn, "Amazing Grace."

Amazing Grace

Amazing grace! (how sweet the sound)
That sav'd a wretch like me!
I once was lost, but now am found,
Was blind, but now I see.

'Twas grace that taught my heart to fear,
And grace my fears reliev'd;
How precious did that grace appear,
The hour I first believ'd!

Thro' many dangers, toils and snares,
I have already come;
'Tis grace has brought me safe thus far,
And grace will lead me home.

Noteworthy

1617 Caspar Fueger, hymnist, died at Dresden.

1819 Josiah G. Holland, American writer and hymnist, was born in Belchertown, Massachusetts (d. October 12, 1881, New York).

1870 John Pelikan, Slovak pastor, Slovak Evangelical Lutheran Church president and writer, was born.

1887 Karl Friedrich Kremmer, missionary to India, died (b. September 8, 1817, Schmalkalden, Germany).

1921 Cyrus Ingersoll Schofiled, editor of the Scofield Reference Bible and defender of dispensational premillennialism, died in Douglaston, New York (b. August 19, 1843).

JULY 25

DAILY READING

I will hasten and not delay to obey your commands. (PS 119:60)

FEAST DAYS

ca. 100	James the Greater	Apostle
ca. 251	Christopher	Patron of travelers
1583	Rudolph Aquaviva	Jesuit missionary to India

ENTRANCE AND EXIT

b. 1848	Sir Arthur James Balfour	British prime minister
b. 1902	Eric Hoffer	American philosopher
b. 1920	Rosalind Franklin	English scientist
d. 1834	Samuel Coleridge Taylor	English author
d. 1843	Charles Macintosh	Scottish inventor
d. 2003	John Schlesinger	English film director

St. James the Greater

James the son of Zebedee and his brother John were among the twelve disciples of the Lord. They, together with Peter, were privileged to behold the transfiguration, to witness the healing of Peter's mother-in-law and the raising of the daughter of Jairus. They were also called aside to watch and pray with Jesus in the Garden of Gethsemane on the night before his death.

James and John were apparently from a higher social level than the average fisherman. Their father could afford hired servants and had connections with the high priest. Jesus nicknamed the two brothers "sons of thunder," perhaps meaning that they were headstrong and impulsive.

On one occasion, Jesus and the disciples were refused the hospitality of a Samaritan village, and James and John proposed to call down fire from heaven on the offenders. On another occasion, they asked Jesus for a special place of honor in the kingdom, and were told that the place of honor is the place of suffering.

About AD 42, shortly before Passover, Acts 12 records that James was beheaded by order of King Herod Agrippa I, grandson of Herod the Great (who tried to kill the infant Jesus), nephew of Herod Antipas (who killed John the Baptist), and father of Herod Agrippa II (who heard the defense of Paul before Festus).

James was the first of the Twelve to suffer martyrdom, and the only one of the Twelve whose death is recorded in the New Testament. James is often called James the Greater to distinguish him from other New Testament persons called James.

Tradition has it that he made a missionary journey to Spain, and that after his death his body was taken to Spain and buried in Santigao de Compostela. This became a major site of pilgrimage in the Middle Ages.

The Balfour Declaration

The British Foreign Secretary, Sir Arthur James Balfour (1848–1930), wrote to Jewish leader Lord Rothschild in 1917 to assure him that the British Government supported the Jewish ideal of providing a permanent homeland for the Jews. The British hoped thereby to win more Jewish support for the Allies in the First World War.

The "Balfour Declaration" became the basis for international support for the founding of the modern state of Israel. The letter was published a week later in *The Times* of London and is reproduced here.

> Foreign Office
> November 2nd, 1917
>
> Dear Lord Rothschild:
>
> I have much pleasure in conveying to you, on behalf of His Majesty's Government, the following declaration of sympathy with Jewish Zionist aspirations which has been submitted to, and approved by, the Cabinet:
>
> His Majesty's Government view with favor the establishment in Palestine of a national home for the Jewish people, and will use their best endeavors to facilitate the achievement of this object, it being clearly understood that nothing shall be done which may prejudice the civil and religious rights of existing non-Jewish communities in Palestine, or the rights and political status enjoyed by Jews in any other country.
>
> I should be grateful if you would bring this declaration to the knowledgeof the Zionist Federation.
>
> Yours,
> Arthur James Balfour

July 26

DAILY READING

Faith is being sure of what we hope for
and certain of what we do not see. (HEB 11:1)

FEAST DAYS

180	Parasceva of Rome	Patron of blind people
1584	Anne	Patron of carpenters
1594	George Swallowell	English martyr

ENTRANCE AND EXIT

b. 1856	George Bernard Shaw	Irish author
b. 1875	Carl Jung	Swiss psychiatrist
b. 1928	Stanley Kubrick	American film director
d. 1680	John Wilmot	Earl of Rochester
d. 1952	Eva Perón	Argentinian reformer
d. 1984	George Gallup	American public opinion pollster

Hinds' Feet on High Places

Hannah Hunard (1905–90), author of the ever-popular *Hinds' Feet on High Places*, found salvation on July 26, 1916, at the Keswick Convention in England. She prayed, "O God, if there is a God anywhere, You must make yourself real to me." There was no answer. She opened her Bible at random, asking God to speak through it. She had opened to 1 Kings and read the story of Elijah, who challenged the people of Israel to choose between Baal and the living God. From that encounter, she realized God wanted her to sacrifice her life to him.

Hurnard was born in England to wealthy Quaker parents. Her training in England was at the Ridgelands Bible College for two years. In 1932 she began missionary work in Haifa, Israel, a work she continued for fifty years. *Hinds' Feet on High Places* was written in 1955 and from all appearances is mainstream and orthodox. It is a classic in the field of Christian publications, with over a million copies in circulation.

Her later works were not as popular, attracting some controversy because critics thought they espoused unorthodox views such as pantheism, universalism, and Gnosticism.

Stanley Kubrick

The innovative filmmaker Stanley Kubrick (1928–99) has been variously described as an intellectual, a recluse, a perfectionist and a tyrant. His body of work remains compelling and many of his movies have been critically acclaimed. His films include:

1950 *Day of the Fight*
1951 *The Flying Padre*
1953 *Fear and Desire*
1957 *Paths of Glory*
1960 *Spartacus*
1961 *Lolita*
1963 *Dr. Strangelove*
1968 *2001: A Space Odyssey*
–Oscar for Special Effects
1971 *A Clockwork Orange*
1975 *Barry Lyndon*
1980 *The Shining*
1987 *Full Metal Jacket*

In 1997, he received the D. W. Griffith Award for Lifetime Achievement from the Directors Guild of America.

His last completed film was *Eyes Wide Shut* (1999). His unfinished project, *AI: Artificial Intelligence* was completed by an admirer, Steven Spielberg, in 2001.

July 27

DAILY READING

Let us fix our eyes on Jesus, the author and perfecter of our faith, who for the joy set before him endured the cross, scorning its shame, and sat down at the right hand of the throne of God. Consider him who endured such opposition from sinful men, so that you will not grow weary and lose heart. (HEB 12:2–3)

FEAST DAYS

250	Maximian	One of the Seven Sleepers
305	Pantaleon	One of the Fourteen Holy Helpers
852	Aurelius	Patron of orphans

ENTRANCE AND EXIT

b. 1824	Alexander Dumas Fils	French author
b. 1929	Jack Higgins	English author
b. 1930	Shirley Williams	English politician
d. 1844	John Dalton	English scientist
d. 1946	Gertrude Stein	American author
d. 2003	Bob Hope	American comedian

Legend of the Seven Sleepers

The legend of the Seven Sleepers relates that around 250, the Emperor Decius, having set up a statue in the city of Ephesus, commanded all the inhabitants to worship it.

Seven young men, disobeying this mandate, fled to Mount Caelius, where they concealed themselves in a cavern. Decius ordered all the various caverns on the mount to be closed up, and nothing was heard of the fugitives till the year 479. A farmer, digging foundations for a stable, broke into the cavern, and discovered them, although they remained asleep.

Eventually, disturbed by the unwanted noise, the young men, who had been asleep all the time, awakened; feeling very hungry, and thinking they had slept but one night, they dispatched one of their number into Ephesus to learn the news and purchase some provisions. The antiquity of the coin proffered by the messenger at a baker's shop attracted suspicion, and the notice of the authorities. After an investigation, the whole affair was declared to be a miracle, and in its commemoration the festival was instituted. The Seven Sleepers are: Maximian, Malchus, Martinian, Dionysius, John Serapion, and Constantine.

Fourteen Holy Helpers

During the fourteenth century, the Black Plague devastated many parts of Europe and many died without receiving the last sacraments. It was a violent time, with those carrying the contagion often isolated and in fear of death.

Many people invoked a group of saints known as the Fourteen Holy Helpers during the Black Plague. Their devotion began in Germany and spread throughout most of Europe during the fourteenth century. Pantaleon was one of this select number and he and his companions were called upon for healing various ailments:

Saint	Condition
Achatius	Headaches
Barbara	Fevers, sudden death
Blaise	Ills of the throat
Catherine of Alexandria	Sudden death
Christopher	Plagues, sudden death
Cyriacus	Temptation
Denis	Headaches
George	Protection of domestic animals
Giles	Plagues
Margaret of Antioch	For safe childbirth
Pantaleon	Protection of domestic animals
Vitus	Epilepsy
Erasmus	Intestinal trouble
Eustachius	Difficult situations

July 28

DAILY READING

I press on toward the goal to win the prize for which God has called me heavenward in Christ Jesus. (PHIL 3:14)

FEAST DAYS

565	Samson	Bishop of Dol, Brittany
1120	Botwid	Swedish missionary
1858	Melchor García Sampedro	Martyr of Vietnam

ENTRANCE AND EXIT

b. 1881	John Gresham Machen	American church leader
b. 1887	Marcel Duchamp	French artist
b. 1929	Jacqueline Onassis	American First Lady
d. 1750	Johann Sebastian Bach	German composer
d. 1794	Maximilien de Robespierre	French Revolutionary politician
d. 1995	Don Carpenter	American author

John Gresham Machen

John Gresham Machen was born in 1881 in Baltimore, Maryland. As a young boy he was taught the Westminster Shorter Catechism, which, by his teen years, had given him a good command of Scripture.

In 1898, Machen went to John Hopkins University in Baltimore, graduating three years later with a BA degree in classics. At the urging of his pastor, he went on to Princeton Seminary in 1902, though at the time he had no intention of entering a vocational ministry. Princeton was renowned for its defense of Reformation theology, biblical inspiration and authority, and the role of the Holy Spirit in religious experience.

Machen embraced the Princeton tradition and in his inaugural address to students, "History and Faith," asserted that a "gospel independent of history is simply a contradiction in terms." Machen was ordained a Presbyterian minister in 1914, and became a leader of the fundamentalists in his denomination. A conservative apologist and theologian with a gift for clarity of exposition, Machen objected to the liberalism of the Presbyterian Board of Foreign Missions. In 1929, he led in the founding of Westminster Theological Seminary, and in 1933 set up an independent board. Suspended from the ministry for this action in 1935, Machen established an independent body, the Presbyterian Church of America (1936), later renamed the Orthodox Presbyterian Church.

Machen died on January 1, 1937, and is buried in his hometown.

Noteworthy

1540 King Henry VIII's chief minister, Thomas Cromwell, was executed. The same day, Henry married his fifth wife, Catherine Howard.

1821 Peru declared its independence from Spain.

1896 The city of Miami, Florida, was incorporated.

1945 A U.S. Army bomber crashed into the 79th floor of New York City's Empire State Building, killing 14 people.

1976 An earthquake devastated northern China, killing at least 242,000 people.

2002 Cycling champion Lance Armstrong won his fourth straight Tour de France.

2004 The Democratic National Convention in Boston nominated Massachusetts Sen. John Kerry for president.

2005 The Irish Republican Army renounced the use of violence against British rule in Northern Ireland and said it would disarm.

*J*ULY 29

DAILY READING

I will never forget your precepts,
for by them you have preserved my life. (PS 119:93)

FEAST DAYS

ca. 80	Martha	Friend of Jesus
950	Olaus	King of Sweden
1832	Joseph Tshang	Chinese martyr

ENTRANCE AND EXIT

b. 1883	Benito Mussolini	Italian dictator
b. 1905	Dag Hammarskjold	Swedish diplomat
b. 1938	Peter Jennings	American television journalist
d. 1833	William Wilberforce	English philanthropist
d. 1890	Vincent Van Gogh	Dutch artist
d. 1983	David Niven	English actor

William Wilberforce—The Great Reformer

William Wilberforce (1759–1833) remains a great example of how a persevering faith can change society. An evangelical Anglican, Wilberforce exhibited a profound faith visible for all to see and appreciate, even when they didn't share it.

Wilberforce also was one of the world's great reformers, spending over twenty years fighting against the scourge of slavery.

On the evening of February 23, 1807, the House of Commons began the second reading of a bill designed to abolish the slave trade throughout the British Empire. Wilberforce had spearheaded the controversial fight against that very profitable business, first almost alone, but then with support that grew slowly.

Those who didn't want to see the trade in slaves come to an end had threatened, more than once, his life. However, by 1807, times had changed, and on the evening of the 23rd the vast majority of the members of the House of Commons rose to give him a standing ovation. He learned just a few days before his death in 1833 that Parliament had voted to fully abolish slavery.

William Wilberforce is buried near his friend Pitt the Younger in Westminster Abbey.

Extract from William Wilberforce's First Abolition of Slavery Speech—1789

When I consider the magnitude of the subject which I am to bring before the House (of Commons)—a subject, in which the interests, not of this country, nor of Europe alone, but of the whole world, and of posterity, are involved: and when I think, at the same time, on the weakness of the advocate who has undertaken this great cause—when these reflections press upon my mind, it is impossible for me not to feel both terrified and concerned at my own inadequacy to such a task.

But when I reflect, however, on the encouragement which I have had, through the whole course of a long and laborious examination of this question, and how much candour I have experienced, and how conviction has increased within my own mind, in proportion as I have advanced in my labours;—when I reflect, especially, that however averse any gentleman may now be, yet we shall all be of one opinion in the end;—when I turn myself to these thoughts, I take courage—I determine to forget all my other fears, and I march forward with a firmer step in the full assurance that my cause will bear me out, and that I shall be able to justify upon the clearest principles, every resolution in my hand, the avowed end of which is, the total abolition of the slave trade.

I wish exceedingly, in the outset, to guard both myself and the House from entering into the subject with any sort of passion. It is not their passions I shall appeal to—I ask only for their cool and impartial reason; and I wish not to take them by surprise, but to deliberate, point by point, upon every part of this question. I mean not to accuse any one, but to take the shame upon myself, in common, indeed, with the whole parliament of Great Britain, for having suffered this horrid trade to be carried on under their authority. We are all guilty—we ought all to plead guilty and not to exculpate ourselves by throwing the blame on others; and I therefore deprecate every kind of reflection against the various descriptions of people who are more immediately involved in this wretched business.

July 30

DAILY READING

"You are the light of the world. . . . Let your light shine before men, that they may see your good deeds and praise your Father in heaven." (MATT 5:14, 16)

FEAST DAYS

ca. 250	Abdon	Patron of coopers
ca. 250	Senen	Patron of coopers
1198	Hatebrand	Benedictine monk

ENTRANCE AND EXIT

b. 1818	Emily Brontë	English writer
b. 1898	Henry Moore	English sculptor
b. 1947	Arnold Schwarzenegger	American actor
d. 1718	William Penn	Founder of Pennsylvania
d. 1771	Thomas Gray	English poet
d. 1784	Denis Diderot	French philosopher

William Penn—Visionary Christian

William Penn was born in 1644 and is known, of course, as the founder of Pennsylvania. He is also known as a famous Quaker and for naming Pennsylvania after his father. He had wanted to call the colony "New Wales" or "Sylvania," but King Charles II intervened, suggesting instead "Pennsylvania."

Penn became a Quaker in his twenties and was loved and memorialized for his treaty with the Leni Lenape (Delaware) colony. "I desire to gain your Love and Friendship by a kind, Just and Peaceable Life," he wrote to them from England. And he followed up with that desire with his "holy experiment."

Penn's holy experiment was idealistic to the point of utopianism. He wanted to establish a society that was godly, virtuous, and exemplary for all of humanity.

By 1681, when he received the charter for the colony, Penn had been an ardent proponent of Quakerism and liberal government, writing numerous political pamphlets, intriguing in the court, and campaigning for favorite candidates. Penn was both idealistic and practical and generally operated by trying for the best he could conceive while pragmatically retreating from these impossible heights.

Political squabbling and health problems meant he did not see the fulfilment of his colonial vision. After his death, the ownership of Pennsylvania passed to his sons, John, Thomas, and Richard.

Emily Brontë

The writer Emily Brontë (1818–48) was born in Thornton, Yorkshire, in the north of England. Her fame rests with the popularity of her only novel, *Wuthering Heights*. However, she was also a poet and published under the pseudonym Ellis Bell.

This poem was one of the last pieces of work ever composed by Emily in 1846.

No Coward Soul Is Mine

No coward soul is mine
No trembler in the world's storm-troubled
sphere
I see Heaven's glories shine
And Faith shines equal arming me from Fear

O God within my breast
Almighty ever-present Deity
Life, that in me hast rest
As I Undying Life, have power in Thee!

Vain are the thousand creeds
That move men's hearts, unutterably vain,
Worthless as withered weeds
Or idlest froth amid the boundless main

To waken doubt in one
Holding so fast by thy infinity
So surely anchored on
The steadfast rock of Immortality

With wide-embracing love
Thy spirit animates eternal years
Pervades and broods above,
Changes, sustains, dissolves, creates and rears

Though Earth and moon were gone
And suns and universes ceased to be
And thou wert left alone
Every Existence would exist in thee

There is not room for Death
Nor atom that his might could render void
Since thou art Being and Breath
And what thou art may never be destroyed.

*J*ULY 31

DAILY READING

To all who received him, to those who believe in his name,
he gave the right to become children of God—children born not of natural descent,
nor of human decision or a husband's will, but born of God. (JOHN 1:12–13)

FEAST DAYS

ca. 370	Germanus	Patron of Auxerre, France
1160	Helen of Skofde	Patron of martyrs
1860	Justin de Jacobis	Missionary to Ethiopia

ENTRANCE AND EXIT

b. 1800	Freidrich Wohler	German scientist
b. 1902	Sir George Allen	English cricketer
b. 1912	Milton Friedman	American economist
d. 1556	Ignatius Loyola	Founder of The Society of Jesus
d. 1875	Andrew Johnson	17th American president
d. 1944	Antoine de Saint-Exupery	French writer

The Society of Jesus

In 1521, Ignatius Loyola assisted in the defense of the Spanish city Pampeluna against the French. A cannonball fractured his right leg, and a splinter injured his left. During his recovery, he read *The Lives of the Saints*.

Inspired by these accounts, Loyola made a pilgrimage to the Holy Land, reaching Jerusalem in 1523, dressed as a beggar. On his return to Spain, at the age of thirty-three, he resumed his education and became a brilliant scholar. The rigor of his life, and the rebukes he administered to lax ecclesiastics, frequently brought him into trouble as a meddler.

He went to Paris in 1528, and at the university he made the acquaintance of Francis Xavier, Peter Faber, James Lainez, Nicholas Bobadilla, and Simón Rodriguez, five students whom he inspired with his own devout fervor. In an underground chapel of the church of Montmartre, the six enthusiasts took the solemn vows of celibacy, poverty, and the devotion of their lives to the care of Christians, and the conversion of infidels. Such was the beginning of the famous Society of Jesus.

Pope Paul III granted them a constitution in a bull, provided they yield obedience to the holy see. In 1540, Loyola was elected president, and was established at Rome as director of the Society of Jesus.

It was the aim of the society to discover and develop the peculiar genius of all its members, and then to apply them to the aggrandizement of the church. Soon the presence of the new order, and the fame of its missionaries, spread throughout the world, and successive popes gladly increased the numbers and enlarged the privileges of the society. Loyola brought more ardor than intellect to the institution of Jesuitism. Loyola died aged sixty-five and was canonized as a saint in 1622.

Prayers of Ignatius Loyola

Teach us, Good Lord,
To Serve Thee as Thou deservest;
To give and not to count the cost;
To fight and not to heed the wounds;
To labor and not to ask for any reward,
save that of knowing that we do Thy will.
Through Jesus Christ Our Lord, Amen.

Dearest Lord, teach me to be generous.
teach me to serve you as you deserve;
to give and not to count the cost;
to fight, and not to heed the wounds;
to labor, and not to seek to rest;
to give of myself and not to ask for reward,
except the reward of knowing that I am
doing your will.

Take, Lord, all my liberty.
Receive my memory, my understanding,
and my whole will.
Whatever I have and possess,
You have given me;
to You I restore it wholly,
and to Your will I utterly
surrender it for my direction.
Give me the love of You only,
with Your grace, and I am rich enough;
nor do I ask anything besides.

August

The sixt was August, being rich array'd
In garment all of gold downe to the ground:
Yet rode he not, but led a lovely mayd
Forth by the lily hand, the which was crown'd
With cares of corne, and full her hand was found.
That was the righteous Virgin, which of old
Liv'd here on earth, and plenty made abound;
But after wrong was lov'd, and justice solde,
She left th' unrighteous world, and was to heav'n extoll'd.

EDMUND SPENSER–*The Shepheardes Calender* (1579)

The Emperor Octavian, called the August,
I being his favorite, bestowed his name
Upon me, and I hold it still in trust,
In memory of him and of his fame.
I am the Virgin, and my vestal flame
Burns less intensely than the Lion's rage;
Sheaves are my only garlands, and I claim
The golden Harvests as my heritage.

HENRY WADSWORTH LONGFELLOW–*The Poet's Calendar* (1882)

Shakespeare ~

Messenger
O, no; wherein Lord Talbot was o'erthrown:
The circumstance I'll tell you more at large.
The tenth of August last this dreadful lord,
Retiring from the siege of Orleans,
Having full scarce six thousand in his troop.
By three and twenty thousand of the French
Was round encompassed and set upon.

–*King Henry VI Part One*–Act One, Scene One

This was one of those perfect New England days in late summer where the spirit of autumn takes a first stealing flight, like a spy, through the ripening country-side, and, with feigned sympathy for those who droop with August heat, puts her cool cloak of bracing air about leaf and flower and human shoulders.

–SARAH ORNE JEWETT, *The Courting of Sister Wisby,* 1887

August ~

This month was originally known as *Sextilis* (sixth) in the old Roman calendar and had twenty nine days and then thirty days during the time of Julius Caesar. However, when the Emperor Augustus renamed it after himself, he took a day from February so that today it has thirty one days.

Proverbs ~

If the first week in August is unusually warm,
the coming Winter will be snowy and long.

For every fog in August,
There will be a snowfall in Winter.

If a cold August follows a hot July,
It foretells a Winter hard and dry.

*A*UGUST 1

DAILY READING

You are my refuge and my shield;
I have put my hope in your word. (PS 119:114)

FEAST DAYS

168 BC	Holy Maccabees	Jewish martyrs
314	Verus	Bishop of Vienne, France
984	Ethelwold	Bishop of Winchester, France

ENTRANCE AND EXIT

b. 1819	Herman Melville	American writer
b. 1930	Lionel Bart	English composer and lyricist
b. 1936	Yves Saint-Laurent	Algerian fashion designer
d. 1137	Louis VI	King of France
d. 1834	Robert Morrison	Scottish missionary
d. 1864	Israel Zangwill	English writer

Ethelwold—the Saint of Wessex

St. Ethelwold (ca. 912–84) did great things for the church at Winchester, in those days part of Wessex. St. Ethelwold began as a simple monk, studying under Elphege the Bald, Bishop of Winchester. Ethelwold was ordained with St. Dunstan and became the dean at Glastonbury Abbey. From there he became abbot of Abingdon Abbey. King Athlestan thought highly of him and asked Ethelwold to teach his son, the future King Edgar.

When in 963 Ethelwold became Bishop of Winchester, he replaced the cathedral canons with monks, thus founding the first monastic cathedral in the land. This was a uniquely English institution, which remained until the Reformation. The monastic reform quickly gained momentum: with the King's support, Ethelwold restored old monasteries such as Milton (Dorset), New Minster, and Nunnaminster in Winchester, while new monasteries were founded and richly endowed at Peterborough (966), Ely (970), and Thorney (972).

When Ethelwold set the monks to work with the masons in the cathedral at Winchester, he built the most powerful organ of its time in England: it was played by two monks, and had four hundred pipes and thirty-six bellows. Ethelwold's monasteries also produced a surpassing new style of illumination, and his school of vernacular writing was the most important of its time. He is famous for producing the *Regularis Concordia*, a monastic decree based on Benedictine Rule. A major event of his episcopate was the consecration of Winchester Cathedral in 980.

Quotes of the Day

"Better to sleep with a sober cannibal than a drunken Christian."

—*Herman Melville*

"No Jew was ever fool enough to turn Christian unless he was a clever man."

—*Israel Zangwill*

"It pains me physically to see a woman victimized, rendered pathetic, by fashion."

—*Yves Saint-Laurent*

August 2

DAILY READING

Do not merely listen to the word, and so deceive yourselves. Do what it says. (JAS 1:22)

FEAST DAYS

371	Eusebius	Bishop of Vercelli, Italy
1073	Gundechar	Bishop of Eichstatt, Germany
1868	Peter Julian Eymund	Founder of Congregation of the Blessed Sacrament

ENTRANCE AND EXIT

b. 1835	Elisha Gray	American inventor
b. 1924	Carroll "Archie Bunker" O'Connor	American actor
b. 1932	Peter O'Toole	Irish actor
d. 1876	"Wild" Bill Hickok	American frontiersman
d. 1923	Warren Harding	29th American president
d. 1936	Louis Bleriot	French aviator

The Apostle to the Mohawks

On this day in 1642, a French Missionary Jesuit called Isaac Jogues was captured on the Lawrence River near Quebec by an Iroquois war party. Hidden in tall grass, Jogues could have avoided capture, but the idea of flight appalled him and he was seized along with his fellow workers.

The prisoners were forced to submit to the Iroquois sport known as "running the gauntlet." This brutal event consisted of having the captives run between two rows of Indians, each beating them furiously with sticks as they passed. Upon reaching their villages on the Mohawk River, the natives again subjected their "guests" to every manner of torture.

After some fourteen months in captivity, Jogues was ransomed back to Quebec, where shortly afterward he sailed to Europe. He petitioned the pope to allow him to celebrate Mass with his deformed hands. Having received this special dispensation from Rome, Jogues then set out back into the land of his abusers on a special "peace mission" to the Mohawk.

Incredibly, the Mohawk received Jogues hospitably, and he set about establishing a mission among them. However, when a plague of caterpillars devastated the Mohawk grain harvest, Jogues was charged with bringing "bad spirits" among the Indians. He and his colleagues were executed. Their decapitated heads were mounted on posts facing north to Canada.

Jogues's testimony led to many conversions among the Mohawk, and eventually even his executioner found Christ. Today a memorial statue shows his peaceful countenance looking over Battlefield Park in Lake George. Jogues was canonized in 1930.

Quotes of the Day

"My hope is in God, who needs not us to accomplish his designs. We must endeavor to be faithful to Him and not spoil His work by our shortcomings."

–Isaac Jogues

"God don't make no mistakes. That's how He got to be God."

–Carroll "Archie Bunker" O'Connor

"The most beautiful dream that has haunted the heart of man since Icarus is today reality."

–Louis Bleriot

August 3

DAILY READING

"Just as Moses lifted up the snake in the desert, so the Son of Man must be lifted up, that everyone who believes in him may have eternal life." (JOHN 3:14–15)

FEAST DAYS

ca. 1st cent.	Nicodemus	Member of the Sanhedrin
ca. 1st cent.	Gamaliel	Jewish Talmudic scholar
ca. 1st cent.	Lydia Purpuraria	Patron of Dyers

ENTRANCE AND EXIT

b. 1867	Stanley Baldwin	British Prime Minister
b. 1887	Rupert Brooke	English writer
b. 1920	Baroness Phyllis Dorothy James	English writer
d. 1792	Sir Richard Arkwright	English inventor
d. 1924	Joseph Conrad	Polish writer
d. 1966	Lenny Bruce	American comedian

Nicodemus

Nicodemus was a prominent and wealthy religious leader among the Jews in Jerusalem in the time of Jesus. He is mentioned only in the Gospel of John, where he appears three times.

In John 3, he speaks privately with Jesus, asking for guidance on whether Jesus is the Messiah. Jesus replies that "no one can enter the kingdom of God unless he is born of water and the Spirit," and "you must be born again." This discourse also contains the most famous verse in the Bible, when Jesus declares: "For God so loved the world that he gave his one and only Son, that whoever believes in him shall not perish but have eternal life."

In John 7, Nicodemus challenges the chief priests and Pharisees who condemn Jesus, "Does our law condemn anyone without first hearing him to find out what he is doing?"

After the death of Jesus, Nicodemus became a disciple of Jesus and joined Joseph of Arimathea in preparing Jesus' body for burial in accordance with Jewish burial customs.

His name occurs later in some of apocryphal writings, including the so-called "Acta Pilati," and the "Evangelium Nicodemi" published in the sixteenth century.

The date of his death is unknown.

Noteworthy

1492 Christopher Columbus set sail from Palos, Spain, on a voyage that would take him to the present-day Americas.

1778 The opera house La Scala opened in Milan, Italy, with a performance of Antonio Salieri's "Europa Riconosciuta."

1852 America's first intercollegiate athletic event was held as Yale and Harvard met for a crew race on Lake Winnipesaukee in Center Harbor, New Hampshire.

1914 Germany declared war on France.

1949 The National Basketball Association was formed.

1981 U.S. air traffic controllers went on strike.

2003 Annika Sorenstam completed a career Grand Slam by winning the Women's British Open.

2004 The Statue of Liberty pedestal in New York City reopened to the public for the first time since the September 11 attacks.

*A*UGUST 4

DAILY READING

"The Lord does not look at the things man looks at.
Man looks at the outward appearance,
but the Lord looks at the heart." (1 SAMUEL 16–17)

FEAST DAYS

ca. 1st cent.	Aristarchus	Fellow worker with Paul
529	Sithney	Patron against rabies
1859	John Vianney	Patron of parish priests

ENTRANCE AND EXIT

b. 1792	Percy Bysshe Shelley	English poet
b. 1901	Louis Armstrong	American musician
b. 1942	David Lange	New Zealand prime minister
d. 1875	Hans Christian Andersen	Danish author
d. 1999	Victor Mature	American actor
d. 2003	Frederick Robbins	American pediatrician

The Cure of Ars

John Mary Vianney (1786–1859), the Cure of Ars in France, was a poor farmer's son who had much difficulty learning Latin and suffered many illnesses. Although he was ordained by the age of thirty, he was considered incapable of leading a parish and needed further training. In short, Vianney had nothing to commend him.

However, St. John had a remarkable healing ministry and attracted many people to his services until his fame spread throughout France. A dedicated priest, he would often spend over fifteen hours a day hearing confession. He conducted a great struggle against the taverns that encouraged drunkenness and eventually succeeded in banning alcohol in his parish. This is an extract from one of his sermons against the evils of drink:

> St. Paul in the Holy Bible, assures us that the drunkard will not enter into the kingdom of heaven; drunkenness, therefore, must be a great sin. If drunkenness is a disease:
>
> It is the only disease contracted by an act of the will
> It is the only disease that requires a license to propagate it
> It is the only disease that is bottled and sold
> It is the only disease that requires outlets to spread it
> It is the only disease that produces revenue for the government
> It is the only disease that is habit forming
> It is the only disease that produces crime
> It is the only disease that is permitted to be spread by advertising
> It is the only disease without a germ or virus and for which there is no corrective medicine
> It is the only disease that will condemn you to eternal separation from God in Hell. (Gal. 5:21)

Vianney was canonized in 1925, and it is said that his body remains incorrupt.

Extract from, "Alastor: Or, the Spirit of Solitude"

Earth, Ocean, Air, belovèd brotherhood!
If our great Mother has imbued my soul
With aught of natural piety to feel
Your love, and recompense the boon with mine;
If dewy morn, and odorous noon, and even,
With sunset and its gorgeous ministers,
And solemn midnight's tingling silentness;
If Autumn's hollow sighs in the sere wood,
And Winter robing with pure snow and crowns
Of starry ice the gray grass and bare boughs;
If Spring's voluptuous pantings when she breathes
Her first sweet kisses,–have been dear to me;
If no bright bird, insect, or gentle beast
I consciously have injured, but still loved
And cherished these my kindred; then forgive
This boast, belovèd brethren, and withdraw
No portion of your wonted favor now!

–Percy Bysshe Shelley

August 5

DAILY READING

The unfolding of your words gives light;
it gives understanding to the simple. (PS 119:130)

FEAST DAYS

350	Cassian	Bishop of Autun, France
642	Oswald	King of Northumbria
1016	Gormeal	Abbot of Ardoilen, Ireland

ENTRANCE AND EXIT

b. 1604	John Eliot	Apostle to the Indians
b. 1850	Guy de Maupassant	French writer
b. 1930	Neil Armstrong	American astronaut
d. 1895	Friedrich Engels	German philosopher
d. 1962	Marilyn Monroe	American actor
d. 2000	Sir Alec Guinness	English actor

The Cane Ridge Revival

On this day in 1801, the remarkable revival at Cane Ridge in Kentucky began under the preaching of young Presbyterian minister, Barton Warren Stone (1772–1844). Rich and poor, slaves and free people, skeptics and believers gathered around the log Cane Ridge Meeting House in rural Bourbon County in what would become the seminal religious event of its day.

The Cane Ridge revival planted religious idealism and was the first great social gathering in a new state emerging from the fearful isolation of its violent frontier days. It also was the biggest, wildest, and most widely publicized event in a broader movement known as the Western Revival, which transformed American religious culture.

An estimated twenty-five thousand people traveled on foot and on horseback, many bringing wagons with tents and camping provisions. Historical accounts recall the contagious fervor that characterized the meetings that continued day and night. Descriptions abound of individuals, taken by great emotion, falling to the ground, crying aloud in prayer and song, and rising to exhort and assist others in their responses to the moment.

With wails and convulsions, thousands lamented their sins. "The noise was like the roar of Niagara," wrote eyewitness James Finley in his biography. "At one time I saw at least five hundred swept down in a moment as if a battery of a thousand guns had been opened upon them, and then immediately followed shrieks and shouts that rent the very heavens."

The Cane Ridge revival became a model for Christian renewal, and for years afterward, preachers would pray, "Lord, make it like Cane Ridge."

The Manifesto of the Communist Party (1848)

Prologue

A spectre is haunting Europe–the spectre
of Communism.
All the Powers of old Europe have entered
into a holy alliance to
exorcise this spectre: Pope and Czar,
Metternich and Guizot,
French Radicals and German police-spies.
Where is the party in opposition that has
not been decried as
Communistic by its opponents in power?
Where is the Opposition
that has not hurled back the branding
reproach of Communism,
against the more advanced opposition
parties, as well as against
its reactionary adversaries?

Two things result from this fact.

1. Communism is already acknowledged by all European Powers to be itself a Power.

2. It is high time that Communists should openly, in the face of the whole world, publish their views, their aims, their tendencies, and meet this nursery tale of the Spectre of Communism with a Manifesto of the party itself.

To this end, Communists of various nationalities have assembled in London, and sketched the following Manifesto, to be published in the English, French, German, Italian, Flemish, and Danish languages.

–Frederich Engels and Karl Marx

August 6

DAILY READING

All your words are true; all your righteous laws are eternal. (PS 119:160)

FEAST DAYS

ca. 500	James	Syrian monk
ca. 291	Justus	Patron Alcala, Spain
1132	Octavian	Bishop of Savona, Italy

ENTRANCE AND EXIT

b. 1504	Matthew Parker	Archbishop of Canterbury
b. 1809	Alfred Lord Tennyson	English Poet Laureate
b. 1881	Alexander Fleming	Scottish scientist
d. 1637	Ben Jonson	English writer
d. 1945	Hiram Johnson	American politician
d. 1978	Giovanni Montini	Pope Paul VI

Matthew Parker

Matthew Parker (1504–75) became Archbishop of Canterbury in 1559, a position he held until his death. He is one of the primary architects of the Thirty-Nine Articles of Religion.

Parker was born in Norwich and in 1537 he was appointed chaplain to King Henry VIII and the King's Chancellor, Thomas Cromwell, reported that, "Parker hath ever been of a good judgment and set forth the Word of God after a good manner."

Although associated with Protestantism, Parker survived Mary's reign without leaving the country. Parker distrusted popular enthusiasm, and he wrote in horror of the idea that "the people" should be the reformers of the church. He was not an inspiring leader, and no dogma, no prayer book, not even a tract or a hymn is associated with his name. He was a disciplinarian, a scholar, a modest and moderate man of genuine piety.

The Thirty-Nine Articles of Religion are the defining statements of Anglican doctrine and an extract is given below:

I. Of faith in the Holy Trinity.
There is but one living and true God, everlasting, without body, parts, or passions; of infinite power, wisdom, and goodness; the maker and preserver of all things both visible and invisible. And in unity of this Godhead there be three Persons, of one substance, power, and eternity; the Father, the Son, and the Holy Ghost.

II. Of the Word, or Son of God, which was made very man.
The Son, which is the Word of the Father, begotten from everlasting of the Father, the very and eternal God, and of one substance with the Father, took man's nature in the womb of the blessed Virgin, of her substance: so that two whole and perfect natures, that is to say, the Godhead and manhood, were joined together in one person, never to be divided, whereof is one Christ, very God and very man, who truly suffered, was crucified, dead, and buried, to reconcile His Father to us, and to be a sacrifice, not only for original guilt, but also for all actual sins of men.

III. Of the going down of Christ into Hell.
As Christ died for us, and was buried, so also is it to be believed that He went down into Hell.

IV. Of the Resurrection of Christ.
Christ did truly rise again from death, and took again His body, with flesh, bones, and all things appertaining to the perfection of man's nature, wherefore He ascended into heaven, and there sitteth until He return to judge all men at the last day.

Noteworthy

1787 The Constitutional Convention in Philadelphia began to debate a draft of the U.S. Constitution.

1806 The Holy Roman Empire went out of existence as Emperor Francis I abdicated.

1890 Convicted murderer William Kemmler became the first person to be executed in the electric chair as he was put to death at Auburn State Prison in New York.

1914 Austria-Hungary declared war against Russia, and Serbia declared war against Germany.

1998 Former White House intern Monica Lewinsky testified before a grand jury about her relationship with President Bill Clinton.

August 7

DAILY READING

The Lord *is our judge, the* Lord *is our lawgiver, the* Lord *is our king; it is he who will save us.* (ISA 33:22)

FEAST DAYS

257	Sixtus II	Pope
362	Donatus	Patron of Arezzo, Italy
1454	Albert of Scilly	Patron of Carmelite schools

ENTRANCE AND EXIT

b. 1876	Mata Hari	Dutch spy
b. 1942	Garrison Keillor	American radio host
b. 1948	Gregg Chappell	Australian cricketer
d. 1941	Rabindranath Tagore	Indian writer
d. 1957	Oliver Hardy	American actor
d. 2004	Bernard Levin	English writer

Bishop Francis Asbury

Francis Asbury (1745–1816), pioneer bishop of American Methodism, was born in Handsworth, near Birmingham, the son of a ordinary gardener He attended the Methodist society, was converted at the age of sixteen, and became a local preacher.

On this day in 1771, Asbury attended a Methodist conference in Bristol. He heard John Wesley's plea, "Our brethren in America call aloud for help. Who are willing to go over and help them?" Asbury stepped forward and committed himself to evangelizing America.

Over the next forty years, he visited Connecticut, Delaware, Georgia, Kentucky, Maine, Maryland, Massachusetts, New Hampshire, New Jersey, New York, North Carolina, Ohio, Pennsylvania, Rhode Island, South Carolina, Tennessee, Vermont, West Virginia, and Canada. He preached nearly seventeen thousand sermons, rode over a quarter of a million miles, ordained three thousand preachers, founded five schools, and distributed thousands of leaflets. Neighborhoods, streets, and even children were named "Asbury" in his honor. When he arrived in 1771, there were just 550 Methodists concentrated in New York and Philadelphia. By 1816, that number had grown to over 250,000.

He maintained a celibate and relentlessly itinerant life to match the rugged terrain and scattered population. Determined to keep the reins in his own hands, he defied the attempts of "Daddy Wesley" to retain remote control of his American followers.

Almost since the moment of his death, American Methodists have been fascinated by his childhood in England. Within ten years of his death, his house in the Black Country began receiving visitors, and nearly two hundred years later, Americans are still visiting.

Asbury never returned to his native land, but died in Spotsylvania County, Virginia, and was buried in Baltimore.

Quotes of the Day

"We should so work as if we were to be saved by our works; and so rely on Jesus Christ, as if we did no works."

–Francis Asbury

"That's another fine mess you've gotten me into."

–Oliver Hardy

*A*UGUST 8

DAILY READING

For the L*ORD takes delight in his people;*
he crowns the humble with salvation. (PS 149:4)

FEAST DAYS

ca. 250	Myron	Greek miracle worker
ca. 1368	Fourteen Holy Helpers	Black Plague Saints
1506	Peter Faber	Apostle of Germany

ENTRANCE AND EXIT

b. 1819	Charles Anderson Dana	American newspaper magnate
b. 1901	Ernest Lawrence	American scientist
b. 1937	Dustin Hoffman	American actor
d. 1827	George Canning	English prime minister
d. 1919	Ernst Haeckel	German scientist
d. 2004	Fay Wray	American actor

Invocation of the Holy Helpers

Fourteen Holy Helpers, who served God in humility and confidence on earth and are now in the enjoyment of His beatific vision in Heaven; because thou persevered till death thou gained the crown of eternal life. Remember the dangers that surround us in this vale of tears, and intercede for us in all our needs and adversities. Amen.

Fourteen Holy Helpers, select friends of God, I honor thee as mighty intercessors, and come with filial confidence to thee in my needs, for the relief of which I have undertaken to make this novena. Help me by thy intercession to placate God's wrath, which I have provoked by my sins, and aid me in amending my life and doing penance. Obtain for me the grace to serve God with a willing heart, to be resigned to His holy will, to be patient in adversity and to persevere unto the end, so that, having finished my earthly course, I may join thee in Heaven, there to praise for ever God, who is wonderful in His Saints. Amen.

Fourteen Holy Helpers

During the fourteenth century, the Black Plague devastated Europe, and many died without receiving the last sacrements. It was a violent time, with those carrying the contagion often attacked and isolated. Many people invoked a group of saints known as the Fourteen Holy Helpers during the Black Plague. Their devotion began in Germany and spread throughout most of Europe during the fourteenth century. The Fourteen Holy Helpers collectively venerated on August 8 every year were:

SAINT	CONDITION
Achatius	Headaches
Barbara	Fevers, sudden death
Blaise	Ills of the throat
Catherine of Alexandria	Sudden death
Christopher	Plagues, sudden death
Cyriacus	Temptation
Denis	Headaches
George	Protection of domestic animals
Giles	Plagues
Margaret of Antioch	For safe childbirth
Pantaleon	Protection of domestic animals
Vitus	Epilepsy
Erasmus	Intestinal trouble
Eustachius	Difficult situations

AUGUST 9

DAILY READING

Are not five sparrows sold for two pennies? Yet not one of them is forgotten by God.
Indeed, the very hairs of your head are all numbered.
Don't be afraid; you are worth more than many sparrows. (LUKE 12:6–7)

FEAST DAYS

ca. 6th cent.	Phelim	Bishop of Kilmore, Ireland
1440	Falco	Italian hermit
1942	Edith Stein	Auschwitz martyr

ENTRANCE AND EXIT

b. 1593	Izaak Walton	English writer
b. 1918	Robert Aldrich	American film director
b. 1922	Philip Larkin	English poet
d. 1962	Hermann Hesse	Swiss writer
d. 1967	Joe Orton	English dramatist
d. 1995	Jerry Garcia	American rock star

Edith Stein

Edith Stein's life seems to be a sign to encourage devotion and faith. She was born on Yom Kippur, the Jewish Day of Atonement, in 1891 in Breslau, Germany. When she was not yet two years old, her father died suddenly, leaving Edith's mother to raise the seven remaining children.

By her teenage years, Stein no longer practiced her Jewish faith and considered herself an atheist, but she continued to admire her mother's attitude of total openness toward God. Like many before and since, Edith Stein came to Christianity through the study of philosophy. She was one of the first women to be admitted to university, and her atheism began to crumble under the influence of her friends who had converted to Christianity. In 1921, she read about St. Teresa of Avila and decided to become a Catholic. Eventually, Stein became a leading voice in the Catholic Woman's Movement in Germany.

By the time Hitler rose to power in early 1933, Stein was well known in the German academic community. Hitler's growing popularity meant increased pressure on Jews and, like Esther in the Bible, she sought to help her people. She wanted a papal encyclical to counteract the mounting tide of anti-Semitism. Unfortunately, due to bureaucratic confusion, her request was not granted.

In 1933, she wrote: "I told our Lord that I knew it was His cross that was now being placed upon the Jewish people; that most of them did not understand this, but that those who did would have to take it up willingly in the name of all. I would do that, but what this carrying of the cross was to consist in, that I did not yet know."

In October 1933 she took the name Teresa Benedicta of the Cross and entered the Carmelite order in Cologne. But in 1942 Edith and her sister Rosa were arrested and deported to Auschwitz. A week later both were executed.

Fellow inmates who survived the Holocaust remarked that Sister Teresa Benedicta in those final days showed remarkable strength, helping to feed and bathe children when even their mothers had given up hope and were neglecting them. One survivor wrote:

> Maybe the best way I can explain it is that she carried so much pain that it hurt to see her smile. . . . In my opinion, she was thinking about the suffering that lay ahead. Not her own suffering–she was far too resigned for that–but the suffering that was in store for the others. Every time I think of her sitting in the barracks, the same picture comes to mind: a Pieta without the Christ.

Although she did not seek death, Stein had often expressed her willingness to offer herself along with the sacrifice of Christ for the sake of her people, the Jews, and also for the sake of their persecutors. She was beatified by Pope John Paul II on May 1, 1987.

*A*UGUST 10

DAILY READING

God is our refuge and strength,
an ever-present help in trouble. (PS 46:1)

FEAST DAYS

258	Lawrence	Patron of comedians
ca. 508	Gerontius	King of Dammonia (Devon)
ca. 6th cent.	Blane	Missionary to Scottish Picts

ENTRANCE AND EXIT

b. 1556	Philipp Nicolai	German theologian and hymn writer
b. 1874	Herbert Hoover	31st American president
b. 1928	Eddie Fisher	American actor
d. 1757	Dr. Benjamin Hoadly	English writer
d. 1759	Ferdinand VI	King of Spain
d. 1945	Robert Goddard	American scientist

The Scheme of the Heavens

On this day in 1675, King Charles II established the foundation stone for the Royal Observatory in Greenwich. The observatory, designed by Sir Christopher Wren, was the abode of the first Astronomer Royal, John Flamsteed (1646–1719). The diagram below shows Flamsteed's description of the night sky at the very minute of the opening ceremony.

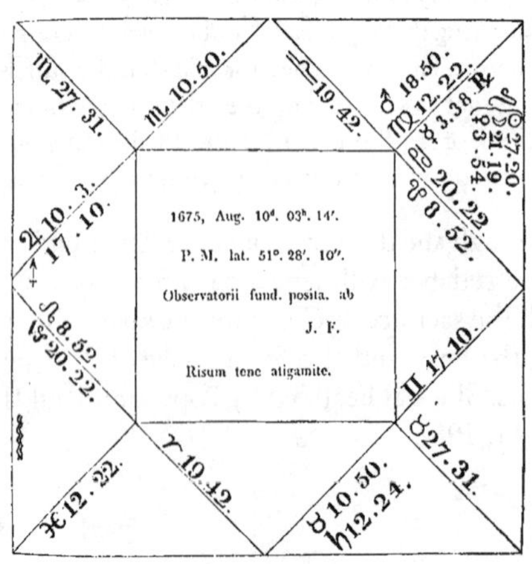

Despite a limited education due to poor health, Flamsteed's legacy to astronomy is an accurate mapping of the skies. A methodical perfectionist, he observed the partial solar eclipse of September 12, 1662, and established a new method of defining the position of stars.

Flamsteed's success aroused the curiosity (and competitiveness) of fellow astronomer Edmund Halley (1656–1742) and physicist Isaac Newton (1643–1727). Halley and Newton conspired to publish Flamsteed's work the *Historia Coelestis* against his wishes (the data was incomplete and not yet up to his high standards of accuracy). The complete, authorized version of Flamsteed's observations was only published posthumously (completed by his assistants) as the *Historia Coelestis Britannica*, including data on the positions of nearly three thousand stars–including a number of sightings of Uranus, which he believed to be a fixed star.

Edmund Halley succeeded Flamsteed as Astronomer Royal.

How Bright Appears the Morning Star

How bright appears the morning star,
With mercy beaming from afar!
The host of Heav'n rejoices!
O righteous Branch! O Jesse's Rod!
Thou Son of man, and Son of God!
We too will lift our voices
Jesus! Jesus! Holy, holy! yet most lowly!
Draw Thou near us:
Great Emmanuel! stoop and hear us!

–Philipp Nicolai

AUGUST 11

DAILY READING

I rejoice in following your statutes as one rejoices in great riches. (PS 119:14)

FEAST DAYS

295	Susanna	Roman noble
1253	Clare of Assisi	Patron of television
1802	Philomena	Patron of lost causes

ENTRANCE AND EXIT

b. 1921	Alex Haley	American author
b. 1897	Enid Blyton	English author
b. 1943	Pervaiz Musharraf	Pakistan president
d. 1890	Cardinal John Newman	English religious writer
d. 1919	Andrew Carnegie	Scottish philanthropist
d. 1994	Peter Cushing	English actor

The Man Who Gave Away $325,657,399

Andrew Carnegie epitomizes the classic American success story. He rose from a $1.20 a week job as a bobbin boy in a cotton mill to the head of a company that sold for the equivalent of $15 billion! Believing that "a rich man who dies rich dies in disgrace," he worked as hard at giving his wealth away as he did to earn it.

The son of a weaver, he came with his family to the United States in 1848 and settled in Allegheny, Pennsylvania. He then moved rapidly through a succession of jobs with Western Union and the Pennsylvania Railroad. In 1865, he resigned to establish his own business enterprises and eventually organized the Carnegie Steel Company, which launched the steel industry in Pittsburgh.

In 1889 he wrote *The Gospel of Wealth*, in which he asserted that all personal wealth beyond that required to supply the needs of one's family should be regarded as a trust fund to be administered for the benefit of the community.

Carnegie set about disposing of his fortune through innumerable personal gifts and the establishment of various trusts. He created philanthropic and educational organizations in the United States and several more in Europe. He established the Carnegie Foundation Peace Prize, the Carnegie Hero Fund Commission, and donated many organs to churches across America.

At age sixty-five, he sold the company to J. P. Morgan for 480 million dollars and devoted the rest of his life to his philanthropic activities and writing, including his autobiography.

Extract From The Gospel of Wealth (1889)

> In Christ's day, it is evident, reformers were against the wealthy. It is none the less evident that we are fast recurring to that position today; and there will be nothing to surprise the student of sociological development if society should soon approve the text which has caused so much anxiety: "It is easier for a camel to enter the eye of a needle than for a rich man to enter the kingdom of heaven." Even if the needle were the small casement at the gates, the words betoken serious difficulty for the rich. It will be but a step for the theologian from the doctrine that he who dies rich dies disgraced, to that which brings upon the man punishment or deprivation hereafter.

[21]

> The gospel of wealth but echoes Christ's words. It calls upon the millionaire to sell all that he hath and give it in the highest and best form to the poor by administering his estate himself for the good of his fellows, before he is called upon to lie down and rest upon the bosom of Mother Earth. So doing, he will approach his end no longer the ignoble hoarder of useless millions; poor, very poor indeed, in money, but rich, very rich, twenty times a millionaire still, in the affection, gratitude, and admiration of his fellow-men, and–sweeter far–soothed and sustained by the still, small voice within, which, whispering, tells him that, because he has lived, perhaps one small part of the great world has been bettered just a little. This much is sure: against such riches as these no bar will be found at the gates of Paradise.

AUGUST 12

DAILY READING

Do you not know that your body is a temple of the Holy Spirit,
who is in you, whom you have received from God?
You are not your own; you were bought at a price.
Therefore honor God with your body. (1 COR 6:19–20)

FEAST DAYS

732	Porcarius	Benedictine monk
792	Jambert	English archbishop
1838	James Nam	Vietnamese martyr

ENTRANCE AND EXIT

b. 1762	George IV	English king
b. 1774	Robert Southey	English writer
b. 1881	Cecil B. deMille	American film producer
d. 1827	William Blake	English mystic
d. 1955	Thomas Mann	German author
d. 1964	Ian Fleming	Scottish author

William Blake

London born poet, artist, and mystic, William Blake (1757–1827) was from earliest youth a seer of visions and a dreamer of dreams. He had religious visions mixed with contemporary life, seeing "Ezekiel sitting under a green bough," and "a tree full of angels at Peckham."

His teeming imagination sought expression both in verse and in drawing, and at age fourteen he was apprenticed to James Basire, an eminent engraver, and thereafter studied at the Royal Academy. Among his chief artistic works were illustrations for Young's *Night Thoughts*, Blair's *Grave*, *Spiritual Portraits*, and his finest work, *Inventions to the Book of Job*, all distinguished by originality and imagination.

In literature his *Songs of Innocence* appeared in 1789, *Songs of Experience* in 1794. These books were literally made by Blake and his heaven-provided wife; poems and designs alike being engraved on copper by Blake and bound by Mrs. Blake. In like fashion were produced his mystical books: *The Book of Thel* (1789); *The Marriage of Heaven and Hell* (1790); *The Gates of Paradise, Visions of the Daughters of Albion, Europe, The Book of Urizen* (1794); *The Book of Los* and *The Book of Ahania* (1795).

His last books were *Jerusalem* and *Milton*. His earlier and shorter pieces, such as "The Chimney-Sweeper," "Holy Thursday," "The Lamb," and "The Sun-flower" have an exquisite simplicity arising from directness and intensity of feeling–sometimes tender, sometimes sublime, always individual.

He lost himself in clouds of mysticism. A truly pious and loving soul, neglected and misunderstood by the world, but appreciated by an elect few, he led a cheerful and contented life of poverty illumined by visions and celestial inspirations.

Jerusalem

And did those feet in ancient time
Walk upon England's mountains green?
And was the holy Lamb of God
On England's pleasant pastures seen?

And did the countenance divine
Shine forth upon our clouded hills
And was Jerusalem builded there
Among those dark Satanic mills

Bring me my bow of burning gold
Bring me my arrows of desire
Bring me my spears o'clouds unfold
Bring me my chariot of fire

I will not cease from mental fight

Nor shall my sword sleep in hand
'Til we have built Jerusalem
In England's green and pleasant land
'Til we have built Jerusalem
In England's green and pleasant land

–*William Blake*

August 13

DAILY READING

We are God's workmanship, created in Christ Jesus to do good works, which God prepared in advance for us to do. (EPH 2:10)

FEAST DAYS

235	Pontian	Pope
675	Wigbert	Missionary to Germany
1943	Jakob Gapp	Nazi martyr

ENTRANCE AND EXIT

b. 1888	John Logie Baird	Scottish inventor
b. 1899	Sir Alfred Hitchcock	English film director
b. 1927	Fidel Castro	Cuban leader
d. 1910	Florence Nightingale	English nurse
d. 1946	Herbert George Wells	English author
d. 1995	Mickey Mantle	American baseball hero

The Lady of the Lamp

Florence Nightingale, the pioneer of modern nursing, was born in 1820 to wealthy British parents traveling in Italy. Named for the city in which she was born, young Florence never quite fit the mold of a Victorian lady. She was well educated in literature, music, drawing, and the domestic arts. Reared in the Unitarian Church, Florence felt an early calling to serve, and refused to marry.

In her diary, an entry shortly before her seventeenth birthday reads: "On February 7th, 1837, God spoke to me and called me to his service."

In 1844 she came to believe that her calling was to nurse the sick. In 1850 her family sent her on a tour of Egypt for her health. Some extracts from her diary follow:

> March 7. God called me in the morning and asked me would I do good for Him, for Him alone without the reputation.
>
> March 9. During half an hour I had by myself in my cabin, settled the question with God.
>
> April 1. Not able to go out but wished God to have it all His own way. I like Him to do exactly as He likes without even telling me the reason.
>
> May 12. Today I am thirty—the age Christ began his mission. Now no more childish things. No more love. No more marriage. Now Lord let me think only of Thy Will, what Thou willest me to do. Oh Lord Thy Will, Thy Will.

When she attempted to go to work as a nurse, her horrified family repeatedly opposed her. Finally, at age thirty-three she was able to obtain some minimal training and begin her career.

Nightingale recruited and equipped a group of nurses and went off to Turkey to help the soldiers injured in the Crimean War. The surgeons there, who resented the interference of a woman, did not celebrate her arrival. Undaunted, she worked tirelessly to improve conditions in the hospital. Her changes revolutionized British military medical care, increasing standards for sanitation and nutrition and dramatically lowering mortality rates. She was called "The Lady of the Lamp," as she worked long into the night to nurse casualties.

Quotes of the Day

"I attribute my success to this—I never gave or took any excuse."

—*Florence Nightingale*

"Go away. I'm all right."

—*H. G. Wells (last words)*

AUGUST 14

DAILY READING

"Here I am! I stand at the door and knock.
If anyone hears my voice and opens the door,
I will come in and eat with him, and he with me." (REV 3:20)

FEAST DAYS

780	Werenfridus	Benedictine monk
1087	Arnoldus	Patron of brewers
1941	Maximilian Maria Kolbe	Nazi martyr

ENTRANCE AND EXIT

b. 1867	John Galsworthy	English writer
b. 1945	Steve Martin	American comedian
b. 1966	Halle Berry	American actor
d. 1956	Bertolt Brecht	German writer
d. 1984	John Boynton Priestley	English writer
d. 1988	Enzo Ferrari	Italian car manufacturer

The Saint from Auschwitz

In the darkness and horror of the Holocaust, Father Maximilian Kolbe (1894–1941) stands as a beacon of light. He was imprisoned in Auschwitz in May 1941. The concentration camp saw daily atrocities and many inmates were left to starve. However, Maximilian carried on his priestly work surreptitiously, hearing confessions in unlikely places and celebrating the Lord's Supper. He pleaded with his fellow prisoners to forgive their persecutors and to overcome evil with good.

To discourage escapes, the camp had a rule that if a man escaped, ten men would be killed in retaliation. In July 1941, a man from Kolbe's bunker escaped. Although he died in the escape attempt, the camp commandant, Karl Fritsch, still demanded ten men be executed.

The men were brought forward, but one prisoner, Franciszek Gajowniczek, couldn't help his cry of anguish. "My poor wife!" he sobbed. "My poor children! What will they do?"

When he uttered this cry of dismay, Maximilian stepped silently forward, took off his cap, and said to Fritsch, "I am a Catholic priest. Let me take his place. I am old. He has a wife and children."

Kolbe's request was granted, and he was led with his fellow victims to Building 13 and left there to starve. One by one, the men died of hunger and thirst. Maximilian Kolbe encouraged the others with prayers, psalms, and meditations on the Passion of Christ. After two weeks, only four were alive. The cell was needed for more victims, and the camp executioner injected a lethal dose of acid into the left arm of each of the four dying men. Kolbe was the only one still fully conscious. With a prayer on his lips, the last prisoner, Father Kolbe, raised his arm for the executioner. His wait was over.

He was canonized by Pope John Paul II in 1982 and declared a martyr of charity.

Noteworthy

1848 The Oregon Territory was established.
1941 President Franklin D. Roosevelt and British Prime Minister Winston Churchill issued the Atlantic Charter, a statement of principles that renounced aggression.
1947 India and Pakistan became independent of British rule.
1969 British troops arrived in Northern Ireland to intervene in sectarian violence between Protestants and Roman Catholics.
1973 U.S. bombing of Cambodia came to a halt.
1997 Timothy McVeigh was sentenced to death for the Oklahoma City bombing.

AUGUST 15

DAILY READING

If we live, we live to the Lord: and if we die, we die to the Lord. So, whether we live or die, we belong to the Lord. (ROM 14:8)

FEAST DAYS

430	Alpius	Bishop of Tasgate, North Africa
1909	Isidore Bakanja	Belgian Congo martyr
1947	Claudius Granzotto	Italian sculptor

ENTRANCE AND EXIT

b. 1769	Napoleon Bonaparte	French emperor
b. 1785	Thomas de Quincey	English author
b. 1888	Thomas Edward Lawrence	English soldier
d. 1557	Agnes Prest	Exeter martyr
d. 1935	Will Rogers	American actor
d. 1951	Artur Schnabel	Austrian composer

Agnes Prest–Exeter Martyr

On this day in 1557, fifty-four-year-old Agnes Prest was led outside the city of Exeter's walls to Southernhay, where she was burned to death. Her last words were from John 11: "I am the Resurrection and the Life. . . . He that believes in me, though he die yet shall he live." Her crime? She refused to renounce her Protestant faith and return to the Catholic fold.

Agnes was poor and illiterate. She was born in Cornwall and worked in Exeter as a domestic servant for a while. Whilst in Exeter she heard things that changed her life. She may have been present in the crowd when Thomas Benet was martyred for refusing to become a Catholic. She wrote in her journal, "I learned such things as are so fixed in my breast that death should not separate them."

Agnes was married to an ardent Papist. They had numerous children, whom he brought up to believe the things he did. They "were much addicted to the superstitious sect of Popery." She was a simple Bible-believing woman, he was an ardent papist; it was not a good match. She wrote, "When I would have him to leave idolatry and to worship God in Heaven, he would not hear me, but he with his children rebuked and troubled me." Prest tried to compel his wife to go to Mass, make her confession, and follow the cross in procession, but Agnes refused to do any of these things. The persecution became so great that finally she fled.

When she returned, Agnes was arrested and kept in gaol at Launceston for three months, and then transferred to Exeter. The charge was, "Heresy chiefly against the Sacrament of the Altar and for speaking against Idols." She was ordered to give up her religion, or be burned as a heretic–she chose the latter.

Extract from Confessions of an English Opium Eater *(1822)*

I here present you, courteous reader, with the record of a remarkable period in my life: according to my application of it, I trust that it will prove not merely an interesting record, but in a considerable degree useful and instructive. In that hope it is that I have drawn it up; and that must be my apology for breaking through that delicate and honourable reserve which, for the most part, restrains us from the public exposure of our own errors and infirmities. Nothing, indeed, is more revolting to English feelings than the spectacle of a human being obtruding on our notice his moral ulcers or scars, and tearing away that "decent drapery" which time or indulgence to human frailty may have drawn over them; accordingly, the greater part of our confessions (that is, spontaneous and extra-judicial confessions) proceed from demireps, adventurers, or swindlers: and for any such acts of gratuitous self-humiliation from those who can be supposed in sympathy with the decent and self-respecting part of society, we must look to French literature, or to that part of the German which is tainted with the spurious and defective sensibility of the French. All this I feel so forcibly, and so nervously am I alive to reproach of this tendency, that I have for many months hesitated about the propriety of allowing this or any part of my narrative to come before the public eye until after my death (when, for many reasons, the whole will be published); and it is not without an anxious review of the reasons for and against this step that I have at last concluded on taking it.

–Thomas de Quincey

AUGUST 16

DAILY READING

Since we have these promises, dear friends, let us purify ourselves from everything that contaminates body and spirit, perfecting holiness out of reverence for God. (2 COR 7:1)

FEAST DAYS

1083	Stephen	Patron of kings
1327	Roch	Patron of epidemics
1618	John of St. Martha	Missionary to Japan

ENTRANCE AND EXIT

b. 1645	Jean de la Bruyere	French scholar
b. 1860	Jules Laforgue	French poet
b. 1911	Ernst Friedrich Schumacher	German economist
d. 1948	George Herman "Babe" Ruth	American baseball star
d. 1949	Margaret Mitchell	American author
d. 1977	Elvis Aaron Presley	American rock star

St. Roch

Born in Montpelier, France, in 1295, St. Roch (or Roche or Roque) was a wealthy nobleman who made a pilgrimage from Montpelier to Rome. He encountered a plague and devoted himself to the sick. Although he was infected, he bore incredible pains with patience and joy. On his return to France, he became noted for his piety and austere penance.

One story related that when infected, a hound belonging to a man called Gotard daily took bread away from his master's board and gave to Roch, whom Gotard thereby discovered, and visited and administered to his necessities. Tradition relates that Roch was healed by revelation of an angel; and with touching and blessing he cured the diseased and sick in the city of Placentia, Italy.

Many churches in Italy, France, and Germany are dedicated to Roch. The English phrase "sound as a roach" may have been derived from familiarity with the legend and attributes of this saint. Plague was a common occurrence in England when streets were narrow, without sewers, and houses were without boarded floors. Those who prayed to him believed that the miraculous intermission of St. Roch could make them as "sound" as himself.

A Lament upon Certain Vexations

Cosmologies, they're not the scene!
And life's routine is such a bore . . .
Never forget, one thing was sure:
Our wit was zilch–man, we were mean!

We'd like to confess to certain things,
Astounding ourselves as on we go,
So, once and for all we get to know
Each other without posturings.

We'd like to bleed sweet Silence white
And have the chattering class demoted;
But no, the ladies are devoted
To getting their precedences right!

With such apt airs they sulk!–They what?
By light of day a guy researches
By what superaesthetic lurches
They are such a delectable lot.

One of them wants us to assist
The search for a ring she cannot place,
(Lost where, in this vast, empty space?)
A token of LOVE, she will insist!

They are such a delectable lot.

–Jules Laforgue (translated by Alan Marshfield)

August 17

DAILY READING

"Let him who boasts boast in the Lord." For it is not the one who commends himself who is approved, but the one whom the Lord commends. (2 COR 10:17–18)

FEAST DAYS

ca. 7th cent.	James the Deacon	York Missionary to Northumbria
1198	Donatus	Benedictine monk
1527	Hyacinth	Apostle to Poland

ENTRANCE AND EXIT

b. 1601	Pierre de Fermat	French mathematician
b. 1930	Ted Hughes	English Poet Laureate
b. 1932	Sir Vidiadhar Surajprasad Naipaul	Trinidadian writer
d. 1969	Mies van der Rohe	German architect
d. 1983	Ira Gershwin	American lyricist
d. 1987	Rudolph Hess	Nazi politician

Dante's Nine Circles of Hell

The Florentine poet Dante Alighieri (1265–1321) was destined for a career as a papal envoy, but he fell out of favor when his supporters were ousted from power and he was banished. On this day in 1301, Dante's glittering career came to an end.

While in exile in Venice, Dante began his epic poetic description of Hell (Inferno), Purgatory (Purgatorio), and Heaven (Paradisio). This is a brief outline of Dante's Inferno:

> Sinners in Dante's nine circles of hell are guilty of one of three types of sin:
>
> **Incontinence**: Evil arising from losing control of natural appetites and desires
>
> **Brutishness**: Evil arising from attraction to things that repulse the healthy soul
>
> **Malice/Vice**: Evil arising from abuse of reason

The downward spiral to hell can be characterized thus:

REGION	STAGE	SIN/SINNERS
The dark wood	Preface to the Journey	Despair
The descent		Fear
Vestibule of Hell	The Gate of Hell	Neutrals
First Circle		Pagans, unbaptized infants
Second Circle (Judgment)		The lustful
Third Circle		Gluttons
Fourth Circle		Prodigals, the avaricious
Fifth Circle		The angry, the sullen
Sixth Circle	Transition to Lower Hell—The Realm of Violence and Fraud	Heretics
Seventh Circle (round 1)		Murderers, war makers
Seventh Circle (round 2)		Suicides
Seventh Circle (round 3)		Blasphemers, sodomites, usurers
Eighth Circle (round 1)	Maleboge—The Realm of Simple Fraud	Seducers
Eighth Circle (round 2)		Flatterers
Eighth Circle (round 3)		Simonists
Eighth Circle (round 4)		Fortune-tellers
Eighth Circle (round 5)		Grafters
Eighth Circle (round 6)		Hypocrites
Eighth Circle (round 7)		Thieves
Eighth Circle (round 8)		Evil counselors
Eighth Circle (round 9)		Sowers of discord
Eighth Circle (round 10)		Alchemists, impersonators, counterfeiters, false witnesses
Eighth Circle (Edge of Pit)		Elemental natures
Ninth Circle (round 1)	The Realm of Compound Fraud	Traitors to the family
Ninth Circle (round 2)		Traitors to the country
Ninth Circle (round 3)		Murderers of guests
Ninth Circle (round 4)		Those who set out to destroy God
Ninth Circle (round 5)		The Ultimate Destroyer—Lucifer

Fermat's Last Theorem

$x^n + y^n = z^n$ has no integer solutions for $n > 2$.

I have discovered a truly remarkable proof which this margin is too small to contain.

Pierre de Fermat (c.1640)

AUGUST 18

DAILY READING

To me, to live is Christ and to die is gain. (PHIL 1:21)

FEAST DAYS

328	Helena	Mother of Constantine
ca. 660	Ronan	Bishop of Lindisfarne, England
1867	Thomas Guengoro	Japanese martyr

ENTRANCE AND EXIT

b. 1807	Charles Francis Adams	American politician
b. 1925	Brian Aldiss	English writer
b. 1927	Rossalyn Carter	American First Lady
d. 1227	Genghis Khan	Mongol leader
d. 1850	Honoré de Balzac	French writer
d. 1940	Walter Chrysler	American car manufacturer

St. Helena

Helena was the mother of Constantine the Great. Little is known about her life, but according to St. Ambrose, Helena was a humble innkeeper when she married Constantius. According to tradition, she was the daughter of a British king, but this does not match up to her innkeeping role. Constantius spent some time in Britain and died at York, but by then he had cast off Helena and taken a new wife.

On the death of his father, the young Constantine brought his mother to live at court at Byzantium, the capital of the Eastern Empire. He honored her by giving her the Roman title of Augusta and also had coins struck bearing her image.

After Constantine's dramatic conversion, he led his mother to faith and ensured his children were raised as Christians. Helena became zealous for the faith, using her influence and wealth to extend Christianity. She built many churches and restored shrines; her name is particularly associated with churches at Rome and at Trier, in Gaul.

In Israel, she ordered the construction of great basilicas at Bethlehem and Jerusalem. By the time she was in her eighties, she cleared the mound that covered the Holy Sepulchre. Thus, tradition holds that she discovered the true cross, on which Jesus was crucified.

Noteworthy

1227 The Mongol conqueror Genghis Khan died.

1587 Virginia Dare became the first child of English parents to be born on American soil, on what is now Roanoke Island, North Carolina.

1958 The novel *Lolita* by Vladimir Nabokov was published.

1988 Indiana Sen. Dan Quayle was nominated as George H.W. Bush's running mate during the Republican National Convention in New Orleans.

1991 Soviet hard-liners launched a coup aimed at toppling President Mikhail S. Gorbachev.

2005 Pope Benedict XVI began his first foreign trip as pontiff in low-key style, returning to his "beloved" German homeland.

*A*UGUST 19

DAILY READING

He who has the Son has life; he who does not have the Son of God does not have life. (1 JOHN 5:12)

FEAST DAYS

304	Timothy	Bishop of Gaza
660	Magnus	Father of St. Agricola
1598	Christopher Robinson	English martyr

ENTRANCE AND EXIT

b. 1631	John Dryden	English Poet Laureate
b. 1871	Orville Wright	American aircraft pioneer
b. 1946	William Jefferson Clinton	42nd American president
d. 14	Gaius Octavius	Roman Emperor Augustus
d. 1662	Blaise Pascal	French mathematician
d. 1936	Federico Garcia Lorca	Spanish writer

Glorious John

The English Poet Laureate, Royal Historiographer, dramatist, and critic John Dryden (1631–1700) is one of the key figures of seventeenth-century literature. Educated at Cambridge University, he first came to public notice with his *Heroic Stanzas* (1659), commemorating the death of Oliver Cromwell. During the Protectorate, he was on the antimonarchical Puritan side, but became a Catholic upon the Restoration of James II. He announced his conversion in 1686 in a 2,500-line poem called *The Hind and the Panther*. The Hind was the Catholic Church pursued by the Anglican Panther. Using imagery from the Song of Solomon, Dryden's poem is a plea for toleration and understanding from both traditions.

In 1662 he was elected to the Royal Society, where he had a long and varied career as a dramatist. His most notable plays include the heroic dramas, *The Conquest of Granada* (2 parts, 1670–71) and *Aurenz-Zebe* (1675); his blank-verse masterpiece, *All for Love* (1677), a retelling of Shakespeare's *Antony and Cleopatra*; and the comedy *Marriage à la Mode* (1672).

With the accession of the Protestant William III, Dryden lost his laureateship and court patronage, but continued writing plays, criticism, and poetry.

An extract from The Hind and the Panther

A milk-white Hind, immortal and unchang'd,
Fed on the lawns, and in the forest rang'd;
Without unspotted, innocent within,
She fear'd no danger, for she knew no sin.
Yet had she oft been chas'd with horns and hounds
And Scythian shafts; and many winged wounds
Aim'd at her heart; was often forc'd to fly,
And doom'd to death, though fated not to die.
Not so her young; for their unequal line
hero's make, half human, half divine.
earthly mold obnoxious was to fate,
immortal part assum'd immortal state.
these a slaughter'd army lay in blood,
Extended o'er the Caledonian wood,
Their native walk; whose vocal blood arose,
And cried for pardon on their perjur'd foes.
Their fate was fruitful, and the sanguine seed,
Endued with souls, increas'd the sacred breed.
So captive Israel multiplied in chains,
A numerous exile, and enjoy'd her pains.
With grief and gladness mix'd, their mother view'd
Her martyr'd offspring, and their race renew'd;
Their corps to perish, but their kind to last,
So much the deathless plant the dying fruit surpass'd.

*A*UGUST 20

DAILY READING

I have set the LORD *always before me.*
Because he is at my right hand, I will not be shaken. (PS 16:8)

FEAST DAYS

662	Haduin	Bishop of Le Mans, France
651	Oswin	Patron of victims of betrayal
1153	Bernard of Clairvaux	Monastery founder

ENTRANCE AND EXIT

b. 1833	Benjamin Harrison	23rd American president
b. 1860	Raymond Poincare	French prime minister
b. 1944	Rajiv Gandhi	Indian prime minister
d. 1818	Emily Brontë	English author
d. 1912	William Booth	Founder of the Salvation Army
d. 1915	Paul Ehrlich	German scientist

St. Bernard of Clairvaux

Towering over twelfth-century society, Bernard of Clairvaux was a brilliant preacher, polished writer, counselor of kings, and adviser to popes. He was an effective and intuitive genius, and a profound mystic.

Born in 1090, Bernard entered the Abbey of Citeaux in 1112, bringing thirty of his relatives with him, including five of his brothers; his youngest brother and his widowed father followed later. In 1115 he was sent to begin a new monastery near Aube: Clairvaux, the Valley of Light. As a young abbot he published a series of sermons on the annunciation. These marked him out as a most gifted spiritual writer.

Bernard's dynamism soon reached far beyond monastic circles. He was sought as an advisor and mediator by the ruling powers of his age. More than any other, he helped to bring about the healing of the papal schism that arose in 1130 with the election of the antipope Anacletus II. It cost Bernard eight years of laborious travel and skillful mediation. At the same time he labored for peace and reconciliation between England and France. In his last years he rose from his sickbed and went into the Rhineland to defend the Jews against a savage persecution.

Bernard died at Clairvaux and was canonized by Pope Alexander III on January 18, 1174. Pope Pius VII declared him a Doctor of the Church in 1830.

Quotes of the Day

"For when God loves, all he desires is to be loved in return. The sole purpose of his love is to be loved, in the knowledge that those who love him are made happy by their love of him."

–St. Bernard

"I see heaven's glories shine and faith shines equal."

–Emily Brontë

"The greatness of a man's power is the measure of his surrender."

–William Booth

August 21

DAILY READING

By day the LORD directs his love, at night his song is with me–
a prayer to the God of my life. (PS 42:8)

FEAST DAYS

ca. 12th cent.	Abraham	Monk of Smolensk, Russia
1786	Joseph Nien Vien	Vietnamese martyr
1879	Our Lady of Knock	County Mayo, Ireland

ENTRANCE AND EXIT

b. 1765	William IV	King of England
b. 1904	Count Basie	American bandleader
b. 1930	Princess Margaret	Sister of Queen Elizabeth II
d. 1940	Leon Trotsky	Bolshevik revolutionary
d. 1947	Ettore Bugatti	Italian car manufacturer
d. 1983	Benigno Aquino	Philippine opposition leader

Marian Apparition at Knock

On this day in 1879, around 8 p.m., Margaret Beirne, a resident of Cnoc Mhuine in County Mayo, Ireland, was sent by her brother to lock up the church for the evening. When she was ready to leave, she noticed a strange brightness hovering over the church. Margaret had other things on her mind, and didn't tell anyone what she saw. Around the same time, another member of the Beirne family, Mary, was leaving from a visit to the church's housekeeper, and stopped with the housekeeper at the gables, where they could see the church. Mary asked: "Oh look at the statues! Why didn't you tell me the priest got new statues for the chapel?"

The housekeeper responded that she knew nothing of the priest getting new statues. So, they both went for a closer look, and Mary Beirne said: "But they are not statues, they're moving. It's the Blessed Virgin!"

Thirteen others also came and saw the beautiful woman, clothed in white garments, wearing a brilliant crown. Her hands were raised as if in prayer. All knew that it was Mary, the Mother of Jesus. On the right of her stood St. Joseph, his head inclined toward her. On her left stood St. John the Evangelist, dressed as a bishop. To the left of St. John stood an altar, which had a lamb, and a cross surrounded by angels on it. The vision lasted about two hours. People who were not at the apparition site reported that they saw a bright light illuminating the area of the church.

As word spread of the apparition, miraculous healings began to occur with some who visited the church–the parish priest recorded three hundred in the first three years.

Today, over one million pilgrims visit the Shrine of Knock each year, making it one of the most popular places in the Emerald Isle.

Noteworthty

1680 Pueblo Indians took possession of Santa Fe, New Mexico, after driving out the Spanish.

1831 Former slave Nat Turner led a violent insurrection in Virginia.

1959 President Dwight D. Eisenhower signed an executive order proclaiming Hawaii the fiftieth state of the union.

2000 Rescue efforts to reach the sunken Russian nuclear submarine Kursk ended with divers announcing none of the 118 sailors had survived.

AUGUST 22

DAILY READING

He who did not spare his own Son,
but gave him up for us all–how will he not also,
along with him, graciously give us all things? (ROM 8:32)

FEAST DAYS

178	Symphorian	French martyr
ca. 877	Andrew of Tuscany	Irish noble
1599	John Kemble	English martyr

ENTRANCE AND EXIT

b. 1862	Claude Debussy	French composer
b. 1893	Dorothy Parker	American writer
b. 1904	Deng Xiaoping	Chinese leader
d. 1485	Richard III	King of England
d. 1922	Michael Collins	Irish politician
d. 1978	Jomo Kenyatta	Kenyan politician

The Battle of Bosworth Field

The Wars of the Roses (1455–85) is the name commonly applied to a series of civil wars that arose out of a dynastic struggle between two main branches of the English royal house–the House of York and the House of Lancaster. The emblem of the House of York was the white rose and the emblem of the House of Lancaster a red rose.

The Battle of Bosworth in Leicestershire marked the end of twenty-four years of Yorkist rule in England. Richard Plantagenet (King Richard III) was struck down while apparently making a final desperate charge against Henry Tudor (House of Lancaster). It is said that he almost succeeded in bringing Henry down, which is evidenced by the death of the young Tudor's standard-bearer. As a standard-bearer of the time invariably stayed close to the commander he was serving, it is generally accepted that Henry was involved in some form of close combat. However, it was Richard who met his demise, and his body was stripped naked and paraded through town slung over the back of a horse. His body was exposed to the public for two days in Grey Friars Church at Leicester. Years later, when this church was destroyed, King Richard's bones were tipped into a river, and the coffin used as a horse trough outside the White Horse Inn in Gallow Tree Gate. Henry Tudor allegedly found Richard's crown under a hawthorn bush near the battle site and was made King of England from that day forward. This marked the beginning of the 120-year Tudor dynasty.

Noteworthy

565 Celtic missionary and abbot Columba (521–97) reportedly confronted the Loch Ness Monster and became the first recorded observer of the creature.

1524 Martin Luther's disputation with Andreas Karlstadt (1486–1541) took place in Jena.

1572 Gaspard de Coligny (ca. 1519–72), a French Huguenot leader, was wounded in an assassination attempt.

1642 The English Civil War began as King Charles I organized an army to fight against the Puritans.

1670 English missionary John Eliot (1604–90) founded a church for Native Americans at Martha's Vineyard, Massachusetts.

1791 Levi Spaulding, missionary to Ceylon, was born in Jaffrey, New Hampshire (d. June 18, 1873).

1791 Johann D. Michaelis, regarded as a founder of Syriac philology, died (b. 1717, Halle).

1948 The first assembly of the World Council of Churches met at Amsterdam.

AUGUST 23

DAILY READING

When I said, "My foot is slipping," your love,
O LORD, supported me. When anxiety was great within me,
your consolation brought joy to my soul. (PS 94:18–19)

FEAST DAYS

ca. 5th cent.	Tydfil	Daughter of Prince Brychan, Wales
ca. 618	Eoghan	Monk of Kilnamanagh Abbey, Ireland
1617	Rose of Lima	Patron of Santa Rosa, California

ENTRANCE AND EXIT

b. 686	Charles Martell	Frankish king
b. 1754	Louis XVI	French king
b. 1912	Gene Kelly	American dancer
d. 1926	Rudolph Valentino	Italian actor
d. 1960	Oscar Hammerstein II	American librettist
d. 1995	Alfred Eisenstaedt	German photographer

The Melody Lingers On

On this day the great American dancer and film director Gene Kelly (1912–96) was born in Pittsburgh, Pennsylvania. His main goal as a young boy was to play baseball for the Pittsburgh Pirates, but encouraged by his mother, Kelly grew to love dance so much that he took it up as a career.

He went to New York City, and in 1940 became a huge success with the film *Pal Joey*, which brought him to the attention of director David O. Selznick. Kelly signed a contract with Selznick, but unfortunately, Selznick didn't have any good parts for him.

He starred in MGM's *For Me and My Gal* and *Cover Girl*, both of which were huge successes. During World War II, Kelly joined the Navy from 1944–46. On his return to Hollywood, he made *Living in a Big Way, The Pirate*, and *The Three Musketeers*. But when Kelly made *On the Town*, he reached a kind of fame he had never had before. It was his directorial debut, and it was a smash hit. *On the Town* was the first musical to be shot on location. In 1950, he became a superstar with *An American in Paris*, which won six Academy Awards, including one for Kelly.

In 1951, Kelly made movie history with *Singin' in the Rain*. Though today it is considered one of the greatest films ever made, at the time it was overshadowed by his previous year's success.

In 1980, Gene made his last film, a musical called *Xanadu*. In 1985, he received a lifetime achievement award from the American Film Institute, and over the years received even more awards for lifetime achievement.

In 1994, Kelly made his last on-screen appearance, hosting *That's Entertainment III*. His last words on the big screen were, "The song has ended, but the melody lingers on."

Noteworthy

1833 Britain abolishes slavery in colonies; seven hundred thousand slaves freed.
1944 Romania liberated from Nazi occupation.
1963 Beatles release "She Loves You" in the UK.

August 24

DAILY READING

I love the L*ORD, for he heard my voice; he heard my cry for mercy.*
Because he turned his ear to me, I will call on him as long as I live. (PS 116:1–2)

FEAST DAYS

ca. 1st cent.	St. Bartholomew	Apostle
253	Massa Candida	300 martyrs of Carthage
ca. 753	George Limniotes	Hermit of Mount Olympus

ENTRANCE AND EXIT

b. 1759	William Wilberforce	English politician
b. 1899	Jorge Luis Borges	Argentinian writer
b. 1957	Stephen Fry	English writer and actor
d. 1680	Thomas Blood	Irish adventurer
d. 1957	Ronald Knox	English theologian
d. 2003	Sir Wilfred Thesiger	English explorer

St. Bartholomew's Day–Associations

There is no scriptural account of the birth or death of St. Bartholomew the apostle, although he is mentioned in the list of apostles in Matthew 10, Mark 3, and Luke 6. He is also identified as Nathaniel in John 1. Tradition holds that he preached in the India and met his death by being flayed alive by order of the King of Armenia in the first century.

This day is also known as Black Bartholomew in recognition of the slaughter of thousands of Huguenots in 1662 in France in the reign of Charles IX. A contemporary account records:

> In that savage scene, the massacre of St. Bartholomew, planned with all the coolness of deliberation, five hundred gentlemen, Protestants, and ten thousand persons of inferior rank were massacred in one night at Paris alone, and great numbers in the provinces. The Roman pontiff, on hearing of it, expressed great joy, announcing that the cardinals should return thanks to the Almighty for so signal an advantage obtained for the holy see, and that a jubilee should be observed all over Christendom.

It was an ancient custom at Croyland Abbey, near Peterborough, until the time of Edward IV to give little knives as gifts on St. Bartholomew's Day. Many of these knives of various sizes have been found in the ruins of the abbey.

St. Bartholomew's Day falls at the end of the forty-day period decreed by St. Swithin for constant rain or sun. For this reason, Bartholomew is known for weather lore: "If St. Bartholomew's Day be fair and clear, then a prosperous autumn comes that year," "St. Bartholomew's mantle wipes dry all the tears that St. Swithin can cry," and "St. Bartholomew brings the cold dew."

A pilgrim called Rahere was healed after seeing a vision of Bartholomew on a trip to Rome in 1123. He founded a St. Bartholomew's priory and hospital in Smithfield, London, and Bart's hospital still occupies the same site.

Ten years later at Smithfield, the first St. Bartholomew's Fair was held to supply food and drink to pilgrims. It grew in popularity and ran until 1855, although some other counties in England still have a St. Bartholomew's Fair on this day.

Quotes of the Day

"Bathe your eyes on Bartimy Day,
You may throw your spectacles away."

–English traditional proverb

"It is stupid of modern civilization to have given up believing in the devil, when he is the only explanation of it."

–Ronald Knox

*A*UGUST 25

DAILY READING

Great peace have they who love your law,
and nothing can make them stumble. (PS 119:165)

FEAST DAYS

ca. 260	Lucilla	Roman martyr
683	Ebbe the Elder	Daughter of King Aethelfrith the Ravager
ca. 690	Hunegund	Benedictine martyr

ENTRANCE AND EXIT

b. 1819	Allan Pinkerton	American private detective
b. 1850	Bill Nye	American humorist
b. 1930	Sean Connery	Scottish actor
d. 1776	David Hume	Scottish philosopher
d. 1900	Friedrich Wilhelm Nietzsche	German philosopher
d. 1984	Truman Capote	American writer

The First Council of Nicea

This day commemorates the conclusion of the First Council of Nicea (Turkey), convened by the Roman Emperor Constantine I in 325. It was the first council to include different wings of Christianity and involved over three hundred bishops from Africa, Europe, and Asia. The purpose of the synod council (also called a synod) was to resolve disagreements in the Church of Alexandria over the nature of the Trinity. The popular leader Arius, for whom the Arian controversy is named, led the party that contended that if Christ is the "Son," then he had a beginning, and there was a time when he was not. Bishop Alexander of Alexandria contended for the position that Christ, the second person of the Godhead, had no beginning and was coeternal with the Father. Athanasius, in his early twenties at the time, accompanied his bishop to the council and became recognized as a chief spokesman for the view that the Son was fully God, coequal and coeternal with the Father.

The principle effort was to find a formula from Scripture that would express the full deity of the Son, equally with the Father. However, the Arians readily agreed to all such formulations, having interpreted them already to fit their own views. Finally, the Greek word *homoousios* (meaning "of the same substance, or nature, or essence") was introduced, chiefly because it was one word that could not be understood to support the Arian view. The first Nicene Creed was therefore drafted with the word *homoousios* and surprisingly endorsed by all but two of the attending bishops.

The result was therefore a ruling against Arianism. The Council of Nicea was historically significant because it was the first effort to attain consensus in the church through an assembly representing all of Christendom.

With the creation of the Nicene Creed, a precedent was established for subsequent ecumenical councils to create a statement of belief and canons that were intended to become orthodox for all Christians. It would serve to unify the church and provide a clear guideline over disputed matters on what it meant to be a practicing Christian, a momentous event in the history.

Noteworthy

National Day, Uruguay
1944 Liberation of Paris by American troops.

Quote of the Day

"In heaven all the interesting people are missing."

–Friedrich Nietzsche

*A*UGUST 26

DAILY READING

Just as each of us has one body with many members,
and these members do not all have the same function,
so in Christ we who are many form one body,
and each member belongs to all the others. (ROM 12:4–5)

FEAST DAYS

247	Zephyrinus	Pope
258	Irenaus	Church father
764	Bregowine	Archbishop of Canterbury

ENTRANCE AND EXIT

b. 1451	Christopher Columbus	Italian explorer
b. 1740	Joseph Montgolfier	French inventor
b. 1875	John Buchan	Scottish writer
d. 1676	Sir Robert Walpole	British prime minister
d. 1743	Antoine-Laurent Lavoisier	French chemist
d. 1975	Haile Selassie I	Ethiopian emperor

John Buchan

Baron Tweedsmuir, better known as Scottish thriller writer extraordinaire John Buchan, was born on this day in 1875. The son of the Rev. John Buchan, he was educated at Glasgow University and Brasenose College, Oxford, where he won the Stanhope historical essay prize (1897) and the Newdigate prize for poetry (1898), and graduating first class in *literae humaniores* (1899). In 1901 he became private secretary to Lord Milner, then High Commissioner for South Africa. His African experiences suggested *The African Colony* (1903), *A Lodge in the Wilderness* (1906), and *Prester John* (1910).

Buchan worked for British intelligence during World War I; served as a member of Parliament; and wrote historical fiction, criticism, poetry, history, and biography.

But it is probably for his novel *The Thirty-Nine Steps* (1915), in which mining engineer Richard Hannay becomes embroiled in espionage, that he is best known because of the Alfred Hitchcock film of 1935 starring Robert Donat and Madeleine Carroll. *The Thirty-Nine Steps* was also filmed in 1959 starring Kenneth More, and in 1978 with Robert Powell. Powell went on to star in a short-lived British television series "Hannay" (1988–89), but the scripts were not based on the other Hannay stories such as *Greenmantle* (1916), *Mr. Standfast* (1919), and *The Three Hostages* (1924). It was rumored that after Hitchcock directed *Family Plot* that he was considering filming *Greenmantle*, but he died before these plans could come to fruition.

Buchan dubbed his thrillers "shockers," which he called "the romance where the incidents defy the probabilities, and march just inside the borders of the possible." He also wrote several novels with lawyer Edward Leithen, such as *The Power-House* (1913), *The Dancing Floor* (1926), and *Sick Heart River* (1941).

He died in 1940 as Governor-General of Canada.

Thirty Nine Steps–Dedication

TO
THOMAS ARTHUR NELSON
(LOTHIAN AND BORDER HORSE)

My Dear Tommy,

You and I have long cherished an affection for that elemental type of tale which Americans call the "dime novel" and which we know as the "shocker"–the romance where the incidents defy the probabilities, and march just inside the borders of the possible. During an illness last winter I exhausted my store of those aids to cheerfulness, and was driven to write one for myself. This little volume is the result, and I should like to put your name on it in memory of our long friendship, in the days when the wildest fictions are so much less improbable than the facts.

–John Buchan

*A*UGUST 27

DAILY READING

Thou wilt keep him in perfect peace, whose mind is stayed on thee: because he trusteth in thee. (ISA 26:3, KJV)

FEAST DAYS

1532	Gabriel Mary	Founder of the Annonciades Order
1582	Transverberation of the Heart of Teresa of Avila	Patron of Spain
1610	Roger Cadwallador	English martyr

ENTRANCE AND EXIT

b. 1770	Georg Hegel	German philosopher
b. 1908	Lyndon Baines Johnson	36th American president
b. 1910	Agnesa Gonxha Bojaxhiu	Mother Teresa of Calcutta
d. 1879	Sir Rowland Hill	English postmaster
d. 1948	Charles Evans Hughes	American secretary of state
d. 1979	Earl Mountbatten	Admiral of the Fleet

Burning Milton's Books

John Milton (1608–74) was one of that century's greatest writers. Although he graduated from Christ's College, Cambridge, in 1632, he undertook a further six years' private study in theology, philosophy, history, politics, literature, and science. He tutored the American theologian Roger Williams in Hebrew in exchange for lessons in Dutch.

In 1638, he embarked on a Grand Tour of France and Italy and met Galileo. He suffered from glaucoma and produced his greatest works, *Paradise Lost* and *Paradise Regained*, through dictation.

In 1660, just before the restoration of the monarchy, Milton added another to his many works against monarchy, *The Ready and Easy Way to Establish a Free Commonwealth*. On this day in that year, King Charles ordered the hangman to burn as many copies of Milton's works as could be found. A House of Commons resolution passed on the 16th of June 1660 attests to this:

> Humbly moved to call in Milton's two books the *Iconoelastes* and the *Defensio*, in justification of the murder of the late king, and order them to be burned by the common hangman; and that the attorney-general do proceed against them by indictment or otherwise.

Milton was fortunate to survive, and it may have been the support of influential friends who prevented the king from taking direct action against the poet.

He is buried in St.-Giles-without-Cripplegate Church in London.

Quote of the Day

"Let nothing trouble you, let nothing make you afraid. All things pass away. God never changes. Patience obtains everything. God alone is enough."

–*St. Teresa of Avila*

August 28

DAILY READING

Jesus answered, "The work of God is this: to believe in the one he has sent." (JOHN 6:29)

FEAST DAYS

430	Augustine of Hippo	Theologian
1821	Elizabeth Ann Seton	First American-born saint of the Roman Catholic Church
1944	Teresa Bracco	Nazi martyr

ENTRANCE AND EXIT

b. 1749	Johann Wolfgang von Goethe	German philosopher
b. 1828	Count Leo Lev Nikolayevich Tolstoy	Russian writer
b. 1906	Sir John Betjeman	English Poet Laureate
d. 1737	John Hutchinson	English mystic theologian
d. 1859	James Henry Leigh Hunt	English writer
d. 1987	John Huston	American film director

Augustine of Hippo

The great theologian St. Augustine remains a central figure, both within Christianity and in the history of Western thought. As he himself was much influenced by Platonism and Neoplatonism, particularly by Plotinus, Augustine was important to the development of Greek thought and its entrance into the Christian, and subsequently the European, intellectual tradition. His early and influential writing on the human will became a central topic in ethics and a focus for later philosophers such as Schopenhauer and Nietzsche. It is largely due to Augustine's arguments against the Pelagians, who did not believe in original sin, that Western Christianity has maintained the doctrine of original sin. Augustine also contended that God exists outside of time in the "eternal present"–time existing only within the created universe.

Augustine was born in North Africa in 354 and lived a wild life, much to the dismay of his mother, St. Monica. However, in 386, in a Rome garden, Augustine underwent a profound personal crisis and decided to convert to Christianity. He abandoned his career in rhetoric, quit his teaching position in Milan, gave up any ideas of marriage, and devoted himself full-time to religion, celibacy, and the priesthood. St. Ambrose baptized Augustine on Easter day in 387, and soon thereafter in 388 he returned to Africa. On his way back to Africa his mother died, as did his son soon after, leaving him relatively alone.

Theologians through the ages have been much influenced by Augustine. Thomas Aquinas developed Augustine's theology and created his own synthesis of Greek and Christian thought. John Calvin's Reformation theology was based on Augustine's writings, and Cornelius Jansen developed a movement inside the Roman Catholic Church.

Augustine was canonized by popular recognition and recognized as a Doctor of the Church in 1303 by Pope Boniface VIII. He is the patron saint of brewers, printers, theologians, and sore eyes.

Noteworthy

1941 Nazi forces began a siege of Leningrad during World War II that lasted nearly two and a half years.

1990 President George H. W. Bush told a news conference that a "new world order" could emerge from the Persian Gulf crisis.

1999 Residents of East Timor voted for independence from Indonesia in a U.N.-sponsored ballot.

2005 A day after Hurricane Katrina hit, floodwaters covered 80 percent of New Orleans.

AUGUST 29

DAILY READING

There is neither Jew nor Greek, there is neither bond nor free, there is neither male nor female: for you are all one in Christ Jesus. (GAL 3:28)

FEAST DAYS

ca. 30	John the Baptist	Cousin of Jesus
670	Fiacre	Irish hermit of Kilfiachra, Ireland
694	Sebbi	Monk of London

ENTRANCE AND EXIT

b. 1632	John Locke	English philosopher
b. 1809	Dr. Oliver Wendell Holmes Sr.	American writer
b. 1936	John McCain	American politician
d. 1930	Rev. William Archibald Spooner	English clergyman
d. 1981	Lowell Thomas	American writer
d. 1982	Ingrid Bergman	American actor

4′33″

On this day in 1952, the American experimental composer John Cage (1912–92) "performed" the debut of his new work, *4′33″*. It was a silent piece lasting 4 minutes, 33 seconds, which elevated incidental, unintended noise in the concert hall to the status of art. His association of coincidental sounds was inspired by the Chinese *I Ching* (*The Book of Changes*), an ancient system of philosophy, folk religion, and astrology. Cage was also influenced by Indian philosophy, Zen Buddhism, and many other Eastern thought systems.

From 1942 onward, Cage collaborated with the choreographer Merce Cunningham and wrote scores for Cunningham's productions.

Also, in 1952 he composed a piece called *Imaginary Landscape No. 4*. This involved twelve radio station sets constantly changing channels while the volume goes up and down. Cage's percussive piano became especially famous, as it was made of pieces of cork, rubber, glass, and wood. In the late fifties, Cage created a composition of six parts called *Variations*. Each part was random. For example, the third part had to be performed by "random amount of people, randomly performing actions."

Another interesting piece Cage wrote was *organ2/ASLSP* (As SLow aS Possible). This work began to be performed in the abandoned Buchardi Church in Halberstadt, Germany, in 2001 and is scheduled to last for 639 years. For the first seventeen months, no notes were sounded. A note was added in July of 2004, and another note was added in July of 2005. The next chord progression took place on March 5, 2006.

Spoonerisms:

Work is the curse of the drinking class.

He was a shoving leopard to his flock.

It is kisstomary to cuss the bride.

In the sermon I have just preached, whenever I said Aristotle, I meant St. Paul.

*A*UGUST 30

DAILY READING

Now therefore ye are no more strangers and foreigners, but fellow citizens with the saints, and of the household of God. (EPH 2:19, KJV)

FEAST DAYS

714	Guthlac	English hermit of Crowland
1259	Bronislawa Odrowaz	Polish hermit
1263	Alexander Nevski	Grand Duke of Novgorod and Kiev

ENTRANCE AND EXIT

b. 1797	Mary Shelly	English author
b. 1871	Lord Ernest Rutherford	New Zealand physicist
b. 1972	Cameron Diaz	American actor
d. 30 BC	Cleopatra	Queen of Egypt
d. 1723	Antonie von Leeuwenhoek	Dutch biologist
d. 2003	Charles Bronson	American actor

Guthlac–Fen Hermit

The little town of Crowland stands in the Fens east of Peterborough and is famous "three-way" medieval bridge. The hermit St. Guthlac (673–714) was its most famous inhabitant.

Today is the feast of the translation of his bones to Crowland Abbey in 1136. As a young man of royal blood from the tribe of Guthlacingas, Guthlac had been a soldier for nine years, fighting for Ethelred, the King of Mercia. At age twenty-four, he renounced both violence and the life of the world and became a monk in Repton, Derbyshire.

On the feast of St. Bartholomew about 701, he found a wet, remote, unloved spot on the River Welland in the Fens, which could be reached only by boat, and lived there for the rest of his life as a hermit, seeking to imitate the rigors of the old desert fathers.

His temptations rivaled theirs. Wild men came out of the forest and beat him. Even the ravens stole his few possessions. But Guthlac was patient, even with wild creatures. A holy man named Wilfrid once visited Guthlac and was astonished when two swallows landed on his shoulders and then hopped all over him. Guthlac told him, "Hast thou not learned, brother, that with him who has led his life after God's will, the wild beasts and birds become more intimate, just as to those who leave the world, the angels approach nearer?"

The exiled prince Ethelbald often came to him for advice, and learned from Guthlac that he would wear the crown of the Mercians. When he was dying, Guthlac sent for his sister, St Pega, and Abbess Edburga of Repton sent him a shroud and a leaden coffin. A year after his death, Guthlac's body was exhumed and found to be incorrupt. A monastery was established on the site of St. Guthlac's hermitage, which developed into the great abbey of Crowland.

Noteworthy

1574 Sri Guru Ram Das becomes the fourth Sikh Guru.
1860 Trains begin running in England.
1901 Invention of the vacuum cleaner by Hubert Cecil Booth.

AUGUST 31

DAILY READING

O come, let us worship and bow down: let us kneel before the LORD our maker.
For he is our God; and we are the people of his pasture,
and the sheep of his hand. (PS 95:6–7, KJV)

FEAST DAYS

258	Cyprian of Carthage	Church father
651	Aidan	Apostle of Northumbria
1537	Richard Bere	English martyr

ENTRANCE AND EXIT

b. 1879	Alma Schindler Mahler	Austrian writer
b. 1918	Alan Jay Lerner	American lyricist
b. 1945	Van Morrison	Irish singer
d. 1688	John Bunyan	English writer
d. 1867	Charles Baudelaire	French writer
d. 1997	Princess Diana Frances Spencer	English royal

William Paley–Natural Theologian

On this day in 1743, William Paley (1743–1805) was baptized in Peterborough, England. The great divine and apologist gave little sign of his genius as a youth, yet today he is celebrated as a brilliant thinker.

After graduating from Christ's College in Cambridge in 1763, Paley trained for the Anglican priesthood. He was appointed a fellow and tutor of his college in 1766, and rose through the ranks of the Anglican Church. Paley wrote several books on philosophy and Christianity, which proved extremely influential. His book *A View of the Evidence of Christianity* (1794) was required reading at Cambridge University until the twentieth century. His most influential contribution to biological thought, however, was his book *Natural Theology* (1802). In this, he laid out a full exposition of natural theology, the belief that the nature of God could be understood by reference to His creation, the natural world. He introduced one of the most famous metaphors in the philosophy of science, the image of the watchmaker:

> When we come to inspect the watch, we perceive . . . that its several parts are framed and put together for a purpose, e.g., that they are so formed and adjusted as to produce motion, and that motion so regulated as to point out the hour of the day; that if the different parts had been differently shaped from what they are, or placed after any other manner or in any other order than that in which they are placed, either no motion at all would have been carried on in the machine, or none which would have answered the use that is now served by it. . . . The inference we think is inevitable, that the watch must have had a maker–that there must have existed, at some time and at some place or other, an artificer or artificers who formed it for the purpose which we find it actually to answer, who comprehended its construction and designed its use.

Living organisms, Paley argued, are even more complicated than watches, "in a degree which exceeds all computation." How else to account for the often amazing adaptations of animals and plants? Only an intelligent Designer could have created them, just as only an intelligent watchmaker can make a watch.

Quotes of the Day

"Some said, John, print it; others said, Not so:
Some said, It might do good; others said, no."

–John Bunyan

"God granted me the privilege of knowing the brilliant works of our time before they left the hands of their creators."

–Alma Schindler Mahler

"Modernity is the transient, the fleeting, the contingent; it is one half of art, the other being the eternal and the immovable."

–Charles Baudelaire

September

Next him September marched eke on foot;
Yet was he heavy laden with the spoyle
Of harvest's riches, which he made his boot,
And him enriched with bounty of the soyle;
In his one hand, as fit for harvest's toyle,
He held a knife-hook; and in th' other hand
A paire of weights, with which he did assoyle
Both more and lesse, where it in doubt did stand,
And equal gave to each as justice duly scanned.

EDMUND SPENSER—*The Shepheardes Calender* (1579)

I bear the Scales, where hang in equipoise
The night and day; and when unto my lips
I put my trumpet, with its stress and noise
Fly the white clouds like tattered sails of ships;
The tree-tops lash the air with sounding whips;
Southward the clamorous sea-fowl wing their flight;
The hedges are all red with haws and hips,
The Hunter's Moon reigns empress of the night.

HENRY WADSWORTH LONGFELLOW—*The Poet's Calendar* (1882)

Proverbs ~

Fair on September first, fair for the month.

September blows soft, 'till the fruit's in the loft.

September dries up wells or breaks down bridges.

A tough apple skin means a hard winter.

September ~

This month marks the end of summer in the Northern hemisphere and the Anglo Saxons referred to it as Gerst-monat (barley month). The name September places this month as the seventh month in the old Roman calendar. It is traditionally a time of reaping the harvest, thanksgiving festivals, and much merrymaking.

Jane Austen ~

Lady Russell, convinced that Anne would not be allowed to be of any use, or any importance, in the choice of the house which they were going to secure, was very unwilling to have her hurried away so soon, and wanted to make it possible for her to stay behind till she might convey her to Bath herself after Christmas; but having engagements of her own which must take her from Kellynch for several weeks, she was unable to give the full invitation she wished, and Anne though dreading the possible heats of September in all the white glare of Bath, and grieving to forego all the influence so sweet and so sad of the autumnal months in the country, did not think that, everything considered, she wished to remain. It would be most right, and most wise, and, therefore must involve least suffering to go with the others.

–*Persuasion*, Chapter Five

SEPTEMBER 1

DAILY READING

Train up a child in the way he should go:
and when he is old, he will not depart from it. (PROV 22:6)

FEAST DAYS

ca. 12th cent. BC	Joshua	Old Testament patriarch
ca. 11th cent. BC	Gideon	Old Testament judge
ca. 710	Giles	Patron of lepers

ENTRANCE AND EXIT

b. 1854	Engelbert Humperdinck	German composer
b. 1866	Jim Corbett	American boxer
b. 1874	Edgar Rice Burroughs	American writer
d. 1159	Nicholas Breakspear	Pope Adrian IV
d. 1715	Louis IV	French king
d. 1948	Charles Beard	American historian

The English Pope

Visitors to St. Alban's Anglican Cathedral may be curious about the figure of a Roman Catholic pope on the great Wallingford screen. The image is of Nicholas Breakspear, the only Englishman elected pope. Little is known about his early life, but it is thought he may have been born within the estates of St. Albans Monastery just thirty-four years after the Norman Conquest. Early records give his name as Briselance (broken spear) in French and Hastafragus (broken lance) in Latin.

Breakspear was born into a poor family and could not afford the time to go to school, but he went to the monastery for his food. The Abbot Richard d'Albini, after examination, found him deficient in knowledge and said to him not unkindly, "Have patience, my son, till you are better fitted for the position you desire."

He studied at Paris University and made friends with the Augustinian Canons, near Avignon. Around 1132 he was transferred from Avignon to Rome, when he was appointed a special advisor to the papal court.

In 1152 Breakspear became papal legate to Scandinavia and restructured the church there. He was elected pope in 1154 and is the only pope to place Rome under interdict. This was withdrawn when Frederick Barbarossa was crowned Holy Roman Emperor.

Breakspear did not get along with Barbarossa and was close to declaring war with him when he died in 1159.

Noteworthy

AD 70 Destruction of Jerusalem under Titus.
1853 The world's first triangular postage stamps issued by the Cape of Good Hope.
1969 National Day, Libya.
1972 Bobby Fischer beats Boris Spassky at Reykjavik, becoming the first U.S. world chess champion.

SEPTEMBER 2

DAILY READING

The earth, O LORD, is full of thy mercy: teach me thy statutes. (PS 119:64, KJV)

FEAST DAYS

420	Castor	Bishop of Apt, France
1067	William of Roskilde	Chaplain to King Canute (England)
1792	Martyrs of September	191 Martyrs of the French Revolution

ENTRANCE AND EXIT

b. 1948	Christa McAuliffe	American astronaut
b. 1952	Jimmy Connors	American tennis star
b. 1964	Keanu Reeves	American actor
d. 1834	Thomas Telford	Scottish engineer
d. 1973	John Ronald Reuel Tolkien	English author
d. 1997	Viktor Frankl	Austrian psychiatrist

The Great Fire of London

> So I rode down to the waterside . . . and there saw a lamentable fire. . . . Everybody endeavouring to remove their goods, and flinging into the river or bringing them into lighters that lay off; poor people staying in their houses as long as till the very fire touched them, and then running into boats, or clambering from one pair of stairs by the waterside to another.

Thus wrote the celebrated diarist, Samuel Pepys, describing the Great Fire of London that started on this day in 1666.Within five days, an area of one and a half miles by half a mile lay in ashes; 373 acres inside the city walls and 63 acres outside, 87 churches destroyed (including St. Paul's Cathedral), and 13,200 houses. In all this destruction, it is amazing that only six people are definitely known to have been killed, but it seems likely that the actual death toll was much higher. In destroying the close-packed houses and other buildings, it is also likely that the fire finally put an end to the Great Plague that had devastated the city in the previous year–killing 17,440 out of the population of 93,000.

It is thought that the conflagration began in the house and shop of Thomas Farynor, baker to King Charles II in Pudding Lane. Fires burned for more than a week, and major areas such as Fleet Street, Old Bailey, Ludgate Hill, and Newgate were all reduced to ashes.

After the fire, Christopher Wren began the reconstruction of London and built forty-nine new churches, together with the great cathedral of St. Paul's that we know today.

Quotes of the Day

"I touch the future. I teach."

–*Christa McAuliffe*

"Since Auschwitz we know what man is capable of. And since Hiroshima we know what is at stake."

–*Viktor Frankl*

"One Ring to rule them all,
One Ring to find them,
One Ring to bring them all
and in the darkness bind them."

–*J. R. R. Tolkein,* The Fellowship of the Ring

SEPTEMBER 3

DAILY READING

Thus saith the LORD, thy Redeemer, the Holy One of Israel;
I am the LORD thy God which teacheth thee to profit,
which leadeth thee by the way that thou shouldest go. (ISA 48:17, KJV)

FEAST DAYS

1326	Herman of Heidelberg	Benedictine monk
1632	Jerome of the Cross	Japanese martyr
1679	Brigida of Jesus	Founder of the Institute of the Ursuline Sisters of Mary Immaculate

ENTRANCE AND EXIT

b. 1728	Matthew Boulton	English engineer
b. 1899	Sir Macfarlane Burnet	Australian scientist
b. 1913	Alan Ladd	American actor
d. 1658	Oliver Cromwell	English Lord Protector
d. 1883	Ivan Sergeyevich Turgenev	Russian playwright
d. 1991	Frank Capra	American film director

England's Lord Protector

This day is memorable in relation to Oliver Cromwell for three reasons: First, in 1650 he gained his first great victory at the Second Battle of Dunbar by defeating the Scotch Presbyterians. Second, a year later Cromwell defeated the Royalists at the Second Battle of Worcester. Third, in 1658 the Lord Protector died on this day. His body was embalmed and wrapped in cloth.

After an elaborate period of state mourning and funeral, Cromwell's son, Richard, became Lord Protector. However, by 1660 the unpopular new Lord Protector was forced to abdicate, leading to the restoration of King Charles II in May of that year.

Upon the restoration, Oliver Cromwell's body was removed from Westminster Abbey on January 26, 1661 (the anniversary of the execution of Charles I), and hung on a pole at Westminster Hall. On January 30, Cromwell's head was severed and put on display as a warning against opposing the king.

After more than twenty years on display at Westminster Hall, Cromwell's head disappeared and turned up in various museums and exhibitions for over two hundred years. Eventually, in 1960 Cromwell's head was buried in a wooden box in Westminster Abbey.

Noteworthy

1189 Coronation of King Richard I at Westminster Abbey.
1783 Britain recognized American Independence at the Paris Treaty.
1916 The first zeppelin shot down over England.
1939 Allies declared war on Germany.
1976 Viking 2 landed on Mars and began sending pictures to earth.

SEPTEMBER 4

DAILY READING

What you heard from me, keep as the pattern of sound teaching, with faith and love in Christ Jesus. Guard the good deposit that was entrusted to you–guard it with the help of the Holy Spirit who lives in us. (2 TIM 1:13–14)

FEAST DAYS

ca. 117	Hermione	Daughter of Philip the Deacon
422	Boniface I	Pope
980	Ida of Herzfield	Patron of brides and widows

ENTRANCE AND EXIT

b. 1736	Robert Raikes	Founder of Sunday schools
b. 1824	Anton Bruckner	Austrian composer
b. 1937	Dawn Fraser	Australian swimmer
d. 1965	Albert Schweitzer	German theologian
d. 1989	Georges Simeon	Belgian author
d. 2006	Steve Irwin	Australian naturalist

The Dandy Reformer

At age twenty-one, Robert Raikes (1736–1811) took over the family business as editor of the *Gloucester Journal.* He was a wealthy man, much given to dressing in a "foppish and dandy manner," seemingly without a care in the world. One day, however, Raikes, while looking for a gardener, found himself in St. Catherine's Street and noticed a group of ragged children playing in the street. He was distressed that there was no one to care for these children and shared his concerns with Rev. Thomas Stock. Together, they came up with the idea of a Sunday school, using laymen and women to teach from the Bible.

The movement began in July 1780, when a Mrs. Meredith conducted a school in her home. Only boys attended, and she heard the lessons of the older boys who coached the younger. Raikes wrote four of the textbooks, but the Bible was the core of the Sunday school. Later, girls were allowed to attend, and Raikes shouldered most of the financial burden in those early years. Within two years, several schools opened in and around Gloucester.

On November 3, 1783, Raikes published an account of the Sunday school in the columns of his paper. Raikes retired in 1801 and died of a heart attack in 1811.

The idea of Sunday schools caught on so much that by 1831 around 1,250,000 children came to the weekly sessions.

Visitors to Gloucester can remember Raikes at his memorial statue in Gloucester Park.

Reverence for Life

The great theologian, philosopher, musician, doctor and Nobel peace prize winner Albert Schweitzer (1875–1965) was born the son of a Lutheran pastor, and brought up in valley villages of the Vosges Mountains, in the Alsace region of Germany.

In his twenties he wrote seminal works on Bach, on the historical Jesus, and on organ building. At the age of thirty, he decided to become a medical doctor and devote the rest of his life to serving the people of Africa. In 1913, he opened a hospital in Lambarene, Gabon, Africa.

As a philosopher, he coined the phrase "Reverence for Life" to sum up his ethical response to all living things. This stressed the interdependence and unity of all life. In 1953, he was awarded the Nobel Peace Prize. During the latter part of his life he warned against the dangers of nuclear weapons and the nuclear arms race between the superpowers, and was instrumental in reversing American military policy on the testing of hydrogen bombs.

By the time of his death, the hospital he founded provided beds for 600 patients, and the staff comprised six doctors and 35 nurses. He passed the administration of the hospital to his daughter Rhena. He is buried in the hospital grounds in Lambarene.

"To the question whether I am a pessimist
or an optimist, I answer that my knowledge
is pessimistic, but my willing and hoping are
optimistic."

–*Life and Thoughts*

SEPTEMBER 5

DAILY READING

And Jesus came and spake unto them, saying, All power is given unto me in heaven and in earth. Go ye therefore, and teach all nations, baptizing them in the name of the Father, and of the Son, and of the Holy Ghost: Teaching them to observe all things whatsoever I have commanded you: and, lo, I am with you alway, even unto the end of the world. Amen. (MATT 28:18–20, KJV)

FEAST DAYS

ca. 700	Bertin	Columban monk
1381	Laurence Giustiniani	Patron of Venice, Italy
1765	Joseph Canh	Vietnamese martyr

ENTRANCE AND EXIT

b. 1187	Louis VII	King of France
b. 1585	Cardinal Richelieu	French minister
b. 1638	Louis XIV	King of France
d. 1877	Crazy Horse	Oglala Sioux leader
d. 1982	Douglas Bader	English airman
d. 1997	Agnes Gonxha Bojaxhiu	Mother Teresa of Calcutta

Marie Curie

On this day in 1910, the great Polish scientist Marya Sklodowska (Marie Curie) (1867–1934) won acclaim at the Academy of Sciences in France by demonstrating the radioactive properties of radium.

Marie and her husband, Pierre, had been at the forefront of physics since 1897, when Marie embarked on her doctorate. She had to overcome male antagonism, racism, personal tragedy, and elitist attitudes to make many discoveries that revolutionized physics at the beginning of the twentieth century.

Marie was raised in Warsaw in a family of teachers and brought up in an environment marked by a sense of duty and a lack of money. However, she was a brilliant student who harbored the dream of a scientific career, a concept inconceivable for a woman at that time.

In 1891, she arrived in Paris, and by 1895 was married to Pierre Curie, who wrote that he wanted to "spend life side by side, in the sway of our dreams: your patriotic dream, our humanitarian dream and our scientific dream." Together, they demonstrated that radioactivity was not the result of a chemical reaction but a property of the element. Marie then studied pitchblende, a uranic mineral in which she measured a much more intense activity than is present in uranium alone. She deduced that there were other substances besides uranium that were very radioactive, such as polonium and radium, which she discovered in 1898.

Tragically, Pierre was killed in a road accident in 1906, and Marie was left to carry on their work alone. Eventually, she took up the position that her husband had finally obtained at the Sorbonne and thus became the first woman to be appointed professor at that august institution.

She remains the only person to be awarded two Nobel Laureates in different sciences, for physics in 1903 and chemistry in 1911. She died in 1934, and in 1995 she became the only woman laid to rest in the Parthenon in Paris, alongside Pierre Curie.

Noteworthy

1174 Fire at Canterbury Cathedral.
1698 Beard Tax imposed by Czar Peter the Great.
1836 Sam Houston elected president of the Republic of Texas.
1905 Ending of Russo-Japanese War.
1972 Palestinian terrorists murder eleven Israeli athletes at the Olympics in Munich.

Quotes of the Day

"If you give me six lines written by the hand of the most honest of men, I will find something in them which will hang him."

—*Cardinal Richelieu*

"I know God will not give me anything I can't handle. I just wish that He didn't trust me so much."

—*Mother Teresa*

SEPTEMBER 6

DAILY READING

Jesus answered and said unto him, If a man love me, he will keep my words: and my Father will love him, and we will come unto him, and make our abode with him. (JOHN 14:23, KJV)

FEAST DAYS

ca. 460	Arator	Bishop of Verdun, France
ca. 666	Magnus of Füssen	Patron against caterpillars
ca. 1571	Thomas Tsugi	Japanese noble

ENTRANCE AND EXIT

b. 1766	John Dalton	English scientist
b. 1869	Felix Salten	American author
b. 1889	Joseph Kennedy	American diplomat
d. 1901	William McKinley	25th American president
d. 1966	Hendrik Verwoerd	South African prime minister
d. 1998	Arika Kurosawa	Japanese film director

The New World

On this day in 1620, 102 Puritans, including three pregnant women (Susanna White gave birth to a son in America), fled religious persecution by boarding the *Mayflower* in Plymouth, England. The *Mayflower* anchored in Provincetown Harbor off the tip of Cape Cod, Massachusetts, on November 11, 1620, a journey of 2,760 miles.

Capt. Christopher Jones and his passengers did not know what lay in this new land. The men of the *Mayflower* wrote "The Mayflower Compact," a set of laws for the new colony. This was the first time that immigrants to the new country had set down rule of the majority. The place they stayed was called the Plymouth Colony.

One of the pilgrims, William Bradford, wrote an account covering the first thirty years of the Plymouth Colony. The extract below is from his journal:

> Being thus arrived in a good harbor and brought safe to land, they fell upon their knees and blessed the God of heaven, who had brought them over the vast and furious ocean, and delivered them from all the perils and miseries thereof, againe to set their feete on the firme and stable earth, their proper element. And no marvell if they were thus joyefull, seeing wise Seneca was so affected with sailing a few miles on the coast of his owne Italy; as he affirmed, that he had rather remaine twenty years on his way by land, then pass by sea to any-place in a short time; so tedious and dreadfull was the same unto him.
>
> Our fathers were English men which came over this great ocean, and were ready to perish in this willdernes, but they cried unto the Lord, and he heard their voice, and looked on their adversity, etc. Let them therefore praise the Lord, because he is good, and his mercies endure for ever. Yea, let them which have been redeemed of the Lord, show how he hath delivered them from the hand of the oppressor. When they wandered in the deserte [and] willdernes out of the way, and found no citie to dwell in, both hungrie, and thirstie, their soul was overwhelmed in them. Let them confess before the Lord his loving kindnes, and his wonderfull works before the sons of men. . . .

Noteworthy

1552 Portuguese sailor Juan Sebastian del Cano made the first circumnavigation of the world.

1852 First free public library opened in Manchester, England.

1941 Jews ordered to wear yellow Star of David in German-occupied Europe.

1968 National Day, Swaziland.

Quotes of the Day

"Dear Jack. Don't buy a single vote more than necessary. I'll be damned if I'm going to pay for a landslide."

–Joseph P. Kennedy writing to his son, John F. Kennedy

September 7

DAILY READING

Whom we preach, warning every man, and teaching every man in all wisdom; that we may present every man perfect in Christ Jesus. (COL 1:28, KJV)

FEAST DAYS

ca. 470	Gratus	Bishop of Aosta, Italy
781	Alcmund	Bishop of Hexham, England
1106	John of Lodi	Bishop of Gubbio, Italy

ENTRANCE AND EXIT

b. 1533	Elizabeth I	Queen of England
b. 1860	"Grandma" Anna Maria Moses	American artist
b. 1913	Anthony Quayle	English actor
d. 1548	Catherine Parr	Queen of England
d. 1910	Holman Hunt	English artist
d. 1978	Keith Moon	Drummer, The Who

Elizabethan Settlement

Queen Elizabeth I, Queen of England, Ireland, and France was the fifth and last monarch of the Tudor dynasty. She ruled from 1588 for a period of forty-five years and is reckoned as one of the most successful rulers of the United Kingdom.

Her father, Henry VIII, had established the Church of England, and Elizabeth continued to replace both the Catholic Church and the Church of England with "reformed Catholicism." This was to be Roman in most doctrines, but national in organization and worship. A new Act of Supremacy made her "Supreme Governor," not "Supreme Head," of the Church of England. Her Act of Uniformity restored the Book of Common Prayer as the standard liturgy, and in 1571 she made the Thirty-Nine Articles the standard doctrine.

Recognizing the ability of "zely people" (fervent Protestants and Catholics) to frighten one another into supporting her moderate approach, Elizabeth replaced numerous bishops with clerics radicalized by exile on the continent. Although they and the more-extreme Puritans preferred the simplicity and "purity" of the first-century church, memories of Mary Tudor's excesses kept them from undermining the status quo. Elizabeth's great popularity and her skill in playing zealots against one another allowed her to keep the several church parties in dynamic balance.

The shortage of qualified lower-ranking clergymen loyal to the Elizabethan Settlement led to lax enforcement of religious conformity laws and the development of "prophesyings," local Bible study groups. The prophesyings caused in turn the rapid evolution of a class of independent preachers and lecturers. Many prophesyings became independent congregations willing to undertake further reform on their own.

However, Elizabeth's middle way did not satisfy extremists, nor did it win many friends among those who had been content with the church under Henry VIII. In the next century the coalition fell apart at last, and England sank into civil war.

Noteworthy

1618 Francis Bacon appointed English Lord Chancellor.
1789 First national presidential elections in America.
1812 Battle of Borodino in Russia.
1822 Brazil declared independence from Portugal.
1901 End of the Boxer Rebellion in China.
1986 Desmond Tutu became Archbishop of Cape Town, South Africa.

September 8

DAILY READING

Teach me to do thy will; for thou art my God: thy spirit is good;
lead me into the land of uprightness. (PS 143:10, KJV)

FEAST DAYS

ca. 1st cent.	Elizabeth	Mother of John the Baptist
ca. 600	Cynfarch the Dismal	Scottish tribal leader
701	Sergius I	Pope

ENTRANCE AND EXIT

b. 1157	Richard the Lionheart	King of England
b. 1841	Antonin Dvorák	Czech composer
b. 1886	Seigfried Sassoon	English poet
d. 1656	Joseph Hall	English bishop
d. 1949	Richard Strauss	German composer
d. 1977	Zero Mostel	American actor

One Nation under God

Francis Bellamy (1855–1931) was a Baptist preacher, Christian Socialist, and educational writer. On this day in 1892, he wrote the original American Pledge of Allegiance, as part of the official program for the National Public School Celebration of Columbus Day.

The pledge was published in a religious magazine called *The Youth's Companion*. It read thus:

I pledge allegiance to my Flag,
and to the Republic for which it stands:
one Nation indivisible,
With Liberty and Justice for all.

On October 21, 1892, the bicentennial of Columbus discovering America, children across the country saluted the flag and recited the Pledge of Allegiance for the first time.

Since then, the Pledge of Allegiance has been altered slightly, for example, in 1924:

I pledge allegiance to the Flag
of the United States of America,
and to the Republic for which it stands:
one Nation indivisible,
With Liberty and Justice for all.

And in 1954 by President Dwight D. Eisenhower:

I pledge allegiance to the Flag
of the United States of America,
and to the Republic for which it stands:
one Nation under God, indivisible,
With Liberty and Justice for all.

In just thirty-one words, this simple statement expresses the American ideals of service, loyalty, liberty, and devotion to God.

Antonin Dvorák

The great composer Antonin Dvorák (1841–1904) was born in Nelahozeves, a small Bohemian village. Dvorák took his formal training at the Organ College in Prague, and found a job as an organist in a small church.

Johannes Brahms, his mentor, introduced Dvorák to a famous publisher, and helped him qualify for an Austrian state fellowship for artists.

Dvorák's *Slavonic Dances* launched his international reputation. Operas and symphonies followed, and he earned enough from his musical compositions to resign his organist job. In 1891, Prague Conservatory prevailed on him to teach composition for one hour a day; his lessons soon stretched out to three or four hours a day.

The following year, he left for a tour of the United States and became the director of the National Conservatory in New York (1892–95). It was here he produced his most famous work, the Ninth Symphony—"From the New World."

1894, Dvorák returned home and for the last ten years of his life he continued to compose and the Austrian government made him a senator. At the end of his life Dvorák was in serious financial straits as he had sold his many compositions for so little he had nothing to live on. He died in 1904.

September 9

DAILY READING

Teach the older men to be temperate, worthy of respect, self-controlled, and sound in faith, in love, and in endurance. (TITUS 2:2)

FEAST DAYS

440	Isaac the Great	Founder of the Armenian Church
ca. 556	Kieran the Younger	One of the twelve apostles of Ireland
1864	Jacques Laval	Apostle of Mauritius

ENTRANCE AND EXIT

b. 1754	William Bligh	English naval captain
b. 1941	Otis Reading	American singer
b. 1960	Hugh Grant	English actor
d. 1583	Sir Humphrey Gilbert	English explorer
d. 1976	Mao Zedong	Chinese leader
d. 2003	Edward Teller	American scientist

The Battle of Flodden Field

Flodden Field, near the village of Branxton in Northumberland, England, was the scene of the last great battle between Scotland and England on this day in 1513. James IV, King of Scotland, with an army of over forty thousand (some from France), invaded Northumbria. This was in support of the "Auld Alliance" between France and Scotland and designed to divert Henry VIII's campaign against the French.

The English army was around twenty-five thousand strong and led by the Earl of Surrey. James, confident of victory, accepted the Earl's challenge to battle. The king was defeated by the lighter English artillery, better tactics, and the poor condition of the Scottish weapons. The Scottish king was probably killed early in the battle. A contemporary account records the English triumph, "our gonnes did so breake and constreyn the Scottische great army, that some part of thaim wer enforsed to come doun towards our army."

The Battle of Flodden Field lasted for just over two hours. As the defeated Scots retreated, they left behind a third of their colleagues, including nine earls, as well as fourteen Lords of Parliament and several Highland chiefs. The English lost around 1,500 men.

The Scots memorialized their losses at Flodden Field with "The Flowers of the Forest"—a poignant verse that remains known to this day.

> We'll here nae mair lilting at our ewe milking,
> Women and bairns are heartless and wae,
> Sighing and moaning on a ilka green loaning,
> The flowers of the forest are a wede away.

St. Peter Claver

According to the hagiographer Alban Butler, Peter Claver (1581–1654), whose feast is celebrated on this day, was a Spanish Jesuit. In Majorca he fell in with the holy lay-brother Alphonsus Rodriguez, who, having already learned by revelation the saintly career of Peter, became his spiritual guide, foretold to him the labors he would undergo in the Indies, and the throne he would gain in heaven. Ordained priest in New Granada, Peter was sent to Cartagena, the great slave-mart of the West Indies, and there he consecrated himself by vow to the salvation of those ignorant and miserable creatures. For more than forty years he labored in this work. He called himself "the slave of the slaves." He was their apostle, father, physician, and friend. He fed them, nursed them with the utmost tenderness in their loathsome diseases, often applying his own lips to their hideous sores. His cloak, which was the constant covering of the naked, though soiled with their filthy ulcers, sent forth a miraculous perfume. His rest after his great labors was in nights of penance and prayer. However tired he might be, when news arrived of a fresh slave-ship, Saint Peter immediately revived, his eyes brightened, and he was at once onboard amongst his dear slaves, bringing them comfort for body and soul. A false charge of reiterating Baptism for a while stopped his work. He submitted without a murmur till the calumny was refuted, and then God so blessed his toil that 40,000 negroes were baptized before he went to his reward, in 1654.

SEPTEMBER 10

DAILY READING

And even to your old age I am he; and even to hoar hairs will I carry you:
I have made, and I will bear; even I will carry, and will deliver you. (ISA 46:4)

FEAST DAYS

257	Jader	Numidian bishop
453	Pulcheria	Patron of exiles
589	Finian	Bishop of Moville, Ireland

ENTRANCE AND EXIT

b. 920	Louis IV	King of France
b. 1771	Mungo Park	Scottish explorer
b. 1938	Karl Lagerfeld	German fashion designer
d. 1935	Huey Long	American politician
d. 1983	John Vorster	South African president
d. 2003	Anna Lindh	Swedish politician

Thomas Sheridan

Irish scholar Rev. Dr. Thomas Sheridan (b. 1687) died on this day in 1738. A Dublin schoolmaster, his caustic wit made and lost friends, and he is chiefly remembered for his close friendship with Jonathan Swift and for being the grandfather of the playwright Richard Brinsley Sheridan.

Swift arranged for his church promotion in South Ireland. However, he lost all chance of further advancement by preaching a sermon on the anniversary of George I's birthday from the text: "Sufficient for the day is the evil thereof." He was struck off the list of the Lord-Lieutenant's chaplains; parents hastened to take their children from his school; and, in short, as Swift said: "He had killed his own fortunes by a chance-shot from an unlucky text."

Sheridan has been described as "cheerful knowing books better than men, and totally ignorant of the value of money. Ill-starred, improvident, but not unhappy, he was a fiddler, punster, quibbler, and wit; and his pen and fiddle-stick were in continual notion."

Swift spent many happy hours at Sheridan's house at Qulica, Ireland, and described it thus:

Let me thy properties explain:
A rotten cabin dropping rain;
Chimneys with scorn rejecting smoke;
Stools, tables, chairs, and bedsteads broke.
Here elements have lost their uses,
Air ripens not, nor earth produces;
In vain, we make poor Shela toil,
Fire will not roast, nor water boil;
Through all the valleys, hills, and plains,
The goddess Want, in triumph reigns,
And her chief officers of state,
Sloth, Dirt, and Theft, around her wait.

Mungo Park

The Scottish surgeon and explorer Mungo Park (1771–ca. 1805) was born in the town of Selkirk in the Scottish Borders. Having served his apprenticeship in Edinburgh, he set off for London and became acquainted with the famous botanist and explorer Sir Joseph Banks, who was treasurer of an organization called the Association for Promoting the Discovery of the Interior Parts of Africa.

With Banks's encouragement, Park was sent to West Africa to find the source of the River Niger. Initially, Park made good progress and by 1795, he had traversed more than two hundred miles up the Gambia River before heading into the uncharted interior. It was here that he encountered a Moorish king who imprisoned him for four months. Although he escaped, having to cover more than three hundred miles of the River Gambia, most of his relatives in Scotland had given him up for dead.

To their surprise, he returned to Scotland in 1797, married in 1799, and set up a medical practice in the town of Peebles in 1801. In September 1804, he accepted an invitation from the government to head a second expedition to find the source of the Niger. Although well provisioned, this time he was not so fortunate and it is thought he either drowned or was killed by native tribesmen. News of his death took several years to reach home when his belongings were discovered down river.

There is a memorial to Mungo Park in Selkirk that commemorates his achievements. The intricate sculpted column with a figure of Park can be found near the Municipal Buildings next to the surgeon's house where Park was apprenticed.

SEPTEMBER 11

DAILY READING

I will lift up mine eyes unto the hills, from whence cometh my help. My help cometh from the L*ORD, which made heaven and earth.* (PS 121:1–2, KJV)

FEAST DAYS

1276	Sperandia	Benedictine mystic
1622	Charles Spinola	Japanese martyr
1802	Jean-Gabriel Perboyre	Chinese martyr

ENTRANCE AND EXIT

b. 1885	David Herbert Lawrence	English author
b. 1887	James Jeans	English scientist
b. 1917	Jessica Mitford	English writer
d. 1994	Jessica Tandy	American actor
d. 2002	Kim Hunter	American actor
d. 2003	John Ritter	American actor

War on America

Extracts from President George W. Bush's speeches on the war on America:

> War has been waged against us by stealth and deceit and murder. This nation is peaceful, but fierce when stirred to anger. This conflict was begun on the timing and terms of others; it will end in a way and an hour of our choosing.
>
> In every generation the world has produced enemies of human freedom. They have attacked America, because we are freedom's home and defender; and the commitment of our fathers is now the calling of our time.
>
> This is a day when all Americans from every walk of life unite in our resolve for justice and peace. America has stood down enemies before, and we will do so this time. None of us will ever forget this day. Yet, we go forward to defend freedom and all that is good and just in our world.
>
> The attacks were meant to bring us to our knees, and they did, but not in the way the terrorists intended. Americans united in prayer, came to the aid of neighbors in need, and resolved that our enemies would not have the last word. The spirit of our people is the source of America's strength. And we go forward with trust in that spirit, confidence in our purpose, and faith in a loving God who made us to be free.
>
> May he bless the souls of the departed, may he comfort our own and may he always guide our country. God bless America.

Noteworthy

1943 Beginning of Jewish family transports from Theresienstadt to Auschwitz.

1944 Third Army captures a large part of Maginot Line intact and reaches the German border at Trier on the banks of the Moselle.

2002 Patriot Day, America.

Coventry Cathedral Liturgy

This is the liturgy spoken on the rubble of the cathedral in Coventry immediately after German bombers destroyed it during World War II:

All have sinned and fallen short of the glory of God
The hatred which divides nation from nation, race from race, class from class,
FATHER FORGIVE.
The greed which exploits the work of human hands and lays waste the earth,
FATHER FORGIVE.
Our envy of the welfare and happiness of others
FATHER FORGIVE.
Our indifference to the plight of the imprisoned, the homeless, the refugee
FATHER FORGIVE.
The lust which dishonors the bodies of men, women and children,
FATHER FORGIVE.
The pride which leads us to trust in ourselves and not in God,
FATHER FORGIVE.

SEPTEMBER 12

DAILY READING

Rejoice in the Lord always.
I will say it again, Rejoice! (PHIL 4:4)

FEAST DAYS

ca. 258	Curonotus	Bishop of Iconium, Turkey
1012	Guy	Patron of Anderlecht, Belgium
1617	Mary Victoria Fornari	Italian mystic

ENTRANCE AND EXIT

b. 1733	François Couperin	French composer
b. 1852	Herbert Henry Asquith	English prime minister
b. 1913	Jessie Owens	American athlete
d. 1977	Steve Biko	South African activist
d. 1992	Anthony Perkins	American actor
d. 2003	Johnny Cash	American singer

Eton College

The King's College of Our Lady of Eton beside Windsor was founded by Henry VI (1421–71) on this day in 1440. The original establishment allowed for a provost, ten priests, four clerks, six choristers, twenty-five poor grammar scholars, and the like number of poor men. Besides the scholars on the foundation, the school always has a larger number of others, called oppidans. The oppidans generally amount to between three and four hundred.

Seventy poor scholars and a provost from Eton were sent to King's College, Cambridge, also established by Henry VI in 1441.

Since the establishment of Eton College, it has been a seat of learning for many famous people, including:

- Prime minsters–Arthur Walpole, Robert Pitt, William Wellington, William Ewart Gladstone, and Harold Macmillan
- Clergy–John Knox, John Charles Ryle, and Charles Studd
- Writers–Ian Fleming, Percyle Shelly, Henry Fielding, and Aldous Huxley
- Fictional characters–Bertie Wooster, Quartermain, James Bond, and Lord Peter Wimsey

It is estimated that there are fifteen thousand old Etonians alive today.

Noteworthy

1609 Henry Hudson discovers Hudson River.
1812 Defenders Day in Maryland.
1878 Cleopatra's Needle erected in London.
1923 Britain takes over South Rhodesia.
1980 Military coup in Turkey.
1988 Hurricane Gilbert devastates Jamaica.

September 13

DAILY READING

Finally, be ye all of one mind, having compassion one of another, love as brethren, be pitiful, be courteous. (1 PET 3:8, KJV)

FEAST DAYS

ca. 347	John Chrysostom	Patron of preachers
630	Amatus	Benedictine monk
887	Hedwig	Benedictine nun

ENTRANCE AND EXIT

b. 1520	William Cecil	English statesman
b. 1894	John Boynton Priestley	English author
b. 1916	Roald Dahl	Welsh author
d. 1806	Charles James Fox	English politician
d. 1944	Heath Robinson	English artist
d. 1996	Tupac Shakur	American rap star

Roald Dahl Day

On this day in 2006, the first Roald Dahl Day was launched to celebrate the life, works, and legacy of the celebrated novelist and short story writer.

Roald Dahl (1916–90) was born in Cardiff and named after the explorer Roald Amundsen–his parents were Norwegian. Throughout his childhood, he spent his holidays in Norway.

While a pupil at Repton School, Derby, he grew to like Cadbury's chocolate and first dreamed of inventing different chocolate confections. This was the genesis of one of his most popular books, *Charlie and the Chocolate Factory*.

Roald Dahl died of leukemia in November 1990 and was buried in Buckinghamshire with his snooker cues, some very good burgundy, chocolates, HB pencils, and a power saw.

A Prayer of St John Chrysostom

O Lord, deprive me not of Thy heavenly blessings;
O Lord, deliver me from eternal torment;
O Lord, if I have sinned in my mind or thought, in word deed, forgive me.
O Lord, deliver me from every ignorance and heedlessness, from pettiness of the soul and stony hardness of heart;
O Lord, deliver me from every temptation;
O Lord, enlighten my heart darkened by evil desires;
O Lord, I, being a human being, have sinned; do Thou, being God, forgive me in Thy lovingkindness, for Thou knowest the weakness of my soul.
O Lord, send down Thy grace to help me, that I may glorify Thy holy Name;
O Lord Jesus Christ, inscribe me, Thy servant, in the Book of Life, and grant me a blessed end;
O Lord my God, even if I have done nothing good in Thy sight, yet grant me, according to Thy grace, that I may make a start in doing good.
O Lord, sprinkle on my heart the dew of Thy grace;
O Lord of heaven and earth, remember me, Thy sinful servant, cold of heart and impure, in Thy Kingdom.
O Lord, receive me in repentance;
O Lord, leave me not;
O Lord, save me from temptation;
O Lord, grant me pure thoughts;
O Lord, grant me tears of repentance, remembrance of death, and the sense of peace;
O Lord, grant me mindfulness to confess my sins;
O Lord, grant me humility, charity, and obedience;
O Lord, grant me tolerance, magnanimity, and gentleness;
O Lord, implant in me the root of all blessings: the fear of Thee in my heart;
O Lord, vouchsafe that I may love Thee with all my heart and soul, and that I may obey in all things Thy will;
O Lord, shield me from evil persons and devils and passions and all other lawless matters;
O Lord, Who knowest Thy creation and that which Thou hast willed for it; may Thy will also be fulfilled in me, a sinner, for Thou art blessed forevermore. Amen.

SEPTEMBER 14

DAILY READING

If you have any encouragement from being united with Christ, if any comfort from his love, if any fellowship with the Spirit, if any tenderness and compassion, then make my joy complete by being like-minded, having the same love, being one in spirit and purpose. (PHIL 2:1–2)

FEAST DAYS

251	Caerealis	Roman soldier
1265	Notburga	Patron of farmers
1850	Gabriel John Tauin Du-Fresse	Chinese martyr

ENTRANCE AND EXIT

b. 1760	Luigi Cherubini	Italian composer
b. 1849	Ivan Pavlov	Russian scientist
b. 1946	Oliver Stone	American film director
d. 1321	Dante Alighieri	Italian writer
d. 1878	Isadora Duncan	American dancer
d. 1982	Grace Kelly	Princess Grace of Monaco

The Messiah *Completed*

George Frederick Handel completed his masterpiece *Messiah*, in the space of just twenty-one days, on this day in 1741. *Messiah* is an oratorio consisting of Old and New Testaments passages, sung by solo voices with orchestral accompaniment. It was a personal triumph for Handel, as he was at a low ebb, having suffered a stroke that led to partial paralysis on his left side.

The most famous movement is the "Hallelujah" chorus, which concludes the second of the three parts. The text is drawn from three passages in the New Testament book of Revelation:

> And I heard as it were the voice of a great multitude, and as the voice of many waters, and as the voice of mighty thunderings, saying, Alleluia: for the Lord God omnipotent reigneth. (Rev 19:6, KJV)
>
> And the seventh angel sounded; and there were great voices in heaven, saying, The kingdoms of this world are become the kingdoms of our Lord, and of his Christ; and he shall reign for ever and ever. (Rev 11:15, KJV)
>
> And he hath on his vesture and on his thigh a name written, KING OF KINGS, AND LORD OF LORDS. (Rev 19:16, KJV)

Handel had been invited to give a series of concerts in Dublin to benefit various charities. The premiere was met with considerable success and served to boost Handel's spirits for a return to London. While it is true that George II stood during the singing of the mighty "Hallelujah" chorus at the second London performance, *Messiah* did not enjoy the popularity of many of Handel's other oratorios during the composer's lifetime. In fact, it was only through Handel's annual Eastertide performances to benefit his favorite charity, the Foundling Hospital, that *Messiah* was heard and gained a considerable following.

The Exaltation of ohe Holy Cross of Our Lord Jesus Christ

Constantine the Great (ca. 280–337) became Roman Emperor in 312 after defeating the Emperor Maxentius at the Battle of Milvian Bridge on the Tiber in Rome. Before the battle, he is reputed to have seen a cross in the sky and heard a voice saying, "By this sign shalt thou conquer."

After the battle, he became a Christian, acknowledging his triumph to this vision.

This feast of the Exaltation of the Holy Cross is the commemoration of the discovery of the cross, on which Christ died, by Constantine the Great, and his mother, Saint Helena.

Legend records that the Emperor Heraclius, recovered the cross from the King of Persia where it had been a prized trophy for fourteen years. At the time of its return to Calvary, a miracle occurred. As Heraclius was about to carry the cross to the proper place on his shoulders, out of veneration for it, he found that while wearing the imperial dress he could not move it. After advice from his priest, he laid aside his royal ornaments, dressed himself plainly, took off his shoes, and in such manner made himself like the humble Savior. Then he was able to carry the cross.

SEPTEMBER 15

DAILY READING

We know and rely on the love God has for us. God is love. Whoever lives in love lives in God, and God in him. (1 JOHN 4:16)

FEAST DAYS

ca. 620	Mirren	Irish missionary
1510	Catherine of Genoa	Patron of widows
1952	Paola Manna	Missionary to Burma

ENTRANCE AND EXIT

b. 1857	William Howard Taft	27th American president
b. 1890	Agatha Christie	English author
b. 1894	Jean Renoir	French film director
d. 1859	Isambard Kingdom Brunel	English inventor
d. 1898	William Seward Burroughs	American inventor
d. 1945	Anton Webern	Austrian composer

St. Catherine of Genoa

The great Catholic mystic Catherine Fieschi was born of a noble family near the historic North Italian port of Genoa in 1447 and at sixteen married, at her family's insistence, a husband who turned out to be unfaithful and usually absent from home. Nevertheless her persistent fidelity and devotion to her faith eventually achieved a change of heart in him. In 1473 they moved to a humble abode and jointly devoted themselves to the sick; Catherine became matron of a hospital, putting her health at risk in a plague in 1493, and again in 1496, one year before her husband died. After his death, she continued her spiritual quest but without becoming a Tertiary of one of the religious orders, as would have been customary at the time. A contemplative and visionary, she shared her experiences with others through her writings, principally on purgatory, and on the soul and the body. She died in 1510 and was canonized in 1740.

In one of her discourses she wrote,

> The love of God is our proper love, for we are created for that alone; the love, on the contrary, for everything beside, ought in truth to be termed hatred, since it deprives us of our proper love, which is God. Love then God, who loves thee, and leave him who does not love thee, namely, everything beneath God; for all things are enemies to that true love. Oh! that I could make this truth be felt as I myself feel it: I am certain that there is no creature who would not love Him; so that if the sea were the food of love, there are no men or women, who would not drown themselves in it, and those who were at a distance from it would always be drawing nearer to it, that they might plunge into it; for every pleasure, when compared to it, is pain, and such riches does it confer on a man, that all beside should seem to him but misery.
>
> It makes him so light that he does not feel the earth beneath his feet; his affections are so fixed on things above that he loses all sense of suffering here below, and he is so free, that there is nothing to keep him from the presence of God. If you asked me: "What dost thou feel?" I should answer thee: "What eye could not see, nor ear hear"; but I am ashamed to speak of it in my poor language, for I am certain that all I can say of God, is not of God, but only fragments that fall from his table.

Noteworthy

1776 British forces occupied New York City during the American Revolution.

1821 Costa Rica, Guatemala, Honduras, Nicaragua, and El Salvador became independent from Spain.

1917 Russia was proclaimed a republic by Alexander Kerensky, the head of a provisional government.

1935 The Nuremberg Laws deprived German Jews of their citizenship and made the swastika the official symbol of Nazi Germany.

1997 The IRA-allied Sinn Fein party entered Northern Ireland's peace talks for the first time.

2004 National Hockey League owners agreed to lock out the players.

2005 President George W. Bush urged Congress to approve a massive reconstruction program for storm-ravaged New Orleans.

SEPTEMBER 16

DAILY READING

Who is wise and understanding among you?
Let him show it by his good life, by deeds done
in the humility that comes from wisdom. (JAS 3:13)

FEAST DAYS

253	Cornelius	Pope
860	Ludmila	Patron of Bohemia
984	Edith of Wilton	Daughter of King Edgar of England

ENTRANCE AND EXIT

b. 1858	Andrew Bonar Law	British prime minister
b. 1893	Sir Alexander Korda	Hungarian film producer
b. 1924	Lauren Bacall	American actor
d. 1932	Sir Ronald Ross	British physician
d. 1976	Marc Bolan	Lead singer, T Rex
d. 1977	Maia Callas	American singer

St. Edith of Wilton

St. Edith of Wilton (961–84) was the illegitimate daughter of King Edgar the Peaceful, son of King Edmund. Edgar kidnapped Edith's mother, Wulfthrith, and imprisoned her at Wilton in Kent. He later did penance for his crime by not wearing his crown for seven years.

Edith became a Benedictine abbess at just fifteen, and her father gave her authority over Winchester and Barking abbeys. When Edgar died, his son Edmund became king but was murdered at Corfe Castle in 979.

Edith built a church under the dedication of St. Denis. Tradition records St. Dunstan was at the consecration of the church and noticed how Edith continuously crossed herself. He caught hold of her right thumb and said, "Never shall this thumb decay."

She was allegedly offered the crown of England by nobles who had supported her brother, Edward the Martyr, against her half-brother, Ethelred, but refused it. Notwithstanding her refusal of all royal honors and worldly power, she always dressed magnificently, and when St. Aethelwold remonstrated, she answered that purity and humility could exist as well under royal robes as under rags.

Edith died at Wilton Abbey, and according to tradition, angels were sighted singing sweetly at the site of her death.

About a month after her death, she appeared to her mother and told her the devil had tried to accuse her, but she had broken his head. Many years after, King Canute laughed at the idea that the daughter of the licentious Edgar could be a saint. St. Dunstan took her out of her coffin and set her upright in the church, whereupon Canute was terrified and fell down in a faint. He had a great veneration for St. Edith ever after.

Noteworthy

1810 National Day, Mexico.
1854 Joshua Norton becomes emperor of the United States.
1859 David Livingston reaches Lake Nyasa.
1919 American Legion incorporated by an act of Congress.
1963 National Day, Malaysia.
1975 National Day, Papua New Guinea.
2004 Hurricane Ivan strikes Alabama.

September 17

DAILY READING

You were once darkness,
but now you are light in the Lord. (EPH 5:8)

FEAST DAYS

ca. 635	Lambert	Bishop of Maastricht, Holland
1179	Hildegard von Bingen	German mystic
1798	Emmanuel Trieu Van Nguyen	Martyr of Vietnam

ENTRANCE AND EXIT

b. 1916	Mary Stewart	English writer
b. 1918	Chaim Herzog	President of Israel
b. 1923	Hank Williams Sr.	American singer
d. 1701	James II and VII	King of England, King of Scotland
d. 1771	Tobias Smollett	Scottish writer
d. 1996	Spiro Agnew	39th American vice president

John Cotton

The Reverend John Cotton became vicar at St. Botolph's Church in Boston, Lincolnshire, in 1612. But over the next two decades he became increasingly critical of the Anglican denomination and began to sympathize with the Puritans.

He published a sermon entitled "The Divine Right to Occupy Land," comparing the Puritans to God's chosen people. Naturally, this aroused contention from the Anglican Church, who were his employers, and Cotton was threatened with legal action. Before this could be started, Cotton sailed to New England and settled in Massachusetts Colony in a place called Trimountain in 1633.

Free to express Puritan views, he became a much loved church leader and wrote several pamphlets, including: *Set Forms of Prayer* (1642); *The Keys of the Kingdom of Heaven and the Power Thereof* (1644); *The Bloody Tenent Washed and Made White in the Blood of the Lamb* (1647); and *Milk for Babes Drawn out of the Breasts of both Testaments Chiefly for the Spiritual Nourishment of Boston Babes in Either England, but May Be of Use for Any Children* (1646).

In New England he introduced the custom of making the Sabbath observances extend from evening to evening, and was largely instrumental in securing Boston Common to posterity.

John Cotton died in Massachusetts on December 23, 1652. On this day, the name of Trimountain was changed to Boston, in honor of his hometown. In 1857, his descendants in Boston erected a tablet to his memory in St. Botolph's Church, Boston, England.

A Prayer of Hildegard of Bingen

O eternal Lord,
it is pleasing to you
to burn in that same fire of love,
like that from which our bodies are born,
and from which you begot your Son
in the first dawn before all of Creation.

So consider this need which falls upon us,
and relieve us of it for the sake of your Son,
and lead us in joyous prosperity.

Noteworthy

1908 Thomas Selfridge becomes the first person to die in an airplane crash.
1920 National Football League formed, United States.
1939 USSR invades Poland.
1944 British airborne invasion of Holland–Operation Market Garden.
1952 Citizenship Day, United States.

SEPTEMBER 18

DAILY READING

But God chose the foolish things of the world to shame the wise; God chose the weak things of the world to shame the strong. (1 COR 1:27)

FEAST DAYS

1555	Thomas the Almsgiver	Archbishop of Granada, Spain
1663	Joseph of Cupertino	Patron of astronauts
1936	Jesus Hita Miranda	Spanish civil war martyr

ENTRANCE AND EXIT

b. 1709	Samuel Johnson	English writer
b. 1905	Greta Garbo	Swedish actor
b. 1961	James Gandolfini	American actor
d. 1721	Matthew Prior	English writer
d. 1830	William Hazlitt	English writer
d. 1970	Jimi Hendrix	American rock star

Patron Saint of Astronauts

Joseph Desa (St. Joseph of Cupertino), patron saint of astronauts, had nothing to commend him as a child. This Franciscan friar, born on June 17, 1603, near Brindisi, Italy, was also known as Joseph the Dunce. As a child, he received ecstatic visions but did not know what to make of them. He was useless at school, absentminded, awkward, a poor speaker, and nervous. He was not wanted as a child, and his slowness made him more and more isolated at home.

Without any hope of a vocation, he tried to become a monk and was initially refused because of his lack of education. When he was accepted as a lay brother in 1620, the monks found they could not do anything with him because of his ecstatic visions that rendered him insensible. When he received a vision, it was as if Joseph turned to stone, and the monks had to prick him with needles to enable him to return to the real world.

He could barely read or write, but his devotion to Christ led to a series of extraordinary visions and miraculous healings. It is said that he would often levitate (hence the connection to astronauts) whilst experiencing these visions and had a deep understanding of the mysteries of faith. He seemed to have a discerning heart and was able to communicate with animals much the same way as Francis of Assisi. Moreover, despite his disadvantages, he was a cheerful soul often caught up in the experience of God.

However, because of the controversy surrounding his ecstasies, he was not allowed to attend choir or eat with the other monks. He was placed in his own cell to stop embarrassing the monks. He was even questioned by the Spanish Inquisition but did not allow their threats to deplete his joyous spirit.

He was canonized in 1767 by Pope Clement XIII.

Quote of the Day

"Your manuscript is both good and original, but the part that is good is not original and the part that is original is not good."

–Dr. Samuel Johnson

September 19

DAILY READING

Do not let any unwholesome talk come out of your mouths,
but only what is helpful for building others up according to their needs,
that it may benefit those who listen. (EPH 4:29)

FEAST DAYS

304	Gennaro	Patron of Naples, Italy
690	Theodore of Tarsus	Archbishop of Canterbury
1852	Emily de Rodat	Religious education pioneer

ENTRANCE AND EXIT

b. 1839	George Cadbury	English confectioner
b. 1911	William Golding	English author
b. 1948	Jeremy Irons	English actor
d. 1812	Mayer Amschel Rothschild	German financier
d. 1881	James Garfield	20th American president
d. 1985	Italo Calvino	Italian writer

International Talk Like a Pirate Day

John Baur (Ol' Chum Bucket) and Mark Summers (Cap'n Slappy), two friends from Albany, Oregon, came up with the notion of this fun day to add "zest, a swagger, to every day conversation," in 1995. International Talk Like a Pirate Day (ITLAPD) is always on this day, in honor of Cap'n Slappy's ex-wife's birthday.

Their efforts went unrecognized until Pulitzer Prize–winning journalist Dave Barry started to promote their event through his newspaper column. From there, the media across the seven seas carried the story, and today thousands of people celebrate ITLAPD from America to New Zealand.

The main activity is to dress like a pirate and use as much pirate slang as possible. The official ITLAPD website (*www.talklikeapirate.com*) contains advice, examples, and "pirate links" to other websites that promote the initiative.

To Autumn

Season of mists and mellow fruitfulness,
Close bosom-friend of the maturing sun;
Conspiring with him how to load and bless
With fruit the vines that round the thatch-eves run;
To bend with apples the moss'd cottage-trees,
And fill all fruit with ripeness to the core;
To swell the gourd, and plump the hazel shells
With a sweet kernel; to set budding more,
And still more, later flowers for the bees,
Until they think warm days will never cease,
For summer has o'er-brimm'd their clammy cells.

Who hath not seen thee oft amid thy store?
Sometimes whoever seeks abroad may find
Thee sitting careless on a granary floor,
Thy hair soft-lifted by the winnowing wind;
Or on a half-reap'd furrow sound asleep,
Drows'd with the fume of poppies, while thy hook
Spares the next swath and all its twined flowers:
And sometimes like a gleaner thou dost keep
Steady thy laden head across a brook;
Or by a cyder-press, with patient look,
Thou watchest the last oozings hours by hours.

Where are the songs of spring? Ay, where are they?
Think not of them, thou hast thy music too,–
While barred clouds bloom the soft-dying day,
And touch the stubble-plains with rosy hue;
Then in a wailful choir the small gnats mourn
Among the river sallows, borne aloft
Or sinking as the light wind lives or dies;
And full-grown lambs loud bleat from hilly bourn;
Hedge-crickets sing; and now with treble soft
The red-breast whistles from a garden-croft;
And gathering swallows twitter in the skies.

–Written by John Keats
on September 19, 1819

SEPTEMBER 20

DAILY READING

Rejoice in the LORD *your God, for he has given you the autumn rains in righteousness. He sends you abundant showers, both autumn and spring rains, as before.* (JOEL 2:23)

FEAST DAYS

1801	Jung Hye	Korean martyr
1839	Paul Chong Hasang	Korean martyr
1846	Andrew Kim Taegon	Korean martyr

ENTRANCE AND EXIT

b. 356	Alexander the Great	Greek leader
b. 1902	Stevie (Florence Margaret) Smith	English writer
b. 1934	Sophia Loren	Italian actor
d. 1863	Jakob Grimm	German writer
d. 1947	Fiorello La Guardia	American politician
d. 1957	Jean Sibelius	Finnish composer

Treaty of Ryswick

> That there be an universal and perpetual peace and a true and sincere friendship, between the Most Serene and Mighty Prince William III King of *Great Britain*, and the Most Serene and Mighty Prince *Lewis XIV* the Most Christian King, their heirs and successors, and between the Kingdoms, states and subjects of both.

Thus begins the text for the first Treaty of Ryswick, signed on this day in 1697. Since 1689, England and France had been at war over the territorial ambitions of King Louis IV. Battles had raged in the Netherlands, the Rhineland, Italy, Ireland, and as far as India and America.

Finally, the King of Sweden mediated between the two parties and arranged a conference at Ryswick in the Netherlands. For the first few weeks no result was reached, and in June William III and Louis XIV appointed one representative to meet together privately. The Earl of Portland, William Bentinch, and Marshall Boufflers soon drew up the terms of an agreement, but Emperor Leopold I and the King of Spain would not agree. Eventually, Spain did assent, and the treaty was signed between France and the Grand Alliance–England, Germany, Spain, and Holland.

The treaty led to France surrendering the towns of Freiburg, Breisach, and Phillippsburg to Germany. France was allowed to keep Strasbourg and regained Nova Scotia and Pondicherry in India. King Louis agreed to recognize William as king of England, and promised to give no further assistance to his rival, James II. Through these means, the complex political, economic, and cultural geography of Europe was established.

Noteworthy

German brothers Jacob Ludwig Carl Grimm and Wilhelm Karl Grimm were German professors who collected folk tales. They compiled 209 stories that are still engage adults and children alike. Some quotes from their works:

> Rapunzel grew into the most beautiful child beneath the sun. When she was twelve years old, the enchantress shut her into a tower, which lay in a forest, and had neither stairs nor door, but quite at the top was a little window. When the enchantress wanted to go in, she placed herself beneath it and cried,
>
> "Rapunzel, Rapunzel,
> Let down thy hair to me."
>
> –*Rapunzel*

> Hard by a great forest dwelt a poor wood-cutter with his wife and his two children. The boy was called Hansel and the girl Grethel. He had little to bite and to break, and once when great scarcity fell on the land, he could no longer procure daily bread.
>
> –*Hansel and Gretel*

> One day an old man and his wife were sitting in front of a miserable house resting a while from their work. Suddenly a splendid carriage with four black horses came driving up, and a richly-dressed man descended from it.
>
> –*The Master Thief*

*S*EPTEMBER 21

DAILY READING

The grace of the Lord Jesus Christ, and the love of God,
and the communion of the Holy Ghost,
be with you all. Amen. (2 COR 13:14, KJV)

FEAST DAYS

ca. 1st cent.	Matthew the Apostle	Apostle of Ethiopia
ca. 1st cent.	Iphigenia	Ehthiopian princess
1799	Francis Jaccard	Missionary to Vietnam

ENTRANCE AND EXIT

b. 1452	Girolamo Savonarola	Italian religious leader
b. 1874	Gustav Holst	English composer
b. 1912	Chuck Jones	American animator
d. 1558	Charles V the Wise	Roman Emperor
d. 1832	Sir Walter Scott	Scottish writer
d. 1860	Arthur Schopenhauer	German philosopher

St. Matthew

Matthew, also called Levi, was the son of Alpheus and brother of the holy apostle James the Less. He worked as a tax collector in the Roman custom house on Lake Tiberias. Such officers were hated by the Jews for their injustice, and were called publicans, or public sinners. While he was sitting at the receipt of custom, he was called by Christ to be one of his disciples, and he immediately left his lucrative office and all that he had tofollow Him. After this incident, recorded in Matthew 9, little is heard about Matthew apart from confirmation that he was one of Jesus' twelve apostles.

Extrabiblical sources, such as the writings of Bishop Papias of Hierapolis from around the end of the first century, state that "Matthew wrote an ordered account of the oracles (of our Lord) and each interpreted these oracles according to his ability."

In Palestine, some time between the years 40 and 50, this ex-civil servant produced the orderly, almost ledgerlike, account, which we know as The Gospel according to St. Matthew. Matthew's mathematical temperament shows itself in his arithmetical neatness. Hence the seven parables of the Kingdom, the seven woes for the Pharisees, seven invocations of the Lord's Prayer, and seven Beatitudes. So, too, with the number five: five disputes with the Pharisees, the five loaves, five talents, and above all the five books into which the body of his Gospel is clearly divided.

Tradition records that Matthew preached the gospel in Ethiopia, and he was killed at the command of King Hutacus for opposing his marriage with the Princess Iphigenia. Relics, purporting to be those of Matthew, were brought to Salermo, Italy in the tenth century.

Girolamo Savonarola

Girolamo Savonarola (1452–98), Italian reformer and martyr, was born at Ferrara, the son of Niccolò Savonarola and of Elena Bonaccorsi. He was educated by his paternal grandfather, Michele, a celebrated doctor and a man of rigid moral and religious principles. From this elderly scholar, whose own education was of the fourteenth century, Savonarola may perhaps have received certain medieval influences. In his early poetry and other adolescent writings the main characteristics of the future reformer are seen. Even at that early date, as he wrote in a letter to his father, he "could not suffer the blind wickedness of the peoples of Italy." He found unbearable the humanistic paganism which corrupted manners, art, poetry, and religion itself.

Beginning in 1493, Savonarola spoke with increasing violence against the abuses in ecclesiastical life, against the immorality of a large part of the clergy, and against the wickedness of many members of the Roman Curia, of Alexander VI, and of numerous princes and courtiers. His preaching began to point plainly to a political revolution as the divinely ordained means for the regeneration of religion and morality.

In 1497, after ignoring the pope's order to stop preaching, he was excommunicated from the Catholic Church in Rome. Fiercely denounced by some Franciscans, he was executed for heresy on May 23, 1498.

SEPTEMBER 22

DAILY READING

Accept one another, then, just as Christ accepted you, in order to bring praise to God. (ROM 15:7)

FEAST DAYS

ca. 287	Innocent	Martyr of the Theban Legion
ca. 287	Exuperius	Martyr of the Theban Legion
ca. 287	Candidus	Martyr of the Theban Legion

ENTRANCE AND EXIT

b. 1694	Philip Stanhope	English statesman
b. 1791	Michael Faraday	English scientist
b. 1931	Faye Weldon	English author
d. 1662	John Biddle	Founder of English Unitarianism
d. 1961	Marion Davis	American actor
d. 1989	Irving Berlin	Russian composer

Caspar von Schwenckfeld

Caspar von Schwenckfeld (1489–1561) was a Silesian courtier who lived in the first generation of the Protestant Reformation. Schwenckfeld rejected the Catholic, Lutheran, and Reformed doctrines of the Eucharist, believing that Christ was spiritually present to believers apart from the elements of bread and wine.

In 1525 Schwenckfeld traveled to Wittenberg to ask Martin Luther for his approval of his "enlightened" views, but found they disagreed on many issues.

In 1541, he published his book, *Great Confession on the Glory of Christ.* He taught that Christ has two natures, divine and human, the human nature being a kind of sinless "celestial flesh." Jesus' human flesh was increasingly divinized while he was on earth, so he was eventually transfigured, resurrected, and taken up to heavenly glory. It was Christ's invisible glorified flesh that Caspar thought believers ate at the Lord's Supper. Because of this view, his followers often called themselves "Confessors of the Glory of Christ."

On this day in 1734, his followers, now known as Schwenckfelders, settled in the Pennsylvania Dutch countryside. Today, there are still five congregations of Schwenkfelders in Pennsylvania, a testament to an original thinker who became a heretic.

Michael Faraday

The English physicist and inventor, Michael Faraday (1791–1867) was born at Newington Butts in London. When thirteen years old, Faraday was apprenticed to a bookseller and bookbinder for eight years.

Faraday's first contact with the Royal Institution was in 1809 when he attended Sir Humphry Davy's last lectures. Faraday took copious notes and sent them to Davy, entreating him at the same time to enable him to quit the book trade, which he detested, and to pursue science, which he loved. Davy, the Professor of Chemistry and Director of the Laboratory, wrote to Faraday and engaged him his assistant.

Faraday is noted as the discoverer of electromagnetic induction, the theory of electrolysis, and the invention of the electric motor. Thus, he has great claim to be characterized as the Father of Electricity.

A keen Christian, Faraday was once questioned on his speculations of a life after death, he replied: "Speculations? I know nothing about speculations. I'm resting on certainties. I know that my Redeemer lives, and because He lives, I shall live also."

Noteworthy

1290 Birth of Bilbo Baggins (Shire reckoning).
1692 Salem witchcraft trials–seven woman and two men executed.
1735 Robert Walpole became the first British prime minister to occupy 10 Downing Street.
1776 American spy Nathan Hale hanged by the British.
1792 French Republic proclaimed.
1955 Start of commercial television in England.
1975 Assassination attempt on Gerald Ford in San Francisco.

September 23

DAILY READING

And not only so, but we glory in tribulations also:
knowing that tribulation worketh patience;
And patience, experience;
and experience, hope. (ROM 5:3–4, KJV)

FEAST DAYS

76	Linus	2nd pope
1253	Clare of Assisi	Founder of the Poor Clares
1968	Padre Pio of Pietrelcina	Italian stimatic

ENTRANCE AND EXIT

b. 63 BC	Caius Octavias	Roman Emperor Caesar Augustus
b. 1800	William Holmes McGuffrey	American children's author
b. 1949	Bruce Springsteen	American rock star
d. 1939	Sigmund Freud	Austrian father of psychoanalysis
d. 1973	Pablo Neruda	Chilean poet
d. 1987	Bob Fosse	American film director

The Concordat of Worms

The relationship between church and state has endured many difficulties through the centuries. Disputes over the balance of power between the two has led to much harm and changed the course of nations over the last 1,500 years.

On this day in 1123 (1122 according to some sources), the city of Worms in Germany was host to a concordat reached between Pope Callistus II and Holy Roman Emperor Henry V. The Concordat of Worms settled the issue of who had the right–clergy or king–to choose replacement clergy for vacant positions. The *Pactum Calixtinum* was a compromise that made a clear distinction between the spiritual side of a prelate's office and his position as a servant of the crown. Bishops and abbots were to be chosen by the clergy, but the emperor was authorized to decide contested elections. The man chosen was first to be invested with the *regalia*, or powers pertaining to his office as servant, for which he did homage to the emperor. Then he was invested with the *spiritualia*, or ecclesiastical powers, symbolized by the staff and ring. He acquired these from his ecclesiastical superior, who represented the authority of the church.

The General Lateran Council of 1123 incorporated the Concordat of Worms, although there were some efforts to challenge it. For example, King Lothair the Saxon demanded the right to reappoint clergy from Pope Innocent II. But the opposition of the clergy was so potent that the king dropped his demand, and Innocent in 1133 confirmed the concordat. Imperial control over the election of bishops in Germany came later to be much curtailed in practice, partly by explicit concessions wrung at various times from individual emperors, such as Otto IV in 1209 and Frederick II in 1213.

However, the principles of the Concordat of Worms continued, if only in theory, to regulate the tenure of bishops and abbots in Germany until the dissolution of the Imperial German Empire in 1806.

Noteworthy

1780 British spy John Andre captured by America.
1846 German astronomer Johann Gottfried Galle discovers Neptune.
1912 Mack Sennett releases first comedy film.
1930 Birth of Ray Charles in Albany, Georgia.
1980 Microsoft Corporation pays $50,000 to Seattle Computer for their QDOS (Quick and Dirty Operating System) system that later became the basis of Windows programs.

SEPTEMBER 24

DAILY READING

Do not throw away your confidence; it will be richly rewarded. You need to persevere so that when you have done the will of God, you will receive what he has promised. (HEB10:35–36)

FEAST DAYS

658	Geremarus	Founder of Flay Abbey, near Rouen, France
718	Rupert	Patron of Salzburg, Austria
1048	Isarnus	Abbot at St. Victor's, Marseilles, France

ENTRANCE AND EXIT

b. 1896	F. Scott Fitzgerald	American author
b. 1936	Jim Henson	American entertainer
b. 1962	Joseph Kennedy II	American politician
d. 1541	Phillippus Paracelsus	German physician
d. 1981	Patsy Kelly	American actor
d. 1991	Dr. Theodore Seuss Geisel	American writer and illustrator

The Muppet Show

The brilliant entertainer Jim Henson created the Muppets, a memorable band of zany character puppets, in the 1950s. They made their debut on the American children's show *Sesame Street* and subsequently made many appearances in their own show, *The Muppet Show*, and other spin-offs.

The name *Muppet* is a combination of marionette and puppet. Every Muppet character is bright, with large eyes and often a large mouth. Muppets are operated from underneath the performance area, with the puppeteer using one hand to operate the mouth and the other for movement. Over the years, Muppet operation has evolved to include motors, radio control, suspended rigs, and computer enhancements.

In addition to shows featuring world-famous actors, singers, and comedians, Muppets have appeared in films such as *A Muppet Family Christmas, Muppets from Space, The Muppets Take Manhattan*, and *A Muppet Christmas Carol.*

England's Nazareth

September 24 is the feast day of the Marian shrine at Walsingham, Norfolk, England. The site is known as England's Nazareth and is regarded as a place of pilgrimage for Catholics and Anglicans.

As popular legend has it, the shrine originated in 1061 when a noble widow, Lady Richeldis was taken, in the spirit, to Nazareth. There the Archangel Gabriel greeted her and the Virgin Mary showed her her home. She directed the widow to take measurements of the house so that she could build one like it at Walsingham. In this spot, the Virgin Mary explained, the people would celebrate the Annunciation, the "root of mankind's gracious redemption," and would find help in their needs.

Three times Richeldis experienced this vision and request. This confirmed her desire to have the chapel constructed, but the directions about the location were unclear to her and to the carpenters. When the carpenters could make no progress in building, Richeldis spent the night in prayer and eventually the shrine was built.

Over the years, many miracles were attributed to Our Lady of Walsingham, including one in which Kind Edward I was saved from a piece of falling masonry.

During the fifteenth and sixteenth centuries, the fervor of Marian devotion waned in England as the Protestant cause gained ground. However, in 1534 the prior and canons of Walsingham signed Henry VIII's Act of Supremacy, placing them among the first to recognize the king's authority.

In the following centuries the shrine fell into ruins and its former glory largely forgotten. But in the nineteenth century, a wealthy Anglican woman, Charlotte Boyd, commenced the restoration of the shrine. However, it wasn't until 1991 when the Pope visited England that the restored shrine of Walsingham regained its popularity. Pope John Paul II celebrated Mass at Wembley with the image of Our Lady of Walsingham on the altar. The image was placed there by the director of the shrine.

SEPTEMBER 25

DAILY READING

My dear children, I write this to you so that you will not sin. But if anybody does sin, we have one who speaks to the Father in our defense—Jesus Christ the Righteous One. (1 JOHN 2:1)

FEAST DAYS

642	Ceolfrid	Benedictine monk
1054	Herman the Cripple	Benedictine monk
1215	Albert of Jerusalem	Bishop of Bobbio, Italy

ENTRANCE AND EXIT

b. 1897	William Faulkner	American writer
b. 1944	Michael Douglas	American actor
b. 1969	Catherine Zeta-Jones	English actor
d. 1680	Samuel Butler	English writer
d. 1872	Peter Cartwright	American evangelist
d. 1987	Mary Astor	American actor

The Lord's Breaking-Plow and Exhorter

Peter Cartwright, "the Lord's breaking-plow" (1785–1872), was born in Amhurst County, Virginia, the son of a Revolutionary War veteran. His family moved to Logan County, Kentucky, where at the age of sixteen he was converted at a camp meeting and joined the Methodist Episcopal Church.

In 1802 this uneducated young man was licensed as an "Exhorter" by Jesse Walker, and four years later he was ordained a deacon by Bishop Asbury. In 1808, Bishop McKendree ordained him an elder.

In 1812 he was appointed a presiding elder and served in that office for fifty years, longer than any other minister in the Methodist Church. Unwilling to see his children grow up in a slave state, Cartwright obtained a transfer and became one of the original members of the Illinois Conference when it was organized in 1824. The previous year he had purchased land on Richland Creek in Sangamon County, where he lived for the remainder of his life. Cartwright was elected a representative to the state legislature in 1828, only four years after he had established residence in Illinois. In his reelection campaign in 1832 he defeated Abraham Lincoln. In 1846 he ran unsuccessfully against Lincoln for Congress.

However, Cartwright's main business was to preach the gospel, which he did from Galena to St. Louis and eastward as far as the prairies extended. Because drunkenness was a problem on the frontier, Peter Cartwright thought he'd demonstrate the danger of strong drink. He placed a worm in a glass of wine. It wriggled. He transferred it to a glass of whiskey. It curled up and died. "There," Cartwright said. "What does that tell you?" A man replied, "It shows that if you drink whiskey you won't have worms."

He was a delegate to twelve General Conferences, once helping to found McKendree College, the Illinois Female Academy (now MacMurray College), and Illinois Wesleyan University.

In 1856 he published his autobiography, a book full of dramatic incident and impassioned spirit. When his fellow ministers paid tribute to him at Lincoln in 1870, he looked back on sixty-five years as a traveling preacher and said simply, "I would take . . . the same track over again, and the same religion, rather than be president of the United States."

Noteworthy

1066 At the Battle of Stamford Bridge, English King Harold II defeats King Harald Hardrada of Norway.
1493 Christopher Columbus starts his second voyage to the New World.
1857 Indian uprising against British rule at Lucknow, India.
1890 Sequoia National Park established.
1973 Skylab 2 returns from its fifty-nine days in orbit.
1979 Bob Dylan releases his first gospel album, *Slow Train Coming.*

SEPTEMBER 26

DAILY READING

We know him who said, "It is mine to avenge; I will repay," and again, "The Lord will judge his people." It is a dreadful thing to fall into the hands of the living God. (HEB10:30–31)

FEAST DAYS

ca. 304	Cyprian the Magician	Bishop of Antioch
910	Nilus The Younger	Hermit from Calabria, Italy
1923	Louis Tezza	Apostle of Lima, Peru

ENTRANCE AND EXIT

b. 1888	Thomas Stearns Eliot	American poet
b. 1898	George Gershwin	American composer
b. 1907	Anthony Blunt	English spy and art historian
d. 1820	Daniel Boone	American pioneer
d. 1915	Keir Hardie	Scottish politician
d. 1917	Edgar Degas	French artist

Thomas Stearns Eliot

The much-loved poet and playwright Thomas Stearns Eliot (T. S. Eliot) was born in St. Louis, Missouri. His mother, Charlotte Stearns Eliot, was a poet, and Eliot's family line can be traced back to the earliest New England settlers. Eliot's paternal grandfather established and presided over Washington University.

In 1906 he was a freshman at Harvard University, having been a pupil at Milton Academy in Massachusetts. He studied philosophy and went to the Sorbonne in Paris for a year.

In 1915, Eliot went to live in London and then studied at Merton College, Oxford. That same year, he married Vivienne Haigh-Wood. Eliot only returned home for occasional visits, and became a British citizen in 1927. After a long period of illness, Vivienne died in 1945, and in 1957, Eliot married Valerie Fletcher.

Eliot's jobs ranged from schoolmaster, bank clerk, freelance writer, assistant editor of the *Egoist*, editor of *The Criterion*, publisher (with Faber and Faber), and even professor of poetry at Harvard.

After much soul-searching and inner turmoil, Eliot was confirmed as a member of the Anglican Church in 1927, although he described himself as an Anglo Catholic. In 1948, T. S. Eliot was made a Nobel Laureate for his services to literature.

His best known works include *Murder in the Cathedral*, "The Love Song of J. Alfred Prufrock," *The Journey of the Magi, The Waste Land*, and *The Four Quartets*.

Eliot died on January 4, 1965. He was a very private man and forbade in his will an official biography.

Extract from the Presentation Speech to T. S. Eliot by Anders Österling, Permanent Secretary to the Swedish Nobel Academy, 1948

Insight into Eliot must always present certain problems to be overcome, obstacles which are at the same time stimulating. It may appear to be contradictory to say that this radical pioneer of form, the initiator of a whole revolution in style within present-day poetry, is at the same time a coldly reasoning, logically subtle theorist, who never wearies of defending historical perspectives and the necessity of fixed norms for our existence.

As early as the 1940's, he had become a convinced supporter of the Anglican Church in religion and of classicism in literature. In view of this philosophy of life, which implies a consistent return to ideals standardized by age, it might seem that his modernistic practice would dash with his traditional theory.

But this is hardly the case. Rather, in his capacity as an author, he has uninterruptedly and with varying success worked to bridge this chasm, the existence of which he must be fully and perhaps painfully conscious. His earliest poetry, so convulsively disintegrated, so studiously aggressive in its whole technical form, can finally also be apprehended as a negative expression of a mentality which aims at higher and purer realities and must first free itself of abhorrence and cynicism. In other words, his revolt is that of the Christian poet. It should also be observed in this connection that, on the whole, Eliot is careful not to magnify the power of poetry in relation to that of religion.

September 27

DAILY READING

But seek ye first the kingdom of God, and his righteousness; and all these things shall be added unto you. (MATT 6:33, KJV)

FEAST DAYS

1360	Delphina	Patron of brides
1571	Gaius	Patron of Milan, Italy
1660	Vincent de Paul	Founder of Congregation of the Daughters of Charity

ENTRANCE AND EXIT

b. 1389	Cosimo de Medici	Italian statesman
b. 1722	Samuel Adams	American revolutionary
b. 1984	Avril Lavigne	Canadian pop star
d. 1915	Remy de Gourmont	French writer
d. 1944	Aimee Semple McPherson	American evangelist
d. 1960	Sylvia Pankhurst	English suffragist

Aimee Semple McPherson

On this day, Aimee Semple McPherson (1890–1944), founder of the Church of the Foursquare Gospel and famous female evangelist, died of a suspected drug overdose.

In the 1920s, McPherson was the first woman to begin a movement of Pentecostal revivals across America. Preaching in Oakland, California, in 1922, she had a vision based upon the prophet Ezekiel's vision of Man, Lion, Ox, and Eagle. She saw four symbols: the cross, the crown, the dove, and the cup. These, she believed, represented Regeneration of the Church, the Second Coming, Baptism in the Spirit, and Divine Healing, respectively. The four symbols created a name for her new movement, the Foursquare Gospel. In 1923, her fame grew after establishing the Angelus Temple, an enormous flagship church building located near Echo Park in Hollywood.

Worldwide attention followed in 1926 when she was kidnapped for thirty-nine days and held for a ransom of $500,000. Months later, Aimee would be tried on charges of adultery and perjury. She was found guilty of "criminal conspiracy to commit acts injurious to public morals and to prevent and obstruct justice" and faced up to forty years in prison. However, after months of reinvestigation and a public outcry this verdict was overturned and McPherson was freed from custody.

McPherson was one of the first to describe the Pentecost "slain in the Spirit" phenomenon, where believers were overcome by the Holy Spirit as in the New Testament.

She was a pioneer in the field of radio evangelism, and on radio station KSFG and in her preaching, McPherson was an innovator, using theatrical style performance techniques to reach her audience.

McPherson mobilized an extensive social ministry from her headquarters at the Angelus Temple. She provided a social and educational center for thousands of Midwestern immigrants.

She also widened the appeal of Pentecostalism to millions of people through her tours and radio broadcasts, and her founding of a Bible College in her name to train missionaries, ministers, and evangelists.

Her tent missions became huge events. For example, on one 150-day tour she traveled over 15,000 miles and delivered 336 sermons to audiences totaling more than two million people.

Noteworthy

1498 Death of Tomas de Torquemada, Spanish Inquisitor.
1825 First public railway started between Stockton and Darlington, England.
1911 First blues song published–"Memphis Blues" by W. C. Handy.
1939 Fall of Warsaw, Poland, to Nazi forces.
1940 Berlin Pact signed between Germany, Italy, and Japan.
1954 *The Tonight Show* made its debut on NBC.

SEPTEMBER 28

DAILY READING

The man without the Spirit does not accept the things that come from the Spirit of God, for they are foolishness to him, and he cannot understand them, because they are spiritually discerned. (1 COR 2:14)

FEAST DAYS

ca. 6th cent.	Baruch the Prophet	Disciple of Jeremiah
929	Wenceslaus	Duke of Bohemia
1900	Regimus Isore	Boxer Rebellion Martyr

ENTRANCE AND EXIT

b. 555	Confucius	Chinese philosopher
b. 1913	Edith Pargeter	English author
b. 1934	Brigitte Bardot	French actor
d. 1891	Hermann Melville	American author
d. 1895	Louis Pasteur	French scientist
d. 1902	Emile Zola	French author

Edith Pargeter

Edith Pargeter (1913–95) is not a familiar name because the reclusive Shropshire author published her books under several pseudonyms. She is better known as Ellis Peters, the creator of one of historical fiction's most memorable characters, the soldier monk Brother Cadfael ap Meilyr ap Dafyd.

Edith was born and lived most of her life in Shropshire, England. As a schoolgirl, she was known as "the girl who never stops writing." She was awarded the British Empire Medal for her work in the Women's Royal Naval Service during World War II.

By May 1945, Edith already had ten novels to her credit, including *She Goes to War* and the *Eight Champions of Christendom*. Many more novels followed, but it is for her historical mystery novels, especially the stories of Brother Cadfael, that she is best remembered.

Commenting on her most famous character creation in 1988, she said:

> Brother Cadfael sprang to life suddenly and unexpectedly when he was already approaching sixty, mature, experienced fully armed and seventeen years tonsured. He emerged as the necessary protagonist when I had the idea of deriving a plot for a murder mystery from the true history of Shrewsbury Abbey in the twelfth century, and needed the high mediaeval equivalent of a detective, an observer and agent of justice in the centre of the action.

The twenty-one Cadfael novels are published in countless languages and the television series, starring Derek Jacobi, is shown in many countries, drawing visitors and fans from all over the world to present-day Shrewsbury.

It is therefore appropriate that Edith is remembered with a permanent memorial in the Abbey Church, which she loved. She was awarded the British Crime Writers Association's Cartier Diamond Dagger Award, the coveted Mystery Writers of America's Edgar, an OBE (Order of the British Empire), an honorary MA from Birmingham University, and numerous other awards.

She died in 1995 at the age of eighty-two in her beloved Shropshire, England.

Brother Cadfael Quotes

There is no profit in ifs. We go on from where we stand, we answer for our own evil, and leave to God our good.

–*The Virgin in the Ice*

For even the pursuit of perfection may be sin, if it infringes the rights and needs of another soul. Better to fail a little, by turning aside to lift up another, than to pass by him in haste to reach our own reward, and leave him to solitude and despair. Better to labour in lameness, in fallibility, but holding up others who falter, than to stride forward alone.

–*The Raven in the Foregate*

Beware how you pass judgement on your superiors at least until you know how to put yourself in their place and see from their view.

–*Monk's Hood*

Penitence is in the heart, not in words.

–*St. Peter's Fair*

But God's justice, if it makes no haste, makes no mistakes.

–*The Potter's Field*

September 29

DAILY READING

Everyone who does evil hates the light, and will not come into the light for fear that his deeds will be exposed. But whoever lives by the truth comes into the light, so that it may be seen plainly that what he has done has been done through God. (JOHN 3:20–21)

FEAST DAYS

n/a	Michael	Archangel
n/a	Raphael	Archangel
555	Kyriakos	Hermit of Palestine

ENTRANCE AND EXIT

b. 1758	Horatio Nelson	English admiral
b. 1901	Enrico Fermi	Italian scientist
b. 1943	Lech Walesa	Polish politician
d. 1890	Alphonse Karr	French writer
d. 1913	Rudolph Diesel	German engineer
d. 1973	Wystan Hugh Auden	English poet

The Feast of St. Michael

Today is Michaelmas Day, or more correctly the day of St. Michael and All Angels, a great festival observed by the Roman Catholic Church and the Church of England. In England, traditionally, it is was one of the four quarter days on which rents were paid. It was the day on which magistrates were elected, and it is also notable for the custom of eating goose at dinner.

Michael is the chief of angels, or archangel. In Scripture, he is mentioned five times, always as a warlike character: namely, by Daniel as fighting for the people of God against Persia; once by St. Jude as fighting with the devil about the body of Moses; and once by St. John as fighting at the head of his angelic troops against the devil.

Sometimes Michael is represented as the sole archangel, sometimes as the head of the archangels, which includes Gabriel and Raphael, and some others. He is usually represented in coat-armor, with a glory round his head, and a dart in his hand, trampling on the fallen Lucifer.

Amongst Catholics, St. Michael is invoked as "a most glorious and warlike prince," "chief officer of paradise," "captain of God's hosts," "receiver of souls," "the vanquisher of evil spirits," and "the admirable general." Magistrates were chosen on this day in recognition of their role, like St. Michael, to protect people against evil and fight for justice.

The custom of eating goose on this day appears to have originated among rural tenants bringing a fattened goose to their landlord, when paying their rent, with a view to making him lenient. Queen Elizabeth I was said to have had this dish when she received news of the defeat of the Spanish Armada.

Michael in the Bible

He said, "Daniel, you who are highly esteemed, consider carefully the words I am about to speak to you, and stand up, for I have now been sent to you." And when he said this to me, I stood up trembling. Then he continued, "Do not be afraid, Daniel. Since the first day that you set your mind to gain understanding and to humble yourself before your God, your words were heard, and I have come in response to them. But the prince of the Persian kingdom resisted me twenty-one days. Then Michael, one of the chief princes, came to help me, because I was detained there with the king of Persia.

–Daniel 10:11–13

In the very same way, these dreamers pollute their own bodies, reject authority and slander celestial beings. But even the archangel Michael, when he was disputing with the devil about the body of Moses, did not dare to bring a slanderous accusation against him, but said, "The Lord rebuke you!"

–Jude 8–9

And there was war in heaven. Michael and his angels fought against the dragon, and the dragon and his angels fought back. But he was not strong enough; and they lost their place in heaven. The great dragon was hurled down–that ancient serpent called the devil, or Satan, who leads the whole world astray. He was hurled to the earth, and his angels with him.

–Revelations 12:7–9

SEPTEMBER 30

DAILY READING

This is my prayer: that your love may abound more and more in knowledge and depth of insight, so that you may be able to discern what is best and may be pure and blameless until the day of Christ. (PHIL 1:9–10)

FEAST DAYS

325	Gregory the Illuminator	Bishop of Armenia
419	Eusebius Hieronymus Sophronius–Jerome	Patron of Bible scholars
653	Honoratus	Archbishop of Canterbury

ENTRANCE AND EXIT

b. 1882	Hans Geiger	German scientist
b. 1924	Truman Capote	American writer
b. 1947	Marc Bolan	Lead singer, T Rex
d. 1770	George Whitefield	English evangelist
d. 1772	James Brindley	English engineer
d. 1955	James Dean	American actor

Judgment at Nuremberg

On November 20, 1945, the Allies convened an International Military Tribunal at the Palace of Justice in Nuremburg, Germany, to prosecute Nazi war criminals. The indictment, which served as the basis for the trials and for charging the defendants contained four counts:

> Count One: The common plan or conspiracy to wage a aggressive war in violation of international law or treaties.
>
> Count Two: Planning, preparation, or waging an aggressive war.
>
> Count Three: War crimes–violations of the international rules of war (mistreatment of prisoners of war or civilian populations, the plunder of private property, and the destruction of towns and cities without military justification).
>
> Count Four: Crimes against humanity–murder, extermination, enslavement of civilian populations; persecution on the basis of racial, religious, or political grounds.

On this day in 1946, the International Military Tribunal found these men guilty of the charges against them:

Hermann Goering	Sentenced to death, but committed suicide
Rudolph Hess	Life imprisonment–committed suicide in 1987
Hans Frank	Sentenced to death
Wilhelm Frick	Sentenced to death
Julius Streicher	Sentenced to death
Walter Funk	Life imprisonment–died in 1960
Fritz Sauckel	Sentenced to death
Alfred Jodl	Sentenced to death
Martin Bormann	Sentenced to death (in absentia)
Franz von Papen	Acquitted
Joachim von Ribbentrop	Sentenced to death
Wilhelm Keitel	Sentenced to death
Ernst Kaltenbrunner	Sentenced to death
Alfred Rosenberg	Sentenced to death
Hjalmar Schacht	Acquitted
Karl Doenitz	10 years imprisonment
Erich Raeder	Life imprisonment
Baldur von Schirach	20 years imprisonment
Artur Seyss-Inquart	Sentenced to death
Albert Speer	20 years imprisonment
Constantin von Neurath	15 years imprisonment
Hans Fritzsche	Acquitted

The Nuremberg Trials concluded on October 1, 1946, the Jewish Day of Atonement.

October

Then came October, full of merry glee,
For yet his noule was totty of the must,
Which he was treading, in the wine-fat's see,
And of the joyous oyle, whose gentle gust
Made him so frollick, and so full of lust:
Upon a dreadfull scorpion he did ride,
The same which by Dianae's doom unjust
Slew great Orion; and eeke by his side
He had his ploughing-share, and coulter ready tyde.

EDMUND SPENSER–*The Shepheardes Calender* (1579)

My ornaments are fruits; my garments leaves,
Woven like cloth of gold, and crimson dyed;
I do not boast the harvesting of sheaves,
O'er orchards and o'er vineyards I preside.
Though on the frigid Scorpion I ride,
The dreamy air is full, and overflows
With tender memories of the summer-tide,
And mingled voices of the doves and crows.

HENRY WADSWORTH LONGFELLOW–*The Poet's Calendar* (1882)

Proverbs

Warm October, cold February.

If in the fall of the leaves in October many of them wither on the boughs and hang there, it betokens a frosty winter and much snow.

When birds and badgers are fat in October expect a cold winter.

October

Fruits continue in abundance during this month, as everybody knows. The wine obtained from the elder-berry makes a very pleasant and wholesome drink, when heated over a fire; but the humbler sloe, which the peasants eat, gets the start of him in reputation, by changing its name to port, of which wine it certainly makes a considerable ingredient.

The mornings and afternoons increase in mistiness, though the middle of the day is often very fine; and no weather when it is unclouded, is apt to give a clearer and manlier sensation than that of October. One of the most curious natural appearances is the gossamer, which is an infinite multitude of little threads shot out by minute spiders, who are thus wafted by the wind from place to place.

The chief business of October, in the great economy of nature, is dissemination, which is performed among other means by the high winds which now return. The changing leaves with all their lights and shades of green, amber, red, light red, light and dark green, white, brown, russet, and yellow of all sorts display their beauty.

–WILLIAM HONE, *The Every-Day Book* (1825–26)

Louisa May Alcott

Once upon a time a farmer planted a little seed. in his garden, and after a while it sprouted and became a vine and bore many squashes. One day in October, when they were ripe, he picked one and took it to market. A gorcerman bought and put it in his shop. That same morning, a little girl in a brown hat and blue dress, with a round face and snub nose, went and bought it for her mother. She lugged it home, cut it up, and boiled it in the big pot, mashed some of it salt and butter, for dinner. And to the rest she added a pint of milk, two eggs, four spoons of sugar, nutmeg, and some crackers, put it in a deep dish, and baked it till it was brown and nice, and next day it was eaten by a family named March.

–*Little Women*, Chapter Ten

OCTOBER 1

DAILY READING

Blessed are you when people insult you, persecute you and falsely say all kinds of evil against you because of me. Rejoice and be glad, because great is your reward in heaven, for in the same way they persecuted the prophets who were before you. (MATT 5:11–12)

FEAST DAYS

ca. 1st cent.	Holy Protection of the Mother of God	Mary, mother of Jesus
ca. 556	Romanos the Melodist	Jewish composer
1897	Therese of Lisieux	Doctor of the Church

ENTRANCE AND EXIT

b. 1207	King Henry III	English king
b. 1885	Louis Untermeyer	American poet
b. 1935	Dame Julie Andrews	English actor
d. 1684	Pierre Corneille	French writer
d. 1893	Benjamin Jowett	English writer
d. 1972	Louis Leakey	English archaeologist

National Day–China

On this day in 1949, as the clock struck three in Tiananmen Square, Beijing, China, Chairman Mao Zedong, leader of the Communist Party of China (CPC), declared the founding of the People's Republic of China (PRC) and waved the first five-star PRC flag.

National Day in China is the start of a "Golden Week" of celebrations marking the founding of the People's Republic. As well as this week, there are two other "Golden Weeks" in the national calendar: Spring Festival Week that takes place during January, and Labor Day Week that begins on May 1.

National Day celebrations are held throughout this vast country, including in Macau and Hong Kong. Festivities include public concerts, fireworks, and school singing events. During National Golden Week, portraits of leaders such as Sun Yat-Sen are publicly displayed. When the anniversary is a multiple of five, 30th or 35th for example, the celebrations are even greater, with special events in the main cities, such as troop inspections by regional and national leaders.

Before the declaration of the Republic, China had suffered under a Japanese invasion that lasted for fourteen years. After World War II, in 1945, the civil war between Mao's CPC and the National Party (or Kuomintang) led by Chiang Kai-shek continued to claim thousands of lives. The CPC eventually prevailed, and Chiang Kai-shek and his followers were forced into exile. In 1949, they established, with their depleted forces, a base in Taiwan and declared Taipei the provisional "capital" of mainland China. The National Party does not recognize the CPC, and for this reason, National Day is not celebrated in Taiwan.

Noteworthy

1529 The Colloquy of Marburg, Germany.
1800 Spain cedes Louisiana to France.
1936 General Franco declared leader of Spain.
1960 National Day, Nigeria.
1960 National Day, Cyprus.
1971 Walt Disney World opens in Orlando, Florida.

*O*CTOBER 2

DAILY READING

Fear of man will prove to be a snare,
but whoever trusts in the LORD is kept safe. (PROV 29:25)

FEAST DAYS

585	Leudomer	Bishop of Chartres, France
616	Leodegarius	Deacon of Poitiers, France
1912	John Beyzym	Jesuit teacher

ENTRANCE AND EXIT

b. 1452	Richard III	English king
b. 1852	Sir William Ramsay	Scottish scientist
b. 1951	Gordon Sumner	English rock star, Sting
d. 322 BC	Aristotle	Greek philosopher
d. 1780	John Andre	English spy
d. 1985	Rock Hudson	American actor

The Father of Modern Missions

On this day, in 1792 a dozen ministers from Kettering in Northamptonshire, England, met and formed the Baptist Missionary Society for Spreading the Gospel Among the Heathen. One of the twelve was a poor cobbler from the nearby village of Moulton. He was William Carey, who was full of zeal to spread the gospel abroad.

William Carey, born in 1761, overcame misunderstanding, hostility, and rejection to take the gospel to India. Carey became known as the Father of Modern Missions. Here are a few brief highlights of Carey's life and achievements:

- In 1785, Carey was appointed the schoolmaster in Moulton and became pastor of Moulton Baptist Church. During this time he read Jonathan Edwards's *Account of the Life of the Late Rev. David Brainerd.* Brainerd was a pioneer missionary to Native Americans, and Carey felt the call to propagate the gospel abroad.
- Though he worked full-time, he mastered Latin, Greek, Hebrew, and Italian in preparation for mission work.
- In 1792, he published his masterpiece *Enquiry Into the Obligations of the Christians to Use Means for the Conversion of the Heathen*, based on "The Great Commission" passage in Matthew 28:18–20.
- In 1793, he arrived in Hooghly, India, but saw no converts for seven years.
- In 1812, the American missionary Adoniram Judson met Carey, and in 1814, Judson formed the first American Baptist Mission. Most American Baptist denominations of today are directly or indirectly descended from this organization.
- In 1834, by the time of his death, Carey had led hundreds to Christ, founded a Christian college at Serampore, translated the Bible into forty languages (including Sanskrit, Bengali, and Hindustani), and saw an end to the heathen practice of suttee (burning of widows on their husbands' funeral pyres).

William Carey died in 1834 in India. The couch on which he died is now housed at Regent's Park College, part of Oxford University.

Quotes of the Day

"Expect great things from God. Attempt great things for God."

—*William Carey*

"Here I am. Send me."

—*William Carey*

OCTOBER 3

DAILY READING

Praise be to the God and Father of our Lord Jesus Christ!
In his great mercy he has given us new birth into a living hope
through the resurrection of Jesus Christ from the dead. (1 PET 1:3)

FEAST DAYS

ca. 96	Dionysios	Greek martyr
695	Edward the Black	Northumbrian martyr
695	Ewald the Fair	Northumbrian martyr

ENTRANCE AND EXIT

b. 1916	James Alfred Wright "Herriot"	English author
b. 1925	Gore Vidal	American writer
b. 1941	Chubby Checker	American rock star
d. 1226	Francesco Bernadone	Italian saint
d. 1906	William Morris	English writer
d. 1967	Woody Guthrie	American folk singer

Francis of Assisi

Francesco Bernadone, St. Francis of Assisi, is one of the Catholic Church's most loved saints. We have many images of him: as a godly man wandering through fields and forests, singing songs and promoting nature worship, fighting in the Crusades, tending to the poor and destitute, writing poetry, and caring for animals.

Francis was born in 1182, and according to legend, when it was time him to be born, the child would not be delivered while his mother Lady Pica stayed her bedroom. Once she was moved to a stable, the child was safely delivered.

Francis fought in the war between Assisi and Perugia, joining a company of lancers, and in some skirmish was taken prisoner. It is said that while in prison, in a dream he received his calling from God. He interpreted this dream as telling him to go to the battlefields of the Crusades, so he joined with others attempting to win back the Holy Land from Muslims.

As a soldier, Francis was praying in the Church of St. Damian, an old shrine of Assisi that had fallen into ruin. He heard a voice saying to him, "Francis, seest thou that my house is in ruins? Go and return it for me." He sold everything and set about rebuilding the church.

Francis was a charismatic figure who drew others to him. Eventually, he formed a mission. Many stories relate his achievements. It is said that one day as Francis and his followers were traveling along, he saw several birds along the way. He reflected that these, too, were God's creatures and stopped and started talking to the birds about God. The birds stopped and listened to him. After he had finished, the birds all flew up and sat on his arms and head. It was as if they had heard and understood what Francis was talking about.

Francis died in 1226 and was canonized on this day in 1228.

Prayer of Francis of Assisi

Lord, make me an instrument of thy peace!
That where there is hatred, I may bring love.
That where there is wrong, I may bring the
spirit of forgiveness.
That where there is discord, I may bring
harmony.
That where there is error, I may bring truth.
That where there is doubt, I may bring faith.
That where there is despair, I may bring hope.
That where there are shadows, I may bring
light.
That where there is sadness, I may bring joy.
Lord, grant that I may seek rather to
comfort, than to be comforted.
To understand, than to be understood.
To love, than to be loved.
For it is by self-forgetting that one finds.
It is by forgiving that one is forgiven.
It is by dying that one awakens to Eternal
Life.

OCTOBER 4

DAILY READING

Do not boast about tomorrow, for you do not know what a day may bring forth. (PROV 27:1)

FEAST DAYS

ca. 350	Ammon the Great	Egyptian Anchorite
445	Petronius	Patron of Bologna, Italy
1470	Julian Majali	Italian hermit

ENTRANCE AND EXIT

b. 1884	Alfred Damon Runyan	American writer
b. 1895	Buster Keaton	American actor
b. 1976	Alicia Silverstone	American actor
d. 1944	Alfred Emmanuel Smith	American politician
d. 1947	Max Planck	German scientist
d. 1970	Janis Joplin	American singer

Alfred Damon Runyan

Gamblers, gangsters, dreamers, and dancing girls populated Damon Runyon's colorful stories of New York nightlife. Larger than life characters emerged from his Prohibition-era tales told in a unique vernacular style that made characters leap out of the page.

Runyon characters were chancers and dancers eager to make a quick buck by staying one step ahead of the law. These streetwise folk were given streetwise nicknames such as "Nathan Detroit," "Big Jule," "Harry the Horse," "Good Time Charlie," "The Lemon Drop Kid," and "Dave the Dude." Such was his success in writing that today the term "Runyonesque" refers to larger-than-life characters in over-the-top situations.

Alfred Damon Runyan (he dropped his first name and altered his surname to Runyon) was born on this day in Manhattan, Kansas. He arrived in New York at the age of thirty to be a sportswriter, and to try out at Mindy's and the Stork Club and any betting window available his crap-shoot worldview: "All of life is six to five against."

In New York, Runyon drank heavily, worked as a newspaper journalist, wrote sports pages, composed poetry, and gambled wildly. Despite, or maybe because of this he wrote engaging stories, many of which have been made into films. For example, *Guys and Dolls, The Lemon Drop Kid, Butch Minds the Baby*, and *Money from Home* were major award-winning films. In the film *Cinderella Man*, the character Sporty Lewis was inspired by Runyon.

Runyon died from throat cancer in 1946. The Damon Runyon Cancer Research Foundation (www.drcrf.org) was established that year by Runyon's friend, Walter Winchell, to fund innovative research into cancer. Over the last sixty years, the foundation has invested nearly two hundred million dollars to support the work of over three thousand scientists.

Noteworthy

1535 Miles Coverdale Bible published in Zurich.

1887 First issue of the *Paris Herald Tribune* published, later retitled *International Herald Tribune*.

1895 Alfred Nobel finalizes plans for prizes for science, literature, and peace.

1931 First appearance of Dick Tracy comic strip.

OCTOBER 5

DAILY READING

Seek the L*ORD while he may be found;*
call on him while he is near. (ISA 55:6)

FEAST DAYS

290	Charitina	Diocletian martyr
1399	Raymond of Capua	Dominican priest
1569	Phillip of Moscow	Primate of the Russian Church

ENTRANCE AND EXIT

b. 1703	Jonathan Edwards	American evangelist
b. 1829	Chester Alan Arthur	21st American president
b. 1936	Vaclav Havel	Czech politician
d. 1967	Clifton C Williams Jr	American astronaut
d. 1984	Leonard Rossiter	English actor
d. 1990	Meir Kahane	Founder of Jewish Defense League

World Teachers' Day

In 1994, the United Nations Educational, Scientific, and Cultural Organization (UNESCO) inaugurated World Teachers' Day (WTD) to "commemorate the signing of the UNESCO Recommendation concerning the Status of Teachers on 5 October 1966."

World Teachers' Day is part of UNESCO's program to ensure that by 2015 every child has access to education.

Each WTD year has a special theme, and previous themes have included:

- Portraits in Courage (1997)
- The Quiet Peacemakers (1998)
- How Teachers Awaken Potential (1999)
- Expanding Horizons (2000)
- Teachers–Opening Doors to a Better World (2003)
- We Appreciate You (2004)
- Training for a Stronger Teaching Force (2005)
- Quality Teachers for Quality Education (2006)

UNESCO seeks to raise the status of teachers and promote the importance of education to personal and economic well-being. World Teachers' Day is celebrated in more than 120 countries in many ways. For example, in previous years Barbados designated the whole month of October to promote education; trade unions in Cameroon used WTD as an opportunity to lobby for more resources; the Canadian Teachers Federation organized an Open House at their offices in Ottawa; in the Ivory Coast the Syndicat National de l'Enseignement Primaire Public organized a large-scale public conference; the Danish Union of Teachers (DLF) decided to sell mints in promotional tins to collect funds for teacher education programs in Northern Ghana; and in the UK, the National Union of Teachers (NUT) held a photo exhibition with Education Action International (a UK-based charity) to celebrate the invaluable contribution made by teachers across the world.

Popular School Pupil Errors

Isosceles triangles are used on maps to join up places that have the same weather.

A triangle with equal sides is called equatorial.

A magnetic force is a straight line, generally a curved one, which would tend to point to where the North Pole comes.

A magnet is a thing you find in a bad apple.

China had confusion as a religion.

By 1930 the Nazis had won approximately 17.5 seats in Parliament.

In March 1936 Hitler sent his troops into the Rainland.

Before the passage of the Repeal of the Combinations Act in Britain in 1824, labor was denied any benefits such as medical and dental.

Hitler first arrived on the political scene in 1923 with the notoriety he gained from his involvement in the French Revolution.

OCTOBER 6

DAILY READING

Trust in the LORD forever, for the LORD, the LORD is the Rock Eternal. (ISA 26:4)

FEAST DAYS

1101	Bruno	Patron of possessed people
1791	Mary Francis of the Five Wounds of Jesus	Italian stigmatic
1916	Isidore of St. Joseph	Passionist lay brother

ENTRANCE AND EXIT

b. 1732	Nevil Maskelyne	English Astronomer Royal
b. 1903	Ernest Walton	Irish scientist
b. 1942	Britt Ekland	Swedish actor
d. 1536	William Tyndale	English Bible translator
d. 1891	Charles Stewart Parnell	Irish leader
d. 1981	Anwar Sadat	Egyptian president

The Uncrowned King of Ireland

Charles Stewart Parnell (1846–91) was the charismatic Irish president of the Nationalist Party and an eloquent voice for the working class against British rule. Although a wealthy Protestant, with little in common with native Irish people, Parnell was looked upon as a Moses-like figure, delivering his people from British enslavement. He seemed destined to become leader of Ireland once Home Rule was achieved. However, a seven-year affair with a married woman ruined him and effectively made the chances of Home Rule a distant prospect, because he lost popular support in a staunchly Catholic country.

On this day in 1891, this "Uncrowned King of Ireland" died in Brighton, England, of rheumatic fever. His funeral was attended by over 150,000 people at Glasnevin cemetery in Dublin.

Many Irish people believed that Parnell alone could have led Ireland to independence, and this day is designated Ivy Day in his honor. Supporters wear a sprig of ivy on their clothing to commemorate Parnell. This celebration has grown over the years thanks to a short story by James Joyce called "Ivy Day in the Committee Room," published in 1914 in his book *Dubliners*. One of the characters, Mr. Hynes, recites a poem entitled "The Death of Parnell" at the end of the story. This is an extract of that poem:

> He is dead. Our Uncrowned King is dead.
> O, Erin, mourn with grief and woe
> For he lies dead whom the fell gang
> Of modern hypocrites laid low.
> He lies slain by the coward hounds
> He raised to glory from the mire;
> And Erin's hopes and Erin's dreams
> Perish upon her monarch's pyre.

Irish Patriots—Easter Uprising

In Dublin in 1916, political activists against British Home Rule led a revolt of over a thousand people. The British authorities eventually regained control and killed the ring leaders who included:

James Connolly, executed 1916

Thomas James Clarke, executed 1916

Padráig Pearse, executed 1916

Joseph Mary Plunkett, executed 1916

Michael Collins, shot dead 1922

Éamonn Ceannt, executed 1916

Cathal Brugha, shot dead 1922

OCTOBER 7

DAILY READING

O God, you are my God, earnestly I seek you;
my soul thirsts for you, my body longs for you,
in a dry and weary land where there is no water. (PS 63:1)

FEAST DAYS

296	Sergius	Syrian martyr
296	Bacchus	Syrian martyr
336	Marcus	34th pope

ENTRANCE AND EXIT

b. 1885	Neils Bohr	Danish scientist
b. 1900	Heinrich Himmler	German Nazi leader
b. 1931	Desmond Tutu	South African archbishop
d. 1849	Edgar Allan Poe	English author
d. 1894	Dr. Oliver Wendell Holmes Sr.	American scientist
d. 1989	Bette Davis	American actor

Battle of Lepanto

On this day in 1571, the naval Battle of Lepanto began at the northern edge of the entrance to the Gulf of Corinth (then the Gulf of Lepanto), off western Greece. A galley fleet of the Holy League–a sometimes flimsy coalition of Pope Pius V, Spain, Venice, Genoa, Savoy, Naples, the Knights of Malta, and others–defeated a force of Ottoman galleys.

The Holy League was led by Don John of Austria (Don Juan) and numbered 212 vessels, including twelve papal ships. The Ottoman forces were led by Ali Pasha and numbered 230 vessels.

During the course of the battle, Spanish forces boarded Pasha's ship, but twice they were repelled. At the third attempt, with reinforcements, the Spanish prevailed and Ali Pasha was killed and beheaded, against the wishes of Don John. However, when his head was displayed on a pike from the Spanish flagship, it contributed greatly to the destruction of Turkish morale. The battle concluded around 4 p.m. The Holy League suffered around nine thousand casualties but freed twice as many Christian prisoners. Turkish casualties were around thirty thousand.

The Battle of Lepanto was a crushing defeat for the Ottomans, who lost all but about fifty of their ships. Despite this, European disunity prevented the allied forces from achieving a lasting supremacy over the Ottomans at this time. The Ottoman Empire immediately began a massive effort to rebuild their navy, and within six months was able to reassert itself. The defeat at Lepanto did not prevent the Ottomans' capture of Cyprus and the forts around Tunis. However, Ottomans lost their control of the seas, especially in the western part of the Mediterranean.

Noteworthy

1555 Charles V calls the Diet of Augsburg.
1769 Capt. James Cook reaches New Zealand.
1777 Second Battle of Saratoga begins in America.
1950 America invades North Korea.
1985 Palestinian hijackers capture the Italian cruise liner *Achile Lauro*.

*O*CTOBER 8

DAILY READING

I, even I, am the L*ORD; and beside me there is no saviour.*
I have declared, and have saved, and I have shewed, when there
was no strange god among you: therefore ye are my witnesses,
saith the L*ORD, that I am God.* (ISA 43:11–12, KJV)

FEAST DAYS

c.461	Pelagia the Penitent	Patron of Actresses
1470	Matthew Carreri	Dominican preacher
1609	John Leonardi	Founder of the Clerks Regular of the Mother of God

ENTRANCE AND EXIT

b. 1895	Juan Perón	Argentinian politician
b. 1941	Jesse Jackson	American politician
b. 1949	Sigourney Weaver	American actor
d. 1754	Henry Fielding	English writer
d. 1869	Franklin Pierce	14th American president
d. 1967	Clement Attlee	British prime minister

Hildegard of Bingen

On this day in 1179 in the Julian calendar, one of the most extraordinary women in history died. Known as the Sybil of the Rhine, Hildegard (1098–1179) was a woman of many talents. In an age when it was almost unheard of for women to pursue education, Hildegard wrote poems and hymns, as well as medical and scientific works. She was one of the first people to unite artistic and scientific thought.

When Hildegard was eighteen, she became a nun. Twenty years later, she was made the head of the female community at the monastery. Within the next four years, she had a series of visions and devoted the ten years from 1140 to 1150 to writing them down, describing them (this included drawing pictures of what she had seen), and commenting on their interpretation and significance. During this period, Pope Eugenius III sent a commission to inquire into her work. The commission found her teaching orthodox and her insights authentic, and reported so to the pope, who sent her a letter of approval.

Hildegard traveled throughout southern Germany and into Switzerland and as far as Paris preaching. Her sermons deeply moved the hearers, and she was asked to provide written copies.

Her major works include *Scivias* (variously *Knowing the Ways of the Lord* or *Let us Know!*), *Liber Vitae Meritorum* (on ethics), and *De Operatione Dei*. She wrote seventy-two songs, including a play set to music. Musical notation had only recently developed to the point where her music was recorded in a way that we can read today. She invented her own language, a blend of Latin and German that had twenty-three letters and nine hundred words. Hildegard also wrote commentary on the Gospels, the Athanasian Creed, and the Rule of St. Benedict, which her nuns followed. She corresponded with Henry II of England, Frederick Barbarrossa, and Bernard of Clairvaux. She also established a daughterhouse at Eibingen, which has claimed her relics since 1632.

Noteworthy

1871 The Great Chicago Fire erupted, killing about 250 people and leaving some 90,000 homeless.

1945 President Harry S. Truman announced that the secret of the atomic bomb would be shared only with Britain and Canada.

1970 Soviet author Alexander Solzhenitsyn was named winner of the Nobel Prize for literature.

1985 The hijackers of the Italian cruise ship *Achille Lauro* killed American passenger Leon Klinghoffer and dumped his body and wheelchair overboard.

2005 A major earthquake flattened villages on the Pakistan-India border, killing an estimated 86,000 people.

OCTOBER 9

DAILY READING

It is the LORD your God you must follow, and him you must revere. Keep his commands and obey him; serve him and hold fast to him. (DEUT 13:4)

FEAST DAYS

ca. 1700 BC	Abraham the Patriarch	Founder of the Hebrew nation
ca. 95	Dionysius	Bishop of Athens, Greece
1059	Aaron the Patriarch	Archbishop of Crakow, Poland

ENTRANCE AND EXIT

b. 1908	Jacques Tati	French actor
b. 1940	John Lennon	English pop star
b. 1975	Sean Ono Lennon	American singer
d. 1958	Eugenio Giovanni Pacelli	Pope Pius XII
d. 1967	Che Guevara	Argentinian revolutionary
d. 1988	Felix Wankel	German engineer

Leif Ericson Day

Contrary to popular belief, Christopher Columbus was not the first European to discover the New World in 1492. Nearly five hundred years earlier, around 1000, the Norwegian explorer Leif Ericson (or Erikson) sailed over six hundred miles along the western coast of Greenland and landed at what he named Helluland, now believed to be Baffin Island.

After resting, he continued along the eastern Canadian coast that he named Woodland. Then Leif sailed southeast for two days and came to an island with a mainland behind it. On this land there were salmon bigger than any the Vikings had ever seen before; there were also very rich pastures there for their cattle and rich forests covering the land. This was New England, and thus Ericson became the first European to set foot in the New World. Norwegians, therefore, can claim that America is actually a colony of their country!

Leif was born in Iceland in about AD 960, and was the second of three sons of Eric the Red. He became a sailor around the age of twenty-four and discovered Greenland using the stars as a guide. He met with King Olaf of Norway, who was impressed with the gifts Ericson brought from Greenland. He became a Christian and was baptized, along with thousands of other converts.

Ericson died in Norway around 1020. In 1964, President Lyndon B Johnson inaugurated Leif Erikson Day to be observed every year on October 9. The date was chosen not because of Ericson, but because the first organized immigration from Norway began on this day in 1825, with the arrival of the ship *Restauration* in New York.

A Norwegian Grace Prayer

I Jesu navn går vi til bords,
In Jesus' name we go to table,

å spise og drikke på ditt ord,
to eat and drink at thy word,

deg Gud til aere oss til gavn;
thou God to honor, us to be gifted;

så får vi mat i Jesu navn.
so receive we food in Jesus' name.

Amen

OCTOBER 10

DAILY READING

Listen to advice and accept instruction, and in the end you will be wise. Many are the plans in a man's heart, but it is the LORD's purpose that prevails. (PROV 19:20–21)

FEAST DAYS

584	Paulinus of York	Missionary to Northumbria
1151	Hugh of Macon	Bishop of Auxerre, France
1572	Francis Borgia	Patron of Portugal

ENTRANCE AND EXIT

b. 1813	Guiseppe Verdi	Italian composer
b. 1877	William Morris	English car manufacturer
b. 1930	Harold Pinter	English writer
d. 1983	Sir Ralph Richardson	English actor
d. 1985	Orson Welles	American film director
d. 2004	Christopher Reeve	American actor

Abraham Kuyper

The Dutch theologian Abraham Kuyper (1837–1920) excelled in many roles, including journalist, politician, academic, publisher, church reformer, and mountain climber. On this day in 1898, he lectured at Princeton University in New Jersey on the theme of a Christian worldview, developing the "Big Picture" so many Christians fail to see. Kuyper was convinced that the Christian faith made sense and could be applied in all areas of modern society.

As a young man, Kuyper studied for the ministry at Leiden University and then became a minister in the rural parish of Beesd. This was a congregation with little spiritual fervor, with the exception of a few "malcontents" among the poorer members. It is among these farmers and laborers that Kuyper was first confronted with a vigorous reformed faith. It is through the influence of these believers that Kuyper rediscovered a biblical faith, lived in real lives and not just in theological texts.

Kuyper believed that the various spheres in society–for example, family, church, school, and politics–are sovereign in relation to one another, while each is subject to the sovereign reign of Christ.

In April 1872, under the editorship of Kuyper, the first issue of the new Christian daily newspaper, *De Standaard* appeared and eventually became an influential channel. Kuyper's stature grew, and in 1874, he was elected to the Dutch parliament.

Due to his numerous commitments, Kuyper suffered a breakdown in 1876. To recuperate, he spent time in Switzerland, developed a liking for mountaineering and eventually became one of the most noted alpinists of the nineteenth century.

Noteworthy

1886 Dinner jacket worn for the first time at Tuxedo Country Club, New York.
1911 Chinese revolution overthrows Manchu dynasty.
1914 Panama Canal opened.
1970 Fiji Independence Day.

Actors Who Have Portrayed Superman

Television: George Reeves, Dean Cain, and Tom Welling

Film: Christopher Reeve, Kirk Alyn, and Brandon Routh

October 11

DAILY READING

Trust in him at all times, O people;
pour out your hearts to him,
for God is our refuge. (PS 62:8)

FEAST DAYS

750	Juliana	Abbess of Plavilly, France
1491	James Grissinger	Patron of glass painters
2000	Angelo Giuseppe Roncalli	Pope John XXIII

ENTRANCE AND EXIT

b. 1821	Sir George Williams	Founder of the YMCA
b. 1884	Eleanor Roosevelt	33rd American First Lady
b. 1937	Sir Bobby Charlton	English footballer
d. 1531	Ulrich Zwingli	Swiss theologian
d. 1837	Samuel Wesley	English composer
d. 1896	Anton Bruckner	Austrian composer

Dorr Eugene Felt

On this day in 1887, the labors of American inventor Dorr Eugene Felt (1862–1930) began to be recognized, as he obtained a patent for the Comptometer–a key-driven calculator. This machine weighed about thirty pounds and required an operator to press numbered keys in each column to display the appropriate number in the display window.

With experience, Comptometer operators could subtract, multiply, divide, as well as add. The advantage of the machine was speed, because the operator could input several digits at the same time by pressing the relevant keys.

Felt's invention had begun on in his Chicago home. He loved mechanical things and produced his first prototype in 1885, a wooden macaroni box with some rubber bands and some meat skewers that turned to display the chosen digit. Next, he replaced the skewers with metal parts and introduced many changes to his original idea. Several thousand prototypes later, he was ready to apply for a patent.

The Comptometer proved popular with the U.S. Treasury Department, and gradually offices across the nation began to use the calculating machine. Felt went into partnership with his financial backer, Robert Tarrant, in 1887. Over the next three decades, the Felt & Tarrant Manufacturing Company made and sold thousands of Comptometers.

Other inventors developed variations of the Comptometer, but generally they were all known by the name of Felts' invention. It wasn't until the 1970s, with the development of office computers, that Comptometers went out of fashion. Today, one of the original Comptometer machines is on display at the Smithsonian Museum in Washington, D.C.

Felt died in 1930, having amassed forty-six domestic and twenty-five foreign patents relating to his calculating machine.

Quote of the Day

"A woman is like a tea bag–you never know how strong she is until she gets in hot water."

–Eleanor Roosevelt

October 12

DAILY READING

Trust in the L*ORD with all thine heart; and lean not unto thine own understanding. In all thy ways acknowledge him, and he shall direct thy paths.* (PROV 3:5–6, KJV)

FEAST DAYS

484	Felix	North African bishop
693	Edwin	King of Northumbria
709	Wilfrid	Bishop of York

ENTRANCE AND EXIT

b. 1537	Edward VI	English king
b. 1872	Ralph Vaughan Williams	English composer
b. 1935	Luciano Pavarotti	Italian opera singer
d. 1845	Elizabeth Fry	English prison reformer
d. 1915	Edith Cavell	English nurse
d. 1997	Henry John Deutschendorf Jr. (John Denver)	American singer

Edith Cavell

Although not involved in espionage, Edith Cavell (1865–1915) was a British nurse tried by German court-martial in Brussels and executed by firing squad on this day in 1915. She was guilty of helping Allied soldiers trapped in German-occupied parts of Belgium escape into neutral Holland. Her case was skillfully used by the British authorities to boost the recruitment of soldiers at a time when there was no conscription.

Several statues have been erected to commemorate Edith Cavell. One is located near Trafalgar Square in London. The statue bears the words, "Humanity, Fortitude, Devotion and Sacrifice." There is also a plaque with the following inscription: "Edith Cavell, Brussels, Dawn, October 12th, 1915. Patriotism is not enough. I must have no hatred or bitterness for anyone." These were Cavell's last words before execution.

The following is an extract of the execution witnessed by Wilhelm Behrens, the chaplin in charge of prison in Brussels where Cavell was held:

> Immediately the sharp commands were given, two salvoes crashed at the same time–each of eight men at a distance of six paces. My eyes were fixed exclusively on Miss Cavell, and what they now saw was terrible. With a face streaming with blood–one shot had gone through her forehead–Miss Cavell had sunk down forwards, but three times she raised herself up without a sound, with her hands stretched upwards. The bulletholes, as large as a fist in the back, proved that without any doubt she was killed immediately. A few minutes later the coffins were lowered into the graves, and I prayed over Edith Cavell's grave, and invoked the Lord's blessing over her poor corpse. Then I went home, almost sick in my soul.

Every year, on the nearest Saturday to October 12, a short service takes place at Edith Cavell's grave at Norwich Cathedral to honor her sacrifice.

John Denver–Achievements

1974 Album of the Year for *Back Home Again*–Academy of Country Music Awards

1975 & 1976 Favorite Male Pop/Rock Artist–American Music Awards

1976 Favorite Country Male Artist–American Music Awards

1976 Favorite Country Album for *Back Home Again*–American Music Awards

1985 NASA Distinguished Public Service Medal

1996 Inducted into the Songwriters Hall of Fame

1997 Best Music Album for Children, Grammy Award for *All Aboard!*

1998 Grammy Hall of Fame Award for "Take Me Home, Country Roads"

October 13

DAILY READING

For I know the thoughts that I think toward you, saith the L*ORD*, *thoughts of peace, and not of evil, to give you an expected end.* (JER 29:11)

FEAST DAYS

1012	Colman of Stockerau	Patron of Austria
1161	Edward the Confessor	King of England
1227	Samuel	Franciscan missionary to Morocco

ENTRANCE AND EXIT

b. 1925	Baroness Margaret Thatcher	British prime minister
b. 1941	Paul Simon	American singer
b. 1959	Marie Osmond	American singer
d. 1890	Austin Phelps	American clergyman
d. 1974	Ed Sullivan	American television presenter
d. 2003	Bertram Brockhouse	Canadian scientist

Touching for the King's Evil

On this day, the pious monarch Edward the Confessor (1003–66) began the tradition of "touching" or laying hands on his subjects to effect a cure for their ailments. According to the *Chronicles of the Kings of England*, a young woman who suffered from "humours collecting abundantly about her neck, she had contracted a sore disorder, the glands swelling in a dreadful manner" had a dream to have the affected area washed by the king. When the lady's neck was washed by Edward, "the lurid skin opened, so that worms flowed out with the purulent matter, and the tumour subsided; but as the orifice of the ulcer was large and unsightly, he commanded her to be supported at the royal expense till she should be perfectly cured. However, before a week was expired, a fair new skin returned, and hid the ulcers so completely that nothing of the original wound could be discovered." The disease was probably scrofula and was difficult to heal at that time.

The practice of "touching for the king's evil" prevailed with subsequent monarchs, and in 1683, King Charles II regulated this curious ceremony. From that time "publick healings" were conducted by the king from All Hallows Eve until a week before Christmas and after Christmas until the first week of March. Each person had to be recommended by their minister and issued with a certificate confirming the individual had an incurable disease and had not been touched for the evil previously.

Many hundreds of cases were recorded of healings being performed by kings from the time of Edward the Confessor onward, but no records have been uncovered of people who were not cured. It is probable that the psychological impact of the attention of a royal personage did much to assuage the tumours associated with scrofula, but no scientific evidence has been produced to explain this phenomenon completely.

Shakespeare

Malcolm–'Tis called the evil; A most miraculous work in this good king; Which often, since my here-remain in England, I've seen him do. How he solicits heaven. Himself best knows; but strangely-visited people, All swoln and ulcerous, pitiful to the eye, The mere despair of surgery, he cures; Hanging a golden stamp about their necks, Put on with holy prayers: and 'tis spoken, To the succeeding royalty he leaves the healing benediction."

–*William Shakespeare,* Macbeth *(act 4, scene 3)*

October 14

DAILY READING

And be not conformed to this world: but be ye transformed by the renewing of your mind, that ye may prove what is that good, and acceptable, and perfect, will of God. (ROM 12:2)

FEAST DAYS

233	Callistus I	Patron of cemetery workers
390	Donatian	Patron of Rheims, France
698	Angadrisma	Archbishop of Rouen, France

ENTRANCE AND EXIT

b. 1644	William Penn	English founder of Pennsylvania
b. 1890	Dwight Eisenhower	34th American president
b. 1940	Sir Cliff Richard	English singer
d. 1944	Erwin Rommel	German Nazi leader
d. 1959	Errol Flynn	American actor
d. 1977	Bing Crosby	American singer

Battle of Hastings

The Battle of Hastings, fought on Saturday, October 14, 1066, was a decisive engagement that marked the commencement of a new epoch. William the Bastard, Duke of Normandy, won mainly through superiority of numbers, and several well-directed feints. The conduct of the English and King Harold was such as to command the highest admiration on the part of their enemies. The result might have been very different had Harold, instead of marching impetuously from London with an inadequate army to repel the invaders, waited a little while to gather strength from the reinforcements that were every day pouring in to his standard. But the signal success that, only a few days previous, he had gained over the Norwegians in the north of England made him overconfident in his own powers, and this proved the principal cause of his overthrow.

On September 28, the Normans, led by William, had landed from their ships, totally unopposed, between Pevensey and Hastings. The future conqueror of England was the last to land, and as he placed his foot on shore, he made a false step and fell on his face. A murmur of consternation ran through the troops at this incident as a bad omen, but with great presence of mind William sprang immediately up and exclaimed: "What now? What astonishes you? I have seized this land with my hands, and by the splendour of God, as far as it extends it is mine and it is yours!"

William of Normandy won England, but it was not until years afterward that he could put away his sword as undisputed sovereign of England. For generations, indeed, the defeated English resisted and for decades maintained that Harold, instead of being killed, had escaped from the field of battle and would one day return to lead them to victory.

Sir Cliff Richard–Summary of Recording Career

Chart	Weeks in Charts
Singles Chart	1,157
Album Chart	808
Video Chart	515
Extended Play Chart	432

Singles	Hits	No. 1s	Albums	Hits	No. 1s
1950s	6	2	1950s	2	-
1960s	43	7	1960s	22	3
1970s	22	1	1970s	10	1
1980s	31	2	1980s	11	2
1990s	20	2	1990s	8	1
2000s	3	-	2000s	3	-
Total	125	14	Total	56	7

Cliff's total worldwide sales now exceed 260 million.

OCTOBER 15

DAILY READING

Wherefore thou art great, O LORD God: for there is none like thee, neither is there any God beside thee, according to all that we have heard with our ears. (2 SAM 7:22, KJV)

FEAST DAYS

970	Bruno	Patron of Prussia
1614	Theresa of Avila	Doctor of the Church
1627	Gaius of Korea	Benedictine monk

ENTRANCE AND EXIT

b. 70 BC	Virgil	Roman poet
b. 1844	Friedrich Wilhelm Nietzsche	German philosopher
b. 1881	Sir Pelham Grenville Wodehouse	English author
d. 1917	Mata Hari	Dutch spy
d. 1946	Herman Goering	German Nazi leader
d. 1964	Cole Porter	American composer

Ten Lost Days

On this day in 1582, France, Spain, and regions of Portugal adopted the Gregorian or "New Style" calendar. This meant that they lost ten days, since the previous day was October 4. When the First Ecumenical Council met in Nicea in 325 to settle the date for celebrating Passover, the church adopted the Julian calendar and ruled that Passover should be observed on the first Sunday after the first full moon after the spring equinox on March 21. This gave a fixed range for the date for Easter from March 22 to April 25.

But over the years, astronomers noticed that the true beginning of spring (when the sun passes through the vernal equinox) moved away from the nominal start of spring on March 21. The Easter date began to lose its intended connection with the Jewish feast of Passover (that is, tied to the true start of spring).

To solve this problem, Pope Gregor XIII in AD 1582 ordered a calendar reform for the domain of the Catholic Church. It consisted of three parts:

- Omission of ten calendar days: October 4, 1582, was followed directly by October 15, 1582, in the new calendar. This brought the start of spring back to March 21. The reckoning of weekdays was not changed.
- Introduction of a new leap year rule according to which no leap days occur in years that are divisible by one hundred but not by four hundred. This reduces the error in the year length and slows down the accumulation of this error. The leap day is inserted at the end of February as in the Julian calendar.
- Modification of the Easter rule to accommodate the new calendar.

The Gregorian calendar is used by the church in the West for both fixed and moveable feasts. Most Catholic countries adopted the new calendar on this day in 1582, but some with Protestant or Islamic leanings were reluctant. For example, Great Britain (1752), Germany (1700), Turkey (1927), and Russia (1914) delayed using the new calendar for many years.

Noteworthy

1880 Grand Cathedral of Cologne, Germany, completed.

1902 "New Orleans Blues" first performed by Jelly Roll Morton.

1945 Pierre Laval, Premier of Vichy, France, executed.

1990 Soviet President Mikhail Gorbachev awarded Nobel Peace Prize.

October 16

DAILY READING

Let the words of my mouth, and the meditation of my heart, be acceptable in thy sight, O Lord, my strength, and my redeemer. (PS 19:14, KJV)

FEAST DAYS

1243	Hedwig	Patron of Germany
1755	Gerard Majella	Patron of expectant mothers
1941	Anicet Koplinski	Auschwitz martyr

ENTRANCE AND EXIT

b. 1854	Oscar Wilde	English writer
b. 1886	David Ben-Gurion	1st prime minister of Israel
b. 1927	Günter Grass	German writer
d. 1555	Nicholas Ridley	English bishop
d. 1555	Hugh Latimer	English bishop
d. 1793	Marie Antionette	French queen

World Food Day

Despite warnings of starvation resulting from overpopulation, there is enough food to provide for every person to live a healthy life. The problem isn't quantity, but lack of willingness to share, as can be gathered from problems of obesity in the developed world and mass starvation in the developing world.

In 1945, the United Nations established the Food and Agriculture Organization of the United Nations (FAO) to promote food availability, research, and distribution to benefit everyone. World Food Day was established in 1979 to commemorate the founding of the FAO. World Food Day aims to "heighten public awareness of the plight of the world's hungry and malnourished and to encourage people worldwide to take action against hunger." First observed in 1981, each year World Food Day highlights a particular theme on which to focus activities.

Themes from recent years are:

2007–The Right to Food

2006–Investing in Agriculture for Food Security

2005–Agriculture and Intercultural Dialogue

2004–Biodiversity and Food Security

2003–Working Together for an International Alliance against Hunger

2002–Water: Source of Food Security

2001–Fight Hunger to Reduce Poverty

2000–A Millennium Free from Hunger

More than 150 countries observe this event every year. In the United States, 450 national and private voluntary organizations sponsor World Food Day, and local groups are active in almost every community. In the UK, UK Food Group organized a conference called, "If Food Could Talk. . . . Hidden Stories from the Food Chain," together with the Guild of Food Writers, ActionAid, Sustain, London Food, and the Food Ethics Council. For further details of activities undertaken by nations on World Food Day, please go to www.fao.org.

"We urge all Nations, International Organisations and Civil Society to join FAO and its partners in an alliance to ensure that humanity can enjoy freedom from hunger."

–World Food Day declaration on the sixtieth anniversary of the FAO

The Wit of Oscar Wilde

A cynic is a man who knows the price of everything but the value of nothing.

A man can't be too careful in the choice of his enemies.

A man's face is his autobiography. A woman's face is her work of fiction.

A true friend stabs you in the front.

Always forgive your enemies–nothing annoys them so much.

Ambition is the last refuge of the failure.

America is the only country that went from barbarism to decadence without civilization in between.

An idea that is not dangerous is unworthy of being called an idea at all.

OCTOBER 17

DAILY READING

The LORD confides in those who fear him; he makes his covenant known to them. My eyes are ever on the LORD, for only he will release my feet from the snare. (PS 25:14–15)

FEAST DAYS

ca. 50	Ignatius of Antioch	Church father
1167	Gilbert the Theologian	Benedictine monk
1604	Serafino of Montegranaro	Capuchin monk

ENTRANCE AND EXIT

b. 1914	Jerry Siegel	American cocreator of Superman
b. 1918	Rita Hayworth	American actor
b. 1972	Marshall Mathers (Eminem)	American rap star
d. 1554	Sir Philip Sidney	English poet
d. 1849	Frederic Chopin	Polish composer
d. 1998	Joan Hickson	English actor

St. Ethelreda

Ethelreda (630–79) was the daughter of Annas, king of the East Angles and St. Hereswyda. As a child, Etheldreda was betrothed to the Gyrvian prince Tondbehrt, who gave her the Isle of Ely in England as a wedding gift; their three-year marriage ended when he died. She retired to Ely and spent five years in prayer before conceding to her family's wishes that she marry Egfrid, the youngest son of Oswiu, king of Northumbria. Her second husband was considerably younger than she, and he eventually consented to her becoming a nun at Coldingham Abbey in Yorkshire under the direction of St. Wilfrid. From Coldingham, she returned to Ely and on this day in 672 established a double monastery that was a popular pilgrim's destination in the Middle Ages.

She is said to have predicted her own death during a plague in 679, and seventeen years later her sister and successor Sexburga translated her incorrupt relics from the graveyard to a shrine inside the church.

Etheldreda is the patron of Cambridge University, and after her death a great medieval fair was held annually in her memory. This was called St. Audrey's Fair, as Audrey was the name by which Ethelreda was commonly known. At the fair, much ordinary but showy lace was usually sold, and from this we get the word "tawdry," a corruption of St. Audrey to denote clothes or objects that look more valuable than their actual worth.

After an absence of many years, St. Audrey's Fair was revived in 1987 and again in 1997 by the Isle of Ely Lions Club. The last time St. Audrey's Fair was held was on June 23, 2000, the feast day of St. Ethelreda.

Noteworthy

1651 King Charles II defeated by Cromwell at the Battle of Worcester.
1777 British forces surrender to American troops in Saratoga.
1902 First Cadillac car comes off the production line in Detroit.
1919 The Radio Corporation of America (RCA) created.
1931 Al Capone convicted of tax evasion and sentenced to eleven years in prison.
1956 First full-scale nuclear power station, Calder Hall in England, opened by Queen Elizabeth II.
1957 French writer Albert Camus awarded Nobel Prize in Literature.
1989 San Francisco shaken by earthquake measuring 7.1 on the Richer scale.

*O*CTOBER 18

DAILY READING

Wait for the L*ORD; be strong and take heart*
and wait for the L*ORD.* (PS 27:14)

FEAST DAYS

ca. 74	Luke	Apostle
1918	Jildo Irwa	Ugandan martyr
1918	Daudi Okelo	Ugandan martyr

ENTRANCE AND EXIT

b. 1785	Thomas Love Peacock	English writer
b. 1865	Henri Bergson	French philosopher
b. 1903	Evelyn Waugh	English writer
d. 1865	Henry John Temple (Lord Palmerston)	English prime minister
d. 1931	Thomas Alva Edison	American inventor
d. 1966	Elizabeth Arden	American business leader

St. Luke's Day

Today is the feast day of St. Luke who wrote two books of the Bible: the Gospel of Luke and the Acts of the Apostles. Luke's writings indicate that he was a physician of Antioch and skilled in Greek.

Unique material found in his Gospel includes much of the account of Jesus' birth, infancy, and boyhood; parables such as that of the Good Samaritan and that of the Prodigal Son; and three of the sayings of Christ on the Cross: "Father, forgive them," "You will be with me in Paradise," and "Father, into your hands I commend my spirit."

Luke's Gospel emphasizes the humanity of Christ; for example, his compassion for sinners, for outcasts such as the Samaritans, tax collectors, lepers, and for the poor. The role of women in Christ's ministry is more emphasized in Luke than in the other Gospel writings.

In the Acts of the Apostles, he shows how the early Christians spread the Gospel from "Jerusalem, and in all Judea and Samaria, and to the ends of the earth" (Acts 1:8).

Luke was buried at Constantinople (Istanbul). In 1562, his relics were transferred to St. Justina's Basilica in Padua in Italy. In 1998, a commission headed by the anatomy and histology department at the University of Padua found a lead box measuring 75 inches by 16 inches and 20 inches in depth resting on a wooden board and sealed with two red wax seals. This box contained the relics of St. Luke.

Traditionally, on St. Luke's Day, girls can gain an insight about their future spouse. Before going to bed, they apply a "love salve" consisting of marigold, thyme, marjoram, honey, and white vinegar to their faces and recite the following; "St. Luke, St. Luke, be kind to me, In dreams let my true love see." Then their dreams are blessed with visions of their husband.

St. Luke's Day is also known as Dog Whipping Day, when all stray dogs in the streets were whipped out of town.

Luke 1:1–4

Since many have undertaken to set down an orderly account of the events that have been fulfilled among us, just as they were handed on to us by those who from the beginning were eyewitnesses and servants of the word, I too decided, after investigating everything carefully from the very first, to write an orderly account for you, most excellent Theophilus, so that you may know the truth concerning the things about which you have been instructed.

OCTOBER 19

DAILY READING

Delight yourself in the L*ORD and he will give you the desires of your heart.* (PS 37:4)

FEAST DAYS

634	Agnes of Jesus	Dominican nun
1605	Charles Garnier	North American martyr
1646	John Lalande	Jesuit missionary

ENTRANCE AND EXIT

b. 1784	James Henry Leigh Hunt	English poet
b. 1862	August Lumiere	French photographer
b. 1931	David John Moore Cornwell (John Le Carré)	English writer
d. 1745	Jonathan Swift	English writer
d. 1937	Ernest Lord Rutherford	New Zealnd scientist
d. 1950	Edna St. Vincent Millay	American writer

Battle of Yorktown

The Battle of Yorktown effectively ended the Revolutionary War and led to American independence. It took place in 1777 in Yorktown, Virginia, where 7,500 British Redcoats, led by Lord Cornwallis, were camped out. Gen. George Washington and Gen. Jean Baptiste Rochambeau led the Americans and French forces consisting of 16,000 men.

They tricked the British into thinking they would be in New York, but actually they went south to Virginia. They surrounded the British by land and cut off their escape route by the York River. Cornwallis was not able to get reinforcements.

On October 14, the Franco-American forces captured two major British redoubts. Cornwallis's options were running out. He even tried sending black prisoners infected with smallpox over enemy lines in an attempt to infect the American and French troops. After a futile counterattack, Cornwallis offered to surrender on October 17. On this day, the papers were signed, and he officially surrendered.

It is said, but never proved, that the British fife and drums played the song "The World Turned Upside Down" when the battle ended because now the colonies belonged to America, not to the British.

Lord North, the British prime minister, quit his job after the defeat at Yorktown. His successor, the Marquis of Rockingham, thought the British should end the war and make peace with America and France. The agreement to end the Revolutionary War was called the Treaty of Paris, signed in that city in 1783. This treaty sealed the peace between Great Britain and the new country of the United States.

"The World Turned Upside Down"

If buttercups buzzed after the bee,
If boats were on land,
Churches on sea,
If ponies rode men,
And if grass ate the corn,
And if cats should be chased
Into holes by the mouse,
If the mammas sold their babies
To the Gypsies for half a crown,
If summer were spring,
And the other way 'round,
Then all the world would be upside down.

*O*CTOBER 20

DAILY READING

Restore to me the joy of your salvation and grant me a willing spirit, to sustain me. (PS 51:12)

FEAST DAYS

ca. 250	Maximus	Deacon of Aquila, Italy
ca. 653	Irene	Portuguese nun
660	Acca	Patron of learning

ENTRANCE AND EXIT

b. 1632	Sir Christopher Wren	English architect
b. 1859	John Dewey	American philosopher
b. 1953	Tom Petty	American singer
d. 1524	Thomas Linacre	English physician
d. 1936	Annie Sullivan	American educator
d. 1964	Herbert Hoover	31st American president

John Dewey–American Pragmatist

John Dewey (1859–1952) was an American psychologist, philosopher, educator, social critic, and political activist. He was born in Burlington, Vermont, and graduated from the University of Vermont in 1879. He received his PhD from Johns Hopkins University in 1884 and began teaching at the University of Michigan that same year. In 1894 Dewey became the chairman of the department of philosophy, psychology, and pedagogy at the University of Chicago.

Dewey made seminal contributions to nearly every field and topic in philosophy and psychology. Besides his role as a primary originator of both functionalist and behaviorist psychology, Dewey was a major inspiration for several allied movements that have shaped twentieth-century thought. Along with Charles Sanders Pierce and William James, Dewey is recognized as one of the founders of the philosophical school of Pragmatism. He also is known as the father of functional psychology; he was a leading representative of the progressive movement in U.S. education; and he was a contributing editor of the *Encyclopaedia for Unified Science*. For over fifty years Dewey was the voice for a liberal and progressive democracy that has shaped the destiny of America and the world.

In 1899, John Dewey was elected president of the American Psychological Association, and in 1905 he became president of the American Philosophical Association. Dewey taught at Columbia University from 1905 until he retired in 1930, and occasionally taught as professor emeritus until 1939. During his years at Columbia, he traveled the world as a philosopher, social and political theorist, and educational consultant.

Among his major travels were his lecture tours to Japan and China from 1919 to 1921, his visit to Turkey in 1924 to recommend educational policy, and a tour of schools in the USSR in 1928. Dewey never ignored American social issues. He was outspoken on education, domestic and international politics, and numerous social movements. Among the many concerns that attracted Dewey's support were women's suffrage, progressive education, educators' rights, the humanistic movement, and world peace. Dewey died in New York City on June 1, 1952.

Noteworthy

1469 Birth of Guru Nanak Dev, founder of Sikh religion.
1714 King George I crowned at Westminster Abbey.
1803 United States Senate ratified Louisiana Purchase Treaty.
1820 United States purchased East Florida from Spain.
1822 *The Sunday Times* first edition.
1955 *The Lord of the Rings* first published.
1973 Sydney Opera House opened by Queen Elizabeth II.

OCTOBER 21

DAILY READING

I desire to do your will, O my God;
your law is within my heart. (PS 40:8)

FEAST DAYS

371	Hilarion	Egyptian hermit
617	Wendelin	Prince of Scotland
1922	Charles	Emperor of Austria

ENTRANCE AND EXIT

b. 1772	Samuel Taylor Coleridge	English writer
b. 1914	Martin Gardner	American scientist
b. 1956	Carrie Fisher	American actor
d. 1805	Horatio Nelson	English admiral
d. 1969	Jack Kerouac	American writer
d. 1984	François Truffaut	French film director

Trafalgar Day

Trafalgar Day in England commemorates Lord Horatio Nelson's great naval victory over Napoleon Bonaparte at the Battle of Trafalgar that concluded on this day in 1805.

In August of that year, Bonaparte, confident of victory, wrote to his admirals: "Come into the Channel. Bring our united fleet and England is ours. If you are only here for 24 hours, all will be over, and six centuries of shame and insult will be avenged."

However, the British blockade of French and Spanish harbors meant that no ships could obey that order, so Napoleon ordered his fleet at Cadiz to sail out and meet the enemy at Cape Trafalgar, some eighty kilometers east of Cadiz. "His Majesty counts for nothing the loss of his ships, provided they are lost with glory," wrote Napoleon.

However, widespread seasickness, the poor morale of French sailors, the poor quality of Spanish sailors (they were mostly beggars press-ganged from the slums of Cadiz), and resentment of the Spanish at being placed under a French admiral meant that Napoleon was facing formidable odds even before the battle began. Moreover, in Nelson, England possessed one of the most skillful and charismatic leaders of all time.

On October 20, 1805, the Franco-Spanish fleet was sighted, and soon afterward the area where the British ships waited became bright with patches of gaudy bunting as each ship broke out strings of flags with the message, "The French and Spanish are out at last, they outnumber us in ships and guns and men: we are on the eve of the greatest sea fight in history."

Although Nelson was fatally wounded in the battle, not one the British Fleets' twenty-seven ships were sunk or captured. Napoleon's losses were heavy: 449 killed, 1241 wounded, and many ships sunk. Victory at Trafalgar established English sea supremacy for the next 150 years.

Naval Terms

Aft: Toward the stern.
Athwartship: At a right angle to the centerline.
Bow: The forward end of a ship or boat.
Bridge: Area in the superstructure from which the ship is operated.
Chow: Food.
Deck: Shipboard floor, with horizontal plating that divides a ship into layers.
Fantail: The after end of the main deck.
Foc'sle: Forward section of the deck on which the anchor handling equipment is located.
Frame: An athwartship beam that provides structural strength to a ship.
Galley: Space where food is prepared. Never called a kitchen.
Mess: 1. Place where meals are eaten, such as Mess Decks, Captain's Mess, etc. 2. A group who takes meals together, such as officer's mess or chief's mess.
Mid Rats: (Midnight Rations) Meal served around midnight for those crewmembers going on or off watch.
Port: To the left of the centerline when facing forward.
Scuttlebutt: 1. Drinking fountain. 2. A rumor.
Square away: To put in proper place.
Starboard: Right of centerline when facing forward.
Stern: The aftermost part of a vessel.
Wake: Trail left by a vessel moving through the water.

OCTOBER 22

DAILY READING

Carry each other's burdens, and in this way you will fulfill the law of Christ. (GAL 6:2)

FEAST DAYS

304	Hermes	Cleric at Heraclea, Turkey
730	Moderan	Bishop of Rennes, France
851	Nunilo	Patron of child abuse victims

ENTRANCE AND EXIT

b. 1844	Sarah Bernhardt	French actor
b. 1920	Dr. Timothy Leary	American academic
b. 1938	Sir Derek Jacobi	English actor
d. 1906	Paul Cézanne	French artist
d. 1935	Lord Edward Carson	Irish statesman
d. 1995	Kingsley Amis	English writer

The Great Disappointment of October 22, 1844

> The day came and passed, and the darkness of another night closed in upon the world. But with that darkness came a pang of disappointment to the advent believers that can find a parallel only in the sorrow of the disciples after the crucifixion of their Lord. The passing of the time was a bitter disappointment. True believers had given up all for Christ, and had shared His presence as never before. The love of Jesus filled every soul; and with inexpressible desire they prayed, "Come, Lord Jesus, and come quickly"; but He did not come. My feelings were almost uncontrollable. I left the place of meeting and wept like a child.

So wrote Washington Morse, one of around fifty thousand followers of Baptist lay preacher and biblical chronologist William Miller.

The reason for their disappointment? Miller had prophesied the Second Advent of Christ, and his followers had gathered in Boston, Hartford, Philadelphia, Cincinnati, Hanover, Montpelier, Portsmouth, Exeter, and Concord to greet the dawn of a new age. Needless to say, Miller proved to be a false prophet, and controversy would dog him until his death in 1849.

William Miller was born in Pittsfield, Massachusetts, in 1782. He grew up on a farm in Hampton, New York, and developed a taste for reading, and much to the distress of his pious mother, was inclined particularly to the fashionable books of Thomas Paine. These cast doubts on the validity of revealed religion and questioned the authority of the Bible. Like many another young man of literary bent, Miller also began to write poetry and to cultivate a way with words. He sought to determine the date of the Second Advent from his own study of the Bible. This led to many inconsistencies, but he announced the date of Christ return initially as "between March 21st, 1843, and March 21st, 1844." When this did not happen, his followers continued to urge him to set a new date, and eventually he came up with this date in 1844. Many theologians believe the Adventist and Jehovah's Witness movements took up Miller's chronology ideas.

The Bible on False Prophets

> Then the LORD said to me, "The prophets are prophesying lies in my name. I have not sent them or appointed them or spoken to them. They are prophesying to you false visions, divinations, idolatries and the delusions of their own minds. . . . Those same prophets will perish by sword and famine." (Jer 14:14–15)

> This is what the LORD Almighty says:
> "Do not listen to what the prophets are
> prophesying to you;
> they fill you with false hopes.
> They speak visions from their own minds,
> not from the mouth of the LORD." (Jer 23:16)

> The word of the LORD came to me: "Son of man, prophesy against the prophets of Israel who are now prophesying. Say to those who prophesy out of their own imagination: 'Hear the word of the LORD! This is what the Sovereign LORD says: Woe to the foolish prophets who follow their own spirit and have seen nothing!'" (Ezek 13:1–3)

OCTOBER 23

DAILY READING

For God did not give us a spirit of timidity,
but a spirit of power, of love and of self-discipline. (2 TIM 1:7)

FEAST DAYS

639	Romanus	Bishop of Rouen, France
877	Ignatius	Patriarch of Constantinople
1794	Josephine Leroux	Ursuline nun

ENTRANCE AND EXIT

b. 1845	George Saintsbury	English historian
b. 1940	Edson Arantes do Nascimento (Pele)	Brazilian footballer
b. 1954	Ang Lee	Chinese film director
d. 1869	Edward Stanley	14th Earl of Derby
d. 1921	John Boyd Dunlop	Scottish inventor
d. 1950	Al Jolson	American actor and singer

The Beginning of Creation

James Ussher (1581–1656), Archbishop of Armagh, was the preeminent figure in the Church of Ireland, and a leading patron of scholarship at Trinity College, Dublin. Ussher is most famous for having dated the start of creation as the evening proceeding October 23, 4004 BC.

Ussher explained his timing in *The Annals of the Old Testament*, a monumental work first published in London in the summer of 1650. In 1654, Ussher added a part two, which took his history through Rome's destruction of the Temple in Jerusalem in AD 70. The project, which produced two thousand pages in Latin, occupied twenty years of Ussher's life.

In the *Annals*, Ussher developed the chronological work of many earlier scholars to provide a framework for dating the whole Bible historically. He argued that although Scripture itself only tended to take notice of entire years, the Holy Ghost had left clues in the Bible that allowed the critic to establish a precise chronology of its events, through the application to the text of the results of astronomical calculations and its comparison with the dates of pagan history. Ussher's system had the advantage of preserving several attractive numerical symmetries–for example, the ancient Jewish notion, adopted by Christians, that the creation anticipated the birth of the Messiah by four thousand years–but it was also heavily dependent on classical chronologies and on an interpretation of the calendar that already seemed outdated to many scholars.

The first paragraph of the first page of *The Annals* says, "In the beginning, God created heaven and earth, which beginning of time, according to this chronology, occurred at the beginning of the night which preceded the 23rd of October in the year 710 of the Julian period." In the right margin of the page, Ussher computes the date in "Christian" time as 4004 BC.

Although Ussher's creation date is much derided in modern times, it is interesting that famous scientists such as Johannes Kepler (1571–1630) calculated a date of 3,992 BC, and Sir Isaac Newton (1643–1727) vigorously defended a creation of about 4,000 BC.

The Message–Modern Bible Paraphrase

First this: God created the Heavens and Earth–all you see, all you don't see. Earth was a soup of nothingness, a bottomless emptiness, an inky blackness. God's Spirit brooded like a bird above the watery abyss.

God spoke: "Light!"
And light appeared.
God saw that light was good
and separated light from dark.
God named the light Day,
he named the dark Night.
It was evening, it was morning–
Day One. (Gen 1:1–5)

OCTOBER 24

DAILY READING

"But you will receive power when the Holy Spirit comes on you; and you will be my witnesses in Jerusalem, and in all Judea and Samaria, and to the ends of the earth." (ACTS 1:8)

FEAST DAYS

527	Martin of Vertou	French miracle worker
1504	John Angelo Porro	Italian hermit
1860	Joseph Thi	Vietnamese martyr

ENTRANCE AND EXIT

b. 1632	Antoni van Leeuwenhock	Dutch scientist
b. 1906	Sir Robert Sainsbury	English businessman
b. 1947	Kevin Kline	American actor
d. 1537	Lady Jane Seymour	English queen
d. 1957	Christian Dior	French fashion designer
d. 1991	Gene Roddenberry	American scripwriter

United Nations Day

The United Nations officially came into existence on October 24, 1945, when the Founding Charter was ratified by China, France, the Soviet Union, the United Kingdom, United States, and by a majority of other signatories.

On April 25, 1945, delegates from fifty countries drove through the rain to meet for the United Nations Conference on international Organization at the Flag-bedecked War Memorial Opera House in San Francisco. Although the delegates came from nations "small, weak, and strong, and in different stages of political and social development," these earnest individuals were "determined to set up an organization which would preserve peace, advance justice, and constitute a permanent structure for international cooperation." This is an extract from the preamble of the Charter:

> WE THE PEOPLES OF THE UNITED NATIONS DETERMINED
>
> To save succeeding generations from the scourge of war, which twice in our lifetime, has brought untold sorrow to mankind and
>
> To reaffirm faith in fundamental human rights, in the dignity and worth of the human person, in the equal rights of men and women of nations large and small, and to establish conditions under which justice and respect for the obligations arising from treaties and other sources of international law can be maintained, and
>
> To promote social progress and better standards of life in larger freedom.

In order to stress the charter's importance, in 1947 the General Assembly of the UN passed a resolution "that October 24 shall hereafter be officially called United Nations Day, and shall be devoted to making known to the people of the world the aims and achievements of the United Nations, and to gaining their support for the work of the United Nations."

United Nations Secretary-General

According to its Charter, the UN Secretary-General is appointed by the General Assembly upon the recommendation of the Security Council. Since its inception, there have been only eight holders of the office of Secretary-General:

Name	Country	Period
Ban Ki-moon	South Korea	2007–
Kofi Annan	Ghana	1997–2006
Boutros Boutros-Ghali	Egypt	1992–1996
Javier Pérez de Cuéllar	Peru	1982–1991
Kurt Waldheim	Austria	1972–1981
U Thant	Myanmar	1961–1971
Dag Hammarskjöld	Sweden	1953–1961
Trygve Lie	Norway	1946–1952

*O*CTOBER 25

DAILY READING

For he chose us in him before the creation of the world to be holy and blameless in his sight. In love he predestined us to be adopted as his sons through Jesus Christ, in accordance with his pleasure and will. (EPH 1:4–5)

FEAST DAYS

283	Daria	Wife of St. Chrysanthus
286	Crispin	Patron of cobblers
535	Hilary	Bishop of Mende, France

ENTRANCE AND EXIT

b. 1800	Lord Thomas Babington MacCaulay	English writer
b. 1825	Johann Strauss the Younger	Austrian composer
b. 1941	Anne Tyler	American writer
d. 1400	Geoffrey Chaucer	English writer
d. 1760	King George II	English king
d. 1993	Vincent Price	American actor

The Feast of St. Crispin

Today is the feast of Crispin and his brother Crispinian (or Crispian), who were Roman nobles martyred by beheading in 286. During the day they preached the gospel, and at night they were shoemakers. They came from Rome to preach at Soissons, in France, and converted many to the Christian faith. In the sixth century a great church was built to their honor at Soissons, and their shrine was richly ornamented.

Crispin's Day is particularly notable because in 1415, the Battle of Agincourt was fought between the English, under King Henry V, and the French on this day. An English force of only six thousand men at arms and twenty-four thousand archers defeated the French, who had nearly a hundred thousand cavalry.

For Henry–wasted with disease, broken with fatigue, and weakened by the privations of a march through a hostile country in the presence of a superior force–this was a night of hope and fear, of suspense and anxiety. They were men who had staked their lives on the event of the approaching battle, and spent the intervening moments in making their wills, and in prayer. Henry sent his officers to examine the ground by moonlight, arranged the operations of the next day, ordered bands of music to play in succession during the night, and before sunrise summoned his troops to attend matins and mass; from there he led them to the field and famous victory.

Shakspeare immortalizes this memorable achievement on Crispin's Day in a speech that he assigns to Henry V before the battle.

This day is called the feast of Crispian:
He that outlives this day, and comes safe
home,
Will stand a tip-toe when the day is named,
And rouse him at the name of Crispian.
He that shall live this day, and see old age,
Will yearly on the vigil feast his neighbours,
And say "To-morrow is Saint Crispian":
Then will he strip his sleeve and show his
scars.
And say "These wounds I had on Crispin's
day."
Old men forget: yet all shall be forgot,
But he'll remember with advantages
What feats he did that day: then shall our
names.
Familiar in his mouth as household words
Harry the king, Bedford and Exeter,
Warwick and Talbot, Salisbury and Gloucester,
Be in their flowing cups freshly remember'd.
This story shall the good man teach his son;
And Crispin Crispian shall ne'er go by,
From this day to the ending of the world,
But we in it shall be remember'd;
We few, we happy few, we band of brothers;
For he to-day that sheds his blood with me
Shall be my brother; be he ne'er so vile,
This day shall gentle his condition:
And gentlemen in England now a-bed
Shall think themselves accursed they were
not here,
And hold their manhoods cheap whiles any
speaks
That fought with us upon Saint Crispin's day.

–Henry V *(act 4, scene 3)*

OCTOBER 26

DAILY READING

Be very careful, then, how you live—not as unwise but as wise, making the most of every opportunity, because the days are evil. (EPH 5:15–16)

FEAST DAYS

99	Evaristus	5th pope
346	Amand	First Bishop of Strasbourg
450	Quodvultdeus	Bishop of Carthage

ENTRANCE AND EXIT

b. 1759	Georges Jacques Danton	French revolutionary leader
b. 1879	Leon Trotsky	Russian revolutionary leader
b. 1916	François Mitterand	French president
d. 1764	William Hogarth	English artist
d. 1944	William Temple	English archbishop
d. 1972	Igor Sikorsky	Russian engineer

St. Anthony Claret

Anthony Claret (1807–70) was a deeply religious Spaniard who became one of his nation's most famous preachers through his itinerant ministry across his native Catalonia—he is said to have preached over ten thousand sermons in his life. In 1849, he established the evangelistic religious order, the "Missionary Sons of the Immaculate Heart of Mary" (C.F.M.), better know as the "Claretians."

After his Spanish ministry, he became Archbishop of Santiago, Cuba, and began many reforms in that violent anti-Catholic society. Not all Cubans warmed to his ministry, and he survived several assassination attempts. One of his assailants was captured and sentenced to death, but Anthony pleaded successfully for his life.

In 1857, he returned to Spain to take up the role of confessor to Queen Isabella II, based at Barcelona. Here he established a vast religious library and gave out thousands of religious pamphlets, many of which he had written. When Isabella was deposed in 1868, he had to flee to Italy, and there he took an active part in the First Vatican Council. From Italy, he settled in Narbonne, France, for eighteen months and died in exile there on this day in 1870.

He was canonized by Pope Pius XII in 1950, and this is part of the proclamation made about St. Anthony on that occasion:

> A great soul born to unite contrasting elements, he was humble in origin, yet illustrious in the eyes of the world. Small in stature, but a giant in spirit. Modest in appearance, but very capable of instilling respect, also in the great ones of the earth. Strong in character, but with the gentleness of someone who knows the restraint of austerity and penance. Always in the presence of God, even in the midst of prodigious activity. Slandered and admired, celebrated and persecuted, and among such great marvels, a gentle light that illumines all, his devotion to the Mother of God.

Noteworthy

1774 The First Continental Congress adjourned in Philadelphia.
1967 The Shah of Iran crowned himself and his queen after 26 years on the Peacock Throne.
1972 National security adviser Henry Kissinger declared "peace is at hand" in Vietnam.
1975 Anwar Sadat became the first Egyptian president to pay an official visit to the United States.
1977 The experimental space shuttle *Enterprise* glided to a successful landing at Edwards Air Force Base in California.
1979 South Korean President Park Chung-hee was shot to death by the head of the Korean Central Intelligence Agency, Kim Jae-kyu.
2004 Israel's parliament approved Prime Minister Ariel Sharon's plan for withdrawing from the Gaza Strip and parts of the West Bank.

October 27

DAILY READING

*Finally, be strong in the Lord
and in his mighty power.* (EPH 6:10)

FEAST DAYS

372	Abraham the Poor	Egyptian hermit
1203	Goswin	Benedictine monk
1270	Bartholomew of Braganza	Dominican priest

ENTRANCE AND EXIT

b. 1728	James Cook	English explorer
b. 1858	Theodore Roosevelt	26th American president
b. 1939	John Cleese	English actor
d. 1505	Ivan the Great	Grand Prince of Moscow
d. 1858	Ida Pfeiffer	Austrian explorer
d. 1953	Eugene O'Neill	American playwright

Ida Pfeiffer

Ida Pfeiffer (1797–1858), the celebrated traveler, was born in Vienna, Italy. By the age of thirteen, she had a great longing for travel. She eagerly read every book of travel that fell into her hands and blamed her sex for preventing her from following their heroic examples.

She was strong, healthy, courageous, and accomplished; and at length, after maturing her plans with anxious consideration, she took up her pilgrim's staff and sallied forth alone–virtually unheard of for a woman in her time.

Her first object was to visit the Holy Land, to tread in the hallowed footsteps of the Lord. For this purpose she left Vienna on March 22, 1842, and embarked onboard the steamer that was to convey her down the Danube to the Black Sea and the city of Constantinople. From there she repaired to Broussa, Beirut, Jaffa, Jerusalem, the Dead Sea, Nazareth, Damascus, Baalbek, the Lebanon, Alexandria, and Cairo, and traveled across the sandy desert to the Isthmus of Suez and the Red Sea. From Egypt the adventurous lady returned home by way of Sicily and Italy, visiting Naples, Rome, and Florence, and arriving in Vienna in December 1842. In the following year she published the record of her experiences under the title *Journey of a Viennese Lady to the Holy Land.* It met with a very favorable reception due to the simplicity of its style and the faithfulness of its descriptions.

An anonymous biographer wrote this about Ida, "Straightforward in character, and endued with high principle, she possessed, moreover, a wisdom and a promptitude in action seldom equalled among her sex. "

Extract From A Visit to the Holy Land

Emerging from St. Stephen's Gate, we pass the Turkish burial-ground, and reach the spot where St. Stephen was stoned. Not far off we see the bed of the brook Cedron, which is at this season of the year completely dried up. A stone bridge leads across the brook; adjoining it is a stone slab where they shew traces of the footsteps of the Saviour, as He was brought across this bridge from Gethsemane, and stumbled and fell. Crossing this bridge, we arrive at the grotto where Jesus sweat blood. This grotto still retains its original form. A plain wooden altar has been erected there, a few years since, by a Bavarian prince, and the entrance is closed by an iron gate. Not far off is Gethsemane. Eight olive-trees are here to be seen that have attained a great age; nowhere else had I seen these trees with such massive trunks, though I had frequently passed through whole plantations of olives. Those who are learned in natural history assert that the olive-tree cannot live to so great an age as to render it possible that these venerable trunks existed at the time when Jesus passed his last night at Gethsemane in prayer and supplication. As this tree, however, propagates itself, these trees may be sprouts from the ancient stems. The space around the roots has been strengthened with masonry, to afford a support to these patriarchal trunks, and the eight trees are surrounded by a wall three or four feet in height. No layman may enter this spot unaccompanied by a priest, on pain of excommunication; it is also forbidden to pluck a single leaf. The Turks also hold these trees in reverence, and would not injure one of them.

–Ida Pfeiffer

OCTOBER 28

DAILY READING

Put on the full armor of God so that you can take your stand against the devil's schemes. (EPH 6:11)

FEAST DAYS

ca. 1st cent.	Simon	Apostle
ca. 1st cent.	Jude Thaddeus	Apostle
1764	John Dat	Vietnamese martyr

ENTRANCE AND EXIT

b. 1585	Cornelius Jansen	Dutch theologian
b. 1820	John Henry Hopkins	American composer
b. 1955	William Gates	American businessman
d. 1485	Rudolphus Agricola	Dutch scholar
d. 1704	Joseph Locke	English philosopher
d. 1998	Ted Hughes	English Poet Laureate

John Henry Hopkins

Clergyman and composer John Henry Hopkins Jr. (1820–91) was born in Pittsburgh, Pennsylvania, and graduated in 1839 from the University of Vermont and the General Theological Seminary, New York City, in 1850. In addition to leading his Baptist congregation, Hopkins was a prolific writer, and his published work includes many pamphlets, review articles, a biography of his father, John Henry Hopkins Sr. (1868), and a book of poems, *Poems by the Wayside* (1883).

However, it is as a composer that he is most well known. Among others, he wrote the hymns:

- Alleluia! Christ Is Risen Today!
- Blow on, Thou Mighty Wind
- Come with Us, O Blessed Jesus
- Glory to God the Father Be
- God Hath Made the Moon Whose Beam
- God of Our Fathers, Bless This Our Land
- Lord, Now Round Thy Church Behold

Most famously, he wrote the words and music of the popular Christmas carol "We Three Kings":

We three kings of Orient are;
Bearing gifts we traverse afar,
Field and fountain, moor and mountain,
Following yonder star.

Refrain
O star of wonder, star of light,
Star with royal beauty bright,
Westward leading, still proceeding,
Guide us to thy perfect light.

St. Simon and St. Jude

Both the Roman Catholic Church and the Church of England maintain a festival to these apostles on this day.

Simon is called the Canaanite, either from Cana, the place of his birth, or from his having been of a hot and sprightly temper. He remained with the other apostles till after Pentecost, and is imagined on slight grounds to have preached in Britain, and there been put to death.

Jude, or Judas, also called Thaddeus and Libbius, was brother to James the brother to Christ (Matt 13:55). Some early writers maintain that he was the son of Joseph by a former wife. Some presume that he suffered martyrdom in Persia, but this is not certain.

OCTOBER 29

DAILY READING

For our struggle is not against flesh and blood, but against the rulers, against the authorities, against the powers of this dark world and against the spiritual forces of evil in the heavenly realms. (EPH 6:12)

FEAST DAYS

99	Narcissus	Bishop of Jerusalem
520	Terence	Bishop of Metz, France
560	Colman	Bishop of Kilmacduagh, Ireland

ENTRANCE AND EXIT

b. 1740	James Boswell	Scottish writer
b. 1837	Harriet Powers	American quilt maker
b. 1897	Paul Joseph Goebbels	German Nazi leader
d. 1618	Sir Walter Raleigh	English explorer
d. 1911	Joseph Pulitzer	American newspaperman
d. 1950	Oscar Gustaf Adolf	King of Sweden –Gustav V

Harriet Powers—Quilting Pioneer

Quilts made by African American folk artist Harriet Powers (1837–1901) are now recognized across America for their quality and unique designs. Using traditional African appliqué technique along with biblical reference traditions, Harriet recorded on her quilts local historical legend, Bible stories, and astronomical phenomena.

Born a slave in Athens, Georgia, in 1837, Harriet Powers created two quilts, which are the best-known and best-preserved examples of Southern American quilting tradition still in existence. They are now on display at the Smithsonian Institution.

In 2005, a doctoral history student at the University of Georgia discovered the grave of Harriet Powers, as well as that of Powers's husband and daughter. The headstone, which was uncovered at the historic Gospel Pilgrim Cemetery in Athens, reveals that Powers died on January 1, 1910.

Sir Walter Raleigh

After a fifteen-year imprisonment in the Tower of London on a charge of conspiracy against King James I, former royal favorite Sir Walter Raleigh was executed by beheading on this day at Whitehall. When he saw the ax that was to behead him, Raleigh said, "This is a sharp Medicine, but it is a Physician for all Diseases."

After the execution, Raleigh's head was embalmed and presented to his wife, who carried it with her at all times for nearly thirty years until her own death. In Raleigh's last letter to his wife, he wrote:

> You shall now receive (my deare wife) my last words in these last lines. My love I send you that you may keep it when I am dead, and my councell that you may remember it when I am no more. I would not by my will present you with sorrowes (dear Besse) let them go to the grave with me and be buried in the dust. And seeing that it is not Gods will that I should see you any more in this life, beare it patiently, and with a heart like thy selfe.
>
> First, I send you all the thankes which my heart can conceive, or my words can rehearse for your many travailes, and care taken for me, which though they have not taken effect as you wished, yet my debt to you is not the lesse: but I pay it I never shall in this world.
>
> Secondly, I beseech you for the love you beare me living, do not hide your selfe many dayes, but by your travailes seeke to helpe your miserable fortunes and the right of your poor childe. Thy mourning cannot availe me, I am but dust.
>
> The everlasting God, powerfull, infinite, and omnipotent God, That Almighty God, who is goodnesse it selfe, the true life and true light keep thee and thine: have mercy on me, and teach me to forgive my persecutors and false accusers, and send us to meet in his glorious Kingdome. My deare wife farewell. Blesse my poore boy. Pray for me, and let my good God hold you both in his arms.
>
> Written with the dying hand of sometimes thy Husband, but now alasse overthrowne.
>
> Yours that was, but now not my own.
>
> —Walter Rawleigh

OCTOBER 30

DAILY READING

You are my hiding place; you will protect me from trouble and surround me with songs of deliverance. (PS 32:7)

FEAST DAYS

250	Besas	Egyptian soldier
1394	Dorothy of Montau	Patron of Prussia
1601	Peter Higgins	Dominican martyr

ENTRANCE AND EXIT

b. 1735	John Adams	2nd American president
b. 1821	Fyodor Dostoevski	Russian writer
b. 1885	Ezra Pound	American poet
d. 1823	Edmund Cartwright	English inventor
d. 1910	Henri Dunant	Swiss founder of the International Red Cross
d. 1923	Bonar Law	English prime minister

Edmund Cartwright

English inventor Edmund Cartwright (1743–1823) would probably have passed a life as a country clergyman had not his attention been accidentally drawn in 1784 to the possibility of applying machinery to the rapidly expanding industry of weaving.

Applying his natural genius, Cartwright fashioned a rough contrivance that was granted a patent in 1785. "It struck me," he wrote, "that as in plain weaving, according to the conception I then had of the business, that as there could only be three movements which were to follow each other in succession, there would be little difficulty in reproducing and repeating them." With subsequent improvements and further patents, he gradually developed his invention into a modern power loom. He also patented a wool-combing machine in 1789 that did the job of twenty workers. Other inventions of Cartwright's included a rope making machine (Cordelier) in 1791 and an engine that used alcohol (1797). In addition to inventing the power loom, Cartwright is also famous for publishing the legendary poems "Armine and Elvira" in 1770 and "The Prince of Peace" in 1779.

He moved to Doncaster from his living in Marwood, Leicestershire, and started one of the first weaving and spinning factories in 1786. However, Cartwright was not good at financial management, and in 1793, the business closed due to bankruptcy, as he owed more than £30,000. A fire at his mill in Manchester in 1791 destroyed his machinery. Although in 1801 his patents were extended by Parliament for another fourteen years, he still could not make his businesses profitable. Eventually, in 1809, after a group of textile manufacturers petitioned the House of Commons on his behalf, he was awarded £10,000 pounds for his contributions to the British textile industry. He used the money to buy a rural estate in Kent, where he spent the rest of his life.

Noteworthy

1811 Jane Austen's *Sense and Sensibility* published.
1938 *The War of the Worlds* radio dramatization causes alarm.
1961 Soviet Union tests hydrogen bomb.
1974 Muhammed Ali regains the world heavyweight boxing title from George Foreman.

Quote of the Day

"I always consider the settlement of America with reverence and wonder, as the opening of a grand scene and design in providence, for the illumination of the ignorant and the emancipation of the slavish part of mankind all over the earth."

–John Adams

OCTOBER 31

DAILY READING

For though we live in the world, we do not wage war as the world does.
The weapons we fight with are not the weapons of the world.
On the contrary, they have divine power to demolish strongholds.
We demolish arguments and every pretension that sets itself up against the knowledge of God, and we take captive every thought to make it obedient to Christ. (2 COR 10:3–5)

FEAST DAYS

287	Quentin	Patron against coughs
665	Follian	Patron of dentists
924	Wolfgang	Patron of carpenters

ENTRANCE AND EXIT

b. 1632	Jan Vermeer	Dutch artist
b. 1795	John Keats	English poet
b. 1962	Peter Jackson	New Zealand film director
d. 1926	Harry Houdini	American magician
d. 1993	Frederico Fellini	Italian film director
d. 1984	Indira Gandhi	Indian prime minister

All Hallow's Eve

According to *Chambers Book of Days* (1869), there is no night in the year that the popular imagination has stamped with a more peculiar character than the evening of the All Hallow's Eve or Halloween. All Hallow's Eve is a relic of pagan times, for there is nothing in the church observance of the ensuing day of All Saints to have originated such extraordinary notions as are connected with this celebrated festival. Halloween is traditionally the night set apart for a universal walking abroad of spirits, both of the visible and invisible world.

Throughout Britain a number of ancient customs were performed. Nuts and apples were consumed in immense numbers. Indeed in northern England, this night is known as Nutcrack Night, when all manner of nuts are cracked and eaten. In Ireland, young women wanting to know if their lovers were faithful would put three nuts upon the bars of the grate, naming the nuts after the lovers. If a nut cracked or jumped, the lover was unfaithful; if it began to blaze or burn, he had a regard for the person making the trial. If the nuts named after the girl and her lover burned together, they would be married.

Another old custom involved snatching apples from a tub of water by people ducking their heads into it. The Three Dishes is another old custom where two dishes are respectively filled with clean and dirty water, and one is empty. They are arranged in a line, and a blindfolded person dips his fingers into one dish. If they dip into the clean water, they are to marry a maiden or man; if into the foul water, a widow or widower; if into the empty dish, they are destined to remain single. Other customs include sowing hemp seed and winnowing corn three times to reveal a future spouse.

The Day Is Gone and All Its Sweets Are Gone!

The day is gone, and all its sweets are gone!
Sweet voice, sweet lips, soft hand, and softer
breast,
Warm breath, light whisper, tender semitone,
Bright eyes, accomplished shape, and
lang'rous waist!
Faded the flower and all its budded charms,
Faded the sight of beauty from my eyes,
Faded the shape of beauty from my arms,
Faded the voice, warmth, whiteness,
paradise–
Vanished unseasonably at shut of eve,
When the dusk holiday -or holinight
Of fragrant-curtained love begins to weave
The woof of darkness thick, for hid delight;
But, as I've read love's missal through today,
He'll let me sleep, seeing I fast and pray.

–John Keats

November

Next was November; he full grown and fat
As fed with lard, and that right well might seeme;
For he had been a fatting hogs of late,
That yet his browes with sweat did reek and steam;
And yet the season was full sharp and breem;
In planting eeke he took no small delight,
Whereon he rode, not easie was to deeme
For it a dreadful centaure was in sight,
The seed of Saturn and fair Nais, Chiron hight.

EDMUND SPENSER–*The Shepheardes Calender* (1579)

The Centaur, Sagittarius, am I,
Born of Ixion's and the cloud's embrace;
With sounding hoofs across the earth I fly,
A steed Thessalian with a human face.
Sharp winds the arrows are with which I chase
The leaves, half dead already with affright;
I shroud myself in gloom; and to the race
Of mortals bring nor comfort nor delight.

HENRY WADSWORTH LONGFELLOW–*The Poet's Calendar* (1882)

Proverbs ~

If there's ice in November to bear a duck
There'll be nothing after but sludge and muck.

On All Hallow's Day cut a chip from the beech tree;
If it be dry the winter will prove warm.

November ~

It is a fact well known to the medical philosopher, that, in proportion as people do not like air and exercise, their blood becomes darker and darker: now what corrupts and thickens the circulation, and keeps the humours within the pores, darkens and clogs the mind; and we are then in a state to receive pleasure but indifferently or confusedly, and pain with tenfold painfulness. If we add to this a quantity of unnecessary cares and sordid mistakes, it is so much the worse. A love of nature is the refuge. He who grapples with March, and has the smiling eyes upon him of June and August, need have no fear of November. –And as the Italian proverb says, every medal has its reverse. November, with its loss of verdure, its frequent rains, the fall of the leaf, and the visible approach of winter, is undoubtedly a gloomy month to the gloomy; but to others, it brings but pensiveness, a feeling very far from destitute of pleasure; and if the healthiest and most imaginative of us may feel their spirits pulled down by reflections connected with earth, its mortalities, and its mistakes, we should but strengthen ourselves the more to make strong and sweet music with the changeful but harmonious movements of nature.

–William Hone, *The Every-Day Book* (1825–26)

In Flanders Fields ~

In Flanders fields the poppies blow
Between the crosses, row on row,
That mark our place; and in the sky
The larks, still bravely singing, fly
Scarce heard amid the guns below.

We are the Dead. Short days ago
We lived, felt dawn, saw sunset glow,
Loved and were loved, and now we lie
In Flanders fields.

Take up our quarrel with the foe:
To you from failing hands we throw
The torch; be yours to hold it high.
If ye break faith with us who die
We shall not sleep,
though poppies grow
In Flanders fields.

–Colonel John McCrae (1915)

NOVEMBER 1

DAILY READING

Do not boast about tomorrow, for you do not know what a day may bring forth. (PROV 27:1)

FEAST DAYS

306	Juliana	Turkish martyr
609	All Saints' Day	Celebration of all Christian martyrs
1560	Peter Paul Novarra	Jesuit missionary

ENTRANCE AND EXIT

b. 1762	Spencer Perceval	English prime minister
b. 1871	Stephen Crane	American writer
b. 1935	Gary Player	South African golfer
d. 1955	Dale Carnegie	American writer
d. 1982	Elbert Vidor	American film director
d. 1985	Phil Silvers	American actor

Jews Expelled from England

In the spring of 1290, King Edward I was severely ill. From his sickbed, he made a solemn vow that if the Almighty should restore him to health, he would undertake another crusade against the infidels. The king recovered, but instead of venturing to Palestine, he sought to dispossess Jews living in England.

Thus, on August 31, 1290, the king issued a proclamation ordering all Jews, under penalty of death, to leave England by the first of November. The Jews were permitted to take with them a small portion of their belongings and as much money as would pay their traveling expenses. Certain ports were appointed as places of embarkation, and safe-conduct passes to those ports were granted to all who chose to pay for them. The passes added more to the royal treasury than to the protection of the fugitives. The people robbed the Jews on all sides, without paying the slightest respect to the dearly purchased protections.

In the years leading up to this proclamation, Jews were imprisoned, tortured, and as much six thousand silver marks were extorted from them. In 1194, English Jewry was called to Northampton to allocate a "tallage" of five thousand marks—their contribution to ransom of Richard I. Also in 1194 the "Exchequer of the Jews" was set up to control money-lending activities. Every Jewish moneylender had to swear an oath on the Torah scrolls that he would register all his bonds. The church forbade money-lending for interest, so the Jews were needed since they did not have such a prohibition. Although many Jews became wealthy through money-lending, their legal status was one of "rightlessness."

Roger of Wendover records the tale of Abraham of Bristol, who refused to pay the tallage. The king ordered his torturers to pull out one of his molar teeth every day until he paid the at least one thousand marks. He stood it for seven days, but paid the ransom when they started on his eighth tooth.

About fifteen thousand Jews were expelled, and English business received a severe shock by this action, as many Jews did traded with them. One of the expelled Jews was an Oxford student called Nicolaus de Lyra. He subsequently wrote a commentary on the Old and New Testaments, a work that prepared the way for the Reformation.

Extract from "All Saints' Day"

Why blow'st thou not, thou wintry wind,
Now every leaf is brown and sere,
And idly droops, to thee resigned,
The fading chaplet of the year?
Yet wears the pure aerial sky
Her summer veil, half drawn on high,
Of silvery haze, and dark and still
The shadows sleep on every slanting hill.

How quiet shows the woodland scene!
Each flower and tree, its duty done,
Reposing in decay serene,
Like weary men when age is won,
Such calm old age as conscience pure
And self-commanding hearts ensure,
Waiting their summons to the sky,
Content to live, but not afraid to die.

–John Keble

NOVEMBER 2

DAILY READING

I will say of the L*ORD*, *"He is my refuge and my fortress, my God, in whom I trust."* (PS 91:2)

FEAST DAYS

303	Victorinus	Bishop of Pettau, Austria
998	All Souls' Day	Commemoration of those in purgatory
1040	Justus	Patron of Trieste, Italy

ENTRANCE AND EXIT

b. 1734	Daniel Boone	American pioneer
b. 1795	James Knox Polk	11th American president
b. 1913	Burton Stephen Lancaster	American actor
d. 1961	James Thurber	American illustrator
d. 1992	Hal Roach	American film director
d. 1996	Eva Cassidy	American singer

The Day of the Dead

The Catholic Feast of All Souls (also known as the Day of the Dead) follows All Saints' Day. Whereas All Saints' Day commemorates all Christian martyrs, on the Day of the Dead the Catholic Church remembers all who have died and are in purgatory.

Catholics offer prayers up on behalf of their departed relatives and friends. This may be done in the form of the *Defunctorum officium*, a prayer service offered in memory of departed friend or relative.

There are many customs associated with All Souls' Day. In Mexico, All Souls' Day is *el dia de los muertos* ("the day of the dead") and customs include going to a graveyard to have a picnic, eating skull-shaped candy, and leaving food out for dead relatives. The practice of leaving food out for dead relatives is not part of Catholic theology.

In the Philippines, "Memorial Day" is based loosely on All Souls' Day. Customs include praying novenas for the holy souls and ornately decorating relatives' graves. On the eve of All Souls' Day, participants go door-to-door, requesting gifts and singing a traditional verse representing the liberation of holy souls from purgatory.

In Hungary, the day is known as *Halottak Napja* ("the day of the dead") and a common custom is inviting orphans into the family and giving them food, clothes, and toys. In rural Poland, a legend developed that at midnight on All Souls' Day a great light shone on the local parish. This light was said to be the holy souls of departed parishioners gathered to pray for their release from purgatory at the altars of their former earthly parishes. After this, the souls were said to return to scenes from their earthly life and work, visiting homes and other places. As a sign of welcome, Poles leave their windows and doors ajar on the night of All Souls' Day. All of these customs show the wide variety of traditions related to All Souls' Day.

Traditional Soul Cakes Recipe

170 g (6 oz) butter, softened

170 g (6 oz) caster sugar

3 egg yolks

450 g (1 lb) plain flour

1 tsp ground mixed spice

1/2 tsp ground ginger

pinch salt

85 g (3 oz) currants

4 to 6 tablespoons warm milk

Preheat oven to 180° C (350° F). In a large bowl, cream the softened butter, gradually adding the sugar, beat until light and fluffy. Beat the egg yolks and add a little at a time while continuing to beat. Fold in the sieved flour, spices, and salt to the mixture. Stir in the currants and enough warm milk to produce a soft dough. Divide into 18 to 24 pieces and shape into flat cakes, marking each with a cross. Place on a greased baking tray and bake for 10 to 15 minutes or until golden.

Makes 18 to 24 pieces.

November 3

DAILY READING

For what the law was powerless to do in that it was weakened by the sinful nature, God did by sending his own Son in the likeness of sinful man to be a sin offering. (ROM 8:3)

FEAST DAYS

ca. 7th cent.	Rumwold	Son of Queen Kynerberga, England
727	Hubert	Bishop of Liege, Belgium
1211	Alphais	Counselor to Queen Adela of France

ENTRANCE AND EXIT

b. 1801	Karl Baedecker	German publisher
b. 1949	Larry Holmes	American boxer
b. 1952	Roseanne Barr	American actor
d. 1864	Antônio Gonçalves Dias	Brazilian poet
d. 1954	Henri Matisse	French artist
d. 1990	Mary Martin	American actor

Karl Baedeker

The German publisher Karl Baedeker (1801–59) produced industry-leading travel guides "to keep the traveler at as great a distance as possible from the unpleasant, and often wholly invisible, tutelage of hired servants and guides (and in part from the aid of coachmen and hotelkeepers), to assist him in standing on his own feet, to render him independent, and to place him in a position from which he may receive his own impressions with clear eyes and lively heart."

Baedeker's travel guides described all of Europe and North America, and much of Asia and Africa. The books were famous not just for their sound travel advice, but they also comforted the timid, encouraged the daring, and explained the proper response to local customs.

Karl Baedeker was born to a line of printers and booksellers in Essen and was fluent in a dozen languages. When he set up shop in Coblenz in 1827, after studying at Heidelberg and working in the book trade at Berlin, he had no intention of providing a guidebook. He published his first book more or less by accident. A bankrupt publishing house that he bought out in 1832 had recently issued a scholarly survey of the history, scenery, and art of the Rhineland by Professor Klein. Baedeker kept Klein's name on the title page, but simplified the text and added practical information on transport and accommodation, enlarging the book so that it extended from Strasbourg to Rotterdam.

The book and subsequent guides covering Belgium, France, and Austria proved to be immensely popular. By the time of Baedeker's death in 1859, largely from overwork, Baedeker guidebooks, with their distinctive red binding and stamped gilt lettering, were instantly recognizable. Today, there are more than 150 Baedeker's guides, and Karl Baedeker's great-grandson manages the business.

St. Hubert

According to the hagiographer Alban Butler, St. Hubert's early life is so obscured by popular traditions that we have no authentic account of his actions. He is said to have been passionately addicted to hunting, and was entirely taken up in worldly pursuits. While hunting a stag on a Good Friday morning, he received a vision of a crucifix between its antlers. A voice warned him, "Hubert, unless you turn to the Lord, and lead a holy life, you shall quickly go down to hell." Thus, he is the patron saint of hunters.

Moved by divine grace, he resolved to renounce the world. His extraordinary fervor, and the great progress which he made in virtue and learning, strongly recommended him to St. Lambert, Bishop of Maestricht, Holland, who ordained him priest and entrusted him with the principal share in the administration of his diocese. That holy prelate being barbarously murdered in 681, St. Hubert was unanimously chosen his successor. With incredible zeal he penetrated the most remote and barbarous places of Ardenne Belgium and abolished the worship of idols; and, as he performed the office of the apostles, God bestowed on him a like gift of miracles. He died on the May 30, 727, reciting to his last breath the Creed and the Lord's Prayer.

November 4

DAILY READING

We believe that Jesus died and rose again and so we believe that God will bring with Jesus those who have fallen asleep in him. (1 THESS 4:14)

FEAST DAYS

ca. 6th cent.	Clether	Welsh hermit
ca. 680	Modesta	Benedictine nun
ca. 1250	Henry of Zweifalten	Benedictine monk

ENTRANCE AND EXIT

b. 1650	William III	King of England
b. 1740	Augustus Toplady	English clergyman
b. 1946	Laura Welch Bush	44th American First Lady
d. 1847	Felix Mendelssohn	German composer
d. 1918	Wilfred Owen	English poet
d. 1995	Yitzhak Rabin	Israeli prime minister

Augustus Toplady

Augustus Montague Toplady (1740–78) is best known for his hymn "Rock of Ages," written two years before his death. He was born in Surrey, the only son of Maj. Richard Toplady, who had died at the battle of Carthagena shortly after his birth, so he never knew his father. We know little about Augustus Toplady, because he lived a largely private and contemplative life.

He was educated at Westminster School and then Trinity College, Dublin, and took his degree there as Bachelor of Arts. He was ordained a clergyman in the year 1762. He was appointed to the living of Blagdon, in Somerset, then Venn-in, Devonshire, and finally to rural parish of Broad Hembury, near Honiton, in Devonshire.

In 1775 poor health compelled him to move to London, but his health continued to deteriorate, and he died at age thirty-eight.

This is an extract from one of his sermons given on Sunday, April 29, 1770, entitled "A Caveat Against Unsound Doctrines," based on 2 Corinthians 3:12:

Heaven must be brought down into the human soul ere the human soul can be fitted for heaven. There must, as the school-men speak, be "a congruity and similitude between the faculty and the object," i.e. there must be an inward meetness for the vision and glory of God, wrought in you by his Holy Spirit, in order to render you susceptible of those exalted pleasures, and that fulness of joy which are in his presence and at his right hand for ever. Was thy soul, O unconverted sinner, to be this moment, separated from thy body, and even admitted into heaven (supposing it was possible for an unregenerate spirit to enter there), heaven would not be heaven to thee. You cannot relish the blessedness of the new Jerusalem, unless God in the meanwhile makes you partaker of a new nature.

Rock of Ages

1. Rock of Ages, cleft for me,
   Let me hide myself in Thee;
   Let the water and the blood,
   From Thy wounded side which flowed,
   Be of sin the double cure,
   Save from wrath and make me pure.
2. Not the labor of my hands
   Can fulfill Thy law's demands;
   Could my zeal no respite know,
   Could my tears forever flow,
   All for sin could not atone;
   Thou must save, and Thou alone.
3. Nothing in my hand I bring,
   Simply to Thy cross I cling;
   Naked, come to Thee for dress;
   Helpless, look to Thee for grace;
   Foul, I to the fountain fly;
   Wash me, Savior, or I die.
4. While I draw this fleeting breath,
   When my eyes shall close in death,
   When I rise to worlds unknown,
   And behold Thee on Thy throne,
   Rock of Ages, cleft for me,
   Let me hide myself in Thee.

–*Augustus Toplady, 1776*

NOVEMBER 5

DAILY READING

If we have been united with him like this in his death, we will certainly also be united with him in his resurrection. For we know that our old self was crucified with him so that the body of sin might be done away with, that we should no longer be slaves to sin. (ROM 6:5–6)

FEAST DAYS

953	Hermengild	Benedictine monk
1123	Gerald	Bishop of Beziers, France
1656	Gomidas Keumurjian	Armenian priest

ENTRANCE AND EXIT

b. 1854	Paul Sabatier	English scientist
b. 1892	John Haldane	English scientist
b. 1941	Art Gunfunkel	American singer
d. 1989	Vladimir Horowitz	Russian composer
d. 1991	Robert Maxwell	English publisher
d. 2005	John Fowles	English writer

Guy Fawkes Night

Guy Fawkes Night is celebrated in Britain and some of its colonies on this day. Fireworks, the lighting of bonfires, and the ceremonial effigy–burning of one Guy Fawkes–mark this night. In 1605 a Catholic plot, led by Guy Fawkes, was discovered to blow up the English parliament along with the ruling monarch, King James I. It was hoped that such a disaster would initiate a great uprising of English Catholics, who were distressed by the increased severity of penal laws against the practice of their religion.

The conspirators secretly stored thirty-six barrels of gunpowder, overlaid with firewood, in the cellars of the Houses of Parliament. However, one of the conspirators, Thomas Wintour, eager to protect a prominent Catholic, Lord Monteagle, sent him a letter warning him not to attend the opening of Parliament on November 5.

This message was revealed to the First Earl of Salisbury and others, and they informed the authorities, who discovered the cache and arrested Fawkes on the night of November 4 as he entered the cellar. The majority of the other conspirators were killed outright, imprisoned, or executed. While the plot itself was the work of a small number of men, it provoked hostility against all English Catholics and led to an increase in the harshness of laws against them. Even to this day, it is the law that no Roman Catholic may hold the office of monarch, and the reigning king or queen remains Supreme Head of the Church of England.

Today, one of the ceremonies that accompanies the opening of a new session of Parliament is a traditional searching of the basement by the Yeoman of the Guard. It has been said that for superstitious reasons, no state opening of Parliament has or ever will be held again on November 5. However, on at least one occasion (in 1957), Parliament did indeed open on November 5. The actual cellar was damaged by fire in 1834, and totally destroyed during the rebuilding of the Palace of Westminster in the nineteenth century.

Traditional Bonfire Night Poem

Remember, remember, the 5th of November
The Gunpowder Treason and plot;
I know of no reason why Gunpowder Treason
Should ever be forgot.
Guy Fawkes, Guy Fawkes,
'Twas his intent.
To blow up the King and the Parliament.
Three score barrels of powder below.
Poor old England to overthrow.
By God's providence he was catch'd,
With a dark lantern and burning match

Holloa boys, Holloa boys, let the bells ring
Holloa boys, Holloa boys, God save the King!

Hip hip Hoorah!
Hip hip Hoorah!

A penny loaf to feed ol'Pope,
A farthing cheese to choke him.
A pint of beer to rinse it down,
A faggot of sticks to burn him.
Burn him in a tub of tar,'
Burn him like a blazing star.
Burn his body from his head,
Then we'll say: ol'Pope is dead.

NOVEMBER 6

DAILY READING

So we say with confidence, "The Lord is my helper; I will not be afraid. What can man do to me?" (HEB 13:6)

FEAST DAYS

ca. 505	Illytd	Welsh monk
716	Winnoc	Patron against fever
1046	Stephen	Bishop of Apt, France

ENTRANCE AND EXIT

b. 1638	James Gregory	Scottish scientist
b. 1814	Adolphe Sax	Belgian inventor–saxophone
b. 1861	James Naismith	American inventor–basketball
d. 1796	Catherine II	Empress of Russia
d. 1836	Charles X	French king
d. 1935	Billy Sunday	American evangelist

Abraham Lincoln

On this day in 1860, Abraham Lincoln, also known as "Honest Abe" and "Illinois Rail-Splitter," was elected as the sixteenth president of the United States. Because of his opposition to slavery, Lincoln's victory changed the racial future of the United States. Southern-sympathizer John Wilkes Booth was agitated enough to first conspire to and then assassinate Lincoln on April 14, 1865.

Lincoln was born in 1809 in a log cabin in Hardin (now Larue) County, Kentucky. In 1834 he became a United States Representative as a member of the Whig Party, and in 1836 Lincoln was elected to the Illinois legislature. He supported the Second Bank of the United States, the Illinois State Bank, government-sponsored internal improvements (roads, canals, railroads, harbors), and protective tariffs.

Lincoln vied for the U.S. Senate in 1855, but eventually threw his support to Lyman Trumbull. In 1856 he joined the newly formed Republican Party, and two years later he campaigned for the Senate against Stephen Douglas. In his senatorial nomination acceptance speech in 1858, Lincoln expressed the view that the nation would become either all slave or all free: "A house divided against itself cannot stand."

In February 1860, Lincoln made his first major political appearance in the Northeast when he addressed a rally at the Cooper Union in New York. He was now sufficiently well known to be a presidential candidate. At the Republican national convention in Chicago in May, William H. Seward was the leading candidate. Seward, however, had qualities that made him undesirable in the critical states the Republicans had lost in 1856: Pennsylvania, Indiana, Illinois, and New Jersey. As a result, Lincoln won the nomination by being the second choice of the majority. He went on to win the presidential election, defeating the Northern Democrat Stephen Douglas, the Southern Democrat John C. Breckinridge, and the Constitutional Union candidate John Bell.

Abraham Lincoln's Address at Gettysburg–November 19, 1863

Four score and seven years ago our fathers brought forth, upon this continent, a new nation, conceived in liberty, and dedicated to the proposition that "all men are created equal."

Now we are engaged in a great civil war, testing whether that nation, or any nation so conceived, and so dedicated, can long endure. We are met on a great battle field of that war. We have come to dedicate a portion of it, as a final resting place for those who died here, that the nation might live. This we may, in all propriety do. But, in a larger sense, we can not dedicate–we can not consecrate–we can not hallow, this ground. The brave men, living and dead, who struggled here, have hallowed it, far above our poor power to add or detract. The world will little note, nor long remember what we say here; while it can never forget what they did here.

It is rather for us, the living, to stand here, we here be dedicated to the great task remaining before us–that, from these honored dead we take increased devotion to that cause for which they here, gave the last full measure of devotion–that we here highly resolve these dead shall not have died in vain; that the nation, shall have a new birth of freedom, and that government of the people by the people for the people, shall not perish from the earth.

November 7

DAILY READING

Each man should give what he has decided in his heart
to give, not reluctantly or under compulsion,
for God loves a cheerful giver. (2 COR 9:7)

FEAST DAYS

658	Willibroad	Bishop of Utrecht, Holland
ca. 693	Florentius	Bishop of Strasbourg, France
1226	Engelbert	Archbishop of Cologne, Germany

ENTRANCE AND EXIT

b. 1917	Helen Suzman	South African politician
b. 1926	Dame Joan Sutherland	Australian opera singer
b. 1941	Joni Mitchell	Canadian singer
d. 1724	John Kyrle	English philanthropist
d. 1910	Count Leo Lev Nikolayevich Tolstoy	Russian writer
d. 1980	Steve McQueen	American actor

The Man of Ross

John Kyrle (1637–1724), known as the "Man of Ross" was a Christian philanthropist from Ross-on-Wye, Herefordshire. He was never weary of doing good, and never too fine for any honest, useful piece of labor–he was truly "of the salt of the earth." His beautiful example teaches and encourages us all to do something, be it little or much, within our sphere, to better our neighbors as well as ourselves.

Educated at Balliol College, Oxford Kyrle succeeded to property at Ross-on-Wye. He had only five hundred a year, yet he managed to greatly benefit the town. He built a marketplace for it, raised money for the construction of the church, apprenticed its sons, was generous to the poor, and spent all he had in good works. If a child was born and no man was willing to be godfather to it, John Kyrle agreed to provide for it. If a townsperson died, John Kyrle attended the funeral and walked in the sorrowful procession with the rest. If the inhabitants had disputes–of rights of way, of leasings, of measurements, of misconstruction, or what else–all agreed to abide by John Kyrle's settling, and he would cool the quarrel down.

In 1876, his memory was preserved by the Kyrle Society to better the life of working people by laying out parks and encouraging house decoration, window gardening, and flower growing. The Society was a forerunner of the National Trust.

Alexander Pope eulogized the Man of Ross in his third *Moral Epistle* (1732):

> Behold the Market-place with poor o'er-
> spread.
> The Man of Ross divides the weekly bread;
> He feeds yon almshouse, neat but void of
> state
> Where Age and Want sit smiling at the gate;
> Him portioned maids, apprenticed orphans
> bless,
> The young who labour and the old who rest.
> Is any sick? The Man of Ross relieves,
> Prescribes, attends, the medicine makes and
> gives.
> Is there a variance? enter but his door,
> Balked are the courts, and contest is no
> more.
> Despairing quacks, with curses fled the place,
> And vile attorneys, now a useless race.
> Thrice happy man! enabled to pursue,
> What all so wish, but want the power to do!

Noteworthy

1917 Bolshevik Revolution begins in Russia.
1918 Billy Graham born in Charlotte, North Carolina.
1990 Mary Robinson first woman president of Ireland.
2000 Hilary Rodham Clinton first First Lady elected to the Senate.

November 8

DAILY READING

If we live, we live to the Lord; and if we die, we die to the Lord.
So, whether we live or die, we belong to the Lord. (ROM 14:8)

FEAST DAYS

ca. 9th cent.	Moroc	Bishop of Dunblane, Scotland
1115	Godfrey	Bishop of Amiens, France
1906	Elizabeth Catez	Patron of illness

ENTRANCE AND EXIT

b. 1656	Edmund Halley	English astronomer
b. 1900	Margaret Mitchell	American writer
b. 1922	Christian Barnard	South African surgeon
d. 1308	John Duns Scotus	Scottish theologian
d. 1674	John Milton	English poet
d. 1998	Lord Henry Cecil John Hunt	English mountaineer

The Subtle Doctor

Outstanding thinker and Franciscan priest John Duns Scotus is perhaps the most important and influential theologian in the history of the Franciscan Order. Founder of the Scotistic School in Theology, his ideas dominated Roman Catholic teaching in nearly all the major universities of Europe. He is remembered for his theology on the Absolute Kingship of Jesus Christ, the Immaculate Conception of the Blessed Virgin Mary, and refutation of what we now understand as evolutionary ideas.

He became known as the Subtle Doctor because of his sophisticated development of philosophic and theological thought. He is said to have "described the Divine Nature as if he had seen God; the celestial spirits as if he had been an angel; the happiness of the future state as if he had enjoyed them; and the ways of Providence as if he had penetrated into its secrets."

John Duns Scotus was born in Duns, Berwickshire, Scotland, around 1265. From an early age, he wanted to read, to write, and to study the profundity of the truths of the faith, but his mind just could not manage to learn or understand anything. He prayed to Mary, asking her to heal his dullness so that he could advance in his studies. Mary is supposed to have appeared to him in a vision.

He entered the Order of Friars Minor (the Franciscans) at Dumfries and was ordained a priest in 1291. Then he traveled between England and France to pursue advanced philosophical and theological studies.

Tradition records that the Virgin Mary appeared to him on Christmas night, 1299, at the Oxford Convent. From this, he developed the doctrine of the Immaculate Conception.

On March 20, 1992, John Duns Scotus was beatified by Pope John Paul II at St. Peter's Basilica in Rome.

Extract from A Treatise on God as First Principle

Although being has many properties it would not be irrelevant to consider, it is to the more fruitful source of the essential order that I turn, proceeding according to the following plan. I shall set forth in this first chapter the four divisions of order. From this one can gather how many kinds of essential orders exist.

For a division to be clear it is necessary (1) that the members resulting from the division be indicated and thus be shown to be contained in what is divided, (2) that the mutually exclusive character of the parts be manifest, and (3) that the classification exhaust the subject matter to be divided. The first requirement will be met in this chapter; the others, in the second. With no attempt at justification, then, in the present chapter I shall simply enumerate the divisions and explain the meaning of the parts.

I do not take essential order, however, in the strict sense as do some who say that what is posterior is ordered whereas what is first or prior transcends order. I understand it rather in its common meaning as a relation which can be affirmed equally of the prior and posterior in regard to each other. In other words I consider prior and posterior to be an adequate division of whatever is ordered, so that we may use the terms order and priority or posteriority interchangeably.

–John Duns Scotus

November 9

DAILY READING

Honor the LORD *with your wealth,*
with the firstfruits of all your crops. (PROV 3:9)

FEAST DAYS

467	Benignus	Bishop of Ireland
ca. 1270	Ilona (Helen) of Hungary	Stigmatic
1610	George Napper	English martyr

ENTRANCE AND EXIT

b. 1818	Ivan Sergeevich Turgenev	Russian writer
b. 1841	Albert Edward Wettin Saxe-Coburg-Gotha	King Edward VII of England
b. 1918	Spiro Theodore Agnew	39th American vice president
d. 1940	Neville Chamberlain	English prime minister
d. 1943	Dylan Thomas	Welsh poet
d. 1970	Charles de Gaulle	French president

Ilona (Helen) of Hungary

Little is known for certain about Blessed Ilona (or Helen) of Hungary. She is thought to have trained the future St. Margaret of Hungary in the ways of holiness and served as the novice mistress of the Dominican convent of Vesprim, Hungary.

From an early age, Ilona displayed a gift for contemplative prayer that often led to ecstasy. Tradition records that she had visible signs of her holiness, which were not always understood by her community.

A story relates that once when deep in prayer, she saw the body of Christ on the crucifix come to life, reach down, and take her hand in His. It took a full day for the sisters to pry her hand from that of the corpus. Another time, the large crucifix from the altar suspended itself over her until she finished her prayer, at which time she replaced it.

Ilona was dearly loved within her Dominican order. Her great desire was that her sisters might remain faithful to the rule and the offering of penance. Ilona is reputed to have been the first Dominican marked with the stigmata. At the feast of St. Francis, around 1237, she received a mark in her right hand. Ten years later, she prayed for some of St. Francis's intense love. As she prayed, she entered into a state of ecstasy and her hand gave off rays of light. In the center of her palm, a circle of gold appeared and from this a bright lily grew. When she returned to a normal state of consciousness, she prayed that the wound would be invisible. Later a similar wound appeared in her left hand. God did not answer that prayer until near the time of her death around 1270.

When Ilona was at the point of death, she was rapt in ecstasy. Her body glowed with a radiance that made it impossible for her sisters to determine the exact moment of her passing. At some point she also received wounds in her side and feet, which healed; however, when her tomb was opened seventeen years after her death, the wound in her side reopened of its own volition.

Noteworthy

1918 Abdication of Germany's Kaiser Wilhelm II.

1938 Kristallnacht, the "night of broken glass," when Nazis looted and burned synagogues and Jewish-owned stores and houses in Germany and Austria.

1989 Fall of the Berlin Wall.

2005 Three suicide bombers carried out nearly simultaneous attacks on three U.S.-based hotels in Amman, Jordan, killing 60 victims and wounding hundreds.

November 10

DAILY READING

Come to me, all you who are weary and burdened,
and I will give you rest. Take my yoke upon you and learn from me,
for I am gentle and humble in heart, and you will find rest for your souls.
For my yoke is easy and my burden is light. (MATT 11:28–30)

FEAST DAYS

627	Justus	Bishop of Rochester, England
1066	John	Bishop of Ratzenburg, Germany
1270	Leo the Great	Pope

ENTRANCE AND EXIT

b. 1483	Martin Luther	German reformer
b. 1730	Oliver Goldsmith	English poet
b. 1759	Friedrich von Schiller	German poet
d. 1938	Mustafa Kemal Atatürk	Turkish leader
d. 1982	Leonid Brezhnev	Soviet 1st secretary
d. 1990	Lisa Kirk	American actor

Martin Luther: Key Dates

1483 Luther was born on November 10 at Eisleben and baptized the following day.

1501 Luther entered the university in Erfurt, and received his bachelor's degree one year later. Three years later, he went on to study for his master's degree.

1505 Vowed to St. Anne that he would become a monk and give his life to the Roman Catholic Church after a brush with death in a thunderstorm. He gave away his earthly possessions and entered the Augustinian monastery in Erfurt. He thought that by making this sacrifice, he would earn peace with God.

1507 Ordained a Roman Catholic priest.

1508 Luther taught philosophy at the University of Wittenberg. Continued to be troubled by his sins, and saw no solution to his guilt and no way to satisfy God's justice but through his own works of merit, sacrifices, and penances.

1510 Made a pilgrimage to Rome hoping there to have his doubts of salvation removed. Shocked by the abuses he saw there, he returned to Wittenberg more confused than ever.

1512 Earned the degree of Doctor of Theology, the highest degree for a student of the Bible.

1514 Luther found salvation by accepting Romans 1:16–17. He knew that poor sinners could never find peace with God by their own works and even saving faith itself was God's gift through the means of the Gospel.

1517 On October 31, Luther nailed 95 Theses or statements to the church door in Wittenberg, questioning the church's sale of forgiveness in letters of indulgence. The start of the Lutheran Reformation.

1520 The pope excommunicated him from the church, branding him a false teacher, a traitor, and a heathen.

1521 Charles V, the emperor, sought to resolve the rift by hauling Luther before a conference of princes, dukes, and bishops of the church in the city of Worms. However, he was sentenced to death. On his way back to Wittenberg, Luther was kidnapped by friends and hidden away safely in a castle called the Wartburg near Eisenach. There he stayed in disguise for almost a year, and translated the New Testament into German for his people–a work that was completed in 1534. He died in 1546.

Quote of the Day

"Faith is a living and unshakable confidence, a belief in the grace of God so assured that a man would die a thousand deaths for its sake."
—*Martin Luther*

NOVEMBER 11

DAILY READING

Accept him whose faith is weak, without passing judgment on disputable matters. (ROM 14:1)

FEAST DAYS

397	Martin of Tours	Patron of soldiers
1952	Peter Vitchev	Bulgarian martyr
1952	Josaphat Siskov	Bulgarian martyr

ENTRANCE AND EXIT

b. 1885	Gen. George Patton	American military leader
b. 1962	Demi Moore	American actor
b. 1974	Leonardo Di Caprio	American actor
d. 1831	Nathaniel Turner	American slave
d. 1855	Søren Kierkegaard	Danish philosopher
d. 2004	Yasser Arafat	Palestinian president

Remebrance Day

On this day in 1918, an armistice agreement was signed between the Allies and Germany, in Paris, France, at 5:00 a.m. local time. Hostilities formally ceased at 11:00 a.m. The guns on the Western Front across Europe fell silent, and one of the bloodiest wars ever came to an end.

On November 6, 1919, Sir George Foster, the acting British prime minister, rose in the House of Commons to read a message from King George V, addressed "to all the peoples of the Empire":

> To all my people:
>
> Tuesday next, November 11th, is the first anniversary of the armistice which stayed the world-wide carnage of the four preceding years, and marked the victory of right and freedom. I believe that my people in every part of the Empire fervently wish to perpetuate the memory of that great deliverance and of those who laid down their lives to achieve it.
>
> To afford an opportunity for the universal expression of this feeling it is my desire and hope that at the hour when the armistice came into force, the eleventh hour of the eleventh day of the eleventh month, there may be for the brief space of two minutes a complete suspension of all our normal activities. During that time, except in the rare cases where this might be impractical, all work, all sound and all locomotion should cease, so that in perfect stillness the thoughts of every one may be concentrated on reverent remembrance of the glorious dead.

Remembrance Day commemorates all those who died or were injured during both World War I and World War II. Until the conclusion of World War II, this day was designated Armistice Day. National ceremonies take place in the United Kingdom, America (Veterans' Day), France, Canada, and many other countries. Many nations hold formal religious services on the Sunday nearest this day and in the UK, wreath-laying ceremonies take place in many towns and cities. The Queen lays a wreath at the Cenotaph in Whitehall and there is a parade of veterans. Poppies are worn as a reminder of the loss of life in the "killing fields" of France and Belgium.

The first two-minute silence took place on November 11, 1919, and was reported by the *Manchester Guardian*:

> The first stroke of eleven produced a magical effect. The tram cars glided into stillness, motors ceased to cough and fume, and stopped dead, and the mighty-limbed dray horses hunched back upon their loads and stopped also, seeming to do it of their volition. Someone took off his hat, and with a nervous hesitancy the rest of the men bowed their heads also. Here and there an old soldier could be detected slipping unconsciously into the posture of "attention." An elderly woman far away, wiped her eyes, and the man beside her looked white and stern. Everyone stood still, the hush deepened and spread over the whole city and became so pronounced as to impress one with a sense of audibility.

Extract from "For the Fallen" by Laurence Binyon

They shall not grow old, as we that are left
grow old:
Age shall not weary them, nor the years
condemn.
At the going down of the sun and in the
morning
We will remember them.

NOVEMBER 12

DAILY READING

May the Lord make your love increase and overflow for each other and for everyone else, just as ours does for you. (1 THESS 3:12)

FEAST DAYS

422	Renetus	Bishop of Sorrento, Italy
ca. 540	Machar	Bishop of Aberdeen, Scotland
ca. 633	Livinus	Patron of Flanders, Belgium

ENTRANCE AND EXIT

b. 1840	Auguste Rodin	French sculptor
b. 1911	Rev. Edward Chad Varah	English founder of the Samaritans
b. 1929	Grace Kelly	American actor
d. 1865	Elizabeth Gaskell	English writer
d. 1035	Cnut	King of England
d. 1993	Harry Robbins Haldeman	American political aide

Rev. Edward Chad Varah

The Rev. Edward Chad Varah has two claims to fame. In 1950 he was the first fiction editor of the famous *Eagle* comic, and in 1953 he founded the world's first suicide prevention helpline, known as the Samaritans.

The *Eagle* was a new children's magazine that quickly became a favorite because of its illustrations and strong characters like Dan Dare and Tintin. In addition to these weekly strips, the back page carried a religious feature bearing the byline "Story by Chad Varah." In 1953, Varah left the magazine to take up his new post as a rector in the Church of St. Stephen, Wallbrook, London.

Samaritans began after Varah had to conduct a burial service for a fourteen-year-old girl who had committed suicide. She believed she had a sexually transmitted disease when all that had happened was that her menstrual cycle had started. Varah noted, "I might have dedicated myself to suicide prevention then and there, providing a network of people you could 'ask' about anything, however embarrassing, but I didn't come to that until later." This led to the start of "a confidential emergency service for people in distress who need spiritual aid." Samaritans has helped many people simply by listening to their concerns. Today over two hundred branches operated by volunteers handle over two million contacts (telephones, emails, letters, and visits) a year. Samaritans operates in the UK and Ireland, and the helpline is run by trained volunteers who provide confidential emotional support to anyone in distress or at risk of suicide.

Varah was a tireless campaigner for people in distress. In his eighties he began a campaign to discourage East African immigrants from continuing their tradition of female genital mutilation.

In 1999, he was made a Companion of Honour.

The Parable of the Good Samaritan
–Luke 10:29–37

But the expert wanting to make himself look good asked Jesus, "And who is my neighbor?" Jesus answered with a story: A man was going down the mountain road from Jerusalem to Jericho, and he was attacked by a gang of robbers who stripped him of everything, beat him up, and ran off, leaving him half-dead. By chance a priest was going down that road. But when he saw the man, he went by on the other side. In the same way a temple official came along. When he saw the man , he also went by on the other side. Then a foreigner from Samaria traveling along that road happened upon the man, and when he saw him, he was filled with compassion and went to help. He treated his wounds with olive oil and wine and bandaged them. He put him on his own donkey and took him to an inn, where he took care of him. The next morning he paid the innkeeper and said, "Take care of this man, and if it costs more than this, I will pay you when I return." Then Jesus asked, "Which one of these three people do you think acted like a neighbor to the man who was attacked by the gang of robbers?" The expert answered, "The one who acted with compassion." Then Jesus said to him, "You go and do the same."

–NIV

For Further information about the work of Samaritans, visit www.samaritans.org.uk

NOVEMBER 13

DAILY READING

Therefore let us stop passing judgment on one another. Instead, make up your mind not to put any stumbling block or obstacle in your brother's way. (ROM 14:13)

FEAST DAYS

444	Brice	Patron of stomach diseases
945	Abbo	Abbot of Fleury, France
1197	Homobonus	Patron of business people

ENTRANCE AND EXIT

b. 354	Augustine of Hippo	Numidian theologian
b. 1312	Edward III	King of England
b. 1850	Robert Louis Stevenson	Scottish writer
d. 867	Nicholas I	Pope
d. 1868	Gioacchino Rossini	Italian composer
d. 1989	Francis Joseph II	Prince of Liechenstein

St. Brice's Day Massacre

On this day in 1002, an appalling example of ethnic cleansing took place when English King Aethelred Unraed II (or Aethelred the Ill Advised), ordered "to be slain all the Danish people who were in England." As it was the feast day of St. Brice, this event became known as the St. Brice's Day Massacre.

According to the historian, John of Wallingford, Aethelred ordered every man, woman, and child of the Danish race in England to be killed at the instigation of one of his advisors, a man called Huna or Eadric. This order was communicated to all the towns around the country, and women were buried up to their waists and attacked by ferocious mastiffs. Children were crushed against doorposts or under rocks, and men were cut down with swords and anything else that came to hand.

In Oxford, some of the Danes escaped to St. Frideswide's Church, where they sought sanctuary. Unfortunately, the townsfolk burnt the Danes inside the church.

John of Wallingford suggests that the Vikings had to be killed because, unlike the English, they combed their hair every day, bathed every Saturday, and regularly changed their clothes, thus making it easier for them to seduce the native women.

Aethelred also felt that Viking raiders were taking over his kingdom, and a massacre would enable him to restore his authority. According to tradition, the massacre took place on a Saturday, because the English were able to surprise the Danes in their baths.

Extract from Augustine's Confessions

Angels fell away, man's soul fell away, and thereby pointed the abyss in that dark depth, ready for the whole spiritual creation, hadst not Thou said from the beginning, Let there be light, and there had been light, and every obedient intelligence of Thy heavenly City had cleaved to Thee, and rested in Thy Spirit, Which is borne unchangeably over every thing changeable. Otherwise, had even the heaven of heavens been in itself a darksome deep; but now it is light in the Lord. For even in that miserable restlessness of the spirits, who fell away and discovered their own darkness, when bared of the clothing of Thy light, dost Thou sufficiently reveal how noble Thou madest the reasonable creature; to which nothing will suffice to yield a happy rest, less than Thee; and so not even herself. For Thou, O our God, shalt lighten our darkness: from Thee riseth our garment of light; and then shall our darkness be as the noon day. Give Thyself unto me, O my God, restore Thyself unto me: behold I love, and if it be too little, I would love more strongly. I cannot measure so as to know, how much love there yet lacketh to me, ere my life may run into Thy embracements, nor turn away, until it be hidden in the hidden place of Thy Presence.

This only I know, that woe is me except in Thee: not only without but within myself also; and all abundance, which is not my God, is emptiness to me.

NOVEMBER 14

DAILY READING

Who are you to judge someone else's servant? To his own master he stands or falls. And he will stand, for the Lord is able to make him stand. (ROM 14:4)

FEAST DAYS

485	Jucundus	Bishop of Bologna, Italy
1511	John Licci	Benedictine priest
1889	Maria Teresa of Jesus	Carmelite nun

ENTRANCE AND EXIT

b. 1650	William III	Prince of Orange
b. 1948	Charles Windsor	Prince of Wales
b. 1954	Condoleeza Rice	American politician
d. 1687	Nell Gywn	English mistress of Charles II
d. 1831	Georg Wilhelm Hegel	German philosopher
d. 1990	Malcolm Muggeridge	English writer

Elizabeth Jane Cochrane

On this day in 1889, pioneer investigative journalist Elizabeth Jane Cochrane (1864–1922) set off on a mission to travel the world in less than eighty days. Cochrane is better known by her pen name, "Nellie Bly," which she took from the Stephen Collins Foster song "Nelly Bly."

She was born in Apollo, Pennsylvania, and started her journalism career in Pittsburgh. She wrote a letter to the editor of *The Pittsburgh Dispatch* in response to a column called "Women's Sphere," and signed the letter "Lonely Orphan Girl." Impressed by her forthright style, editor George Madden published an announcement asking "Lonely Orphan Girl" to send her name and address to the office. Instead, she showed up in person and persuaded him to let her write for the paper. Not interested in writing pleasant social pieces, Nellie immediately tackled social issues in her columns on working women, reform of divorce laws, and factory conditions. After her first few columns, she was hired by the *Dispatch* as a staff member at $5 a week. She was assigned to "women's interest" stories on fashion, gardening, and culture. Frustrated, she quit her job, but was persuaded to return with an assignment to write from Mexico. She spent six months in Mexico, and sent back stories published under the headline "Nellie in Mexico."

She was inspired to fly round the world by Jules Verne's fictional character Phileas Fogg, who covered the globe in eighty days. She left from New York in 1889 and visited England, Italy, Japan, China, and Hong Kong on her 24,899-mile journey. She returned to New York seventy-two days, six hours, eleven minutes, and fourteen seconds later on January 25, 1890.

She was the first woman to travel around the world unaccompanied at all times by a man, and became a role model for women everywhere.

Nelly Bly

Nelly Bly! Nelly Bly! Bring the broom along,
We'll sweep the kitchen clean, my dear,
And have a little song.
Poke the wood, my lady love,
And make the fire burn,
And while I take the banjo down,
Just give the mush a turn.
Heigh, Nelly! Ho, Nelly!
Listen, love, to me,
I'll sing for you and play for you
A dulcet melody.

–Stephen Collins Foster (1826–64)

November 15

DAILY READING

"Sirs, what must I do to be saved?" They replied, "Believe in the Lord Jesus, and you will be saved–you and your household." Then they spoke the word of the Lord to him and to all the others in his house. At that hour of the night the jailer took them and washed their wounds; then immediately he and all his family were baptized. (ACTS 16:30–33)

FEAST DAYS

520	Malo	Bishop of Aleth, France
1136	Leopold III	Patron of Austria
1539	John Rugg	English martyr

ENTRANCE AND EXIT

b. 1708	William Pitt the Elder	1st Earl of Chatham
b. 1739	William Herschel	English astronomer
b. 1919	Veronica Lake	American actor
d. 1280	Albertus Magnus	German theologian
d. 1630	Johanes Kepler	German astronomer
d. 1958	Tyrone Power	American actor

William Cowper

Poet and hymn writer William Cowper (1731–1800) was born at his father's rectory in Berkhampstead. His mother died when he was six and it affected him profoundly. He wrote about her funeral in a poem written when he was sixty:

> I heard the bell tolled on thy burial day,
> I saw the hearse that bore thee slow away,
> And turning from my nursery window drew
> A long, long sigh and wept a last adieu!
> But was it such? It was. Where thou art gone
> Adieus and farewells are a sound unknown.

He was educated at Westminster and a promising career as a lawyer awaited him. But he had a nervous breakdown and attempted three times to commit suicide. However, Cowper came under the guidance of John Newton at Olney in Northamptonshire and found salvation on this day in 1761. Of this experience, he wrote:

> I found my heart at length so powerfully drawn towards the Lord, that having a retired and secret nook in the corner of a field, I kneeled down under a bank and poured forth my complaints before Him. It pleased my Saviour to hear me so that the oppression was taken off and I was enabled to trust in Him that careth for the stranger, to roll my burden upon Him and to rest assured that wheresoever He might cast my lot, the God of all consolation would still be with me. But this was not all. He did for me more than either I had asked or thought.

The next day, after church, Cowper returned to the place where his prayer had been answered. He wrote:

> I went immediately after church to the place where I had prayed the day before and found the relief I had there received was but the earnest of a richer blessing. How shall I express what the Lord did for me, except by saying that He made all His goodness to pass before me. I seemed to speak to Him face to face, as a man conversing with his friend, except that my speech was only in tears of joy and groanings which cannot be uttered. I could say indeed with Jacob not how dreadful, but how lovely is this place; this is none other than the House of God.

In 1781, he began writing poetry and published his great poem "The Task" the following year. He is also famous as a hymn writer, and his works include such favorites as "God Moves in a Mysterious Way," and "There Is a Fountain Filled with Blood."

NOVEMBER 16

DAILY READING

Be joyful always, pray continually; give thanks in all circumstances, for this is God's will for you in Christ Jesus. (1 THESS 5:16–18)

FEAST DAYS

759	Othmar	Benedictine abbot
1093	Margaret	Patron of Scotland
1302	Gertrude the Great	Patron of West Indies

ENTRANCE AND EXIT

b. 42 BC	Tiberius Claudius Nero	Roman Emperor
b. 1896	Sir Oswald Mosley	British Fascist Party leader
b. 1908	Burgess Meredith	American actor
d. 1960	Clark Gable	American actor
d. 1961	Samuel Rayburn	American politician
d. 1981	William Holden	American actor

Tiberius Claudius Nero

Roman Emperor Tiberius Claudius Nero began his military career as an officer under Julius Caesar, sought to honor his assassins, and then joined with Mark Antony's brother to overthrow Octavian. He was exiled, but returned to Rome under the general amnesty.

From 22 to 6 BC, Tiberius served as a tribune in the Spanish peninsula war. In 20 BC, Tiberius crowned Tigranes the Parthian King of Armenia, and he gave up the spoils and the standards of three Roman armies. The Roman senate ordered a thanksgiving to celebrate this victory.

For his victories in the Danube regions, Augustus conferred on him a triumphal entry, taking the form of an ovation, into the capital. Subsequent triumphs and promotions marked him out as the heir to the throne. However, as his star was rising, Tiberius suddenly begged permission to retire to Rhodes to study the works of Horace.

At Rhodes Tiberius lived simply, passing his time mainly in the company of Greek professors. He acquired considerable proficiency in the study of astrology, prose, and poetry.

Eventually, at the age of fifty-six Tiberius became emperor. What struck his subjects was his cold intellect, tenacity, sternness, silence, simplicity of life, and frugality. Pliny the Elder called him "the gloomiest of mankind," and he was prone to be superstitious.

When he died, he left the empire in a condition of unparalleled prosperity. Officials governed without favor, taxation was light, and security maintained by a strong armed presence at home and abroad. Tiberius ruled with a firm will, and this made many enemies and few friends.

Noteworthy

532 Francisco Pizarro captures Inca chieftain Atahualpa in Caxamalca, Peru.
1665 *London Gazette* (originally *The Oxford Gazette*) first published.
1750 Westminster Bridge opens for traffic in London.
1776 British forces capture Fort Washington, New York.
1824 Longest river in Australia–Murray River–discovered by Hamilton Hume.
1855 Missionary David Livingstone discovers, and names after his Queen, Victoria Falls.
1869 Formal opening of Suez Canal at Port Said.
1907 Oklahoma becomes forty-sixth state admitted to Union.
1918 Hungary proclaimed an independent republic.

NOVEMBER 17

DAILY READING

The LORD your God is with you, he is mighty to save.
He will take great delight in you, he will quiet you with his love,
he will rejoice over you with singing. (ZEPH 3:17)

FEAST DAYS

ca. 270	Gregory the Wonderworker	Bishop of Caesarea, Turkey
594	Gregory	Bishop of Tours, France
1220	Hugh of Lincoln	Patron of swans

ENTRANCE AND EXIT

b. 1790	August Ferdinand Mobius	German mathematician
b. 1937	Peter Cook	English actor
b. 1942	Martin Scorsese	American film director
d. 1093	Margaret	Queen of Scotland
d. 1588	Mary Tudor	Queen of England
d. 2002	Abba Eban	Israeli politician

Queen Elizabeth's Day

This day celebrated the accession to the English throne of Queen Elizabeth in 1558. She was also Queen of Ireland and Queen of France. She was the only surviving child of Anne Boleyn and King Henry VIII and reigned for forty-five years.

The Elizabethan Age included luminaries such as Shakespeare, Christopher Marlowe, Ben Johnson, Francis Bacon, Walter Raleigh, and Francis Drake. The State of Virginia is named after Queen Elizabeth.

She was a popular and pious ruler, and the common people welcomed her accession. There has been much speculation about why she never married: was she disfigured from smallpox; perhaps she could not marry Robert Dudley (First Earl of Leicester) because of his political connections; and perhaps she did not want to unite the English crown with other nations. Elizabeth was a strong character who saw her role as a divine calling, and therefore she resisted Parliament's attempts to force her to marry.

Queen Elizabeth's Day included processions throughout many towns and cities across England that became more and more anti-Catholic. Effigies of the pope were burned, Catholic rites and traditions were parodied, and religious riots led many Catholics to fear for their safety. Eventually, in 1698, these activities were banned with the accession of King George I to the throne.

Queen Elizabeth died in 1603. Her embalmed body was placed in a lead coffin in Westminster. It had been a long reign, and many of her subjects had not been ruled by anyone other than Elizabeth. She lay in state for over a month and was given a magnificent funeral at Westminster Abbey. A contemporary account records that "there was such a general sighing, groaning and weeping as the like hath not been seen or known in the memory of man, neither doth any history mention any people, time or state to make like lamentation for the death of their sovereign."

Extract from the speech of Queen Elizabeth I at Tilbury, 1588, on the eve of the war with Spain

My loving people,

I am come amongst you, as you see, at this time, not for my recreation and disport, but being resolved, in the midst and heat of the battle, to live and die amongst you all; to lay down for my God, and for my kingdom, and my people, my honour and my blood, even in the dust. I know I have the body but of a weak and feeble woman; but I have the heart and stomach of a king, and of a king of England too, and think foul scorn that Parma or Spain, or any prince of Europe, should dare to invade the borders of my realm; to which rather than any dishonour shall grow by me, I myself will take up arms, I myself will be your general, judge, and rewarder of every one of your virtues in the field.

NOVEMBER 18

DAILY READING

But grow in the grace and knowledge of our Lord and Savior Jesus Christ. To him be glory both now and forever! Amen. (2 PET 3:18)

FEAST DAYS

690	Mummolus	Abbot of Lagny, France
777	Constant	Hermit of Lough Erne, Ireland
942	Odo	Abbot of Cluny, France

ENTRANCE AND EXIT

b. 1787	Louis Jacques Daguerre	French inventor
b. 1923	Alan Shepherd	American astronaut
b. 1968	Owen Wilson	American actor
d. 1886	Chester Alan Arthur	21st American president
d. 1962	Niels Bohr	Danish scientist
d. 1965	Henry Agard Wallace	24th American vice president

Odo of Cluny

St. Odo was the second abbot of Cluny, born 879, probably near Le Mans. From his childhood the saint was much given to prayer, and piety made him regret the time that he threw away in hunting and other amusements and exercises of a court life.

He was in the households of the Count of Anjou and Duke William of Aquitaine and became a student of Remigius at St. Martin's in Tours.

Odo became a monk in 909 and was named director of the Baume Monastery school by Berno, who became abbot of the newly founded Cluny, in 910. In 924, Odo was named abbot of Baume. He reformed the monasteries in Aquitaine, northern France, and Italy.

Pope Leo VII called Odo to Rome in 936 to arrange peace between Alberic of Rome and Hugh of Provence. He succeeded temporarily by negotiating a marriage between Alberic and Hugh's daughter. He visited Italy several times, founding in Rome the monastery of Our Lady on the Aventine, and reforming several convents, such as Subiaco and Monte Cassino.

In addition to being entrusted with important political missions, Odo wrote epic poems, three books of moral essays, a biography of St. Gerald of Aurillace, and twelve choral antiphons in honor of St. Martin.

He died at Tours on the way back to Rome on this day in 942. He was buried in the church of St. Julian, but it is thought that the Huguenots burnt the greatest part of his remains.

Noteworthy

1626 St. Peter's Church in Rome consecrated.
1883 Standard time introduced in the United States; four time zones established: eastern, central, mountain, and pacific.
1918 Latvian Independence Day.
1978 Mass suicide of 913 cult members of Jim Jones's People Temple.
1991 British Hostage Terry Waite released by Islamic Jihad for the Liberation of Palestine.
2001 Lennox Lewis regains world heavyweight title by knocking out Hasim Rahman.

NOVEMBER 19

DAILY READING

Let us therefore make every effort to do what leads to peace and to mutual edification. (ROM 14:19)

FEAST DAYS

373	Nerses the Great	Father of St. Isaac the Great
694	Ebbe of Minster in Thanet	Wife of King Merewalh of Magonset
885	James of Sasseau	Benedictine soldier

ENTRANCE AND EXIT

b. 1831	James Garfield	20th American president
b. 1885	Haldor Lillenas	American hymn writer
b. 1962	Jodie Foster	American actor
d. 1828	Franz Schubert	Austrian composer
d. 1976	Sir Basil Unwin Spence	Scottish architect
d. 1988	Christina Onassis	American heiress

Haldor Lillenas

The hymn writer Haldor Lillenas (1855–1959) was born on Stord Island, near Bergen, Norway. He grew up in the Lutheran Church and came to America. His parents brought him to the United States as a child, and he was confirmed at the age of fifteen.

Haldor Lillenas wrote the words and music to well-known hymns such as "Wonderful Grace of Jesus" and "The Bible Stands." He also wrote music to others' words, including the hymn "It Is Glory Just to Walk with Him."

He trained at Deets Pacific Bible College in Los Angeles and became a pastor in the Church of the Nazarene. He received his musical training through personal study and correspondence courses. Haldor married Bertha Mae Wilson, who was also a song writer, and they traveled as evangelists for many years.

In 1925, while pastor of the First Church of the Nazarene in Indianapolis he founded the Lillenas Publishing Company, which was later purchased by the Nazarene Publishing House, and became its music division. Over his lifetime, Lillenas wrote more than four thousand hymn texts and tunes, many of which are still in use today.

"Wonderful Grace of Jesus" combines doctrinal truth with a buoyant melody and serves as a good vehicle for teaching the doctrine of grace. It touches on the availability, sufficiency, and efficacy of the salvation offered by grace through faith in Christ, and so carries an appropriate message for believer and unbeliever alike.

"Wonderful Grace of Jesus"

Wonderful grace of Jesus, greater than all my sin;
How shall my tongue describe it, where shall its praise begin?
Taking away my burden, setting my spirit free,
For the wonderful grace of Jesus reaches me!

Wonderful grace of Jesus, reaching to all the lost,
By it I have been pardoned, saved to the uttermost;
Chains have been torn asunder, giving me liberty,
For the wonderful grace of Jesus reaches me!

Wonderful grace of Jesus, reaching the most defiled,
By its transforming power, making him God's dear child.
Purchasing peace and heaven for all eternity;
And the wonderful grace of Jesus reaches me!

REFRAIN: Wonderful the matchless grace of Jesus,
Deeper than the mighty rolling sea;
Higher than the mountain, sparkling like a fountain,
All-sufficient grace for even me;
Broader than the scope of my transgressions,
Greater far than all my sin and shame;
O magnify the precious name of Jesus, praise His name!

–Haldor Lillenas

NOVEMBER 20

DAILY READING

When anxiety was great within me, your consolation brought joy to my soul. (PS 94:19)

FEAST DAYS

870	Edmund	King of East Anglia, England
1212	Felix of Valois	Cofounder of the Trinitarians
1922	Maria Fortunata Viti	Patron against poverty

ENTRANCE AND EXIT

b. 1889	Edwin Hubble	American astronomer
b. 1925	Robert Francis Kennedy	American senator
b. 1929	Kenneth DeWitt Schermerhorn	American conductor
d. 967	Abu al-Faraj al-Isbahani	Iraqi writer
d. 1806	Isaac Backus	American Baptist leader
d. 1975	Francisco Franco	Spanish dictator

Isaac Backus

> All my past life was opened plainly before me, and I saw clearly that it had been filled up with sin. I went and sat down in the shade of a tree, where my prayers and tears, my hearing of the Word of God and striving for a better heart, with all my other doings, were set before me in such a light that I perceived I would never make myself better, should I live ever so long. Divine justice appeared clear in my condemnation, and I saw that God had a right to do with me as He would. My soul yielded all into His hands, fell at His feet, and was silent and calm before Him. . . . The Word of God and the promises of His grace appeared firmer than a rock, and I was astonished at my previous unbelief. My heavy burden was gone, tormenting fears were fled, and my joy was unspeakable.

Thus wrote Isaac Backus (1724–1806) about his conversion experience. Backus became an influential figure in the Baptist movement, arguing for religious liberty and separation between the church and state. Backus's thoughts and beliefs can be seen echoed in much of the Constitution and Bill of Rights. Backus was a spiritual child of the Great Awakening, and his conversion is directly linked to the work of Jonathan Edwards and George Whitefield.

Backus fought against the desire by some Baptist churches to be incorporated by the state. This desire for civil recognition derived from the early American policy of taxing citizens to provide salaries for ministers. Backus was totally opposed to this practice. Incorporation gave the state authority over the church, and this was unacceptable.

Backus offered a Bill of Rights for consideration to friends at the time of the writing of the American Constitution. His second right read:

> As God is the only worthy object of all religious worship, and nothing can be true religion but a voluntary obedience unto His revealed will . . . every person has an unalienable right to act in all religious affairs according to the full persuasion of his own mind, where others are not injured thereby.

Much of his latter life was given to writing against the inroads of Arminianism, which ultimately led to Universalism.

Backus also helped found the United States' first Baptist school of higher learning, Rhode Island College, subsequently known as Brown University.

Noteworthy

1272 Edward I proclaimed King of England.
1759 British navy defeats French at Battle of Quiberon Bay.
1776 British forces take Fort Lee (Revolutionary War).
1818 Simón Bolívar declares Venezuela independent of Spain.
1866 Pierre Lallemont of Paris patents bicycle with rotary crank.
1906 Rolls Royce motor company formed by Charles Stewart Rolls and Frederick Henry Royce.
1920 America's first municipal airport inaugurated in Tucson, Arizona.
1992 Fire breaks out at Windsor Castle, causing enormous damage.

November 21

DAILY READING

Whatever town or village you enter, search for some worthy person there and stay at his house until you leave. As you enter the home, give it your greeting. (MATT 10:11–12)

FEAST DAYS

496	Gelasius I	Pope
1045	Hilary	Benedictine monk
1166	Albert of Louvain	Bishop of Liege, Belgium

ENTRANCE AND EXIT

b. 1694	François-Marie Arouet de Voltaire	French writer
b. 1702	Philip Doddridge	English hymn writer
b. 1863	Sir Arthur Quiller Couch	English writer
d. 1624	Jakob Bohme	German writer
d. 1899	Garret Hobart	24th American vice president
d. 1916	Franz Josef I	Austrian emperor

World Hello Day

Today is "World Hello Day," a wonderful opportunity for people throughout the world to learn about different cultures by simply saying "hello!"

World Hello Day began in 1973 in response to the war between Israel and Egypt. Its goal is to promote peace through increased communication, simply by asking people all over the world to say "hello" to at least ten people!

Since then, World Hello Day has been observed by people in over 180 countries.

People around the world use the occasion of World Hello Day as an opportunity to express their concern for world peace. Beginning with a simple greeting on World Hello Day, their activities send a message to leaders, encouraging them to use communication rather than force to settle conflicts.

Here are some versions of hello in other languages:

Nation	Greeting	Pronounciation
Bulgarian	Zdraveite	ZZ-DRA-veyt
Cantonese	Nei Hou	Nay Hoe
Czech	Dobry den	DO-bry den
Danish	Goddag	Go dah
Estonian	Tere	TER-e
Finnish	Terve	TER-vey
French	Bonjour	Bohn-ZHOOR
German	Guten Tag	GOOT-en Tahk
Greek	Kalimera	Kah-lee-MEH-rah
Hawaiian	Aloha	Ah-LOH-hah
Hebrew	Shalom	Sha-LOHM
Hindi	Namaste	Nah-mah-STAY
Italian	Buon giorno	Bwohn JOR-noh
Japanese	Konnichiwa	Kon-NEE-chee wah
Mayan	Ba'ax ka wa'alik	BAH-ah shko-WAH al-LEEK
Mohawk	Sekoh	SHE-goh
Navajo	Ya at eeh	YAH-AHT-AY
Norwegian	God dag	Goo-dagh
Persian	Selam	She-lam
Polish	Czesc	Chesht
Portuguese	Oi	Oy
Romanian	Buna ziua	BOO-nuh ZEE-wa
Russian	Zdraustvuite	ZzDRAST-voyt-yah
Serbian	Zdravo	ZDRAH-vo
Slovak	Dobry den	Dobree den
Spanish	Hola	OH-la
Swedish	God dag	Goo dag

Noteworthy

1620 Pilgrims in *Mayflower* first land at Cape Cod.
1789 North Carolina twelfth state admitted to Union.
1918 Surrender of German battle fleet to Allies.
1934 Cole Porter's *Anything Goes* opens at Alvin Theatre, New York.
1962 End of Cuban missile crisis.
1974 IRA bombs in Birmingham, England, killing nineteen.

NOVEMBER 22

DAILY READING

Having therefore these promises, dearly beloved, let us cleanse ourselves from all filthiness of the flesh and spirit, perfecting holiness in the fear of God. (2 COR 7:1, KJV)

FEAST DAYS

ca. 1st cent.	Philemon	Christian convert
ca. 117	Cecilia	Patron of music and musicians
1895	Dimbalac Oghlou Wartavar	Armenian martyr

ENTRANCE AND EXIT

b. 1890	Charles de Gaulle	French president
b. 1819	Mary Ann Evans (George Eliot)	English writer
b. 1913	Benjamin Britten	English composer
d. 1963	John Fitzgerald Kennedy	35th American president
d. 1963	Clive Staples Lewis	English writer
d. 1963	Aldous Huxley	English writer

The Patron Saint of Music

The story of St. Cecilia, like that of many of the saints venerated throughout history, is a romantic one. According to church history, Cecilia was a maiden of noble birth, and at early age, she dedicated her life to God with a vow of chastity. Against her will, she was later betrothed to a young noble named Valerian. However, on her wedding day, as instruments were playing, she was singing in her heart to God, saying, "Make my heart and my body pure that I may not be confounded." It is thought this led to the eventual naming of Cecilia as the patron of music. In the original Latin, the term for musical instruments is *cantantibus organis*, and in later texts it was translated that she was playing an organ instead of listening to music as she prayed. Valerian was willing to take her as his wife without forcing her to break her vow. Not only did he accept her vow of chastity, he and his brother Tiburtius were both converted to Christianity and were baptized by Pope Urban I.

However, all three were soon discovered as Christians and were martyred in Rome. Cecilia's martyrdom required two attempts. First she was condemned to be suffocated in the Roman baths. She was shut in for a night and a day, and the fires were heaped up and made to glow and roar their utmost, but Cecilia did not even break out into perspration through the heat. Next, she was ordered beheaded. A soldier struck at her neck three times, and she was left dying on the floor. She lingered for three days, during which time the Christians thronged to her side, and she formally made over her house in Trastevere, Rome, to Pope Urban I.

Until the Middle Ages, Pope St. Gregory had been the patron of music and musicians, but when the Roman Academy of Music was established in 1584, it was put under the protection of St. Cecilia; thus, her patronage of music originated.

In 1687, the poet John Dryden wrote a "Song for Saint Cecilia Day," and in 1739 George Handel composed an "Ode for Saint Cecilia's Day."

St. Cecilia, virgin and martyr, was held in high honor by Christians in the West. Her legend was the basis for the "Second Nun's Tal" in Chaucer's *Canterbury Tales*.

NOVEMBER 23

DAILY READING

Love the LORD, all his saints! The LORD preserves the faithful, but the proud he pays back in full. Be strong and take heart, all you who hope in the LORD. (PS 31:23–24)

FEAST DAYS

101	Clemens Romanus	Pope
ca. 7th cent.	Trudo	Apostle of Hasbein, Belgium
1927	Miguel Augustin Pro	Mexican martyr

ENTRANCE AND EXIT

b. 912	Otto I	Holy Roman Emperor
b. 1804	Franklin Pierce	14th American president
b. 1888	Adolph Arthur "Harpo" Marx	American actor
d. 1585	Thomas Tallis	English composer
d. 1910	Dr. Hawley Crippen	American murderer
d. 1979	Merle Oberon	American actor

Blaise Pascal

On this day in 1654, the French mathematician, physicist, theologian, inventor, and writer Blaise Pascal (1623–62) had a brush with death that led to an intense religious conviction. He was in an accident where the horses carrying his coach plunged over a bridge. In desperation he clung onto the coach, fainted, and remained in a coma for some days. About two weeks later, he saw a vision that he recorded as: "Fire. God of Abraham, God of Isaac, God of Jacob, not of the philosophers and the scholars." The words of Psalm 119:16: "I delight in your decrees; I will not neglect your word," were given him, and he found great assurance in them.

Although Pascal struggled to understand his faith, his spirit and mind convinced him that there was a God and He desired all people be saved. Pascal sought to answer the big question of why we are here in his famous work, *Pensees*.

Pascal suffered much ill health, but possessed a precocious intellect. At just sixteen, he wrote papers on mathematics and went on to work with Pierre de Fermat on the calculus of probabilities. He invented the calculating machine, the barometer, the hydraulic press, and the syringe.

In 1646 Pascal joined the Catholic Jansenist movement, which enjoyed the support of the king, Louis XIV. Pascal examined the problems of human existence from both psychological and theological points of view. He wrote, "The heart has its reasons which reason knows nothing of." Against the immensity of the universe, he measured the fate of human beings—"Man is but a reed, the weakest thing in nature; but he is a thinking reed."

In his famous "Pascal's wager," he argued that it was rational to believe in God. If this turns out to be true, then an eternity of bliss is the reward, but even if belief in God was false, then nothing was lost since belief provided a firm foundation for a contented life.

Films Featuring All Four Marx Brothers

1926 *Humor Risk*—never released
1929 *The Cocoanuts*
1930 *Animal Crackers*
1931 *The House That Shadows Built*
1931 *Monkey Business*
1932 *Horse Feathers*
1933 *Duck Soup*

NOVEMBER 24

DAILY READING

If the LORD *delights in a man's way, he makes his steps firm; though he stumble, he will not fall, for the* LORD *upholds him with his hand.* (PS 37:23–24)

FEAST DAYS

489	Kenan	Bishop of Duleek, Ireland
ca. 700	Eanfleda of Whitby	Daughter of King Edwin
1839	Joachim Ho	Chinese martyr

ENTRANCE AND EXIT

b. 1505	John Knox	Scottish theologian
b. 1632	Barouch Spinoza	Dutch philosopher
b. 1784	Zachary Taylor	12th American president
d. 1963	Lee Harvey Oswald	Assassin of President Kennedy
d. 1980	George Raft	American actor
d. 1991	Freddie Mercury	English rock star

The Hollywood Ten

On this day in 1947, the American Congress' House of Un-American Activities Committee (HUAC) cited for contempt ten members of the entertainment industry who refused to testify about people suspected of being Communist sympathizers. The ten were thought to have had links with the American Communist Party, and the Motion Picture Association of America fired them. According to the association, this action was taken so that the entertainment industry would not "knowingly employ a Communist or a member of any party or group which advocates the overthrow of the government of the United States by force or by any illegal or unconstitutional methods."

The Hollywood ten were:

- Lester Cole, famous screenwriter of well-known films such as *Born Free* (1966), *The Invisible Man Returns* (1940), and *Charlie Chan's Greatest Case* (1933). He avoided the blacklist by using an assumed identity.
- Ringgold Wilmer Lardner Jr., screenwriter who spent a year in prison and wasn't able to work until the 1960s. In 1970, he wrote the screenplay for *M*A*S*H.*
- Albert Maltz, screenwriter who contributed to the Clint Eastwood epic, *Two Mules for Sister Sara.*
- Edward Dmytryk, film editor of movies such as *Bulldog Drummond's Peril* (1938). He moved to Europe, but returned to America in 1951 and directed four films for Stanley Kramer.
- Samuel Ornitz, screenwriter who was imprisoned for a year, during which time he wrote the novel *Bride of the Sabbath.*
- Herbert Biberman, actor, director, and screenwriter. He worked in Mexico and throughout Europe.
- Dalton Trumbo, screenwriter who served ten months in prison and moved to Mexico.
- John Howard Lawson, screenwriter and playwright who spent a year in prison.
- Adrian Scott, producer and screenwriter who never worked again.
- Alvah Bessie, screenwriter who never worked in Hollywood again. Just two years earlier he had been nominated for an Oscar for Best Original Story for the film *Objective Burma* (1945).

Quotes of the Day

"Peace is not an absence of war, it is a virtue, a state of mind, a disposition for benevolence, confidence, justice."

–Baruch Spinoza

"A man with God is always in the majority."

–John Knox

NOVEMBER 25

DAILY READING

The LORD is my light and my salvation—whom shall I fear?
The LORD is the stronghold of my life—of whom shall I be afraid? (PS 27:1)

FEAST DAYS

ca. 251	Moses of Rome	Jewish martyr
1420	Elizabeth the Good	Stigmatic
1965	Maria Corsini	Red Cross nurse

ENTRANCE AND EXIT

b. 1844	Karl Friedrich Benz	German engineer
b. 1900	Helen Gahagan Douglas	American politician
b. 1914	Joe Di Maggio	American baseball star
d. 1748	Isaac Watts	English hymn writer
d. 1974	Pantanaw U Thant	Burmese diplomat
d. 1993	Anthony Burgess	English writer

Carrie Nation

The militant crusader and driving force behind Prohibition in America, Carrie Nation was born on this day in Kentucky in 1846. Although she was born Carrie Moore, she used the name Carry A. Nation to signify her calling to free America from the temptations of liquor.

During her childhood, she was often ill and her family moved around the country several times, before settling in Belton, Missouri. Her mother was delusional and declared that she was Queen Victoria on numerous occasions. During these bouts of insanity, Carrie was taken care of by the family's slaves.

She was the jail evangelist of the Women's Christian Temperance Union and challenged many drunks in the county jail at Kiowa, Kansas. She found out which bars supplied most of the liquor for the prisoners. She claimed that she heard a voice telling her to go to Kiowa and smash the saloons. In 1900, she attacked three "joints" in Kiowa, using stones, brickbats, full malt bottles, and one billiard ball as ammunition. Carry's attack surprised local officials, but because of the fact that the operation of such "joints" was illegal, she was not jailed as she would be later in other communities. The Kiowa attack quickly received national attention and instigated great debate even among the temperance organizations.

Carrie then undertook a series of national crusades to smash saloons and became famous for using a hatchet to carry out her work. At one point, she described herself as "a bulldog running along at the feet of Jesus, barking at what he doesn't like."

Despite her unpopularity with people that frequented saloons, she gained a large amount of recognition from Christians and prohibitionists. As a result, she was able to pay for all of her fines by giving paid lectures and selling souvenir hatchets to fans. Later, an opera was made based on her life story.

After being hospitalized for some time, she died in Leavenworth, Kansas, on June 9, 1911.

Noteworthy

1783 British troops evacuate New York.
1865 Lewis Carroll's *Alice in Wonderland* published.
1882 Gilbert and Sullivan's *Iolanthe* first performed.
1952 *The Mousetrap* opens in London.
1963 Funeral of President John F. Kennedy.
1965 Joseph Mobutu assumes presidency of the Congo.
1975 Surinam Independence Day.

NOVEMBER 26

DAILY READING

"No weapon forged against you will prevail, and you will refute every tongue that accuses you. This is the heritage of the servants of the LORD, and this is their vindication from me," declares the LORD. (ISA 54:17)

FEAST DAYS

ca. 311	Peter	Bishop of Alexandria, Egypt
975	Conrad	Patron of Constance, Switzerland
1585	Hugh Taylor	English martyr

ENTRANCE AND EXIT

b. 1731	William Cowper	English hymn writer and poet
b. 1922	Charles Schulz	American illustrator
b. 1938	Tina Turner	American singer
d. 1876	Karl Ernst von Baer	German scientist
d. 1939	James Naismith	American inventor of basketball
d. 1956	Tommy Dorsey	American bandleader

Thanksgiving Day

The American Thanksgiving holiday takes place on the fourth Thursday in November. The tradition goes back to 1621 when the Puritan pilgrim settlers in Plymouth, Massachusetts, set aside a day of thanks for a bountiful harvest.

On June 20, 1676, the governing council of Charlestown, Massachusetts, held a meeting to determine how best to express thanks for the good fortune that had seen their community securely established. By unanimous vote they chose June 29 as a day of thanksgiving. This thanksgiving celebration probably did not include the Indians, as the celebration was meant partly to be in recognition of the colonists' recent victory over the "heathen natives."

October of 1777 marked the first time that all thirteen colonies joined in a thanksgiving celebration.

On October 3, 1789, Thanksgiving Day was proclaimed as the first official holiday by a president. This is part of the text of George Washington's proclamation:

Whereas it is the duty of all Nations to acknowledge the providence of Almighty God, to obey his will, to be grateful for his benefits, and humbly to implore his protection and favor, and Whereas both Houses of Congress have by their joint Committee requested me "to recommend to the People of the United States a day of public thanks-giving and prayer to be observed by acknowledging with grateful hearts the many signal favors of Almighty God, especially by affording them an opportunity peaceably to establish a form of government for their safety and happiness." Now therefore I do recommend and assign Thursday the 26th day of November next to be devoted by the People of these States to the service of that great and glorious Being, who is the beneficent Author of all the good that was, that is, or that will be.

I Will Praise the Lord at All Times

Winter has a joy for me,
While the Saviour's charms I read,
Lowly, meek, from blemish free,
In the snowdrop's pensive head.

Spring returns, and brings along
Life-invigorating suns:
Hark! the turtle's plaintive song
Seems to speak His dying groans!

Summer has a thousand charms,
All expressive of His worth;
'Tis His sun that lights and warms,
His the air the cools the earth.

What! has autumn left to say
Nothing of a Saviour's grace?
Yes, the beams of milder day
Tell me of his smiling face.

Light appears with early dawn,
While the sun makes haste to rise;
See His bleeding beauties drawn
On the blushes of the skies.

Evening with a silent pace,
Slowly moving in the west,
Shews an emblem of His grace,
Points to an eternal rest.

—William Cowper

NOVEMBER 27

DAILY READING

Whatever happens, conduct yourselves in a manner worthy of the gospel of Christ. Then, whether I come and see you or only hear about you in my absence, I will know that you stand firm in one spirit, contending as one man for the faith of the gospel without being frightened in any way by those who oppose you. This is a sign to them that they will be destroyed, but that you will be saved–and that by God. (PHIL 1:27–28)

FEAST DAYS

ca. 730	Fergus	Patron of Wick, Scotland
1619	John Ivanango	Japanese martyr
1619	John Montajana	Japanese martyr

ENTRANCE AND EXIT

b. 1701	Anders Celsius	Swedish astronomer
b. 1862	Adelaide Pollard	American hymn writer
b. 1942	Jimi Hendrix	American rock star
d. 8 BC	Quintus Horatius Flaccus Horace	Italian writer
d. 1953	Eugene O'Neill	Irish playwright
d. 1988	John Carradine	American actor

Adelaide Addison Pollard

Adelaide Addison Pollard (1862–1934), writer of the popular hymn, "Have Thine Own Way, Lord!" was born Sarah Pollard in Bloomfield, Iowa. She adopted the name Adelaide because she disliked her given name.

She had a strong faith from her early years, and in the 1880s she worked as an itinerant Bible teacher around Chicago as part of the ministry of evangelist Alexander Dowie. She became convinced that God wanted her to serve in Africa and spent several years at the Missionary Training School at Nyack-on-the-Hudson. However, these plans failed because of lack of money, and Adelaide felt depressed and useless to God.

One night in 1902, she attended a prayer meeting and was moved by the prayer of an old lady, "Lord, it doesn't matter what you bring into our lives–just have your way with us." She went home and meditated on this and the text from Jeremiah 18 that refers to God as the potter and people as his vessels, molded by Him for His glory. She was greatly uplifted and wrote the four stanzas of the hymn that night.

Adelaide Pollard wrote at least another hundred other hymns and eventually served in Africa for a short time. She spent most of World War I in Scotland and then returned to New England, where she continued to serve many people as a faithful minister of Christ.

"Have Thine Own Way, Lord!" is still a popular consecration hymn, and Adelaide's experience is a reminder of God's sovereignity.

"Have Thine Own Way, Lord!"

Have Thine own way, Lord!
Have Thine own way!
Thou art the potter; I am the clay.
Mold me and make me after Thy will,
While I am waiting, yielded and still.

Noteworthy

1095 Pope Urban begins to preach the First Crusade at Clermont.
1582 William Shakespeare marries Anne Hathaway.
1676 First major fire in America occurs in Boston.
1885 First photo taken of a meteor shower.
1895 Arms dealer Alfred Nobel establishes his Nobel Prize.
1942 French fleet at Toulon scuttles cruisers, destroyers, and submarines to prevent them from falling into Nazi hands.
1989 First successful living donor liver transplant at the University of Chicago.
2005 First ever face transplant operation in Amiens in northern France takes four hours.

NOVEMBER 28

DAILY READING

Her children arise and call her blessed; her husband also, and he praises her: "Many women do noble things, but you surpass them all." (PROV 31:28–29)

FEAST DAYS

714	Stephen the Younger	Patron of coin collectors
ca. 1000	Simon the Logothete	Secretary to Emperor Constantine VII
1582	James Thompson	English martyr

ENTRANCE AND EXIT

b. 1688	John Bunyan	English writer
b. 1757	William Blake	English poet
b. 1820	Freidrich Engels	German philosopher
d. 1694	Matsuo Basho	Japanese poet
d. 1952	Enrico Fermi	Italian scientist
d. 1960	Richard Wright	American writer

Stir Up Sunday

The last Sunday before the season of Advent is traditionally known as Stir Up Sunday. This is the last Sunday of the Anglican year, and the phrase "Stir Up Sunday" comes from the words of the 1549 Book of Common Prayer for this day: "We beseech thee, O Lord, the wills of thy faithful people; that they, plenteously bringing forth the fruits of good works, may of thee be plenteously rewarded; through Jesus Christ, Amen."

Spiritually, this is a day to revive flagging spirits by reminding ourselves of God's promises and calling upon our lives.

Traditionally, this is the day for "stirring up" and making Christmas pudding, when everyone in the family takes a turn to stir up the Christmas plum pudding.

Tradition dictates that the Christmas pudding is stirred from the east to the west in honor of the Wise Men who came from the east in the Christmas story. The Christmas pudding should have thirteen ingredients to symbolize Christ and his disciples, and coins, rings, or thimbles can be included to signify wealth, marriage, and good luck.

The British love affair with Christmas pudding is hard to overestimate. In 2005, the world's oldest and largest manufacturer of Christmas puddings, Matthew Walker, sold forty million puddings, and Queen Elizabeth II spent ten thousand pounds on Christmas puddings for her household staff.

Traditional Christmas Pudding Recipe

4 oz. shredded suet
2 oz. self-rising flour, sifted
4 oz. white bread crumbs
1 tsp. mixed spice
1/4 tsp. freshly grated nutmeg
A large pinch of cinnamon
8 oz. dark brown sugar
4 oz. sultanas
4 oz. raisins
10 oz. currants
1 oz. mixed candied peel, finely chopped
1 oz. blanched almonds, chopped
1 small cooking apple, peeled, cored, and finely chopped
Grated zest of 1/2 a large orange
Grated zest of 1/2 a large lemon
2 1/2 oz. barley wine
2 1/2 oz. stout
2 large eggs
2 Tbsp. rum

Mix the suet, sifted flour, bread crumbs, spices, and sugar. Gradually mix in all the dried fruit, mixed peel, and nuts, followed by the apple and the grated zests.

In a small basin, measure out the barley wine, rum, stout, and eggs. Beat thoroughly together. Next, pour this over all the other ingredients and mix all together very thoroughly. Cover the bowl and set aside overnight.

The next day, pack the mixture in the lightly greased basin, cover with a double sheet of greaseproof paper (waxed paper) and a sheet of foil. Tie securely with string.

Place the pudding in a steamer set over a saucepan of simmering water and steam for eight hours. Remove greaseproof paper and foil and replace with fresh ones. Keep the pudding in a cool place away from light until required. Before serving, the pudding will be required to be resteamed for about an hour.

NOVEMBER 29

DAILY READING

For it has been granted to you on behalf of Christ not only to believe on him, but also to suffer for him. (PHIL 1:29)

FEAST DAYS

573	Brendan of Birr	Apostle of Ireland
917	Radbod	Benedictine monk
ca. 1250	Julitta of Heiligenthal	Benedictine nun

ENTRANCE AND EXIT

b. 1799	Louisa May Alcott	American writer
b. 1898	Clive Staples Lewis	English writer
b. 1932	Jacques Chirac	French president
d. 1530	Thomas Wolsey	English cardinal
d. 1924	Giacomo Puccini	Italian composer
d. 2001	George Harrison	English rock star

Lemuel Haynes

On this day in 1780, Vermont clergyman Rev. Lemuel Haynes (1753–1833) became the first African American licensed to preach. Haynes had an inauspicious beginning. He was the illegitimate son of an African father and a middle-class white woman, born in Hartford, Connecticut. Abandoned by his family, he was indentured (a limited and temporary form of slavery) to a white family in Massachusetts from the age of five months to twenty-one years.

After obtaining his freedom in 1774, he enlisted in the local militia and took part in the attack on Fort Ticonderoga under Ethan Allen. At the end of the Revolutionary War, Haynes studied independently for the ministry. After obtaining his license to preach, he became the first African American pastor of a white congregation in 1785 when he was ordained by the Congregational Church.

In a forty-year career, Haynes served in an integrated church in Rutland, Vermont, and in 1804 was the first African American to be awarded an honorary degree from Middlebury College in 1804. He became famous for his preaching despite enduring racism from a few white-only congregations. During his leadership of the church in Rutland, the congregation grew from under fifty people to over three hundred. Haynes also emerged as a defender of Christian orthodoxy, opposing the encroachment of Arminianism, Universalism, and other errors.

Haynes seven-year–successful–fight for the freedom of two wrongly convicted murderers in Vermont resulted in a best-selling book in 1820 entitled *Mystery Developed.*

Haynes was passionate about manifesting Christ-like character to his congregation. He identified five key traits for a Christian minister: to love Christ, to be wise, to be patient, to be courageous, and to be alert.

C. S. Lewis Quotes

"If God is satisfied with the work, the work may be satisfied with itself."

–*The Weight of Glory*

"The Moral Law tells us the tune we have to play: our instincts are merely the keys."

–*Mere Christianity*

"The surest way of spoiling a pleasure is to start examining your satisfaction."

–*Surprised by Joy*

"The claim to equality, outside the strictly political field, is made only by those who feel themselves to be in some way inferior."

–*The Screwtape Letters*

"'You would not have called to me unless I had been calling to you,' said the Lion."

–*The Silver Chair*

NOVEMBER 30

DAILY READING

Charm is deceptive, and beauty is fleeting; but a woman who fears the LORD is to be praised. (PROV 31:30)

FEAST DAYS

ca. 60	Andrew the Apostle	Patron of Scotland
1835	Joseph Marchand	Vietnam martyr
1941	Ludwig Gietyngier	Holocaust martyr

ENTRANCE AND EXIT

b. 1667	Jonathan Swift	Irish writer
b. 1835	Samuel Clemens (Mark Twain)	American writer
b. 1874	Winston Churchill	English prime minister
d. 1016	Edmund II	King of England
d. 1900	Oscar Wilde	Irish writer
d. 1977	Sir Terence Rattigan	English playwright

Andrew the Apostle

The Apostle Andrew was the first to be called by Jesus, and so his feast is the first to be celebrated at the beginning of the new church year. He is associated particularly with Scotland because tradition records that his relics were taken to Scotland by a missionary called Rule or Regulus. This monk brought Andrew's tooth, arm bone, kneecap, and some fingers, but he was shipwrecked on the coast of Fife at Kilryment, now St. Andrews, at some point in the eighth century.

In the Bible, Andrew is mentioned in all four Gospels and in the Acts of the Apostles. He was the son of Jonah or John, born in Bethsaida of Galilee, and the brother of Simon Peter. Both were fishermen and lived in the same house at Capernaum. From the Gospel of John 1:35–40, we learn that Andrew was a disciple of John the Baptist, whose testimony led him to follow Jesus. Andrew was first to recognize Jesus as the Messiah, and hastened to introduce his brother Peter to Him. Thereafter, the two brothers were disciples of Christ and gave up all things to follow Him. Andrew was chosen as one of the twelve disciples. Where he is mentioned in the Gospels, he is mostly listed with Peter, James, and John as being one of the four main disciples. It was Andrew, before the miraculous feeding of the five thousand, who found the boy with the five loaves and two fishes.

Andrew was close to Jesus during his public life, and was present at the Last Supper, saw the risen Lord, witnessed the Ascension, shared in the gifts of Pentecost, and helped establish the Christian faith thereafter.

Traditionally, he is said to have preached in Greece. He was put to death in Patrae, in Achaia, Greece. He was crucified, on the orders of the Roman Governor Aegeas, on a Saltire cross. He was bound, not nailed, in order to prolong his suffering. His martyrdom took place during the reign of Nero, on November 30, AD 60.

"St. Andrew the King, three weeks and three days before Christmas comes in."

–English traditional proverb

Noteworthy

1782 Britain signs Treaty of Paris, recognizing U.S. independence.
1804 Impeachment trial of Supreme Court Justice Samuel Chase begins.
1936 London's Crystal Palace (built 1851) destroyed by fire.
1939 USSR invades Finland over a border dispute.
1966 Barbados National Day.
1975 Dahomey changes its name to Benin.
1988 Cyclone lashes Bangladesh, eastern India; 317 killed.
1990 Actor Burt Lancaster suffers a stroke.
1990 George H. W. Bush proposes U.S.-Iraq meeting to avoid war.

December

And after him came next the chill December;
Yet he, through merry feasting which he made
And great bonfires, did not the cold remember;
His Saviour's birth so much his mind did glad.
Upon a shaggy bearded goat he rode,
The same wherewith Dan Jove in tender years,
They say was nourisht by the Idæan mayd;
And in his hand a broad deepe bowle he beares,
Of which he freely drinks an health to all his peers.

EDMUND SPENSER–*The Shepheardes Calender* (1579)

Riding upon the Goat, with snow-white hair,
I come, the last of all. This crown of mine
Is of the holly; in my hand I bear
The thyrsus, tipped with fragrant cones of pine.
I celebrate the birth of the Divine,
And the return of the Saturnian reign;–
My songs are carols sung at every shrine.
Proclaiming "Peace on earth, good will to men."

HENRY WADSWORTH LONGFELLOW–*The Poet's Calendar* (1882)

Shakespeare ~

ARVIRAGUS
What should we speak of
When we are old as you? when we shall hear
The rain and wind beat dark December, how,
In this our pinching cave, shall we discourse
The freezing hours away? We have seen nothing;

–*Cymbeline* Act 3, Scene III

HENRY BOLINGBROKE
O, who can hold a fire in his hand
By thinking on the frosty Caucasus?
Or cloy the hungry edge of appetite
By bare imagination of a feast?
Or wallow naked in December snow
By thinking on fantastic summer's heat?
O, no! the apprehension of the good
Gives but the greater feeling to the worse:
Fell sorrow's tooth doth never rankle more
Than when he bites, but lanceth not the sore.

–*Richard II,* Act 1, Scene III

December ~

December is the twelfth and final month of the Gregorian calendar and the first month of winter. It derives its name from the Latin word *decem*, meaning ten, as December was the tenth month of the oldest Roman calendar. The Franks call it Heilagmanoth, or Holy Month, because of its large number of sacred festivals. In the old Tibetan calendar, December 1 was the beginning of the new year.

Proverbs ~

A green Christmas; a white Easter.

If there's thunder during Christmas week,
The Winter will be anything but meek.

The nearer the New Moon to Christmas Day, the harder the Winter.

If Christmas day be bright and clear
There'll be two winters in the year.

Thunder in December presages fine weather.

Like in December like all the year long.

December 1

DAILY READING

In the beginning was the Word, and the Word was with God, and the Word was God. He was with God in the beginning. . . . The Word became flesh and made his dwelling among us. We have seen his glory, the glory of the One and Only, who came from the Father, full of grace and truth. (JOHN 1:1–2, & 14)

FEAST DAYS

680	Botulph	Patron of Huntingdonshire, England
1637	Nicholas Ferrar	Founder of the Little Gidding community
1916	Charles de Foucauld	Founder of the Little Brothers of Jesus and the Little Sisters of Jesus

ENTRANCE AND EXIT

b. 1798	Albert Barnes	American theologian
b. 1935	Allan Stewart Konigsberg (Woody Allen)	American director, actor, and writer
b. 1945	Bette Midler	American actor
d. 1135	Henry I (Beauclerc)	King of England
d. 1521	Giovanni di Lorenzo de Medici	Pope Leo X
d. 1947	Aleister Crowley	English Satanist

Albert Barnes

Presbyterian minister Albert Barnes (1798–1870) was born on this day in Rome, New York. A gifted scholar, he attended Princeton Theological Seminary. He was ordained as a minister in 1825 and served in Philadelphia for forty-seven years.

Today he is chiefly remembered for his Bible notes, particularly *Notes on the New Testament* (1870), which sold more than a million copies. Barnes was an eloquent preacher and a dedicated student and writer. He arose early in the morning and studied by lamplight—a discipline that almost cost him his eyesight. He also wrote expository works on Job, the Psalms, Isaiah, and Daniel.

His *Notes on Romans* (1835) were controversial within his denomination and led to a charge of heresy, because he maintained that man possessed free will—a view at odds with the tenets of Calvinism espoused by Presbyterians. The issues stirred by his trial led to widening the breach between the conservative and the progressive elements in the church, and he was eventually identified as one of the leaders of the liberal Presbyterians.

Barnes had a strong sense of morality and was much opposed to the practice of slavery. In 1846, he wrote a book, *An Inquiry into the Scriptural Views of Slavery*. He also preached against the use of alcoholic beverages, urging total abstinence.

Extract from the Preface to Barnes's Notes on the New Testament—*Romans:*

The Epistle to the Romans has been usually regarded as the most difficult portion of the New Testament. It is from this cause, probably, as well as from the supposition that its somewhat abstruse discussions could not be made interesting to the young, that so few efforts have been made to introduce it into Sunday Schools and Bible Classes. It will doubtless continue to be a fact, that Sunday School instruction will be confined chiefly to the historical parts of the Bible. In the Sacred Scriptures there is this happy adaptedness to the circumstances of the world, that so large a portion of the volume can thus be made interesting to the minds of children and youth; that so much of it is occupied with historical narrative; with parables; with interesting biographies of the holy men of other times, and with the life of our blessed Lord. But still, while this is true, there is a considerable portion of the youth, in various ways under the instruction of the Bible, who may be interested in the more abstruse statements and discussions of the doctrinal parts of the Holy Scriptures. For such—for Sunday School teachers; for Bible Classes; and for the higher classes in Sabbath Schools—these Notes have been prepared. The humble hope has been cherished that this epistle might be introduced to this portion of the youth of the churches; and thus tend to imbue their minds with correct views of the great doctrines of the Christian Revelation.

DECEMBER 2

DAILY READING

In the past God spoke to our forefathers through the prophets at many times and in various ways, but in these last days he has spoken to us by his Son, whom he appointed heir of all things, and through whom he made the universe. (HEB 1:1–2)

FEAST DAYS

363	Bibiana	Patron of Los Angeles
ca. 450	Silvanus	Bishop of Troas, Turkey
1910	Channing Moore Williams	Missionary to India

ENTRANCE AND EXIT

b. 1831	Francis Nathan Peloubet	American clergyman
b. 1860	Charles Thomas Studd	English cricketer and missionary
b. 1981	Britney Spears	American pop star
d. 1814	Marquis de Sade	French writer
d. 1859	John Brown	American abolitionist
d. 1990	Aaron Copland	American composer

Dedication of St. Paul's Cathedral

The principal church of the great city of London had its service of dedication on December 2, 1697. There has been a place of worship on the site of St. Paul's since 604. Services were sung by canons who lived on site, and there was provision for "almonry boys" (poor children) to serve at the cathedral.

Another, larger building was erected by the Normans in 1087. This was extensively restored by Inigo Jones in 1621. However, in 1666 the Great Fire of London destroyed 80 percent of the city, including St. Paul's, eighty-seven parish churches, and over thirteen thousand houses. The debris was so thick that the streets beneath were invisible, and the lead in St. Paul's roof ran in streams as the fire took hold.

Christopher Wren was appointed to design a new cathedral just eight days after the conflagration had ceased. He submitted three designs to the clerical authorities–the Greek Cross Design, the Warrant Design (both of which are on display in the Cathedral), and the Great Design, which was finally accepted.

When building began in 1675, it was marked by an auspicious omen: tradition records that a workman sent to find a suitable spot to begin the work found a piece of rubble with the word *Resurgam* ("Rise again") inscribed upon it. Today, the pediment near the South Door has this word and a phoenix rising from the flames as a reminder of this incident.

Although the new cathedral began services in 1697, the building itself was not completed until 1710. In 1997, the tercentenary was marked by a service of thanksgiving attended by the Queen.

Noteworthy

1873 The Reformed Episcopal Church was organized in New York City under the leadership of Bishop George David Cummins of Kentucky.

1971 Independence Day, United Arab Emirates.

1985 The International Bible Society occupied its new headquarters in Carter House in New York City.

2001 American corporation Enron filed for bankruptcy.

DECEMBER 3

DAILY READING

Jesus declared, "I am the bread of life.
He who comes to me will never go hungry,
and he who believes in me will never be thirsty." (JOHN 6:35)

FEAST DAYS

ca. 318	Mirocles	Bishop of Milan, Italy
1552	Francis Xavier	Spanish Jesuit missionary
1860	Johann Nepomuk	Bishop of Innsbruck, Austria

ENTRANCE AND EXIT

b. 1838	Octavia Hill	English reformer
b. 1857	Joseph Conrad	Polish novelist
b. 1902	Mitsuo Fuchida	Japanese military leader
d. 1888	Carl Zeiss	German optician
d. 1910	Mary Baker Eddy	Founder of Christian Science Church
d. 1980	Oswald Moseley	English fascist leader

Octavia Hill

The Victorian housing and social reformer Octavia Hill (1838–1912) was born in Wisbech, Cambridgeshire, on this day in 1838. Today she is chiefly remembered for restoring over six thousand dilapidated homes in the poorest districts of London. She was a great help to poor people whose needs were often neglected by avaricious landlords. An assidious worker who pioneered partnership working, under her careful supervision, "repairs [were] promptly and efficiently attended to, references completely taken up, cleaning sedulously supervised, overcrowding put an end to, the blessing of ready-money payments enforced, accounts strictly kept, and, above all, tenants so sorted as to be helpful to one another."

Octavia Hill was much influenced in her work by the Christian Socialist movement and the theologian and reformer Rev. Frederick Denison Maurice. Her other great influence was the poet and artist John Ruskin, who was her dance partner and helped to finance her initial housing reform ventures.

Seeing her success in housing improvement, Octavia's help and advice were often sought by charities and governments in connection with the promotion of social reform by legislation. In 1873, she supported the Charity Organization Society, which was lobbying for new laws on artisans' dwellings, and in 1893 she gave valuable evidence to the Royal Commission on the Aged Poor.

Octavia had a great love of open spaces, and in 1895, she was one of the three cofounders of the National Trust (along with Sir Robert Hunter and Canon Hardwicke Rawnsley). This body, today regarded as one of the nation's defining charities, was established to acquire and protect land against the onslaught of industrialization.

Novels by Joseph Conrad (1857–1924)

1895 *Almayer's Folly*
1896 *An Outcast of the Islands*
1897 *The Nigger of the Narcissus*
1900 *Lord Jim*
1902 *Heart of Darkness*
1903 *Romance*
1904 *Nostromo*
1907 *The Secret Agent*
1909 *The Nature of a Crime*
1911 *Under Western Eyes*
1913 *Chance*
1915 *Victory*
1917 *The Shadow Line*
1919 *The Arrow of Gold*
1920 *The Rescue*
1923 *The Rover*

DECEMBER 4

DAILY READING

When Jesus spoke again to the people, he said, "I am the light of the world. Whoever follows me will never walk in darkness, but will have the light of life." (JOHN 8:12)

FEAST DAYS

217	Clement	Bishop of Alexandria, Egypt
ca. 235	Barbara	Patron of Santa Barbara, California
ca. 750	John of Damascus	Church father

ENTRANCE AND EXIT

b. 1795	Thomas Carlyle	English writer
b. 1866	Wassily Kandinsky	Russian artist
b. 1949	Jeff Bridges	American actor
d. 1131	Omar Khayyam	Persian writer
d. 1976	Benjamin Britten	English composer
d. 1993	Frank Zappa	American rock star

The Icon Defender

St. John of Damascus (c.676–749) came from an Arab Christian family. In 717 he became a monk in the Lavra of St. Sabbas in Palestine, where he spent the rest of his life in study and writing.

He is acknowledged as the last Father of the Eastern Church and is renowned as an eminent thelogian and passionate defender of icons.

During the eighth century, the church was split between those who rejected images of the Divine (the Iconoclasts) and those who venerated them (the Iconodules). The Iconoclasts maintained that the use of religious images was a violation of the Second Commandment, but the Iconodules argued the Christ had dwelt among men so it was fine to have religious images. The incarnation had changed everything. The Roman Emperor Leo II supported the Iconoclasts, but John favored the Iconodules. He could oppose the Emperor because he enjoyed the protection of the Moslem Khalif Abdul Malek.

In the *Fount of Knowledge*, John wrote an exposition of the Orthodox faith and established a theological system based on the writings and teachings of the church fathers and councils from the fourth to the seventh century. It thus embodies the finished result of the theological thought of the early Greek Church.

John is also known as a hymn writer. Two of his hymns are sung are still popular at Easter: "Come Ye Faithful, Raise the Strain" and "The Day of Resurrection! Earth, Tell It Out Abroad!" Many more are sung in the Eastern Church.

Extract from The Rubaiyat *by Omar Khayyam*

I

Wake! For the Sun, who scatter'd into flight
The Stars before him from the Field of Night,
Drives Night along with them from Heav'n, and strikes
The Sultan's Turret with a Shaft of Light.

II

Before the phantom of False morning died,
Methought a Voice within the Tavern cried,
"When all the Temple is prepared within,
Why nods the drowsy Worshipper outside?"

December 5

DAILY READING

Therefore Jesus said again, "I tell you the truth, I am the gate for the sheep. . . .
Whoever enters through me will be saved. He will come in and go out
and find pasture. The thief comes only to steal and kill and destroy;
I have come that they may have life, and have it the full." (JOHN 10:7, 9–10)

FEAST DAYS

ca. 750	John the Wonder Worker	Bishop of Polybatum, in Phrygia
1025	John Gradenigo	Benedictine monk
1612	John Almond	Catholic martyr

ENTRANCE AND EXIT

b. 1830	Christina Georgina Rosetti	English poet
b. 1901	Walter Elias "Walt" Disney	American animator
d. 1985	Frankie Muniz	American actor
d. 1057	Macbeth	King of Scotland
d. 1791	Wolfgang Mozart	Austrian composer
d. 1926	Claude Oscar Monet	French artist

Christina Georgina Rosetti

The much loved Victorian poet Christina Rosetti (1830–94) was born into a literary and artistic family. The youngest of four children, Christina's brother Dante Gabriel was a noted painter and poet. Her other brother, William Michael, was a leading art critic and editor–he edited Christina's works after her death. Both brothers became founder members of the Pre-Raphaelite Brotherhood, a movement dedicated to studying nature and promoting moral values.

In 1848 Christina was briefly engaged to another member of the Pre-Raphaelites, James Collinson, but when he became a Roman Catholic, the engagement was terminated. She never married but devoted her efforts to education and the arts. She mixed with many celebrated artists such as Whistler, Swinburne, and the Rev. Charles Dodgson.

Her most popular works include the lyrics to the carol "In the Bleak Mid-Winter," a long poem called "Goblin Market," and "Remember."

She continued to write poetry throughout her life, and in the 1870s she worked on a voluntary basis for the Society for Promoting Christian Knowledge. Her poems express feelings of love and religious ecstasy. She remained close to her family and was deeply affected by Dante Gabriel's nervous breakdown in 1872. After his death in 1882, she lived as a recluse at home, concentrating on her religious life. She died of cancer in 1894, having been diagnosed with the disease in 1891.

"Remember" by Christina Rosetti

Remember me when I am gone away,
Gone far away into the silent land;
When you can no more hold me by
the hand,
Nor I half turn to go yet turning stay.
Remember me when no more day by day
You tell me of our future that you planned:
Only remember me; you understand
It will be late to counsel then or pray.
Yet if you should forget me for a while
And afterwards remember, do not grieve:
For if the darkness and corruption leave
A vestige of the thoughts that once I had,
Better by far you should forget and smile
Than that you should remember and be sad.

December 6

DAILY READING

"I am the good shepherd; I know my sheep and my sheep know me—just as the Father knows me and I know the Father—and I lay down my life for the sheep." (JOHN 10:14–15)

FEAST DAYS

326	Nicholas	Bishop of Myra, Turkey
ca. 558	Abraham	Bishop of Kratia, Turkey
1865	Adolph Kolping	Patron of World Youth Day

ENTRANCE AND EXIT

b. 1421	Henry IV	King of England
b. 1920	Dave Brubeck	American musician
b. 1958	Nick Park	English animator
d. 1882	Anthony Trollope	English writer
d. 1988	Roy Orbison	American singer
d. 2000	Werner Klemperer	American actor

St. Nicholas of Myra

There are many stories about St. Nicholas and his generosity. He is most well known as the model for our modern-day Santa Claus. St. Nicholas grew up to become the Bishop of Myra in modern-day Turkey.

Nicholas is the national saint of Russia and Greece, and churches named after him number in the thousands—more than four hundred in Great Britain alone. He is the patron saint of judges, murderers, pawnbrokers, thieves, merchants, paupers, scholars, sailors, bakers, travelers, maidens, and poor children.

The most famous story about Nicholas tells of how he helped three unfortunate young sisters who all had suitors but had no dowries because their father, a poor nobleman, could not raise the money. Because of this, they could not marry.

Bishop Nicholas, being a shy man, thought of a way to help them anonymously. When the first daughter was ready to marry, Nicholas tossed a bag of gold into the house at night. Later, when the second daughter prepared to marry, she too received a mysterious bag of gold. When the third daughter prepared to marry, the poor nobleman and father of the three girls was determined to find out who had been so generous. So he kept watch and saw the bishop drop another bag of gold into the house.

It has been said that St. Nicholas climbed on the roof and dropped the third bag of gold down the chimney, where it landed in a stocking hung to dry, giving us a reason to hang up Christmas stockings today.

Noteworthy

1492 Columbus discovers the island of Hispaniola.
1877 Thomas Alva Edison records first song on his phonograph machine, "Mary Had a Little Lamb."
1917 Independence Day, Finland.
1917 City of Halifax, Nova Scotia, destroyed by ship explosion and tidal wave.
1921 Anglo-Irish treaty signed, setting up Irish Free State.
1952 The Great Smog of London reduces visibility to ten yards, over four hundred killed.

December 7

DAILY READING

"I am the resurrection and the life. He who believes in me will live, even though he dies; and whoever lives and believes in me will never die. Do you believe this?" (JOHN 11:25–26)

FEAST DAYS

375	Victor	Bishop of Piacenza, Italy
397	Ambrose of Milan	Church father
1148	Humbert	Benedictine monk

ENTRANCE AND EXIT

b. 1598	Gian Lorenzo Bernini	Italian artist
b. 1928	Noam Chomsky	American writer
b. 1932	Ellen Burstyn	American actor
d. 43 BC	Cicero	Roman writer
d. 1985	Robert Graves	English writer
d. 1992	Vincent Gardenia	American actor

Attack on Pearl Harbor

On this day in 1941, the United States of America entered World War II following the Japanese attack on Pearl Harbor. The Japanese Imperial Navy attacked the American fleet at Oahu, Hawaii. The attacking planes came in two waves; the first hit its target at 7:53 a.m., the second at 8:55 a.m. An hour later the planes departed, and by 1:00 p.m., the carriers that launched the planes from 274 miles away were heading back to Japan. The surprise attack consisting of 353 Japanese aircraft was led by Commander Mitsuo Fuchida, who in 1950 converted to Christianity and became a well-known evangelist.

Of the over one hundred ships attacked at Pearl Harbor, the battleships *Arizona, Utah*, and *Oklahoma* were completely destroyed. Other battleships severely damaged in the attack included the *California, Nevada*, and *Pennsylvania*. At the same time, the nearby base at Hickam Field was also victim of the surprise Japanese attack.

The destruction was immense: 2,341 naval, marine, and army personnel were killed, another 1,178 were wounded; 21 ships were sunk or damaged, and 323 aircraft were destroyed or damaged. Just 29 Japanese aircraft were shot down.

On the following day, Japanese planes eliminated much of the American air force in the Philippines, and a Japanese army was ashore in Malaya.

These Japanese strikes, achieved without any declaration of war, shocked and enraged the American people to a new purpose that eventually led to the devastation of Japan four years later.

Today, the anniversary of the Pearl Harbor attacks is marked throughout America by services of remembrance and civic ceremonies.

Extracts from President Franklin D. Roosevelt's "Day of Infamy" Speech to the Congress of the United States, December 8, 1941

Yesterday, December 7, 1941—a date which will live in infamy—the United States of America was suddenly and deliberately attacked by naval and air forces of the Empire of Japan.

Japan has, therefore, undertaken a surprise offensive extending throughout the Pacific area. The facts of yesterday speak for themselves. The people of the United States have already formed their opinions and well understand the implications to the very life and safety of our Nation.

As Commander-in-Chief of the Army and Navy I have directed that all measures be taken for our defense.

I ask that the Congress declare that since the unprovoked and dastardly attack by Japan on Sunday, December seventh, a state of war has existed between the United States and the Japanese Empire.

DECEMBER 8

DAILY READING

Jesus answered, "I am the way and the truth and the life. No one comes to the Father except through me." (JOHN 14:6)

FEAST DAYS

ca. 1st cent.	Eucharius	Bishop of Trier, Germany
ca. 7th cent.	Patapius	Hermit
653	Romaric	Merovingian monk

ENTRANCE AND EXIT

b. 65 BC	Quintus Horatius Flactus	Roman writer
b. 1865	Jean Sibelius	Finnish composer
b. 1939	James Galway	Irish flutist
d. 1903	Herbert Spencer	English philosopher
d. 1978	Golda Meir	Israeli prime minister
d. 1980	John Lennon	English pop star

The Feast of the Immaculate Conception

On this day in 1854, Pope Pius IX issued a papal encyclical that formally defined the Roman Catholic doctrine of the Immaculate Conception (*Ineffabilis Deus*). This established December 8 as a holy day of obligation, requiring all Catholics by the first Precept of the Church to attend Mass.

Put simply, the doctrine of the Immaculate Conception maintains that:

1. The entire being of the Blessed Virgin Mary, her physical and spiritual natures, were created by God Himself at her conception; and,
2. She was never subject to original sin, but was completely preserved from all the effects of the sin of Adam.

This notion of Immaculate Conception poses difficulties for many Christians who claim that it makes Mary into a god, since only God is without sin. However, others point out that Adam and Eve were without sin in Eden. Another objection is that if Mary was truly sinless, then she would have no need of a savior, but Catholics maintain Mary was saved by anticipation rather than through forgiveness.

Catholics maintain that the Feast of the Immaculate Conception was observed as early as the sixth century in the Greek Church as a celebration in honor of the conception of St. Anne. By the tenth century, it had become a holy day, and by way of Naples it came to the West, where it first took root in Ireland and Normandy. All through the Middle Ages the dogmatic foundation of the mystery was contested.

Noteworthy

1862 First postage stamp issued in Hong Kong.
1914 Irving Berlin's first musical, *Watch Your Step*, opens on Broadway.
1914 Naval Battle of the Falkland Islands; British fleet destroy several German ships.
1941 The day after Pearl Harbor with 2,400 dead Americans, U.S. declares war on Japan.
1987 America and Russia sign a treaty to destroy intermediate-range nuclear missiles.
1991 Russia, Ukraine, and Byelorussia announce commonwealth.
1992 NASA takes first photo of four-mile long speeding asteroid "Toutatis" only 2.2 million miles from Earth.

DECEMBER 9

DAILY READING

"I am the vine; you are the branches. If a man remains in me and I in him,
he will bear much fruit; apart from me you can do nothing. . . .
This is to my Father's glory, that you bear much fruit,
showing yourselves to be my disciples." (JOHN 15:5, 8)

FEAST DAYS

297	Philotheus	Martyr of Samosata, Turkey
ca. 320	Proculus	Bishop of Verona, Italy
ca. 7th cent.	Budoc	King of Brittany

ENTRANCE AND EXIT

b. 1608	John Milton	English writer
b. 1848	Joel Chandler Harris	American writer
b. 1934	Dame Judi Dench	English actor
d. 1814	Joseph Bramah	English inventor
d. 1994	Kim Il Sung	President of North Korea
d. 1996	Mary Leakey	English archaeologist

Joel Chandler Harris

The famous children's writer and folklorist Joel Chandler Harris (1848–1908) was born in Eatonton, Georgia. He became famous over a century ago as the creator of popular children's stories written in the dialect of the South, told by Uncle Remus, a slave who entertained his master's son with his folktales.

During his formative years, Harris befriended elderly slaves George Terrell and Old Harbert, who entertained him with trickster tales about Brer Rabbit and Brer Fox and the other critters in the Briar Patch. This was the genesis of his stories.

In 1862, Harris became a journalist working on *The Countryman*–he also had newspaper jobs in New Orleans and Savannah before landing at the *Atlanta Constitution* in 1879.

His first collection of folk poems and proverbs was published in 1881 as *Uncle Remus: His Songs and Sayings*. Further collections included *Nights with Uncle Remus* (1883), *Uncle Remus and His Friends* (1892), and *Uncle Remus and the Little Boy* (1905). These dialect stories are engaging because they serve as morality tales and highlight the importance of actions matching intentions. Uncle Remus as the narrator is the reader's best friend, and the charming nature of the tales have ensured their popularity.

Joel Chandler Harris died at his home in Atlanta, but his stories attracted further attention in 1946 with the Walt Disney film *Song of the South*.

Extract from The Wonderful Tar Baby Story *(1881)*

"Didn't the fox never catch the rabbit, Uncle Remus?" asked the little boy the next evening.

"He come mighty nigh it, honey, sho's you born–Brer Fox did. One day atter Brer Rabbit fool 'im wid dat calamus root, Brer Fox went ter wuk en got 'im some tar, en mix it wid some turkentime, en fix up a contrapshun w'at he call a Tar-Baby, en he tuck dish yer Tar-Baby en he sot 'er in de big road, en den he lay off in de bushes fer to see what de news wuz gwine ter be. En he didn't hatter wait long, nudder, kaze bimeby here come Brer Rabbit pacin' down de road–lippity-clippity, clippity-lippity–dez ez sassy ez a jay-bird. Brer Fox, he lay low. Brer Rabbit come prancin' 'long twel he spy de Tar-Baby, en den he fotch up on his behime legs like he wuz 'stonished. De Tar Baby, she sot dar, she did, en Brer Fox, he lay low.

"'Mawnin'!' sez Brer Rabbit, sezee–'nice wedder dis mawnin',' sezee.

"Tar-Baby ain't sayin' nuthin', en Brer Fox he lay low.

"'How duz yo' sym'tums seem ter segashuate?' sez Brer Rabbit, sezee.

"Brer Fox, he wink his eye slow, en lay low, en de Tar-Baby, she ain't sayin' nuthin'.

"'How you come on, den? Is you deaf?' sez Brer Rabbit, sezee. 'Kaze if you is, I kin holler louder,' sezee.

"Tar-Baby stay still, en Brer Fox, he lay low."

DECEMBER 10

DAILY READING

The LORD your God will raise up for you a prophet from among your own brothers. You must listen to him. (DEUT 18:15)

FEAST DAYS

ca. 290	Eulalia	Patron of Merida, Spain
ca. 700	Deusdedit	Bishop of Brescia, Italy
741	Gregory III	Pope

ENTRANCE AND EXIT

b. 1830	Emily Dickinson	American poet
b. 1851	Melvil Dewey	American librarian
b. 1960	Kenneth Brannagh	English actor and director
d. 1896	Alfred Nobel	Swedish inventor
d. 1968	Karl Barth	Swiss theologian
d. 1968	Thomas Merton	French theologian

The First Nobel Prizes

When the Swedish inventor and chemist Alfred Nobel died in 1896, he left instructions in his will that his estate be used to establish annual prizes to "those who, during the preceding year, shall have conferred the greatest benefit on mankind." The first Nobel Prizes were awarded in 1901, in the fields of Chemistry (Jacobus H. van't Hoff), Physics (Wilhelm C. Röntgen), Physiology or Medicine (Emil A. von Behring), Literature (Rene F. A. Sully Prudhomme), and Peace (Jean H. Dunant Frédéric).

Nobel stated that the awards should be decided by the Royal Swedish Academy of Sciences for the Nobel Prize in Physics and Chemistry, the Karolinska Institute for the Nobel Prize in Physiology or Medicine, the Swedish Academy for the Nobel Prize in Literature, and a committee of five persons to be elected by the Norwegian Parliament (Storting) for the Nobel Peace Prize. In 1968, the Sveriges Riksbank established the Prize in Economics. The Royal Swedish Academy of Sciences was given the task to select the Economics Prize Laureates starting in 1969.

The five years between his death and the first Nobel prizes were taken up by relatives contesting the will and establishing how to execute Nobel's wishes. Notable winners of the Nobel Prize include: Pierre and Marie Curie (Chemistry, 1903), Ivan Pavlov (Medicine, 1904), Theodore Roosevelt (Peace, 1906), Rudyard Kipling (Literature, 1907), Ernest Rutherford (Chemistry, 1908), William Butler Yeats (Literature, 1923), Sir Alexander Fleming (Medicine, 1945), Albert Camus (Literature, 1957), Desmond Tutu (Peace, 1985), and Jimmy Carter (Peace, 2002).

Extract from the Will of Alfred Nobel

The whole of my remaining realizable estate shall be dealt with in the following way: the capital, invested in safe securities by my executors, shall constitute a fund, the interest on which shall be annually distributed in the form of prizes to those who, during the preceding year, shall have conferred the greatest benefit on mankind. The said interest shall be divided into five equal parts, which shall be apportioned as follows: one part to the person who shall have made the most important discovery or invention within the field of physics; one part to the person who shall have made the most important chemical discovery or improvement; one part to the person who shall have made the most important discovery within the domain of physiology or medicine; one part to the person who shall have produced in the field of literature the most outstanding work in an ideal direction; and one part to the person who shall have done the most or the best work for fraternity between nations, for the abolition or reduction of standing armies and for the holding and promotion of peace congresses.

DECEMBER 11

DAILY READING

The LORD himself will give you a sign: The virgin will be with child and will give birth to a son, and will call him Immanuel. (ISA 7:14)

FEAST DAYS

342	Barsabas	Persian abbot
493	Daniel	Stylite monk
1371	Hugolino Magalotti	Hermit

ENTRANCE AND EXIT

b. 1918	Aleksandr Isayevich Solzhenitsyn	Russian writer
b. 1931	Rosita Dorores Alverio (Rita Moreno)	American singer and dancer
b. 1943	John Kerry	American politician
d. 1718	Charles XII	King of Sweden
d. 1910	Lars Olsen Skrefsrud	Norwegian missionary to India
d. 1964	Alma Schindler Mahler	Austrian writer

The Root and Branch Petition

On this day in 1640, a petition signed by fifteen thousand London citizens was debated in the House of Commons. The petition called for the system of church government to be swept away "root and branch."

The Root and Branch Petition was an instrument of the Puritans designed to urge Parliament to reform the established church. Among the many reasons for reform cited by the petition were:

- The faint-heartedness of ministers to preach the truth of God, lest they should displease the prelates
- The encouragement of ministers to despise the temporal magistracy, the nobles and gentry of the land; to abuse the subjects, and live contentiously with their neighbors
- The restraint of many godly and able men from the ministry, and thrusting out of many congregations their faithful, diligent and powerful ministers, and
- The great increase of idle, lewd and dissolute, ignorant and erroneous men in the ministry, which swarm like the locusts of Egypt over the whole kingdom; and will they but wear a canonical coat, a surplice, a hood, bow at the name of Jesus, and be zealous of superstitious ceremonies, they may live as they list, confront whom they please, preach and vent what errors they will, and neglect preaching at their pleasures without control.

The petition was accepted by the Long Parliament, called by King Charles I. However, for the proposal to be made law, the petition also had to be approved by the House of Lords. As many members of the House of Lords were bishops who resented any pressure from the common people, the Root and Branch Petition was narrowly defeated.

Noteworthy

1719 First recorded display of aurora borealis in America in New England.
1816 Indiana nineteenth state admitted to Union.
1848 Louis Napoleon elected president of the Republic of France.
1936 Edward VIII abdicated English throne and George VI becomes king.
1941 U.S. declared war on Germany and Italy.
1946 United Nations International Children's Emergency Fund (UNICEF) founded.
1961 John F. Kennedy ordered first U.S. military intervention in Vietnam.

DECEMBER 12

DAILY READING

But when the time had fully come, God sent his Son,
born of a woman, born under law, . . .
that we might receive the full rights of sons. (GAL 4:4–5)

FEAST DAYS

549	Finian	Bishop of Clonard, Ireland
490	Corentin	Bishop of Cornouaille, France
1531	Our Lady of Guadalupe	Mexican festival

ENTRANCE AND EXIT

b. 1630	Erasmus Darwin	English naturalist
b. 1775	William Henry	English scientist
b. 1821	Gustave Flaubert	French writer
d. 1889	Robert Browing	English poet
d. 1917	Andrew Taylor Still	American founder of osteopathy
d. 1999	Joseph Heller	American writer

The Father of Osteopathy

> In the past I stood and watched four physicians, the best the medical schools could furnish, battle with all their skill against the dread disease of cerebro-spinal meningitis in my family. I found prayers, tears, and medicine all unavailing. The war between life and death was a fierce one, but at the close of it three lifeless bodies lay in my desolate home. In my grief the thought came to me that Deity did not give life simply for the purpose of so soon destroying it–such a Deity would be nothing short of a murderer. I was convinced there was something surer and stronger with which to fight sickness than drugs, and I vowed to search until I found it.

Thus wrote Andrew Taylor Still in his autography (1828–1917) about his motivation for researching the techniques of manipulative medicine that laid the foundations of osteopathy. The son of a Methodist minister and a physician, Still had witnessed the death of three of his children from spinal meningitis in 1864.

Still served as a surgeon in the American Civil War as part of the Union forces and afterward developed his understanding of bone manipulation through tending to injured soldiers. His success, compared with traditional methods, became rapidly evident as he concentrated on treating the whole body, not just the area of injury. Indeed, his new methods earned him the title of the "lightning bone setter."

Still's approach divided the body into three parts; chest (head, neck, chest, abdomen, and pelvis), upper limbs (head, neck, lower and upper arm, and hand) and lower limbs (foot, leg, thigh, pelvis, and lumbar vertebra). Each division was important in the diagnosis and treatment of injury, regardless of the site of the injury. The expertise of the osteopath lay in correctly surmising the root cause and then applying the appropriate manipulation.

In a Gondola

The moth's kiss, first!
Kiss me as if you made me believe
You were not sure, this eve,
How my face, your flower, had pursed
Its petals up; so, here and there
You brush it, till I grow aware
Who wants me, and wide ope I burst.

The bee's kiss, now!
Kiss me as if you enter'd gay
My heart at some noonday,
A bud that dares not disallow
The claim, so all is render'd up,
And passively its shatter'd cup
Over your head to sleep I bow.

–Robert Browning

DECEMBER 13

DAILY READING

When [King Herod] had called together all the people's chief priests and teachers of the law, he asked them where the Christ was to be born. "In Bethlehem in Judea," they replied, "or this is what the prophet has written: 'But you, Bethlehem, in the land of Judah, are by no means the least among the rulers of Judah; for out of you will come a ruler who will be the shepherd of my people Israel.'" (MATT 2:4–6)

FEAST DAYS

304	Lucy	Italian martyr
669	Aubert	Bishop of Cambray, France
669	Jodoc	French prince

ENTRANCE AND EXIT

b. 1818	Mary Todd Lincoln	American First Lady
b. 1925	Dick Van Dyke	American actor
b. 1929	Christopher Plummer	English actor
d. 1204	Moses ben Maimon	Spanish philosopher
d. 1466	Donato di Niccolò di Betto Bardi (Donatello)	Italian sculptor
d. 1784	Samuel Johnson	English writer

St. Lucy

Tradition holds that St. Lucy was born in Syracuse, Sicily, early in the fourth century, the child of wealthy Christian parents. Her father died while she was an infant, and Lucy was raised by her widowed mother, Eutychia, who was noted for her piety. Lucy is the patron of light and eye ailments, possibly because her name means "light." Sometimes she is portrayed holding two eyes in a dish. Because her intercession saved Sweden from a famine, she is also the patron saint of Sweden.

Throughout Sweden the feast day of Lucia, or Lucy, is celebrated as a festival of lights. Early in the morning a young woman, dressed in a white gown and wearing a red sash and a crown of lingonberry twigs and blazing candles, would go from one farm to the next, carrying a torch to light her way, bringing baked goods, stopping to visit at each house, and returning home by break of day. Every village had its own Lucia. The custom is thought to have begun in some of the richer farming districts of Sweden and still persists, although the crowns are now electric lights.

In Norway and Sweden, it is still a custom on December 13 for a girl in a white dress to bring a tray of saffron buns and steaming coffee to wake the family. She is called the *Lussibrud* (Lucy bride) and her pastry (saffron buns) is *Lussekattor*. Today many families have a Lucia-Queen in their own home, often the youngest daughter, who wakes the rest of the family with song.

Lucy is said to have been beheaded by the sword during the persecutions of Diocletian at Catania in Sicily. Her body was later brought to Constantinople and finally to Venice, where she is now resting in the church of Santa Lucia.

Ember Days

The Ember Days are four series of Wednesdays, Fridays, and Saturdays that correspond to the natural seasons of the year. Thus autumn brings the September, or Michaelmas, Embertide; winter, the Advent Embertide; Spring, the Lenten Embertide; and in summer, the Whit Embertide (named after Whitsunday, the Feast of Pentecost).

Wednesday, Friday, and Saturday after St. Lucy's Day mark the first Ember Days in the church year. These Embertides are periods of prayer and fasting, with each day having its own special service.

In the Old Testament, a "fast of the fourth month, and a fast of the fifth, and a fast of the seventh, and a fast of tenth" (Zech 8:19, KJV) was observed. In the New Testaments, the first Christians fasted on every Wednesday and Friday: Wednesday in recognition of the day that Christ was betrayed, and Friday because it was the day that Christ was crucified. The Ember Days thus perfectly express and reflect the essence of Christianity. Christ does not abolish the Law, but fulfills it (Matt 5:17) by following the spirit of the Law rather than its letter. Thus, not one iota of the Law is to be neglected (Matt 5:18), but every part is to be embraced and continued, albeit on a spiritual, or figurative, level.

DECEMBER 14

DAILY READING

God sent the angel Gabriel to Nazareth, a town in Galilee, to a virgin pledged to be married to a man named Joseph, a descendant of David. The virgin's name was Mary. The angel went to her and said, "Greetings, you who are highly favored! The Lord is with you." (LUKE 1:26–28)

FEAST DAYS

348	Spiridion	Bishop of Tremithous, Cyprus
ca. 5th cent.	Nicasius	Bishop of Rheims, France
1591	John of the Cross	Carmelite friar

ENTRANCE AND EXIT

b. 1503	Michael Nostradamus	French astrologist
b. 1836	Frances Ridley Havergal	English writer
b. 1935	Lee Remick	American actor
d. 1417	Sir John Oldcastle	English Lollard leader
d. 1799	George Washington	1st American president
d. 1989	Andrei Sakharov	Russian scientist

Frances Ridley Havergal

Poet, hymn writer, musician, and linguist Frances Ridley Havergal (1836–79) was the youngest child of Canon W. H. Havergal, from Astley, Worcestershire. A gifted child, she suffered from poor health and was discouraged from study.

Nevertheless, Frances persevered and began writing short stories and verses to *Good News* magazine and other Christian publications. As a result, her fame spread and she was much in demand as a speaker and correspondent.

She published her first anthology *The Ministry of Song* in 1869, and after her father's death, she edited his work *Havergal's Psalmody* and included her own compositions for publication. Most of her royalties went to support the Church Missionary Society.

In 1878 she moved to Mumbles, Swansea, where on June 3, 1879, she died of hepatitis at age forty-two. The plaque outside the house (now named "Havergal") where she died describes her as a "Christian Poetess and Hymnwriter." She was buried beside her father's grave in Astley.

Her best known hymns include the consecration hymn "Take My Life and Let It Be" (1874), "I Am Trusting Thee, Lord Jesus" (1874), and "Who Is on the Lord's Side?" (1877).

Take My Life and Let It Be

Take my life and let it be
consecrated, Lord, to thee.
Take my moments and my days;
let them flow in endless praise.

Take my hands and let them move
at the impulse of thy love.
Take my feet and let them be
swift and beautiful for thee.

Take my voice and let me sing
always, only, for my King.
Take my lips and let them be
filled with messages from thee.

Take my silver and my gold;
not a mite would I withhold.
Take my intellect and use
every power as thou shalt choose.

Take my will and make it thine;
it shall be no longer mine.
Take my heart it is thine own;
it shall be thy royal throne.

Take my love; my Lord, I pour,
at thy feet its treasure store.
Take myself, and I will be
ever, only, all for thee.

–Frances Havergal, 1874

DECEMBER 15

DAILY READING

The angel said to Mary, "Do not be afraid, you have found favor with God. You will be with child and give birth to a son, and you are to give him the name Jesus. He will be great and will be called the Son of the Most High." (LUKE 1:30–32)

FEAST DAYS

ca. 320	Nino	Apostle of Georgia
1005	Adalbero	Benedictine monk
1349	John Discalceat	Franciscan priest

ENTRANCE AND EXIT

b. 1832	Gustave Eiffel	French engineer
b. 1859	Ludvic Lazarus Zamenhof	Polish philologist
b. 1932	Edna O'Brien	Irish writer
d. 1890	Sitting Bull	Sioux Indian chief
d. 1916	Grigori Rasputin	Russian mystic
d. 1962	Charles Laughton	American actor

Bill of Rights Day

On this day in 1791, the document listing ten amendments to the American Constituition, known as the Bill of Rights, was formally adopted by the legislature following ratification by the required minimum of 75 percent of the Union. The ten amendments ensure freedom of speech, the right to bear arms, the right to private property, protection against self-incrimination, trial by jury, and fair treatment for the accused.

The Bill of Rights was influenced by the English Magna Carta, drawn up in 1215 to offer similar rights and protections to the common people.

A day to commemorate the Bill of Rights adoption was announced by President Roosevelt in 1941, just days after the Pearl Harbor attack by Japan had threatened the freedoms espoused by the Bill of Rights.

Bill of Rights Day is a civc holiday in America. In 2006, President Bush announced that it would form part of Human Rights Week, starting with Human Rights Day on December 10. The presidential proclamation noted that "Americans are committed to the God-given value of every life, we cherish the freedom of every person in every nation and strive to promote respect for human rights. By standing with those who desire liberty, we will help extend freedom to many who have not known it and lay the foundations of peace for generations to come."

The day is marked by civil ceremonies, school competitions, and religious services across America.

Esperanto

Esperanto (the word means "one who hopes") was invented in 1887 by a gifted intellectual, Ludvic Lazarus Zamenhof (Dr. Esperanto). He was a Jew of German origin living in what is now Poland, then Czarist Russia, and bordering on Lithuania, steeped in the Lithuanian Jewish tradition.

In his hometown of Bialystok, four "native" languages–Polish, Russian, German, and Yiddish–competed for local dominance, exacerbating the already sharp tensions between the ethnic groups. Thus Bialystok was a perfect microcosm of the world Zamenhof wanted to help heal.

Zamenhof was inspired to create an easy, logical second language that all could learn and use profitably. When he was twenty-seven, his project was ready to be unveiled to the world. The new language grew by leaps and bounds, and by the turn of the century already had an international following. By 1905 the movement was ready for its first international congress–which has become an annual event. Today millions of people worldwide speak and enjoy this ingenious language.

DECEMBER 16

DAILY READING

Mary said, "My soul glorifies the Lord and my spirit rejoices in God my Savior. . . . The Mighty One has done great things for me—holy is his name." (LUKE 1:46–47, 49)

FEAST DAYS

ca. 6th cent.	Haggai	Old Testament prophet
875	Ado	Archbishop of Vienne, France
999	Alice or Adelaide	Empress of Germany

ENTRANCE AND EXIT

b. 1485	Katharine of Aragon	English Queen
b. 1775	Jane Austen	English writer
b. 1867	Amy Beatrice Carmichael	Scottish missionary
d. 1965	William Somerset Maugham	English writer
d. 1980	Col. Harlan Sanders	American chef
d. 1989	Lee Van Cleef	American actor

Amy Carmichael of Dohnavur

The much-loved missionary Amy Carmichael (1867–1951) was an unlikely candidate to serve God overseas. She suffered from severe neuralgia, a disease that often put her in bed for weeks on end. However at the 1887 Keswick Convention, she heard Hudson Taylor speak about missionary life and the need for workers to serve in India. She felt called to serve, and despite her weakness she soon left for Japan, where she served for fifteen years. However, her lifelong vocation was in India, and she founded the Dohnavur Fellowship in the state of Tamil Nadu at the southernmost tip of India. Here she continued to serve without a furlough for fifty-six years and became known as "Amma" (mother) in the native language.

A prolific writer, she wrote over thirty books, including *Things as They Are: Mission Work in Southern India* (1903), *His Thoughts Said . . . His Father Said* (1951), *If* (1953), and *Edges of His Ways* (1955).

Amy's main work was to rescue young girls from temple prostitution—a widespread practice at the time. The Dohnavur Fellowship became a place of sanctuary for more than one thousand children who would otherwise have faced a bleak future. Members of the organization respected local culture by wearing Indian dress, and Amy dyed her skin with coffee. She often traveled long distances on India's hot, dusty roads to save just one child from suffering.

Despite being badly injured by a fall in 1931, Amy continued her work although she was often bedridden. She left instructions that no stone be put over her grave; instead, the children she had cared for put a birdbath over it with the single inscription "Amma."

Noteworthy

431 Henry VI crowned King of France.
1631 Mount Vesuvius eruption kills eighteen thousand.
1653 Oliver Cromwell becomes Lord Protector of the Commonwealth of England, Scotland, and Ireland.
1773 Boston Tea Party begins U.S. War of Independence—342 chests of tea dumped in Boston harbor.
1893 Dvorak's "New World Symphony" premieres at Carnegie Hall, New York.
1944 Battle of Ardennes; Battle of the Bulge; last major German offensive begins.
1953 Chuck Yeager sets new airborne speed record, flying Bell X-1A rocket-fueled plane 1,600 mph.

DECEMBER 17

DAILY READING

An angel of the Lord appeared to him in a dream and said, "Joseph, son of David, do not be afraid to take Mary home as your wife, because what is conceived in her is from the Holy Spirit. She will give birth to a son, and you are to give him the name Jesus, because he will save his people from their sins." (MATT 1:20–21)

FEAST DAYS

627	Briarch	Welsh monk
779	Sturmi of Fulda	Apostle of the Saxons
1283	Yolanda	Dominican nun

ENTRANCE AND EXIT

b. 1770	Ludwig von Beethoven	German composer
b. 1837	Dwight Lyman Moody	American evangelist
b. 1944	Bernard Hill	English actor
d. 1830	Simon Bolivar	South American revolutionary
d. 1957	Dorothy Leigh Sayers	English writer
d. 1992	Dana Andrews	American actor

Dwight Lyman Moody

Dwight Lyman Moody (1837–99) was one of the most influential figures in American Evangelicalism. Born in Northfield, Massachusetts, Moody was only four years old when his father died, leaving his mother to raise the large family on her own. The family struggled to make ends meet, but this taught Dwight the value of hard work and determination.

At the age of seventeen, Moody started working in his uncle's shoe store in Chicago and became a successful businessman. He wrote to his family in Massachusetts that "God is the same here as in Boston." He became very involved and interested in Chicago's Protestant evangelism, which was becoming increasingly popular among the city's Christians. In 1860, he abandoned his profitable career as a shoe salesman, saying, "I am at work for Jesus Christ now."

In 1886, he founded the Chicago Evangelization Society, later called the Moody Bible Institute. Today, the Moody Bible Institute has major ministries in the fields of broadcasting, education, and publishing.

Moody was a tall, thin, earnest figure, scarcely unwilling to stop his good works even to sleep. He had many stories of the impact of the gospel, stories of drunkard's children, wives, sisters, aunts, grandmothers, of atheist soldiers dying on the battlefield, that bore testimony to the love of God for sinners. There were many stories about Moody, too. For example, once he stopped a man on the street and asked, as was his custom, "Are you a Christian?" "It's none of your business," the offended pedestrian replied. "Yes, it is," insisted Moody. "Then you must he Dwight L. Moody," said the man. Eventually the stranger found salvation. Moody's followers stated that he "saved a million souls from descending into hell."

Beethoven's Ninth Symphony in Popular Culture

Beethoven's Ninth Symphony has been used many times in films, television drama, and pop music. Examples include:

- In 1989 Leonard Bernstein conducts a Berlin Philharmonic performance of the symphony in celebration of the fall of the Berlin Wall.
- Nicaragua's national party has adopted it as its unofficial anthem.
- The film *Immortal Beloved* about Beethoven features the symphony.
- The 1987 movie *Raising Arizona* used the final movement, and it was also featured in the 1989 film *Die Hard.*
- Andy Williams's song "Words" uses original lyrics set to the melody of the fourth movement.
- The rock group Rainbow feature the Ninth Symphony on their album *Difficult to Cure.*
- The second movement is used as a sample by Microsoft in its Windows XP operating system.

DECEMBER 18

DAILY READING

"Praise be to the Lord, God of Israel, because he has come and has redeemed his people. He has raised up a horn of salvation for us in the house of his servant David (as he said through his holy prophets long ago)." (LUKE 1:68–70)

FEAST DAYS

ca. 700	Desiderius of Fontenelle	Son of St. Waningus
761	Winebald	Son of King Richard I
1838	Peter Truat	Vietnamese martyr

ENTRANCE AND EXIT

b. 1879	Paul Klee	Swiss artist
b. 1943	Keith Richards	English rock star
b. 1947	Steven Spielberg	American film director
d. 1737	Antonio Stradivari	Italian violin maker
d. 1971	Bobby Jones	American golfer
d. 1993	Sam Wanamaker	American film director

The Battle of Verdun

The Great War of 1914–18 is acknowledged by many historians as the bloodiest conflict in the history of war. The most prolonged battle in that war was the Battle of Verdun between German and French forces, which took place on the Western Front from February 21 to December 18, 1916.

The German Fifth Army, under the command of General Erich von Falkenhayn, wanted the battle to be a long one, with the intention of inflicting as many casualties on the French as possible. Thus they began with a twenty-one-hour artillery bombardment all along the eight-mile front.

France's Field-Marshal Joseph Joffre, who was himself concentrating on the battle of the Somme, entrusted the defense of Verdun to General Henri Petain and the Second Army. On June 23, the Germans attacked the heights that commanded the Verdun and Meuse bridges. They were repeatedly repulsed, with both sides losing hundreds of thousands of men.

Exhaustion combined with the increased demands for extra men for the Russian Brusilov offensive and the Somme offensive finally stopped the German advance. On October 24, the French launched a counterattack and the Germans began to withdraw. The French recaptured Douamant and Vaux, and by December had regained almost all the positions lost in February.

Victory by the French was at tremendous cost: 120,000 died and there were 258,000 casualties. The Germans lost at least 100,000 men and suffered over 250,000 casualties.

Directed By Steven Spielberg

1964 *Firelight*
1968 *Amblin'*
1971 *Duel*
1974 *The Sugarland Express*
1975 *Jaws*
1977 *Close Encounters of the Third Kind*
1979 *1941*
1981 *Raiders of the Lost Ark*
1982 *Poltergeist*
1982 *E.T. The Extra-Terrestrial*
1984 *Indiana Jones and the Temple of Doom*
1985 *The Color Purple*
1986 *An American Tail*
1987 *Empire of the Sun*
1988 *The Land before Time*
1989 *Indiana Jones and the Last Crusade*
1989 *Always*
1991 *Hook*
1993 *Jurassic Park*
1993 *Schindler's List*
1997 *The Lost World: Jurassic Park*
1997 *Amistad*
1998 *Saving Private Ryan*
2001 *AI: Artificial Intelligence*
2002 *Minority Report*
2002 *Catch Me If You Can*
2004 *The Terminal*
2005 *War of the Worlds*
2005 *Munich*
2007 *Transformers*

DECEMBER 19

DAILY READING

"You, my child, will be called a prophet of the Most High; for you will go on before the Lord to prepare the way for him, to give his people the knowledge of salvation through the forgiveness of their sins, because of the tender mercy of our God." (LUKE 1:76–78)

FEAST DAYS

540	Gregory	Bishop of Auxerre, France
790	Ribert	Abbot of Saint Oyend, France
1122	Bernard Valeara	Bishop of Teramo, Italy

ENTRANCE AND EXIT

b. 1498	Andreas Osiander	German theologian
b. 1790	Sir William Parry	English explorer
b. 1980	Jake Gyllenhaal	American actor
d. 1848	Emily Brontë	English writer
d. 1851	Joseph Mallord William Turner	English artist
d. 1996	Marcello Mastroianni	Italian actor

Poor Richard's Almanac

The first edition of *Poor Richard's Almanac* appeared on this day in 1732. It's author was the celebrated American inventor and statesman Benjamin Franklin, who continued to produce this digest of witty sayings, seasonal weather forecasts, practical household hints, puzzles, and wordplay until 1757. The first edition was an instant hit and went on to sell over ten thousand copies in a pamphlet form.

Benjamin Franklin adopted the name Richard Saunders as a pseudonym and continued to use it for every annual edition. Franklin stated that his *Almanac* was written because:

> "The plain Truth of the Matter is, I am excessive poor, and my Wife, good Woman, is, I tell her, excessive proud; she cannot bear, she says, to sit spinning in her Shift of Tow, while I do nothing but gaze at the Stars; and has threatned more than once to burn all my Books and Rattling-Traps (as she calls my Instruments) if I do not make some profitable Use of them for the good of my Family. The Printer has offer'd me some considerable share of the Profits, and I have thus begun to comply with my Dame's desire.

Poor Richard's Almanac contained many sayings that have endured such as:

> Eat to live, and not live to eat.
>
> There are no gains without pains.
>
> God gives all things to industry.
>
> Plough deep while sluggards sleep and you shall have corn to sell and to keep.

Noteworthy

1154 Henry II becomes King of England.
1783 William Pitt the Younger becomes youngest prime minister at age twenty-four.
1842 U.S. recognizes independence of Hawaii.
1843 Six thousand copies of Charles Dickens's *A Christmas Carol* are sold in five days.
1957 Air service between London and Moscow inaugurated.
1972 Moon program ends as Apollo 17 splashes down in the Pacific
1984 Britain and China sign agreement to return Hong Kong to China in 1997.

DECEMBER 20

DAILY READING

In those days Caesar Augustus issued a decree that a census should be taken of the entire Roman world. So Joseph also went up from the town of Nazareth in Galilee to Judea, to Bethlehem the town of David, because he belonged to the house and line of David. He went there to register with Mary, who was pledged to be married to him and was expecting a child. (LUKE 2:1, 4–5)

FEAST DAYS

249	Ammon	Roman soldier
249	Ingen	Roman soldier
1073	Dominic of Silos	Founder of the Order of Preachers

ENTRANCE AND EXIT

b. 1576	Edmund Grindal	Archbishop of Canterbury
b. 1863	Charles Cutler Torrey	American Bible scholar
b. 1952	Jenny Agutter	English actor
d. 1968	John Steinbeck	American writer
d. 1973	Bobby Darin	American singer
d. 1996	Dr. Carl Sagan	American scientist

The Louisiana Purchase

On this day in 1803, the treaty completing the transfer of Louisiana from France (it had been a French colony since 1699) to the United States was completed. The cost of the Louisiana Purchase was about sixty million francs or about fifteen million dollars (of which $11,250,000 was paid directly). The money bought 828,000 square miles of land west of the Mississippi River stretching from the Mississippi River to the Rocky Mountains and from the Gulf of Mexico to the Canadian border. Thirteen states were created from the Louisiana Territory.

The Louisiana Purchase nearly doubled the size of the United States, making it one of the largest nations in the world, and secured free navigation of the Mississippi River. Special Envoy James Monroe had been instructed by Thomas Jefferson to secure New Orleans. The president wanted to ensure it did not become Spanish territory, as he anticipated that Napoleon was about to transfer the city and its environs. He was therefore surprised when Napoleon offered to sell not only New Orleans, but the whole state as well. The territory actually belonged to the Indian tribes, and this agreement gave the United States freedom to negotiate with them to ensure ownership.

In 1804, Thomas Jefferson authorized Meriwether Lewis and William Clark to explore the newly acquired Louisiana Territory. A forty-five-strong expedition took three years to map the area.

Today, the original documents relating to this historic purchase can be viewed in the Old State Capitol in Baton Rouge, Louisiana.

Edmund Grindal (1517–83)

Edmund Grindal, Archbishop of York (1570–75) and Archbishop of Canterbury (1575–83), came from the small West Cumbrian village of St. Bees. He lived at Cross Hill House, St. Bees, where his father, William Grindal, was a tenant farmer of St. Bees Priory. Remarkably for such a small place, Grindal's childhood friend was Edwin Sandys, who also became Bishop of London and Archbishop of York.

Two stories remain from Grindal's childhood: one, that he was saved from a stray arrow piercing his heart by a thick book under his cloak; another, that he saved his father from drowning by pulling him back over a bridge that soon after collapsed into a raging torrent.

DECEMBER 21

DAILY READING

While Joseph and Mary were in Bethlehem, the time came for the baby to be born, and she gave birth to her firstborn, a son. She wrapped him in cloths and placed him in a manger, because there was no room for them in the inn. (LUKE 2:6–7)

FEAST DAYS

ca. 3rd cent.	Honoratus	Bishop of Toulouse, France
609	Anastasius II the Younger	Bishop of Antioch, Syria
1597	Peter Canisius	Patron of Germany

ENTRANCE AND EXIT

b. 1804	Benjamin Disraeli	English prime minister
b. 1937	Jane Fonda	American actor
b. 1948	Samuel Jackson	American actor
d. 1375	Giovanni Boccaccio	Italian writer
d. 1940	Francis Scott Key Fitzgerald	American writer
d. 1945	George Smith Patton Jr.	American general

St. Thomas's Day

St. Thomas's Day falls on the winter solstice, the shortest day in the year, as expressed in the following couplet: "St. Thomas gray, St. Thomas gray, / The longest night and the shortest day."

In some parts of England this day was marked by a custom, among poor persons, of going a "gooding," that is to say, making the round of the parish in calling at the houses of their richer neighbors, and begging a supply either of money or provisions as a means of enjoying themselves at the approaching festival of Christmas. From this circumstance, St. Thomas's Day was in some places designated "Doleing Day," and in others "Mumping [begging] Day." In Warwickshire, the custom used to be called "going a corning," from the poor people carrying with them a bag in which they received a contribution of corn from the farmers.

In Germany there are lots of traditions associated with this day, for instance:

- *Thomasfaulpelz* or *Domesel* (lazybone or donkey of St. Thomas Day) were names given to the last person to get out of bed and for the last student to appear in class.
- The *Rittburgische Hochzeit* (Rittberg wedding), also in Westphalia, was an opulent meal served in the belief that if you ate well on St. Thomas Day, you could expect to do so all of the next year.
- Trying to steal a farmer's *Weihnachter* (Christmas pig), either alive or when it was butchered, worked about the same way as stealing the Maypole, only stealth and cunning were allowed, not bodily force. Very cautious owners slept in the pig sty so they could better guard their *Weihnachter.*

Noteworthy

1118 Thomas a Becket, the Archbishop of Canterbury who clashed with England's King Henry II, was born in London (d. 1170).

1521 The Zwickau Prophets–Muenzer, Storch, and Stuebner–arrived at Wittenberg.

1620 The Pilgrims, English separatists known as Puritans, landed at Plymouth Rock when the *Mayflower* anchored off Plymouth, Massachusetts, and there founded the first Congregational Church on American soil.

1913 *The New York World* newspaper printed the first modern crossword puzzle in the United States.

1937 The animated motion picture *Snow White and the Seven Dwarfs* premiered.

1956 The U.S. Supreme Court ruled segregation on public buses unconstitutional.

1968 Apollo 8, the first manned mission to the moon, was successfully launched from Cape Canaveral, Florida, with astronauts Frank Borman, James Lovell Jr., and William Anders aboard.

1988 Bomb killed 259 in Lockerbie as London/NY Pan Am flight 103 crashes.

2005 First civil marriages for same-sex couples performed in register offices in England and Wales.

December 22

DAILY READING

And there were shepherds living out in the fields nearby, keeping watch over their flocks at night. An angel of the Lord appeared to them, and the glory of the Lord shone around them, and they were terrified. But the angel said to them, "Do not be afraid. I bring you good news of great joy that will be for all the people. Today in the town of David a Savior has been born to you; he is Christ the Lord." (LUKE 2:8–11)

FEAST DAYS

ca. 250	Chaeremon	Bishop of Nilopolis, Egypt
303	Zeno of Nicomedia	Roman soldier
362	Flavian of Acquapendente	Father of St. Bibiana

ENTRANCE AND EXIT

b. 1789	Ann Hasseltine Judson	American missionary
b. 1839	John Maskelyne	English magician
b. 1858	Giacomo Puccini	Italian composer
d. 1885	August Yulevich Davidov	Russian mathematician
d. 1989	Samuel Beckett	Irish writer
d. 2002	Joe Strummer	English rock star

The Dreyfus Trial

On October 15, 1894, Capt. Alfred Dreyfus, the sole Jewish member of the French Army General Staff, was detained on charges of spying for Germany. Dreyfus was wrongly blamed on all accounts. Unfortunately, the Dreyfus trial was confidential, and no one other than French military officers was allowed in the courtroom except for two days–the first and last day (December 22, 1894) of the trial. Therefore, the French public never knew of any evidence presented against Dreyfus. He was sentenced to life in prison and sent to Devil's Island in French Guyana.

Why was Alfred Dreyfus charged with this crime? It quickly became apparent that there was little objective evidence against him, and the main reason was because Dreyfus was a Jew.

The founder of the Zionist movement, Theodore Herzl, attended both open sessions of the trial. From Dreyfus's attitude in the courtroom and by the look in Dreyfus's eye as Dreyfus shouted, "I am innocent," Herzl was convinced by Dreyfus. Herzl carried out his own research, which proved there was no motive other than anti-Semitism.

As Dreyfus was carried off, the hateful words "Death to the Jews" were heard from the gallery. Herzl, filled with great fury, determined that the fate of the Jewish population would never be the same. Following the trial, Herzl labored intensely to make the case for a new nation for the Jews, "where we can live without being despised."

Herzl died in 1897. On May 14, 1948, the independent nation of Israel was established. Dreyfus was eventually vindicated in 1906.

Five Kernels of Corn

The Canadian tradition of placing five kernels of corn at each plate on this day first started at Plymouth on Forefather's Day, December 22, 1820, on the occasion of the bicentennial of the landing of the Pilgrims.

The first Thanksgiving in the fall of 1621 was a bountiful feast, but an inventory taken afterward in preparation for winter proved that the Pilgrims had grossly overestimated their harvest.

They struggled through the winter, but in May 1622, their food supply was completely gone and the harvest was four months away. The long-awaited harvest of 1622 was a dismal failure.

For months at a time the Pilgrims' diet consisted of fish, clams, groundnuts, and whatever deer or waterfowl could be hunted. They would live four or five days at a time on a few grains of corn.

Again their hopes rested on a good fall harvest, but the harvest of 1623 was almost wiped out. A six-week drought began in June, and the crops turned brown and were slowly withering away. They turned to the only hope they had–intervention by God–and assembled one July morning under a hot, clear sky and prayed for nine hours. Their prayers were answered the next morning, and for the next two weeks it rained heavily.

The harvest of 1623 proved to be one of their best. Our Pilgrim ancestors never again faced starvation.

December 23

DAILY READING

"This will be a sign to you: You will find a baby wrapped in cloths and lying in a manger." Suddenly a great company of the heavenly host appeared with the angel, praising God and saying, "Glory to God in the highest, and on earth peace to men on whom his favor rests." (LUKE 2:12–14)

FEAST DAYS

250	Victoria	Sister of St. Anatolia
679	Dagobert II	Patron of kings
766	Frithbert	Bishop of Hexham, England

ENTRANCE AND EXIT

b. 1648	Robert Barclay	Scottish theologian
b. 1790	Jean François Champollion	French Egyptologist
b. 1948	Jack Ham	American footballer
d. 1834	Thomas Malthus	English clergyman
d. 1948	Hideki Tojo	Japanese prime minister
d. 2000	Victor Borge	Danish pianist

Robert Barclay

The Scottish theologian Robert Barclay (1648–90) was one of the earliest and most energetic champions of the newly emerging Quaker Church. Robert received his first religious training in the strict school of Scottish Calvinism, but having been sent to Paris to study in the Scots College there, he converted to the Roman Catholic Church. However, when he returned to Scotland, he found his father had joined the Quakers. He followed his father and became an ardent advocate of the Quaker Church. Both father and son were imprisoned for promoting what the establishment regarded as a dangerous sect.

Barclay spent the rest of his life furthering the Quaker cause and enjoyed the patronage of King James II, and had frequent interviews with him during his visits to London. Barclay's great work, *An Apology for the True Christian Divinity*, was first published in Latin and afterward translated by the author into English. It is a passionate exposition of fifteen religious propositions maintained by the Quakers, and forms the ablest and most scholarly defense of their principles that has ever been written. The leading doctrine pervading the book is that of the internal light revealing to man divine truth, which it is contended cannot be attained by any logical process of investigation or reasoning.

Barclay was not just an able writer–he lived his faith and on one occasion walked through the streets of Aberdeen clothed in sackcloth and ashes, urging everyone to repentance.

Halcyon Days

According to legend, the two-week period on either side of the winter solstice is associated with unusually calm seas in the Mediterranean region. Ovid recounts the story of the goddess Alcyone (or Halcyone), daughter of Aeolus, god of the winds. Alcyone married a mortal king named Ceyx, who drowned at sea in a storm. Such was Alcyone's love for her husband that she threw herself into the ocean after him. Seeing this, the gods transformed Alcyone and Ceyx into birds.

The Latin name for the belted kingfisher is *Megaceryle alcyon*, and by legend, this bird builds its nest on the water as Aeolus keeps the winds calm on the sea for a week before and a week after the solstice. Hence Halcyon Days are also known as Kingfisher Days.

Today, the expression "halcyon days" recalls a bygone time remembered for its peace and tranquillity, an apt reminder at this time of festive rush.

December 24

DAILY READING

But Mary treasured up all these things
and pondered them in her heart. (LUKE 2:19)

FEAST DAYS

385	Venerandus	Bishop of Clermont, France
735	Adela of Pfalzel	Daughter of Dagobert II
1898	Joseph Zaroun Makhlouf	Lebanese hermit

ENTRANCE AND EXIT

b. 1698	William Warburton	English bishop
b. 1822	Matthew Arnold	English writer
b. 1905	Howard Hughes	American businessman
d. 1524	Vasco da Gama	Portugese navigator
d. 1982	Louis Aragon	French poet
d. 1984	Peter Lawford	American actor

The Festival of Nine Lessons and Carols

For many people Christmas is not Christmas without the Festival of Nine Lessons and Carols. This annual service broadcast from the Chapel of King's College, Cambridge, was inaugurated on Christmas Eve 1918. The chapel was commissioned by King Henry VI, and finished by King Henry VIII. The order of service since 1919 has remained the same (apart from some carols) and is based upon the design of Edward White Benson, Archbishop of Canterbury. His son, the poet Arthur Christopher Benson, noted that the order came from ancient sources revived by his father and influenced by the Rev. George Henry Somerset Walpole, later the Bishop of Edinburgh.

The choir of fourteen men and sixteen boys sings carols, interspersed with lessons from the Old and New Testaments read by members of the community. Prayers are offered by the Dean of the Chapel at the beginning and end of the service.

Today many Anglican Churches have their own Festival of Nine Lessons and Carols, but the King's College service gains in popularity every year. The service is broadcast to millions by radio and is open to the public with free admission.

Since the early 1930s, the BBC has broadcast the service, and since 1963 a shorter service has been filmed periodically for television. Recordings of carols by Decca and EMI have also served to spread its fame.

The order of the Nine Lessons is as follows:

- First Lesson from Genesis 3
- Second Lesson from Genesis 22
- Third Lesson from Isaiah 9
- Fourth Lesson from Isaiah 11
- Fifth Lesson from Luke 1
- Sixth Lesson from Luke 2
- Seventh Lesson from Luke 2
- Eighth Lesson from Matthew 2
- Ninth Lesson from John 1

Lord of Misrule

In medieval times at Christmas time, every grand house and institution had a Lord of Misrule, or master of merry disports. In the University of Cambridge, the functions of the Lord of Misrule were performed by one of the Masters of Arts, who elected to lead the annual representation of Latin plays by the students, besides taking a general charge of their games and diversions during the Christmas season. A similar Master of Revels was chosen at Oxford. But it seems to have been in the Inns of Court in London that the Lord of Misrule reigned with the greatest splendor, being surrounded with all the parade and ceremony of royalty, having his lord-keeper and treasurer, his guard of honor, and even his two chaplains, who preached before him on Sunday in the Temple Church.

DECEMBER 25

DAILY READING

For to us a child is born, to us a son is given, and the government will be on his shoulders. And he will be called Wonderful, Counselor, Mighty God, Everlasting Father, Prince of Peace. (ISA 9:6)

FEAST DAYS

303	Martyrs of Nicomedia	20,000 Christians martyred in the reign of Diocletian
810	Alburga	Patron of Wilton Abbey, England
1231	Folquet the Minstrel	Bishop of Toulouse, France

ENTRANCE AND EXIT

b. 1698	William Warburton	English bishop
b. 1822	Matthew Arnold	English writer
b. 1905	Howard Hughes	American businessman
d. 1524	Vasco da Gama	Portugese navigator
d. 1982	Louis Aragon	French poet
d. 1984	Peter Lawford	American actor

The Nativity of Our Lord Jesus Christ

This ancient festival, today known as Christmas, celebrates the coming of the Savior into this world 5,000 years after the creation of the world (according to some Christians), 3,000 years after the Flood, 1,500 years after Moses, 1,000 years after King David, in the sixty-fifth "week" according to the prophecy of Daniel (9:25), and 750 years from the foundation of the city of Rome.

> In the forty-second year of the reign of Octavian Augustus, the whole world being at peace, in the sixth age of this world, God sent His Son Jesus Christ the eternal God to earth. He did this to sanctify the world by his most merciful coming, being conceived by the Holy Spirit, and nine months having passed since his conception, was born in Bethlehem of Judea of the Virgin Mary, being made flesh.
>
> This feast of Nativity of our Lord is one of the greatest feasts of all the year, and for to tell all the miracles that our Lord hath showed, it should contain a whole book; but at this time I shall leave and pass over save one thing that I have heard once preached of a worshipful doctor, that what person being in clean life desire on this day a boon of God, as far as it is rightful and good for him, our Lord at the reverence of this blessed high feast of his Nativity will grant it to him. Then let us always make us in clean life at this feast that we may so please him, that after this short life we may come unto his bliss. Amen.
>
> –*Extracts from* The Golden Legend

Scriptures Relating to the Birth of Jesus Christ

Born in Bethlehem

Micah 5:2: But you, Bethlehem Ephrathah, though you are small among the clans of Judah, out of you will come for me one who will be ruler over Israel, whose origins are from ancient times.

Matthew 2:1: After Jesus was born in Bethlehem in Judea, during the time of King Herod, Magi from the east came to Jerusalem.

To be born of a virgin.

Luke 1:26–35: In the sixth month, God sent the angel Gabriel to Nazareth, a town in Galilee, to a virgin pledged to be married to a man named Joseph, a descendant of David. The virgin's name was Mary. The angel went to her and said, "Greetings, you who are highly favored! The Lord is with you."

Mary was greatly troubled at his words and wondered what kind of greeting this might be. But the angel said to her, "Do not be afraid, Mary, you have found favor with God. You will be with child and give birth to a son, and you are to give him the name Jesus. He will be great and will be called the Son of the Most High. The Lord God will give him the throne of his father David, and he will reign over the house of Jacob forever; his kingdom will never end."

"How will this be," Mary asked the angel, "since I am a virgin?"

The angel answered, "The Holy Spirit will come upon you, and the power of the Most High will overshadow you. So the holy one to be born will be called the Son of God."

DECEMBER 26

DAILY READING

"For my eyes have seen your salvation." (LUKE 2:30)

FEAST DAYS

ca. 35	Stephen	Deacon and Proto martyr
400	Zeno	Bishop of Gaza, Palestine
1659	Gabriel	Patriarch of Serbia

ENTRANCE AND EXIT

b. 1194	Frederick II	German king
b. 1792	Charles Babbage	English mathematician
b. 1893	Mao Zedong	Chinese leader
d. 1957	Charles Pathé	French film producer
d. 1972	Harry Truman	33rd American president
d. 2001	Sir Nigel Hawthorne	English actor

The Feast of St. Stephen

An account of the life and death of St. Stephen is given in the Acts of the Apostles. Following the death and resurrection of Jesus, the early Christians preached the gospel with great boldness, much to the anger of the Jews. Stephan gave an outstanding defense of the Christian gospel and was stoned to death by an angry mob incited by religious Jews in Jerusalem.

St. Stephen's Day is a national holiday in Ireland, where it is also known as Wren Day. Originally, groups of small boys would hunt for a wren, and then chase the bird until they either caught it or it died from exhaustion. The dead bird was tied to the top of a pole or holly bush, which was decorated with ribbons or colored paper.

Early in the morning of St. Stephen's Day, the wren was carried from house to house by the boys, who wore straw masks or blackened their faces with burnt cork and dressed in old clothes (often women's dresses).

There are different legends about the origin of this custom. One is that St. Stephen, hiding from his enemies in a bush, was betrayed by a chattering wren. The wren, like St. Stephen, should be hunted down and stoned to death. Another legend holds that during the Viking raids of the 700s, Irish soldiers were betrayed by a wren as they were sneaking up on a Viking camp in the dead of night. A wren began to eat breadcrumbs left on the head of a drum, and the rat-a-tat-tat of its beak woke the drummer, who sounded the alarm and woke the camp, leading to the defeat of the Irish soldiers and the continuing persecution of the wren.

The Feast of St. Stephen is celebrated in the traditional English Christmas carol, "Good King Wenceslaus" (1853):

Good King Wenceslaus went out
On the Feast of Stephen,
When the snow lay round about
Deep and crisp and even.

Boxing Day

The feast of St. Stephen is celebrated as Boxing Day in the United Kingdom, Australia, Canada, and in other commonwealth countries. The name refers to the practice, as legend has it, of nobles and other wealthy Britons "boxing up" and distributing food and other gifts to their servants and to the poor on the day after Christmas. Boxing Day was traditionally when the alms box at every English church was opened and the contents distributed to the poor. Servants by custom were also given the day off to celebrate Christmas with their families.

DECEMBER 27

DAILY READING

Praise the L*ORD*, *O my soul; all my inmost being, praise his holy name.*
Praise the L*ORD*, *O my soul, and forget not all his benefits.* (PS 103:1–2)

FEAST DAYS

ca. 1st cent.	John the Divine	Apostle
399	Fabiola	Patron of widows
1944	Sára Schalkház	Hungarian martyr

ENTRANCE AND EXIT

b. 1630	Johannes Kepler	German astronomer
b. 1822	Louis Pasteur	French scientist
b. 1948	Gerard Depardieu	French actor
d. 1814	Joanna Southcott	English prophetess
d. 1974	Jack Benny	American comedian
d. 1974	Amy Vanderbilt	American writer

Joanna Southcott

The Devon-born prophetess Joanna Southcott (1750–1814) was eighteen when she maintained that the "Spirit of Truth" became her guide and guard. From 1772 to 1792 her whole life was thus directed, and in 1792 she claimed a divine visitation to "warn her of what was coming upon the whole earth." In this year she began writing prophecies in verse that were placed in the Great Box in the custody of one of her friends.

These prophecies were sealed in packets and not opened until 1801, when Joanna was examined by the clergy. She wrote over thirty pamphlets, and it is difficult to decipher her prophecies and apply them to a particular time or circumstance. Take for example, this extract from her first "book," *The Strange Effects of Faith; With Remarkable Prophecies* (1792):

> I have been led on from 1792, to the present day; whereby the mysteries of the Bible, with the future destinies of nations have been revealed to me, which will all terminate in the Second Coming of Christ; and the Day of Judgment, when the seven thousand years are ended.

"Now, should men say, all this by thee is done,
Thy head is wiser than each mortal's son.
And if they say it cometh from the Devil,
Then plainly tell them, that their thoughts are evil;
For Satan's wisdom never lay so deep;
Yet to thyself thou must the secret keep.
But if men say, it cometh from on high,
My judges shall appear, the truth to try.
Then in thy faith be steadfast still,
With salt be season'd well.
Remember thy baptismal vow,
And triumph over hell.
Your Captain too shall quickly come
And bring all to an end,
And fix his glorious Empire o'er
The wise, whose hearts will bend.
As in a humble manger here,
Kings did their Sovereign see,
So my low handmaid doth appear
To all a mystery.
Now, can you longer make dispute,
From whence you hear the sound
Thus Satan must henceforth be mute,
Nor talk the faithful down.
The reasons all are none at all
Of those that won't believe:
Thus when the Bible forth I call,
What answer will you give?"

Johannes Kepler Quotes

"I used to measure the Heavens, now I measure the shadows of Earth. The mind belonged to Heaven, the body's shadow lies here."

"I wanted to be a theologian; for a long time I was unhappy. Now, behold, God is praised by my work even in astronomy."

"My aim is to say that the machinery of the heavens is not like a divine animal but like a clock (and anyone who believes a clock has a soul gives the work the honour due to its maker) and that in it almost all the variety of motions is from one very simple magnetic force acting on bodies, as in the clock all motions are from a very simple weight."

DECEMBER 28

DAILY READING

"Come to me, all you who are weary and burdened, and I will give you rest." (MATT 11:28)

FEAST DAYS

ca. 1st cent.	Holy Innocents	Massacre of Bethlehem boys under 2
ca. 5th cent.	Gowan of Wales	Wife of King Tewdrig of Glamorgan
520	Anthony	French hermit

ENTRANCE AND EXIT

b. 1856	Woodrow Wilson	28th American president
b. 1934	Dame Maggie Smith	English actor
b. 1969	Linus Torvalds	American computer engineer
d. 1859	Lord Thomas Babington MacCaulay	English historian
d. 1984	Sam Peckinpah	American actor
d. 1999	Clayton Moore	American actor

Childermas

Childermas, or the Holy Innocents' Day, has been observed from an early period in the history of the church as a commemoration of the barbarous massacre of children in Bethlehem, ordered by King Herod, with the view of destroying among them the infant savior, as recorded in the Gospel of St. Matthew.

Because of this horrific edict, Childermas Day is reckoned to be unlucky. To marry on Childermas Day was especially inauspicious. It is said of the equally superstitious and unprincipled monarch, Louis XI, that he would never perform any business, or enter into any discussion about his affairs, on this day. This vulgar superstition reached the throne; the coronation of King Edward IV was put off till the Monday, because the preceding Sunday was Childermas Day. In Victorian times, housewives in Cornwall, and probably also in other parts of the country, refrained scrupulously from scouring or scrubbing on Innocents' Day.

It was also an unlucky day for children. It was customary to whip children on Innocents' Day morning, in order that Herod's murder of the Innocents might be physically remembered.

On a lighter note, in Spain and other hispanic countries like Mexico, Childermas is rather like April Fools' Day. Tricks are played, and the one tricked is called "Innocente!" rather than an "April Fool!" In many places, it is the young who play tricks–on their elders, whom they often lock inside rooms and such until the oldsters pay a ransom!

Noteworthy

1065 Construction began on Westminster Abbey.

1594 Shakespeare's *The Comedy of Errors* performed as part of Christmas celebrations at Gray's Inn, London.

1694 Queen Mary II of England died after five years of joint rule with her husband, King William III.

1846 Iowa becomes twenty-ninth state admitted to Union.

1869 Chewing gum patented by William Finley Semple of Mt. Vernon, Ohio.

1908 Earthquake struck Messina in Italy, killing two hundred thousand.

1945 The Pledge of Allegiance adopted by Congress.

1973 Alexander Solzhenitsyn published *Gulag Archipelago*, an exposé of the Soviet prison system.

1974 Earthquake measuring 6.8 on the Richter Scale killed 5,200 in Pakistan.

2007 Incwala Day, Swaziland.

December 29

DAILY READING

"Do not let your hearts be troubled. Trust in God; trust also in me. In my Father's house are many rooms; if it were not so, I would have told you. I am going there to prepare a place for you. And if I go and prepare a place for you, I will come back and take you to be with me that you also may be where I am." (JOHN 14:1–3)

FEAST DAYS

ca. 1st cent.	Trophimus	Missionary with St. Paul
706	Ebrulf of Ouche	Merovingian courtier
1170	Thomas Becket	Archbishop of Canterbury

ENTRANCE AND EXIT

b. 1808	Andrew Johnson	17th American president
b. 1809	William Gladstone	British prime minister
b. 1972	Jude Law	English actor
d. 1952	Fletcher Henderson	America bandleader
d. 1967	Paul Whiteman	American bandleader
d. 1986	Harold Macmillan	British prime minister

Grigory Yefimovich Rasputin

The Russian mystic and healer Grigory Yefimovich Rasputin was born in the Siberian town of Pokrovskoye on January 10, 1869, into a peasant family. He grew up to have the ear of the Russian Imperial Family—Emperor Nicholas II and his wife Empress Alexandrina.

At around eighteen years of age, Rasputin spent three months in the Verkhoturye Monastery and experienced a religious transformation. He was summoned to the royal palace in 1908 because of stories about his healing powers. The Emperor's son Alexis suffered from hemophilia, and Rasputin succeeded in healing him. His fame was secured, but his closeness to the czar also meant he had many enemies.

In December 1916, he was lured to the palace of Prince Yusupov in St. Petersburg and poisoned. Seeing the poison had little effect, Yusupov then shot Rasputin several times and dumped his body in the Neva River.

The injuries eventually killed Rasputin, and his body was discovered on January 2. He foresaw his death and wrote prophetically to czarina Alexandra, December 7, 1916:

> I write and leave behind me this letter at St. Petersburg. I feel that I shall leave life before January 1st. I wish to make known to the Russian people, to Papa, to the Russian Mother and to the children, to the land of Russia, what they must understand. If I am killed by common assassins, and especially by my brothers the Russian peasants, you, Tsar of Russia, have nothing to fear, remain on your throne and govern, and you, Russian Tsar, will have nothing to fear for your children, they will reign for hundreds of years in Russia. But if I am murdered by nobles, their hands will remain soiled with my blood, for twenty-five years they will not wash their hands from my blood. They will leave Russia. Brothers will kill brothers, and they will kill each other and hate each other, and for twenty-five years there will be no nobles in the country. Tsar of the land of Russia, if you hear the sound of the bell which will tell you that Grigory has been killed, you must know this: if it was your relations who have wrought my death then no one of your family, that is to say, none of your children or relations will remain alive for more than two years. They will be killed by the Russian people. . . . I shall be killed. I am no longer among the living. Pray, pray, be strong, think of your blessed family.

Nineteen months after Rasputin's death, the emperor and his family were murdered by a revolutionary mob, and the imperial reign of the czars was over.

Noteworthy

1170 Archbishop Thomas Becket murdered in Canterbury Cathedral in England.
1845 Texas was admitted to the union as the twenty-eighth state.
1851 The first American Young Men's Christian Association was organized in Boston.
1890 Battle of Wounded Knee—four hundred Sioux Indians killed.
1989 Playwright Vaclav Havel was elected president of Czechoslovakia.

DECEMBER 30

DAILY READING

"I have told you these things, so that in me you may have peace. In this world you will have trouble. But take heart! I have overcome the world." (JOHN 16:33)

FEAST DAYS

ca. 410	Anysius	Bishop of Thessalonica, Greece
717	Egwin	Bishop of Worcester, England
2006	Frances Joseph Gaudet	American education and prison reformer

ENTRANCE AND EXIT

b. 1691	Robert Boyle	English scientist
b. 1865	Rudyard Kipling	English writer
b. 1975	Tiger Woods	American golfer
d. 1892	Andrew Bonar	Scottish clergyman
d. 2002	Mary Wesley	American writer
d. 2006	Saddam Hussein	Iraqi leader

Frances Joseph Gaudet

The American prison reform worker and educator Frances Joseph Gaudet (1861–1934) was formally recognized by the Episcopal Church in 2006 when Bishop Jenkins lead the first official commemoration of the feast day of Frances Joseph Gaudet in New Orleans.

Frances Joseph Gaudet dedicated her life to social work. She assisted the Prison Reform Association by aiding unjustly accused prisoners with prayer meetings, letter writing, and clothing. She was also the first woman in Louisiana to support juvenile prisoners. She founded the Gaudet Normal and Industrial School in New Orleans in 1902 to help house and reform former juvenile prisoners.

Frances, the daughter of a former slave, was born in a log cabin in Mississippi. She was a seamstress by trade, but dedicated much of her time to prayer and social reform. After the death of her second husband, she pursued these aims full time, working with the Prison Reform Association, both on behalf of those unjustly accused and also writing letters and providing clothing for prisoners. Initially her efforts were on behalf of black prisoners, but they expanded to include white inmates as well. She was recognized by the mayor and the governor for her truly heroic efforts.

Following her return from a Women's Christian Temperance Union convention in Scotland in 1900, Frances worked to reform the juvenile justice system in Louisiana. She purchased a farm and founded the Colored Industrial Home and School, an innovative boarding school for the children of working mothers. Until 1921 she served as principal, and she gave the facility to the Episcopal Diocese on the condition that they continue it or use the proceeds from its sale to promote the education of African American children.

Books by Rudyard Kipling

1888 *Plain Tales from the Hills*
1888 *Wee Willie Winkie*
1890 *Indian Tales*
1890 *The Story of the Gadsbys*
1892 *Barrack-Room Ballads*
1894 *The Jungle Book*
1897 *Captains Courageous*
1899 *Stalky and Co*
1899 *From the Sea to Sea*
1901 *Kim*
1902 *Just So Stories*
1903 *The Five Nations*
1915 *The Fringes of the Fleet*
1918 *The Eyes of Asia*
1918 *To Fighting Americans*
1931 *East of Suez*

DECEMBER 31

DAILY READING

"Forget the former things; do not dwell on the past. See, I am doing a new thing! Now it springs up; do you not perceive it? I am making a way in the desert and streams in the wasteland." (ISA 43:18–19)

FEAST DAYS

ca. 300	Potentian	Bishop of Sens, France
335	Sylvester I	Pope
ca. 383	Melania the Younger	Patron of exiles

ENTRANCE AND EXIT

b. 1491	Jacques Cartier	French explorer
b. 1720	Charles Edward Stuart	Bonnie Prince Charlie–the Young Pretender
b. 1937	Sir Anthony Hopkins	Welsh actor
d. 1384	John Wycliffe	English reformer
d. 1877	Gustave Courbet	French painter
d. 1997	Michael Kennedy	Son of Robert F. Kennedy

Hogmanay

While New Year's Eve is celebrated around the world, the Scots have a long rich heritage associated with this event–and have their own name for it, Hogmanay. There are many theories about the derivation of this name. The Scandinavian word for the feast preceding Yule was *hoggo-nott* while the Flemish phrase *hoog min dag* means "great love day." In Anglo-Saxon, *haleg monath* means "holy month," and the Gaelic *oge maiden* means "new morning." Or it could be derived from the French *homme est né* or "man is born."

Hogmanay in Scotland is a great festive time, seeped in many customs and traditions. Friends and strangers are warmly welcomed, and it is customary to bestow a kiss to wish everyone a Guid New Year.

During the day the household would be busy cleaning so that the New Year could be welcomed into a tidy and neat house. It is considered ill luck to welcome in the New Year in a dirty, unclean house. Fireplaces would be swept out and polished, and some people would read the ashes of the very last fire of the year, to see what the New Year would hold. The act of cleaning the entire house was called "the redding," that is getting ready for the New Year.

Pieces from a Rowan tree would be placed above a door to bring luck. In the house would be placed a piece of mistletoe, not for kissing under like at Christmas, but to prevent illness to the householders. Pieces of holly would be placed to keep out mischievous fairies, and pieces of hazel and yew, which were thought to have magical powers and would protect the house and the people who lived in it. Juniper would be burnt throughout the house, then all the doors of the home would be opened to bring in fresh air. The house was then considered ready to bring in the New Year.

Debts would be paid by New Year's Eve because it was considered bad luck to see in a new year with a debt.

"First footing" (that is, the "first foot" in the house after midnight) is still common in Scotland. To ensure good luck for the house, the first foot should be male, dark (believed to be a throwback to the Viking days when blond strangers arriving on your doorstep meant trouble), and should bring symbolic coal, shortbread, salt, black bun, and whisky.

"Handselling" was the custom of gift giving on the first Monday (Handsel Monday) of the New Year, but this has died out.

Acknowledgments

The main sources consulted in the production of this book include:

Organizations

Gideons International
The Nobel Foundation
The Society of Friends
The United Nations
The White House
United Methodist Church of America
Westminster Abbey

Books

Richard Bentley, *Bentley's Miscellany* (1836–68)
Robert Chambers, *Book of Days* (1869)
Encyclopedia Press, *Catholic Encyclopedia* (1913)
Matthew Easton, *Easton's Bible Dictionary* (1897)
Encyclopedia Britannica Inc., *Encyclopedia Britannica* (1911)
William Hazlitt, *Faith and Folklore: A Dictionary of National Beliefs* (1905)
Oxford University Press, *Helps to the Study of the Bible* (1905)
G. M. Trevelyan, *History of England* (1926)
Harold Wheeler, ed., *How Much Do You Know?* (1915)
H. Pickering, *A Thousand Tales Worth Telling* (1918)
Alban Butler, *Lives of the Saints* (1894)
John Aubrey, *Miscellanies upon Various Subjects* (1890)
Benjamin Franklin, *Poor Richard's Almanac* (1732–58)
E. A. Greene, *Saints & Their Symbols* (1913)
Horace Porter, *Saints of the Church* (1906)
William Hone, *The Every Day Book* (1825–26)
Hodder & Stoughton, The Holy Bible, New International Version (1983)

Websites

bibliomania.com
birthdaze.com
born-on-this-day.com
born-today.com
catholic-forum.com
ccel.org
chi.gospelcom.net
classicauthors.net
cofe.anglican.org
crwflags.com
datedex.com
goarch.org
heartlight.org
holytrinityorthodox.com
justus.anglican.org
kirjasto.sci.fi
newble.co.uk
on-this-day.com
qppstudio.net
safran-arts.com
satucket.com
scopesys.com
thisdays.info
tnl.net
todayinsci.com
victorianweb.org
woodlands-junior.kent.sch.uk
wholesomewords.com